AMERICA MOVES WEST

THE DRYDEN PRESS INC.

THE DRYDEN PRESS INC.
HINSDALE, ILLINOIS

Fifth Edition

AMERICA MOVES WEST
ROBERT E. RIEGEL/ ROBERT G. ATHEARN
Dartmouth College   *University of Colorado*

Cover illustration: San Xavier del Bac Mission, Arizona.
Painting by Pedro A. Noa.
Photographs following half title, from left: Moki Pueblo, Arizona
(State Historical Society of Colorado).
Montana Cowboys, 1890s (Minnesota Historical Society).
Arizona, 1909 (Library of Congress).
Title-page photograph: Frontier Town (Library of Congress).

Photo research by Donna Friedman

Copyright 1930, 1947, © 1956, 1964, 1971 by Holt, Rinehart and Winston, Inc.
All Rights Reserved
Library of Congress Catalog Card Number: 72–113832
ISBN 0-03-084316-2
Printed in the United States of America
234567890 074 98765432

To G.S.R.

PREFACE

The United States has been distinguished during most of its history by a population frontier that moved mainly from east to west until the limits of the continent were reached. The land the migrants entered was to them a wilderness, but it was in fact already sparsely populated by native Indians, who came to be overwhelmed by the more complex culture of the newcomers. The moving frontier has been labeled the most American part of America. While the extent of the influence of the pioneers has been much debated, certainly the frontier was one of the important factors in the development of a distinctive nation.

The study of the nature and importance of the westward movement of population was introduced in a scholarly way by Frederick Jackson Turner, particularly in his paper "The Significance of the Frontier in American History," which was read to a group of historians in 1893. Turner's ideas were accepted widely and often uncritically by some, disputed by others. After a period during which historians argued vigorously and often bitterly over the Turner thesis, a new generation of historians of the West has appeared. These scholars are not emotionally involved with the Turner propositions, are diligent in research, and look at the material with fewer preconceptions. Their studies have produced different interpretations in many areas, and it is hoped that in the not too distant future a new general interpretation, or even several, will appear.

The fifth edition of *America Moves West* incorporates recent new materials and interpretations, but the general outline of the book remains as in earlier editions. The suggested readings have been reconsidered and updated, and existing paperbacks noted. Over a hundred pictures have been added, and the fifty-three maps and two charts redrawn.

Any text must be based largely on the research of others. We are grateful for the published work of many scholars and for the suggestions, verbal or written, of many others. Particular gratitude goes to Professor Harry Scheiber of Dartmouth College. The final result is of course our own, for which we take complete responsibility.

Hanover, New Hampshire
Boulder, Colorado
September 1970

Robert E. Riegel
Robert G. Athearn

CONTENTS

MAPS AND CHARTS

Maps

xi

Charts

AMERICA MOVES WEST

Arrival of the English in Virginia. A sixteenth-century artist depicts the hazards of westward passage. A profusion of sunken ships, an apparently aroused sea monster, and canoe-paddling natives whose intentions are not revealed greet the newcomers. Palisaded fortifications suggest that the problems of the emigrants are not yet over. (New York Public Library)

Chapter 1/THE FIRST FRONTIER

For approximately three hundred years after the first English settlement at Jamestown the irresistible attraction of land somewhere "beyond" pulled Americans westward. As they conquered the frontier, plowed their fields, and built their cities, they wrote the American story.

1

That these people should use the word frontier so frequently was only natural, for during most of their history a large area of undeveloped country stretching out toward the Pacific Ocean beckoned, and in answering the challenge many of them lived constantly in that forward population wave described by the term. As it does today, when applied to such fields as science, industry, education, or religion, "frontier" meant something new, relatively unknown, but always promising. To the pioneers the word came to suggest the West, but beyond that it had no specific geographical definition. One cannot pinpoint the frontier on a map. Unlike the European concept of the frontier as a national boundary, it was vague and ever moving, a shadowy thing that combined physical characteristics with mental attitudes. That great exponent of the American frontier, Frederick Jackson Turner, could come no closer than explaining it as a place "between civilization and savagery."

The American frontier movement was part of a much larger development, one that was launched from western Europe and fanned out across the entire western hemisphere. Just as the European impact influenced hemispheric development and was in turn affected by the flood of resources discovered in the new lands, so the vast and seemingly illimitable domain that lay before the colonists along the Atlantic seaboard molded the kind of nation that was to grow in the latitudes between the Rio Grande and the 49th parallel.

Other peoples had pressed forward at other times and in far-flung reaches of the globe, but no other has ever been as successful as the invasion begun on Virginia beaches in the early seventeenth century. That this particular frontier developed differently from the others was due to climate, geography, the reaction of the natives, the mixture of European bloods, and the elements of chance. Within a relatively short time this population surge welded itself into a nation that had a powerful role in global affairs.

EUROPE MOVES WEST   In many ways the dawn of the sixteenth century was not a time of optimism for Europe. The rise of the national states threatened to fragment the continent as their jealous monarchs fought one another for ascendancy. Society's stratification, born of medieval times, was beginning to crumble as the young nations passed through a transitional stage whose outcome was in question. The situation did not offer much promise to the common man. With a minimum of precious metals available and a limited supply of raw materials at hand, his opportunities were limited. As if this were not disturbing enough, his church was in the throes of a reformation that would cause division among men and warfare among nations. What the average European needed most at this time was an economic miracle.

The miracle that happened was the discovery of the western hemisphere and the opening of a whole new world. Almost overnight a people who had developed a number of skills and techniques, but who were sorely in need of a wide variety of cheap raw materials, were handed the key to the treasure house. What they did with their new-found riches was an important part of European history for several hundred years after the discovery. In turn, the coming of the European made an enormous change in the new, unexploited land. Spain, in particular, saw its entire course altered, as countries that traded with or fought against the Spanish soon discovered. France, Holland, and Sweden experimented with New World colonization in more northerly regions; but of these only the French became very deeply involved, and their effort proved generally unprofitable.

Of all the people interested in North American real estate the English, who entered the race belatedly, were the most successful. On the face of it this is surprising, especially when one considers that in 1607 these people established that very weak toehold, Jamestown, well over a century after Columbus made his first voyage. Tardiness, however, did not prove to be a major drawback, for during the sixteenth century England's rapid and widespread commercial development provided valuable schooling in international trade. In those years the Muscovy Company was founded to secure a profitable Russian trade, after which the Cathay Company, the Levant Company, and the East India Company were formed to tap Middle and Far East sources. In each of these ventures hardy English seamen delved more deeply into maritime mysteries, seeking out new routes, learning advanced methods of navigation, and increasing their geographical knowledge.

While perfecting their system of international trade Englishmen developed an efficient commercial structure at home. The coincidence of the Reformation and the rise of capitalism blended fortuitously with the age of discovery and colonization, for the ambitious English businessmen much preferred the Puritan doctrine "work and save" to an older, Catholic attitude that found excessive profits sinful. The growing middle class, freed from the strictures of the Catholic Church and in an independent political mood, became well knit and powerful. Joint stock companies multiplied rapidly on a broad background of highly speculative enterprises as their projectors, the rugged individualists of the day, undertook increasingly complex commercial operations. The application of these commercial techniques to the American frontier at a later date would be a relatively simple operation.

ENGLISH PIONEERS   The English appeared to be in no hurry to enter the business of colonizing. The Elizabethan seadogs, those nautical frontiersmen who ranged the seven seas, had only a passing interest in the new lands along North Atlantic shores. They much preferred to attack Spanish shipping and colonies, an activity that at once satisfied their monarch's commercial and anti-Catholic urges. In an era when British maritime development was in full bloom there was much more emphasis on exploration than on settlement. By the 1570s Sir Martin Frobisher was probing North Atlantic waters for a passage to the Pacific Ocean making three unsuccessful attempts. Sir Humphrey Gilbert agreed with those who believed in the existence of a sea passage and in 1583 he landed a large expedition on New Foundland shores. His efforts to establish a staging area for further exploration were frustrated when storms destroyed part of his small fleet. In a similar try two years later, John Davis found only a strait—Davis Strait between Greenland and Baffin Island.

Hunting for new routes of commerce was only one of the motives that sent the English to America. As the threat of open warfare with the Spanish heightened, it became obvious that the enemy's great economic resources were coming from the western hemisphere, and in order to cut into that preserve a foothold along American shores would be desirable. John Cabot's transatlantic claims for England, which had gathered dust for nearly a century after his voyage in 1497, were now put into play as a strategic weapon against Spain. Gilbert's appearance at New Foundland, in 1583, with his elaborate ceremonial rite of discovery—the formal excavation of a piece of turf, accompanied by an announcement that he was taking possession in the queen's name— signified his nation's intent to capitalize on its earlier claim. Onlooking fishermen, who had worked those waters for decades, must have thought his performance quaint.

Despite their unquestioned abilities in overseas operations, the first English efforts in America were uncertain and fumbling. Gilbert was lost at sea on his return trip, and his half brother, Sir Walter Raleigh, took his place in the colonial effort. In 1584 the queen

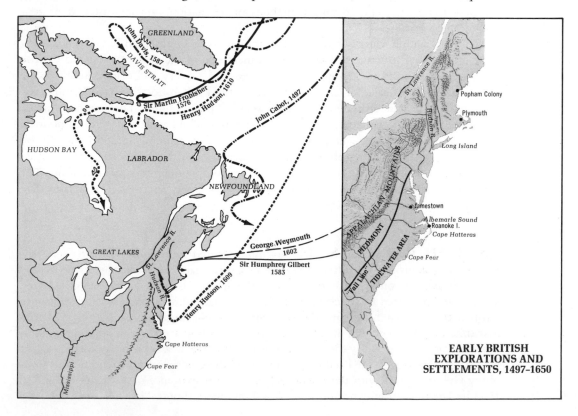

EARLY BRITISH EXPLORATIONS AND SETTLEMENTS, 1497-1650

granted Raleigh a charter to found a colony south of Newfoundland. The place would be named Virginia, in honor of the Virgin Queen, and during the following year a small settlement was established on Roanoke Island at the mouth of Albemarle Sound. After spending one winter there the colonists wanted to go home. When Sir Francis Drake, returning from one of his raiding trips, stopped off to see them they clambered aboard, glad to leave their new western homes. Raleigh sent out another group, in 1587; but he was unable to look after it because of the events at home (the Spanish Armada), and by the time a relief ship arrived in 1591 not a settler was to be found. As the seventeenth century neared, the British westward movement appeared to be stalled.

The emptiness of the effort was illusory. Even in failure Raleigh's attempts at colonization were sufficiently publicized to arouse interest among those who saw possibilities abroad. Moreover, his charter contained a significant provision: all those who left home for America would carry with them their traditional rights, the legacy of common law, and the liberties thus far accumulated. The inclusion of this provision was to have a far-reaching effect, not only on English colonial settlement in America, but on the continued westward movement of that nucleus. Attracted by the Raleigh venture, others followed. In 1605 Captain George Weymouth examined the coast of Maine and returned home with five Indians, whom he had taught enough English to be able to praise the climate and the economic potential of their homeland. Such testimonials, coupled with the fact that the Frenchman Champlain was exploring the country close to Maine, further stimulated the interest of government and private circles in the British Isles. Consequently, the Virginia Company of London found it surprisingly easy to finance a three-ship expedition which sailed for Virginia, under the command of Captain Christopher Newport, in the spring of 1607.

In many ways the tidewater frontiersmen who laid out the little community of Jamestown were typical of millions who followed them. Captain Newport went home to report that the place was so very rich in gold and copper that his passengers had remained to extract the precious resources as quickly and as painlessly as possible. These adventurers, who thought in terms of a quick return and were interested in agriculture only as a means of subsistence, resembled the army of miners on later frontiers. Characteristically, they showed their extreme individualism when John Smith attempted to weld the group into something resembling a civil society. Only under protest did they go forth to hack down trees with which to erect buildings, instead of digging for the gold they so desired, and when their oaths became too obvious Smith declared that any offender would receive a can of cold water poured down a sleeve to cool his temper. Even under such rigorous leadership the colony barely survived the first years in the wilderness, and many disillusioned colonists longed to return home. However, the arrival of more ships and supplies from time to time helped to ameliorate their hardships.

In the year that Jamestown was settled, Englishmen established a temporary beachhead farther north. This expedition, headed by George Popham (a brother of one of the promoters) and Raleigh Gilbert (son of Sir Humphrey), landed 120 settlers on the coast of Maine. After spending a winter at these latitudes the colonists decided they had over-looked some opportunities at home, and Gilbert agreed to take them back in the summer of 1608. Several other small efforts were made during the next few years—little establishments chiefly engaged in fishing these northerly waters—but there was no solid colonial effort until the *Mayflower* brought approximately a hundred Pilgrims to Cape Cod late in 1620.

In addition to the fact that the settlement of Pilgrims at Plymouth was a permanent one, from whose roots grew an important part of British America, the group made a significant contribution to what later came to be called the American heritage. Finding themselves beyond the jurisdiction of their homeland, or of Virginia, they drew up the famed Mayflower Compact, a declaration designed to provide self-government until English legal machinery could be imported. In this act they established a frontier custom that would be many times repeated in western mining camps, cattle towns, wagon trains criss-crossing the uncharted prairies, or in any other isolated group that found itself temporarily in a political vacuum.

The movement of peoples from the British Isles, and later from other European countries, to the seaboard of North America and from the low-lying tidewater area up to the line of falls that barred navigation, beyond to the Piedmont, then finally, across the Appalachian barrier, furnishes a great part of what we call our colonial history. The growth of American political, social, and economic institutions during these years was shaped by frontier conditions found in a raw and undeveloped America. Out of this experience came the refinement of old knowledge and the origination of native-born ideas employed in continuing a westward movement that had commenced in the British Isles. The westward projection of this force over nearly three centuries produced a new and powerful nation.

EARLY FRONTIER CHARACTERISTICS   The westward advance, in any of its many stages, was not something that "just happened." The first seaboard settlers had to be furnished transportation, supplied with enough food until they could raise their own, and reinforced with more men and necessities from the main base before the operation could be termed successful. To accomplish these aims businessmen were required to perfect extensive plans and to raise relatively large sums of money. These entrepreneurs were necessary to those who wanted to emigrate, whether they were families able to cover their own expenses or poor workers with little to offer but their labor. Even the wealthier who wanted to take advantage of the frontier boom economy tended to approach the organizers of frontier projects. To a degree this would be true on later American frontiers, although by that time the average American farmer moving west often accumulated his own capital and undertook his own moves.

As a rule European emigration to the Americas was sponsored and closely controlled by home governments. Spain and France furnish good examples. The English were unique in the use of private enterprise, the chartered companies that founded early

Virginia and Massachusetts settlements being typical, and the aim was profit for the investors who put up the risk money. In the proprietary colonies an investor supplied passenger fare to help settlers make the journey, after which they paid him back in rent or services. Much later, railroad companies would be selling immigrants their lands on time payments under much the same conditions. Whatever frontier one considers, whether it was exploited by the miner or the cattleman or the farmer, land was the dominant factor. Generally speaking, the principal goal was to get labor onto the limitless western acres. This process, begun on Virginia shores, was repeated with variations all the way to the Pacific Ocean. Even the Pilgrims of Massachusetts, whose prime motive for moving was religious, bought out the merchants who had financed their venture so that they might have title to their own lands.

Economic conditions in seventeenth-century England plus an almost limitless area of available American land provided the circumstances for a great migration. As a result of the enclosures, thousands of acres of land in the British Isles were turned into sheep runs, setting adrift a large population of laborers to whom a seven-year indenture service in the colonies looked better than a debtor's prison. After 1665 the imbalance in the supply of and demand for labor was somewhat corrected; a plague reduced the population, and gradually England's infant industrial structure assimilated English laborers. American colonial proprietors and entrepreneurs responded to the consequent decline in immigration by making more attractive the terms under which men might move. Indentured servants were promised bonuses in land on completing their obligations; freedom of worship was assured for all; and there was a general political liberalization characterized by promises of representative government empowered to pass upon taxation. The newer and less-developed colonies vied with older ones by offering more generous inducements, particularly in land; and here the "pull" of the frontier movement, as opposed to the "push" from England, came into play. This economic pendulum, once set in operation, did not lose its momentum until the frontier movement was completed.

TIDEWATER FRONTIERSMEN Modern Americans visualize the frontiersman as a man who lived off the land, cleverly utilizing nature's resources to provide food and shelter, prospering where less ingenious souls perished. This was a trait that developed slowly, for the first residents along the Atlantic seaboard found great difficulty in adjusting to their new environment. Englishmen to the core, they found themselves shackled by tradition, by the habits of their municipal way of life, and by the strictures of a rigid class society. It is quite understandable that they moved inland, away from a sea connection with the old country, slowly and cautiously. In this new, strange, forbidding country they tried to plant a European society, to shape rough logs into clapboards for the construction of traditional housing, to raise crops as before, and to carry on the only kind of life they knew. They went hungry while food abounded all around them; their clothes wore out and they patched the patches; they were cold when they might have been warm.

It was the grandson and the great-grandson of the early settler who moved on, learning how to build a snug log cabin and how to utilize timber in making furniture, fences, and clay-lined fireplaces, who became the prototype for later pioneers. The trout-filled streams, the wild life of the forests, and the native plants fed and clothed the practical pioneers. They discovered the utility of deerskins, the medicinal value of roots and herbs, and the wonderful versatility of the long rifle. As the Englishmen "went native," a new breed began to emerge, one that would call itself "American," and take pride in its citizenship in the state of nature.

The first colonists also had to cut away some of the political traditions that entwined them if they were going to enjoy any kind of equality in their new country. Despite a surprising liberality on the part of the mother country, these people were a long way from achieving anything like a political democracy. Officials still wore gold braid to denote their rank, the governor's council was exempt from taxation, and in the royal colonies most of the important appointments were made subject to the approval of the home government. The custom of primogeniture kept estates together by allowing only the eldest son to inherit property if his father died without a will; to prevent him from subdividing his inheritance, another custom, entail, was followed. These laws and customs tended to perpetuate class distinctions and to make it difficult for anyone to rise above the circumstance of his birth. The main abrasive that finally wore away such traditional strictures was the existence of limitless cheap land. Its extent, and its availability, lessened the need of men to seek security in time-encrusted tradition and privilege; there was sufficient security in the promise of the soil.

Officers of the Virginia Company were not long in learning that they must liberalize their land restriction. As early as 1613 Governor Thomas Dale decreed that each of the older settlers should have 3 acres for his own use, a privilege that was extended three years later when those purchasing £12 10s. worth of stock in the company were given 50 acres. By 1618 anyone who emigrated to Virginia at his own expense received a "headright" of 50 acres for himself and a like amount for each member of his family, servants included. As the better lands were claimed, newcomers were obliged to move deeper inland, or farther back from the navigable rivers.

The first American frontier, that which succeeded the original English settlement, tended to bulge westward, pressing first against the fall line and then against the Appalachian Mountains. As long as they could these people clung to the rivers that connected them with the sea, regarding these threadlike waterways as a type of umbilical cord that kept alive economic embryos still tied to the mother country. When they moved onto the Piedmont the land seekers found themselves west of the fall line and closer to a subsistence kind of economy. Once the Appalachians were crossed they had, in effect, passed the point of no return. This was the step they resisted so long.

Nearly a hundred years passed before differences between the prosperous governing classes along the coast and the small farmers who had moved farther inland began to produce repercussions. During this period the ordinary farmer recognized the fact that the wealthier tidewater residents ran things, that they dominated not only the economic and political scene but the religious and cultural aspects of society. Cities were separated by great distances and the family unit tended to concentrate on affairs in its own neighborhood, making it very difficult for anyone with notions of reform to get an audience. Those who were dissatisfied with conditions were so ingrained with the notion of "the classes" that they seldom did more than grumble. Besides, most of the offices were held by the aristocrats and to defy them would be to break the law. Those in power correctly judged this attitude and there was little trouble. From time to time they flattered the lower classes with some small attention, enough to give the aggrieved a sense of some importance. Moreover, the increasing numbers of Negro slaves appearing on plantations tended to throw the white classes together. Society continued to be stratified, but it was a condition that everyone recognized, something that had prevailed for a long time, and there was little disposition to upset the established order. Until men went farther west, by choice or by necessity, and until that western balance became more important politically, gentlemen along the seacoast could assure themselves that the status quo was not in danger.

Life on the First Frontier. These Virginians, defending themselves against the natives, engaged in a struggle for survival that would be repeated over and over again as the frontier pushed westward. (Brown Brothers)

A MILD CASE OF INSURRECTION   Before the seventeenth century ended, some fissures began to show in the political and social strata that the early colonial leaders had maintained from the outset. By this time the shortage of good farm sites near the coast had forced latecomers farther back into the hinterland. Some of these were indentured servants who had moved on after working off their obligations and now took back seats, so to speak, on farms in the fringe area, where they made unkind remarks about those farther east who held the reins of political power.

Discontent commonly smolders until some precipitating event, not necessarily directly related, sets off an explosion. In Virginia the uproar centered around a young man named Nathaniel Bacon, a relative newcomer, who was a member of Governor Berkeley's Council. The "rebellion" that occurred was not staged by frontiersmen and was aimed at the governor rather than at London's officialdom; but it is of interest here because its origin sprang from frontier conditions. In the spring of 1676 Indians living along the edges of settlement in Virginia and Maryland killed a number of settlers with muskets and ammunition purchased from traders who were sposored by the governor. Berkeley seemed undisturbed by these events and refused to call out the militia because, as the rumor went, he did not want to disturb the fur trade in which he was financially interested. Without consulting the governor, young Bacon gathered together some volunteers and drove off the Indians, much to the pleasure of the frontiersmen, who were angry over eastern disinterest in their welfare. Hard times, induced by low tobacco prices, and the levying of a poll tax added to the discontent of western farmers. The rest of the story, which did not concern the frontiersmen particularly, involved Bacon's demands for further reform, resultant warfare that sent Governor Berkeley fleeing, and the anticlimatic illness and death of Bacon that ended the insurgency.

Rebellion in Virginia stirred insurrectionary sentiments in neighboring Maryland. Josias Fendall and John Coode, whom Lord Baltimore called Rank Baconists, were strongly opposed to the proprietor and to the extent of his power. In a feud that periodically flared during the 1680s against Baltimore's Catholic management, the two men leaned heavily upon frontiersmen, who were largely Protestant. Although there was not the violence that occurred in Virginia, and nothing that might be termed a revolt, the simmering discontent reflected the rise of a western attitude and a growing ideological "apartness" from the East.

SETTLEMENT ADVANCES   As the Virginia frontiersmen moved toward the Appalachian Mountains, it was natural for them to veer either north or south rather than to continue westward. By moving in a southerly direction, along the mountain front, they were able to keep in touch with the coastal areas by means of the many streams that emptied into the ocean. The land known vaguely as Carolina was thought of as a part of the Virginia claim, whereas the Spanish regarded it as theirs. The British government, therefore, was not displeased to see the settlers advance in that direction, and in this instance the area was a frontier in both the European and the American senses.

Although the eight lords proprietors were not awarded their grants in Carolina until 1663, emigration from Virginia commenced a decade earlier with the establishment of a settlement on Albemarle Sound. In 1664 Governor Berkeley (one of the eight lords proprietors) severed the little colony from Virginia and appointed William Drummond as its governor. Albemarle is particularly interesting to students of the American frontier because of its extremely liberal legislation, enacted to attract settlers, and the subsequent history of that practice. For example, in 1669 a law provided that after five years of residence no man could be sued for any cause that originated outside the colony, a provision that must have proved interesting to many a man on the move. Attractive also was the exemption from taxes accorded to new settlers during their first year, as well as the outlawing of all debt contracted elsewhere. A further incentive was provided businessmen by guaranteeing the Indian trade to residents and denying it to transients. That the liberal legislation tended to attract quantity rather than quality is seen in the sobriquet given it by Virginians: Rogues' Harbour. But then there was very little blue blood anywhere on the frontier.

Into this backwoods country around Albemarle Sound and beyond, across what was to become North Carolina, pushed a group of hardy individuals who either could not adjust to Virginia society or did not find there the land they desired. As on later frontiers, the initial attempts to establish a civil society were rough around the edges, and these people were regarded by members of more settled areas as rather lawless. Frontier justice, often dispensed across a tavern table and frequently without any kind of written record, was sufficiently unsophisticated to give the impression of lawlessness when, actually, these people were attending their legal needs as best they could under rather crude circumstances. Similarly, the absence of much religious machinery made the Carolina frontiersmen appear to be godless (a situation repeated many times in the Far West), but time would bring churches and organized worship.

The spread of population to unsettled areas, this dilution of its density, tended to break down the traditional class structure and bring out the individual's importance in society. It was, for the moment, a rampaging democracy that made the more conservative talk about anarchy, irreligion, and the "wild West." These people were not necessarily the dregs of Virginia society, but were often hardworking, thrifty small farmers who opposed the large plantation owners and the power they represented. Typically, the group appeared to be poor, but it was not poverty-stricken. Although there was as yet no great wealth, there was no real suffering; and in the economic leveling there lay the elements of an egalitarian society, one whose members found equality in their common situation. In their very "sameness" they stood apart from others huddled along the coastal areas; America's first real sectionalism began to take shape.

NEW ENGLAND'S "WEST"   As the southern frontier bulged against the Appalachian barrier, swelling north and south before bursting through the mountain gaps to flood into the Mississippi Valley, the Puritan pioneers also felt a westward pull. As always, the nature of the land shaped the ways of men. On the relatively thin soil of New England there sprang up a trading and commercial community unlike the planter society in the South. The commercial or shipbuilding towns tended to preserve the English village system. Even the purely agricultural communities of the New England backcountry were inclined to keep the village type of life they knew in old England, which permitted the church and community fathers to keep track of their flocks and to develop a more tightly knit kind of settlement. Although this had its restrictive qualities, it also permitted the growth of a democratic type of government. Proximity meant the feasibility of the town meeting—that nursery of popular government—out of which grew representative government. On its westward march this small political and economic unit—the town—made a considerable impact upon American development.

As early as 1629 a number of little settlements lay sprinkled along the New England coast and in that year began the "great migration" from England, pouring forth more home seekers, many of whom were obliged to move inland to find suitable sites. Settlement along the coast was attractive to newcomers for about the first fifteen years after the 1620 landing at Plymouth Rock; then they began to look elsewhere. In 1635 the authorities of Massachusetts Bay Colony made a grant of land to a small group of men to found the town of Concord. Recognizing the hardships of this first New England frontier community, the founding fathers exempted the pioneers from taxes for three years. In the next few years others undertook new settlements inland, particularly along the rich Connecticut River Valley, and again, as in the Virginia area, the frontier movement veered off in a southerly direction before heading west.

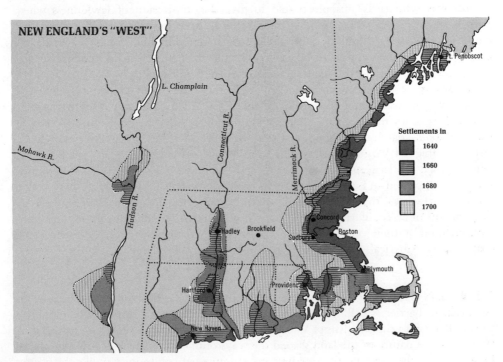

By 1660 there was an irregular frontier line in New England. Generally it ran from the Penobscot River of Maine down to Manhattan Island, hugging the coast fairly closely except for the occasional bulges westward into little valleys or along rivers that were attractive to the more adventurous frontiersmen. In addition to the advanced settlements that identified the frontier line there was also something of a legal frontier. For example, in 1645 the General Court of Massachusetts officially designated such villages as Concord, Dedham, and Sudbury as frontier towns and prohibited their residents from moving without permission. During the 1670s, particularly in times of Indian troubles, the word frontier was used as a term of law and into the American language came a word that meant "edge of settlement" rather than the designation of a line separating two nations. The military line of defense and the frontier of settlement were already coinciding, a condition that would exist in many parts of the West in later times.

After 1660 development proceeded much more rapidly. Although dates are often used arbitrarily to designate a general time of change, this one has a special significance, for in that year the Stuarts were restored to the English throne in the person of Charles II. When the new monarch began to enact despotic policies that harked back to an earlier day of oppression, a number of those who disagreed with him were inclined to emigrate. A more positive factor, one that attracted emigrants to America, was the stimulus lent by the king's efforts to pay off old obligations in the form of huge proprietary grants in the colonies. New York, Pennsylvania, and the Carolinas are good examples of the results. Not to be overlooked is the benefit gained by all the American colonies in the renewal of British commercial efforts under the Restoration. Trade warfare with the Dutch and the institution of the Navigation Acts had their restrictive aspects, but the boom that resulted was highly beneficial to the economy of the colonies. As land seekers migrated to take up these new opportunities, pressure against the Appalachians increased until it became so great that not even mountains, distances, or Indians could hold back the westward push.

READINGS   *Paperbacks are marked with an asterisk.*

Introductory   Walter P. Webb, *The Great Frontier* (1952) concerns the projection westward from Europe of the American frontier. *Edward P. Cheyney's older work, *European Background of American History 1300–1600* (1904) is still widely used. The first four chapters of Ralph H. Brown, *Historical Geography of the United States* (1948) should be read.

The Colonies   Max Savelle, *History of Colonial America* (rev., 1964) and Curtis P. Nettels, *The Roots of American Civilization* (1938) are comprehensive, one-volume colonial histories that touch on the frontier movement. For more detail see *Charles M. Andrews, *The Colonial Period of American History* (4 vols., 1934–1938). *Wallace Notestein, *The English People on the Eve of Colonization, 1603–1630* (1954) is valuable. More recent is David Hawke, *The Colonial Experience* (1966).

Northern Frontiers   Douglas Leach, *The Northern Colonial Frontier 1607–1763* (1966) is the most recent account. Alternative reading is provided in Alden Vaughan, *The New England Frontier: Puritans and Indians, 1621–1675* (1965). E. Douglas Branch, *Westward: The Romance of the American Frontier* (1930), interesting; see particularly chap. 1. More detail is in Lois K. Mathews, *The Expansion of New England* (1909), which has not been superseded. Excellent is *Louis B. Wright, *The Atlantic Frontier* (1947); see chap. 2. Alternative is Roy V. Coleman, *The First Frontier* (1948). See also William Bradford, *History of Plymouth Plantation* (1856, 1952); the 1952 edition has notes and an introduction by Samuel Eliot Morison.

Southern Frontiers   Thomas P. Abernethy, *Three Virginia Frontiers* (1940) is of prime importance. It should be supplemented by Thomas J. Wertenbaker, *The Old South: The Founding of American Civilization* (1942), which treats tidewater frontiersmen, or Wesley F. Craven, *The Southern Colonies in the Seventeenth Century, 1607–1689* (1949). Harold R. Shurtleff, *The Log Cabin Myth: A Study of the Early Dwellings of the English Colonists in North America* (1939) is an interesting commentary.

Bacon's Rebellion   *Wilcomb E. Washburn, *The Governor and the Rebel* (1958) is the most satisfactory account. Mary Johnston, *Pioneers of the Old South* (1918), chaps. 1, 2, 13, and Thomas J. Wertenbaker, *Torchbearer of the Revolution* (1940) are pertinent. Richard L. Morton, *Colonial Virginia* (2 vols., 1960) has several good chapters in vol. 1.

A Birch Canoe Going Upstream. Maneuvering the craft by pole and paddle testifies to the difficulty of using water transportation. Years later, and farther west, frontiersmen would encounter much the same problem. (New York Public Library)

Chapter 2 / WESTERN BARRIERS

While the New Englanders edged their way inland, cautiously probing unsettled land and attempting to maintain a more traditional kind of frontier, those who lived along the southern seaboard roamed the backcountry in a more adventurous spirit. The Virginians and Carolinians were particularly curious about "the other side of the mountain," a trait that was to send many a man west for more than two centuries.

Almost from the first, the colonists heard interesting tales about strange and mysterious things out west, stories that titillated the imagination and stirred ambitions. In 1649, for example, Governor Berkeley was said to have learned from the Indians that only a few days' travel into the interior lay a great mountain whose watershed drained into a large sea, and from across that body of water came shiploads of quaintly garbed men who brought with them animals that resembled horses. During the next summer Captain Abraham Wood was sent forth to investigate these stories and although he found nothing resembling the description, or, for that matter, anything that was not already known to fur traders, the urge to explore was stimulated. Within a decade most of the western area of Virginia and the Carolinas was fairly well known. In 1670, twenty years after his first efforts, Wood was still examining the backcountry of Virginia while the German adventurer John Lederer was trying to find a pass across the Blue Ridge Mountains.

None of the early Virginia explorers found the great river of the West, the South Sea, or acres of gold nuggets; but they did learn about the wilderness and how best to penetrate it. Lederer advised others to notch trees on their westward travels to avoid becoming lost on the return trip. He pointed out that small groups could move in greater safety because the Indians were not afraid of them and were inclined to do battle only with larger and more threatening expeditions. Of economic interest was his report that the Indians wanted to trade furs for guns, knives, hatchets, and other articles. "Sometimes you may with brandy or strong liquor dispose them to an humour of giving you ten times the value of your commodoty," he wrote, thus laying down a principle upon which many a subsequent transaction was made. His admission that the more remote Indians still could be separated from their goods with beads, mirrors, and trinkets, but that the nearer and more knowledgeable natives were demanding hardware, was another indication of the frontier's progress westward.

Undeterred by their relatively fruitless efforts at finding great wealth in the woodlands, the Virginians persisted in their explorations. In the spring of 1673 Abraham Wood sponsored another expedition, this time under the leadership of James Needham, whose purpose was to establish trade with the Cherokee in the Tennessee River country. The venture was successful despite the fact that Needham was killed by the jealous Occaneechi, who wanted to stop any such dealings with the rival Cherokee. The appearance of the white man had already sharpened the Indian's business acumen and he was prepared to deal with interlopers in a manner both sides understood.

Proprietors of the Carolina grant showed an interest similar to that of Governor Berkeley in the economic possibilities of the western lands. Anxious for a financial return from the Carolina venture, Lord Ashley and his associates did not overlook the rich fur trade deep in the new land. Within a few years more than 50,000 deerskins a year were being sent to London from a country that was described as "one continued park." One of Ashley's friends posed the central question when he asked: "If the Porch be so beautifull, what must the Temple be?" The search for the Temple, sought by so many men in later years, began at once. In 1671 the Carolina proprietors voted a sum of £100 to Henry Woodward to explore the interior of their holdings. So curious were men about the land beyond that some of the more conservative colonists began to worry about draining off the population to a danger point. Their concern must have had some basis, for Ashley instructed the governor to "bind the peoples mindes wholly to planting and trade" and to discount rumors about gold in the backcountry. But, being a man of many parts, Ashley overlooked no possibilities and agreed upon a secret code with Woodward whereby the explorer could send back any word of gold discoveries or other information that would profit the proprietor without disturbing the settlers.

INDIANS   The American frontier did not have to move very far inland before the white and red races came into close contact. In New England that contact began almost at once, and within fifteen years there was trouble. By 1637 the Pequot Indians rose up and tried to hurl out the white newcomers. Thanks to joint action by several villages, and the fact that Roger Williams persuaded the Narragansett to keep the peace, the disturbance was quelled. So effective was the chastisement that the Pequot posed no threat to Massachusetts and Connecticut villages for nearly forty years. That well-known religious thinker must have been dismayed at the enthusiasm with which his fellow Christians went about the business of putting down the native insurrection. The Indians, regarded as children of the devil, were shown no mercy; as William Bradford later described the slaughter: "Those that escaped the fire were slain with the sword: some hewed to pieces, others run through with their rapiers, so as they were quickly dispatched, and very few escaped. It was conceived they thus destroyed about 400 at this time. It was a fearful sight to see them thus frying in the fire, and the streams of blood quenching the same, and horrible was the stink and scent thereof." But, as Bradford said, the soldiers were grateful for the victory and "gave the praise thereof to God who had wrought so wonderfully for them."

A much more serious Indian war broke out in 1675, one that kept the frontier from Maine to Connecticut in a state of turmoil for two years. The story of its causes, to be told many times in the years to come, was that of white encroachment, of "purchases" of Indian lands under terms the natives did not understand, and of the rise of a capable leader who organized his forces and fought them well. "King" Philip persuaded most of the New England Indians, including the peaceful Narragansett, that the oncoming frontier must be rolled back; and in the effort that followed, scalps were lifted and blood flowed in the outlying white settlements. By this time there were about 120,000 white residents in New England, of whom some 16,000 were fighting men, but it took all the strength they could muster to put down a threat that really did not end even after Philip's death in 1676.

Such periods of strife tended to dramatize the existence of a frontier in that the line of demarcation between civilization and savagery stood out with greater clarity. The recognition of this condition is seen in an order by the General Court of Massachusetts, set forth in 1703, for 500 pairs of snowshoes and moccasins to be used in counties "lying Frontier next to the Wilderness." Also, there were numerous demands made by outlying villages for soldiers to "scout the towne while wee get in our hay," demands that would be echoed in Colorado and in Montana in the 1860s.

Pressure against the southern frontier resulted in trouble with the Indians of that region. Despite Lord Ashley's expressed desire to proceed slowly and in an orderly manner, neither he nor his followers could resist the lure of the backcountry. During the 1670s explorers probed deeper while traders negotiated a treaty of alliance and friendship with the Westo Indians. The agreement was commercial and military in that the Westo agreed to help make war on Indians living farther south under Spanish control. Aside from an occasional white murder the Indians kept their agreement until 1680, when the alliance gave way to open warfare with the settlers. The Carolinians enlisted the help of the Savannah Indians, who campaigned with such vigor that by 1683 the proprietors were informed that only fifty Westo remained.

So anxious were the Carolinians to trade in the backcountry, and so assiduous were they in capturing natives for sale as slaves, that the need for some kind of governmental

The Deerfield Massacre, February 1704. The French and their Indian allies raided unprotected outlying settlements in harassing attacks that were vicious but not of great military consequence. (Fruitlands Museum)

intervention came early to this part of the land. The small landholders who moved out to the frontier paid a heavy penalty for the recklessness with which traders dealt with the Indians, and to alleviate their difficulties the colonial government was obliged to formulate an Indian policy. In 1707 the South Carolina legislators set up a board of nine commissioners empowered to issue annual trading licenses. The key figure in this new regulatory structure was the Indian agent, who was paid £250 a year and was to live for at least ten months of that period among the Indians. In addition to being the principal adviser to the local government with regard to Indian matters, he was endowed with a considerable power over those who wanted to trade among the natives. As a contemporary remarked, the enterprising drummers had made it a practice to meet with the natives and "by giving rum and making them Drunk get their Slaves or Skinns for little or nothing, to the great dissatisfaction of the Indians when they are Sober. . . . " It was the agent's duty to eliminate such unsavory commercial methods and, if possible, to prevent the Indians from being swindled.

EARLY WESTERN SETTLEMENTS   Typical of later frontiers, the acceptance of this early West by small farmers was relatively slow to develop. By the turn of the eighteenth century explorers and traders were generally familiar with the area east of the Appalachians, but the average householder was reluctant to move away from the coastal areas any farther than necessary. The colonial population of 1690 is estimated at about 213,000; within twenty years it had jumped to around 357,000. But despite that rapid growth the line of frontier settlement remained almost fixed. Such events as King Philip's War discouraged the movement westward and in some cases drove back the frontier line, so that considerable population pressures had to build before the movement was resumed.

Distances, isolation, Indians, and other dangers were not a sufficient deterrent to the more adventurous. Many a small farmer might hang back, unwilling to risk his possessions and perhaps his life, but there had developed as early as 1675 a class of men in Virginia that came to represent the prototype of the "frontiersman" in later American history. Some of these were men like Abraham Wood, who examined the land and kept a close account of his findings, but most of the vanguard lacked either the ability or the desire to set down much of what they saw. Some years before 1700 the traders, large and small, were familiar with the land beyond the mountains, that country of the "beautiful river" (Ohio) so familiar to the early French trappers. They searched for furs, and even for gold; and even though they were sometimes disappointed in the material aspects of their search, they contributed to a growing store of information about the West.

The pattern of the past—and of the future—was followed in that the quest of riches, so often frustrated, led to an interest in the soil itself. The returning explorers, literate or illiterate, tended to talk about the land and its possibilities. These men came largely from a planter class and recognized a crop potential when they saw one. Out of their various sojourns in the West came the desire to speculate in land, particularly in view of the pressures being exerted by land-hungry Germans and Scotch-Irish immigrants who crowded in from the seacoast.

By 1730 the frontier line was again on the move, and such places as the Shenandoah Valley began to fill up. It was said that Governor Gooch of Virginia was handing out land grants so generously that one Jacob Stover became a man of much property by giving human names to his cattle and using them to take land titles. In another instance a young woman, adept at disguise, presented herself in several variations of male attire and laid claim to an immoderately large acreage. A century and a half later, in Nebraska and Colorado, stockmen engaged in similar subterfuges.

After New Englanders had recovered from the effects of King Philip's War, their frontier once more edged forward. Francis Parkman, in describing that frontier of two or three hundred miles in length, said it was largely agricultural and its settlements were widely scattered. When the villagers could, they fortified themselves with some kind of palisade; and in larger communities much more secure fortifications, replete with blockhouses, afforded protection in times of extreme danger.

In the second quarter of the eighteenth century these settlements crept along river valleys into the Berkshires and other mountains, little clusters of people carrying their Puritan ideals, moral codes, and notions about education, deeper into the new land. Instead of offering large grants of land to individuals, as was common on the southern frontier, the New Englanders continued their system of group allotments, after which town proprietors might make individual assignments of acreages, and thereby control the nature of the expansion.

By this time the social and religious ideas characteristic of Puritan society were beginning to be set aside in favor of economic and political considerations. Massachusetts illustrated the change when, to protect its boundary claims, it began to locate towns in advance of settlement. In 1736, for example, it laid out five towns on the New Hampshire border; in the years that followed, more grants were made in what is now Vermont. These were cash deals, and the rush of speculators who bought up favorable sites for future subdivision indicated a modification of the older religious ideal. As the economic aspects of town-building grew in importance, the grasp that community leaders once exercised over their flocks diminished and the "moral police," as Turner called them, began to lose their grip. The result was an increased individualism, one that operated within the framework of the town settlement system, but did not necessarily erode its many virtues.

By the middle of the eighteenth century the emergence of two New Englands was apparent: one a coastal area wedded to the commercial ideal, and the other a more primitive hinterland dominated by agriculture and peopled by men with democratic ideals unafraid of change. Although the development was north and south, running up little valleys, the fact that it was not moving west in no way meant that it lacked the qualities of a frontier movement.

In nearby New York, the spread of settlement up the Hudson River valley provided another example of the "northward movement." From a very early date Albany was an important fur-trading post, and despite the restrictiveness of the Dutch land system a group of small farmers worked its way to the backcountry. After the British took custody of New York, in 1664, and cultivated friendly relationships with the Iroquois Indians, there was much more inducement for the farmers to take up lands on the fringes of settlement.

Refugees from the strife-torn continent of Europe were welcomed in England and often were sent on to the American colonies. In 1709 Protestant Germans fleeing the troubled Palatinate were given shelter by Queen Anne. Some of them were sent on to North Carolina, where an unsuccessful attempt was made to form a colony, but a much larger group—some 3000—were settled along the Hudson River. The British government, which anticipated the policies of private societies at a later date, advanced the necessary funds for travel, tools, and provisions. It was hoped that these people would produce naval stores for "Mother England," but the immigrants became dissatisfied with the project and turned to farming, with which they were much more familiar. The availability of large amounts of unclaimed land on the frontier made it difficult to discipline the newcomers, who drifted off, many into Pennsylvania, to take up individual farmsteads.

The movement into Pennsylvania's backcountry was westward. Into the great

Penn's Treaty with the Indians. The proffered bolt of cloth, eyed with some interest by the natives, became a basic part of later negotiations with the tribesmen, although as time passed their demands became somewhat more sophisticated. (Collection of Edgar William and Bernice Chrysler Garbisch)

valleys poured thousands of Germans and Scotch-Irish. The movement picked up speed in the late 1720s and by the time of the American Revolution perhaps a third of the Pennsylvania population was German, or "Pennsylvania Dutch" as they were mistakenly called. Some 200,000 of these people were strung out along the frontier line of the thirteen colonies at the time independence was declared, about half of them living in Pennsylvania. Too poor to pay the going price for available land, they headed for the fringe of settlement: north into New York's Mohawk Valley, south into the Georgia mountains, and westward along a line between these regions. They were good farmers, men who knew how to produce the most from the soil, wedded to the land, and little interested in politics or warfare.

The Scotch-Irish were equally attracted to the new country. Pennsylvania, founded by William Penn in 1681, appealed to them because of its agricultural possibilities and because its proprietor was more interested in economic development than in religious hairsplitting. These were rough-minded people, willing to put up with the hardships of frontier life but unwilling to be interfered with. James Logan, one of Penn's agents, characterized them well when he used the term "bold and indigent strangers." He remarked that when questions arose over land titles—a frequent occurrence—the Scotch-Irish stood by their claims, holding that it was against the laws of God and Nature that Christians who wanted to work should be denied the use of idle acres. Stubbornly squatting on their claims, they refused to move or to pay quitrents.

When it came to dealing with the Indians the Scotch-Irish took up the challenge much more quickly than the peace-loving Germans. As Logan wrote, "The Indians themselves are alarmed at the swarms of strangers, and we are afraid of a breach between them—the Irish are very rough to them." The Indians, or anyone else blocking their westward push, found these independent, militant frontiersmen ready to settle matters by a test of arms. Along with other dissident factions, such as the Irish Quakers and the French Huguenots, the Scotch-Irish were a hard-fighting, individualistic, and frequently quick-tempered people ever ready to take up any challenge to their assertion of individual rights. Perhaps more than any other group they came to epitomize the typical frontiersman in the minds of their contemporaries and of later generations.

THE OLD WEST These early western settlements furnish excellent examples of initial frontier influences. Virginia was not very old before the settlements in the Shenandoah Valley began to have a pronounced effect on the coastal area. At the outset the colony was primarily English, Episcopal, and aristocratic; but before long Scotch Presbyterianism and German Lutheranism, small farms, and democratic tendencies began to reduce the influences of the privileged class. In the House of Burgesses the representatives of these upcountry folk ran head on into eastern ideologies and the result was then, and much later, conflict. The privileged class managed to keep its grip for some time; but when the changes came in revolutionary days, when church and state were separated and such feudal vestiges as primogeniture and entail were erased, the changes were, in part, the result of backcountry pressures. As one historian has remarked,

Jefferson has been called the father of democracy, but there is some validity to the notion that the Shenandoah Valley was one of its cradles.

All along the frontier, from the Carolinas northward to New England, old customs and distinctions gradually wore away under the pressures of emphasis upon social equality. Westerners from Massachusetts and Connecticut traded among the New York Dutch, and frequently their children intermarried. The same mingling took place on other parts of the frontier, and as time passed, a new generation grew up, one that had moved several times, had associated with other religions and languages so much that these were no longer significant distinctions among people—and from it had come a people simply known as westerners. While no frontier society could be called classless, these pioneering families enjoyed the open, relatively unfettered life they lived far away from the strictures of tradition that shackled older communities along the coast. When these western notions filtered eastward, they appealed to people of ordinary means, and men of substance who had ruled so long with so little opposition were concerned. Ideas of social and political equality gradually spread to the eastern parts of the colonies, and to a degree that cannot be measured they affected later thinking.

It is possible, however, to examine some of the more concrete results of the population movement into the backcountry, or what Turner called "the Old West." Along the outer edge of colonial settlement, from New England to Georgia, there lay a picket line of men who carried their rifles with their axes, ready to exchange one instrument for the other on a moment's notice as the day's work proceeded. This fighting frontier was tangible and unmistakable, and its residents stood out in sharp contrast to the tidewater folk. Out on the "front" lived men and women who knew adversity, who frequently had experienced hardships in the old country, and whose environment molded them into a hardheaded people, highly individualistic, ever jealous of their rights. Into this first "melting pot" came immigrants from various European trouble spots, tired of religious persecution, political suppression, and economic inequalities. In their common situation they found a new fellowship, new allegiances, a new unity, and for these they shed old loyalties. When this occurred a new kind of man was bred, and the name American became more meaningful.

Not all frontier communities intermixed freely. Those that tended to cluster together in linguistic groups were easy to identify. The Dutch, for example, tended to stay together; so did the Germans. This tendency persisted, and much later, Russians, German Mennonites, Swedes, Norwegians, and other nationalities clustered in their own settlements out on the high plains. In nearly all cases, however, time and the pressures of frontier movement would break down these religious or national groupings, and parents would lament the fact that their children had lost their pride in the native tongue. Intermarriage, economic opportunities elsewhere, and in some cases an overweening pride in the new national allegiance eroded older attachments.

As new settlements were made farther away from the Atlantic seaboard, there was a tendency for local industry to develop and an internal trade to spring up. Thus the dependence on European products lessened in favor of local or American seaboard goods. Rising eastern commercial firms recognized the importance of these embryonic frontier business communities, and rivalries for their attentions soon became apparent. However, the chronic indebtedness of the westerners tended to set them apart, and animosities between the sections became so permanent that they are today regarded as traditional.

With economic sectionalism came a demand for political and religious independence. Residents of this thinly peopled land resented the power wielded by those from the more heavily populated portions of the country, whether the resentment emanated from the backcountry of the Carolinas or Virginia and was directed toward legislatures, or from a later West that felt neglected in national legislative concerns. As Turner pointed out, these dissatisfactions as well as the shift in political centers of gravity due to the movement westward resulted in the relocation of capital cities in Virginia, South Carolina, North Carolina, New York, and Pennsylvania. Similarly, political and economic demands of the westerners were revealed in their constitution-making where mortgage stay laws or paper money came under consideration, and in their state-making, where a continual splitting off of territories occurred as a result of growing population needs. The religious splintering that accompanied this political development assured westerners that their society would be religiously tolerant as well as secular. Continual fragmentation prevented any church from becoming powerful enough to dominate the others.

It was this "Old West" that furnished the manpower for later and distant frontiers. These men, with their notions about individual enterprise, landownership, social, religious, and political independence, were the shock troops that led the westward attack; after them came their sons and grandsons. Time bred a frontiering group, and as they moved across the land, bound for new and more promising places, these peculiarly American people left their mark on the institutions of every community through which they passed.

FRONTIERS IN COLLISION   As the British colonial frontier edged forward, a competitor flanked it and preempted much of the desirable land that lay between the claimants. In 1605 the French made their first permanent settlement in North America, at Port Royal (now Annapolis Royal) in Nova Scotia, and in 1608 founded Quebec. Although their colonial attempts in America also came relatively late, the French moved much more rapidly than the English. Shortly after he founded Quebec Samuel de Champlain moved into the American interior, finding the lake that now bears his name, and encountering the Iroquois with whom he fought. During that encounter the natives were introduced to gunfire, or the "white man's thunder," and it helped to establish their undying hatred for the French. Since these Indians soon were to become friends of the English, a foundation for the Anglo-French antagonism in the West was laid.

The French penetration continued. In 1613 Champlain explored along the Ottowa River; two years later he returned, going farther up that waterway and then crossing overland to Georgian Bay on Lake Huron, to find a westward passage that avoided the hostile Iroquois. Jean Nicolet, one of Champlain's lieutenants, pushed even deeper into the interior in 1634, moving to Lake Michigan and as far west as the Green Bay region of present Wisconsin. The next decades were spent in consolidating early French gains, after which, in 1673 the Jesuit Jacques Marquette found the Mississippi River and descended it as far as modern Arkansas. A few years later the explorer LaSalle reached the Gulf of Mexico, completing the great arc that had begun at the St. Lawrence River. From a commercial point of view a line of battle had been drawn, and in the years to come it would be the scene of conflict between the French and the English, each supported by Indian allies.

In 1687 the Marquis de Denonville, governor of New France, directed an attack against the English-sponsored Iroquois Indians. Two years later that visit was repaid when approximately 1500 of those Indians swept into the village of Lachine, a few miles from Montreal. The Comte de Frontenac quickly organized a force that included the friendly Huron and directed a triple-headed invasion of the English colonies. This was in 1690, and by now the French and English were at war in Europe over the French failure to recognize England's new monarch, William of Orange. Frontenac's war parties struck hard at New York, New Hampshire, and Maine frontier settlements, leaving a trail of blood and terror behind them. Sir William Phips, governor of Massachusetts, countered with a strike against Port Royal and won an easy victory. The victorious governor celebrated his triumph by "liberating" everything he could get his hands on, including silver, the French governor's shirts, nightcaps, garters, and even his wigs. It was a clean sweep. In the following year the English invaded Canada by way of Lake Champlain and almost reached Montreal before turning back. In 1696 Frontenac, now so old he had to be carried, directed a counterattack against New York in which the Iroquois allies of the English lost their main village by fire. The Peace of Ryswick, signed the next year, ended the phase of French-English colonial warfare known as King William's War.

The uneasy peace was broken by French refusal to approve Queen Anne's succession to the English throne (1702) and by the stand taken by Louis XIV over succession to the Spanish throne. In the general war that resulted in Europe—the War of the Spanish Succession (1702–1713)—fighting again broke out along the American frontier. During 1703 and 1704 the French raided outlying villages in Massachusetts, the famous Deerfield massacre of February 1704 being the bloodiest of several attacks. The killing of some 40 or 50 settlers in this affair so enraged the people of Massachusetts that their authorities offered a bounty for every Indian scalp brought in.

An invasion of Canada in 1710 that led to the capture of Port Royal so encouraged the English that the next year they gathered a large military and naval force designed to take Quebec. Wind, fog, and bad luck in the Gulf of St. Lawrence so disrupted the expeditionary force that the whole scheme was abandoned, and no more attacks were tried upon the city before the conclusion of Queen Anne's War in 1713. By the settlement, called the Peace of Utrecht, the British gained from France in America the Hudson Bay region, Newfoundland and Acadia, and a recognition of the special relationship existing between the English and the Iroquois Indians. The principal problem left

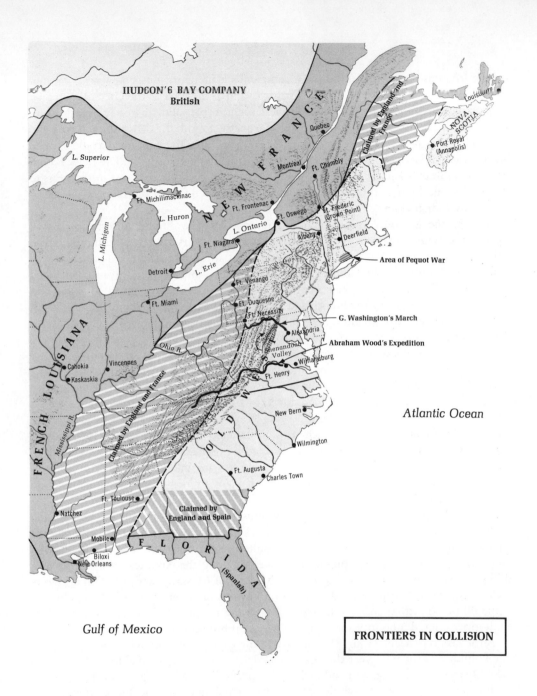

HUDSON'S BAY COMPANY
British

NEW FRANCE

L. Superior

Quebec

Montreal

Ft. Chambly

L. Huron

Ft. Michilimackinac

Ft. Frontenac

Ft. Oswego

Ft. Frederic
(Crown Point)

Claimed by England and France

NOVA SCOTIA

Louisburg

Port Royal
(Annapolis)

L. Michigan

L. Ontario

Ft. Niagara

Albany

Deerfield

Detroit

L. Erie

Ft. Venango

Area of Pequot War

Ft. Miami

Ft. Duquesne

Ft. Necessity

G. Washington's March

Alexandria

Abraham Wood's Expedition

Ohio R.

Shenandoah
Valley

Williamsburg

FRENCH LOUISIANA

Cahokia

Vincennes

Kaskaskia

Ft. Henry

Claimed by England and France

OLD W

New Bern

Atlantic Ocean

Mississippi R.

Wilmington

Ft. Augusta

Charles Town

Ft. Toulouse

Claimed by
England and Spain

Natchez

FLORIDA
(Spanish)

Mobile

Biloxi
New Orleans

Gulf of Mexico

FRONTIERS IN COLLISION

unsettled was the disposition of the vast interior, particularly the Ohio Valley, and it was the jockeying for position there that helped to spark the next conflict.

An indication of England's expansive mood is seen in a 1721 Board of Trade statement to the effect that although the Appalachians served as a "very good frontier," there should be no thought of limiting the western boundary to them. On the contrary, said the board, settlements might well be founded west of the mountains and a few forts should be established along the Great Lakes "in proper places." If such posts should be established where they would interrupt French communications between Quebec and the Mississippi, so much the better. Thus in 1726 Fort Oswego was built near Lake Ontario on land claimed by the French; there would be others. By the end of the 1730s the British frontier bristled with outposts, pinpoints of irritation thrust at the French from the Alabama River to Crown Point on Lake Champlain.

The French countered these moves by strengthening their existing posts in the Mississippi Valley and by adding new ones at strategic points. During the 1720s they erected a line of defenses between New Orleans and the Great Lakes that effectively challenged the aggressive British. In addition, the French and their Indian allies carried out sporadic raids against outlying British settlements, particularly in Massachusetts, that kept the frontier in a continual uproar for two decades after 1720. Formal war was carried on after 1744 when France and England were once again locked in a conflict known in America as King George's War. After a naval-military struggle in which the English captured the great French fortress of Louisbourg in Nova Scotia, peace was once again restored in 1748. New Englanders, who had contributed much to the expedition against Louisbourg, were astonished and angry when the Treaty of Aix-la-Chapelle handed back that prize at the end of the war.

The indecisiveness of the war was demonstrated by an immediate renewal of French activity in the West. Led by Celeron de Blainville, who moved through the disputed Ohio country burying lead plates to establish a claim to the land, the French once again were on the march. But later, aggressive traders such as Irish George Croghan extended operations into Ohio, trading with the Indians as far west as the Miami Indian country. Croghan paid for his audacity in 1752 when the French struck the little British trading post of Pickawillany, killing its defenders and hauling off a large store of goods. Encouraged by the victory, and the subsequent desertion of part of the Indians under British sponsorship, the French stepped up their endeavors to secure the fur-trading country that lay within their grasp.

Governor Robert Dinwiddie of Virginia, a tough-minded Scot who saw his colony's western claims threatened, not to mention his own trading interests, ordered young George Washington to go out and warn off the intruders. The officer did as he was told, but the Frenchmen flatly refused to move. Returning home, Washington reported that the French were well entrenched, particularly at Fort Venango on the Allegheny River, and that in his opinion it would take more than words to move them. Dinwiddie agreed and sent Washington back to build a fort at the forks of the Ohio in the vicinity of modern Pittsburgh; but again there was disappointment when Washington found that the French had anticipated him by erecting Fort Duquesne at the desired location.

Instead of abandoning his mission Washington engaged the French, defending himself behind a hastily built fortification dubbed "Fort Necessity," only to be defeated and driven out of the western country.

By now France and England were again at war on the Continent and the sparring that had taken place in America turned into full-scale combat. British strategists, anxious to tighten their American defenses, held a conference at Albany in the summer of 1754, whose purpose it was to consolidate colonial efforts and to reassure the Indians—the Iroquois in particular—of British friendship. (The fact that the struggle was called the French and Indian War in America indicates the importance of participation by the natives.) The Iroquois contended that although their friendship for the British had not diminished, they were worried by the continual white advance westward and by the French-English struggle for land they regarded as belonging to the tribes. They asked that their friend Sir William Johnson be made their representative and empowered to represent the northern Indians in dealings with the British government. The request was granted. Similarly, Edmund Atkin was put in charge of the Indians to the south, and the first real semblance of a comprehensive Indian policy in America began to emerge.

To integrate defenses in the forthcoming war the home government suggested that intercolonial cooperation be increased. Benjamin Franklin submitted his well-known Albany Plan of Union in which he foresaw a single general government for the American colonies presided over by a president-general and operated by a representative council. Into this organization's hands would go the disposition of all Indian matters affecting the American colonies. The proposal was endorsed enthusiastically by the delegates, and just as vigorously rejected by the individual colonies who were asked to approve it.

The first serious challenge to France's military establishment across the mountains came in the spring of 1755 with the arrival of General Edward Braddock in Virginia. With more than 1500 regulars, militiamen, and Indian scouts he marched on Fort Duquesne, only to be severely repulsed (July 9) by a much smaller French and Indian force using ambush tactics. The English reeled back upon Virginia, demoralized and disorganized, their commander mortally wounded, while the French retained complete control of the Ohio River country. About the same time another expedition, aimed at Crown Point and headed by Sir William Johnson, succeeded in establishing two forts in the Lake George area, thus checking the French on the north. For more than two years the holding operation continued. By 1758, under William Pitt's political leadership, the English had moved ahead on all fronts. In America the principal strategy involved a two-pronged attack upon the French: one against the great Canadian fortress at Louisbourg and a second up the Hudson River valley past Lakes George and Champlain into St. Lawrence River country.

One element of the grand assault proposed was a return to the headwaters of the Ohio, where the British had been so consistently defeated at the outset of the hostilities. The legislatures of both Virginia and Pennsylvania were anxious to eradicate this stubborn French barrier to their plans for expansion and to repair their tarnished military reputation in that region. This time there was to be no chance of falling into an ambush; the preparations were extensive and complete. A force of more than 6000 men under the command of General John Forbes marched resolutely upon Fort Duquesne, only to find that its pitifully weak garrison of some 200 men had decided to burn the place rather than surrender it. Taking over the smoldering ruins, Forbes, who had been ill during most of the campaign, notified the home government that the French had departed, and the place was renamed "Pittsbourgh" after the great war minister.

The loss of such western outposts as Duquesne was followed by a general contraction of French holdings, particularly during 1759. In September of "the wonderful year," as the British called it, the mighty fortress of Quebec fell. At the battle fought on the Plains of Abraham, General Montcalm, the French commander, and General Wolfe, who headed the invading force, both fell mortally wounded. Within a year the American aspect of the war was over.

In 1763, when the European phase was concluded and the diplomats sat down to write the Treaty of Paris, the formalities of the French demise in America were carried out. That document, signed February 10, had worldwide repercussions. At the stroke of a pen France surrendered all of Canada to the British, with the exception of some small

A Ferry Crossing the Susquehanna. All across the country westward-moving emigrants would find rivers and streams that blocked their way until some enterprising person provided ferry service, usually at a price that brought considerable complaint from the travelers. (Courtesy, The Metropolitan Museum of Art, Rogers Fund, 1942)

islands in the Gulf of St. Lawrence, and everything east of the Mississippi except the immediate vicinity of New Orleans. The remainder of the terms involved a division of claims around the globe, ranging from Caribbean islands to the Philippines, Africa, and India. For the Americans, by far the most important stipulation was that which lowered the French ensign beyond the Appalachians and cleared the way for uninterrupted expansion westward.

READINGS   *Paperbacks are marked with an asterisk.*

The Old West   John A. Caruso, *The Appalachian Frontier: America's First Surge Westward* (1959) treats the early trans-Appalachian settlements, as does *Frederick Jackson Turner, *The Frontier in American History* (1920, 1962). Thomas P. Abernethy, *Three Virginia Frontiers* (1940) treats the preparation for the transmontane move; also recommended is Herbert L. Osgood, *The American Colonies in the 18th Century* (4 vols., 1924). Westward movement by the southerners is described fully in *Verner W. Crane, *The Southern Frontier, 1670–1732* (1928) and John R. Alden, *John Stuart and the Southern Colonial Frontier . . . 1754–1775* (1944). Works mentioned for Chapter 1 of the present book—Savelle, Mathews, Branch, Wright—all contain pertinent sections. Oliver P. Chitwood, *A History of Colonial America* (3 vols., 1960) has a good chapter (17), "The Old West."

Struggles with the French   George M. Wrong, *The Rise and Fall of New France* (2 vols., 1928) remains the classic; see also his *The Conquest of New France* (1918). L. H. Gipson, *The British Empire Before the American Revolution* (9 vols., 1936–1956), vols. 5 and 6. French encirclement is also discussed in *Harold A. Innis, *The Fur Trade in Canada* (1930). See also Louise P. Kellogg, *The French Regime in Wisconsin and the Northwest* (1925). For the general reader is *Dale Van Every, *Forth to the Wilderness: The First American Frontier, 1754–1774* (1961). The French penetration is also discussed in John A. Caruso, *The Mississippi Valley Frontier* (1966).

Indian troubles along Pennsylvania's frontier are well covered in Robert L. D. Davidson, *War Comes to Quaker Pennsylvania, 1682–1756* (1957); briefer is George A. Cribbs, *The Frontier Policy of Pennsylvania* (1919). John W. Harpster (ed.), *Pen Pictures of Early Western Pennsylvania* (1938) is an informative collection from contemporary journals.

Stagecoach Travel. These fragile-looking vehicles changed very little in appearance over the years and provided the most popular means of passenger transportation until the coming of the railroads. (Virginia State Library)

Chapter 3/ BEYOND THE MOUNTAINS

The peace that came after 1763 presented problems not uncommon in a postwar era. As always, each of those who participated had his own ideas about the rewards of victory and about new economic directions. To the Americans the coming of peace meant the departure of the French from

North America; this thought naturally led to the conclusion that those lands so recently left vacant would be occupied by colonials, who were already indulging in western real-estate speculation. But empire planners, viewing the situation from remote London, saw it otherwise. In the new order of things there must be exercised a greater measure of control. Now the British flag flew over more of the earth's surface than ever before, and to manage properly such far-flung possessions stricter regulations were called into being. In America, for example, there were not only the upstart colonials who had plunged ahead pretty much on their own for years past; there were also some 60,000 residents of New France to be governed—people of a different language, different customs, and different religious faith. In the preceding turbulent decades the English, French, and Indians had become accustomed to warfare against each other and now, if British North America were to prosper, this would have to cease. One of the simplest ways to deal with the matter of quarreling children seemed to be to separate them. This the British tried to do by the Proclamation of 1763.

THE PROCLAMATION OF 1763   Despite the fact that their traders had been buying furs in the Ohio Valley for about seventy-five years, the British knew very little about the land beyond the mountains. The war had aroused considerable interest in the region, but such knowledge as had been gained from the western campaigns was limited to the upper reaches of the rivers flowing into the great valley. Although that part of the country was well known for its furs, there was little reason to suppose that it had any agricultural promise. Dr. Samuel Johnson, who knew no more about it than the next man, wrote that large tracts of land acquired as a result of the war were "only the barren parts of the continent, the refuse of the earlier adventures, which the French, who came last, had taken only as better than nothing." The doctor may be forgiven for his ignorance. Even William Knox, a long-time undersecretary for the colonies and a man who might be expected to know something about them, wrote as late as 1789 that the Americans would not settle western areas for years and that it would be best to assign such lands to the savages. It was a nation that would be current for nearly a hundred years, about other Wests, farther "beyond."

Undoubtedly the average American knew little more about the west beyond the mountains than did Johnson or Knox, but he exhibited a great deal more enthusiasm over the presumed potentialities of the new country. The eighteenth century was one of bold speculation, and land fever was rampant in America. Of the many promotional ventures undertaken, the Ohio Company, formed in 1748, was the best known. A group of wealthy English and Virginia investors was granted 200,000 acres of land along the upper Ohio River, provided a hundred families were located there within seven years. The promoters hoped to profit from the sale of lands and from the Indian trade; the home government saw it as an opportunity to shove back the French. Virginia's interest in the transmontane area was shared by other colonies, particularly Pennsylvania, whose people were concerned about the aggressiveness of the Virginians. Benjamin Franklin openly interested himself in various settlement schemes. Governor

Thomas Pownall, of Massachusetts, was another whose advocacy of western development by means of such grants was well known in America. The coming of the French and Indian War temporarily quieted such activities, but did not kill the keen speculative interest that had been generated.

The return of peace brought an immediate renewal of interest in the vast western country. The Virginians, always alert to the possibilities of westward expansion, promised to reward veterans with transmontane homesites; and Colonel George Washington, who had an interest in some real estate in that area, was a strong advocate of this policy. Early in 1763 land claims were being made, individually and collectively. Some prominent men of Maryland and Virginia (including Washington) founded the Mississippi Land Company and asked for a land grant at the junction of the Ohio and Mississippi Rivers. In 1770 the company renewed its request, this time asking for 2,500,000 acres in the Ohio country, only to be thwarted by rival speculators with more influence in London. Such pressures, so apparent at the close of the French and Indian War, prompted the home government to reevaluate its American colonial land policies.

In the spring of 1763 governmental officials in London began to ask each other a number of questions about the American trans-Appalachian West. Turning to the Board of the Trade, the British ministry asked for recommendations. How should the Indians of this unsettled land be governed? How fast and how far ought the whites be allowed to proceed? Should the older colonies govern these new settlements, or would it be better to found new colonies? To what jurisdiction should the Ohio Valley belong —seaboard British America or Quebec?

During the months that answers to such questions were being sought, developments in America suggested the need for an early decision. The British government's concern over the westward press of frontiersmen was shared by the Indians, who not only resented the intruders but who were also annoyed at the London policy makers for their lack of interest in making gifts to the natives. An Ottawa tribesman named Pontiac, who had assembled a large Indian confederation, decided to keep his people free from the British who were in the process of acquiring Canada and eastern Louisiana. After an unsuccessful attack upon Fort Detroit, early in 1763, Pontiac sent his warriors against other British posts in the country north of the Ohio River. One by one the forts at Michilimackinac, Sandusky, St. Joseph (Niles, Michigan), and Miami fell before the attackers. By June only Fort Detroit, manned by a relatively small force, remained as a British bastion in the West; closer to the more settled areas, forts Niagara and Pitt alone withstood the assaults.

During the summer of 1763 the tide of battle turned. Failure of the southern Indians to carry out their part of Pontiac's grand plan, coupled with an aggressive thrust by British troops under Colonel Henry Bouquet, blunted the Indian offensive. On August 6, at a place called Bushy Run, not far from Fort Pitt, Bouquet's soldiers soundly defeated the enemy. Sporadic fighting continued throughout the West in the ensuing months, during which time British forces suffered some sharp reverses, but the weight of arms finally pressed the tribes to such an extent that by late autumn the principal Indian threat had been extinguished.

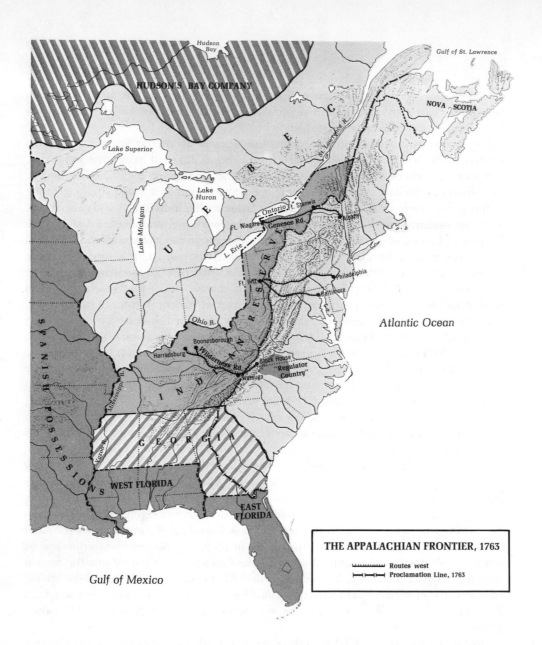

Hudson
Bay

HUDSON'S BAY COMPANY

Gulf of St. Lawrence

NOVA SCOTIA

Lake Superior

St. Lawrence R.

Q
U
E
B
E
C

Lake
Huron

Lake Michigan

Ontario Ft. Stanwix

Ft. Niagara

Genesee Rd.

Albany

L. Erie

I
N
D
I
A
N

R
E
S
E
R
V
E

Ft. Pitt

Philadelphia

Baltimore

Atlantic Ocean

Ohio R.

Boonesborough

Harredsburg

Wilderness Rd.

Block House

Watauga

"Regulator Country"

S
P
A
N
I
S
H

P
O
S
S
E
S
S
I
O
N
S

Mississippi R.

Yazoo R.

G E O R G I A

WEST FLORIDA

EAST
FLORIDA

Gulf of Mexico

THE APPALACHIAN FRONTIER, 1763

⊥⊥⊥⊥⊥⊥ Routes west
⊢▬⊣⊢▬⊣ Proclamation Line, 1763

The turmoil surrounding Pontiac's rebellion pointed up the necessity of formulating a policy that would minimize future conflicts between whites and Indians in remote and unsettled parts of British North America. Separation of the two races had been suggested in the earlier Treaty of Easton (1758) when Pennsylvanians had relinquished their claims to land west of the mountains in return for Indian cooperation. Now, in 1763, planners at London sought to extend this notion by establishing a boundary that would be understood by both parties, one that would be practical. Since there were few settlements beyond the mountains and since most of the claims in that area were held by speculators, the obvious answer appeared to be the crest of the Alleghenies.

By a proclamation, signed October 7, 1763, the crown attempted to set at rest several western problems. As an immediate answer to Indian complaints, a line was drawn along the crest of the mountains, west of which was to be the domain of the natives. Equally important as the segregation of races was the establishment of a new policy that took Indian affairs from the hands of the colonies and gave them to imperial agents. Henceforth, trading was to be carried on only by those licensed for such purposes and their relations with the Indians were carefully controlled. The idea anticipated later efforts made by the American government. The Indian reserve was flanked to the south and north by the new colonies of East and West Florida and Quebec, comprising a vast domain lying between the 45th and 31st parallels. Colonial governors were prohibited from issuing any more land grants, and individuals were warned against making individual purchases from the Indians.

The pressure under which the Proclamation of 1763 was formulated resulted in some important errors of omission. A glaring oversight was the lack of any provision for civil government for the French, many of whom had settled along the lakes and in the Ohio Valley. Not until 1774, by the Quebec Act, would this omission be corrected. Again, provision was made to arrest and punish anyone fleeing into unorganized Indian country, but there was nothing to cover crimes committed in that part of the land. More serious was the replacement of French law with English law in Quebec, a move that not only aroused the American French but was, in fact, a direct violation of the Treaty of Paris (1763). So great was the uproar over the proclamation that no one was willing to identify himself as its writer, and there were loud outcries from the speculators. Calmer investors, such as George Washington, took a view that such a restriction was only temporary, a gesture toward the irate Indians, and that the westward march would not be delayed for very long.

Washington's assumption was correct. During 1764 the Indian confederation was crushed by British troops, and the press of settlement beyond the mountains was renewed. By 1766 loud complaints by settlers and speculators were heard on both sides of the Atlantic. The new Indian trade policies were not working as well as had been expected. Benjamin Franklin was a personal friend of the Earl of Shelburne, who had drawn up the original plan, and it was to Shelburne, now secretary of state for the Southern Department in charge of American affairs, that the prominent Pennsylvanian turned for help. American arguments must have been powerful, for Shelburne recommended that trade in the Indian country be turned over to the individual colonies and that troops be withdrawn. Before any orders to this effect could be given, Lord Hillsborough took over such American affairs and a compromise measure was enacted. The Treaty of Fort Stanwix, formulated by the shrewd Sir William Johnson in 1768, extended the line drawn by the Proclamation of 1763 to such an extent that the northern Indians gave up claims to all the country south and east of the Ohio River, while the Treaty of Hard Labor (also 1768) similarly extended the southern portion of the line. Thus the notion of Indian country, open only to licensed settlers, was preserved but at the same time another area of fresh land was opened to the clamorous settlers.

OBJECTIONS TO IMPERIAL POLICY The westering tendencies of American real-estate promoters were more powerful than British politicians imagined. Although the speculators, particularly those of Virginia, were deeply disappointed by the home government's restrictive policies, as enunciated in the Proclamation of 1763, they found some hope in their remoteness and in the traditional lethargy of London administrators. As later westerners were to discover, there was some virtue in a convenient breakdown in communications and a general misunderstanding of orders. For those who were of this mind, the appointment of Lord Dunmore as governor of Virginia, in 1771, was indeed a happy circumstance.

Dunmore, who had been governor of New York, and had opposed such expansion, now displayed a surprising interest in the West. In 1770 the old Ohio Company of Virginia had been merged into the Grand Ohio Company, whose managers had gained permission from the crown to purchase 2.5 million acres of western land. The new group proposed to create a colony to be named Vandalia in honor of Queen Charlotte because the lady was said to have descended from the Vandals. Although the name was meant to be applied to the colony, the sponsoring organization became known popularly as the Vandalia Company. Unfortunately for the Virginians its claims in the Ohio country overlapped theirs.

While Dunmore had once argued that such a colony as Vandalia, located so far from the coast, would complicate the matter of defense and even contribute to the depopulation of the East, his mood changed when he arrived in Virginia. Local land speculators, who opposed the Vandalia scheme for reasons of their own, may have convinced him that despite his earlier concern over the danger of pushing too far west, the governor's fortune lay in that direction. In any event, he became one of the most reckless of plungers among his associates.

A group of Virginians, organized by Colonel George Washington, maintained that in 1754 veterans of the recent war had been promised lands by Governor Robert Dinwiddie and that the promise should be kept. The colonel, who foresaw great profits in such development, wrote to Dunmore in the autumn of 1773 and urged him to recognize veterans of both the regular and the provincial branches of the service. When the request was granted, there ensued a considerable land rush across the mountains, with Washington among those advertising lands in the new country. Several new little towns sprang up in 1774, the most important of which was Harrod's Town (later Harrodsburg). The site of present Louisville, platted during the previous year, soon would contain a thriving community. The West was beginning to find its place on the map.

The Vandalia Company, upon whose lands the Virginians had encroached, registered such a protest that the British government ordered Dunmore to cease and desist. It was here that the governor showed his real abilities. He not only denied any knowledge of the boundaries of the Vandalia Company but blandly asserted that he had no notion that the Proclamation Line of 1763 was in force. He cited the Treaty of Lochaber (1770) with the Cherokee as his authority and held that under its terms the expanded boundaries of Virginia put him quite within his rights. While making such bold assertions to British officials, he sent one of his agents to take possession of Pittsburgh on the assumption it also was within his realm. Pennsylvania officials reacted by throwing the agent into jail and registering a strong complaint to the home government.

About the time the Virginia-Pennsylvania uproar reached its height, matters were further complicated by the outbreak of another Indian war. The Shawnee, unhappy with the Treaty of Fort Stanwix and resultant frontier pressures, launched attacks upon white settlements during 1774. The home government was dismayed at such a turn of events, but Lord Dunmore looked upon the development as the answer to his problems. What he could not take in time of peace he could claim by virtue of conquest in war. What is known as "Lord Dunmore's War" was staged that autumn and was climaxed by the Battle of Point Pleasant, near the mouth of the great Kanawha River, where the Indians were turned back. To this "one-battle war" are attributed the opening of Kentucky and the quelling of the Shawnee, but the best that can be said is that it only

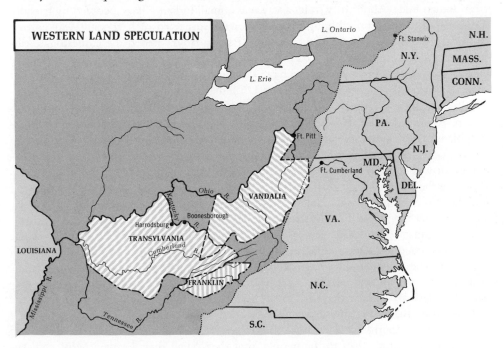

temporarily removed obstacles to white settlement. The Indians would be back. Dunmore's activities and the resultant quarrels over land were stifled by the coming of the Revolutionary War. He did prove, however, that the British government's western land and the Indian policy had its weaknesses and that the Treaty of Fort Stanwix was a failure. However, the same point was to be demonstrated over and over again in later American history.

FRONTIER DISCONTENT Turbulence in the colonial West was not confined to squabbles among speculators. Even before the restrictive Proclamation of 1763 frontiersmen had registered a number of complaints, not so much against imperial control as that of alleged injustices by colonial governments. It was only coincidental that in the year of the proclamation there occurred a disturbance in the Pennsylvania backcountry that almost erupted into civil war.

Thousands of Germans had settled along the western fringes of the middle colonies, along with large numbers of Scotch-Irish. The Ulstermen of Pennsylvania not only complained that the pacific Germans and the "Indian-loving" Quakers did not share their views with regard to a hard-line policy with the natives, but also that they were very poorly represented at the seat of government. It was this combination of resentment toward the "easterners" and a natural proclivity of westerners to deal harshly with the natives that led to what became known as the Paxton riots.

The hamlet of Paxton, located on the banks of the Susquehanna River, had suffered from Indian raids. About fifty miles away was a small Indian village peopled by friendly Conestoga Indians who, although harmless, were suspected of harboring war parties. In mid-December 1763 an armed group of "Paxton Boys" raided the Conestogas, killing a half dozen of them. Fourteen Indians who escaped were taken into protective custody at nearby Lancaster, only to have Paxton Boys break into the jail and kill all of them. The raiders then learned that some 125 Indians were being given shelter at Philadelphia and they promptly marched upon that city, determined to do away with this group. About six miles from the city the militants were met by a deputation of Philadelphians that included Benjamin Franklin who persuaded them to give up their mission of vengeance. A list of grievances was submitted by the frontiersmen but, to their frustration, it was debated for over a decade before any action was taken in the matter.

While the Paxton affair dealt largely in Indians, who were the victims, the uprising had far larger implications; namely the long list of grievances and irritations felt by those frontiersmen who thought that the scales of government were tilted against them.

Later in that same decade settlers along the Carolina frontier evinced many of the same dissatisfactions, and once again the situation resulted in what amounted to a small civil war. These people, who had gathered along the outer edge of settlement, demonstrated an increasing independence as their contact with both home and colonial governments lessened. Since they had little influence with the bureaucracy that ran the colony from the coast, their grievances tended to go unanswered. Such officials as county justices, sheriffs, and even militia officers were appointed by the governor and it was to him, rather than to the people, that they owed their loyalty. Most civil appointees were interested primarily in the fees they collected and the percentage that was turned back to them as pay.

Settlers in remote areas often complained that civil officials not only exacted excessive fees but withheld a much higher portion of the receipts than was due them. Governor William Tryon of North Carolina asserted in 1767 that his colonial sheriffs were embezzling over half the funds they collected. Westerners further complained that a badly apportioned tax load put the heaviest burden on the poor. Scarcity of money in the region, coupled with such resentment, made the life of the tax collector difficult.

Document Signed by Chiefs of the Six Nations, July 28, 1769. This early record acknowledges receipt of money paid to them by Thomas and Richard Penn, through Sir William Johnson, for lands sold under the Treaty of Fort Stanwix. (Granger)

As early as August 1766 some of the settlers in Orange County agreed to meet "at some place where there is no liquor" to discuss their grievances. It was the conclusion of that assemblage that officeholders were responsible to the voters, a point of view that was not entirely shared by the appointed officials. In the spring of 1768 it was announced that sheriffs would collect taxes at specified locations, and delinquents could expect to be fined. The challenge was met by the formation of a group of men calling themselves Regulators, who pledged organized resistance to taxes they regarded inequitable.

Colonel Edmund Fanning, of the Orange County militia, tried to ignore this informal group, but when they called on him and shot the roof of his house full of holes he appealed to the governor for aid. Governor Tryon played a double-dealing game, telling the dissidents to submit a petition containing their grievances, while at the same time ordering Fanning to arrest two leading Regulators named Hermon Husband and William Butler. When the angry mob frightened the officers into giving up the two men, the governor's secretary persuaded the group to ask Tryon for redress, and again he revealed his double-dealing by disavowing the secretary. However, the petitioners received assurances that there would be no more illegal fees, and with this they were temporarily satisfied. Only when these promises were broken did the Regulators again defy the law; Tryon then resolved to use force.

Toward the end of September the governor, with about 1400 men, appeared before Hillsboro, where Husband and Butler, who had not yet cleared themselves in the eyes of the law, were about to be tried. After an inconclusive parley between the two forces the Regulators quietly returned to their homes. That both sides wanted peace was indicated by the result of the trials that followed: Husband was acquitted and Butler received a sentence of only six months. Fanning was tried, found guilty on five counts, and fined one penny on each.

The Regulators, far from satisfied, pressed for the election of their friends to the legislative assembly, only to see the governor dissolve that excessively liberal body in November 1769. This was too much for the Regulators, who told themselves that every peaceful avenue had been explored in vain. When the superior court met at Hillsboro in the autumn of 1770, they presented it with one last petition, determined to use force if their demands were not answered. Judge Richard Henderson, who shortly would be involved in western land speculation, attempted to put off the petitioners. A mob scene took place in which Henderson was threatened, his law partner was driven into hiding, and Colonel Fanning was beaten. Henderson appeased the mob with promises, but his own duplicity was revealed when he fled, leaving Fanning to fend for himself. After threatening the colonel with death, the angry farmers ran him out of town and burned his house to the ground.

That autumn the assembly charged Hermon Husband with "false and seditious libel" and ordered him imprisoned. Only the rumor that the Regulators would march on his jail moved the governor to release the prisoner, after which Tryon gathered up another army, this time numbering about a thousand men, and once more headed for Hillsboro. About 2000 Regulators waited for him in the vicinity of the Alamance

River where, on May 16, 1771, the two forces met. During a two-hour battle in which each side lost 9 killed, the rebels were defeated. Those who took Tryon's proffered oath of allegiance—some 6000 did—were pardoned, and the remainder fled westward beyond the pale of the governor's law.

Those who moved on, about 1500 of them, had registered a strong protest against arbitrary government and had put their demands for reform into action. They offered no resistance to the home government and were in no way disloyal to the crown; in fact, some of them later became Loyalists during the Revolution. In this instance, however, they fought for their traditional rights as freemen. Their resistance had nothing to do with the coming Revolution except that it nearly coincided in point of time. The difficulty, however, demonstrated that the colonists were prepared to use armed resistance in the defense of their rights, and from this the mother country might have drawn a lesson it appears to have overlooked.

THE WAY WEST   The blandishments of speculators in western lands, who sang the glories of their new-found agricultural paradise, the diminishing supply of first-rate farmsteads east of the Appalachians, and conditions such as those faced by the Regulators blended into a powerful westering urge among small farmers living along the Piedmont. After more than a century and a half of hesitancy the frontier farmer took his courage in hand and headed for the mountain passes. When he reached the western slope he had, in effect, passed the point of no return, for this big step, one that he had avoided for so many years, put him into a new ideological, economic, social, and political world.

The assault on the western lands was frontal and direct. There was no other way. The French had circled to the north, skirting the British settlements, and had moved along the Great Lakes before penetrating the Mississippi Valley. The Spanish made their approach to the West from the South, probing at Florida, the lower Mississippi, and what would one day be the American Southwest. For the British colonials there were several points at which the great Appalachian front might be pierced. In the north, the most desirable route followed the Hudson and Mohawk rivers, and then through central New York from Fort Stanwix beyond Oneida to Lake Erie, whence it was easy to follow the Great Lakes, then to ascend some river flowing into one of the lakes, and eventually to portage to the Ohio-Mississippi system. Unfortunately for the early traveler, the Iroquois Indians were a more effective barrier than mountains, and before 1800 their friendship was never sufficiently assured to permit safe traveling by the Hudson-Mohawk route.

Farther south there were two routes in Pennsylvania. The first of these, the Kittanning Path, ran along the Susquehanna and Juniata rivers to the mountains, and then crossed the Appalachians to Fort Pitt (Pittsburgh) on the Ohio River; today the Pennsylvania Railroad follows this route. In southern Pennsylvania was the Forbes Road, opened between Philadelphia and Fort Pitt in 1758; the modern Pennsylvania Turnpike follows most of this route.

Along the Potomac River lay another possibility—Braddock's Road, opened in 1755. This route followed the Potomac as far as the town of Cumberland, and then cut overland to Fort Pitt. Later, when the National, or Cumberland, Road was built, it followed the old trail west to Cumberland and then branched out for a terminus at Wheeling.

Still farther south was the Cumberland Gap—a beautiful pass through the main range of mountains in the extreme southwestern corner of present Virginia. As a pass through the mountains it was excellent and much used in Revolutionary days. No important settlements arose at either end of the gap, owing largely to the absence of navigable rivers and to the existence of other mountains to the east and west, so that the importance of this route tended to decrease with time.

A final important passage into the heart of the continent skirted the Appalachians to the south through Georgia. Here the mountains no longer offered a barrier to travel, but in earlier days other handicaps were just as potent. Georgia was still in the earliest

River Flatboating. Crude vessels, little better than large rafts, were guided downriver by large "sweeps." (Library of Congress)

stages of its development, and no considerable bodies of people were interested in going farther west. More important, powerful Indian tribes, including the Creeks, lay to the west and they barred travel just as effectively as did the Iroquois in New York.

Most of these routes at one time had been game trails, and all of them were known and used by the Indians. Before the French and Indian War the trails were exceedingly primitive, being only unblazed footpaths. Whenever possible they followed the uplands to avoid the spring floods. A few logs enabled the traveler to pass the worst places. Rivers were crossed on sandbars, which shifted from time to time, so that a crossing could only be made after some experimentation. During the French and Indian War Braddock's Road and the Forbes Road were opened for wagons, but this merely meant that enough trees were felled and brush removed to allow the passage of crude carts. Time and the passage of thousands of families westward would wear away nature's impediments and afford well-marked and widened roadways that, despite considerable improvement, continued for years to be called trails. That they went west fascinated more adventurous Americans.

FIRST SETTLEMENTS   The end of the French and Indian War, and the opening of western lands by the Treaty of Fort Stanwix (1768), attracted settlers to the Fort Pitt region. Aware that at least two passable roads led to the headwaters of the Ohio River and encouraged by the Iroquois land cession, settlers moved west in considerable numbers during the 1769 travel season. They were ordinary farm folk, searching out new homes in a country familiar principally to fur traders and explorers in previous years. It is estimated that by 1770 some 5000 of them had made the mountain crossing to become "men of western waters," as they called themselves. Within the next few years the figure mounted to around 30,000.

Early Pittsburgh was the first permanent British settlement west of the Allegheny front in the present United States, and it immediately assumed a vital importance in business between East and West. At the head of the Ohio River, it was on the natural route of travel for all men and materials moving across the mountains, and it more than earned the appellation "gateway of the West." In its early years it was a commercial rather than a manufacturing center, although it did some manufacturing. Until 1790 all the iron used in Pittsburgh was hauled over the mountains from the East.

The Virginians, many of whom migrated to the headwaters of the Ohio, had an alternate route across the mountains. From the western edge of Virginia or North Carolina, passage into eastern Tennessee by the Cumberland Gap was relatively easy, and the headwaters of streams that fed into the Tennessee River were close. One of these, the Watauga, was a branch of the Holston, itself a principal tributary of the Tennessee River. Daniel Boone first saw the attractive Watauga country in 1769, and before long a permanent settlement was located in the area. James Robertson, who came in 1770, also liked the place and returned east to get his family and a group of settlers. He was back in 1771 with sixteen families, some of whom were disgusted Regulators who had lost their bid at the recent Battle of Alamance. They thought they were in Virginia and safe from the North Carolina authorities. Close behind them came Jacob Brown, who marked off a little settlement along the Nolichucky, a branch of the Holston. Another newcomer was Anthony Bledsoe, a surveyor who came up with information that disheartened the migrating Regulators: the place was within the charter limits of North Carolina, not Virginia.

The result of the survey presented a number of disturbing problems. The settlers from North Carolina were in no mood to yield to its authority; the settlement was geographically out of touch with both the Virginia and North Carolina seats of government; there was doubt that the little communities were within the area ceded by the Cherokee. In a sense the colonists were in a position similar to that in which the passengers on the *Mayflower* had found themselves more than a century and a half earlier. The solution to the problem was the same: the formation of a temporary government of their own. In 1772 Robertson, a dour, taciturn Scot, put his talents to work in the formation of the Watauga Association, an organization that included several of the nearby settlements. Here the frontiersmen studied the constitutions of similar groups. In search of a model that would satisfy their own administrative needs, the association provided authority for making laws, negotiating with the Indians, registering deeds and wills, solemnizing marriages, and performing the other essential functions of government. It was particularly important as the first in a long series of transmontane efforts to set up a governing body when the regularly constituted authorities would not act. As would be true of later experiments, the Watauga Association was temporary, lasting about six years, after which the colony was incorporated into North Carolina as Washington County. So faithfully had the constitution makers followed precedent that no basic changes of law were necessary and, in fact, most of the old officers were retained.

KENTUCKY   The growth of the settlement at Watauga encouraged many people to look farther west and to covet the fertile plans of the Kentucky, the Tennessee, and the Cumberland. One of these visionaries was Judge Richard Henderson of North Carolina, who organized the Transylvania Company (not chartered) to buy land from the Indians and then sell it to white settlers—a procedure that was illegal under the terms of the Proclamation of 1763. In March 1775 he and eight others from North Carolina met the Indians at Sycamore Shoals, on the Watauga, and concluded a treaty with the Cherokee that assigned the promoters about half the modern state of Kentucky. For this they paid about £10,000 worth of goods.

The Transylvania Company at once opened this huge tract of land to purchase on easy terms, and sent Daniel Boone to mark off a trail from the eastern settlements through the mountains and down the Kentucky River to the Ohio. This route, as marked by the famed frontiersman, took the name Wilderness Road. It was the only practical passage through the mountains in that region and it was used extensively by early westbound settlers. In addition, Boone established a small fort (Boonesborough) on the Kentucky River, near the present city of Lexington. As soon as the trail was opened, many settlers began to pour into the Kentucky region, going not only to Boonesborough, but also to nearby places such as Harrod's Town, Boiling Springs, and St. Asaph's. Some of them held Virginia grants, since Virginia did not recognize Henderson's ownership. In consequence, Henderson received but little for his land, and his settlement at Boonesborough was not very successful; his company store charged high prices and drove the settlers to other trading centers.

The Transylvania Company's political origins were similar to those of Watauga. Not only was the whole project in direct violation of the Proclamation of 1763, but its membership was willing to proceed independently, hopeful that theirs would be accepted as the fourteenth colony. Consequently, elections were held in May 1775, and residents of four small settlements—Boonesborough, Harrod's Town, Floyd's Settlement, and Boiling Springs—all cast their votes. Judge Henderson announced the existence of local sovereignty in his opening speech before the House of Delegates: "We have the right to make laws for the regulation of our conduct without giving offense to

The Wilderness Road Through the Cumberland Gap. The pass, or the gap as it was sometimes called, was a prominent route in westward travel. Such funnels in the mountains became well-known landmarks, familiar to thousands of emigrants. (Culver)

Great Britain or any of the American colonies." This fact established, the delegates proceeded with their endeavors, enacting legislation that established criminal and civil courts, provided for a militia, and—with an eye upon community morals—an "act to prevent profane swearing and Sabbath breaking."

Henderson's promotional schemes caused considerable turmoil in the East. Colonel William Preston warned his friend George Washington that the Transylvania project had its dangers, "for it is certain that a vast number of people are preparing to go out and settle on this Purchase; and if once they get fixed there, it will be next to impossible to remove them or reduce them to Obedience; as they are so far from the Seat of Government." Governor Josiah Martin, of North Carolina, called Henderson a "famous invader" and labeled his followers "an Infamous Company of Land Pyrates." Lord Dunmore, royal governor of Virginia (who was deeply involved in land speculation himself) demanded that "one Richard Henderson and other disorderly persons, his associates" immediately relinquish their land claims, but "one Richard" ignored the warning. Dunmore, whose thinking appears to have suffered from a lack of logic, complained that Henderson's activities were in violation of the Proclamation of 1763, a document with which he had earlier professed to have only the haziest acquaintance.

With the view of circumventing objections by Virginia and North Carolina, Transylvania's founders approached the recently convened Continental Congress and requested admittance as the fourteenth colony. New England's John Adams quickly pointed out to his colleagues the fact that any solution to differences with the mother country would not be made easier by sanctioning a colony whose very existence violated the King's Proclamation of 1763. Thus, in the autumn of 1775, the colony continued its career as a political orphan and, after bickering between some of the residents and proprietor Henderson, the scheme fell through. In December 1776 the Virginia assembly made Kentucky one of that state's counties.

The failure of Henderson's Transylvania project marked the disappearance of the notion of government under a proprietorship on American soil. Although his promotional efforts were frowned upon by coastal authorities and doomed to failure in the West the development publicized the existence of rich lands beyond the mountains and brought forth those restless, adventurous souls who would never have accepted the proprietor's authority for any length of time. Their presence beyond the mountains, irritating to future speculators who objected to squatters, was turned to good use before long. The American Revolution was at hand and these stubborn, hard-fighting, independent souls registered a strong objection to British plans for pushing back the frontier as one means of crushing the colonies.

READINGS   *Paperbacks are marked with an asterisk.*

   Land Speculation   Kenneth P. Bailey, *The Ohio Company of Virginia and the Westward Movement, 1748–1792* (1939), detailed. A detailed treatment of the Vandalia project is in chap. 3 of Thomas P. Abernethy, *Westerlands and the American Revolution* (1959). W. S. Lester, *The Transylvania Colony* (1935). George E.

Lewis, *The Indiana Company, 1763–1798* (1941). More general are A. M. Sakolski, *The Great American Land Bubble* (1932); Shaw Livermore, *Early American Land Companies* (1939); *Everett Dick, *The Dixie Frontier* (1948).

Individuals and the Westward Movement Albert T. Volwiler, *George Croghan and the Westward Movement, 1742–1782* (1926), a classic biography; an alternate is Nicholas B. Wainwright, *George Croghan* (1959). Howard Peckham (ed.), *George Croghan's Journal of His Trip to Detroit in 1767* (1939). Less satisfactory is Thomas A. Boyd, *Simon Girty, the White Savage* (1928). Sewell E. Slick, *William Trent and the West* (1947), Pittsburgh area. John Bakeless, *Daniel Boone* (1939), well written; Carl S. Driver, *John Sevier: Pioneer of the Old West* (1932), pedantic; W. H. Masterson, *William Blount* (1954); Louis K. Koontz, *Robert Dinwiddie: His Career in American Colonial Government and Westward Expansion* (1941), colonial governor.

The Way West Two good accounts of well-used roads are Robert L. Kincaid, *The Wilderness Road* (1947) and Philip D. Jordan, *The National Road* (1948). *Solon J. and Elizabeth H. Buck, *The Planting of Civilization in Western Pennsylvania* (1939) and John E. Wright and Doris S. Corbett, *Pioneer Life in Western Pennsylvania* (1940) are very informative. Life in the trans-Appalachian West is well described in a number of works. See Temple Bodley, *Our First Great West* (1938); Louis K. Koontz, *The Virginia Frontier, 1754–1763* (1925); Thomas P. Abernethy, *From Frontier to Plantation in Tennessee* (1932); Charles H. Ambler, *West Virginia: The Mountain State* (1958); Thomas D. Clark, *A History of Kentucky* (1937); John R. Alden, *The South in the Revolution, 1763–1789* (1957).

Frontier Discontent E. Douglas Branch, *Westward* (1930); Richard M. Brown, *The South Carolina Regulators* (1963); Hugh T. Lefler and Albert R. Newcome, *North Carolina* (1954); Duane Meyer, *The Highland Scots of North Carolina, 1732–1776* (1961); Robert O. Demond, *The Loyalists in North Carolina During the Revolution* (1940), includes Regulator movement; Richard J. Hooker, *The Carolina Back Country on the Eve of the Revolution* (1953); Wilbur R. Jacobs (ed.), *The Paxton Riots and the Frontier Theory* (1967), good, brief; "How Quakers Misjudged the Indians," in Daniel J. Boorstin, *The Americans: The Colonial Experience* (1958).

Chapter 4 / THE REVOLUTIONARY WEST

The outbreak of the American Revolution found a relatively small group of colonists nestled along the western slopes of the Appalachians, practically cut off from the eastern settlements, threatened from the west by British-sponsored Indians, unsure of their political status, and, in a sense, forgotten people. The preoccupation of the new American government with the desperate military situation it faced made it unlikely that any substantial aid could be sent to more remote regions. The frontiersmen had a choice between falling back upon settled areas or making a stand in the new country; most of them chose the latter. The decision meant that for seven years they lived in constant apprehension of attack. Eastern burghers experienced a civilized kind of warfare with formal battles, the taking of prisoners, the occupation of cities; but for those along the fringes of settlement it was a savage conflict in which men, women, and children died at the hands of raiding Indians, a struggle in which no quarter was given and none was expected.

COLONIES AT TIME OF REVOLUTION The American Revolution was a dramatic indication of the rapidly increasing gap between European and American conditions and points of view. Americans had been conditioned by a century and a half of contact with an untamed wilderness. They had begun to realize their own potentialities—that they could provide their own economic, social, and religious necessities for which they had depended upon Europe for so many years. The Revolution was an indication of a definite cleavage already in existence between the Old and the New World.

Self-confidence and youthful enthusiasm did not necessarily imply strength: when viewed realistically, the English colonies at the time of the Revolution were far from being an awe-inspiring factor in the affairs of the world. Thirteen small colonies straggling along the Atlantic seaboard had a population of only some 2,600,000 persons; Virginia was the most populous, and after Virginia followed, in order, Massachusetts, Pennsylvania, North Carolina, and Maryland. Philadelphia was the largest colonial city, its competitors being Boston, Newport, New York, and Charleston. Today, cities of the size these were then would not be regarded as large. Every important city was either on the seaboard or on some large river that afforded good communication with the sea.

Outside the larger towns, population tended to concentrate along the rivers so that produce could be shipped to market more easily. The inland limit of civilization was in general the Appalachians, but few people had gone even that far west. To the north and south, settlement became more sparse and finally gave way to the wilderness. In the North, a small fraction of Maine was settled; central and northern New Hampshire and Vermont were just being opened; in New York, adventurous German immigrants were pushing out along the Mohawk. In the South, Georgia was still largely unpopulated.

Agriculture was the predominant pursuit. Everywhere there were small farms, but south of the Potomac were also large plantations using slave labor to grow tobacco, indigo, and rice. Slavery, however, seemed to be an uneconomic and declining institu-

---

Indians Attacking a Cumberland Valley Settlement, Late 1700s. The palisaded fort, developed early, was employed throughout most of the American frontier experience. The frequency of Indian attacks was less than is generally supposed. (Granger)

tion, and many of the farseeing planters looked forward to the day when slavery would cease to exist. North of the Potomac small farms were almost universal, with the owner, his wife, and his children doing most of the work, and now and then a hired laborer to help with planting and harvesting.

Manufacturing remained largely in the home, since the mother country discouraged any competition with its own new and struggling industries. Here and there iron forges, hat factories, and other small enterprises gave a faint promise of future industrialization.

Shipping was an item of major interest to the northern colonies. The Yankee shipper was a well-known figure on the seas. His business was expanding rapidly, and he was soon to talk of Canton, Singapore, Oregon, the Sandwich Islands (Hawaii), and other far places of the world. South of New England the ports did most of their business in foreign bottoms. The plantation owner tended to deal directly with his European connections, thereby eliminating American middlemen.

Intercolonial business by land was small and unimportant. The first good improved road was not built until after the Revolution. For the most part people depended on the rivers as their best means of communication, most of which flowed from west to east, with the result that trade between the colonies never assumed large proportions. So miserable were the roads that as late as 1803 John Quincy Adams needed twenty days to ride his horse to Washington from his home at Quincy.

Although the population of the American seaboard area was predominantly English in the seventeenth century, the heavy influx of other racial stocks that flooded in during the early part of the next century effected a radical change in the composition of colonial society. In the years that followed the Peace of Utrecht (1713) the flow of German immigrants increased until, by mid-century, their arrivals were numbered in thousands. Likewise, the Scotch-Irish arrived in ever-increasing waves until, by the Revolution, more than a quarter million of them were to be found in the backcountry of Pennsylvania and the colonies to the south. Meantime, the landed Dutch aristocracy strengthened its foothold in the Hudson and Mohawk River valleys, Swedes were in evidence along the Delaware River, and a scattering of French Huguenots lived along the Atlantic coast. Despite what might be regarded as dilution, from the English point of view, the language, laws, customs and heritage remained largely English.

REDSKINS AND REDCOATS   In 1775 the transmontane West was a very thinly populated area. Its largest town, Pittsburgh, was no more than a collection of some thirty log houses, and Wheeling could barely call itself a village. Scattered along streams and rivers were widely separated homes whose connection with the western villages was very slight. A majority of the settlers had little interest in British imperial problems, except, of course, for such things as the Proclamation of 1763, which touched them directly. Commercial restrictions that brought forth loud complaints from seaboard merchants provoked little talk among westerners. In all probability they were quietly amused at outcries of easterners who objected to what they called "taxation without representation." The backcountry people had for years submitted to a political imbalance in colonial legislative houses, and complaints about inequitable taxation were nothing new to them. The main thing the Revolutionary movement meant to these people along the outskirts of colonial settlement was that the Indians would play a prominent part in the coming hostilities and would be allied with the British, who could pay more for their friendship. Frontiersmen also knew that their traditional independence of eastern colonials would be costly and that they could expect little help from that source.

When the American colonists announced their decision to fight, at Lexington and Concord, reverberations were heard in more remote parts of the land. Among other things, the British now had to reverse their old Indian policy and convince the natives that they should fight the colonists. Sir William Johnson had spent a good many patient years weaning away from the French the northern tribes and persuading them to live at peace with the English frontiersmen. John Stuart, working among the southern Indians, had performed a similar task. Now these men, and their associates, had to convince the Indians that they should do the opposite, a shift in policy many of the unsophisticated savages had difficulty in understanding. The Creeks, for example, who had been friendly to the settlers, were mystified by this sudden shift in the attitude of the British administrators.

As word spread across the frontier the tribes made their decisions. In 1776, when the Cherokee informed Stuart that they would stay with the British, that agent at once warned such settlements as Watauga of the consequences they invited by deserting the mother country. The response was not long in coming: the settlers strengthened their fortifications and asked Virginia for help. In June and July the blows began to fall: raiding parties struck at scattered settlements, including Watauga, where James Robertson and John Sevier headed a small corps of riflemen that drove off the invaders. Stuart, acting under orders from Lord George Germain, had sent his Indian allies against the colonials at a time when a frontal attack was to be made on Charleston. Not only did the sea invasion fail, when Admiral Peter Parker's forces were repulsed, but so did the diversionary attacks staged by the Indians. The result was so favorable to the colonials that both South Carolina and Georgia were in a position to lend help to the western settlers.

General Charles Lee, in command of American forces at Charleston, invited Virginians to join in an expedition against the Indians. Moved by encouragement from the Continental Congress, and by an enthusiastic response from Thomas Jefferson (who wanted to drive the Indians beyond the Mississippi River), a force of some 2000 colonials was raised in the latter part of 1776. The force, under the command of Colonel William Christian, marched to the Holston River, scattered the Cherokee, and burned the Indian villages and the harvested crops. Not a soldier was lost during the operation. Simultaneously another force, from North Carolina, attacked some of the Cherokee villages, and after suffering a few losses burned more dwellings and crops. The campaign was costly to the Indians, not only in the seriousness of the attacks, but because in 1777 they were obliged to cede additional lands to Georgia, South Carolina, North Carolina, and Virginia. The Cherokee holdings were generally rolled back, some Indians withdrawing as much as a hundred miles.

THE REVOLUTION IN THE NORTHWEST

While the Americans punished the Indians on the southern frontier, the British went ahead with their plans to enlist the aid of the natives in the Northwest. This theater of war was one of vast distances and widely separated objects of attack. Except for a few settlements around Pittsburgh, there were few English colonists in the region. From the viewpoint of overall strategy there seemed to be little profit in sending British troops, so hard to

THE WEST
IN THE AMERICAN REVOLUTION

□ British outposts
■ American outposts
△ Spanish outposts

provide, across hundreds of barren miles to attack a few scattered white settlements. On the other hand, it was desirable to harass the western fringe of the colonies to force the withdrawal of some colonial troops from the more important operations in the East, or at least to prevent the westerners from joining the eastern forces.

An effective weapon for the attack on the outlying settlements was available for immediate use—the Indians. Since many of the tribesmen bitterly resented white encroachments, there was little need of urging by their British sponsors for them to harry white squatters. Major Henry Hamilton, lieutenant governor of New France, directed operations from his headquarters at Detroit. In long councils with the natives, in which lavish gifts were forthcoming, the "Hair Buyer" urged his allies to strike at any and all outlying settlements. He emphasized the psychological value of terror tactics to frighten off the settlers. One British official objected to the slaughter of innocent families by warriors who were reluctant to face armed opponents; but Hamilton persisted, arguing that only these methods would succeed among the tough-minded American frontiersmen. In the warfare that ensued, the westerners struck back with equal viciousness, scalping and torturing in the Indian fashion, until the war took on a degree of barbarity rarely witnessed in the New World.

Although the American defense against these raids was bitterly executed, in general it was not very well organized. The states most subject to attack—particularly Pennsylvania, Virginia, North Carolina, and Georgia—made some provision for their own defense, but were usually glad to let the settlers themselves or the central government assume the main burden. The settlers were few and poor, so that providing men and materials for extensive operations proved an almost insurmountable task. The Continental Congress was more than busy in the East and could be persuaded to furnish troops and supplies only when the danger was extremely pressing.

By a law of 1775 three Indian departments were created by the Congress. Commissioners from each of them undertook to win over the Indians with gifts and formal treaties, but they were not very successful. An example of the difficulties faced by these men was the murder of a friendly chief named Cornstalk and three of his warriors by some Pennsylvania frontiersmen in the autumn of 1777. The chief's Shawnee followers immediately took to the warpath and engaged in a number of bloody raids on settlements in Kentucky and western Virginia.

The "year of the three sevens," as it has been called, is remembered as the bloodiest and gloomiest of the war in the West. Hostile Indians, particularly the Shawnee and other Ohio tribes, drove back or killed settlers, and even attacked such fortified communities as Boonesborough. The situation was so obviously serious that Congress sent Brigadier General Edward Hand to strengthen Fort Pitt, lest this key position fall to the British and Indians. The reinforcements were so weak and their supply problems so great that the Indians were only emboldened by the move. During the following year the fact that Washington sent some of his badly needed troops, under General Lachlan McIntosh, from Valley Forge indicates something of the vital urgency of the danger. Both Hand and McIntosh led expeditions against the Indians, but neither accomplished more than irritating the tribes.

THE AGGRESSIVE GEORGE ROGERS CLARK   Out of this desperate situation came one of the outstanding exploits of the war—the expedition of George Rogers Clark to the Illinois country. It was his conviction that the only effective way to protect the scattered settlements from Indian raids was to undertake offensive operations. He realized that security could be obtained only by convincing the Indians of American superiority, and he felt that the English posts, particularly the one at Detroit, should be captured if peace were to come to the frontier. Conditions were at their worst in Kentucky in 1777—even Boonesborough was attacked twice—but Clark sent scouts to investigate British western military strength in the Illinois country. In two months they returned with word that the outposts were virtually unprotected, particularly Kaskaskia, near the junction of the Kaskaskia and Mississippi rivers.

Obviously the West itself could not furnish the men, supplies, and munitions necessary for an extensive expedition into enemy country; hence late in 1777 Clark again made the long trip back to Virginia to request assistance. Immediately upon his arrival he called upon Governor Patrick Henry and outlined his ambitious plans for the conquest of the Northwest. Governor Henry was reluctant, as well he might be, in view of the situation in the East; on the other hand, such a conquest, if successful, would be of advantage in the prosecution of the war in the East, would greatly enhance Virginia's prestige, and might reinforce its claims to western lands. Clark was given two sets of orders. The first, which contained the ostensible reason for his activities, authorized him to raise seven companies (350 men) for the defense of Kentucky, and to purchase arms, ammunition, and supplies on the credit of the state of Virginia. The second set of orders, which was to remain secret, empowered Clark to undertake offensive operations and to capture "Kaskasky."

Armed with these instructions, Clark made his way to Pittsburgh, the logical gathering place for any expedition planning to descend the Ohio River, where he gathered men and supplies for the campaign. Finding it impossible to recruit the desired 350 men, he set off with only 175. The group was heterogeneous: the men dressed as they pleased, carried a wide assortment of arms, and were unwilling to obey any command they thought unreasonable. Some were frankly homeseekers accompanied by their families in order to take up desirable land at the first favorable opportunity.

The first part of Clark's plan was to descend the Ohio as far as the mouth of the Kentucky and there disembark and drill his men. The topography of the land led him to change his mind and to camp instead at the falls of the Ohio. Here some of the homeseekers built houses and began farming, thus founding the first white settlement at present-day Louisville. Here also Clark divulged his larger plans to his followers. At first there was much grumbling and dissent; but eventually objections were silenced and the expedition was ready to begin its real work.

KASKASKIA AND VINCENNES   On June 24, 1778, the little army shot the rapids at Louisville and started to float down the Ohio River. Nine miles below the mouth of the Tennessee the party left its boats and started overland. After a rigorous march the group arrived at Kaskaskia on July 4. Sufficient speed and secrecy had been maintained, so that the invasion was a complete surprise; Clark and his men met no resistance on entering the town. The residents, largely French, were so thoroughly imbued with the notion that all Americans were barbarians that they prostrated themselves on the ground, convinced that the end was near. Clark, who was anxious to have their friendship, explained his mission and told his listeners about the Franco-American alliance. Their emotions changed instantly from terror to unrestrained joy and the conquered at once prepared a party for the Americans, decking the streets with flowers and swearing oaths of loyalty to the United States as fast as their sentiments could be recorded.

As Clark established himself at Kaskaskia, Captain Joseph Bowman took over nearby smaller settlements. Cahokia fell without a murmur. Bowman simply rode up to the commanding officer's house and demanded the town's surrender, a request that the surprised officer granted at once. Clark, meanwhile, spread the idea of American military strength in the West by circulating a rumor that the force in Illinois was only a small part of a large army, which even then was encamped at the falls of the Ohio.

Meanwhile, Governor Hamilton at Detroit had begun to hear disturbing reports about American activity in the West. What had been a leisurely plan to attack Pittsburgh was now abandoned in favor of one that would turn back the invading Clark. His new plans were to establish himself at Vincennes, from which point he could recapture the Illinois settlements. After hurried preparations he left Detroit on October 7, 1778, with a small force of soldiers and Indian auxiliaries. His army was augmented on the way, mostly by Indians, so that by the time he arrived at Vincennes he had over 500 men. Here he established himself for the winter, erecting fortifications, drilling his men, planning to move in the spring when the weather permitted. It seemed both to Hamilton and to his staff that there was no danger of an attack from Clark at a time when cold weather and flooded rivers made the drainage basin of the Wabash a veritable swamp.

Clark was placed in an exceedingly awkward position by Hamilton's expedition. He was several hundred miles from home and could hope for no reinforcements. His men were on short-term enlistments that would soon expire. The Indians were not friendly, and the French had little genuine interest in the success of their new master. If Clark stayed at Kaskaskia until spring it seemed evident that Hamilton, aided by the Indians, could defeat him and would then have no difficulty in conquering Kentucky at his leisure. And so Clark again decided to move forward; the march on Vincennes was to begin at once. The main body of 170 men was reenlisted and left Kaskaskia on February 5, 1779, for the march across the wilderness. Much of the country traversed was flooded, and for days at a time everyone was soaking wet. For hours they waded through swamps and creeks, with the water at times to their shoulders, so that the shorter drummer boy had to float on his drum. Food was scarce and many times a tightening of belts took the place of a meal. When fires were impossible because of the wetness of the wood, everyone had to sleep in his wet clothes. As they neared Vincennes conditions became worse. The country was practically one large lake, and both fires and shooting for game were out of the question because of the danger of making their presence known. All this, too, in the depths of winter, when cold weather intensified all of the other discomforts.

The approach to Vincennes raised new problems. It seemed somewhat doubtful if a small, wet, hungry, poorly armed band of Americans could capture a fortified post garrisoned by upward of 600 fighting men. Again Clark proved himself equal to the emergency. His first effort was to impress the French villagers to keep them neutral. A letter was sent to them offering peace and good treatment if they refrained from participating in the hostilities, but promising severe treatment otherwise. Then Clark marched and countermarched his men as fast as possible to give an impression of a large force. The result was that the French remained neutral.

Upon gaining entrance to the town the Americans at once threatened the fort within it. Clark's ammunition was insufficient for a protracted siege, but, as luck would have it, Hamilton was so impressed by the supposed size of the attacking force that he immediately asked for a truce. Clark audaciously refused the request and insisted upon unconditional surrender. On February 25, 1779, the Americans took complete possession of Vincennes, agreeing to some conditions. The French volunteers in Hamilton's army were permitted to return to Detroit, but Hamilton and some of his officers were sent to Virginia for imprisonment.

Clark's capture of Vincennes was not without its bloody side. Even as he and Hamilton negotiated the terms of surrender, a Frenchman hired by the British marched into town with his Indian followers, unaware of recent developments. Having just returned from raiding the frontier, they brought with them two prisoners and a number of fresh scalps. Their hopes for a hearty welcome vanished when it was revealed that the Americans now commanded Vincennes. To teach a lesson to the neighbor Indians, and to any of the French onlookers whose new-found American loyalties might waver, Clark lined up the Indians of the raiding party and had them tomahawked in full view of the garrison.

The American soldiers were well paid for their recent privations. The goods that Hamilton had so recently brought down from Detroit proved to be a rich haul. Still better, another consignment of goods came in a few days after the fall of Vincennes, word of the event not yet having reached Detroit. Forty more prisoners were taken along with seven boatloads of goods valued at about $50,000.

With the capture of Vincennes, Clark apparently was in a secure position. The Northwest had been subdued, and Detroit, the center of British influence, lay open to easy conquest. Yet the way was not as clear as it seemed. Clark's men had no stomach for further hardships, and as fast as their enlistments were completed they went home. Despite the small fortunes in booty that the men had acquired, war supplies and ammunition were insufficient for a major campaign. Clark had no choice but to settle down at Vincennes and wait until spring brought him new men and supplies. When the expected reinforcements did not appear, Clark made a trip to Kaskaskia to seek help. By July some 350 men had gathered at Vincennes, but the lack of stores and provisions continued to plague the Americans, making the proposed attack on Detroit too hazardous to risk. Eventually all plans for offensive operations were given up for the year, and Clark moved his headquarters to the falls of the Ohio.

The whole western campaign was characterized by audacity on the part of the Americans, who relied on the element of surprise, and by administrative ineptitude on the part of the British, who supplied their outposts with forces and supplies that barely missed being adequate. There were no major battles, and no territory of immediate consequence changed hands. It is impossible to measure the morale value or the extent to which the expedition warded off Indian and British pressures on the northwestern frontier. Another imponderable is the weight the American campaign might have lent to territorial considerations at the peace table in 1783. It can be said, however, that Clark saw an opportunity to strike at a weakly defended region, and did so, with courage and perseverance that must have thrilled a war-weary American public east of the Appalachians.

KING'S MOUNTAIN   By 1780 the British evolved plans of their own for the reconquest of the West. During that year both Charleston and Augusta fell, adding to a list of British-held southern cities that already included Savannah. With the view of making a complete conquest of the southern colonies, London strategists now hoped to

Battle at King's Mountain. This scene of preparation or departure shows the informality of western warfare during the American Revolution. Long rifles and buckskin seem to have been the order of the day. (Tennessee State Museum)

capitalize on what they believed to be a western loyalty to the crown. Since the back-country Scots, in particular, had shown little cooperation with the Revolutionary movement, it was mistakenly supposed that they would welcome the Redcoats. Major Patrick Ferguson, known as the best shot in the British army and a man highly regarded by his fellow Scots, was given the new western assignment.

As word spread along the mountain range, the Americans began to gather in preparation for the next move. Colonel William Campbell, a Virginia westerner, joined with the followers of John Sevier, Isaac Shelby, Benjamin Cleveland, and other local leaders to gather an army of frontiersmen who fought as informally as they lived. By common consent, Campbell took command of the group of some 1500 volunteers and marched against Ferguson, who had around 1100 men. Ferguson, with the inferior force, picked his way along the eastern base of the mountains in search of a site that would offer both a satisfactory defensive terrain and one within reach of reinforcements by Lord Cornwallis. He decided upon a wooded area on the southern edge of King's Mountain, just south of the boundary separating North Carolina from South Carolina.

On October 7, in a driving rain, approximately a thousand horsemen from the American group reached the site that Ferguson had chosen to do battle. As the forces readied themselves for the ensuing engagement the sun came out, creating a steamy atmosphere that shrouded the ground and provided a cover for the attackers. In a battle that lasted less than an hour the Americans gave way to bayonet attacks only to spring back, in frontier fighting style, sniping from behind wooded cover, and won their fight. As British men and officers fell, one of Ferguson's subordinates urged him to surrender. "To those damned banditti? Never!" was the resolute answer. Leading his men in one last charge, the leader went down, riddled with bullets. White flags now emerged, but the confused fighting could not be halted at once and a great many more casualties occurred.

The surrender lacked the usual formalities of organized warfare. Ferguson's body was stripped of its uniform and thrown into a ditch while the victors divided his personal belongings. Although a number of the wounded British troops were left to die on the field of battle, the remainder were marched off for further punishment. By the light of pine-knot torches there commenced the systematic program of hanging 38 prisoners summarily adjudged guilty of recent atrocities. After 9 of them were executed the westerners decided to call off the proceedings, and 29 were granted reprieves. In the fray the British had lost 225 killed, the Americans 28; the rest of the British force, including a large number of wounded, became prisoners of war.

King's Mountain did not mean that the war was over, but it had several lessons for the Americans. In a battle where no Indians were involved on either side, westerners met a British armed force and defeated it completely. The backcountry, lacking any formal military organization, had gathered men for its own defense and had demonstrated a regional unity that the coastal region lacked. Coupled with Clark's successful campaign in the Northwest, this southern success was enormously heartening, not only to westerners, but to the rest of the young nation. It was, as General Washington put it, "proof of the spirit and resources of the country." As is true of Clark's expedition, there has been some tendency to exaggerate the importance of King's Mountain, but most authorities agree that its contributions, somewhat difficult to assess, were directly related to the general movement that now began against Cornwallis and ended with his defeat at Yorktown.

LAST YEARS OF THE REVOLUTION Individual American victories in the West did not mean the end of British pressure in that region. Sharply stung by their reverses, the king's troopers resolved to renew their attacks upon the Northwest and to drive out the intruder Clark. Plans were also made for attacks on New Orleans and the lower Mississippi Valley now that Spain had elected to join France in its American alliance. So thorough were preparations that General Frederick Haldimand, governor general of Canada, registered an objection. When the officials at Detroit handed out Indian gifts amounting to more than £84,000, he called the sum "amazing." He was answered with the argument that the pressure of American settlers upon the West was great and that only terror tactics would repel that kind of invasion. It was a simple economic fact that the scalps brought in cost money, and the crop was large. As the Delaware and Shawnee employees of the British continued their work among the American settlers, there were loud outcries from the frontier for assistance. Clark, to whom appeals were made, had only a small force and did not want to disperse it to protect scattered settlements. He feared that he might end by giving up the entire Mississippi Valley to the enemy.

The latest British plan called for General Patrick Sinclair to start from Michilimackinac, to capture the Illinois towns of Kaskaskia and Cahokia, and then to take St. Louis. Three smaller forces were to keep Clark engaged and to punish the Indians: the first was to advance from Detroit toward Vincennes, the second was to watch the plains between the Wabash and the Mississippi, and the third was to move down the Illinois River and chastise the Sauk and Fox Indians. All these plans eventually failed. The British commander in the South never felt he had a sufficient force to move north, and finally was forced to surrender Pensacola to Bernardo de Gálvez, the Spanish commander. The Illinois River expedition burned a few Indian towns and then returned. The Detroit expedition heard rumors of a superior American force and so retreated, leaving Clark free to go westward and defeat Sinclair near St. Louis. In 1781 Spain undertook a retaliatory expedition against England, and succeeded in advancing as far as the present Niles, Michigan.

After the defeat of Sinclair there again seemed to be an excellent opportunity for the conquest of Detroit, and so Clark hurried to Virginia to obtain support for his plans. He found little difficulty in getting encouragement; but unfortunately such aid was almost entirely verbal, and words would not pay troops or feed hungry men. Clark organized a new expedition at Pittsburgh, but when the commander of one division of the little force was defeated overwhelmingly by Indians under Joseph Brant, the entire plan had to be abandoned.

Fortunately for the American cause, British campaigns in the West were never particularly successful. During 1781 and 1782 the West hung in the balance; neither side was prepared to put a military force of any size into the area, rationalizing that the outcome in the eastern theater of war would probably govern the fate of the West anyway. The frontier war continued as a fluid campaign in which the Indians played a prominent part. In June 1782 an expedition under Colonel William Crawford fought a sharp engagement at Sandusky in which the colonel and some of his men were made captive. Crawford was burned at the stake. About the same time a body of 300 militiamen captured a group of 90 friendly Delaware Indians who made no effort to escape, and were methodically executed—men, women, and children. It was a vicious, merciless kind of warfare in which the torture of prisoners was the general rule and simple death the exception. George Rogers Clark, goaded by constant appeals for help, struck into the Ohio country several times in an effort to relieve the pressure on Kentucky, but as long as the British were paying their Indian allies there could be no cessation of constant isolated attacks upon the frontier. By the end of the war it had become a western way of life.

TREATY OF PEACE   At the conclusion of active fighting the statesmen of the East had the task of confirming the conquests that Clark had made in the West. The commissioners were instructed to make peace only with the concurrence of our principal ally, France, but they soon discovered that this procedure contained an almost fatal error. France was not primarily interested in the United States; instead, it supported Spain, and Spain was opposed to American expansion. As Vergennes, the French foreign minister, admitted: "We have no interest whatever to see America play the part of a power." France and Spain agreed on a plan: Spain would take the Floridas, the Indians would be guaranteed the country between the Appalachians and the Mississippi south of the Ohio under the joint protection of Spain and the United States, and Britain would retain the country north of the Ohio or—better—divide it with the United States.

When the American commissioners heard of these plans of France and Spain, they cast their instructions to the winds and independently formulated a treaty with Great Britain. They were favored in this procedure by the British attitude, which preferred American to Spanish expansion. The provisions of the Treaty of Paris as they related to the West were as favorable as the United States had any reason to expect. The entire region south of the Great Lakes went to the United States. The northwestern boundary was to run from Lake Superior to the Lake of the Woods and then directly west to the Mississippi (actually such a line was impossible to run, because a line directly west from the Lake of the Woods would not touch the Mississippi). From this point the boundary was to follow the Mississippi south to 31° north latitude and then along the 31st parallel and the present northern boundary of Florida to the Atlantic coast. A secret agreement provided that if Britain retained West Florida, its northern boundary would be the parallel of the mouth of the Yazoo River (32°28'). These terms were eminently satisfactory to the United States except for the slowness with which Great Britain evacuated the Great Lakes posts that were within the limits of the United States.

AFTERMATH   But what happened to George Rogers Clark, the chief actor of the drama, and the one man to whom the conquest of the Northwest was due? His principal reward was the gift of some 6000 acres of land in the wilderness of southern Indiana. In addition to the land, he received a letter of thanks from the governor of Virginia, and an ornamental sword. These gifts of a grateful commonwealth had been won by Clark at the cost of the best years of his life, and the undermining of his health by the privations he had experienced. Both he and his friends were weighted with debts contracted during the Revolution, when they had dug into their own pockets to make up the gap between the appropriations of Virginia and the cost of carrying on the war.

When Virginia removed Clark from his command in 1783, the sad spectacle of a

Clark's March on Vincennes, 1779. Privation, hostile terrain, and a paucity of numbers characterized the attack.

hero without a job led Jefferson to make the suggestion that Congress commission the conqueror to explore the Far West. Congress failed to act (it was Clark's younger brother William who would explore the West), but a renewal of Indian warfare again called the campaigner into the field during the middle 1780s. After his return from fighting the red men, he was drawn into intrigues with the government of Spain, during which he received some funds from the Spanish commander at New Orleans (1787). A little later he was involved in an effort to free Louisiana from Spanish control, but the expedition never materialized. The remainder of his life was a losing struggle to develop his Indiana land, and he died in 1818, poor and discouraged.

The close of the Revolution found an ever-increasing number of settlers pouring into the West, and with the larger population the problem of government immediately became more difficult. The simple local government that had sufficed in an earlier day would not meet the needs of a larger and more intricate social group. Even the county governments established by Virginia and North Carolina did little to alleviate the confusion. Such governments were far from their seaboard sources of power, and they lacked authority to solve the very definite and pressing needs of the West.

Peace and order had to be produced from the chaotic conditions created by recent political changes. Marriages, deeds, and wills had to be made legal and to be made uniform. Land titles had to be more easily obtainable and more exact, for land had been sold in the East upon the vaguest kind of identification, and consequently many of the claims overlapped. Some provision had to be made for the families that came west without land claims. Squabbles among land companies, deferred only by the war, needed solution.

Furthermore, the Indian problem that once had perplexed British statesmen was now handed to a new and inexperienced American government whose leaders had no ready answers. For the want of a better solution, Patrick Henry suggested an amalgamation of the two races and recommended a cash bounty for half-breed children. Defense against the Indians remained a problem, for they continued to attack outlying groups and individuals from time to time. The joint action of all the settlers in the region menaced was not a good substitute for effective action by an active government. In warfare against the Indians the best form of defense was always offense, and unorganized settlers found sustained offensive operations difficult. Another menace that required unified action was the possibility of a Spanish advance up the Mississippi Valley.

NOTION OF AN AMERICAN EMPIRE While a more popular conception of war aims during the American Revolution bespoke of independence and freedom from tyrannical rule, the notion that the leaders had in mind the erection of an American empire was not entirely obscured in the turmoil of events. Since the land beyond the Mississippi appeared to be the most available for inclusion in the plan, it was to this vast and undeveloped region that the planners of empire looked for material with which to fulfill their dreams.

Westward expansion was not only inherent in the thinking of the times, but it had been so for decades. The old savant, Benjamin Franklin, had talked of it for nearly forty years. Now, during these early postwar years, as the new nation set its course for the future, the prospect became even more exciting, for the possibility of its realization appeared to be much more real. George Washington, the war hero, foresaw a rising empire emerging from the successful struggle for independence and before long he would comment upon his membership in it. In 1789, the year the federal government was created, Bostonian Jedidiah Morse published his *American Geography*. Although he praised the productivity of eastern lands, as compared to those farther west, he could not help but dream a little as to the nation's potential. Casting an eye westward he predicted that in the foreseeable future the American realm would "comprehend millions of souls." Even Gouverneur Morris, one of the fathers of the Constitution and a man who advocated supremacy for the Atlantic seaboard states in the new government, had to admit that the dream of American empire lay westward. In 1801 he remarked: "As yet we can only crawl along the outer shell of our country. The interior excells the part we inhabit in soil, in climate, in everything. The proudest empire in Europe is but a bauble compared to what America will be, must be, in the course of two centuries, perhaps of one."

As learned men viewed the geographical gains of the Revolution and speculated over the potential of the land beyond the Appalachians, small farmers took up the advance that they, the outriders of empire, would continue until the shores of the Pacific Ocean came into view.

READINGS   *Paperbacks are marked with an asterisk.*

General   Jackson Turner Main. "English Colonial Society in the Eighteenth Century," in John J. Tepaske, *Three American Empires* (1967) contains some interesting passages dealing with pioneer society of the Revolutionary period. Allan W. Eckert, *The Frontiersman* (1967), semifiction, but interesting and factually based.

Northwest   Regional and state studies of the West in the Revolutionary period include Charles H. Ambler, *West Virginia: The Mountain State* (1958); Beverley W. Bond, Jr., *The Foundations of Ohio* (1941) and *The Civilization of the Old Northwest* (1934); E. H. Roseboom and F. P. Weisenburger, *A History of Ohio* (1953), brief and factual; Theodore C. Pease, *The Story of Illinois* (rev., 1949); *Solon J. and Elizabeth H. Buck, *The Planting of Civilization in Western Pennsylvania* (1939); John E. Wright and Doris S. Corbett, *Pioneer Life in Western Pennsylvania* (1940); Logan Esarey, *A History of Indiana* (3 vols., 1923). Walter Havighurst, *Land of Promise* (1946) reads well. A fine regional study is Louise P. Kellogg, *The British Regime in Wisconsin and the Northwest* (1935).

Western Warfare   *Jack M. Sosin, *The Revolutionary Frontier, 1763–1783* (1967). Natalie M. Belting, *Kaskaskia Under the French Regime* (1948) considers a pivotal point in the Clark strategy. Milo M. Quaife (ed.), *The Capture of Old*

Vincennes (1927). J. F. McDermott, et al. (eds.), *Old Cahokia* (1949). Leland D. Baldwin, *Pittsburgh: The Story of a City* (1937) contains pertinent chapters, as does the excellent *Randolph C. Downes, *Council Fires on the Upper Ohio* (1940). Dale Van Every, *A Company of Heroes: The American Frontier, 1775–1783* (1962).

Personalities   Among the better biographies of Clark are John E. Bakeless, *Background to Glory: The Life of George Rogers Clark* (1957); James A. James, *The Life of George Rogers Clark* (1928); Theodore C. and Marguerite J. Pease, *George Rogers Clark and the Revolution in Illinois, 1763–1787* (1929); F. Palmer, *Clark of the Ohio* (1929). John A. Caruso, *The Great Lakes Frontier* (1961) treats Clark. John D. Barnhart, *Henry Hamilton and George Rogers Clark in the American Revolution* (1951) includes Hamilton's journal.

Ceremonies Marking the Transfer of Louisiana to the United States. (Louisiana Historical Society, courtesy Louisiana State Museum)

Chapter 5 / THE WEST ACQUIRES PATRIOTISM

Westerners of the late eighteenth century did not possess the kind of patriotism that within a few years led Stephen Decatur to vow allegiance to "my country right or wrong." They were risking their lives to advance their personal fortunes, and not to promote the power of a young and relatively unknown central government Government to them was meant to serve the interests of the individual, and not to be a supreme end in itself.

As westerners considered their situation they found little about which to be grateful to any eastern government. Problems were numerous and difficult, with seaboard aid small or nonexistent. Land titles were chaotic, the Indians were dangerous, and transportation was practically impossible. Not only were the refinements of life unprovided, but even the necessities were frequently lacking. The eastern states that exercised control did little more than create county organizations from time to time. The federal government under the Articles of Confederation was too weak to be effective. Theoretically it controlled the Indians, but in actuality such control was negligible. Land disposition was completely unsatisfactory, as the states were dilatory in transferring their claims to Congress. The only effective action of the central government was in providing government, and even this was long delayed. Little wonder the West felt it must assume responsibility for its own improvement.

IMPORTANCE OF SPAIN The West could survive and prosper only if it succeeded economically, and economic progress depended on the Ohio-Mississippi River system. Since connections between the West and the Atlantic seaboard were tenuous, with travel slow and expensive, the main western trade outlet was the Mississippi, on which one could float in relative comfort to New Orleans, where he could transship his raw materials to foreign markets. In consequence, the control of the Mississippi, and particularly its mouth, was vital to the West, and at times seemed more important than any possible connections with the East.

The end of the Revolution found Spain in control not only of the vital mouth of the Mississippi but also of the entire border area to the south and west—East Florida, which was present Florida extending as far west as St. Marks on the Gulf; West Florida, roughly from St. Marks to Baton Rouge on the Mississippi, but with the northern boundary in dispute; Louisiana, including not only the present state of that name, but also a vast domain from the Mississippi to the Rockies. Of greatest immediate importance to the West was the Gulf Coast with its control of the outlets of various rivers, particularly the Mississippi.

Spain worried the West during the 1780s because it showed no enthusiasm for the United States. In 1784 Spain tried to weaken the American West by closing the Mississippi to all but Spanish traffic. Spain's negotiations with the southwestern Indians brought some success with the Creeks, who were hostile to the United States. New frontier posts brought Spanish garrisons to the Yazoo River (present-day Vicksburg) in 1791 and Chickasaw Bluffs (near present-day Memphis) in 1795. Farther north was St. Louis, which helped to encircle western settlements. These developments, and particularly the closing of the Mississippi, seemed ominous to all westerners.

The Spanish show of vigor tended to obscure the essential weakness of their position. The Floridas and Louisiana were only the extreme outposts of a vast empire; and although Spain desired to halt Anglo-American advance, it had neither men nor money for an effective job. West Florida and Louisiana were under a single governor, who was an army officer; these areas contained almost all the white population, with four-fifths in the towns from Mobile to New Orleans. The governor of Louisiana in 1780 commanded less than 1400 effective troops, of whom about half were at New Orleans and St. Louis; New Orleans was the only fortified southern post. The governor of East Florida was stationed at St. Augustine, and his realm included few white settlers and fewer troops. Both governors were starved financially, and reinforcements had to be brought from Cuba or Mexico.

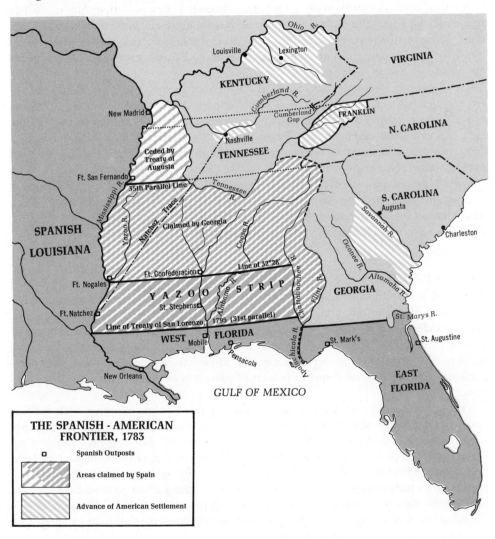

SPANISH POLICY   To secure Spain's possessions against aggressive Americans the obvious Spanish policy was to strengthen its military position, to close the river against American trade, and to exclude American settlers. The most immediate drawback of this policy was that closing the river hurt New Orleans as much or more than it did the Americans. Louisiana produced primarily tobacco, indigo, furs, and lumber for export; these products had limited markets and hence New Orleans prosperity depended on American trade. In consequence, there was strong local pressure to reopen the river, which was done in 1788; American goods for export could be sold in New Orleans with a 15 percent tax, which was later reduced.

Another great difficulty with a restrictive Spanish policy was that Americans had already trickled into the Gulf region in considerable numbers and might revolt if irritated. Moreover, the American settlers of Kentucky and Tennessee vastly outnumbered the Spanish to the south, and there were insufficient Spanish troops to resist a determined advance from the north.

These and other complexities caused Spanish policy to fluctuate. Part of the time the river was closed, and American settlers were excluded. More usually the river was open, and American settlers were encouraged—provided they swore loyalty to the Spanish king and embraced Catholicism. The policy was a sad mistake, just as later it was in Texas. Americans tended to prefer connections with the home folks over loyalty to a remote Catholic king.

Spanish policy, no matter how wisely or foolishly conceived, was badly damaged in its administration. Spanish officials were notoriously corrupt, with the bribe a recognized institution. The closing of the Mississippi never really stopped trade because enforcement officers frequently winked at violations—for a consideration.

THE STATE OF FRANKLIN   Westerners confronted by a menacing Spain and hostile Indians, and with little prospective help from eastern governments, which seemed either uninterested or impotent, fell back on their own resources. Many favored independence, and then perhaps an alliance, or even union, with Spain. The idea of independence appealed to Spanish governors, who were glad to help potential seceders. The stage was thus set for a plethora of plots by westerners who saw in independence an advantage in terms of power, of payments by Spain, and of land speculation.

That western independence was not merely idle talk became apparent with the formation of the independent state of Franklin. The source of this development in the early 1780s was a strong drive for effective government by the frontiersmen south of the Ohio River. Appeals for statehood were made to the Confederation Congress, but that body found difficulty in taking effective action on any subject, and in this case was particularly handicapped because various states were being asked to cede their western land claims. Any congressional action that violated presumed rights and powers of such important land-claiming states as Virginia and North Carolina would hardly speed land cessions; hence Congress did nothing.

Western pressure for effective government was strongest in the Holston River region, claimed by North Carolina. Long debates in the North Carolina legislature on what to do with westerners, who wanted so much and who paid so little taxes, resulted in North Carolina ceding its western lands to Congress in 1784 by a narrow vote. When Congress dawdled as usual, North Carolina repealed its act of cession before the end of the same year.

Westerners rapidly grew impatient with the indecision of Congress and North Carolina. Interest in independence grew, and involved two groups of land speculators with different ideas of which government would be the more useful to them. The freedom movement culminated in the Jonesboro convention, which on December 14, 1784, declared the independence of the Holston region by a vote of 28 to 15. The new nation was named Franklin, in honor of Benjamin Franklin. A temporary constitution provided for a senate and house of representatives, which jointly elected a governor. The first legislature met in March 1785 and passed laws about such matters as land titles, education, militia, county divisions, taxation, and elections. A permanent constitution, based on that of North Carolina, was adopted in March 1785. The first governor was John Sevier, who was elected by acclamation.

Internal affairs of the new nation progressed satisfactorily under the able administration of Sevier, but foreign affairs did not run as smoothly. The Indians were a continual danger, forcing Sevier to take the field several times; when the Franklinites expanded their territory at the expense of the Cherokee (1785), they became embroiled in trouble both with the majority of the tribe and with the United States. Spain was approached for recognition and assistance. Congress was asked for recognition, but as usual was weak and unwilling to meddle, and Benjamin Franklin refused to aid his namesake. The Kentucky area was asked to join the venture, but decided it had more to gain from Congress and Virginia than from independence. Georgia gave the new nation its greatest success, granting recognition and expressing willingness to cooperate in fighting the Indians. North Carolina naturally objected vigorously to the actions of its ungrateful progeny, but had neither the force nor the desire to conquer the back-country. After the failure of efforts at reconciliation, the two states issued manifestos and countermanifestos as fast as they could concoct and print them.

The trouble that finally destroyed Franklin was internal. Sevier's chief rival was John Tipton; and when Tipton failed to win the ascendancy in Franklin, he obtained recognition and authority from North Carolina. Then followed a comic-opera war between the followers of Sevier and those of Tipton, with Tipton receiving some aid from North Carolina, which outlawed Sevier in 1786. Sevier was finally captured by the Tipton forces in 1788. He was rescued by his friends before he could be brought to trial; but the affair resulted in the collapse of Franklin, with North Carolina resuming control. Sevier was pardoned immediately, and participated in the North Carolina convention of 1788, which considered the adoption of the new federal constitution. During the next year North Carolina ceded its western lands to Congress by a decisive vote, but the action was little more than a gesture, since most of the land had been sold.

WESTERN INTRIGUES AND WILKINSON   The state of Franklin included only a small part of the area west of the mountains, and elsewhere there occurred various plottings, usually with the idea of independence and alliance with Spain, and almost always involving land speculation. Dr. James White, a former congressman, was particularly active in present-day Tennessee, having associations with such prominent men as Sevier, William Blount, and James Robertson. White proposed to the Spanish minister in 1786 that the West declare its independence and then be taken under the protection of Spain. The minister was at first interested, but his ardor soon cooled, and he suggested that any westerner who really liked Spain could move into Spanish territory.

James O'Fallon, a brother-in-law of George Rogers Clark, developed an even more impressive plan in 1790. He talked of a large army under Clark to occupy the lower Yazoo River Valley and create a new state, allied with Spain, and of course offering free land for the adventurers. Those who feared that Spain might be unfriendly were assured that he was on good terms with the Spanish; in fact, O'Fallon had written to the Spanish governor of Louisiana concerning his "ardent views of promoting the interests of his Catholic majesty." As was true of so many similar plans, those of O'Fallon never materialized.

Most spectacular were the activities of the adventurer William Augustus Bowles, Maryland-born, who had held a British army commission during the Revolution. After the war he sought to exploit the troubled conditions in Florida. His manifold activities took him in time over much of the world, with dealings with several countries; but his center of operations was near St. Marks, Florida, and his main objective was an independent nation, protected by Britain, yielding profits from Indian trade and land speculation. Actually he produced a Creek-Seminole nation of Muskogee, with a constitution and a flag, and himself as probably the self-appointed director general. In a "war" with Spain he captured the fort at St. Marks, but ultimately found the contest a mismatch, was captured, and died (1805) in a Havana prison.

Best known of the plotters of the 1780s and 1790s was James Wilkinson, son of a Maryland planter, who had volunteered for the Continental Army and by 1777 had risen to the rank of brevet brigadier general at the age of twenty. After the Revolution Wilkinson settled in Pennsylvania—he had married the daughter of a well-known Philadelphia family—and for a time sat in the Pennsylvania legislature. Finding economic success elusive, he moved to Kentucky in 1783 as the representative of several Philadelphia merchants. Immediately he was outstanding in Lexington, where he built a large house and entertained lavishly. As a youthful retired general, as a suave and persuasive man, and as a trader and land speculator, he was soon well known. He was active in several Kentucky statehood conventions, even though he preferred independence, as did many of his friends.

In 1784, the year that Spain closed the Mississippi, Wilkinson took two flatboats to New Orleans, detouring to St. Louis to tell the Spanish commander that he carried important information concerning an expedition by George Rogers Clark to take Natchez. At New Orleans he talked long and earnestly with the governor, Esteban

Miró, warning him of a potential attack from Kentucky. Motivated by his characteristic affinity with the pen, he also addressed a memorial to Spain suggesting that a western revolt be fomented or that American settlers be encouraged to come to Louisiana. In either event he would be willing to become chief Spanish agent.

Spain was soon paying Wilkinson, thanks to his persuasiveness or to Spanish credulity, and by 1791 he was receiving a regular pension. Whether Wilkinson believed his own tales may be doubted, and particularly after they became more complex and contradictory. In Kentucky he worked publicly for independence and an alliance with England if Spain would not open the Mississippi. To Miró he talked of union with

Royal Decree Regulating Commerce Between Spain and Its New Territory, Louisiana. (Historical Pictures Service, Chicago)

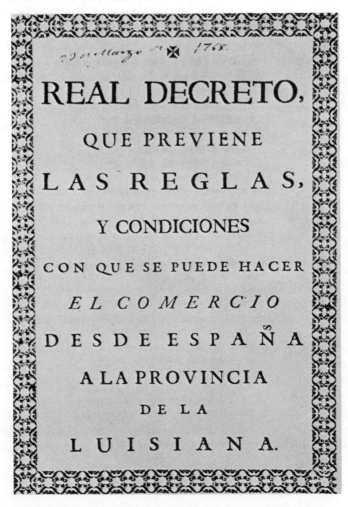

Spain, and advocated that the Mississippi be kept closed. To complicate his plans further he also memorialized England, suggesting that he be made British agent to work for independence and that an attack be made on New Orleans if Spain did not open the river; to his disappointment the English were not as gullible as the Spanish. The conclusion seems inescapable that toward the end he was milking Spain for everything he could get, and had no intention of carrying out his side of any bargain.

STATEHOOD FOR KENTUCKY AND TENNESSEE   The extension of statehood to Kentucky and Tennessee upset the plans for an independent West during the 1790s. Kentucky had long been dissatisfied with its position as a Virginia county: Richmond was remote and the Kentuckians wanted to run their own affairs. Virginia had no great objection, but mutually agreeable terms were necessary. Kentucky had nine statehood conventions during the years 1784 through 1790, while Virginia passed four enabling acts. Ultimately agreement was reached, and Kentucky was admitted to the Union in 1792—the first of the trans-Appalachian states.

Tennessee did not attain statehood so promptly. After the North Carolina land cession, Congress created a territorial government corresponding to that of the Northwest. The governor was William Blount, prince of land speculators, who filled the offices under his control with friends, relatives, and business associates, with special reference to men formerly connected with the state of Franklin. The speculators remained firmly in control until the arrival of statehood in 1796, at which time Sevier became governor and Blount went to the United States Senate.

GENÊT   By the 1790s opportunities for western intrigue seemed to be declining. Statehood came to Kentucky and Tennessee, and all states but Georgia ceded their western land claims to Congress. The federal government was perceptibly stronger. Wilkinson, with his usual debts and his Spanish intrigues less lucrative, returned to the army with a commission issued by Washington despite rumors of Spanish payments. Wilkinson was for a time in command at Fort Washington (Cincinnati), and he fought acceptably in the Indian wars of the 1790s while continuing to receive his Spanish pension and to ask for more.

A new complication arose in 1793 with the arrival in the United States of Citizen Edmond Charles Genêt as an emissary of France. The Genêt mission, as it concerned the West, was to raise an American frontier army, pay it with money that the United States still owed France, and capture Florida and Louisiana, where presumably the oppressed inhabitants were panting for an opportunity to accept the ideas of the French Revolution.

Genêt's representative in the West was André Michaux, French scientist and explorer, who commissioned George Rogers Clark as major general of the expedition. Clark, resentful of the smallness of his rewards for war service, was interested. Moreover, he was in financial difficulties from his land speculation, and his Spanish intrigues had not proved lucrative. He advertised for men at the princely pay of a dollar a day plus 1000 acres of land for each year's service. To the south, an expedition was collected in Georgia under Major General Elijah Clarke, presumably to take St. Augustine and Pensacola.

The promising Genêt plans collapsed in 1794 when President Washington prohibited enlistments and ordered the governor of Kentucky to stop George Rogers Clark. In the South, Elijah Clarke crossed the St. Marys River with some 150 men and established a "Trans-Oconee Republic," but was forced to withdraw when Governor George Mathews of Georgia closed the river to needed supplies. Wilkinson took advantage of the excitement by warning Spain of the potential invasion, and by asking for a reward; but his compensation was seized by bandits on its way to him. Wilkinson remained in the American army, participating in various Indian campaigns, and serving as second in command to Anthony Wayne at the battle of Fallen Timbers.

ENGLISH AND SPANISH TREATIES   The western uproar made the federal government keenly aware of problems of the area, and Washington was worried over the possibility of independence. A real effort was made in the mid-1790s to improve the situation by sending expeditions against the Indians and by negotiating treaties that would remove at least some frontier grievances. The Jay Treaty with England in 1794 provided for the transfer of the western posts to American control—a transfer that occurred the following year. At this time Anthony Wayne commanded the western army, and when he died in December 1796, Wilkinson succeeded him. By then Wilkinson had received some $30,000 from Spain, and the story had not ended.

The treaty with England opened the way for an agreement with Spain, which was no longer allied with England and feared a joint English-American occupation of its North American possessions. By the Treaty of San Lorenzo, negotiated by Thomas Pinckney in 1795, Spain agreed to accept the boundary of 31° north latitude, and to withdraw its troops from north of that line. Even more important, Spain agreed to the free navigation of the Mississippi and to a three-year right of deposit at New Orleans: the privilege of landing and storing goods for reshipment without paying duties. This right of deposit was to be continued later, but not necessarily at New Orleans.

Spanish authorities were slow in carrying out the terms of the Pinckney Treaty, hoping that the West might be detached from the Union; the change of times was evident, however, when Wilkinson jailed Thomas Power, the Spanish agent. Free navigation of the Mississippi went into effect in December 1796, but the right of deposit was not accorded for another two years. Transfer of the territory north of 31° was also delayed, and when Andrew Ellicott, the American representative, arrived to accept and survey the boundaries of the accession, he soon became impatient. Gathering a small armed force, he engineered a "revolution" by American settlers, after which the actual power was exercised by a committee of citizens, even though the Spanish commander remained in nominal control. When the Spanish posts were surrendered in 1798, Wilkinson was on hand to extend all possible courtesies to the departing Spaniards.

FURTHER IDEAS OF EXPANSION   With the settling of the Spanish boundary and the statehood of Kentucky and Tennessee, western conditions might theoretically have been presumed stabilized. But they were not. William A. Bowles, as described earlier, invaded Florida. Philip Nolan, a Wilkinson protégé and adventurer, tried his luck in Texas. William Blount was involved in a plot (1796) to gather an army of whites and Indians, and, with the help of a British fleet, to capture the Floridas and Louisiana for Britain; the reward was to be land. The plot was exposed prematurely, and Blount was expelled from his office in 1797. An even more impressive plan was concocted by Alexander Hamilton, who had been disappointed by his failure to obtain military glory in the Revolution. Hamilton envisioned an alliance with England, and war with France and Spain. He himself would lead an army to conquer Florida and Louisiana, and possibly Mexico and Central America, or even more remote areas. Failing to attract support in the West, his expedition never materialized.

Aggressive plans such as those of Blount and Hamilton indicated an attitude that was typical of the period. The principal motive of the leaders was probably the hope of personal gain in plunder, trade, or land, but patriotism was also claimed as a justification. The authors talked of freeing oppressed peoples and of adding territory to the United States. Whatever their real motives, they were developing a procedure that the United States was to use frequently in its expansion of the next half century.

THE LOUISIANA PURCHASE   The United States was not the only nation interested in Spanish territory; it was France that first succeeded in detaching a piece of it. While Americans talked and plotted, France negotiated to obtain Louisiana—partly because revolutionary France felt it had a world mission and partly because of less laudable colonial motives. Spanish diplomats were superficially coy and reluctant, but had no real objection to selling Louisiana any time after 1795 if the price was right. They saw the immense wilderness of Louisiana, inhabited by only some 50,000 people, as nothing but a drain on the Spanish treasury. The French-Spanish dickering produced in 1800 the Treaty of San Ildefonso, by which France received Louisiana. This treaty was secret, and for the time being the actual transfer of Louisiana was not made.

When Napoleon signed the Peace of Amiens in March 1802, he was freed for an American colonial venture. Immediately he pushed for a quicker transfer, and sent a sizable army to Santo Domingo as a start for operations on the American continent. French plans envisioned a resurrection of their colonial ambitions in the western hemisphere, and a lucrative trade primarily between the homeland and the French West Indies sugar islands. Rumors of the impending transfer distressed the Americans, who regarded France as a more objectionable neighbor than Spain. Suspicions grew when the French army arrived in Santo Domingo, and when in October 1802 the Intendant of Louisiana stopped the right of deposit at New Orleans. The stoppage was brief and did not prevent American navigation of the Mississippi, but it roused the West and there was talk of war. Incidentally, the assumption that Napoleon had ordered the end of the right of deposit, although a reasonable one, was not true.

President Thomas Jefferson was in a difficult position. His old hope that the advance of American settlement would solve the Spanish difficulties was less easy to hold, and he appreciated the willingness of the West to act on its own initiative, even to the point of independence. Furthermore he was sensitive to political factors, and the Federalists were making capital by urging immediate and forceful action. Finally, Jefferson had

WESTWARD EXPANSION
1783 - 1800

1. Western Reserve
2. Seven Ranges
3. Ohio Company
4. Scioto Company
5. Virginia Military Reserve
6. Symmes' Purchase

Darker shaded areas show overlapping cessions of western lands previously claimed by the original states

grave doubts as to the constitutional right of the federal government to acquire new territory.

Jefferson put pressure on France by suggesting that its American adventure might push the United States into alliance with England. At the same time the American minister, Robert R. Livingston, was trying unsuccessfully to buy New Orleans and possibly additional territory. When American sentiment increased in vigor, Jefferson appointed a special emissary, James Monroe, who was popular in the West, and provided him with a $2 million fund voted by Congress. Monroe was instructed to buy the Floridas and the Island of Orleans (New Orleans) for not over $10 million; he also had permission to promise favored treatment to French vessels and trade, and even to guarantee French possession of the remainder of Louisiana. Alternate instructions envisioned the purchase of less territory, even to a single town on the Mississippi for deposit. Finally, if Napoleon would sell nothing, Monroe and Livingston were authorized to cross the Channel and make an English alliance.

Before Monroe arrived in France, Napoleon had abandoned his American plans. The heroic resistance of natives under Toussaint L'Ouverture had supplemented the yellow fever in producing thousands of French graves; but Napoleon as a soldier was not deterred by casualties, and in the fall of 1802 gathered a new army to occupy New Orleans. His armada failed to sail because of the cold winter, and then the colonial project was pushed into obscurity by the prospective renewal of war with England in the spring of 1803. Napoleon exclaimed pettishly: "Damn sugar, damn coffee, damn colonies," and planned to obtain funds for the English war by selling Louisiana—of course he could reconquer it if he changed his mind.

While Monroe was en route to France, the French offered to sell to Livingston all of Louisiana, and he reluctantly postponed a decision until Monroe arrived. The bargaining was brief, and in 1803 the final treaty transferred all of Louisiana to the United States for approximately $15 million, about a quarter of which was used to settle United States claims on France. The boundaries of the acquisition were stated vaguely, opening the way for future disputes. His constitutional scruples overcome, Jefferson seemed untroubled by the earlier promise of France to Spain never to dispose of the country.

The change of masters occurred late in 1803 at New Orleans, then a dilapidated community of some 8000 inhabitants. On November 30 Louisiana was formally transferred from Spain to France, and on December 20 from France to the United States. The American commissioners who accepted the cession were William C. C. Claiborne, the prospective governor, and James Wilkinson, head of the western army and future governor of upper Louisiana Territory. Wilkinson must have regretted the disappearance from New Orleans of his paymaster, but his sorrow was abated by a Spanish payment of $12,000 for his lengthy "Reflections," a modified version of which he sent to Jefferson.

Provision for the government of the new region came early in 1804. All the portion outside the present Louisiana was called Louisiana District, with Wilkinson as governor, but with judicial administration by Indiana Territory. The present Louisiana was constituted Orleans Territory; its eastern boundary fluctuated during the next eight years.

Governor Claiborne was received by the French and Spanish with a considerable skepticism that produced serious administrative difficulties in the early years. In 1805 Orleans was given a government like that of the neighboring Mississippi Territory, and with the passage of years the administration came to operate smoothly. American occupation brought an immediate increase in population, so that in 1812 Louisiana could be admitted to the Union.

BURR   The acquisition of Louisiana seemed on its face to satisfy all current American desires and hence to end American plans to invade Spanish territory; but within the next few years occurred the best advertised of all such expeditions—that under the brilliant, restless, ambitious, dapper, and spendthrift Aaron Burr. The promising political career of Burr appeared to be approaching an end with the completion of his vice-presidency (1801–1805). Jefferson had never forgiven him for failing to withdraw from the presidential voting in 1800, and refused him any important appointment; and his killing of Hamilton in a duel further hurt his political chances. On the other hand, he was still under fifty, active and vigorous, and in need of money. Like many other men looking for opportunity, Burr turned his eyes to the West, where his killing of Hamilton would be a positive advantage to his reputation.

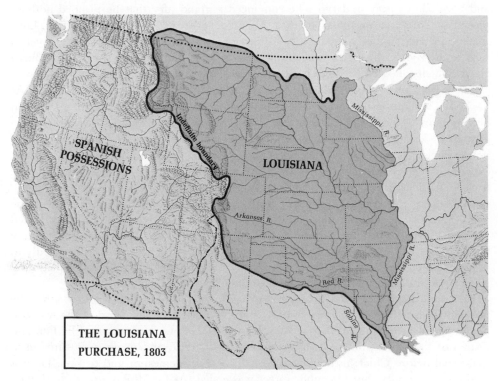

THE LOUISIANA
PURCHASE, 1803

Burr tried to raise money from both the English and the Spanish ministers. To the former he suggested an independent western state, with England providing $500,000 and a fleet at the mouth of the Mississippi. To the latter he outlined a fantastic scheme for capturing both New Orleans and Washington, kidnapping high executives, and taking the contents of an arsenal and bank. Burr's persuasiveness was demonstrated when he convinced both men, but unfortunately for his bank account their home governments were too far distant to be impressed.

Soon after Burr completed his duties as vice-president he and his beloved daughter Theodosia toured the West, where they were greeted with vast enthusiasm. Inevitably Burr talked to hundreds of men, including Jackson and Clay, but what he said is uncertain, since he varied his story to appeal to each listener. Possibly he did not advance the wild proposals he had used as bait for the Spanish and English ministers. Perhaps he talked of colonization. Later he indicated an interest in becoming emperor of Mexico. Among the men to whom he talked was his old friend James Wilkinson, with whom he had long corresponded in code—not unusual in a day when carriers frequently read the dispatches entrusted to them. Burr and Wilkinson spent four days in earnest conversation, but the contents of their talks remain unknown.

Burr was again in the West in August 1806, collecting men and supplies for a rendezvous late in the year on an island in the upper Ohio River. Twice he was arrested and tried for treason, and twice he convinced a grand jury that he planned nothing more than colonization. Jefferson heard the rumors of treason, but took no action. Ultimately a disappointingly small party of thirty men started the trip down the river in nine boats. By this time Jefferson had become alarmed and issued a warrant for Burr's arrest, which followed the expedition down the river.

The actions of Wilkinson during 1806 are as difficult to explain as those of Burr. At St. Louis, Wilkinson had been in perpetual trouble as governor, and in June 1806 had been ordered to move to the vicinity of New Orleans. These orders he obeyed with the greatest of leisure, detouring from Natchez to Natchitoches on the pretext of a slight border incident. At Natchitoches he enquired among his men concerning a possible expedition against Mexico, but could discover no enthusiasm. By September he was back in Natchez, leaving his army to make its own way to New Orleans.

At Natchez, Wilkinson apparently finally made up his mind. Rather belatedly he sent a note to Jefferson warning him of the Burr expedition, which he said was headed for Vera Cruz. At the same time he warned Spain and Mexico. Then he rushed to New Orleans, and to the surprise of everyone urged martial law and worked frenziedly to prepare the city against an attack. Apparently the pathetic Burr expedition had now become an imposing menace to the United States.

Meantime Burr had been floating leisurely down the river, unaware of either the warrant for his arrest or the actions of Wilkinson. Ultimately he heard of the warrant, became panic-striction, and fled overland in disguise. He was apprehended by Edmund Gaines of the United States Army on February 19, 1807, and taken to Richmond to stand trial before Chief Justice John Marshall for a misdemeanor and treason. He was adjudged not guilty, but his public career was ended. As for Wilkinson, his testimony in the Burr trial was vague and inconclusive—after all, he had to consider his own vindication. In fact, his conduct was so suspect that he was investigated by congressional and military committees. His explanations of peculiar letters and actions were thin; but the evidence was inconclusive, and he was exonerated in each case.

The Burr episode was only one of many plans made by Americans to invade neighboring lands, but it at least marked a temporary halt to western plans for independence. By the early nineteenth century there was no longer any question that the Mississippi Valley would remain a part of the United States. In fact, the West was in the process of becoming as vocally patriotic as the East, with a deep and intense love of the United States, a belief in its superiority, and a desire to expand the Union to bring the blessings of its institutions to neighboring peoples.

READINGS   *Paperbacks are marked with an asterisk.*

Spanish Intrigues   The general story is covered in Thomas P. Abernethy, *The South in the New Nation* (1961) and Francis S. Philbrick, *The Rise of the West, 1754–1830* (1965). Smaller parts of the situation are presented in Thomas P. Abernethy, *From Frontier to Plantation in Tennessee* (1932); John W. Caughey, *Bernardo de Gálvez in Louisiana, 1776–1783* (1934). Standard on the relations with Spain are *Arthur P. Whitaker, *The Spanish-American Frontier 1783–1795* (1927, 1962) and *The Mississippi Question 1795–1803* (1934).

The Louisiana negotiations can be followed in Elijah W. Lyon, *Louisiana in French Diplomacy, 1759–1804* (1934). The previous British occupation is treated carefully in Clinton N. Howard, *The British Development of West Florida, 1763–1769* (1947) and Cecil Johnson, *British West Florida, 1763–1783* (1943).

State of Franklin   Samuel C. Williams, *History of the Lost State of Franklin* (1924) is standard. Considerable material appears in John A. Caruso, *The Appalachian Frontier* (1959) and Carl S. Driver, *John Sevier* (1932).

Wilkinson   Best on Wilkinson is James R. Jacobs, *Tarnished Warrior* (1938) and the pertinent parts of the same author's *The Beginning of the United States Army, 1783–1812* (1947). Also useful are Royal O. Shreve, *The Finished Scoundrel* (1933), popular in tone; and James Wilkinson, *Wilkinson* (1935), a justification by a grandson. William Blount is covered clearly in William H. Masterson, *William Blount* (1954). Kentucky events are presented interestingly in Thomas D. Clark, *A History of Kentucky* (1937). For Bowles, see J. Leitch Wright, *William Augustus Bowles* (1967), good.

Burr   Thomas P. Abernethy, *The Burr Conspiracy* (1954) is excellent. The best Burr biography is *Nathan Schachner, *Aaron Burr* (1937). Also good are Herbert S. Parmet and Marie B. Hecht, *Aaron Burr* (1967) and Holmes M. Alexander, *Aaron Burr* (1937), the latter adverse in tone.

Chapter 6 / GOVERNMENTAL PROBLEMS

The first settlers who crossed the Appalachians were confronted by a virgin wilderness where even the simplest necessities to which they were accustomed did not exist. To fulfill their varied desires, which ranged from the basic needs of survival to complicated cultural ambitions, the new inhabitants had to conquer a strange environment. Quite naturally they tried to retain the customs and ideals that had characterized their life in the East, but these were necessarily modified by western conditions.

CHARACTER OF WESTERN MIGRANTS   Methods of solving western problems depended on the character of the new inhabitants. Most obviously, the usual migrant had not been successful in the East; the well-established farmer, businessman, or professional man was more likely to stay in the community of his success. The most important exceptions were slaveowners looking for more fertile land, and financiers or land speculators—not infrequently combined in one man—who saw opportunities for gain in a new and expanding community. Of course the land speculator might either lose his money and become like his neighbors, or make large profits and move back East.

Unsuccessful easterners were not for the most part completely poverty-stricken easterners. Most migrants took up farms, which was far from costless, particularly if families were involved. Even if a man took up land without immediately paying for it, he still needed sufficient resources to make the trip west, to obtain necessary tools and seed, and to live until he harvested his first crop. If the man were unmarried, he might plan to work for wages in the West before starting his own farm; but if he were married this procedure was more difficult.

Lack of success in the East did not necessarily imply that westerners lacked ability. Frequently they came from desirable but unfavored portions of the communities of their origins. Young members of large New England farming families sought more opportunity than their few relatively infertile acres provided. Slaveowners sought replacements for their worked-out land. Established farmers and artisans sought to improve their conditions of life. Immigrants from Europe were attracted by opportunities for employment or by cheap land. Along with these and other desirable groups came a sprinkling of the less desirable—criminals seeking to escape the law, possibly to start new lives or perhaps to resume old ways in a new setting; the reckless and the footloose who would probably never become adjusted satisfactorily to any settled society.

Migration to the West implied that the prospective frontiersman had a little more intellectual dissatisfaction, a little greater willingness to take a chance, than his friends and neighbors. Psychologically he was more restless, perhaps somewhat maladjusted in his relations with family and friends. Normally he said—and believed—that his motives were economic, but behind these very real economic desires may well have been psychological dissatisfactions that were basically noneconomic.

The greatest single group of migrants was composed of young, unmarried farm boys. The usual age was twenty-one, which meant that they were legally free to seek their

View from Bashongo Tavern, 5 miles from York Town on the Baltimore Road. This is the "wooden" frontier: housing, fuel, bridging, and fencing are of lumber. The scene would change dramatically as the wooded area gave way to the Great Plains. (New York Public Library)

fortunes. Frequently they worked for a time in the West, returned to the East to marry their childhood sweethearts, and then went back to the West to take up farms in the new country. When a family migrated, its head might make a preliminary trip to discover a suitable place to settle; otherwise, he depended on reports from friends and neighbors who had gone west earlier. In any case he preferred a fairly definite objective before he moved.

Western migrants tended to travel by the most easily available routes, and as directly west as possible; thus they expected to find themselves in something like the geographical and climatic conditions to which they were accustomed, and near people from their own part of the country. During the Revolutionary years most of the migrants came from the South, passed through the Cumberland Gap, and settled in Kentucky or Tennessee, or went up the Potomac and then overland to the Pittsburgh area. Eventually these streams of settlement overflowed into the region just north of the Ohio River—what is now southern Ohio, Indiana, and Illinois. Later they occupied Missouri, and even reached Iowa. Settlers from the Middle Atlantic states went west by way of Pittsburgh and mixed with the southern stream in the Ohio Valley. New England migrants of the eighteenth and early nineteenth centuries flowed largely into New York State, with the farthest advance reaching the Great Lakes; a few New Englanders, however, went into the Ohio Valley, usually by way of Pittsburgh but sometimes through southern New York State.

MAIN WESTERN PROBLEMS   Several of the most serious problems facing these new settlers were of continuing importance throughout the entire history of the West. Of first concern were the Indians. During the period of the Revolution most Indians were hostile; hence the few whites tended to huddle together in fortified settlements, while the isolated settler feared to leave his cabin unprotected, and seldom had the temerity to travel at night. The outlook at the end of the war was extremely discouraging because neither the national government, the states, nor the settlers had the manpower and resources to prosecute successful Indian wars. Almost the only hopeful element was that a few leaders such as Washington saw the importance of the area, and maintained a continuing interest in it.

A second problem of the West was the method by which a settler might obtain land that was good, cheap, and easily available. During and immediately after the Revolution all western lands were claimed by some states, and conditions were chaotic. State claims overlapped, procedures for surveying and marking individual claims were not uniform, prices fluctuated, and the recording of claims was often difficult. The state claims were eventually released to the national government, but with considerable reservations that frequently were confusing. Congress then had the problem of devising an adequate plan for the disposition of western lands. Its difficulties were increased by the fact that most of the lands were not actually unoccupied. Should the Indian claims be respected and illegally settled whites removed? Such a problem was difficult for a white government.

A third big problem confronting the West was that of money and credit, for the

West lacked both. Individual settlers strained their resources in going west, and needed credit to buy land and tools, to say nothing of meeting current expenses. Communities wanted roads, bridges, schools, jails, churches, and the other trappings of civilization. Large amounts of credit were obviously desirable, and for many years western attitudes were influenced strongly by the fact that the West was a debtor community.

A fourth problem was transportation, which was the very foundation of future prosperity. Western products must be carried to market quickly and cheaply, and news and goods must be brought from the East and from Europe. Each transportational innovation that became popular in the East found a host of ready supporters in the West. The great difficulties were the long and rugged routes between East and West, the lack of available capital, and the paucity of traffic. Various more or less ingenious solutions for these difficulties were tried.

A fifth problem was the development of good and effective government, which was essential to make life and property secure, to defeat the Indians, to record wills, deeds, and marriages, to build roads and bridges. The first efforts to solve the governmental problem were local and spontaneous, but such sporadic efforts proved unsatisfactory. A good many troubles, such as Indians, finance, and transportation, were insoluble on the local level. State and federal action were essential.

In addition to these five large problems were innumerable others of less pressing urgency. Religion, education, literature, art, medicine, law, and all the other attributes of civilization had to be developed from relatively simple beginnings. As matters turned out, however, the first two problems to be dealt with constructively were land and government.

LANDOWNERSHIP   The ability to acquire land in the West during the years after the Revolution was of vital importance. Most Americans were farmers, and because of the lack of industries, fishing, and shipping in the West, men concentrated on farming even more than in the East. The typical farmer owned his own land rather than rented it, and one important reason for western migration was men's hopes of securing land of their own.

Most of the land of the present United States east of the Mississippi had been granted originally to proprietors or to companies that wanted to exploit or colonize the New World. Because geographical knowledge was inadequate, boundaries specified in charters were often inexact and frequently overlapped, causing colonial disputes over dividing lines. Some charters granted land beyond the mountains. As settlement expanded, the original grantee would sell or give away such land as was needed for the increase of population. The limits of such sales or donations were sometimes so ill defined that they were impossible to mark; and frequently two or more grants overlapped, while the Proclamation of 1763 forced all claims to lapse for some years.

The outbreak of the Revolution revived the aspirations of each colony to western territory. Virginia was the most active and fortunate, for it was under its auspices that George Rogers Clark conquered much of the Northwest. Virginia organized Kentucky and the region north of the Ohio into counties; North Carolina did the same for the

Tennessee country. Settlers had not yet moved into the Georgia claim. This situation had some advantages for the states with western counties, but it also had drawbacks. Other states also had western claims, and what was to become of them if Virginia and North Carolina monopolized almost the entire West? Furthermore, the West itself was not fully satisfied, for it wanted cheap land and a government that would spend money freely to fight the Indians and to make public improvements: Virginia and North Carolina not only had no money to spend, but were desirous of increasing their revenues.

Just at the time that the central government needed unusual powers to deal with western problems it was at the nadir of its effectiveness. The Continental Congress, from its first meeting in 1774, was a purely voluntary and noncoercive body, with little power and an aversion to arousing enmities by interfering with the West. The new Articles of Confederation finally went into effect with the ratification by Maryland on March 1, 1781, after having been before the states since 1777, but here again was an incredibly weak central authority: there was no executive branch with power to enforce legislation and no central national court. But in spite of the serious handicaps surrounding Congress, it succeeded in putting into force legislation that was exceedingly important for the West.

STATE CESSIONS   Even before the Articles of Confederation were adopted by Maryland it was proposed by some states (those not having land claims) that all claims to western land be surrendered to the central government. The states with land claims could see quite obvious objections to such a proposal, but, on the other hand, they could also see good reasons for making the cessions. Conflicting state claims made problematical the amount of land any one state would be able to hold. The Indians were in the main hostile, and their subjugation would be long and arduous. All kinds of public improvements would have to be constructed with eastern money, while the poor westerners would not be able to pay any considerable taxes for many years. Altogether, it seemed to many persons that the disadvantages of holding western territory far outweighed the future benefits that might accrue from land sales.

In view of these various factors the states began to cede their western claims to Congress. New York had the honor of being the first (1780)—possibly in part because its claim as heir of the Iroquois pretensions was scarcely tenable. Other states followed, the last being Georgia in 1802. Some of them, such as Virginia and North Carolina, had already sold considerable shares of the lands they theoretically were ceding to Congress. Others made reservations. The unsold lands of Kentucky and Tennessee never came under congressional control. The "Connecticut Reserve," including the present Cleveland, Ohio, was retained by Connecticut for the benefit of certain sufferers from the Revolution. Virginia withheld large amounts of land, the greater share of which was to go to its Revolutionary soldiers. The Georgia cession actually cost the United States more in settling conflicting claims than it received from the lands remaining unsold at the time of the transfer.

LAND DEBATES   As a result of these cessions Congress was endowed with an immense public domain; and a continually increasing influx of population meant that immediate provision must be made for the survey, sale, and government of the regions attractive to settlers. Many of these settlers had paid no attention to legal ownership, merely occupying and beginning to cultivate whatever land seemed to them good. What should be done with such "squatters"? Furthermore, soldiers of the Revolutionary army had been promised land as part payment for their war services, and their Newburgh petition of 1783 demonstrated that at least some of them had a real desire for the land. What, if anything, should be done for them? Here were two classes that were insistent upon virtually free land—but free land did not sound attractive to a government that was desirous of collecting every possible cent of revenue. Furthermore, both East and West were agreed that some sort of action would have to be undertaken immediately to protect the white man from red depredations. And finally, men such as Washington realized that if the United States did not act immediately and effectively, there was a real possibility that the West might either try to settle its own affairs as an independent state or to appeal for protection to some foreign power such as Spain.

The debate in Congress on the disposition of the public lands was long and acrimonious. New England practice, in which each township was sold as a unit and then subdivided by its purchasers, was compared with the southern procedure, in which each man picked his land, fixed his own boundaries, had his title recorded at the county seat, and then paid a lawyer to fight the cases that rose over disputed boundaries and ownership. The argument between indiscriminate and exact location was won by New England. There were other debates as to whether the new land should be plotted in large or small townships, and whether large or small tracts should be offered for sale. In both cases compromises eventually were effected. The progress of the discussion can best be understood by reading the reports made to Congress in 1784 and 1785.

THE LAND ORDINANCE OF 1785   Out of the welter of proposals emerged the Ordinance of 1785, which applied to the region north of the Ohio and was designed primarily to obtain revenue from the public domain. The survey system established by the act became universal for all public lands, and continues today to remain the practice in most of the United States. Townships 6 miles square were to be surveyed prior to sale; each township was to be divided into 36 sections, each section thus being 1 mile square and containing 640 acres. Since the earth is round, these amounts actually varied slightly. The land was to be sold in the eastern states at auction, with a minimum price of one dollar an acre plus the cost of survey. Half of the land was to be sold in townships, and the remainder in sections. Reservations were made for Revolutionary soldiers and for schools.

Sales of land under the new ordinance were disappointingly slow to a government badly in need of funds. Seven ranges of townships adjacent to the western boundary of Pennsylvania were surveyed in the years 1785–1787 and put on the market. Auctions were held in the city of New York, but only a few speculators attended and little land was sold. Most of the settlers merely squatted and hoped that Congress would some day take pity on their plight; certainly they had no money to go east and buy land at auction.

THE GOVERNMENTAL ORDINANCE OF 1784 Efforts to solve the problem of the survey and sale of the public domain were paralleled by discussions about the form of government to be given the West; in fact, the first governmental legislation came a year earlier than the Land Ordinance of 1785. The Ordinance of 1784 was based on a report made by Jefferson to Congress earlier the same year; kind critics have called it a temporary aberration. The report suggested limited local self-government for the West until its population was sufficiently large to justify the creation of states. To produce areas of sizes appropriate for statehood, the land west of the mountains and north of the Ohio was to be divided in a checkerboard fashion on every other degree of latitude, with a transverse line through the center of the territory. The result would have been ten approximately equal divisions, to be given such mellifluous names as Cherronesus, Polypotamia, Pelisipia, Metropotamia, and Assenisippia. When any of these regions had a population as large as the smallest state of the United States, it was to be admitted to the Union under whatever government it desired. When the report was finally put into law, the boundaries were changed, Jefferson's names were abandoned, and provision was made for each region to send a delegate to Congress as soon as it had attained a population of 20,000.

The ordinances of 1784 and 1785 were not final solutions of the land and government problems, but they were important steps in that direction. Most observers agreed that these ordinances were unsatisfactory. Land was not being sold, and consequently no revenue was being produced. There was still no real provision for government before statehood.

THE OHIO COMPANY While Congress was trying to make up its mind, a movement started that had an important influence both on Congress and on the settlement of the West. As previously mentioned, the soldiers of the Revolutionary army had long been interested in obtaining western land as part of their reward for services in the war, and in 1786 Brigadier Generals Rufus Putnam and Benjamin Tupper called a meeting of all interested parties at the Bunch of Grapes Tavern in Boston. At this meeting the Ohio Company, with a nominal capital of $1 million, was formed. Each member was to subscribe $1000 in depreciated Continental currency, which was easy to obtain, and $10 in cash, which was more difficult. The $10 subscriptions were to be used for immediate expenses, and it was hoped that Congress would accept the paper money in payment for western lands. General Samuel H. Parsons was delegated to present the proposition to Congress.

When Parsons arrived to talk with Congress he found no Congress in session—a quorum failed to appear from May 12 to July 5, 1787. He finally succeeded in presenting his petition; but any action seemed unlikely since Congress was only marking time, waiting to see what was to happen in the Constitutional Convention, which had begun its meetings May 25.

The gloomy outlook in Congress caused the Ohio Company to take further thought, and to send a new representative, the Reverend Manasseh Cutler, who had been a chaplain in the Revolutionary army and had wide interests and broad culture. He immediately mounted his horse and rode to New York to see what might be done. His first efforts seemed so fruitless that he took a vacation and rode down to Philadelphia to attend some of the meetings of the Constitutional Convention. When he returned to New York he found his prospects more promising, and so embarked on a strenuous program of calling on members of Congress, attending clambakes and receptions, and of cultivating particularly the friendship of the president of the Congress, Arthur St. Clair.

The petition of the Ohio Company for land was but one of the matters pressing on Congress for attention. The necessity of providing a better government for the West was a paramount problem, and it was but natural that Cutler, in lobbying for his own

At the Bunch of Grapes Tavern: Forming the Ohio Company. (Bettmann Archive)

measure, should become interested in the governmental legislation and have a hand in both affairs. Another modifying factor was the speculative interest of many members of Congress and their friends in western lands. In fact, one of these men, William Duer, was so influential that Cutler felt it necessary to come to an understanding with him; Cutler promised to buy extra land for Duer and his associates in return for their support of the proposed Ohio Company purchase. But the congressional committee that was considering Cutler's proposal remained hesitant. Thereupon Cutler grew impatient and threatened to buy his land from the individual states if Congress did not act. According to his statement his threat "appeared to have the effect I wished"; the committee was "mortified," and eventually the grant was made.

The final grant in July 1787 included 6.5 million acres of Ohio land—1.5 million acres for the Ohio Company and the remainder for Duer and his associates. The price to the Ohio Company was one dollar an acre, with one-third off for bad lands, to be paid in Continental currency, which was then worth twelve and a half cents on the dollar. The actual price was therefore about eight cents an acre, which certainly was not excessive for good Ohio land, even when the land was in a state of wilderness. According to the terms of the contract, $500,000 was to be paid immediately and the remainder when the surveys were completed.

The grant to the Ohio Company immediately stirred that organization to activity. The down payment was made, and plans for settlement were drawn up. In 1788 a group of New Englanders made the trip across New York and northern Pennsylvania, and then floated down the Ohio River to the mouth of the Muskingum, where they founded the town of Marietta near Fort Harmar, which had been established three years earlier. Being confirmed New Englanders they produced a good New England village, including the usual Congregational Church. When the Ohio Company ultimately found itself unable to pay the remainder of the purchase price, Congress remitted it and cut the grant in half.

THE SCIOTO COMPANY   Meantime the Duer group (usually known as the Scioto Company, although not organized formally) went ahead with plans to settle its land. Joel Barlow, the well-known author of the *Columbiad*, was sent to France to sell potential American farms. While in France he became associated with William Playfair, an Englishman who took the initiative in organizing a French company to do the actual selling. The wild land of the Scioto Company was advertised as very fertile, well populated, and suited particularly to artisans and mechanics of all kinds; no mention was made of the lack of a final title by the company. Soon the company's office was crowded with hopeful buyers, and 3 million acres were sold. In 1790 some 600 of the purchasers started for America. For the most part they were of the upper-middle class, including professional men, artisans, wood-carvers, watch- and clockmakers, tailors, wigmakers, and dancing masters. There was something pathetically humorous in the idea of wigmakers and dancing masters migrating to the untamed wilderness of Ohio.

Duer and his friends were both pleased and embarrassed by the success of Barlow and Playfair. They were particularly concerned over their ability to make the necessary payments on their grant, for the cost of 5 million acres was a huge sum, even though the price was only two-thirds of a dollar an acre and payments could be made in six installments. When they tried to obtain the proceeds of the French company, it was found to be insolvent due to the manipulations of Playfair. The result was the bankruptcy of the Scioto Company, and by the time the French settlers landed in Virginia their prospects were exceedingly gloomy. Eventually the migrants were escorted to the West and there, instead of finding populous towns and plenty of work, they discovered a wilderness containing a few partly completed log cabins. Some drifted away to other parts of the country, while others stayed to form the town of Gallipolis. Actually they were on Ohio Company land, where most of them remained in spite of a congressional donation of land in the present Scioto County.

In addition to the Ohio Company and the Duer group many other individuals and companies applied to Congress for the purchase of large areas in the West. The only other sale was to John Cleves Symmes, a member of Congress from New Jersey. Symmes received in 1788 a grant of 1 million acres west of the Little Miami. The terms were similar to those made to the Ohio Company; he was to pay $82,198 down and the remainder in seven installments. He made the down payment, but defaulted on the remainder, and the grant ultimately was reduced to 300,000 acres along the Ohio River.

THE NORTHWEST ORDINANCE   While these various tracts of land were being granted, the matter of government was finally settled by an ordinance that probably was the most remarkable piece of legislation passed by Congress under the Articles of Confederation, particularly in view of the fact that the old government was giving its last feeble gasps of life before the new Constitution was completed and put into effect. True it is that the act was mixed with the lobbying efforts of Cutler, Duer, and others, that Cutler himself had a hand in the final outcome, and that Arthur St. Clair aided it partly because he had been promised the governorship of the new territory; and yet the Northwest Ordinance of 1787 was a remarkable bit of constructive legislation, whose principles were to remain in effect during the entire process of frontier advance from the Appalachians to the Pacific. Any act used successfully for a century and a half under varying conditions is worthy of respect.

The Ordinance of 1787 applied only to the Old Northwest. This territory was to be divided into three, four, or five states. If three, the dividing lines were to be approximately the present boundaries on the east and west of Indiana. If four or five states were to be created, then an additional line was to be drawn directly east and west through the tip of Lake Michigan. This last line was later modified.

More important than the division of territory were the provisions for government that remedied the defects of the Ordinance of 1784 by providing an effective administration before statehood. Three stages of government were provided. The first, which was to go into effect immediately, gave administration of the Northwest Territory to a governor, a secretary, and three judges, all appointed by the Congress of the Confederation, which maintained control. When the population of the territory attained 5000 free males of voting age, the second type of government was to go into effect: all the old officers and provisions remained, but the settlers might elect a legislature, thus giving the electorate its first taste of self-government, and they might also elect a delegate to represent them in Congress. Finally, when the population of any part of the territory reached a total of 60,000 free inhabitants, a constitutional convention could be held and the prospective state could apply for admission to the Union. In addition to these provisions there was also a bill of rights similar to that of the federal government, and a prohibition of slavery, except for those slaves already in the territory.

Immediately following the passage of the Ordinance of 1787 Arthur St. Clair was appointed first governor of the Northwest Territory. After a leisurely trip he arrived at Marietta on July 9, 1788. He had little to govern, in terms of land or population, and as a man of ambition was anxious to increase both, which meant that he was particularly desirous of pushing back the Indians.

The fact that the Ordinance of 1787 applied only to the Old Northwest is sometimes forgotten. A similar act of 1790 made provision for the territory south of the Ohio. In later years the principles of the Ordinance of 1787 were reenacted many times to provide for all the new regions west to the Pacific, excepting only Texas and California.

FURTHER DEBATES ON LAND If anyone believed that making large grants such as that to the Ohio Company would replace the necessity for smaller sales to individuals, he was soon disillusioned by the difficulties which appeared before the large grants were adjusted. For the most part, existing congressional legislation had no effect whatever: settlers continued to go where they pleased regardless of the law. Certainly it seemed an imposition to ask a poor land seeker to make the long trip east to have a chance to bid at auction for the land he had already improved. If the prospective settler bought before he moved West, he found himself in equally bad circumstances; either he must buy his land unseen or he must make an expensive and time-consuming trip to the West before he bought. The only logical solution was to establish land offices reasonably near the land that was to be sold.

The question of price also disturbed Congress. Everyone agreed that the land should produce revenue to the central government, but here unanimity ceased. What sort of price would produce a maximum return? Too expensive land would mean that the poorer settlers could not afford to buy, and would simply squat; whereupon the government would be faced with the unpleasant necessity of either ejecting large numbers of settlers from their homes or giving them the land. Closely allied with this problem was that of deciding the minimum size of a tract that would be sold to one person. Too large a minimum would mean that only the speculator could buy, but a very small one would raise the cost of administration to a prohibitive figure. These and other phases of the land situation were debated continually by Congress after 1789.

Alexander Hamilton contributed to the discussion in 1790 by a report to Congress in which he suggested a policy designed to increase the stability of the nation. He recommended that preference in land sales be given to large companies, and that the small settler be pacified by being permitted to buy tracts of not over 100 acres at 30¢ an acre. Branch land offices would supply local needs. Influenced to some extent by this report, Congress eventually passed the Land Act of 1796, which represented one more step toward a solution of the land problem. There were a few main changes from the Ordinance of 1785: the minimum price was set at $2 an acre, payments could be spread over twelve months, and land offices were to be opened in Pittsburgh and Cincinnati.

LAND ACT OF 1800

The most significant legislation of this period came in 1800, when Harrison's frontier bill became law. William Henry Harrison was the first congressional delegate from the territory of Ohio, and his measure represented western desires of the time—modified to some extent by the necessities of practical politics. Most of the provisions were not novel, having long been discussed and having been expressed in considerable part in the Land Act of 1796. Local land offices were established at Cincinnati, Chillicothe, Marietta, and Steubenville; each office was manned by a registrar (for drawing up the deeds) and a receiver (to control the finances). East of the Muskingum the land was to be sold entirely in tracts of a section apiece (640 acres); west of that river half was to be sold in sections and half in half sections. The auction system was retained, with a minimum price of $2 an acre, the purchaser also paying the

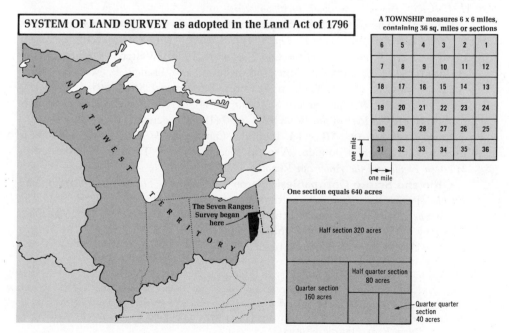

SYSTEM OF LAND SURVEY as adopted in the Land Act of 1796

A TOWNSHIP measures 6 x 6 miles, containing 36 sq. miles or sections

The Seven Ranges: Survey began here

One section equals 640 acres

Half section 320 acres

Quarter section 160 acres

Half quarter section 80 acres

Quarter quarter section 40 acres

cost of survey. Any land remaining unsold after the auction was open to private entry at the minimum price. Only about one-twentieth of the purchase price was due at the time of the sale, the remainder of the first quarter being due in forty days, and the other three quarters in three annual payments, the last payment coming due at the end of four years. Interest was charged on the deferred payments, and a discount was given for an earlier settlement.

The Land Act of 1800 fulfilled the general desires of the West. The size of the individual purchase had been reduced, although even 320 acres of uncleared land proved a large amount, and was reduced in 1804 to 160 acres and in 1817 to 80 acres. The price was still high from the standpoint of the westerner, but this trouble was alleviated by the credit system; the westerner might now make the first payment on twice the amount of land that before 1796 he could have bought at $1 an acre; true, he was in debt, but few worried when almost everyone expected that within a few years he would be rich.

With the passage of the Land Act of 1800 two of the important western problems had been settled for the time being. No other important land legislation was passed for another twenty years. A scheme of government had been devised that was to last throughout the entire period of the continental expansion of the United States. In view of these accomplishments it becomes possible to consider some of the other problems and conditions of life that surrounded the people of the West in the period immediately after the Revolution.

READINGS   *Paperbacks are marked with an asterisk.*

   General   The topics of this chapter are covered in various state histories. Useful are Clarence W. Alvord, *The Illinois Country, 1673–1818* (1920); Beverley Bond, Jr., *The Civilization of the Old Northwest* (1934); Walter Havighurst, *Land of Promise* (1946), readable; Eugene Roseboom and Francis P. Weisenburger, *A History of Ohio* (1953); William T. Utter, *The Frontier State 1803–1825* (1941), Ohio. Frazer E. Wilson, *Arthur St. Clair* (1944) is highly sympathetic. Francis S. Philbrick, *The Rise of the West, 1754–1830* (1965) is general.

   Land Legislation   *Roy M. Robbins, *Our Landed Heritage* (1942) is the best history of the public domain. A good special study is Thomas P. Abernethy, *Western Lands and the American Revolution* (1937).

   Ohio and Scioto Companies   Aaron M. Sakolski, *The Great American Land Bubble* (1932) deals generally with land speculation. Theodore T. Belote, *The Scioto Speculation* (1907) remains the best on Gallipolis. Alfred P. James, *The Ohio Company* (1959) is best on that subject, and *Stewart H. Holbrook, *The Yankee Exodus* (1950) has material on Marietta.

Fort Harmar, Ohio, 1790. The palisades appear to be little more than a closely woven picket fence. The traditional blockhouse is missing, a fact the onlooking natives might well be discussing. (New York Historical Society)

The American Indians

Although they were once the only inhabitants of the land, the American Indians yielded place to newcomers from abroad. With the onrush of white settlers and the inroads made by the white man's diseases, they were reduced to a distinct minority.

The popular image of the Indian in the days of westward expansion—and the view often accepted by the artist—portrayed him as a proud horseman and great nomadic warrior who dominated the limitless stretches of the frontier.

Actually, Indians were members of nations that were made up of tribes and subtribes, each with different cultures and modes of living.

But regardless of their economies, viewpoints, or methods of warfare, the Indians were engulfed by the flood tide of white settlers.

Indian Village. These are Crow Indians of Montana, and their encampments of tepees, or lodges as they were also called, were small, mobile cities. Mobility was one factor that contributed to keeping the Indian groups intact and difficult for the whites to subjugate. (Museum of the American Indian, Heye Foundation)

Arapaho Camp. Meat, normally buffalo meat, was the mainstay of the Indian diet. Here it is hung out to dry. When cured and packed for future use it made a highly nourishing diet. (Smithsonian Institution, National Anthropological Archives)

A Southwest Indian Home. Not all Indians were tepee dwellers. Rough lodges made of sticks or brush, somewhat similar to rude dwellings first used by the whites on earlier frontiers, provided some shelter from the elements. (California Historical Society)

Potters at Work. These Arizona Indians are renowned for their skill in this field of endeavor. They represent the sedentary segment of the native population. (Smithsonian Institution, National Anthropological Archives)

Interior of a Zuni Indian Pueblo, 1897. The apartment dwellers of the Southwest were a far cry from the roaming Indians of the northern plains. (Los Angeles County Museum of Natural History)

The Kiaha, or Carrying Basket. This photograph was taken on the San Xavier Reservation, Arizona in 1894. (Smithsonian Institution, National Anthropological Archives)

Preparing a Buffalo Hide. From hoofs to horns the buffalo was the Indians' major resource. Here a hide is being stretched and prepared for future use. Hides were used for clothing, robes, the making of tepees and even shields. (Granger)

Blanket Weavers, Arizona, 1893. This family is at work looming, carding, and spinning. (Smithsonian Institution, National Anthropological Archives)

The Care and Feeding of the Young. Here a Hopi mother feeds her apparently contented offspring. (Vroman Collection, Courtesy Southwest Museum)

The Travois. This crude trailer made of light poles was a common means of transportation among the Indians. These are Montana Cheyenne. (Museum of the American Indian, Heye Foundation)

The Indian and the Horse. When the Indian acquired the horse, he achieved a new mobility. He could now pursue buffalo herds with greater ease and became a formidable warrior on the plains. The United States Army undertook the subduing of a fleet, ever-elusive tribesman who could strike his tepee and be miles away in very little time. (Bettmann)

Chapter 7/ THE ADVANCE INTO INDIAN COUNTRY

By no means the least of the dangers facing the western settler was the Indian, who was viewed somewhat contemptuously as "uncivilized" because he was still in the stone age, seminomadic, and had no written language except pictographs. The Indian's friends have drawn him as an impossibly noble savage, always brave, generous, wise, and sensitive; his enemies have painted him as sly, cruel, bloodthirsty, untrustworthy, and depraved. Actually he was a man like other men, by turns generous and selfish, kind and cruel. He was sometimes able and sometimes stupid. Generally he was fun loving and reasonably garrulous, with strong family devotion.

The original Indian culture was finally almost eliminated, but the Indian himself had numerous effects on his conquerors. Indian names such as Oshkosh, Winnebago, and Arkansas are found throughout the United States. Indian plants such as maize, potatoes, tobacco, pumpkin, squash, and tomato have been estimated to constitute over half of all agricultural production. Other white adaptations have ranged from lacrosse to scalping.

INDIAN TRIBES, 1800

Major Northern Indian
—— Treaty Lines before 1800

- - - Southern Indian Nations

///// Southern Indian Cessions
before 1800

NORTHERN TRIBES   To the north, centering in present New York State, lived the ten to twelve thousand of the Iroquois or Six Nations—a confederation that represented the highest type of political organization ever developed by North American Indians. They claimed a nominal overlordship of the tribes as far west as the Mississippi, and now and then enforced part of their claims. During the Revolution the Iroquois were powerful and important, but their power then waned and after 1800 they were no longer significant.

A second important group of Indians west of the Appalachians and east of the Mississippi was composed of tribes located between the Ohio River and the Great Lakes. Foremost were the Shawnee in present Ohio, the Wyandot near Detroit, the Miami in present Indiana, the Illinois in present Illinois, the Sauk and Foxes north of the Illinois River, and the Potawatomi, Winnebago, Ottawa, and Chippewa in the upper Great Lakes region. Most of them were Algonquian, and in contrast to the Iroquois of the Six Nations they seldom acted together. This group totaled possibly 50,000 persons, but in all probability not over 3000 warriors were on the warpath at any one time.

The Indians north of the Ohio were normally peaceful, but could on occasion be warlike and cruel. Each tribe, each group, and often each individual acted independently in war; each warrior sought whatever shelter he could find, did his fighting, and then went home. Pitched battles were rare. The dead were scalped, with the scalp a sort of trophy. Prisoners were sometimes adopted by the tribe, particularly if they were women or children; now and then a captive was tortured, but such incidents were unusual.

Landownership among the Algonquians existed only through use: whoever planted a crop of corn possessed that piece of land until the corn was harvested, and not longer. Agriculture was limited usually to the raising of corn, and sometimes squash and beans. More important was the fishing and hunting land, for the Indians lived mostly on fish and game. Here also was a rough ownership through use. Each tribe had vague limits to the land over which it could hunt, and invasion by other tribes might mean war. These tribes were not truly nomadic, but a hunting life meant much movement; consequently their housing was a simple wigwam—usually a dome-shaped framework, overlaid with bark, hides, or rush mats. Here and there permanent towns were constructed at strategic points.

At the time the whites arrived all the clothing of these Indians was of leather. The man ordinarily wore a breechcloth, moccasins, leggings, and a hunting shirt; on the warpath he limited his attire to a breechcloth and plenty of bright paint. The woman wore a skirt extending below her knees, and sometimes a jacket. Polygamy was usually permitted, for there was no large surplus of women, but it was never widely practiced. Infidelity by the wife was punished by cutting off the end of her nose or by killing her. Such punishment was meted out by the injured husband, since all punishment was a matter of individual vengeance. A woman's life was difficult and arduous. It was she who usually did the planting and cultivating, gathered herbs and firewood, cooked, dressed the leather, sewed the clothes with sinew, made the utensils, constructed the wigwam, and cared for the children. The men confined their activities mainly to hunting, fishing, and fighting.

Sickness was considered supernatural and due to evil spirits. The Indian medicine man depended heavily on elaborate rituals designed to drive out the wicked spirits. Also he used simple herbs, which may have had some effect. Frequently the medicine man would suck the part affected, and then spit out of his mouth hair, stones, sticks, or similar material; these articles were supposed to have come from the ailing member, and their absence was expected to relieve the patient. Wonderful cures were often made, particularly with wounds, probably because of the sucking, the herbs, and the outdoor life of the patient, but functional disorders and contagious diseases frequently were fatal.

The treatment of sickness was to the Indian but one phase of the continual process of placating the innumerable spirits, both good and bad, that were thought to inhabit the world. There were hundreds of ceremonials to gratify the various Indian desires, such as getting rain, securing good hunting, curing disease, overcoming enemies, and producing brave warriors. Each of these ceremonials had a complicated ritual, with specified ceremonial actions, decorations, fire, and speeches. Usually it included some kind of instrumental music (drum or whistle), singing, and dancing. Often particular animals, such as the snake and the bear, were mimicked. In addition to the hundreds of small good and bad spirits that had to be placated, most tribes believed in one more important good and one more important bad spirit. Usually they also believed in a future life in which the good Indian would live at his ease, with much fine hunting and fishing, and no accidents or disease.

THE OLD SOUTHWEST   South of the Ohio River were the large loose confederations of the Five Civilized Nations—Cherokee, Choctaw, Creeks, Chickasaw, and Seminole—whose destinies in the decade after the Revolution were controlled to some extent by the unusually able Creek half-breed Alexander McGillivray. The Cherokee lived in the mountainous parts of the present states of Tennessee, Alabama, Georgia, and North and South Carolina. They were an industrious and intelligent group, tilling the land, hunting, raising horses, dogs, and poultry, and developing many picturesque dances—ceremonial, erotic, and warlike. One of their amusements was an early form of the present lacrosse, but the field was larger, the players unlimited in number, and the game even rougher. The Indian seldom lost his temper, even though he might lose in a bet his entire possessions.

West of the Cherokee, and extending to the Mississippi, were the Chickasaw. Most warlike of the Five Nations, they usually acted together in case of trouble. South of the Chickasaw were the Choctaw, the least important of the groups. They were commonly reported as treacherous, and did not act together. East of them (in present Florida) were the Seminole, who were really a branch of the Creeks.

Strongest of the Five Nations were the Creeks, living south of the Cherokee. They were probably the most civilized of the Indians within the present boundaries of the

United States. Their fields were extensive and sometimes fenced, were worked by communal effort, and produced rice, corn, tobacco, beans, and potatoes. They hunted and fished, and also raised horses, hogs, and poultry, and sometimes owned Negro slaves. Their clothing, blankets, and wigwams were well made and beautifully trimmed. Their pottery was of clay, and glazed to give it a hard surface.

The Creeks had permanent towns. In the center of each town was an open square surrounded by four long low buildings in which the warriors were housed according to rank. The families of the warriors lived in lodges built around the central square and up and down a river or creek; from fifteen to two hundred lodges constituted an ordinary village. For each town there was a head man in addition to the war chiefs, and each town sent representatives to general tribal councils. This rough confederation sometimes took common action.

As was true of all Indians, the Creeks had elaborate rituals and ceremonials. Their principal festival was the green-corn dance, at which the first ear of corn was burned with intricate rites. For three days the men stayed in the square and fasted, while the women bathed frequently. The big ceremony came on the fourth day, when both sexes mingled in the open square. As was usual such ceremonies were connected with the belief in a good and a bad spirit, and in a time of future reward or punishment.

The marital customs of the Creeks were slightly unusual. Sexual relations before marriage were quite free. Courtship was carried on by a female friend of the male suitor. Both marriage and divorce were easy, either party being permitted to leave his or her mate at any time without warning. The family centered in the woman; the husband moved to his wife's home. Adultery by the wife was punished by whipping or by cutting off the hair or ears, and was inflicted either by the husband or by male relatives of the wife.

ATTITUDE TOWARD THE INDIANS

The first problem of the white settler in regard to the Indian was protection, for from time to time and without announcement the Indian went to war, and no settlement was safe. But of almost equal importance was the fact that the Indians possessed land that the frontiersmen wished to occupy, and that the federal government recognized as belonging to the Indians. The westerner, however, was not deterred from claiming rights to the land either by the attitude of the government or that of the Indians, for to him landownership meant small individual holdings for the purpose of farming. The Indians, from this point of view, were only savages whom God for some inscrutable reason had allowed to hinder the progress of his chosen white people, and had no rights against those of the superior white civilization; killing them was much like killing poisonous snakes. Some whites held that if the game were killed off, the Indians would be forced to accept farming and be absorbed by white civilization.

Religious easterners often saw the Indians as "heathen" ripe for conversion, and devoted missionaries spent their lives in bringing them the gospel. They were deeply disappointed when the Indian did not recognize immediately the superiorities of

Christianity; in fact, the Indian clung to his own practices and found it difficult to understand such concepts as "sin" and "total depravity," particularly when explained in imperfectly understood English.

The missionaries were certain that accepting Christianity involved adoption of white ways of life, but the Indian was not enthusiastic about such ideas as private property, a permanent home, monogamy, observing the Sabbath. He objected to being called lazy because he spent his life in hunting, fishing, and fighting. The brave rejected agriculture, which he considered squaws' work. Moreover, the Indian observed that the behavior of most of the whites he saw—soldiers, trappers, and traders—did not exemplify the virtues of sobriety, honesty, peacefulness, and chastity which were preached by the missionaries, while the bitter feeling between Catholic and Protestant failed to exemplify the ideal of brotherly love.

Finding the older generation unresponsive, the missionaries tended to emphasize education of the children. Here again they had troubles, for they persisted in teaching in English, using white methods and materials. Indian parents were hard to convince that white education was better for their children than Indian play. Higher education began with the Foreign Missionary School, opened at Cornwall, Connecticut, in 1817 by the American Board of Foreign Missions. Other schools followed, and a few Indians attended white schools, where they frequently had language difficulties. Altogether, the results of the missionary efforts were decidedly disappointing.

The federal government approved and sometimes subsidized the work of the missionaries. In a long series of laws it made every effort to treat the Indian with the "utmost good faith," as promised by the Northwest Ordinance. Traders in the Indian country presumably were brought under control by a licensing system. Private land purchases were forbidden, and settlers in the Indian country were to be removed—by force if necessary. Agents were sent and gifts were provided, as in the Intercourse Act of 1793, to try to persuade the natives to adopt settled farming. The enforcement of such legislation was almost impossible. Federal forces were too small to police the Indian country properly. Illegal settlers might be removed from time to time but soon returned. Persuading the Indian to become a farmer on the white model had little success except among some of the southern tribes. Friction was continual as Indians visited white settlements, whites invaded Indian country, and frontier cattle roamed freely.

From the standpoint of the federal government the Indians were in an anomalous position. On the one hand, they were considered as independent nations exercising the rights of sovereignty; they owned the land they occupied, and land cessions or other agreements had to be in the form of treaties made by the executive power and ratified by the Senate. On the other hand, it was evident that, regardless of any legal fiction, Indian tribes were not in fact free and independent states. They lived within the territorial limits of the United States, were not recognized by foreign nations, and were subject to controls imposed without their consent, and often without their knowledge.

Both the nation and the Indians suffered from the attempts to maintain an unrealistic theory of Indian independence. The federal government was in a perpetual quandary as to how to treat frontier advance. If Indian rights were maintained rigidly, there would be no white advance; and a white government could hardly view this prospect with equanimity, particularly when white westerners could vote and Indians could not. At the same time the federal government had every intention of treating the Indians fairly. The fluctuations and inconsistencies of white policy are understandable, if not always admirable.

INDIAN TREATIES   The method usually followed in settling a conflict between Indian rights and white desires was to buy the disputed land and open it formally to white settlement. The Indians were summoned to a council at some central spot. Government agents mixed cajolery, threats, food, clothing, and liquor to obtain a treaty of cession. Orinarily the compensation to the Indians included blankets, cloth, weapons, jewelry, annuities, and frequently aid to settled agriculture. After the signing by Indians and whites, the treaty went to the Senate for approval. In many cases the Senate modified its terms, necessitating an effort, usually futile, to have the modifications accepted by the original signatories. As soon as the treaty was made and ratified, it was considered by the United States as permanently binding on all members of the tribes represented, and on their descendants. The ceded land was formally surveyed and opened for settlement; usually the original settlers, who had come while the land still technically belonged to the Indians, had their possessions confirmed.

Not only was the treaty policy of the federal government based on an unrealistic theory, but it involved all sorts of practical difficulties. The Indians never really understood the white concept of permanent individual ownership and sale. In a vague way they recognized ownership by use, but even here their concepts were not clear-cut. They often failed to appreciate that the land they sold was closed to them forever. Land was like air and water—plentiful enough for the use of everyone—and it was a perpetual surprise to the Indian that he was prohibited from returning to the land on which he had formerly hunted.

Moreover, the Indians never saw eye to eye with the whites concerning treaties. Both the Indians and the whites agreed in theory that a treaty must be signed by authorized representatives, and then ratified by proper authority—tribe and Senate, respectively. But here agreement ended. Indian signatories frequently had no official status, but were just random braves rounded up by the whites; many times they were befuddled by whiskey when they placed their marks at the bottom of words they could not read. The affected tribe might or might not accept the agreement, and in either case the terms might well not be understood. As for the whites, they assumed that a treaty was binding on the Indians as soon as it was signed, regardless of technicalities. The possibilities for trouble were obviously unending.

When the Indians violated a treaty, possibly because of lack of understanding, a failure of ratification, or complete unawareness of its existence, further differences between red and white ideology developed. The violation was usually committed by an individual, or by one or more small groups acting independently. The tribe as a whole might have no knowledge of these acts, and feel no responsibility, but the federal government professed to see no difference between the part and the whole. It was difficult to discover and punish the real offenders; hence the punitive expedition waged war on any group of Indians within the district in which the trouble had occurred.

These differences in attitude between white man and red made conflict inevitable as settlers continued to view Indian land with covetous eyes. The clashes should be blamed as much on unavoidable differences of viewpoint as on bad faith on either side. Some of the disastrous results of the conflict might have been avoided if the federal government had abandoned earlier the effort to treat Indian tribes as independent nations, but the removal of the Indians would still have brought them untold misery and heartbreak.

THE WEST AT THE END OF THE REVOLUTION The end of the Revolutionary War found the frontier in turmoil; never had there been a decisive and large-scale defeat of the Indians. For the Indians the war continued, and they harried outlying settlements, killing individuals, capturing families, driving off stock, stealing crops, and destroying improvements. Arguments that the war was over because a few far distant whites had uttered the magic word peace carried little conviction. White intruders were still arriving, and their increasing number made conflict with the reds unavoidable. Indians loved their homes and would not leave voluntarily. In the South the expansion was from Georgia and the infant state of Franklin. In the North the occupation of Ohio had begun, with streams of settlement converging from Kentucky and western Pennsylvania. A sprinkling of towns such as Marietta had appeared on the northern bank of the Ohio River.

Foreign powers complicated the situation. In the South, Spain was anxious to keep the Indian trade and to provide a buffer against United States expansion. To accomplish these ends it was cordial toward the Indians and friendly toward Franklin, which it even talked of attaching to itself. In the North, England continued to hold such western posts as Detroit and Mackinac, and to cultivate friendly Indian relations, with the object of retaining the fur trade. A gesture was made toward restraining the Indians from active war, for American goodwill was desired, but an Indian confederation was encouraged, and British statements at least implied that assistance would be forthcoming for the Indians in any future trouble with the United States.

Northwest and Southwest were similar in another matter: in each area there was an Indian confederation. The southern combination was inspired by Alexander McGillivray, and the northern one by the equally able Joseph Brant. Each federation was hostile to any further land cessions to the whites and agreed not to consider such cessions valid.

INDIAN TREATIES AFTER THE WAR The central government under the Articles of Confederation was unduly optimistic about the Indians. Flushed with success, Congress held in 1783 that the Indians, as unsuccessful British allies, had lost the war and thereby forfeited all claim to their land—a proposition impossible to maintain.

During the same year Congress ordered all white intruders off the Indian lands, even though it had insufficient power to enforce the order, and sent commissioners to obtain treaties of peace and friendship with the various tribes. In 1786 it provided for the administration of Indian affairs through two departments that divided their duties at the Ohio River; both were subject to the secretary of war.

When the congressional commissioners went west they found their job extremely difficult. Most Indians had little desire to talk and even less to sign treaties—particularly treaties involving land cessions. Ultimately the southern Indians were brought into line by treaties with the Cherokee (1785), the Chickasaw and Choctaw (1786), and the Creeks (1790). Of these tribes the Chickasaw and Choctaw were generally friendly to the whites, and the Cherokee and Creeks generally hostile—a hostility not alleviated either by treaties or by military operations, including those of Georgia and of the state of Franklin.

In the North the congressional commissioners made a parallel series of treaties but with even poorer results, if that were possible. By the Treaty of Fort Stanwix (1784) the Iroquois once more promised to give up their western claims. By the treaties of Fort McIntosh (1786) and Fort Finney (1786) most of the northwestern tribes agreed to accept American sovereignty and to cede their claims to most of Ohio. The trouble with these treaties was that many groups were not represented, and most Indians considered them not binding. The commissioners tried to show their good faith by ordering Colonel Josiah Harmar in 1785 to eject all unauthorized white settlers in the Indian country. Harmar made a few feeble gestures, and constructed Fort Harmar at the mouth of the Muskingum, but he then decided quite wisely that his force was too small to accomplish the task with which it was charged.

All these treaties made a brave show on the statute books but produced little change in western conditions. Indian raids continued. At this juncture the problem was transferred to the hands of the new government established under the Constitution. Some sort of action was inevitable, especially since President Washington had long been concerned with the West.

HARMAR   Arthur St. Clair, as governor of the Northwest Territory, tried his hand at Indian affairs by concluding a treaty with all available Indians at Fort Harmar in January 1789. Again the Indians bound themselves to keep earlier treaties of peace, but again they showed little enthusiasm for keeping their agreements. The consequence was that Brigadier General Harmar (his rank had been raised by this time) was sent on a raiding expedition against the hostile tribes. In spite of some minor successes, Harmar's expedition was a failure; instead of pacifying the Indians it made them more hostile.

Harmar's failure moved Congress in the summer of 1790 to empower President Washington to call out the militia of Kentucky, Virginia, and western Pennsylvania to defend the frontier. General Harmar, who was placed in command, was at Fort Washington (Cincinnati), and the new troops were allowed to straggle down the Ohio River at their own convenience.

The army at Fort Washington was composed of 1453 men, of whom 320 were federal troops who had had experience in the Revolutionary War. The others were militiamen who were far from satisfactory fighters. They ranged in age from the very young to the very old. Many were physically incompetent; few had even an elementary idea of how to care for and use a gun. Supplies were poor, clothing was inadequate and shoddy, and food was bad. The militiamen had the usual resentment toward military control; disciplining a western company of militiamen was almost as difficult as controlling the Ohio River. In addition, the militiamen and the regulars looked on each other with contempt, and came to the assistance of the other only in dire necessity.

Late in September, after desultory training, this ill-assorted army left Fort Washington to fight the Indian confederation, of which the most hostile were the Shawnee, the Miami, and the Kickapoo. Soon the militia threatened mutiny; some of the volunteers actually started to go home, and force was necessary to recall them. After the army had covered some 170 miles, it accidentally encountered a small group of Indians. Both parties were surprised and alarmed, but the militiamen were more quick witted and started to run first. Again they had to be brought back ignominiously.

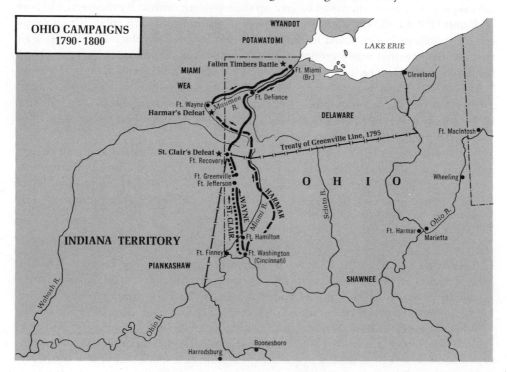

The general route of Harmar's slow and badly organized march was up the Little Miami and then north near the present Ohio-Indiana boundary. Supplies were inadequate and the men were discontented, but luckily no considerable body of Indians appeared. Finally the army reached one of the more important Indian towns, at the site of the present Fort Wayne; the Indians fled, and Harmar's men had the satisfaction of destroying the Indian lodges and crops.

This "brilliant victory" was followed by less satisfactory engagements. On September 19 a detachment was surprised and overwhelmed. Two days later a general engagement brought the disorganization and hurried retreat of Harmar's army; 200 whites were killed and 35 wounded, the proportion of killed to wounded showing the thoroughness of the Indian operations. More men would have been killed if the Indians had not been occupied taking scalps and loading themselves with plunder. Eventually Harmar's army was restored to partial order, but it was thoroughly disheartened. On November 4 the survivors arrived at Fort Washington.

Harmar's operations were unsuccessful, but a court of inquiry exonerated the general. He had probably shown considerable personal bravery and had done the best he could; but the net result was that a white expedition had been defeated disastrously, and that the Indians continued their depredations with increased self-assurance. Two smaller expeditions were sent early in 1791, one of them led by Wilkinson. They succeeded in doing some damage, but not enough to frighten the red man.

ST. CLAIR   In this emergency President Washington ordered Governor St. Clair to take personal command. St. Clair was a high-minded gentleman of the Federalist school with noble ideals and great personal courage. But he was also elderly and choleric; his strength was waning, his fat was increasing, he was troubled periodically by gout, and he overrated his military ability. In spite of these handicaps he developed a good campaign plan, with the principal objective of constructing a line of forts from the Ohio River to Lake Erie.

St. Clair's men, like Harmar's, were poor material. They were gathered largely from the cities, often from the poorhouses and prisons. Most of them were six months' militia, poorly paid, lacking military experience, and thriving on dissipation and disorder. This nondescript array came west by way of Pittsburgh, following its own pleasure in descending the Ohio to Fort Washington. Theoretically St. Clair had some 3000 men, but his actual effectives were never more than 2000. All the bad conditions that had bothered Harmar also harassed St. Clair.

St. Clair first dispatched an advance guard to build a fort on the Great Miami about twenty-five miles from Cincinnati. The main army started its advance early in October 1791, with much grumbling at leaving the pleasures of garrison life. The wilderness, however, was made endurable by continued gambling and drinking, as well as by the presence of many women camp followers. On October 12 Fort Jefferson was built six miles south of the present Greenville, Ohio, and here the army rested twelve days before advancing. November 3 saw the expedition camped on a plateau of the Wabash a hundred miles north of Cincinnati, on the present Ohio-Indiana line.

At daybreak of November 4 the soldiers were startled from their slumbers by Indian war whoops and a shower of arrows coming from the surrounding forest. When the partially clothed whites rushed from their tents they had to fire at an unseen foe. The resulting engagement included many feats of bravery, but no effective resistence. St. Clair was so weak he had to be lifted to his horse; three horses were shot from under him, eight bullets went through his clothes, and one clipped his hair. His best efforts, however, failed to produce any semblance of order among his troops. The Indians lurked in the forest, shot down the easily visible whites, and now and then rushed forth to take a scalp. The troops, unaccustomed to Indian fighting, probably never saw their foes. Soon they began to retreat and shortly their walk turned into a run. As had occurred with Harmar's troops, the Indians were so busy collecting booty that they did not pursue their defeated adversaries.

When St. Clair's army had recovered enough to count its losses, it found 630 killed and 283 wounded—approximately half the total force had been put out of action. Many of the bodies were left on the field of battle, and these were mutilated by the Indians; a later investigation showed a considerable number of females among the dead. The remnants of the so-called army gradually straggled back to Cincinnati, thoroughly beaten and demoralized. Congress investigated the conduct of the expedition and exonerated St. Clair, but his resignation from the army was accepted in April 1792.

WAYNE   President Washington's choice to turn defeat into victory was a former Revolutionary hero, Anthony Wayne, even though "Mad Anthony's" daring exploits during the Revolution raised some question as to his caution in fighting Indians. A new army was gathered at Pittsburgh, and again it was composed of the kind of men who had "fought" under Harmar and St. Clair. But at this point all similarity to preceding expeditions ended. Wayne joined his command at Pittsburgh and immediately started to drill his 2500 infantry, cavalry, and artillery.

Wayne desired to win the war in a hurry and return to the pleasures of the East, but the secretary of war, backed by the President, vetoed the plan. Accordingly, Wayne moved twenty miles down the river in the fall of 1792 and spent the winter at Legionville doing more drilling. By this time the West was becoming impatient with a "mad" general who spent his time in the barracks while his enemies were laying waste the settlements he was supposed to protect. But Washington insisted that no offensive action be undertaken until after the Indian councils of 1793. In April of that year Wayne moved his camp to a point near Cincinnati, where he devoted the summer and early fall to still more drilling. Undoubtedly this was the best-prepared and -drilled army that had ever existed in the West. "Mad Anthony" was in a fair way to lose his hard-earned nickname, although not entirely through his own desire.

While Wayne drilled his men, American commissioners suffered the ignominy of following the Indians to Detroit to try to make peace. They were authorized to make real concessions, even to the extent of restoring all Indian lands except the Ohio Company and Symmes grants, or to make large additional payments. But the Indians, arrogant and intractable, refused any compromise and insisted on recovering all their land north of the Ohio. The humiliated commissioners returned home without an agreement.

Upon the failure of negotiations, Wayne was given the signal to advance. During the fall he moved north slowly, acclimating his men to actual campaigning. At the present Greenville he built Fort Greenville, an imposing stockade, did more drilling, sent out spies, and started road construction. An advance guard was dispatched late in the year to construct Fort Recovery on the scene of St. Clair's defeat. The Indians gathered some 2000 warriors in the spring of 1794, but made the mistake of attacking Fort Recovery instead of confining themselves to cutting off isolated parties and interfering with supply trains. Discouraged by the failure of their attack on the fort and by the lack of expected British aid, many of them returned home, so that only 1300 remained when Wayne started to move.

Wayne's advance, beginning late in July, was slow and impressive. Fort Adams was built on the St. Marys River and Fort Defiance at the junction of the Maumee and Auglaize. The main body of Indians was encountered August 20 at a place called Fallen Timbers because of the presence of trees overturned by a heavy storm. Amazingly enough, the Indians were willing to fight one of their rare pitched battles. Wayne repulsed the attack but won no clear-cut victory; the Indians lost only some 50 braves and were by no means demoralized. The decisive nature of the battle lay in the Indian realization that they were to receive no active English aid; the silence of the guns at nearby Fort Miami (British) was more significant than the actual battle.

After Fallen Timbers Wayne returned to Fort Defiance, from which base he destroyed the nearby Miami towns and built Fort Wayne. The winter of 1794–1795 was spent in Greenville. Wayne's objective had been attained. The Indians had come to realize the futility of further immediate resistance, and for the first time in many years the frontier was relatively free from the menace of Indian attack.

Wayne finished his work in the West by putting the results in a treaty. Starting early in 1795 he called the Indian chiefs to a large conference at Fort Greenville. By June there had arrived 1130 Delawares, Potawatomi, Wyandot, Shawnee, Miami, Chippewa, Ottawa, Wea and Piankashaw, Kickapoo, and Kaskaskia. Fifty days were taken up with feasts, speeches, and ceremonies before any action was taken. The resulting Treaty of Greenville settled the status of the Indians of the Old Northwest for the time being—not because it was the first and only treaty of its kind, but because it was the first to be based on a thorough intimidation of the Indians. By its terms a definite line was drawn between red and white territory. The whites received approximately the southeastern two-thirds of the present state of Ohio and the southeastern corner of present Indiana, while the rest of the Northwest was left to the Indians. In return for these land cessions the Indians were to receive immediately goods to the value of $20,000 and then about half that amount annually. As soon as the treaty was signed Wayne returned to the East, to be received as a hero.

JAY'S TREATY   While Wayne was engaged in his victorious campaign in the West, there was in progress another mission of a far different nature, in which the west was also vitally interested. In June 1794 John Jay was sent on a special mission to England to carry on direct negotiations concerning English-American difficulties. The final treaty (November 19, 1794) was intensely unpopular in the United States, but it did provide for the surrender of the Northwest posts that England had not evacuated at the end of the Revolution. The surrender actually took place in June 1796, and it was only fitting that Anthony Wayne should be the man to accept the most important of them—Detroit.

  With the surrender of the Northwest posts and the submission of the Indians, the trans-Appalachian region was more available for settlement than it had ever been. The Indians were not again to be ready for any widespread hostilities until the period of the War of 1812. With American possession of the Great Lakes posts the likelihood of

The Treaty of Greenville, 1795. The artist is believed to have been one of General Wayne's staff officers. (Chicago Historical Society)

English encouragement of the Indians was decreased, and more freedom was possible for American traders, trappers, and settlers.

The result of these developments was an ever-increasing flow of migration to the West. Whereas most of the early settlers had come from the South by way of the Cumberland Gap, now they began to come in large numbers from the central and northern states. The inevitable cycle of Indian relations was soon completed, and almost before the ink of the Greenville treaty was dry new settlers were again pushing into the Indian country. And again the government followed these pioneers, forcing the Indians back still farther. Half a dozen new cessions in the ten years after Greenville emphasized the ephemeral nature of Indian treaty lines and promises.

READINGS   *Paperbacks are marked with an asterisk.*

Indian Description   Among the more useful works are H. Wendell Oswalt, *The Land Was Theirs* (1966); Flora W. Seymour, *Story of the Red Man* (1929), popular in tone; Alpheus H. Verrill, *The Real Americans* (1954), interesting; *Harold E. Driver, *Indians of North America* (1961), anthropological; Clark Wissler, *The American Indian* (1917, 1957), and *Indians of the United States* (1940), good anthropology; Ruth M. Underhill, *Red Man's America* (1953); D'Arcy McNickle, *They Came Here First* (1949), early Indian culture; *Roy H. Pearce, *The Savages of America* (1953), white ideas about them.

Specifically on the northern tribes see *Randolph C. Downes, *Council Fires on the Upper Ohio* (1940), excellent; Arthur Pound and Richard E. Day, *Johnson of the Mohawks* (1930), fair. On the southern tribes see Robert S. Cotterill, *Southern Indians* (1954), good; Angie Debo, *The Rise and Fall of the Choctaw Republic* (1934) and *The Road to Disappearance* (1941), both very good; David H. Corkran, *The Creek Frontier, 1540–1783* (1967); Grace S. Woodward, *The Cherokees* (1963); Henry T. Malone, *Cherokees of the Old South* (1956); Merritt B. Pound, *Benjamin Hawkins, Indian Agent* (1951). A more specialized topic is Robert F. Berkhofer, Jr., *Salvation and the Savage: An Analysis of Protestant Missions and American Indian Response, 1787–1862* (1965). Two useful books on the effect of disease are Percy M. Ashburn, *The Ranks of Death* (1947), mostly before 1700; Esther A. Stearn, *The Effect of Smallpox on the Destiny of the Amerindian* (1945).

Indian Policy   Several monographs, although sometimes not easy to read, cover the subject well: Walter H. Mohr, *Federal Indian Relations, 1774–1788* (1933); *Francis P. Prucha, *American Indian Policy in the Formative Years . . . 1790–1834* (1962) and *The Sword of the Republic: The United States Army on the Frontier, 1783–1846* (1969); George D. Harmon, *Sixty Years of Indian Affairs, 1789–1850* (1941); James R. Jacobs, *The Beginning of the U.S. Army, 1783–1812* (1947); Reginald Horsman, *Expansion and American Indian Policy, 1783–1812* (1967).

Ohio Wars   Histories of Ohio always cover the subject, as, for example, Beverley W. Bond, Jr., *The Civilization of the Old Northwest* (1934) and *The Foun-*

dations of Ohio (1941); John A. Caruso, *The Great Lakes Frontier* (1961); Randolph C. Downes, *Frontier Ohio, 1788–1803* (1935); Walter Havighurst, *Land of Promise* (1946), reads well. Accounts of the military leaders include Thomas Boyd, *Mad Anthony Wayne* (1929), reads well; Harry E. Wildes, *Anthony Wayne* (1941), more detailed; Gayle Thornbrough (ed.), *Outpost on the Wabash, 1787–1791* (1958), includes the letters of Harmar; Frazer E. Wilson, *Arthur St. Clair* (1944), overly eulogistic.

Erecting a Log Cabin. While this type of structure was not used by the earliest settlers, its adoption from the European proved very useful. Throughout frontier history this method of construction varied little. (Library of Congress)

*Chapter 8/*ADVANCING SETTLEMENT

The first really large flow of settlers across the Appalachians came in the twenty years after the Revolution. The number of migrants tended to increase with the years, with a slowing down in periods of depression, of war, and of Indian troubles; for example, the Old Northwest could not compete equally with the Old Southwest for new population until after the Treaty of Greenville (1795). Moreover, the new people did not spread equally over the West. Certain areas were more attractive if they had more fertile land and better transportation.

The vast majority of these self-elected westerners were native-born. Throughout the late eighteenth and most of the nineteenth century the United States doubled in population each generation, somewhat from immigration, but much more from the native birth rate. These extra people sought economic opportunity either in eastern cities, which grew during the period, or in the farms and towns of the West. Foreign immigrants joined the western shove, but in relatively small numbers, preferring the opportunities of the East; a town like Gallipolis, which was settled by French migrants, was exceptional.

The eastern states viewed the departure of their sons and daughters with mingled pride and alarm. The expansion of the American people increased American power and prestige, demonstrating the virility of a young and ambitious people, and increasing trade between East and West to the profit of both sections. On the other hand, the departure of many young vigorous citizens was viewed regretfully by those who had visions of local greatness, and particularly by those who wanted labor for expanding eastern stores and mills, for domestic service, or for the construction and operation of roads and canals. American labor was in general scarce, and hence highly paid, producing difficulties in competing with European production; migration to the West further increased the scarcity of eastern labor.

Westward-bound settlers were of all ages and both sexes but, as already mentioned, the largest single element was young men who had just attained their majority and were traveling alone or in small groups. Such a man might be sufficiently lucky to be able to buy a farm immediately, after no more than a brief exploratory trip. More likely he possessed only a few dollars and planned to do farm work, storekeeping, boating, trapping, surveying, schoolteaching, or some other work until he acquired needed capital. Although he might squat on unsurveyed land, he still needed capital to purchase supplies, animals, implements, and seed. Before setting up as an independent farmer, he might well return to the East to marry his boyhood sweetheart. A frontier farmer's wife was a person to love and cherish, but also a needed companion and co-worker on the farm.

THE PROCESS OF MIGRATION   When an entire family moved, the process was more complicated, since a family wanted a more definite idea of where it was going. Possibly relatives or friends had moved earlier and had found a desirable region, or else the father or an older son would make a preliminary tour. In any case a man seldom took his wife and children across the mountains without confidence that he could provide for them; there must have been many evenings of earnest conversation before a family decided to leave old friends and surroundings for the newness of the West.

The migrating family sold its eastern possessions before it departed—partly because few articles could be packed into a single farm wagon, and partly because funds would be required to start farming and to tide them over the first year until crops could be harvested and marketed. Frequently the father enlarged his own small funds by borrowing from family and neighbors, for he realized that even with the greatest frugality moving was costly. Every westerner advised migrants to bring a good supply of cash, but the eastern family seldom was able to follow this advice; indeed, if the family had been well-to-do, it would have stayed in the East.

Only the bare necessities of life could be given space in the one farm wagon that was the sole means of transportation. Of first importance were implements for erecting a home and for farming—particularly an ax, an auger, an adz, a hammer. Guns and ammunition were necessary. Food consisted primarily of such staples as flour, bacon, sugar, salt, yeast, and vinegar. A spinning wheel was vital, and seeds for the first planting might be taken. Other desirable articles were almost innumerable, and might include clothes, cloth, needles, thread, pots and pans, dishes, and cutlery. Possibly some of the precious space was taken by a clock, a bureau, a bedstead, or some other specially prized family possession.

The westward-bound wagon was usually protected from sun and rain by canvas stretched tightly over curved strips of wood. Sometimes it was drawn by horses, but more frequently by the more useful and hardy oxen. Mother and the younger children might ride in the wagon, while father plodded beside the team and the older children followed to the rear. A cow or two or an extra horse might be part of the caravan, and it was not unknown to have the children chase chickens along the road. The speed was that of men and animals walking. At night the family camped by the side of the road and fried bacon and cooked its biscuits over an open fire. Rain slowed the trip and made life miserable.

SOUTHERN SETTLEMENT   People moving to the farming frontier moved as directly west as possible. Belts of settlement were created in which time after time the culture of a particular section of the East was reproduced. The bulk of the Virginia and Carolina migration went to Kentucky and Tennessee, Pennsylvania migration to Ohio, and New England migration to central New York and the region of the Great Lakes.

The most popular mecca for the earliest trans-Appalachian settlers was Kentucky. Its population of 74,000 in 1790 tripled within the next ten years and almost doubled again in the succeeding decade. Although almost all early settlers came over the mountains through the Cumberland Gap, later arrivals traveled more frequently by way of Pittsburgh or Wheeling and then down the Ohio River. Louisville was the most important of the river towns of Kentucky; its chief rival was Maysville, lying across the river from the terminus of Zane's Trace, which originated at Wheeling.

Lexington was the great interior metropolis of Kentucky, even though it claimed fewer than two thousand inhabitants in 1800. It dominated the blue grass country, overshadowing such rivals as Frankfort, Paris, and May's Lick. Lexington, the trading center for nearby farmers, could boast such varied industries as ropeworks, tanneries, potteries, and powder mills. It was proud of its literary and cultural achievements, being a publishing center of importance and the home of Transylvania, the first western college. Little wonder that an energetic and ambitious lawyer like Henry Clay picked Lexington as the proper place to settle during the 1790s.

The population of Tennessee was about half that of Kentucky, although in the generation after 1800 the difference decreased. The earliest settlements were, naturally, near the Cumberland Gap, in the eastern part of the state, and the road through the Gap was improved for wagon traffic in the 1790s. Eastern Tennessee, with its mountains and valleys, was particularly attractive to small farmers practicing a diversified agriculture. The center of population came to be Knoxville, founded in 1789.

Central Tennessee was topographically a continuation of the blue grass region of Kentucky; it was suitable for cotton culture and the profitable use of slaves, although there were few slaves in the early days. Nashville was the metropolis of the area, and experienced a boom after the opening of a wagon road in 1795. Industries, lawyers, doctors, ministers, churches, and comfortable homes soon appeared, and slavery increased. Cumberland College was organized in 1806. West of the Nashville area, in western Tennessee, little settlement existed before 1810.

South of Tennessee, restless Georgians pushed into the central and northern parts of the present state, with a roving and avaricious eye cast as far west as the Mississippi, since Georgia claimed land to the river. The state had been exceedingly reluctant to grant this immense empire and possible source of wealth to the federal government, even though powerful Indian groups made immediate settlement impossible. Georgia's policy shortly after the Revolution had been to grant western land as a reward to people who had served the state, and to prospective settlers; it early developed a sort of homestead policy. These early grants seldom produced settlement. The grantees tended to sell their claims to speculators, and in some cases a single person amassed a million or more acres. In addition, warrants were issued for several times the amount of land existing in several counties, and these warrants were then resold to unsuspecting buyers in Philadelphia and elsewhere. All such practices meant future trouble.

The Georgia land situation was further confused by several large sales (the Yazoo grants), made ostensibly to help the precarious Georgia finances, but inspired, often through questionable means, by speculators who looked hopefully at the lands near the Mississippi. Particularly attractive was the mouth of the Yazoo River, which in time was the location of Vicksburg. Four companies were given grants in 1789, and each made a down payment and tried unsuccessfully to encourage settlement. Three new companies were given additional land in 1795. All told, some 50 to 70 million acres were granted at prices that were ridiculously low even for wild western land, not considering that some of the payments were in worthless Georgia currency. Then in 1796 the state had a change of heart and repealed the grants, holding quite correctly that they had been acquired by fraud and bribery, and that in any case the lands belonged to the Indians and the state had no right to dispose of them.

Confusion became even greater when the companies brought court action to get the act of repeal declared illegal, while those to whom they had sold land sold it to others. Georgia solved its embarrassment by turning over its claims to the federal government in 1802. The federal government ordered all Yazoo claimants ejected, and had the land surveyed with the object of sale. This sweeping solution turned out to be impossible, not only because the government was tender of the feelings of settlers, but also because the Supreme Court decided in *Fletcher* v. *Peck* (1810) that the first grants were valid contracts and could not be abrogated by the action of one party. Before the affair ended, the government bought off the claiming companies for more money than it received from land sales. The only positive accomplishment was the expansion of Mississippi Territory.

Along the Gulf Coast and up the Mississippi as far as Natchez settlers had come after the region was acquired by England at the end of the Seven Years' War. Many of these people had obtained grants from the English government. The growth of population was slow, and up to 1810 these small communities continued to cling to the coast and the lower river. Spain reconquered the whole area during the Revolution, and then argued with the United States as to the proper boundary. When Spain withdrew its troops from the disputed area, the United States set up the Mississippi Territory (1798). In 1804 Mississippi was enlarged to include the Georgia cessions, and other changes came with the acquisition of Louisiana.

NORTHERN SETTLEMENT   North of the Ohio River, settlement came slowly until the Wayne campaign ended the Indian menace. Present Ohio had a negligible population in 1790 and only 45,000 in 1800; but by 1810 the number had jumped to an impressive 231,000—almost as many people as in Tennessee. Early settlements clung closely to the banks of the Ohio, but after 1800 they began to fill the area of the cessions made at Greenville. A surplus of settlers drifted farther down the Ohio into present southern Indiana and Illinois, but prior to 1810 few men were sufficiently courageous to venture far from a river; population generally followed the Ohio and the Wabash, particularly in the area of Vincennes.

The earliest migrants to the Old Northwest were predominantly southern in origin, and this southern flow continued into the nineteenth century, coming either by way of the Potomac or through Kentucky. By the later period, however, other population elements were becoming more important. The New England settlement at Marietta, the New Jersey settlement at Cincinnati, and the foreign settlement at Gallipolis were symptomatic of the change.

The most important Ohio metropolis was Cincinnati, even though it could boast but 500 residents in 1800. Cincinnati had been founded in 1789 on the Symmes purchase and was a product of land speculation, as were many other Ohio towns, such as Dayton (1795) and Chillicothe (1796). It soon outdistanced its nearest competitors, although it had no great geographic advantage over the many other towns on the

Ohio River. Most significant was the favor of Governor St. Clair, who moved his capital from Marietta to Cincinnati in 1790.

Settlers bound for the Ohio Valley tended increasingly to come by way of Pittsburgh. The population of this thriving potential city was little over 1500 in 1800, but the next few years saw Pittsburgh grow rapidly and outdistance such competitors as Steubenville, Wheeling, and Marietta. Early Pittsburgh was primarily a commercial rather than a manufacturing center. Its most important early industries were milling, and ship building for ocean as well as for river trade. The coal and iron business was growing, so that within a few years Pittsburgh was to become known as "the Birmingham of America," manufacturing products that ranged from nails and other iron articles to leather, paper, glass, hats, and rope.

Another and more northern stream of migration began to flow into the region of the Great Lakes by 1800. Settlement had been expanding through central New York State after the Holland Land Company had planned the town of New Amsterdam (Buffalo) in 1799. This young village was to become the northern entry to the West, and thus similar to Pittsburgh, but for a time growth was small. During the War of 1812

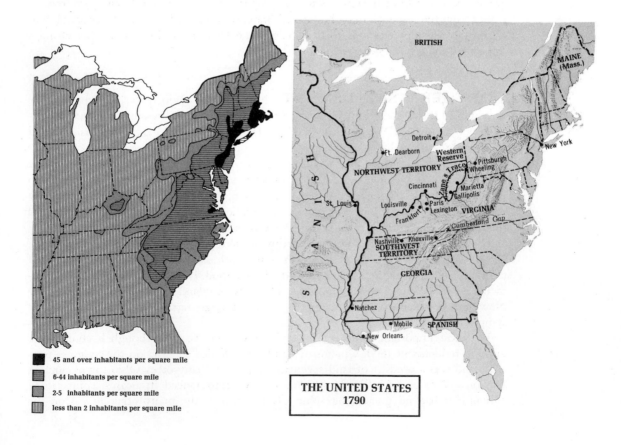

45 and over inhabitants per square mile

6-44 inhabitants per square mile

2-5 inhabitants per square mile

less than 2 inhabitants per square mile

**THE UNITED STATES
1790**

the village was burned, and it was not until after the war, and particularly after the opening of the Erie Canal, that real expansion came.

West of Buffalo a string of hamlets was coming into existence along the southern shore of Lake Erie. Most important of them was Cleaveland, which was a speculation of the Connecticut Land Company. The area of the city was in the "Connecticut Reserve," which had been retained by the state for sufferers from the Revolution. The city, whose name was soon modernized, was founded in 1796 by Moses Cleaveland and a group of settlers from Connecticut. At first it had to provide its own government, but in 1800 administration was assumed by the Northwest Territory. West of Lake Erie the most important town was Detroit, a small trading settlement.

TOWNS AND CITIES   Any description of settlement makes apparent that although most of the new arrivals were farmers, some were interested in town life. Among the migrants were merchants, small manufacturers, lawyers, doctors, millers, shoemakers, and others who gravitated toward the urban areas. A number of migrants called themselves artisans, but this term did not describe the skilled labor of today: the artisan of 1800 had some skill, such as carpentry or ropemaking, but he probably also could farm. His occupation in the West depended on the opportunities offered; a carpenter might run a livery stable, and a doctor might farm. Occupations tended not to be highly specialized.

Certain cities occupied locations that were obviously well suited geographically for their growth. Examples are Pittsburgh at the head of the Ohio River, Louisville at the falls of the Ohio River, and St. Louis just below the junction of the Missouri and Mississippi rivers. Other towns had less obvious geographical advantages. Lexington, Kentucky, was merely in the center of a rich farming area. Cincinnati had unfavorable terrain, and its growth can be credited primarily to speculation. With the speculative factor frequently looming large there were bound to be many mistakes, including such towns as New Athens, New Lisbon, Palermo, and others that failed to grow. Most disappointing was Town of America at the junction of the Ohio and Mississippi; the location seemed perfect, but the overflow of the rivers made impossible any considerable settlement.

The new towns of the West had all sorts of obvious troubles. Such problems as street paving and lighting, fire protection, and sanitation were particularly difficult in a new community that lacked adequate wealth. Then too there had to be developed such necessary institutions as newspapers, churches, saloons, libraries, and schools, which were more urban than rural. In general, political, social, and economic innovations came to the cities before they did to the countryside. Also, social distinctions were greater, since almost immediately considerable differences in wealth appeared. The merchant's wife and the wife of the livery stable worker hardly met on a plane of social equality. In other words, the western town reproduced on a smaller scale the conditions of the larger eastern city.

CONDITIONS OF TRAVEL Roads connecting East and West were in general bad, being improved only enough to permit wagons on the main thoroughfares. In the West, roads were being opened during the 1790s and later to connect the principal towns, such as Lexington and Nashville. Smaller inland towns had to be content with blazed trails or, at most, paths that were passable only for pack animals.

Road construction meant cutting the trees, but leaving the stumps, and clearing away most of the brush. Grades were not improved, and no roadbed was constructed except for a few specially difficult places; a swampy sector, for example, might be overlaid with a few logs over which the wagons could jolt to higher land. Such roads were bad at any time of the year, but were particularly atrocious during wet weather. Streams were ordinarily forded, but a few of the larger ones could be crossed by private ferries operated at the caprice of their owners, who charged all the traffic would bear.

Bad roads meant that whenever possible the migrant moved by water, and water transportation meant that the heaviest movement of population was down the Ohio River. The obvious point of embarkation was one of the most easterly towns, which increasingly meant Pittsburgh. Here a westward-moving family acquired a rough and boxlike flatboat, which served two functions. First and most obviously it was a means of transportation, carrying the entire possessions of the family. Second, it was an important source of planed lumber and nails for a future home. Both articles were scarce, and hence the flatboat was carefully disassembled so that wood and nails could be used again.

CHOOSING A HOME Upon arriving in the West, the migrant found nothing so important as his choice of land. Of obvious importance was fertility, which was surprisingly difficult to recognize. One sure test seemed to be whether the land in its native state produced luxurious vegetation. This criterion explains in part why frontiersmen preferred the densely wooded land near the rivers and why the ring of the woodman's axe was the most characteristic sound of the new settlement. Houses, barns, and fences were ordinarily of wood. The new settler did not, however, find himself attracted by the overflow land of the river bottoms. The other common test for a new settler was to find land that looked similar to that which he had found good in his old home, and here he made many mistakes: the New Englander who looked for oak clearings or the Pennsylvanian who sought reddish soil was starting his western life under a severe handicap.

Practically as important to the settler as good land was the availability of water, both for drinking and for transportation. A spring or a small brook sufficed for drinking, but a navigable stream was necessary for transportation and could also be used for drinking; true, it might be dirty, but the dirt would settle; and no one worried about bacteria, since no one had heard of them.

Finally, the migrant preferred to be reasonably near a settlement—not only for protection from the Indians, or to be able to buy and sell easily, but also for human companionship and assistance. The transplanted easterner was no hermit, and his family had no desire to be lost in a wilderness. He was a farmer looking for greater opportunity and wanted eastern advantages as soon as possible. If he had sufficient funds, he bought land that had been cleared and improved; if not, he still sought to reproduce his old surroundings with the greatest possible speed. The frontiersman who made the original clearings at the very tip of civilization frequently sold out and moved to a newer frontier, which meant that a large share of arrivals took land that had been at least partially cleared and transformed into productive farms.

ACQUIRING LAND   The land selected by the settler might be acquired in any one of several ways. Rather frequently it was bought from the original frontiersman or from a speculator. The speculator was ubiquitous, including not only such outstanding men as Clark, Boone, Sevier, and Blount, but thousands of lesser known persons down to the poorest frontiersman who acquired unneeded land in the hope that it would inflate in value with the increase of settlement. Eastern speculators were also numerous. The companies obtaining Yazoo grants, the Ohio Company, Symmes, and the rest were merely the outstanding illustrations of eastern land speculation. Although eastern speculators might buy their land in the West, the large companies in the early

Cincinnati in 1800. Note the passing flatboat carrying family, farm wagon, and belongings. This river town grew to be of considerable importance. (Cincinnati Historical Society)

years were more likely to operate from the East. Some bought directly from the United States government or from states with western claims. Others collected land warrants issued by the federal government for Revolutionary veterans, or by such states as Connecticut, Virginia, North Carolina, and Georgia. Apparently a large proportion of the land donated to veterans eventually got into the hands of the speculators. The veteran seemed to be more interested in immediate cash than in a prospective farm.

Speculators were interested in good agricultural land, but even more in water power, millsites, and townsites, for here lay the best chance of large profits. An impressive proportion of western towns represented the work of speculators. Marietta, Cincinnati, Chillicothe, Dayton, Boonesborough, and Nashville were but a few of the hundreds that received their original impetus from speculators. But for each successful settlement there were a dozen that remained entirely in their originators' minds or that eventuated only in a few log cabins. Probably the majority of speculators lost money, with only enough successes to keep the will-o'-the-wisp of huge profits glowing to attract other adventuresome souls.

The alternative to buying from a original settler or from a speculator was to purchase from the government. Legally the settler could not occupy land until it had been surveyed and he had bought it at auction, but thousands of settlers started farming without the formality of purchase. They hoped that the government would later confirm their occupancy or that they could buy the land they had occupied at the minimum price when the auction took place. This frequently occurred, possibly because of the assistance of neighbors similarly situated.

Once a man had picked his land or bought it, he started the arduous labor of making it into a real farm. Ordinarily he arrived in the spring to give himself the maximum time to prepare for the winter. For every settler arriving around 1800 the process of starting a farm was similar, regardless of whether he lived in the North or in the South. If in the South, he might have a slave or two, without thereby changing the picture radically. The movement of large slave coffles, with the establishment of big western plantations, was not common until after the War of 1812.

BUILDING A HOUSE   The first requirement for a family was shelter. A temporary, open, three-sided camp might be constructed from poles, and thatched; the front was higher than the back, and the fire was built before the open front. The labor of erecting such a camp might be avoided if some neighbor offered his hospitality. Father and the older sons immediately got out their axes and started to chop down the trees on the site of their future home and garden. These trees were transformed into a house, a barn, and rail fences, for the wooden rail fence was practically universal. In the meantime the smaller children collected brush and grubbed out small trees and bushes. Ultimately the whole mass of trash was burned in large bonfires.

The construction of the permanent house was a community undertaking, since seldom had a family enough grown sons to perform the necessary backbreaking work. On the day of the house-raising neighbors gathered from miles around. The logs were rolled to the site of the cabin, notched or dovetailed at each end, and lifted into place; they were placed first on one pair of opposite sides and then on the other pair. Meantime the women cooked a feast, which was probably followed by a dance in the new home. A little later the family might aspire to a cabin of squared logs, which shut out more of the weather and permitted better interior and exterior finishes. The ultimate goal was, of course, a house of planed lumber or brick or stone.

The construction of the roof represented a considerable problem as long as nails remained a luxury. The frame of rafters was held in place by wooden pins driven into auger holes. Over the rafters might be placed bark or rude shingles, but more frequently the roof was of clapboard construction, with the boards held in place by saplings fastened with wooden pegs.

After the frame of the house was completed, various openings were cut for doors, windows, and fireplace. All doors were wooden, and swung on leather or wooden hinges. Security could be attained by a heavy wooden bar fitted into brackets on the inside. A simple iron lock or a swinging wooden bar could be opened from the outside by means of a leather thong passed through an auger hole in the door; the latch string hanging outside was an indication of hospitality.

The fireplace was constructed of stone or of logs or of sticks covered with clay, depending on the region; the chimney was ordinarily built of logs, and but rarely of stone. The earliest cabins had no windows, but by 1800 most of them had at least small openings, sometimes barred to exclude wild animals, to admit light and air. Window glass was a rarity in the North and somewhat more frequent in the South; a more or less satisfactory substitute was oiled paper. The floor of the log cabin was ordinarily hardpacked earth, but the more particular and industrious frontiersman used puncheons—that is, logs that had been split in the middle and whose relatively flat surfaces were placed uppermost. The finishing touch for the cabin was filling the chinks between the logs with moss or dirt or clay.

The usual log cabin was neither beautiful nor commodious, and could boast but little comfort. It had the one artistic value of being appropriate to its surroundings. Its materials and method of construction made unlikely any great size; the usual cabin was no larger than a moderate-sized modern living room—say 15 to 18 feet long and 12 to 14 feet wide. A partition might create two rooms, but generally there was no such division. A windowless loft could be used as a storeroom and as sleeping quarters for the children. Now and then two such cabins were built side by side with a common roof. In the South the two-room and even the two-story log cabin soon appeared; the kitchen might be in an ell, and other rooms were added as the family grew.

CLEARING THE LAND   The building of the cabin entailed clearing a portion of the land, but in many cases little more than enough for a garden and chicken yard. Further efforts were necessary before a crop could be planted. The really radical method was to cut down all trees and use oxen to pull the stumps, but in actual practice this procedure was seldom used. Most common was the cutting of girdles around the trees, thus killing them; in time they were probably burned. Corn, which was tilled poorly because of the multiplicity of tree roots and which received only the sparse sunlight filtering between the dead trees, could not be luxuriant; but some corn was better than none.

The process of conquering a wilderness was slow and laborious. Even though the family left the East in the spring as soon as the roads dried and grass was available for the stock, so much time was consumed that first year in making the trip west, in selecting land, in building a cabin, and in clearing the land that nothing more than a small garden could be grown. In fact, with girdled trees, the crops of the first few years might all be very small. The interval between migration and marketable crops emphasized the need for a cash reserve. Even though the father shot game and everyone went on starvation rations, money was necessary to permit survival. The traditional hospitality of the West was of little advantage, since everyone in a particular region was in similar circumstances. Well over a year had to elapse before the family could again be self-supporting.

READINGS   *Paperbacks are marked with an asterisk.*

North   Among the general accounts are Beverley W. Bond, Jr., *The Civilization of the Old Northwest* (1934); John A. Caruso, *The Great Lakes Frontier* (1961), somewhat episodical; *Stewart H. Holbrook, *The Yankee Exodus* (1950), more so. Walter Havighurst, *Land of Promise* (1946) is readable, but his *Wilderness for Sale* (1956) is not. Lewis D. Stilwell, *Migration from Vermont 1776–1860* (1937) is an excellent monograph on a subject treated too infrequently. Useful are state histories, as Beverley W. Bond, Jr., *The Foundations of Ohio* (1941); Randolph C. Downes, *Frontier Ohio* (1935); Eugene H. Roseboom and Francis P. Weisenburger, *A History of Ohio* (1953); William T. Utter, *The Frontier State* (1941); Harlan Hatcher, *The Western Reserve* (1949), reads well; Clarence W. Alvord, *The Illinois Country* (1920), careful. Western Pennsylvania receives interesting treatment in *Solon J. and Elizabeth H. Buck, *The Planting of Civilization in Western Pennsylvania* (1939); John E. Wright and Doris S. Corbett, *Pioneer Life in Western Pennsylvania* (1940); John W. Harpster (ed.), *Pen Pictures of Early Western Pennsylvania* (1938); Paul D. Evans, *The Holland Land Company* (1924), a fine monograph on the Buffalo region.

South   Good general accounts are Thomas P. Abernethy, *The South in the New Nation, 1789–1819* (1961); Harriette L. S. Arnow, *Seedtime on the Cumberland, 1763–1803* (1960); *Everett Dick, *The Dixie Frontier* (1948); the last two are heavily social and read very well. Kentucky is well covered in Thomas D. Clark, *A History of Kentucky* (1937) and Francis G. Davenport, *Ante-Bellum Kentucky* (1943). Two good original accounts are Daniel Drake, *Pioneer Life in Kentucky, 1785–1800* (1948), and Harry Toulmin, *The Western Country in 1793* (1948), edited by Thomas D. Clark.

Cities *Richard C. Wade, *The Urban Frontier* (1959) is a fine study of five western cities between 1780 and 1830. Individual cities are covered in Frederick C. Bald, *Detroit's First American Decade, 1796 to 1805* (1948); Leland D. Baldwin, *Pittsburgh* (1937), good; Robert W. Bingham, *The Cradle of the Queen City* (1931), Buffalo. Harold R. Shurtleff, *The Log Cabin Myth: A Study of Early Dwellings of the English Colonists in North America* (1939) treats the origin of the log cabin.

Chapter 9 / LIFE IN THE WEST

Newly established western families were confronted with the problem of building a civilization with simple materials and tools. Most migrants were in no sense revolters from the traditional ways of life, desiring a new, different, and simpler environment. They sought only economic opportunity, and were anxious to reproduce the familiar trappings of eastern society as soon as possible. Crude houses and furniture, linsey-woolsey clothes, and bear steaks were only makeshifts until better things could be acquired.

HOUSE FURNISHINGS   While the new civilization was in the making, the settler lived in the simplest of home surroundings. The crude, homemade furniture consisted mainly of a rough plank or puncheon table and a few three-legged stools, which stood more solidly on the rough floor than did the four-legged kind. The absence of closets was compensated in part by pegs in the wall, and perhaps a few shelves. Beds were built against the walls, preferably in the corners; the walls furnished the main supports, but needed the supplement of forked stakes driven into the ground. A lattice work of leather thongs, rope, or slats served as springs. Mattresses were filled with straw until enough feathers were collected to produce the favored featherbeds, which were most comfortable if resting on straw ticks. Covers consisted of bear or buffalo robes or a second featherbed. All reports indicated that in the average cabin these articles were filthy and full of vermin. If cleanliness is next to godliness, these people deserved the fears for their spiritual welfare that the East entertained for them.

Privacy in a frontier cabin was practically impossible: the entire family dressed, undressed, and carried on most of its activities in the one room. Here occurred everything from spinning and making bread to childbirth. Some saving of modesty was possible as cold weather deterred one from removing all his clothes at night, while the all-over bath was ordinarily reserved for warm weather and the neighboring stream. Favorite western stories dealt with the embarrassment that resulted when a group of travelers of both sexes spent the night with a large family in a log cabin.

Of the varied activities that made the cabin a busy workshop, none was more important or more frequent than the preparation of food. Cooking was done at the fireplace, and therefore most of the food was either boiled or fried. A crane or iron hook held the pot for boiling, and the three-legged frying pan or spider was either held over the coals or allowed to rest on them. Some of the more elaborate fireplaces included ovens, but this was unusual. Roasting could be done on a spit. Frequently the baking was done in a skillet with a tight cover or in a Dutch oven, a large cast-iron pot with a tight lid, pushed into the coals and then covered with them. Sometimes the article to be baked was wrapped in cabbage leaves and pushed directly into the coals. The fireplace, in addition to being used for cooking, furnished the only heat for the cabin in winter, and light at night. Tallow candles were made by the women, but the light of the fire was used whenever possible to save labor.

Cooking and eating utensils were simple. The family brought from the East a few skillets, pots, and pans, as well as pewter dishes, plates, and spoons. Additional utensils were homemade, and the men spent many a long winter evening carving wooden bowls, trenchers, and noggins (cups). Gourds were used as cups and other containers.

Preparing Tobacco for Market. Drying and packing the product for shipment and sale required several steps, as the illustration shows. (New York Public Library)

FOOD AND CLOTHES The food was limited largely to the products the family raised. Wild game was available in the early days, and a deer or some wild ducks or turkeys were welcome additions to the family menu; bears were plentiful, but their meat was coarse and greasy. A staple article of diet was corn, which was used in every conceivable form, including johnnycake, pone, and mush. Mush and milk was a favorite supper; the heavy meal of the day was eaten at noon. Equally universal was pork. Hog and hominy was a better known combination than ham and eggs, for eggs were scarce. The pigs were allowed to run wild in the forest and were shot like wild animals. The meat had to be dried, smoked, or salted for summer use, since there was no ice available. The resulting demand for salt encouraged the development of western salt manufactories at the important saline springs.

Cane sugar was always scarce on the frontier, white sugar being rarer than brown; frequently maple sugar, honey, or molasses was used instead. Milk was at times limited in supply, and whenever possible, as on mush, it was replaced by such liquids as gravy or bear's oil. Tea and coffee were luxuries for which the westerners discovered some substitutes. On the other hand, vegetables, including corn, beans, potatoes, peas, squash, and pumpkins were plentiful. Within a few years supplies of peaches, melons, apples, cherries, plums, and grapes were adequate. All in all, the frontiersman had a plentiful variety of good food—at least in the summer. In the winter his diet was more monotonous, for then he depended on such staples as cornmeal and salt pork. The only methods of preserving fruits and vegetables were covering them with sand or pine needles, pickling, or drying, which produced a leathery, tasteless substance that may have been nourishing but certainly was not appetizing.

One of the commonest articles of western diet was corn whiskey, which was drunk by everyone upon any or no pretext. A hospitable home kept a jug of whiskey and a gourd near the door to refresh visitors. Much western corn was made into whiskey because the decreased bulk and increased value were an advantage in transporting it to market. Distilleries were an early and important feature of western life. Tobacco, almost as widely used as whiskey, was raised and consumed at an early date. Tobacco chewing became as universal in the West as in the East, and very few travelers failed to comment on the common art of chewing and the lack of delicacy in disposing of the surplus juice.

Frequently shoes or moccasins were made at home by the father with tools he had brought from the East. But the tanning of leather was a difficult operation for the individual family, and so the tanning industry, carried on by professionals, soon made its appearance in the West. To save shoes members of the family went barefoot whenever possible.

Clothes were nearly all homemade. Flax, hemp, and wool were all produced on the farm; consequently, linen cloth was cheaper than cotton. The various processes of home manufacture included combing, carding, spinning, dyeing, weaving, cutting, and sewing the garments. The cloth (usually linsey-woolsey) was heavy and strong, but colors were limited and the finish was not professional: garments were more practical than beautiful. The frontiersman tended to copy his costume from the Indians, even to the extent of leather hunting shirt, leggings, moccasins, and breechcloth; although he might have a cloth shirt and pantaloons. A prosperous westerner might buy broadcloth to be made into a suit by a tailor, but such a suit was worn only on special occasions, and would last for years. A woman was adequately but not elegantly clothed in a loose, plain dress something like a modern smock; one or more better dresses for churchgoing or other important events followed eastern styles. A small child's wardrobe was usually limited to a simple, loose shirt.

The activities of the interior of the cabin, including preparing the food and making the clothes, were the particular domain of the woman. Her many duties ranged from making soap and candles and caring for small children to acting as family physician. Lest she have any spare moments she usually tended a garden; it was not unknown for her to work in the fields. Men worked hard but women, if anything, worked harder; indeed the operation of a farm was almost impossible without the presence of a woman.

FARMING The main business of farming was the province of the man, and he would have been justified if he had frequently felt discouraged. Not only was he confronted with the prodigious task of clearing and breaking the virgin land; even after he cleared the land he was handicapped by poor tools and methods. Foremost among his tools was a plow, which might be nothing more than a forked stick, and which at best was a straight wooden implement, sometimes tipped with iron, that needed at least two yoke of oxen in an operation that was man killing. A harrow was a wooden triangle fitted with wooden or iron teeth to be dragged through the ground.

All grain was planted by hand. Cutting was done by a scythe; the greatest farm improvement of the period was the introduction of the cradle scythe in the late eighteenth century. The grain was separated from the chaff either by driving horses over it or by using a hand flail composed of two sticks connected by a leather thong. Considerable dexterity was necessary if the wielder was to avoid cracking his own skull. The grain was then tossed in the air; if no timely breeze was present to blow away the chaff, a sheet flapped by two men created one.

Simple tools used on fields filled with dead trees could not be expected to produce a large crop; in fact the first corn crop was seldom as much as 15 bushels an acre. As time passed and the fields were better cultivated, the corn crops on the more fertile Ohio and Kentucky land averaged 40 to 50 bushels an acre, with some yielding as high as 75. Even at best, however, work was hard and yields were low. Tools remained poor, and no proper rotation of crops was practiced; the same crop was grown year after year on the same field. Chemical fertilizers were unknown, and manure was generally unavailable because the animals were allowed to roam freely.

The dominant western crop was corn, which was planted in checkrows about 3 feet apart. Seven or eight kernels were planted at each intersection, and all but two or three were weeded out when they started to grow, at which time there was one additional plowing. Ultimately the corn was picked, shucked, and shelled by hand. For home use it was either ground in a handmill or treated with homemade lye to produce the ubiquitous hominy. If marketed, it never brought over twenty-five cents a bushel. Sometimes it was shipped as kernels, but more frequently it was ground into meal, packed into small barrels, and loaded on flatboats for shipment to New Orleans.

Although corn was the important western crop, such grains as wheat, oats, barley, rye, and buckwheat were grown in considerable amounts. Wheat was the usual cash crop of the Northwest. Tobacco was widely cultivated, particularly in Kentucky; much of it was used in the West, but shortly after 1800 several thousand hogsheads were floated down the river every year. Hemp was exported both raw and as rope; every western town of importance had one or more ropewalks. Flax was grown primarily for home use, but a marketable excess was sold mainly as rough cloth. A considerable variety of poor fruit was produced, particularly peaches, possibly because westerners were told that peach trees became productive within two years. A large share of the peach crop was transformed into brandy, which sold commonly at a dollar a gallon. Vegetables were grown mainly for home use; a few were sold to the residents of the towns.

Western livestock was never impressive. Oxen, horses, beef cattle, pigs, and sheep were kept for home use. Many times they were branded and allowed to forage for themselves, which explains why their quality was generally poor and tended to deteriorate, and why fences were necessary for the cultivated fields. The pig was supreme from the standpoint of numbers. Surplus hogs were marketed as ham and salt pork, but at times were driven across the mountains to be fattened in Pennsylvania for the eastern market. The raising of blooded horses soon became a recognized Kentucky industry, but semiwild horses remained so common that they furnished skins for export.

The Harvest, 1788. Before the day of the reaper and thresher, most field labor was done by hand, as it had been for thousands of years. (New York Public Library)

As usual, the West, and particularly Ohio, raised many cattle. Ordinarily they were branded and allowed to roam freely, only returning to be milked and to obtain salt. Some of the milk was made into butter for sale in New Orleans. Herds of cattle were often driven to nearby forts or over the mountains to be fattened for market, but the profits seem to have been questionable. With the passage of time, fences were built, special food was used, and improved stock was introduced. By this time Ohio served as a feeding ground for stock coming from farther west. This typical frontier cycle was to be repeated in later years as population moved westward.

MERCHANDISING   The western family's agricultural surplus was usually bartered, and hence little money changed hands. The family with extra cloth or corn or pigs took them to the nearest store and traded with the merchant for salt, spices, iron implements, window glass, cloth, or whatever else it wanted. Even in the early days the western stores had a surprising array of commodities, ranging from coffee to flutes and from nails to Havana cigars. This variety increased rapidly with time.

The business of the frontier merchant was by no means uncomplicated. Ordinarily he had but little capital, and consequently did most of his business on credit. The articles he sold came from some eastern city, usually Philadelphia, but possibly Baltimore, Richmond, or elsewhere. These goods were purchased on credit, which meant that the merchants of Philadelphia financed a large part of western business. Eastern merchandise was hauled over the mountains by wagon and bartered for western products, which were then loaded on flatboats and floated down the river to New Orleans, where they were resold, frequently to the West Indies but sometimes to other parts of the world. Often this sale was again barter, as for sugar or molasses, which was then sailed to the eastern seaboard, thus completing the circle.

This circular trade meant that the great majority of the movement of western business within the United States was from east to west. Manufactured articles moved in this direction because few of the bulky western products could stand the high freight charges for the eastward trip; moreover, most of them were also produced in the East. As a result, most of the wagons returned empty. Furs and whiskey were prominent among the few articles that were shipped east. Obviously both East and West were anxious for improved transportation, which was expected to reduce costs and to increase the traffic both ways.

Exports from the trans–Appalachian West moved west and south, since that was the direction in which the rivers flowed. Not until after the War of 1812 was there a cheap way to reverse the trip; before this time the keelboat was too expensive to operate for cheap, bulky products, and overland traffic was almost impossible. The usual method of hauling goods was by flatboat, which could move only with the stream. For example, a flatboat would be built on the Ohio, loaded possibly with 300 barrels of cornmeal, and placed in the charge of a supervisor and four boatmen. After about a month the boat would reach New Orleans, where the meal was sold and the boat broken up and the wood sold. The men then returned overland.

MONEY   The lack of currency always seriously hindered western business. What little money there was came largely from new migrants, from New Orleans sales, and from the army as it bought supplies and paid its members—which was one reason why every western community was delighted to have an army post. Even these small amounts of currency tended to be drained back to the East, with the result that the average westerner seldom saw even a few dollars in cash during the course of a year. Barter was necessary but far from satisfactory; paying the schoolteacher in corn or the Yankee peddler in pork was at best cumbersome.

The necessity for an expanded medium of exchange encouraged the use of anything that came to hand. Foreign coins, and particularly Spanish, were in common use; a "piece of eight" was roughly equivalent to an American dollar; "four bits" to a fifty-cent piece; and "two bits" to a quarter. Westerners also circulated a great variety of eastern banknotes, many of dubious validity. Likewise they began to circulate currency of their own, issued by such organizations as the Kentucky Insurance Company (1802) and the Miami Exporting Company (1803). Such currency was not well backed, and its existence showed clearly the pressing western need for more circulating medium.

MANUFACTURING   As the West continued to develop, many of the functions that at first were performed by individual families were taken over by commercial enterprises. Among the earlier industries were mills for grinding corn, salt manufactories, distilleries, flour mills, tanneries, ropewalks, boatyards, sawmills, textile mills, glass factories, paper mills, shoe factories, and tobacco-processing concerns. The desirability of and even necessity for professional production in these fields were quite evident, even though most of the new shops were quite small, consisting of little more than the master and a handful of apprentices and workmen. In time some of these enterprises became important in favorable places, as did iron at Pittsburgh and pork packing at Cincinnati. Consolidations, with price-fixing tendencies, began to appear by the 1820s in such fields as salt, iron, cotton, glass, and transportation. Water furnished the early power, but the steam engine began to be used before the nineteenth century was very old.

Obtaining the necessary labor was always a difficult problem for the western manufacturer. Most men moving to the West were farmers, and even those who called themselves artisans were not highly skilled and tended to become farmers. At times workmen were bribed to come from the East, and at times women and children were used, but in any case both apprentices and skilled workmen were hard to find. The result was that wages, both money and real, were high, and that early nineteenth-century strikes had more than normal success in comparison with eastern and European strikes of the same period.

In addition to the employees of manufacturing enterprises, the towns contained a host of independent professional and business men. As the communities grew, there appeared the usual collection of doctors, lawyers, ministers, and teachers, with the lawyers and ministers outnumbering their professional colleagues. Shopkeepers and clerks furnished a perceptible part of the population. Blacksmiths, shoemakers, tinkers, seamstresses, and tailors were soon performing functions difficult for the untrained man. Some of them were itinerant, taking the job to the customer, which was a desirable procedure for a sparse population unconnected by good roads.

GOVERNMENT   One occupation that was not generally considered as a full-time job was that of politician. Many men considered politics an avocation, even a sport. Any average adult male was assumed to be competent to fill any public office within the gift of his fellow citizens, and in the early communities the politician might also be a farmer or lawyer, land speculator, trader, or miller. Quite naturally the West accepted the most democratic egalitarianism then in existence, for the feeling of equality was stronger in western society than in any other society in the world. It is not surprising, therefore, that in the 1790s they accepted Jefferson's agricultural democracy and that

Clearing the Land, 1793. Timber, so useful for building and fencing, nevertheless posed problems for the plowman, as this maze of stumps indicates. A lifetime could be spent in digging out the last stubborn roots. (New York Public Library)

later they became enthusiastic supporters of Jackson. Only very gradually, and after the government became much more complex, did the West begin to think of politics as a full-time and moderately specialized occupation.

The earliest of the western governments were frequently extralegal, if not actually illegal. These were occasioned by the failure of eastern government to bring law and order as fast as settlement expanded. Watauga, Nashville, Cleveland, and the state of Franklin come quickly to mind, but there were hundreds of other cases. Even in the Northwest Territory, counties were formed slowly, and many communities established their own organizations before the properly constituted authorities began to function.

The need for governmental organization was particularly evident in the newer and wilder sections of the country, which gave visible proof that the West attracted the lawless and dissolute as well as the sober and industrious. Without direct law enforcement the strong and well-armed man could dominate his region, and bullies were never lacking to take advantage of more timorous men. Personal violence, ranging from fist fights and gouging matches to punctilious duels, was common in the West for a long time.

Best-known evidence of western lawlessness were the bandits who preyed along the routes of travel, as they were to continue to do until the disappearance of the frontier. Western criminals were sometimes eastern criminals who had escaped justice, but were often the restless and adventurous who found outlawry more interesting and exciting—and only a little more dangerous—than cutting trees and plowing virgin soil. Some were fascinated by adventure, but others were simply trying to avoid continuous hard work.

Several of the early nineteenth-century bandits attained enough notoriety to keep their names alive, although often in legendary form. Colonel Fluger, commonly known as "Colonel Plug," kept a tavern near Cairo, Illinois. His chief stock-in-trade was his wife, "Pluggy," who bestowed her favors freely on boatmen and traders while her husband robbed them. James Girty, nephew of the notorious Simon Girty, claimed without serious dispute that he could beat any man in the West; one of his paramours provided an explanation by asserting that his chest was solid bone. Micajah and Wiley Harpe, usually called Big and Little Harpe, roamed Kentucky and Tennessee, robbing and murdering in a casual and insensitive fashion. Legend has it that Big Harpe was ultimately killed by a posse and that his head was removed and nailed to a tree as a warning to other evildoers, thereby giving the name to Harpe's Head, Kentucky.

Most notorious of the western bandits of the early nineteenth century was John A. Murrell, "The Great Land Pirate," who operated during the 1820s and 1830s. Murrell was both picturesque and able. Tall, muscular, handsome, and an excellent leader of men, he was everything that an outlaw of fiction should be. His early crimes were simple holdups or horse thefts, but later he preferred to steal Negroes, whom he ordinarily sold and recovered several times before he finally killed them to destroy incriminating evidence. His greatest achievement was the formation of the Mystic Clan—which he organized on his many trips along the Ohio and Mississippi—a secret criminal organization specializing in Negro stealing. It had secret grips, a code, passwords, and all the other fraternal symbols. At its height it had possibly 1500 members, of whom a small inner group was cognizant of all the more important plans; the rank and file did specified jobs for which they were paid. It also had the luxury of a legal staff, with lawyers retained at strategic points to be ready to defend any member accused of a crime.

Murrell's early success led him to conceive the idea of a general slave rebellion in the South to create a Negro empire of which he would be emperor. Unfortunately Murrell was but human and liked admiration and praise. He talked too freely to a spy, was captured, brought before the court on the charge of stealing Negroes, convicted, and incarcerated. While in prison he contracted the "prison sickness" and died at the age of forty-three.

NEW STATES   The earliest governmental interests of the West centered largely on the actions of the eastern states, but attention was later turned to the legislation of Congress. The provisions of the Northwest Ordinance and those of its counterpart in the Southwest had to be tried in practice. The performance of a governor with practically dictatorial powers, the change to partial self-rule, and the ultimate transformation to a state of the Union were all matters of intense interest to the westerner.

Actually it was not a western but a New England state that became the fourteenth member of the Union. Northern New England remained a frontier approximately as long as Ohio. The Vermont district had long been in dispute between New Hampshire and New York, and both were making land grants in this intervening area. Upon the outbreak of the Revolution Ethan Allen and his Green Mountain Boys engineered an independence movement, which cynics have held was concerned primarily with land speculation. At any rate, independence was achieved in 1777, and Vermont became an independent republic, carrying out all the functions of a sovereign state, including negotiations with Congress and intrigues with England. Ultimately, in 1791, Vermont became the first state admitted to the Union after the adoption of the Constitution by the original thirteen states. This event at least recalls the existence of a frontier that stretched from Maine through central New York, and was the New England equivalent of the Kentucky and Tennessee frontier.

Following Vermont in the procession of states admitted to the Union came Kentucky and Tennessee, as described earlier. Neither was a typical "public land state" any more than Vermont had been, because in each case the available land had been practically exhausted before Congress took control. Kentucky never came under direct congressional regulation before its admission as the fifteenth state in 1792, but Tennessee experienced the territorial form of government before it was admitted as the sixteenth state in 1796.

The experiences of Ohio in its progress toward admission to the Union were more significant than those of its predecessors, since Ohio represented more nearly the usual process of development that was to take place in the great majority of the future states to the west. Governor Arthur St. Clair arrived in 1788 at Marietta, which was the only settled community in present Ohio. The remainder of the officials appointed by Congress under the terms of the Ordinance of 1787 were three judges and a secretary of the territory. St. Clair created one county immediately and others as settlement progressed. A code of laws was promulgated, courts were established, and efforts were made to increase the land open to the whites by purchases from the Indians.

The affairs of the Northwest Territory never proceeded smoothly. Governor St. Clair, Scottish-born, was an intelligent and well-educated man, with a degree in medicine. He had high ideals of public service, but his aristocratic federalism conflicted sharply with the prevailing Jeffersonian republicanism of the territory. Wealthy by virtue of marriage, formerly president of Congress, he despised democracy and described himself in the West as "a poor devil banished to another planet." This attitude partly explains why he was so frequently absent from the seat of government—in the East, or treating with the Indians, or prosecuting an Indian war. During his absences the secretary acted in his place, and Winthrop Sargent was even more objectionable than St. Clair. Ultimately Sargent was advanced to the governorship of the newly created territory of Mississippi in 1798.

The second stage of government became possible for the Northwest Territory when a census of 1798 showed the requisite 5000 adult white males. Governor St. Clair immediately called for the election of a legislative lower house of twenty-two, which met

House Raising, 1810. Group efforts such as this somewhat belie the notion of frontier individualism. (The Metropolitan Museum of Art, The Edward W. C. Arnold Collection of New York Prints, Maps, and Pictures. Bequest of Edward W. C. Arnold, 1954)

the following year. This body nominated ten men, of whom five were picked by the President of the United States to form an upper house. St. Clair and his legislature never saw eye to eye. Frequently he acted on his own initiative, to the loudly expressed rage of the representatives. In turn he found much of their legislation displeasing and vetoed it. He obtained the nomination of his son to be the territorial representative in Congress, but William Henry Harrison won the election. Ultimately St. Clair's irritation overcame his discretion and he publicly criticized both Congress and the President, whereupon the President removed him.

The growth of the population of the Northwest Territory led many people to think of statehood, but for this purpose some reduction in boundaries was necessary. After many suggestions and much discussion, Indiana was finally sheared away in 1800, with the dividing line the present Indiana-Ohio boundary, except that it was continued north to the international boundary. The section that is now a part of Michigan was later removed, but the boundary was sufficiently uncertain to cause a near war. The new Territory of Indiana included at first all the remainder of the Old Northwest, and to this lordly domain was added, for a short time in 1804–1805, the vast bulk of the Louisiana Purchase, exclusive of Louisiana. Gradually this mass was reduced by eliminating the region west of the Mississippi (1805), Michigan (1805), and Illinois (1809), thus fixing the present boundaries of Indiana.

As for the future Ohio, a strong statehood movement received added impetus from the disputes between the legislature and St. Clair. Congress from 1801 was quite willing to have more Republican votes, and on April 30, 1802, passed the Ohio Enabling Act to permit the region to construct a constitution and apply for admission. (The Ohio Enabling Act of 1802 was the first of a long series passed for later areas farther west.) Under its terms Ohio formed a constitution, and early in 1803 was admitted by Congress to the Union as the seventeenth state. Not surprisingly the new Ohio constitution gave the governor no power of veto.

Ohio furnished the prototype for other states that were later to be carved from the public domain. Each state participated successively in the three stages of government outlined by the Ordinance of 1787. The territorial legislature had the seemingly inevitable quarrels with the governor. Surplus lands were removed to make new territories. A state constitution was formed under the authority of an enabling act and the state was admitted to the Union. At this point a few states varied from the pattern by not waiting for the enabling act, but the general process soon became so standardized that only exceptions seem worthy of notice.

READINGS   *Paperbacks are marked with an asterisk.*

Political   See the regional and state histories listed for Chapter 8 under Caruso, Bond, Havighurst, Clark, Davenport, Downes, Utter, Roseboom and Weisenburger. See also Thomas P. Abernethy, *From Frontier to Plantation* (1932), Tennessee; John D. Barnhart, *Valley of Democracy* (1953), giving Ohio a Turnerian interpretation; Frazer E. Wilson, *Arthur St. Clair* (1944).

The political accounts given above also contain economic material. For regional presentations see Harriette L. S. Arnow, *Seedtime on the Cumberland* (1960) and *Flowering of the Cumberland* (1963); *Everett Dick, *The Dixie Frontier* (1948); James M. D. Miller, *The Genesis of Western Culture: The Upper Ohio Valley 1800–1825* (1938). City histories listed in the previous chapter apply, as does the readable Harold Sinclair, *The Port of New Orleans* (1942). Travel accounts always contain much economic material, as does John W. Harpster (ed.), *Pen Pictures of Early Western Pennsylvania* (1938); John E. Wright and Doris S. Corbett, *Pioneer Life in Western Pennsylvania* (1940); *Solon J. and Elizabeth H. Buck, *The Planting of Civilization in Western Pennsylvania* (1939); Daniel Drake, *Pioneer Life in Kentucky* (1948); Harry Toulmin, *The Western Country in 1793* (1948); Reuben G. Thwaites (ed.), *Early Western Travels* (31 vols., and atlas; 1904–1907), particularly vols. 3 and 4. Best on the history of the raising of cattle, pigs, and sheep are, respectively, Charles W. Towne and Edward N. Wentworth, *Cattle and Men* (1955) and *Pigs* (1950); Edward N. Wentworth, *America's Sheep Trails* (1948).

Bandits Accounts of outlaws are always questionable, but worth consideration are Robert M. Coates, *The Outlaw Years* (1930) and Ross Phares, *Reverend Devil* (1941), concerned with Murrell. Walter Blair and F. J. Meine, *Mike Fink* (1933) is good on the semilegendary riverman.

The One-room Schoolhouse, 1805. In this Lutheran school a respite from the three R's is enjoyed by all scholars but one, a young man apparently consigned to punishment under the teacher's desk. (Historical Society of York County, Pa.)

Chapter 10 / REPRODUCING A CULTURE

Westerners in the years near 1800 did not devote their entire time to earning their livings and to providing a government for themselves. Even the most ambitious and hardworking man needed periodic relaxation, while the majority desired to cultivate literature, the arts, and religion. In such aspirations westerners were children of the East; practically no one thought of a unique western culture; in fact one easy way of making a westerner fighting mad was to accuse him of being deficient in any of the traits that distinguished the East. The only difference he was willing to accept with pleasure was one that implied superiority. Buildings must be as impressive, canals as long, women as charming, penitentiaries as depressing, horses as fast, and parties as magnificent as those in the East.

In the development of interest in sports, the arts, education, and religion, the West was under obvious disadvantages. Population was sparse and generally deficient in money and leisure, even in the towns. Furthermore, few westerners were thoroughly familiar with the contemporary intellectual contributions of the East or of Europe. Migrants were not drawn from the leisured and cultured classes, but from less prosperous farmers and artisans. They had perfectly adequate native intelligences, but they lacked the background, time, and funds that could have provided an excellent education and encouraged wide reading. Many of them were illiterate, and their children were equally handicapped.

LITERATURE Although westerners were generally deficient in literary interests, there were exceptions. European visitors periodically marveled when they visited a rough log cabin in the wilderness and discovered a collection of books, newspapers, and magazines, plus a frontiersman owner who could talk informatively on national and international politics. Thousands of families had at least the minimum of the Bible, *Pilgrim's Progress*, and the poems of Milton. Well-known English authors included Goldsmith, Pope, Shakespeare, Scott, and Maria Edgeworth; Byron was the first of the romantic poets to become popular. As early as 1788 the town of Lexington, Kentucky, with a population of no more than 700, had at least six merchants who handled books; schoolbooks were the most numerous, but there were also volumes on religion, law, physics, and the classics. Most books originated in Philadelphia, but the West itself did more publishing than might have been expected.

Of the western literary productions almanacs and newspapers were the most widely circulated. The almanac by no means confined itself to the calendar and the weather, but printed all kinds of advice and information, from the proper season for planting various crops to medical advice and moral precepts. The first to receive wide circulation was the *Kentucky Almanac*, which started publication in 1794.

Newspapers appeared quite early in most western towns, but their mortality rate was frightful: subscription lists were small, and many of the subscribers forgot to pay. The first paper west of the mountains (except in New York State) was the *Pittsburgh Gazette* (1786), which was soon followed by the *Kentucky Gazette* (1787) at Lexington. First in the Old Northwest was the *Centinel of the North-Western Territory* (1793) at Cincinnati. Early newspapers usually consisted of four pages. Their contents were almost entirely national and European news, partly because the editors felt that everyone in a small western town knew all the local gossip, but more because of the ease with which a paper could be filled with items clipped from the eastern and European press. Nearly every western paper was issued weekly; the daily paper was unknown. More frequent issues were impossible because of the lack of good communication, the paucity of subscriptions, and the shortage of advertising.

Western books and magazines were scarce but not unknown. The first book printed west of the mountains was a third volume of *Modern Chivalry*, published at Pittsburgh in 1793. The author, Hugh Henry Brackenridge, was a prominent resident of Pittsburgh. The story was a long and rambling account of the troubles of an illiterate Irish servant, Teague O'Regan, who perpetually was being rescued from distressing and precarious situations by his master, Captain Farrago. *Modern Chivalry* is no masterpiece of fiction, but it does contain interesting comments on western life. Much more widely sold and read was that eminently practical book, Zadock Cramer's *The Navigator*, the first edition of which appeared in 1801. The most important early publishing center west of Pittsburgh was Lexington, Kentucky.

Most of the other western literary productions consisted of ephemeral religious and political pamphlets. The first magazine to be published in the West was *The Medley, Or Monthly Miscellany*, begun at Lexington in 1803. Probably the earliest poem to be written and published in the West was The *Kentucky Miscellany*, written by Thomas Johnson some time before 1800; Johnson disliked Kentucky heartily and made his views known with more force than beauty.

Lack of funds and interest meant that libraries were few and small. Many a family had a handful of books, but a collection of as many as a hundred was rare. Booksellers made precarious livings in the larger towns. Here and there a subscription library was established—Lexington in 1795, Belpre (Ohio) in 1796, and Cincinnati in 1802; the famous "Coonskin Library" of Athens County, Ohio, was opened in 1804.

EDUCATION   Lack of writing and printing could be traced largely to meagerness of education. Few people could write effectively; more important, few could read with sufficient ease to bring pleasure. Most farmers of the early nineteenth century approved education in theory, but felt skeptical of the practical advantages of anything more than an irreducible minimum. Education beyond the three R's seemed an unnecessary luxury when every penny loomed large. Furthermore, westerners (like easterners) quite generally agreed that the operation of schools at public expense meant an unjustified increase of taxes. To them it seemed obvious that parents should pay for whatever education they wanted their children to have. The orator's panegyrics about the necessity of an educated population were accepted by the mass of farmers as true, but with various practical limitations.

Every school was private, and the teacher was paid by the parents of his students. Since the parents had little or no cash, the teacher frequently received his compensation in the form of pigs, vegetables, and corn. Ordinarily he "boarded around," staying for a short time at the home of each of his students. Such a life did not attract capable and dedicated teachers, particularly because they were poorly paid on the common assumption that anyone who could read and write was competent to teach. The teaching profession had no important standing in the community and therefore was a haven for many misfits, men without steady occupations who found schoolteaching the path of least resistance. However, it also attracted a more desirable group of young New England men who used it as a means of becoming acquainted with the country while saving a little money before they began their chosen work.

Instruction, usually limited to the three R's, was given to children only when they could not be employed usefully on the farm, which meant a few weeks or months in the winter for the older children and a little additional summer work for the younger ones. Many children never attended school at all. The "little red schoolhouse" was an institution of the future, for the best the West could afford in 1800 was a small, log, single-room schoolhouse. The children were ungraded and studied aloud simultaneously, after which they recited the lessons from memory. Texts were scarce, and father's books were considered good enough for little John. The diversity of population sometimes meant that no two books in the school were alike. Paper was scarce and consequently little used; its substitute was slate, on which marks were made with a piece of soapstone. The summit of education for most children was a knowledge of the elementary rules of reading, writing, spelling, and ciphering.

Secondary and higher education in the West were almost nonexistent prior to 1800. Here and there were a few seminaries (sometimes called colleges) for either boys or girls. For the girls they offered polite "finishing" courses in such subjects as fancy needlework, deportment, and painting. For the boys they offered the classical subjects necessary for entrance to an eastern college. The only institution of higher education in the West prior to 1800 was Transylvania University at Lexington. Its requirements were not high, and it had a hard struggle to stay alive; eventually it became important. Between 1800 and 1810 a few other institutions appeared, such as Jefferson College and Washington College (later united) in Pennsylvania, Ohio University (Athens) and Vincennes University in the Old Northwest, and Cumberland College in Tennessee.

SOCIAL GATHERINGS   Western life was frequently lonely, but few people desired continual solitude. Moreover, a number of tasks could not be performed by the family without outside help. The result was that the West grasped eagerly every opportunity for common action, including some that were not really essential. Work was combined with play so that the work was submerged in the general fun and merrymaking. Such an occasion as a logrolling, house-raising, cornhusking, maple-sugar gathering, a wedding, a funeral, harvesting, quilting, fulling, sewing, or weaving attracted the entire neighborhood. The singing school and the spelling bee brought similar gatherings.

A community enterprise attracted everyone within traveling distance. The men spent the day in raising the house, husking the corn, or doing whatever had been planned, while the women prepared an immense feast. Neither sex was mute during these activities. Then everyone ate and drank all he could, told jokes (often crude), gossiped, and debated politics and religion. In the evening the older folk continued their conversations while the young people danced to the music of a fiddle. Square dancing was the rule, with some stentorian-voiced male calling off the figures. Although dancing was rather general in the backcountry, it had opponents; some of the more religious felt it to be immoral, and in this attitude they were supported by most of the churches.

Western parties tended to be boisterous, earthy, even crude. These were vigorous and hardworking people, who had not as yet arrived at the Victorian period. Kissing games were frequent. For example, a cornhusker who found a red ear could kiss the girl of his choice; the kiss was by no means a perfunctory peck, and it was rumored that the fore-sighted boys brought red ears with them to the party. Lovemaking was frequently coarse, with vigor replacing finesse when youthful couples strolled into the moonlit woods. A wedding was a time of riotous fun and pointed jokes. Frequently the happy couple was put to bed in the loft to the accompaniment of ribald remarks while the party continued downstairs. When to the natural relief from backbreaking toil was added the consumption of too much whiskey, the festivities might turn into a near-riot. Westerners lived close to the basic facts of nature, and were not oppressed by the prud-ishness of a later generation.

DRAMA   One amusement largely absent from the West was the drama. A few theaters were constructed before 1810, as at Pittsburgh and Cincinnati, but there were no regular professional companies of actors. Amateurs presented a few plays, as at Lex-ington before 1800, but the performances were bad. Many people throughout the country felt that the theater was basically immoral, and an even greater number held that professional actors, and certainly actresses, led lives of sin. The general feeling that the theater had a contaminating effect on women influenced the amateur actors to use men in all female parts. The performances may have been highly moral, but they had no other virtues to recommend them.

ATHLETIC CONTESTS   The West was always interested in athletic contests, which it commonly combined with gambling. Horse racing was highly popular, with race tracks in operation at various towns, both in the North and the South, before 1800. Shooting matches, foot races, and wrestling, all had their devotees, each of whom usu-ally had a bet on the outcome. The stake was probably more than the bettor could af-ford, which of course made the event more exciting. Each contest was accompanied by copious drinking, and sometimes the drinking occurred without the excuse of the contest. Shooting was possibly the most utilitarian of these sports, and each westerner was proud of his prowess with a gun. Although the shooting was not remarkably good from a modern standpoint, it was next to miraculous when the heavy gun, the poor powder, and the small and often irregular shot are considered.

Athletic contests were frequently highly objectionable from the point of view of a later and more squeamish generation. Rough-and-tumble fistfights had no Marquis of Queensberry rules. The contestants kicked, butted, bit, and gouged, and the loss of an eye, an ear, or a finger was not uncommon. Even making allowances for the tall stories that the West liked to impose on credulous easterners, the fact still remained that the West was tough and uncouth, and that its fun was boisterous.

RELIGION   No cultural development in the West was more important than the growth of religious denominations. The best-informed guess is that in 1800 fewer than half of western families were affiliated with any church, which did not necessarily mean irreligion. Money to build and repair churches and to pay ministers was hard to obtain. In fact, ministers themselves were difficult to find; all divinity schools were in the East, and a graduate needed considerable fervor and missionary zeal to forgo a comfortable eastern living for the hardships of the frontier. A special western disadvantage was the multiplicity of sects. In the East these sects tended to congregate geographically, but in the West a dozen or more might exist more or less equally in a single small community —not only larger churches such as the Methodist, Presbyterian, Congregational, Roman Catholic, Episcopal, and Lutheran, but also such small groups as the Moravian, Dunkard, United Brethren in Christ, Anabaptists, Quakers, and Shakers. Few groups had sufficient strength to build churches and support ministers, and the idea of a community church would have been viewed with horror.

The religious lag of the West greatly distressed thousands of people, both East and West. In the East, men feared that irreligion would grow in the West, infect the East, and destroy one of the foundations of the Republic. To avert this potential tragedy, proselyting groups were formed. Home missionary societies mushroomed during the 1790s, including notably the Missionary Society of Connecticut (1798), the Massachusetts Missionary Society (1799), and the Boston Female Society for Missionary Purposes (1800). Various "female cent institutions" collected a cent a week from each member. These societies sent a considerable number of men on missionary tours of the West. In addition, tract societies provided religious pamphlets and books without charge, and Bible societies distributed the "Word of God." Each denomination of any size devoted part of its funds to work in the West.

Thousands of westerners were similarly concerned with the dangers of irreligion; reared in religious eastern homes, they wanted their children to have the benefit of church teaching. They realized that worship could be an individual matter, but that for most people group worship was important, and they made every effort to organize and maintain churches in the West.

The various denominations exercised considerable control over the morals of their members; any man leaning toward such temptations as lying, slander, cheating in business, fighting, or illicit sex adventures might be deterred by the considerable chance of being ejected from church membership if he succumbed. Education was supported by most churches, regardless of the educational background of their own clergy. Churches were responsible for the founding of many western colleges designed to prepare for the ministry.

The church helped to give meaning to western life. The hazards and hardships of frontier farming became more tolerable to one who believed that God watched over him and would make him successful. Hence a devout Christian could feel that the destruction of the Indian, an unbeliever, was a victory of right over the powers of darkness. The westerner was no turn-the-other-cheek type of Christian, but one that believed in a positive, vigorous, and aggressive brand of Christianity.

Organized religion also offered westerners important social and emotional outlets. On Sunday the whole family walked or rode to church to spend the entire day. Sunday school was followed by a morning service, then dinner, and finally an afternoon service. Sermons were long and seats hard, but hymns gave a joyous occupation to the lungs; hymns were "lined out" two lines at a time, since many people could read neither words nor music. The noon dinner provided an opportunity to hear the latest news of crops, of politics, and of new babies. Religious emotionalism gave a welcome release from the hard and prosaic task of earning a living.

A church with real hope of success in the West needed an optimistic faith, with stress on the importance of the individual. It needed social and emotional content. It needed an organization adapted to the widely scattered western population. It needed a clergy that could speak the language of the crude and hardworking West; the refined and sophisticated product of the eastern theological seminary was no doubt satisfactory to an educated audience, but his appeal to a relatively uncultured West was slight.

METHODISTS   One church well fitted to western needs was the Methodist. The best-known and most effective leader was Francis Asbury, usually called by the unmerited title of Bishop, who disregarded his feeble body to travel widely. Under his guidance Methodism became important in the religious life of the United States. Methodism crossed the mountains in the early 1780s. The Western Conference, organized in 1800, included some 2500 members in Kentucky and Tennessee; an additional 350 members belonged to three circuits north of the Ohio; and Methodist ministers had pushed into Missouri. By 1811 western Methodists numbered 30,000 (including 1500 Negroes) and were at least as numerous as any other denomination.

The Methodist doctrines of free will, free grace, and individual responsibility appealed to the westerner. Furthermore, the church organization was adapted admirably to the West. Instead of devoting his entire time to the care of one church, a minister might "ride circuit," thus distributing his attention over a considerable region. During his absence from any community the work was continued by lay members, called exhorters," or "local preachers," who both preached and conducted religious services. Methodist ministers tended to be particularly effective because the church was willing to use forceful men regardless of their education. They talked in the strong and vivid language of the frontier, and although they might be confused by the subtleties of theological disputation and be entirely ignorant of Latin and Greek, they could paint the terrors of hell in compelling terms, and could call upon sinners to repent with a vigor, earnestness, and pathos that put their more learned brethren to shame.

The circuit rider ordinarily went on horseback, and his circuit required continuous traveling for four or five weeks. He preached daily at noon in any convenient place, such as a cabin or clearing. His salary in 1784 was $64 a year, out of which he paid his own traveling expenses, but in 1800 it was advanced to $80 and traveling expenses for himself, plus an allowance for his family. This stipend often took the form of agricultural products, and was frequently supplemented by entertainment and gifts from parishioners. The circuit rider usually wore a straight-breasted waistcoat, a high collar, and a plain necktie. Suspenders were a luxury. His hair was allowed to grow to his shoulders, according to western custom; barbers were rare, and the man with long hair, or his wife, could do any needed trimming.

The Methodist circuit rider threw his influence in the direction of culture in spite of his own crudities and lack of education. Often he carried books in his saddlebags, and lent them to the people with whom he stayed. On many occasions he was the only visitor a family would entertain for months, and to such a family he would bring news of the outside world—tales of wondrous cities, new styles of dress and social intercourse, marvelous mechanical improvements, and neighborhood gossip. His advent was awaited eagerly, for he was more informative than the newspaper.

BAPTISTS The chief frontier rivals of the Methodists were the Baptists, who believed in immersion and in close communion. Great freedom was allowed the individual churches, which varied widely in their practices. Instead of having a circuit system the Baptists licensed local preachers. Like the Methodists, they were more interested in fervor than in education of the ministry, and favored rapid evangelization by emotional pleas. Also like the Methodists, they established their first trans-Appalachian churches in the 1780s and then expanded rapidly, until by 1800 they had crossed the Mississippi.

The Baptists were the unwilling parents of the Disciples of Christ, commonly known as "Christians" or "Campbellites." The originator of this new sect was Thomas Campbell, who migrated from Scotland to western Pennsylvania in 1807; but the important leader was the founder's son Alexander. The Disciples favored a "purer," more primitive Christianity, to combine the true believers of all churches. After flirting with the Presbyterians they joined the Baptists (1813) and grew within that church. Ultimately, in the late 1820s, they withdrew from the Baptist Church to establish, rather ironically, a new sect.

PRESBYTERIANS AND CONGREGATIONALISTS Third in size among the western Protestant sects was the Presbyterian, which was handicapped by the gloomy doctrines of Calvin, the lack of an effective frontier organization, the insistence on an educated clergy, and a reluctance to accept revival methods. On these issues there occurred two southwestern schisms in the years immediately after 1800. One, the "New Lights," raised doubts about the doctrines of election and predestination, but soon died out. The Cumberland Presbyterian Church (1810), with reservations about the Calvin doctrines, seceded largely on the educated ministry issue, holding that piety was more important than book learning and that high educational qualifications meant a deplorable lack of ministers in the West. The parent church tried to fill western needs by promoting western colleges, but this procedure was too slow for many impatient westerners.

Closely allied with the Presbyterians were the Congregationalists. These two churches were in such community of feeling that in 1801 they adopted a plan of union by which they collaborated in founding new churches and then allowed these churches to decide for themselves whether their services, church rules, and ministers would be Presbyterian or Congregational. This cooperation tended to develop Presbyterian rather

A Philadelphia Anabaptist Immersion During a Storm. This watercolor by the Russian artist Pavel Petrovich Svinin depicts an event that occurred frequently on the American frontier. (The Metropolitan Museum of Art, Rogers Fund, 1942)

than Congregational churches. Congregationalism became more important when an increased flood of New Englanders carried it to Michigan, Wisconsin, Iowa, Minnesota, and other regions of the Far West.

EPISCOPALIANS   The Episcopal Church had more difficulties in appealing to the West than any of the larger Protestant sects. As an integral part of the Church of England, it had suffered severely during the Revolution; and though the English connection was broken with the Convention of 1789 the old reputation lingered. Furthermore, the scarcity of its ministers, due in part to the high educational requirements, the lack of a system of itinerancy, and the reluctance to use emotionalism, all made work in the West more difficult. Even the development of a strong evangelical, Low Church, group that accepted the universal possibility of salvation rather than predestination did not correct the situation entirely.

The slowness of Episcopalian expansion was evident to everyone. Here and there was a man such as Philander Chase, who worked effectively in Ohio after his arrival in 1817, but by 1820 there was only a handful of ministers west of the mountains, with none in Indiana, Illinois, Tennessee, or Mississippi. During this same year the Domestic and Foreign Missionary Society of the Protestant Episcopal Church was organized, but it did little work until its reorganization fifteen years later. In 1840 the Missionary Society was helping to support 64 western ministers, or over a third of those west of the mountains (152). The smallness of the Episcopal strength is indicated by the fact that its total number of western ministers in 1840 was approximately equal to the number of Baptist clergy in the one state of Missouri.

ROMAN CATHOLICS   The Roman Catholics did the earliest missionary work west of the Appalachians. Jesuit priests had long labored among the Indians and with the French and Spanish settlers, but these efforts had practically no influence on the American West of 1800. Catholicism expanded from east to west in the period after the Revolution in the same way as did other faiths. The Diocese of Bardstown (Kentucky) was established in 1808, and Joseph Flaget arrived to take charge of it three years later. By 1815 there were probably 10,000 Catholics among the white settlers west of the mountains. Later migration was to increase Catholic membership, to the great distress of many Protestant Americans who questioned whether Catholicism was not worse than paganism.

CAMP MEETINGS   The frontier community needed vital religious experiences that could not be satisfied by the occasional preachings of a peripatetic Methodist minister. Emotional outpourings could alleviate the deadly seriousness of daily life. All believers must at times be assembled to gain consciousness of common purpose and strivings. The institution that ultimately met this need was the camp meeting. In its original form as an emotional expression of religious strivings, the camp meeting was not distinctively western, but in its increased use and in its typical later form it was a western contribution to the religious life of the nation.

As early as 1796 James McGready, a Presbyterian minister inspired by eastern revivals, arrived in Kentucky. Personally unprepossessing and with a coarse, tremulous voice, he nevertheless created a curious and unearthly effect. He held a series of emotional meetings in which hell was pictured frequently and vividly, and in which there was much weeping and ecstasy. The unusual effectiveness of these meetings aroused widespread interest, and among the people attracted were the McGee brothers—William, a Presbyterian, and John, a Methodist. The McGees were so impressed that they held similar meetings throughout the West. Of William it is related that "he would sometimes exhort after the sermon, standing on the floor, or sitting, or lying in the dust, his eyes streaming, and his heart so full he could only ejaculate, 'Jesus! Jesus!' "

Emotional religious meetings had a profound appeal for westerners. Soon the attendants became too numerous to be accommodated by the small country churches. Tents and cabins were found necessary; tents were probably first used in 1800. The length of the meetings increased until it became common for a meeting to occupy an entire weekend from Friday until Tuesday. The largest of such meetings, and possibly the height of the "Great Revival," was at Cane Ridge, Kentucky, in August 1801; the attendance was variously estimated at between ten and twenty thousand. Although the Great Revival ended by 1805, the camp meeting continued to be used frequently and successfully.

Whole families traveled twenty, thirty, or even a hundred miles to attend a camp meeting. They brought with them tents, food, cooking utensils, clothes, and even furniture. Upon their arrival they raised their tents or constructed rude log cabins on the edge of the cleared space that was used for the larger meetings. Furniture was crude, and cooking was done over open fires.

The main meetings were held in the large clearing at the center of the camp ground. A high platform at one end served as a pulpit, and eight, ten, or even more ministers served in relays. Most of the participating clergy were Methodists, but there was a sprinkling of Baptists and Presbyterians; the number of Presbyterians, however, decreased with time. Seats for the congregation were usually the halves of split logs arranged in parallel rows. Between the congregation and the platform was a litter of loose straw to ease pressure on the knees of repentant sinners. Meetings were held morning, afternoon, and evening, pine torches providing the illumination after dark. Along the sides of the cleared space smaller meetings in tents were usually held simultaneously with the larger meeting.

The camp meeting stressed the emotional appeal of religion. Songs by the congregation and prayers were prefaces and interludes to the main business of exhorting. The appeals included lengthy descriptions of the horrors of hell, with less stress on the glories of heaven, and included many admonitions for sinners to repent. Frequently they were punctuated by shouted "Amens" and "Yes, Lords" and "Glories."

Bombarded by soul-harrowing discourses, "sinners" came forward to repent of their sins, and the ministers "labored" with them individually. Flaming calls for repentance inspired even the purest woman or most innocent girl to feel a conviction of deadly sin that must be acknowledged and repented; adolescent girls seemed to be particularly affected. The response of a few people was contagious, and soon the whole meeting was raised to a pitch of hysteria, particularly because the ministers knew by experience the psychological appeals of maximum effect. Conditions for emotional release were most favorable at night, when the wild flare of the torches contrasted dramatically with the blackness of the surrounding forest and when the description of other-worldly subjects was particularly impressive. Of almost equal effectiveness were the small tent meetings, where aided by the hot, stuffy air, the exhortations for repentance were difficult to resist.

The intensity of the emotional strain of a camp meeting was shown by the convulsive and involuntary actions of those people most affected. They leaped, ran, jumped, laughed, sang, sobbed, shouted, and beat the ground in agony; others barked like dogs or emitted the "holy laugh." Many twitched in every joint with the "jerks," reputed to be so contagious that even scoffing onlookers were similarly affected. Trances and visions, in which conversations were held with Christ or His apostles or the dear departed, were not unusual. The more powerful the reaction the more the Lord had worked, and the more the sanctification of the person affected.

The emotional displays of the camp meeting were desired and carefully planned, but other results were achieved less consciously. The camp meeting was incidentally an opportunity for meeting friends and neighbors. Families came in part to see other families, and in intervals between meetings and while food was being prepared, gossip was exchanged and old friendships renewed. The small children played together during the day, and it was not unknown for the elders to miss meetings to discuss crops or the latest candidate for the legislature.

The social intercourse of the camp meeting was generally good, but also had its less desirable aspects. People not interested in the religious exercises would come for the excitement, and their presence would detract from the sincerity of the worship. Large numbers of people required an immense supply of food, necessitating the establishment of small stores on the edge of the grounds. Among other merchandise, these stores frequently handled whiskey, which attracted a rowdy element from the nearby towns. Sometimes friction between the religious and nonreligious elements ended in a free-for-all fight. The westerner, even the religious westerner, was not docile.

The camp meeting encountered another difficulty in the tendency of some of the young people to confuse human and divine love and to obey too literally the injunction to "love thy neighbor as thyself." Some meetings posted guards at night to prevent young couples from wandering into the surrounding woods. In the emotional orgy of a meeting women at times threw themselves upon the ground in suggestive attitudes, tore open their clothes, and hugged and kissed everyone they met. Observers commonly noted that adolescent boys and girls were most subject to religious exaltation, and it is easy to believe that at times sex was not sublimated, but took direct and earthy means of expression.

In spite of minor difficulties, the camp meeting was useful to the West both as a social meeting place and as an occasion for the emphasis on religious idealism. It provided a socially accepted vehicle for the expression of emotions that were frequently given no outlet on the frontier. Friendships were made or renewed, common problems discussed, courtships begun or continued, information and experiences exchanged, and the inhabitants of the region given a feeling of unity and religious fellowship that helped to make more bearable future months of isolation. Many of the people were influenced to lead more socially desirable lives, although of course there was the inevitable backslider who was "saved" at each successive meeting. In consequence, the camp meeting must not be considered as a picturesque but unimportant western eccentricity; rather, it was an institution that added necessary elements to western life.

READINGS   *Paperbacks are marked with an asterisk.*

Social   The nonpolitical readings of the previous chapter are almost all applicable to this one; to the state histories add Francis P. Weisenburger, *The Passing of the Frontier, 1825–50* (1941), concerning Ohio. Particularly interesting are *Arthur K. Moore, *The Frontier Mind* (1957), an interpretation based on Kentucky, and James McD. Miller, *The Genesis of Western Culture* (1938). John F. McDermott, *George Caleb Bingham* (1959) is a good biography of the West's most eminent artist. *Thomas D. Clark, *The Rampaging Frontier* (1939) treats western humor.

Religion   Most diligent and useful of the religious historians has been William Warren Sweet; his *The Story of Religions in America* (1930) and his *Religion in the Development of American Culture, 1765–1840* (1952) are good for background; see also Walter B. Posey, *Frontier Mission: A History of Religion West of the Southern Appalachians to 1861* (1966) and *Religious Strife on the Southern Frontier* (1965); T. Scott Miyakawa, *Protestants and Pioneers* (1964). On missions consult Wade C. Barclay, *History of Methodist Missions* (3 vols., 1949–1957); confined to the West is Colin B. Goodykoontz, *Home Missions on the American Frontier* (1939). Most useful for the camp meeting are *Bernard A. Weisberger, *They Gathered at the River* (1958); Charles A. Johnson, *The Frontier Camp Meeting* (1955); Catharine C. Cleveland, *The Great Revival in the West, 1797–1805* (1916).

Baptists: William W. Sweet (ed.), *Religion on the American Frontier*, vol. 1: *The Baptists* (1931), largely documents. **Catholics:** Theodore Maynard, *The Story of American Catholicism* (1941); Joseph H. Schauinger, *Cathedrals in the Wilderness* (1952). **Congregationalists:** William W. Sweet, *Religion on the American, Frontier*, vol. 3: *The Congregationalists* (1939). **Disciples of Christ:** Winfred E. Garrison and Alfred T. De Groot, *The Disciples of Christ* (1948). **Episcopalians:** William W. Manross, *A History of the American Episcopal Church* (1935) and *The Episcopal Church in the United States 1800–1840* (1938). **Methodists:** Wade C. Barclay, *Early American Methodism* (2 vols., 1949), long and informative; William W. Sweet, *Methodism in American History* (1933), *The Rise of Methodism in the West* (1920), and *Religion on the American Frontier*, vol. 4: *The Methodists* (1946);

good special studies are Elizabeth K. Nottingham, *Methodism and the Frontier* (1941), concerning Indians, and Walter B. Posey, *The Development of Methodism in the Old Southwest* (1933); an interesting biography of Francis Asbury is Herbert Asbury, *A Methodist Saint* (1927). **Presbyterians:** William W. Sweet (ed.), *Religion on the American Frontier*, vol. 2: *The Presbyterians* (1936); Walter B. Posey, *The Presbyterian Church in the Old Southwest* (1952). **Shakers:** Julia Neal, *By Their Fruits* (1947) describes Shaker communities in Kentucky.

Battle of the Thames. This primitive print was intended to show the death of the Indian leader Tecumseh at the hands of the Kentucky Mounted Volunteers. (Library of Congress)

Chapter 11/THE WAR IN THE NORTHWEST

The surging of white population into the West during the opening years of the nineteenth century was impressive but limited; in the Old Northwest the whites occupied little more than the land cessions of the Treaty of Greenville. The Indians were generally hostile to the advancing Americans and friendly to the British, who retained a considerable interest in the area despite their evacuation of posts south of the border. The British desired to retain the lucrative Great Lakes fur trade, and were glad to keep aggressive American frontiersmen as far from Canada as possible. The Indians preferred trading with the British to trading with the Americans, and felt no danger from Canadian expansion; whereas the Americans were becoming more menacing year by year. The Indians had been overawed temporarily by the Wayne campaign, but the memory of white military power was fading, and again they had hopes of resisting white aggression successfully, and even of expelling the intruders.

INDIAN GRIEVANCES   The Indian had many rankling and irritating grievances to arouse his hatred of the whites. He realized that the contact of the two civilizations always meant eventual supremacy of the white, with decay and destruction of the red, and that his total elimination was not far distant if he did not fight back. He could see clearly the increasing numbers of whites driving off his game and taking possession of his land. The federal government continued to give lip service to the fiction of Indian independence and landownership, but the Indian was more impressed by the rapidity with which the whites obtained any area they coveted. No opposition short of war seemed to have the least chance of damming the white flood.

The Indian was also increasingly resentful of the many other ways in which he suffered at the hands of the white man. He was cheated at the trading posts. He was plied with whiskey until his reasoning powers were gone. He traded a year's catch of furs for a few trinkets and a little bad whiskey. He gave the trinkets to his wife and drank the whiskey, with the result that his season's work gave him only a dark brown taste and impaired health, after which the white man's diseases completed the havoc. The white had taught him new and more expensive ways of eating and dressing; with his money gone for bad liquor, the Indian was often reduced to slinking about white settlements and resorting to petty pilfering, which damaged his self-respect and could put him in jail. The crimes committed by the Indians were always punished if the culprits were detected, but those of the whites against the Indians might be overlooked. Furthermore, Indian women were comparatively easy prey for the aggressive frontiersmen. The result was the introduction and spread of venereal disease, which further sapped the strength of the Indians.

The Indian who best exemplified the growing rancor toward white civilization was Tecumseh, probably the ablest leader the Shawnee ever produced. Tecumseh was born in 1768 of a Shawnee father and a Creek mother. His father was killed by a white hunting party, and his mother instilled vengeance in his youthful mind. As a young man he fought against St. Clair and then at Fallen Timbers against Wayne. He was married at the rather advanced age of twenty-eight, but soon separated from his half-breed wife; then he fell in love with a white girl, but refused to adopt the white ways upon which the girl insisted, and did not marry her. Tecumseh was five feet ten inches but looked taller. He was exemplary in habits and never drank liquor. Physically he was powerful in spite of a slightly bent leg that had been broken in a buffalo hunt and never set properly. His mind was keen and his speech convincing. His brother, called the Prophet, had been a drunken and worthless young man who had lost an eye in an accident, but after his conversion by the Shakers he was transformed, and was felt by other Indians to have magical powers.

Tecumseh watched the advance of the whites and the progressive deterioration of the reds with ever-growing anger. He was certain in his own mind that the land belonged to the Indians forever, no matter by what show of legality it might be taken away from them, and that they should cling to their traditional ways of life. He concluded that the only possible method of opposing the white advance successfully was to obtain the cooperation of all Indians and to have them act in concert. To further this plan he traveled widely, particularly in the first decade of the nineteenth century, talking with Indians both north and south. In 1808 he and his brother had their headquarters at the confluence of Tippecanoe Creek and the Wabash; here was built Prophetstown, with its extensive agricultural fields and large herds—and no whiskey.

WILLIAM HENRY HARRISON   The white man who best represented the point of view diametrically opposed to that of Tecumseh was William Henry Harrison who had been born in Virginia on February 9, 1773, to a family that had lived in Virginia for over a century. He was given a good education in the expectation that he would enter the medical profession, but military life attracted him more and in 1791 he joined the army. His command was ordered west, and arrived at Fort Washington just as the remnants of St. Clair's defeated army were returning. Harrison subsequently took part in Wilkinson's campaigns against the Indians and then distinguished himself at Fallen Timbers with Wayne. Returning to Fort Washington in 1796, he was given command of the fort with the rank of captain. Two years later he resigned because of lack of action.

Harrison spent much of his life in seeking remunerative positions through political influence. In 1798 he obtained the job of secretary of the Northwest Territory, but proved more interested in farming and distilling than in keeping records. The following year he took advantage of a factional fight in the Ohio Legislative Council to get himself elected as delegate to the United States House of Representatives. His victory was by the close vote of 11 to 10, and was probably due to the fact that his opponent was the son of the unpopular Governor St. Clair. In Congress Harrison supported a revision of the land laws and the division of the Northwest Territory to permit statehood to Ohio, playing an active role in the construction and passage of the Land Act of 1800 and in the formation of Indiana Territory. Then once more he pulled all the political strings within his reach to obtain the appointment as governor of Indiana.

When Harrison arrived at his new post early in 1801, he found himself with but few people to govern in spite of his nominal control of a large area. The total white population of the present states of Indiana, Illinois, Michigan, and Wisconsin was little more than 5000; the most populous town, Vincennes, had 700 residents. Consequently the new governor had plenty of spare time in which to try a little farming, dabble in land speculation, and take an interest in the schemes of Aaron Burr. He was personally ambitious; as governor of Indiana he desired to enlarge his constituency by buying Indian land for the benefit of white settlers. On the other hand, his immediate aim was to continue in office; and since he felt that Jefferson favored a policy of benevolent noninterference in Indian affairs, he was content for the time being to sit idle and do nothing.

Harrison was soon freed to follow his own desires by a plain intimation from President Jefferson that new land acquisitions would not be looked on with disfavor. Immediately (1802–1803) he entered negotiations with the Indians, and another million acres were added to the land available for white settlement. Other treaties followed; and the resulting Indian resentment was attributed by the governor to British influence, which since the surrender of Detroit centered at Malden (Amherstburg) across the river. Harrison had some sympathy for the Indians, for they suffered from "unprovoked wrongs," but he nevertheless was convinced that the only possible way to deal effectively with them was to destroy them. He had visions of himself as a second Wayne, and read such classic war narratives as those of Herodotus, Thucydides, Caesar, and Sallust. He mapped out wonderful prospective campaigns, and felt that all he needed was an opportunity to exhibit his military abilities.

Harrison's attention was not called to Tecumseh until 1806, but the succeeding years saw the men come into closer and closer contact. In 1808, the year that Tecumseh took up his residence in Prophetstown, he had an interview with Harrison in which he promised peace if the United States did not make further treaties involving land cessions; if such cessions were made, Tecumseh threatened a British alliance and war. A similar interview was held the following year, but by this time events made peace impossible. Illinois Territory was created, leaving Indiana with its present boundaries. Harrison received permission from the secretary of war to buy more Indian land; the purchase of 2.5 million acres in the fall of 1809 increased the number and wrath of the hostile Indians. Rumors of war became current on the frontier.

TIPPECANOE   The new land purchase led Tecumseh in his conversations with Harrison in 1810 to insist more strongly that Indian land was held in common and could not be alienated by a few individuals. Harrison might well have commenced war at this time if the government had not been busy in West Florida, but he waited until August 1811, at which time he felt that his opportunity had come. Tecumseh, after an interview in which he had asked that no immediate action be taken, departed on a tour to the south to talk with the southern Indians. As soon as he had gone, Harrison gathered 1000 men (mostly volunteers) and, with a well-planned campaign already formulated, prepared to annihilate his unsuspecting enemies. Possibly he was absentminded—at least he forgot to report his plans to the President.

When Harrison left Vincennes on September 26, 1811, his objective was to crush Shawnee power by destroying Prophetstown. Moving up the Wabash he paused only long enough to build Fort Harrison on the present site of Terre Haute, and on the night of November 6 encamped on Tippecanoe Creek. Although he stated that he did not intend to attack Prophetstown, the Indians quite rightly feared treachery and under the leadership of the Prophet attacked the white camp early on the morning of November 7. Despite this surprise attack, Harrison maintained his position. The white casualties were 61 killed and 127 wounded; the Indian losses were unknown. Both sides claimed victory, but popularly Harrison received the credit. He became a military hero largely because he had the foresight to dispatch messengers to the East immediately after the battle with reports of an overwhelming defeat of the Indians. In later years there was much controversy as to whether or not Harrison had actually won. He had repulsed the Indians, but, on the other hand, he had found it necessary to retreat almost immediately, stopping only long enough to destroy Prophetstown. He was back in Vincennes on November 18.

The battle of Tippecanoe had far-reaching effects, though somewhat different from those that Harrison had anticipated. Prophetstown did not disappear; the Indians immediately rebuilt it. Indian troubles did not stop; new depredations occurred at once. From a larger point of view, however, the Indians suffered greatly. Tecumseh lost some of his prestige, and plans for a general Indian alliance never again came so near to success as they had in the years just prior to 1811. The United States encountered no further resistance in expanding its land purchases to Lake Michigan after the War of 1812. For Harrison's personal benefit the encounter inspired the battle cry of "Tippecanoe and Tyler too," which was an important factor in his successful presidential campaign of 1840.

WESTERN WAR SENTIMENT   Scarcely had Harrison returned from his Indian campaign than the War of 1812 took the center of the stage. The stated causes of the war were freedom of the seas and the impressment of American seamen; although rather curiously the Federalist Northeast, which should have been most concerned, was actually least in favor of the war. The Republican South and West were more bellicose, partly on nationalistic grounds, but partly for other reasons. Both had been experiencing a depression from about 1808, and a curtailment of trade by British restrictions on exportation of such products as cotton, corn, tobacco, and hemp. The West also blamed its Indian troubles on British incitement, and expected that a British defeat would give Americans the Great Lakes fur trade and sap the power of the Indians. Then too the West coveted Canada and Florida; waging two major wars simultaneously would obviously be foolhardy, but at least Canada might be taken. England was the traditional enemy, and the stronger and more objectionable neighbor.

War sentiment was brought to the boiling point in Congress by the "War Hawks," mostly from the South and West. One of them, Henry Clay, became Speaker of the House. The War Hawks shouted vigorously in the session of 1811 for a larger army and navy for "defense," and for the armed protection of American rights. They called for the annexation of Florida and Canada as "natural" parts of the United States, which would benefit by superior American civilization. Clay thundered that the Kentucky militia alone could conquer Canada. This attitude showed at least that the West was no longer attracted by separatist ideas, but had become as patriotic as the rest of the United States. With greater population it realized that its influence in the councils of the nation was ever increasing.

HULL'S OPERATIONS The West, having obtained its war, looked forward eagerly to the immediate conquest of Canada. The first campaign in the Northwest was undertaken by General William Hull, then governor of the comparatively new Michigan Territory, which had been created in 1805. Hull did not feel competent to undertake a military expedition, opposed his own appointment as commander, and finally accepted only under protest. His orders were to reinforce Detroit and then to invade Canada, with aid to be provided by an offensive movement at Niagara by General Henry Dearborn. From the very beginning Hull's plans went wrong, when his boat containing supplies and orders for Detroit was captured by the British under Major General Isaac Brock at Malden. On July 5, 1812, Hull and his army of 1600 men arrived at Detroit. A week later he crossed the Detroit River and entered Canada, issuing a proclamation promising real freedom to the British inhabitants of the region; he delayed, however, in his attack on Malden.

General Hull has been criticized severely for his failure to attack Malden when his effectives outnumbered the British three to one, but Hull realized his own incompetence as leader of the expedition. Entirely lacking in military ability—by nature he was timid and fearful, leaning toward persuasion rather than force. He was opposed by Major General Brock, a comparatively young man with a background of active military life, and the traditions of a British family of soldiers. In addition, Hull was hampered by the necessity of using part of his men to keep open his communications to the rear.

Hull suffered further by not receiving the cooperation he expected. The Niagara offensive failed, the eastern invasion of Canada did not materialize, and Lake Erie remained in English hands. In the West, Mackinac was lost, and the troops from Fort Dearborn (present-day Chicago) were annihilated in their effort to join Hull. These factors led him to decide that he was too weak to advance farther, and so he recrossed the river and returned to Detroit. In fact, he wanted to evacuate Detroit and retire to the Maumee, but his officers, led by Lewis Cass, effectively opposed any such retreat.

Hull's timidity encouraged Brock to cross the river and lay siege to Detroit. On August 15 he demanded the surrender of the city, and the next day, much to Brock's surprise, Hull acceded to the ultimatum. News of this ignominious capitulation was received in the East with amazement and chagrin. Without even attempting to defend themselves, a considerable body of American troops that had been expected to capture Canada had been taken prisoner by a numerically smaller body of British. Hull was immediately court-martialled and sentenced to be shot, but his sentence was later remitted. His punishment was not only unnecessarily harsh but did not advance the American cause. The hostile Indians were lined up solidly with the British, and for the time being the frontier of defense had to be withdrawn to the line of the Wabash and Maumee. General James Winchester was sent with a relief army to recover some of Hull's losses.

HARRISON'S CAMPAIGNS   While these events were occurring in the North, William Henry Harrison was forced to remain in a position not at all to his liking. He had expected that upon the outbreak of the war he would be made a major general and given charge of offensive operations, for had he not shown his military acumen by his successful campaign against the Indians? When no such appointment

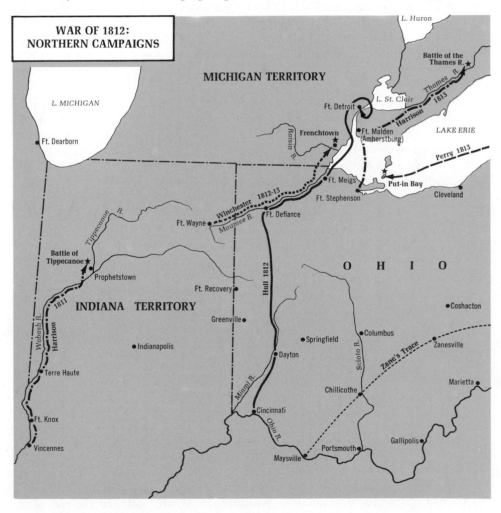

WAR OF 1812:
NORTHERN CAMPAIGNS

was made, Harrison deserted his Indiana job and went to Cincinnati to use his political influence to obtain a high army command. He was successful in raising a body of Kentucky militia and in persuading his friend the governor of Kentucky to commission him major general of the Kentucky militia, even though he was not an inhabitant of the state.

Harrison's first offensive operation was to move on Cincinnati, where he found Brigadier General Winchester with a mixed army of militia and regulars, and with orders to reinforce Hull. Harrison browbeat Winchester and took control of the whole army. With the news of Hull's defeat and with definite orders from Washington for Winchester to lead the relief army, Harrison was in an embarrassing position, and found it necessary to say, possibly with his fingers crossed, that he would restore Winchester's army immediately. He interpreted this "immediately" to mean after the capture of Terre Haute, which had been taken by the Indians. Just at this time he received some measure of justification for his delay with the news that he had finally been appointed a brigadier general of the United States Army, largely through the influence of his friend Henry Clay.

Harrison advanced upon Fort Wayne with his borrowed army, and entered it on September 12, 1812. The victory actually was barren, since the Indians had already departed. Winchester now demanded the return of his army, and even Harrison could no longer find a reason for refusal, since he was the junior officer. To add to his annoyance he received orders from the War Department to support Winchester with his Kentucky militia; such action would make him distinctly a subordinate. Actually he kept control of his militia and decided to act independently and capture Detroit. Meanwhile the influence of Henry Clay had been at work in Washington, with the result that President Madison came to appreciate the merits of Harrison and to give him complete charge of the armies of the West. It is not recorded what Winchester thought when these new orders reached him, but he had had a good army training, and obeyed the commands of his superiors.

As soon as Harrison took command, he decided to divide the 10,000 men into three armies and advance toward Detroit at once. Both decisions were probably bad; the army should have been kept united and given more training before it undertook offensive operations. As it was, roads were either nonexistent or nearly impassable, supplies were poor and inadequate, the leaders were jealous, and the army showed its disaffection by desertions and threats of mutiny. Harrison thereupon became less sure of the desirability of an advance, and corresponded voluminously with the secretary of war on the subject. While the troops under the immediate command of Harrison were thus loitering in October and November, the column under Winchester continued to advance—on the assumption that it was being supported by the rest of the army. On the Raisin River, January 22, 1813, Winchester was attacked by a small force under Henry Proctor, who had succeeded Brock in command of the British troops, and was defeated completely, in part because of the lack of expected support by Harrison. If Proctor had continued to advance, he probably would have defeated the rest of the army under Harrison; but his force was so small that he grew timorous and hurried back to defend Malden.

Winchester's defeat caused Harrison to abandon his plans temporarily, and to retreat to the Portage River, where he established winter quarters, explaining that the support of the West for his campaign had been lukewarm and ineffective. While the men were in winter quarters, the enlistments of many of the six months' militiamen expired, and most of them went home. Thus Harrison found it necessary to postpone his advance still longer while he spent the summer of 1813 in raising new troops in Ohio and Kentucky. It was at this time that he learned that his rank had been raised to that of major general. Lucky for his leaderless force, it was not attacked during his absence.

Activities on the northern frontier were resumed in the late summer. Both Proctor and Harrison advanced, and fought a number of indecisive skirmishes. Then came the news of Oliver Hazard Perry's victory on Lake Erie on September 10, 1813, and Harrison was encouraged to move more rapidly. In the latter part of September he embarked for Malden. When he arrived there on September 27, he found the town deserted. The greatly outnumbered Proctor had felt that discretion dictated a retreat rather than a battle. Harrison, after some hesitation, decided to follow his retreating enemy. By means of forced marches he overtook Proctor at the Thames River on October 5, 1813, where the numerically superior Americans defeated the British decisively. The Indian allies deserted the British cause, although Tecumseh remained to end his life fittingly on the field of battle.

After the Battle of the Thames, Harrison was again a hero and could enjoy the fruits of his victory. Returning by way of Detroit and the southern shore of Lake Erie, he eventually reached the East, where the "hero of the Thames" was given a proper reception of parades, banquets, speeches, toasts, and eulogies. American victories had been so infrequent that even the least of them was the occasion for enthusiasm that approached adoration of the victor.

Harrison returned to Cincinnati in January 1814, but finding that interest in the war had given way to boredom, resigned his army position. Although technically still in progress, the war was at an end as far as the Northwest was concerned. The easy victories that had been expected at the opening of hostilities had failed to materialize. Hoped-for glory had been reduced to one small victory and a number of defeats, resulting in the loss of several posts in the Far Northwest. Since the war had brought no advantages, and the conquest of Canada was now recognized as impossible, the West regarded a continuation of hostilities as pointless.

EFFECTS OF THE WAR   The results of the War of 1812 were mixed in value. Several ignominious defeats had injured patriotic confidence. The expected conquest of Canada had not materialized. Men had been killed, property had been destroyed, and agricultural production had been reduced because of the absence of manpower. On the other hand, the power of the Indians had been broken. Tecumseh had been killed, and the possibility of a general Indian confederation had vanished. No further Indian outbreak was to occur until the Black Hawk War, a minor episode twenty years later. The subjection of the Indian inevitably meant new purchases of land in the succeeding years. Some of the cessions were engineered by Harrison, as was only fitting. In all, he bought some 33 million acres.

The war was also responsible for the first real beginnings of settlement in Michigan, which from 1818 to 1834 included not only the present state but also the region west to the Mississippi. Returned soldiers advertised the opportunities in the vicinity of Detroit when they told their friends of their war experiences and observations. People from farther south moved north in increasing numbers, although it was another decade before large-scale immigration came to Michigan.

The development of Michigan was closely associated with the life and work of Lewis Cass. Cass had commanded an Ohio regiment in Hull's army in the early stages of the war. He opposed Hull's strategy and advocated the defense of Detroit, but his efforts were unavailing. In the general capitulation there, he was taken prisoner, but was later paroled. His parole was removed in January 1813, at which time he gathered a new army and joined Harrison, whom he followed through the succeeding campaigns. When Harrison occupied Detroit, Cass was placed in command of the fort and the town.

Cass was appointed governor of Michigan on October 29, 1813, and immediately set to work to rehabilitate his territory, which had seen rough usage up to that time. For twenty years he was active in developing and advertising Michigan. He traveled widely, both on exploring trips and on missions to deal with the Indians, covering the territory as far west as the Mississippi. He was also instrumental in influencing Henry Schoolcraft to explore the area. In recognition of his abilities and services, Cass was appointed secretary of war by Andrew Jackson in 1831.

The end of the War of 1812 marked a definite stage in the development of the Old Northwest. The early hunters, trappers, and explorers had long been giving way to the advancing frontiersmen; but now, with the removal of the last Indian barrier, the way was opened for a still more rapid increase of white settlement. Frontier conditions were soon to be replaced by the development of a more peaceful, stable society.

READINGS   *Paperbacks are marked with an asterisk.*

    General   Pertinent regional and state histories include Clarence W. Alvord, *The Illinois Country* (1920); Frederick C. Bald, *Michigan in Four Centuries* (1954); John A. Caruso, *The Great Lakes Frontier* (1961); Logan Esarey, *A History of Indiana* (1923); Louise P. Kellogg, *The British Regime in Wisconsin and the Northwest* (1935), very scholarly. *Dale Van Every, *The Final Challenge: The American Frontier, 1804–1845* (1964), places war in western context; Francis P. Prucha, *The Sword of the Republic: the United States Army on the Frontier, 1783–1846* (1969).

    Causes of the War   Long standard has been Julius W. Pratt, *The Expansionists of 1812* (1925), which stresses western land hunger and Indian danger. *Bradford Perkins, *Prologue to War* (1961) reverts to older concepts; *Reginald Horsman, *The Causes of the War of 1812* (1962) stresses trade factors and minimizes western influences.

Harrison and Tecumseh   Harrison is best treated in Freeman Cleaves, *Old Tippecanoe* (1939). Tecumseh is well covered in Glenn Tucker, *Tecumseh: Vision of Glory* (1956) and John M. Oskison, *Tecumseh and His Times* (1938).

Chapter 12/THE SOUTHWEST AND JACKSON

A rough similarity existed between the Northwest and the Southwest before and during the War of 1812. Both regions were most thickly populated near the Ohio River, and was less densely settled away from the river banks. The Algonquian tribes harassed the northern frontier, and the southern tribes were only slightly less hostile. The frontiersmen coveted English Canada in the North and the Spanish Floridas in the South. But here the similarity ceased. American leadership, action, and accomplishments in the South were entirely different from those in the North.

The history and situation of the Floridas were unlike those of Canada. The portion of the Floridas east of the Perdido River had been Spanish, and the portion west of that river, French, until the end of the Seven Years' War (1763), when both areas went to England. Under English rule immigration was encouraged by liberal land grants, and new settlements appeared. During the Revolution these settlements provided bases for expeditions into Georgia and havens for Tory refugees. At this time the northern boundary of the Floridas was the parallel of the mouth of the Yazoo River (32°28′).

The end of the American Revolution saw Britain in the role of the vanquished, and the Floridas were ceded to Spain. The Spanish holdings in Florida and Louisiana were continual sources of irritation to the United States, for they included control of the mouths of the Mississippi and other important rivers such as the Tombigbee, the Alabama, and the Apalachicola. For the time being the navigation of the Mississippi overshadowed all other considerations, taking preference both in private plots and in governmental negotiations. The results, as described earlier, were the Pinckney Treaty of 1795 and the subsequent purchase of Louisiana.

EFFORTS TO ACQUIRE THE FLORIDAS   The acquisition of Louisiana soon proved an altogether too meager morsel for the appetites of American expansionists, and agitation for the taking of the Floridas continued. The Americans who had settled on the Gulf Coast and the lower Mississippi did not thereupon become loyal Spaniards. The outlets of the principal southern rivers began to look more important as Georgia and Tennessee settlements pushed toward the southwest. Because of the weak Spanish administration fugitive slaves, bands of hostile Indians, and outlaws of all kinds found safety in the Florida swamps.

American desire for the Floridas went much further than mere dreaming. Pinckney made an effort to buy them in 1797 but failed. This failure, together with increased western irritation, brought frequent rumors of war in 1803–1806 and thus furnished part of the background for the Burr plans. After 1806 the talk of war decreased. Negotiations for the purchase of the Floridas were reopened, but Spain proved adamant. However, Napoleon conquered Spain in 1808. Thereupon Jefferson turned to France, for having bought one property from a country with dubious title he saw no reason why he might not again do business that way. His idea was sound, but Napoleon asked more money than Congress was willing to appropriate.

Failure to buy the Floridas led people to consider other methods of acquisition. Most convenient and satisfactory was the supposition that at least West Florida had been included in the Louisiana Purchase. Truly, no one had thought of this possibility

Fort Mellon, Lake Monroe, East Florida. More of an encampment than a fort, this base represents the temporary nature of this military frontier. (Library of Congress)

when the purchase was made; but when Napoleon's delightfully vague boundaries were reconsidered, it seemed only reasonable to make them cover as much ground as possible. As early as 1803 Robert Livingston came to the conclusion that his earlier ideas of the boundaries of Louisiana were wrong and that the United States had also bought part of West Florida. In the next year Congress agreed with this pleasant theory and provided for the establishment of custom houses as far east as the Mobile River. Naturally, Spain protested, and since the United States did not want war at this particular time, the objectionable act was held in abeyance.

ACQUISITION OF WEST FLORIDA While the United States was making efforts to buy the Floridas, American citizens were filtering into the coveted region, and soon there were rumors that the settlers planned to revolt from Spain and either set up their own government or ask to be annexed to the United States. West Florida was particularly attractive because it included both Gulf ports and land along the Mississippi. Jefferson talked of seizing the territory as far east as the Perdido, and Madison suggested to Governor Claiborne of Mississippi that Claiborne hint to a friend the desirability of a revolution in the Baton Rouge area, with subsequent annexation by the United States.

The rumors of trouble in West Florida were confirmed when a convention of settlers met in 1810. Although these men were thinking of a revolt and then annexation to the United States, and actually had prepared a declaration of independence, they at first declared their allegiance to the Spanish king and petitioned for a redress of their grievances. To no one's surprise the Spanish governor failed to act; whereupon Philemon Thomas, as commandant of militia, took some eighty men, seized Baton Rouge, captured the Spanish military commander, and declared West Florida independent. The "State of Florida" adopted a constitution based on that of the United States, designed a flag with a white star on a blue field, elected a president, and applied to the United States for annexation.

Here was the plum that the United States had so long desired, now ripe for the plucking. President Madison refurbished his claims to the territory and issued a proclamation announcing that West Florida from the Mississippi to as far east as the Perdido River was part of the United States. He received the necessary support from Congress in the act of January 15, 1811. The western army was dispatched to the south and seized all of West Florida except Mobile, which was held by a fairly strong Spanish garrison. Upon the admission of Louisiana to the Union in 1812 it was given the portion of West Florida west of the Pearl River, and the remainder was added to Mississippi Territory. This acquisition of West Florida was interesting in part because of its immediate effects, but more because it served as a startling parallel to later expansions of the United States.

EAST FLORIDA After the acquisition of West Florida, East Florida became the center of interest. President Madison decided that the pattern of events of the earlier acquisition might well be repeated, and sent to the scene of prospective expansion the seventy-two-year-old, short, stocky, red-haired, and aggressive George Mathews, brigadier general of Georgia militia and a former governor of Georgia. He was instructed that he could accept any territory offered by local authorities or threatened by a foreign power, and he interpreted these instructions as giving him a free hand to take East Florida.

General Mathews established himself on the St. Marys River, where he collected "Florida patriots," largely from Georgia, many of whom had never been in Florida. The invasion of the "homeland" was begun in March 1812, supported by an American naval squadron that cooperated reluctantly, and by a regular army group that required a change of commanders before it would act. Amelia Island and Fernandina were taken, and siege was laid to St. Augustine. Freedom was declared for East Florida, a constitution was adopted, and a flag was designed with a blue soldier presenting a fixed bayonet against a white background. John H. McIntosh became Director of the Territory of East Florida. The obvious implication was early annexation to the United States.

Unfortunately for Mathews' plans, the administration then had a change of heart because of pressing war difficulties farther north. Mathews was dismissed on the pretext that he had exceeded his instructions—a repudiation that practically killed the old man, who died August 30, 1812, on his seventy-third birthday. After a brief period in which it seemed that Congress might authorize the military occupation of Florida, and after

Georgia Militia Under General Floyd, November 1813. Rarely did the opposing forces fight at close quarters in the manner shown; the picture is an artist's conception of an Indian battle on the southern frontier. (New York Historical Society)

Andrew Jackson had been sent toward the border, more moderate counsels prevailed. American troops were removed on the promise of the Spanish governor to grant amnesty to all rebels, and the "revolution" contracted to a few guerrilla groups that looted the countryside. The West Florida technique had failed in East Florida, and other measures had become necessary.

ANDREW JACKSON   In the Southwest the War of 1812 was notable principally because of the activities and rise to power of one man—Andrew Jackson. Jackson was Scotch-Irish by descent. In 1763 his parents had moved west to the Catawba region, where Andrew was born two years later. His father died before Andrew's birth, and his mother when he was fourteen; hence for most of his life he was forced to depend on his own resources. He spent his youth and early manhood among rough and uneducated people, and it is therefore not remarkable that he swore fluently, drank liquor, chewed tobacco, fought duels, gave way to violent fits of temper, and never had a good command of English. In contrast to these less desirable traits, he had the frontier virtues of straightforwardness, trustworthiness, self-sufficiency, truthfulness, and loyalty to his friends.

Andrew Jackson began his mature life with the study of law in North Carolina, and in the latter 1780s moved to the Tennessee frontier, where he developed a successful legal business and entered local politics. He was a member of the state supreme court, and after 1802 held the rank of major general of militia. When the war with England began, he immediately raised an army and offered his services to the government. His offer was accepted, and early in 1813 he received orders to move south and help capture Florida. His best route lay down the Mississippi, so he marched his troops to Natchez, preliminary to following the river to New Orleans. He was willing to promise with easy confidence the capture of Mobile, St. Augustine, Pensacola, or any other place that was desired. While at Natchez he quarreled with Wilkinson over the question of who was superior in rank, and then he quarreled with Thomas H. Benton because Benton thought Wilkinson was right. At a later time Jackson engaged in a tavern brawl with the Bentons (the future Missouri senator and his brother) and received a serious arm wound.

Jackson's orders to move south were part of a general plan that included three armies and presumably was designed to conquer all of the Floridas. The ostensible purpose was to prevent a Spanish invasion, Spain then being an ally of England. Whatever the general plans may have been, they were not put into operation, since the Senate would authorize no more than the occupation of Mobile. General Wilkinson obtained the honor of investing that city on April 13, 1813, thus rounding out the American control of West Florida.

By the time Jackson arrived in Natchez, the government had changed its mind about the advisability of a Florida expedition, and ordered him to disband his troops. This order displeased Jackson intensely. Not only did it destroy his hopes of a successful military expedition, but the volunteers would have to make their way as best they could over several hundred miles of wilderness, since no provision was made for returning the men to their homes. For a person of Jackson's temperament there was only one thing to do: disobey orders. Disregarding his instructions, he marched his men home over the Natchez Trace making himself responsible for the necessary expenses. It was a brave and humane act—bad military etiquette but good politics. Eventually he was paid for his expenses.

CREEK WAR The return of Jackson to Tennessee coincided with a new outbreak by the Indians of the Southwest. These tribes had long resented white aggression, and now were heartened by Hull's defeat in the North. More important at the time, however, were internal conflicts, particularly between those who favored adopting

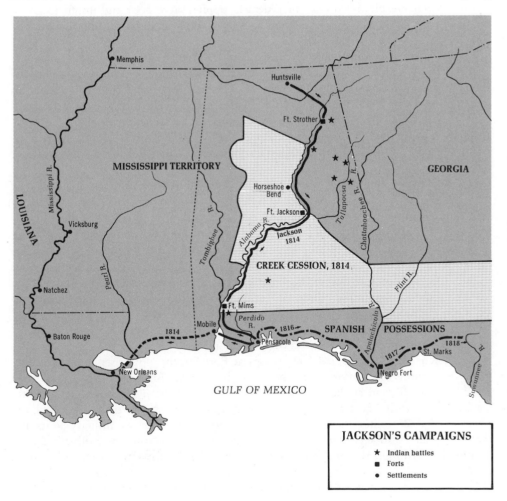

white methods of life and those who preferred traditional Indian customs, and even the peace tour of Tecumseh could not allay the dispute. As part of this intratribal struggle, Creek primitives on August 30, 1813, attacked the half-breeds at Fort Mims, which lay at the junction of the Alabama and the Tombigbee. In the ensuing battle the attackers were carried away by their martial enthusiasm, and ended by killing all the people at Fort Mims, white as well as Indian.

Almost before the last of the scalps had been torn from the heads of the slaughtered whites at Fort Mims, plans were made for a punitive expedition into the territory of the hostile Indians. As a matter of fact, such an expedition had been planned earlier and needed only the finishing touches. Three armies were to take the field—one from Georgia under John Floyd, a second from Louisiana under W. C. C. Claiborne, and a third from Tennessee under Jackson. The three divisions failed to cooperate according to plans: the generals quarreled over precedence, supplies were poor and insufficient, and the troops were disaffected. The Jackson column was by far the most important of the three.

The orders for Jackson to take the field against the Indians arrived while Jackson was confined to his bed as the result of his shooting fray with the Bentons. Despite his disability he assumed command of the army at once, and conducted the early part of his campaign when he could scarcely sit on his horse. His plan called for a movement down the Coosa and Alabama rivers, and the establishment of permanent forts along the route. As Jackson progressed, he found himself opposed by the Indians in continual skirmishing, with here and there a more important engagement that did not always turn out favorably to him.

Jackson's major difficulty was not with the Indians but with his own men. Most of them were new recruits, not anxious to fight the Indians at any time, but particularly reluctant to fighting on empty stomachs. From time to time, as portions of them started to desert, Jackson had to use one part of the army to keep the remainder from going home, and subsequently to use the second group to keep the first in camp. To preserve discipline he punished infractions of all rules severely, almost unknown with frontier militia. On one point, however, the men succeeded in having their own way. In the middle of the campaign the enlistments of most of them expired and they decided to go home. Jackson blustered and raged, but still the men went home. Left with only 1000 men, most of whom were enlisted for terms that would soon be over, he found it necessary to return to civilization to gather more troops.

By March 1814 Jackson had 5000 troops at Fort Strother in present northern Alabama. Resuming his movement to the south, he won decisive victories at Horseshoe Bend (March 27) and at the junction of the Coosa and the Tallapoosa; on the latter battlefield he erected Fort Jackson, where in August he dictated a treaty by which the Creeks ceded 22 million acres of land, permitted construction of military posts and roads, and agreed to keep the peace in the future. In the meantime his militia had been dismissed (April 21, 1814) and had marched home. The southwestern Indians had been crushed.

Jackson was rewarded for his successful Indian campaign with the major-generalship in the regular army left vacant by the resignation of Harrison. He made his headquarters in Mobile so as to be ready for either a recurrence of Indian trouble or an attack by the British. Having some leisure, he entered into an acrimonious dispute with the governor of Florida over the return of fugitive Indians; he also built a fort west of Pensacola which was clearly within Spanish territory. Finally, becoming impatient at the slowness with which the war was being fought, he asked permission of the War Department to take Pensacola, justifying his proposed action by the presence of British troops, whose capture he felt would be a "defense" of Spain. The War Department denied his request, whereupon Jackson captured Pensacola in November 1814. Desk generals could not prevent Jackson from doing what he considered desirable.

BATTLE OF NEW ORLEANS   By this time it had become fairly certain that the British contemplated a southern invasion, which would begin at New Orleans, and so as soon as Jackson had completed his occupation of Pensacola, he hurried west to the hitherto defenseless New Orleans. Arriving on December 2, 1814, he displayed his usual energy in completing the defenses, in collecting supplies, and in recruiting and training soldiers. Unified action was obtained by placing the city under martial law. As Jackson's preparations were nearing completion, the British arrived, making a careful landing below the city. They were led by General Edward M. Pakenham, an able soldier who had seen service under Wellington.

After preliminary skirmishing the final attack on New Orleans was launched on January 8, 1815, and resulted in a complete victory for Jackson, who lost only 6 men while his opponents lost 2000. The British advance was halted, Pakenham was killed, and soon the invading troops took to their boats and sailed away. It was a glorious victory for Jackson, who was thereupon toasted throughout the United States as the "hero of New Orleans." A picture of him riding a hypothetical white charger came to be a commonplace in the barrooms of the country. The glory of the feat was in nowise dimmed by the fact that it occurred two weeks after the signing of the Treaty of Ghent. Carping critics have insisted that Jackson's troops were superior in number and equipment and had their choice of a position to defend, while Pakenham's men were confused by the terrain. Even admitting these conditions, the credit that Jackson received for his effective handling of the defense of New Orleans was well deserved.

After the victory at New Orleans Jackson continued to rule despotically. Military discipline was enforced vigorously and the unusual punishment of death was given for desertion. New Orleans remained under martial law, and Jackson's word was supreme. Such a situation was endurable in time of imminent danger, but now that peace had returned, the people of New Orleans became restive. Collisions between civil and military authority were increasingly frequent and acrimonious. Jackson involved himself in disputes with many people, including a federal judge, Governor Claiborne, and the state legislature of Louisiana. The situation did not improve until the spring of 1815, when the army was restored to a peacetime basis. At this time Jacob Brown was placed in command north of the Ohio, Jackson in the Southwest, and Edmund Gaines on the

Florida border. Jackson felt himself sufficiently relieved of military duties to travel in the East, where he was acclaimed as the outstanding hero of the late war, and where his exploits would help him become President.

FLORIDA TROUBLES   While Jackson was receiving a deserved ovation from his admiring countrymen, the Florida situation remained as troublesome as ever. Although active operations in that region had been curtailed for the duration of the war, the United States had by no means lost its interest in annexation. Now new sources of irritation made the acquisition of Florida still more desirable. The Indians who had

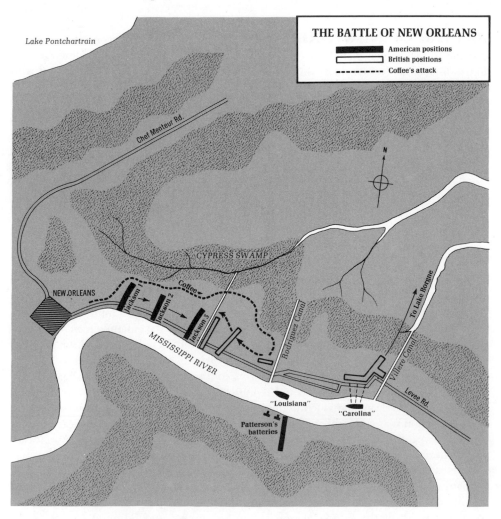

been defeated farther north found an asylum in the Florida swamps, from which they emerged to harass the border settlements. Escaped Negro slaves also went to Florida, where they could not be recaptured. Both groups remained actively hostile, partly because of the English traders who operated south of the borders of the United States.

The center of the East Florida trouble was the so-called Negro Fort on the Apalachicola River. Here the escaped Negroes rallied and showed their disdain of their pursuers by desultory firing at the Americans on the other side of the river. The situation was no more pleasing to the Spanish governor of Florida than it was to the Americans, so he gave permission for the capture and destruction of the fort. After a brief attack it was demolished by hot shot on July 27, 1816.

Negotiations for the purchase of Florida were resumed by President Monroe after the War of 1812, but by the latter part of 1817 he felt so doubtful of the possibilities of peaceful purchase that he sent troops to the border to invade the territory if the occasion demanded. Gaines was ordered early in December to capture Amelia Island, which was a well-known rendezvous of smugglers, and Jackson was put in charge of border operations. When Gaines arrived at Amelia Island he found a body of American filibusters in control, and consequently his occupation was bloodless.

When Jackson took control of the border late in 1817 he had a not unreasonable feeling that the administration might be pleased if he conquered the desired territory. Before acting on his own authority, he took the precaution of writing to Monroe, asking for at least tacit permission. Under normal conditions he would have written to the secretary of war, but in this case he disliked Secretary Calhoun even to the extent of forbidding his subordinates to obey any orders coming directly from the Department of War. This action was called treason by General Winfield Scott, whom Jackson immediately challenged to a duel, which Scott refused on religious and patriotic grounds. Jackson's letter to Monroe was never read by the President, who was ill at the time. The President's friend Congressman John Rhea, however, wrote to Jackson intimating that the President approved of the general's plans—or, at least, this was the tenor of the letter according to Jackson's later statements. Unfortunately, Jackson had burned the original document before he quoted it to others.

With these hypothetical instructions Jackson raised troops in Tennessee and marched to a position near the site of the Old Negro Fort, arriving in March 1818. Then, pusuing some fleeing Negroes, he crossed the border into Florida. Later he supported his action on the grounds that hostile Indians were given encouragement from Florida, and that the British in the region were a continual source of trouble to the United States. In his advance into Florida he pushed the Indians ahead of him, killing a few of them and also executing two British subjects accused of furnishing military supplies to the Indians. The latter act caused the United States some diplomatic trouble. Eventually Jackson captured St. Marks, and at the same time ordered Gaines to take St. Augustine. On his way home he made a final gesture by recapturing Pensacola, which had been returned to Spain.

Jackson's operations in Florida threw the government at Washington into turmoil.

Spain was angry and asked that Jackson be punished, and the captured territory returned. The negotiations for the purchase of Florida, which had been progressing fairly well, came to an end. Long cabinet meetings debated whether or not Jackson should be upheld; President Adams backed the general while Calhoun was his chief opponent. Congress was restive, and Henry Clay brought in a motion censuring Jackson for his precipitous action. Apparently Jackson himself was amazed and resentful at all this hubbub. In respect to the cabinet he was completely in error, for he credited Calhoun with his defense and for many years hated Adams because of his supposed opposition. Jackson also missed the political significance of the move by Clay, who had the presidency in mind, and considered it a personal affront.

Eventually the cabinet adopted a compromise position. Pensacola and St. Marks were returned to Spain as requested, but Adams intimated plainly that the presence of Florida as a constant source of irritation was bound to produce just such invasions unless Spain sold the territory to the United States. The soundness of this attitude was demonstrated later in Spain's sale of Florida, but at the time it served only to infuriate the irascible Jackson, who was certain in his own mind that he had obeyed orders. The compromise also displeased the people of the United States, who admired the spectacular exploits of the impetuous general. Monroe attempted to placate Jackson by a friendly letter, and the general public by an open communication to the *National Intelligencer*.

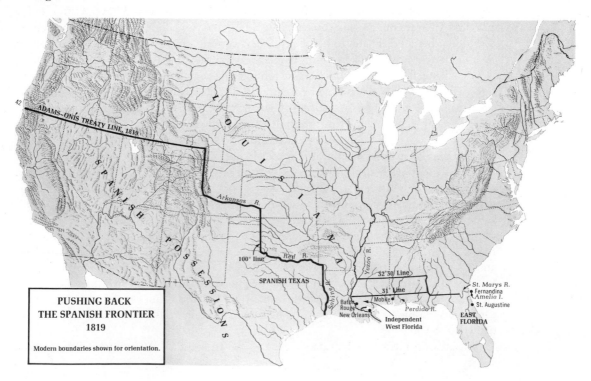

PUSHING BACK
THE SPANISH FRONTIER
1819

Modern boundaries shown for orientation.

PURCHASE OF FLORIDA   The results of Adams' diplomacy came in the purchase of Florida in 1819, with the Adams-Onís Treaty being ratified two years later. In addition to transferring title to Florida, the treaty also settled definitely the northern limits of Spanish claims in the Southwest. Starting at the mouth of the Sabine, the boundary followed that river to its intersection with 32° north latitude, then due north to the Red River, up the Red to 100° west longitude, north to the Arkansas River, along the Arkansas to its source, north to 42° of latitude, and thence along that parallel to the Pacific. In view of later developments it is interesting that not even Jackson desired to acquire Texas at this time.

After the acquisition of Florida, Jackson was finally and completely vindicated by being appointed governor of the new territory. As in previous similar situations, he at once involved himself in quarrels with many of the people with whom he had dealings; this time his chief opponent was the former Spanish governor. Jackson's temper was further ruffled by the scarcity of offices that he could bestow on his relatives and friends. Soon he came to the conclusion that his health was not adequate for the governorship of Florida, and therefore resigned.

The series of events in the Southwest that terminated with the acquisition of Florida had many results: the United States acquired a considerable body of new territory, rounding out its possessions east of the Mississippi, and many people thought that the end of expansion had been reached. The Indians had been defeated and were to remain harmless for another generation. A new figure from the West, Andrew Jackson, had achieved distinction and assumed an important role on the national stage, while two of his principal rivals, Henry Clay and William Henry Harrison, also westerners, were brought into prominence by the war. Possibly most significant was the method used for expansion—a method that was to appear again and again with but minor variations.

READINGS   *Paperbacks are marked with an asterisk.*

    General   Best for the entire subject are Thomas P. Abernethy, *The South in the New Nation* (1961) and John A. Caruso, *The Southern Frontier* (1963); shorter but also good is E. Merton Coulter, *A Short History of Georgia* (1933)—1960 edition is titled *Georgia, A Short History*. See also Francis P. Prucha, *The Sword of the Republic: The United States Army on the Frontier, 1783–1846* (1969). Julius W. Pratt, *The Expansionists of 1812* (1925) describes the revolts in both East and West Florida. Rembert W. Patrick, *Florida Fiasco* (1954) is excellent on Mathews. Isaac J. Cox, *The West Florida Controversy, 1798–1813* (1918) is complete but not exciting. Philip C. Brooks, *Diplomacy and the Borderlands* (1939) is best in its field.

    Indians and Jackson   The best complete story of the Indian troubles is Robert S. Cotterill, *The Southern Indians* (1954). Angie Debo, *The Road to Disappearance* (1941) is excellent on the Creeks. Marion L. Starkey, *The Cherokee Nation* (1946) is good on the Cherokee. Biographies of Jackson are almost endless, but among the useful ones in connection with the Indians are *Marquis James, *Andrew Jackson, the Border Captain* (1933) and David Karsner, *Andrew Jackson* (1929).

Chapter 13 / THE GREAT MIGRATION

The end of the War of 1812 cleared the way for a vastly increased influx of settlers from the East. As with all population movements, people were both propelled and attracted; they had to find their home conditions in the East less desirable than their prospects in the West.

PROSPERITY AND MIGRATION The period of the Napoleonic Wars was generally one of depression in America, particularly as Britain tightened its control over ocean shipping and as the United States replied with self-imposed limitations. New England shipping was badly damaged, while the markets for western and southern products declined. Depression in the East could theoretically have meant an increase in the movement to the West, but the costs of moving and settling could not be dismissed lightly, and where was a man to obtain the necessary capital in hard times? The truth was that people found more difficulty in moving during hard times; migration slowed, even though it never stopped. The other side of the story was that the attractive pull of the West also declined in bad times when western agricultural prices fell, work was scarce, and wages were low. Westerners wrote to their eastern friends advising them to defer moving until times were better. Any potential migrant found the West much less attractive in bad times than in good.

Several types of evidence support the generalization that the heaviest western movements occurred during periods of prosperity. Census figures are disappointing because a decennial count has no useful correlation with the business cycle; but here and there a state has helpful figures, particularly when a western territory counted its inhabitants several times in the hope of obtaining statehood. The dates of the admissions of the various states are in themselves useful when ranged alongside the business cycle, since normally admission occurred at the time of the first big influx of people. Accounts of westerners give clues to the time when migration was heaviest, as do the toll receipts of roads and canals used heavily in travel to the West. Land sales can be tabulated, but with the reservations that all sales did not mean settlement and all settlement did not mean sales. But no matter the method used, the conclusion emerges that the great flow of migration came in prosperous times.

Although the depressed decade of 1805–1815 discouraged migration, it also contained seeds that germinated a little later into a large-scale growth of population. Various striking events gave the West effective advertising. The purchase of Louisiana, the Lewis and Clark and other explorations, the boundary disputes, the Florida disturbances, the Indian wars, and the War of 1812, all helped to arouse interest in the West. Then too the West was becoming more attractive and accessible. The Indian menace was practically eliminated with the operations of Harrison and Jackson. The National Road was under construction, and the first steamboats were appearing on western waters. More land was available with new land purchases and surveys. Land was becoming cheaper because of the land bonuses given to the soldiers of the War of 1812. These grants were made in the form of scrip, which most soldiers sold instead of exchanging for land, thus making available large quantities of good land at comparatively low prices.

The Land of Promise, late 1830s. In each of the great waves of migration westward there were "go-backers." While promoters were reluctant to admit this, others, who thought the East was being "depopulated," publicized it. The print warns that Illinois is not necessarily a land of milk and honey. (Library of Congress)

Increased movement to the West after the War of 1812 came to a peak in the years 1818–1819 and ended with the panic of 1819. So great was the movement that it came to be known as the Great Migration. Over 1 million acres of land were sold in 1814, more than in any one previous year; by 1818 and 1819 yearly sales reached 3.5 million acres, but then the figures decreased.

ACQUIRING LAND   The land settled during the Great Migration was theoretically occupied under the provisions of the Land Act of 1800, which provided for local land offices, the auction system, and then private sale at two dollars an acre, with possible credit payments for most of the purchase price. Surveys of the new land were made as rapidly as possible, and local land offices were opened as needed; by 1820 there were thirty-four western land offices, of which fourteen were in Ohio. The auction system did not prove profitable, since the average selling price remained very near the legal minimum.

Settlers frequently paid little attention to government surveys and sales. Surveys were

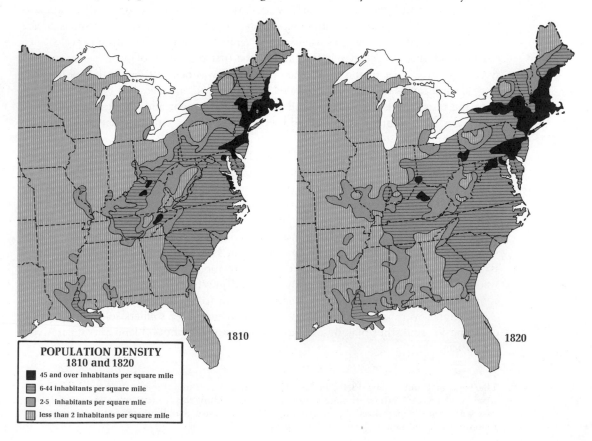

1810

1820

**POPULATION DENSITY
1810 and 1820**

■ 45 and over inhabitants per square mile

▨ 6-44 inhabitants per square mile

▨ 2-5 inhabitants per square mile

▥ less than 2 inhabitants per square mile

made slowly and systematically, and included all the land, good and bad. Settlement, on the other hand, skipped the apparently poorer sections and took only the best land. The result was that some of the settlement was always ahead of the surveys and many new inhabitants took up unsurveyed land to which they had no legal right and trusted to luck that they would be able to buy it later. Their number was increased by those who lacked funds and sought to elude the governmental land system.

The subdivision of the government that handled land sales prior to 1812 was a bureau in the Department of the Treasury, but a more effective control of the public domain was provided by a law of April 25, 1812, creating a General Land Office. The new bureau remained a part of the Treasury Department until it was transferred to the Department of the Interior when that department was organized in 1849.

LAND ACT OF 1820   The Great Migration brought to light glaring faults in the public land system. Outstanding were the difficulties produced by the credit feature of the Land Act of 1800. Western farmers were always too optimistic, and wanted to buy all the land on which they could make the down payment. Frequently their optimism was unjustified, and they could not meet succeeding installments. Theoretically they should then have been dispossessed and their first payments forfeited. Actually it was difficult to evict thousands of farmers when they became obstinate and bitter; moreover, such a procedure was politically dangerous. Not only the delinquent farmers but all the West was opposed to dispossession and forfeiture, for each westerner realized that at some time he might have the same sort of trouble. And what would happen to the dispossessed families?

The credit situation became worse when hard times swept the country during the Napoleonic Wars, the Indian troubles in the West, and the War of 1812. Not only was depression general but the use of a farmer militia meant that many westerners were in the army rather than farming. The immediate result was a flood of petitions asking congressional assistance. Congress responded with a long series of relief bills that aided particular persons or localities by postponing or omitting payments, or by alloting reduced amounts of land to correspond with the money already paid. In spite of such relief, $21 million was still overdue and unpaid in 1820, and with the panic of 1819 the future looked dark.

The failure to modify the Land Act of 1800 earlier was due in part to a very real division of opinion. The East continued to feel that western land was a trust fund for the nation, and should produce the largest possible revenue. Furthermore, many easterners favored a high price to discourage western migration so that the new manufacturing establishments of the East would have more labor. The West, on the other hand, felt that the price should be decreased to benefit the people who worked the land and gave it value. A further argument stressed that a reduced price would encourage settlement and thus add to the wealth and strength of the United States.

Out of this sea of conflicting interests and arguments eventually emerged the Land Act of 1820. The credit system was abolished by general agreement. The smallest unit to be sold was to be 80 acres. The auction system was retained, and was to be followed, as before, with private entry at the minimum price, but now the price was reduced to the compromise figure of $1.25 an acre. Defaulters under former legislation were to be aided by being given outright the amount of land corresponding to the money they had already paid.

The Land Act of 1820 was a real watershed in the history of the public domain because it changed the emphasis from producing revenue to getting land into the hands of actual settlers. The credit idea was never revived. The smaller minimum unit was found desirable and retained. On the other hand, the auction system continued to prove less and less satisfactory. The settler wanted the right to settle on the land before it was surveyed and then to be assured that a speculator could not bid it away from him at an auction. The most pressing demand of the West, however, continued to be low-priced land. These western desires came to be mixed with various sectional disagreements, and remained a continual source of trouble for Congress.

REGIONS OF SETTLEMENT The greatest flow of settlers during the Great Migration followed the central route through either Pittsburgh or Wheeling and then down the Ohio River. The state of Ohio received more population than any other region, so that by 1820 its nearly 600,000 residents made it the most populous state west of the mountains. Farther to the west new families occupied southern Indiana and Illinois, followed the Mississippi both north and south, and pushed up the Wabash and the Missouri. To the north a string of settlements blossomed along the entire southern shore of Lake Erie and as far west as Detroit. Detroit at the end of the War of 1812 numbered fewer than 1000 people; in 1820 the entire Michigan Territory (which included the present Wisconsin) contained fewer than 9000 persons. Migrants clung closely to navigable waters and wooded land, and hence did not touch central and northern Illinois and Indiana or the great bulk of the present Michigan and Wisconsin.

To the south additional migration flowed into Kentucky and Tennessee, so that by 1820 the former was almost as large as Ohio, while the latter had over 400,000 residents. In general the land extending north and south through the central section of the two states attracted most people. The real beginnings of Memphis came in 1819, but the first growth was small. Still farther south the largest concentration of population was in Louisiana, where 150,000 people made it the fourth largest of the western states. Mississippi was settled almost exclusively in the southern part. Alabama had a sprinkling of farms covering most of the western half of the state, but with the greatest concentration in the region of the great bend of the Alabama River. West of the Mississippi, and in addition to the Louisiana and Missouri settlements, were a few residents in Arkansas Territory, particularly along the Mississippi and Arkansas rivers.

Even though most of the West in 1820 was sparsely settled, the new states and territories west of the mountains had a total of some 2,225,000 people, which was almost a quarter of the total population of the United States. Here lies the reason for the ever-increasing power of the West in the federal government. In the House its votes might be decisive, but in the Senate its proportional strength was even greater. Consequently the West had better than an even chance of obtaining any legislation that it desired wholeheartedly. The great limitation was that the West was not always itself united. Clay and Jackson were both westerners, but not necessarily in accord for that reason. The more highly developed states such as Ohio and Kentucky by no means always agreed with the smaller and younger communities.

THE NEWER SOUTHWEST   The most distinctive characteristic of the Great Migration was the changing character of the people going to the Southwest, which was making this region far different from the Northwest. The change was due largely to two important developments. The first was the invention of the cotton gin by Eli Whitney in 1793 and its subsequent rapid development after 1800, which made practicable the large cotton plantation operated by slave labor. The second was the opening of large quantities of virgin soil in the Southwest by Jackson's successful operations against the Creeks. As a result of these two factors there was a westward push by the cotton planters with their slaves. The movement first became noticeable about 1810, and then grew rapidly.

The new southern migration resembled that of the North in its early stages. The trapper and hunter was usually followed by the herdsman and then by the farmer who cleared the land; sometimes he had one or two slaves. As the country developed, the small white farmer tended to concentrate in the more difficult up-country in a subsistence economy, while some of them acquired slaves and stayed on the plains, and others sold out to the larger planters from the East. As compared with the North, fewer industrial towns developed, while the farms tended increasingly to be one-crop operations rather than being diversified. The one-crop system tended to exhaust the soil, whereupon a share of the planters moved to newer land farther west.

By the end of the War of 1812 the southern roads to the west were so crowded with planters and gangs of Negroes that there was a scarcity of provisions. The Negroes, sometimes shackled, traveled on foot while the planters rode. Most groups went overland, although a few moved to the lower Mississippi Valley either by ocean or by way of the Ohio and Mississippi rivers. The roads, as elsewhere, were very bad, often little more than bridle paths. The most important one in the Far South was the Federal Road, authorized by Congress in 1806, which ran from Athens, Georgia, by way of the Tombigbee settlements to New Orleans; in the east it connected Athens with Greenville, Charlotte, Salisbury, Fredericksburg, Washington, and Baltimore. A few slaves appeared in Kentucky and Missouri, and more went to Tennessee, but the main migration was to the lower South.

The majority of the planters who moved west came from the Piedmont of the East rather than from the coastal plain, and carried with them the customs with which they were familiar. They soon constructed large, ramshackle "mansions" in which they dispensed southern hospitality. They raised almost exclusively cotton and corn, which meant that the plantation frequently depended on the outside world even for necessary food and clothing. By far the most important crop was cotton, which was particularly profitable in the period immediately after the War of 1812. The first plowing came in

February, and the cotton was planted in March. Later the plants required thinning and frequent cultivation. Picking started late in August and continued into the winter. After picking, the cotton was ginned, although a certain number of impurities had to be removed by hand; it was then pressed into 350-pound bales. Because there was no fertilization of the soil and no rotation of crops, the land was soon exhausted.

The labor of the southern plantation was performed by Negro slaves, who were worked in large gangs under continuous supervision. Each slave was given clothing twice a year, in the spring and the fall. With full-time work he was supposed to cultivate from 5 to 6 acres of cotton or corn, with the result that for each slave there was a production of about a thousand pounds of ginned cotton. On some plantations the slave was given a limited area of land to cultivate for himself. The planter seldom rolled in wealth; normally his profits were put back into the business to purchase new land and more slaves, so that he seldom had reserve capital and was frequently in debt. When a dwindling yield threatened disaster he might move his laboring force and equipment farther west.

The most obvious characteristics of southern agriculture were the increasing importance of cotton and the rapid exhaustion of the soil. In the decade 1811–1821 only one-third of the value of crops raised west of Georgia came from cotton, but by 1831 the proportion had grown to one-half and by 1834 to two-thirds ($75 million). As for soil depletion, older communities such as Virginia had shown evidences as early as colonial times, and districts farther west soon exhibited the same tendency; hence a decrease of population and wealth in the older communities was by no means unusual.

Another characteristic of the southern system was a continued and increasing demand for slaves. The institution of slavery, far from dying as southern colonial leaders had predicted, grew progressively stronger. The demand for additional western labor was filled in part by the increase of illegal slave trading, but more important, by the purchase of Negroes from the worn-out farms of the East. Eastern slaveowners had exhausted lands and an oversupply of Negroes, whereas the West was willing to pay high prices for eastern slaves. The result was a recognized and lucrative business of buying Negroes in the East, shipping them to the West, and selling them to western plantation owners. The traffic was so profitable that slaveowners were sometimes accused of breeding their slaves like cattle. To the Negro, being sold to the West was the acme of misfortune, and many humane owners refused to sell their slaves for the western trade. The West meant hard work, poor food, inadequate clothes, and an excessive amount of sickness. The swampy cotton plantations of Mississippi and the sugar plantations of Louisiana, where slaves died by the hundreds, were especially dangerous.

Free Negroes were not numerous in the West except in New Orleans, where they included many artisans and small shop owners. Generally they were quiet and peaceful, although periodic rumors of slave revolts made the whites fearful. Curiously enough, Negroes in New Orleans approved of slavery, and themselves had slaves. City life produced some unusual situations for the Negro. Many mulatto girls became the mistresses of white men, and likely looking female slaves had a good market among the "sporting class."

METHOD OF SETTLEMENT   The process of hewing homes from the wilderness during the Great Migration was very similar to that of twenty years earlier. There was the same long and tedious trip to the West, the same effort to pick out good land near friends from home, the same clearing of a plot of land, the same community house-raising, and the same girdling of trees and planting. Amusements were still dances, house-raisings, singing schools, weddings, camp meetings, and husking bees. Life had changed but little since the first pioneers had followed Daniel Boone into the wilderness.

The crops in the newly settled lands of the Ohio Valley were, as before, chiefly corn, wheat, rye, oats, tobacco, hemp, and flax. Prices were comparatively high, but it was difficult to get the goods to market. Labor was scarce and expensive, and difficult tasks were done by community effort. The homemade clothing, as earlier, was made of linsey-woolsey from the wool and flax grown on the farm. The materials from which clothes were made continued to be raised, carded, spun, woven, and sewed at home. Even shoes were still made at home by the frontier farmer, although the tanning of leather was becoming a commercial process. Both clothing and shoes were saved as much as possible, particularly in the summer.

Towns with centralized industry continued to develop slowly. Pittsburgh, with its

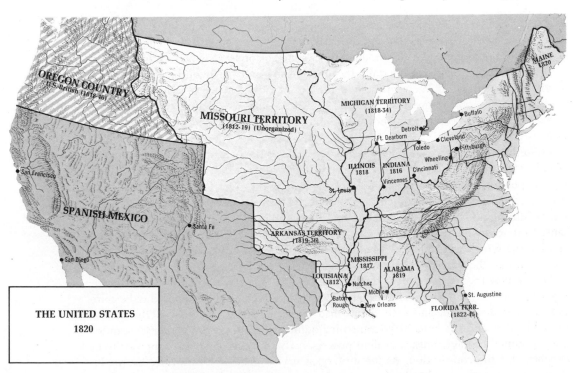

THE UNITED STATES
1820

manufacture of iron, glass, and rope, and its building of boats, still grew and prospered. Farther west, Cincinnati was attaining commercial importance, particularly with the development of pork packing; the farmers were learning that it was more profitable to drive their hogs to a central slaughtering and packing plant than to do the work themselves. St. Louis was coming into prominence as a center of the fur business and as a distributing point for the Far West. New Orleans, with the increase of the steamboat traffic, continued to maintain its commercial dominance. Other smaller but bustling centers contained water-driven lumber mills, grist mills, distilleries, and tanneries.

The growing towns were divorced to some extent from the rural countryside, even though their main functions were as commercial centers. City dwellers usually came from the East rather than from the surrounding countryside. They tended to look down on the country people, who in turn were becoming suspicious of city folk. City residents frequently specialized in their work, whereas the farmer continued to be a jack-of-all-trades. Cultural life in the cities became incomprehensible to many of the poorly educated of the country, and the prosperous lawyer or businessman increasingly sent his son to an eastern college and his daughter to an eastern finishing school. Class divisions, both within the cities and between city and country, were clearly sharpening.

HEALTH   One of the most unsatisfactory conditions of western life was the lack of adequate medical facilities. During the early nineteenth century there were few properly trained doctors west of the mountains. Competent physicians preferred to remain in the East rather than to undertake the poorly paid and hardworking life that was inevitable farther west. Western medical life meant riding many miles over atrocious roads, day and night, in good weather and in bad, to serve a widely scattered and poor population. Good hospitals did not exist, and medical schools and publications were rare.

Westerners were not exceedingly healthy in spite of the outdoor life and hard work. Accidents were common as long as hunting, felling trees, and fighting Indians were regular pursuits. Fever and ague were omnipresent in the river lowlands. Scarlet fever was frequent and at times epidemic. Yellow fever was prevalent in the New Orleans region during the summer, killing its hundreds and thousands. A typhoid epidemic caused numerous fatalities all over the West in 1816–1817. Cholera had periodic epidemics, the worst being in 1832. In addition to these serious diseases the westerner suffered from all the other common human ailments.

The earliest medical treatment on the frontier was given by anyone with even the simplest knowledge of drugs and surgery. Every educated man was supposed to be competent to treat disease, and each family had its own supply of simple herbs such as calomel, jalap, and cinchona bark (containing quinine). The seventh son of a seventh son was presumed to have unusual healing powers; early morning dew was supposed to be excellent for the complexion. As for surgery, it was as gruesome as torture by the Indians. For example, the details of an amputation without anesthetics (ether and chloroform were not used until the 1840s) and performed with a butcher knife, a meat saw, and a hot iron are best left to oblivion.

The ministrations of the early pioneer doctor were little better than those of kind friends, for such a practitioner ordinarily had little formal education, having learned his trade from his predecessors and by experience. His equipment, which he carried in his saddlebags, consisted of a few simple drugs, roots, herbs, calomel, a lancet, cupping glasses, and possibly a few other crude surgical implements and a supply of leeches. He compounded all his own medicine, and a particularly bitter dose was concealed in a piece of apple or dough. The western physician had two principal cures for all disease—calomel and bleeding. Calomel (sometimes jalap) was prescribed for every known disease, and often given in such large doses that it caused intense salivation and loosening of the teeth. Bloodletting was almost equally universal, being ordinarily accomplished either by cupping or by the use of leeches. The leeches were put into a tumbler and the open end of the tumbler was then placed over the skin. Cupping consisted of opening a vein and covering the opening with a glass from which the air had been expelled by the burning of alcohol. Such bloodletting was done in reckless amounts, and was considered especially efficacious for any illness that involved a fever.

Early medical methods produced results that were marvelous for the size of the group that remained alive. Fresh air was taboo; in a case of fever or inflammation the patient was placed between featherbeds, and the doors and windows of the sickroom were tightly closed. Cautery was performed with a white-hot iron. Wounds were encouraged to discharge pus by being kept irritated with threads or a pea. Hemorrhages were treated by bloodletting.

Epidemics ordinarily just ran their courses because there was no knowledge of their causes. The usual bloodletting and calomel were none too helpful for such plagues as yellow fever. Some public health measures were introduced, as cleaning the filth off the streets, possibly burning tar, or quarantining groups such as immigrants and the sick. Quite a few people felt that an epidemic was a sign of God's wrath, and that the best answer was cleaner living and prayer, which in fact may have been at least as effective as the ordinary remedies.

Western doctors were bad, and western health was poor, but these facts lose some of their force in view of generally poor American health and generally badly trained American doctors. Western epidemics were national and world epidemics, while western remedies were also general American remedies. Furthermore the West had some of the nation's more progressive doctors. Dr. William Goforth introduced vaccination to the West at the early date of 1801. Dr. John Sappington of Missouri popularized the use of quinine, particularly for malaria, in the 1830s with "Dr. Sappington's Anti-Fever Pills." Dr. Crawford Long, a small-town Georgia doctor, probably made the first medical use of ether as an anesthetic in 1842 for the removal of a neck tumor.

Curiously enough several medical operations were first performed in the West. Dr. Francis Prevost of Louisiana claimed the use of the rare Caesarian section in four cases prior to 1832, with three of them successful. The best-authenticated of the early Caesarean operations was performed by Dr. John L. Richmond in 1827 in rural Ohio. Dr. Richmond, who was also a Baptist minister, was called to the rude shack of a Negro woman late one night, and there he performed the operation by the light of candles and with only his pocket case of instruments; the child died, but the woman returned to work in twenty-four days. Most amazing of all was the ovariotomy performed by Dr. Ephraim McDowell of Danville, Kentucky, in 1809. Without special training or equipment, and of course without anesthetics, Dr. McDowell was the first man in the world to remove an ovarian tumor successfully; his operation marked the real beginning of abdominal surgery.

After about 1820 medical science west of the mountains gradually improved. Here and there promising young men attended medical schools in the East, while more and better doctors moved to the West as the population grew large enough to support them. Medical schools were established in the West; earliest was the medical department of Transylvania, which attained an excellent reputation by the 1830s. Other schools such as the Ohio Medical College (1819) and the Worthington Medical College (1832) helped raise the level of medical practice. Magazines such as the *Ohio Medical Repository* (1826), which later became the *Western Journal of the Medical and Physical Sciences* under the editorship of Daniel Drake, provided mediums for disseminating the latest scientific advances.

NEW STATES AND TERRITORIES   Advancing settlement brought agitation for statehood, since most westerners desired greater self-government than existed under territorial organization. Each region followed the steps outlined in the Northwest Ordinance—congressional control, limited self-government, and finally statehood. In each case a congressional enabling act and a constitutional convention preceded admission to the Union. The state conventions showed the democratic tendencies of the times, with limitations on executive power, removal of religious and property qualifications for voting, and the election of judges by the legislature. These trends were not original with the West, but had their fullest expression in that region.

North of the Ohio the western fruits of the Great Migration in terms of new states were Indiana and Illinois. Indiana Territory had come into existence in 1800, and with the arrival of settlers its size was reduced by the creation of Michigan (1805) and Illinois (1809) territories. The second stage of territorial government came in 1805, and ten years later an Indiana census showed the 60,000 people necessary for statehood; the statehood came in 1816. A strict adherence to the boundaries stated in the Northwest Ordinance would have meant that Indiana touched Lake Michigan at only a single point, but the extension of the northern boundary at the expense of Michigan produced the lake frontage that now includes the city of Gary. Indianapolis, founded in 1819, became the state capital in 1825 for no better reason than that it was approximately the geographical center of the state.

The first governor of Illinois Territory was Ninian Edwards, who remained in office until statehood. The second stage of territorial government was achieved in 1812, and a growing movement for statehood reached its goal in 1818, even though the population was then considerably less than the required 60,000. As had been done for Indiana, the new state was given a lake frontage—this time by extending the northern boundary some sixty miles; in consequence many Wisconsinites have protested that Chicago should be in Wisconsin. North of Indiana and Illinois the country to the international boundary was reallotted several times. From 1818, when Illinois was admitted, until Wisconsin became a territory, present Michigan and Wisconsin were combined as Michigan Territory.

South of the Ohio River the first new state of the nineteenth century was Louisiana, which had been populated largely before the Americans took control, and hence should not be considered a result of the Great Migration. Its admission in 1812 was opposed bitterly by New England Federalists, who foresaw dire results if the entire Louisiana Purchase, with its semiwild people, were to be carved into states and admitted to the Union. The eastern boundary of the new state was extended to the Pearl River, thus including part of West Florida.

Mississippi Territory had come into existence in 1798 to provide for the region between the 31st parallel and the mouth of the Yazoo, which had been evacuated reluctantly by Spain. The addition of the Georgia land cession of 1802 expanded the new territory to the present size of Mississippi and Alabama, except for the Gulf Coast,

Settlers in the Ohio Country, Early 1800s. Here the wooded land shows that the pioneers are still in the "tree belt." (New York Historical Society)

which was not added until 1812. After Jackson crushed the Indians, settlement increased, particularly in the rich black land of the Mississippi, the Gulf Coast, and the valleys of the Alabama and Tombigbee rivers. Expanding population brought a division of the territory in 1817, the year in which Mississippi became a state. Two years later Alabama followed into the Union; by 1820 the population of Alabama was about 128,-000, which was over half again as large as that of Mississippi.

The last two states to be produced by the great Migration were Maine and Missouri, admitted respectively in 1820 and 1821. Maine had been a part of Massachusetts, but in 1820 was separated from it by mutual agreement. Missouri, which had a more checkered career, had been something of an administrative problem, since for many years the St. Louis settlement had been the only important area of population west of the Mississippi. The entire Louisiana Purchase, exclusive of the prospective state of Louisiana, had been successively Louisiana District (1804) attached to Indiana Territory, Louisiana Territory (1805), and Missouri Territory (1812). In 1819, two years before Missouri became a state, Arkansas Territory was created to include not only present Arkansas but also the land west to the existing international boundary.

The application of Missouri for statehood called attention to the fact that with the admission of Alabama in 1819 the slave and free states each numbered eleven. This equality of sectional interests seemed important because it ensured for the South half of the votes of the Senate in a day when its influence in the House was declining. Consequently Congress, after a heated debate, accepted (1820) the admission of Missouri and Maine as compensating states, but with the proviso that no later state formed from the Louisiana Purchase and north of the principal southern boundary of Missouri (36°30′) should have slavery. This "Missouri Compromise" led to the immediate admission of Maine, but Missouri was delayed until the following year (1821). The delay was caused by Missouri's adoption of an extremely proslavery constitution to demonstrate its independence, which made a new compromise necessary. Missouri was the twenty-fourth state to enter the Union. Of the twenty-four states nine were west of the Appalachians.

The Great Migration was significant in carrying settlers to, and even beyond the Mississippi, although large areas remained unsettled farther east, both in the North and in the South. Half a dozen new states had been added to the Union, until the older West was no longer the frontier of settlement. Ohio, Kentucky, and Tennessee were soon to consider themselves old and well-settled regions, and to resemble seaboard communities more than they did a new frontier. The conquest of the continent had well begun.

READINGS   *Paperbacks are marked with an asterisk.*

North   General accounts include Roscoe C. Buley, *The Old Northwest* (2 vols., 1950), a prize-winning book, but long and detailed. Albert L. Kohlmeier, *The Old Northwest* (1938); John A. Caruso, *The Great Lakes Frontier* (1961); Walter Havighurst, *Wilderness for Sale* (1956). More localized accounts include Clarence W. Alvord, *The Illinois Country* (1920); John D. Barnhart, *Valley of Democracy* (1953), good on Indiana and Illinois; Floyd R. Dain, *Every House a Frontier* (1956),

Detroit; Logan Esarey, *History of Indiana* (1923); Theodore C. Pease, *The Story of Illinois* (1949); William T. Utter, *The Frontier State* (1941), Ohio; Charles Boewe (ed.), *Prairie Albion* (1962), contemporary Illinois settlement of 1817; *Richard C. Wade, *The Urban Frontier* (1959), excellent on specific cities. Lewis D. Stilwell, *Migration from Vermont* (1937) is first rate. *Stewart H. Holbrook, *The Yankee Exodus* (1950) is episodical.

South   Best general account is Thomas P. Abernethy, *The South in the New Nation* (1961). More specific accounts include Thomas P. Abernethey, *The Formative Period in Alabama, 1815–1828* (1922); Thomas D. Clark, *A History of Kentucky* (1937); Samuel C. Williams, *The Beginnings of West Tennessee* (1930); Floyd C. Shoemaker, *Missouri and Missourians* (5 vols., 1943).

Medicine   Medical histories generally give little attention to the West, but two interesting accounts are Madge E. Pickard and Roscoe C. Buley, *The Midwest Pioneer* (1945) and Erwin H. Ackerknecht, *Malaria in the Upper Mississippi Valley* (1945).

Land Act of 1820   Best is *Roy M. Robbins, *Our Landed Heritage* (1942). See also the scholarly Malcolm Rohrbough, *The Land Office Business* (1968).

Chapter 14 / THE PERMANENT
INDIAN FRONTIER

The increase of the white population between the Appalachians and the
Mississippi presaged the elimination of the Indian tribes still there. The
Indians had been squeezed into smaller and smaller areas with each advance.
Futile efforts had been made to keep whites out of the Indian country and

to persuade the Indians to adopt a settled agriculture. Now the time was fast coming when these delaying measures were obviously inadequate.

THE NEW INDIAN HOME   Provision for the eastern Indians seemed simple to most Americans. West of the Mississippi lay millions of acres of wild land that everyone felt would never be desired by white farmers, and hence would be perfect as a home for the eastern Indians. Lewis and Clark described much of the region as "desert and barren." Pike likened the Southwest to the African deserts. In 1820 Stephen H. Long found the area "wholly unfit for cultivation." In fact, even the plains areas east of the Mississippi were viewed doubtfully, Southeastern Wisconsin was found to be laboring under permanent defects of coldness of soil and want of moisture" (1817), while northern Illinois was described by Horace Greeley as late as 1847 as having "the great, formidable, permanent" drawback of "deficiency of water." School geographies labeled the vast western plains as "The Great American Desert," and almost everyone agreed that they would support only prairie grass, buffalo, and Indians.

The idea of moving eastern Indians to the western plains went back as far as Jefferson; eastern groups who had no homeland acceptable to the whites were moved west. This idea was gradually generalized. The Senate Committee on the Public Lands urged exchange of eastern for western land in its report to Congress in 1817, arguing that such action would remove the Indians from demoralizing white influences. Six years later Secretary of War Calhoun made the same recommendation to Congress. President Monroe followed similar reasoning in his congressional message of 1824. By this time an increasing number of treaties had removal as their objective. A law of 1830 accepted this procedure as general American policy. The objectors were mainly philanthropists, influenced by the large mission establishments, particularly in the South, who feared that they would lose patronage if the Indians went west.

New western homes for eastern Indians involved persuading them to move and western Indians to make room for them, neither of which was simple to do, but was assumed to be the permanent solution of the Indian problem. The important congressional act of 1830 authorized the President to make the necessary treaties and "solemnly to assure the tribe . . . that the United States will forever secure and guarantee to them, and their heirs or successors, the country so exchanged with them." Nearly every treaty had a similar provision; one of 1838, for example, gave the Cherokees "a permanent home, and which shall, under the most solemn guarantee of the United States, be, and remain, theirs forever." The "forever" that the United States so solemnly promised actually turned out in most cases to be less than a generation.

The Trail of Tears by Robert Lindneux. While most westward migrations were, presumably, undertaken with optimism, the removal of the Indians was characterized by bitterness and sadness. (Woolaroc Museum)

NORTHERN INDIANS The removal of the northern Indians was relatively easy, since no strong and warlike tribes remained to oppose the will of the United States. A long series of treaties indicated that the eastern tribes accepted the necessity of moving. Another series produced western land for them to occupy; most noteworthy was a St. Louis treaty of 1825 with the Kansa and Osage, which together with other agreements provided space between the Platte and the present Oklahoma.

The Northwestern Indians were a trifle more vigorous, but still comparatively peaceful and inoffensive. The earlier efforts, such as the Prairie du Chien agreement of 1825, were merely to get the Iowa, Sauk, Foxes, Sioux, and Chippewa to agree to boundary limitations. The negotiations at Prairie du Chien were among the most notable of western gatherings, with the white negotiators including such well-known men as William Clark, Lewis Cass, Henry Schoolcraft, and Lawrence Taliafero. White advances soon made necessary further agreements, particularly a new Prairie du Chien treaty five years later.

BLACK HAWK WAR The one outbreak that resulted from northern removals was the Black Hawk War, which has been better advertised than its importance warrants. The disturbing nations were the allied Sauk and Foxes, some 5400 strong, seminomadic, and noted for their fighting ability. Their resistance to the whites was entirely justified from a legal standpoint. By a treaty made with Harrison in 1804 and reaffirmed several times they had sold their land east of the Mississippi between the mouths of the Illinois and Wisconsin, retaining only the right to use it until it should be demanded by white settlers. Finally in the 1820s the first settlers came, and their number increased yearly. Relying on the old Indian treaty, they paid no respect to their red neighbors, but plowed up Indian villages and graveyards to plant their fields of corn.

The Indians were surprisingly mild and docile in their reaction to white encroachment, particularly since the squatters had no more legal right than the Indians to be there. Keokuk, the principal chief, counseled moving west of the Mississippi. The war chief Black Hawk, now sixty years old, wanted to resist, but he was persuaded to go west with Keokuk and the rest of the tribe. Then Black Hawk visited Malden and was advised by the British that he could not be forced to leave. When he returned home he ordered the white settlers to depart. They immediately petitioned Governor John Reynolds of Illinois for assistance, and in response the governor declared Illinois "invaded" and called for volunteers. Almost at once General E. P. Gaines of the United States Army moved to the scene of the trouble with 600 volunteers, including the youthful Abraham Lincoln, and 10 companies of regulars. As soon as Gaines arrived the Indians deserted their villages and fled across the Mississippi. The new treaty signed in the same year—1831—confirmed the old agreement of 1804.

Unfortunately for the Indians, they crossed the Mississippi too late to grow crops of corn before winter, and were soon near starvation. In this extremity some of them stole back across the river and pilfered corn they had planted in the spring. Immediately there was another loud outcry from the settlers, who had visions of being murdered and scalped in their beds. Conditions among the Indians continued to get worse, where-upon Black Hawk concocted a wild plan to cross the river in the spring, join the Winnebago and jointly raise a crop of corn. Probably he also hoped to secure British aid. Certainly he had a childish faith that he would not be harmed if he did not enter his old village.

To carry out these vague plans Black Hawk and 400 warriors with their families crossed the Mississippi in April 1832 and started up the river toward the Winnebago country. Colonel Henry Atkinson immediately sent orders for him to return, which he

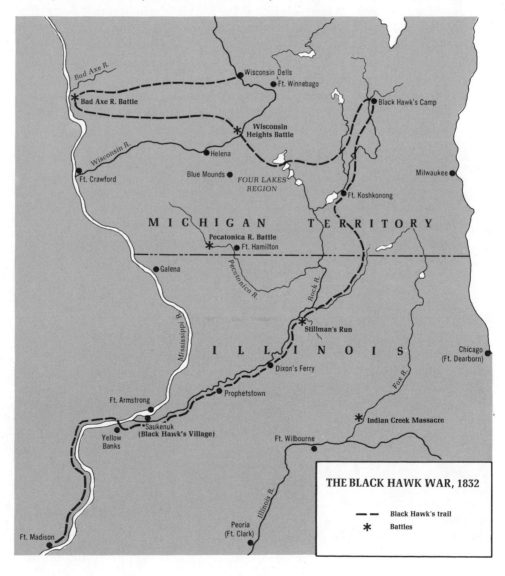

THE BLACK HAWK WAR, 1832

- - -   Black Hawk's trail
*   Battles

refused to do. The frontier was once more in an uproar. Volunteers were gathered in Illinois amid scenes of wild excitement, with the men enlisting for adventure and fun. General Winfield Scott started from the East with some 1000 regulars, including the West Point cadet corps; these troops never saw action because of a cholera epidemic that held them at Fort Dearborn (Chicago).

The gathering of these hundreds of white soldiers surprised and worried Black Hawk. Then, too, his reception by the Winnebago was far from cordial, and no encouragement came from the British. In consequence he dispatched a small party with a flag of truce to arrange for a surrender. When the white volunteers saw the Indians they disregarded the white flag and started firing; some of the Indians were killed, others were captured,

The Dogs of War. In this satirical cartoon the Secretary of War is presenting a stand of colors to the "First Regiment of Republican Bloodhounds," a criticism of the army's use of bloodhounds to track Indians in the Seminole campaign. (Granger)

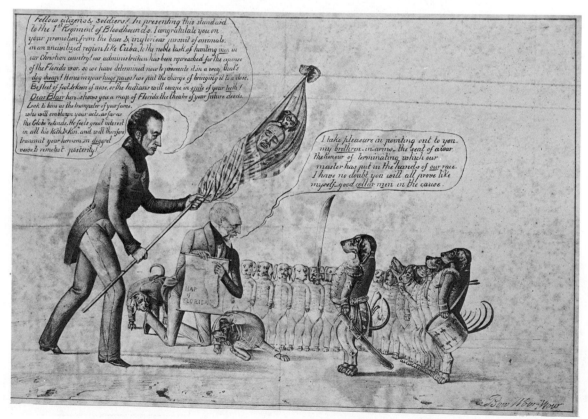

and the whites made a wild scramble to take part in the complete destruction of Black Hawk's band. Black Hawk was naturally amazed at this reception of his flag of truce and decided that he would at least die fighting; hence with 40 warriors he awaited the oncoming rush of the whites. When the whites came within range the Indians rushed from the woods, uttering death cries of defiance, and as soon as they charged the white troops ran. Again the Indians were astonished—so astonished that when they started to pursue the fleeing troops, the whites were out of range.

After the white troops had returned to safety they told awe-inspiring stories of battling with 1500 to 2000 bloodshirsty and ferocious savages led by that military genius, the crafty Black Hawk. As for Black Hawk, he was elated by his easy and un-expected victory. The whites were, after all, not invulnerable, and so the Sauk and Fox warriors attacked the frontier at various unprotected spots, keeping the outlying settle-ments in continual apprehension.

One victory did not make a successful war, and Black Hawk soon had to retreat before the superior white force. Up the Rock River he went, his flight hampered by the presence of women, children, the aged, and the sick; provisions became scarcer each day. Finally the Indians were reduced to eating horseflesh and whatever barks and roots they could find. As the situation became worse, Black Hawk's one thought was to re-turn to the main part of the tribe, and so he crossed to the Wisconsin River and de-scended it toward the Mississippi. Most of the women and children were put on rafts to float down the Wisconsin, while the warriors followed on foot to cover the retreat of their dependents.

The pursuing white army floundered and grumbled through the woods. Fighting Indians was exciting, but pursuing them through hundreds of miles of wilderness was not a holiday excursion. For a long time the troops moved rather blindly, depending largely on a general impression of the direction in which the Indians were going, but in the Four Lakes region of Wisconsin the whites finally discovered the trail, and there was a small engagement with the Indians who were acting as a rear guard for the cross-ing of the river. As luck would have it, some of the white troops blundered on a party of woman and children floating down the river on rafts. The troops had great sport shooting at these open targets until the entire party had been either shot, drowned, or captured.

Eventually Black Hawk and the remnants of his party reached the Mississippi. Here he again tried to surrender, this time to a steamboat which happened to be passing. And again the whites failed to respect a flag of truce and fired on the Indians. About this time the white troops also reached the Mississippi, and partly by accident discovered a band of 300 men, women, and children. The ensuing slaughter continued for three hours until all but 50 women and children had been killed. Black Hawk was captured, and the remainder of his force was taken back to Iowa; only 150 of the original 1000 Indians survived the expedition.

General Scott finally arrived and took command on August 7, 1832. Under his auspices a new treaty was signed, in which the Indians agreed to remain west of the Mississippi, but to cede a fifty-mile strip along the west bank of the river as expiation for their sins. Not surprisingly, other treaties and land cessions soon followed. Game was not available, the demoralized tribe spent altogether too much time drinking and gambling, and its numbers declined by over half. The Sauk and Foxes were put on a reservation in present Oklahoma in 1867, and their land was allotted to individuals in 1891.

Black Hawk himself was taken east and exhibited to throngs of thrill-hungry easterners. Elderly, hollow-cheeked, and pale, he proved a great disappointment to those who had expected a fierce savage of bright copper color. He was released in June 1833 and sent back to Iowa. His comment was terse: "Rock River was a beautiful country. I loved my towns, my cornfields, and the home of my people. I fought for it. Now it is yours. Keep it as we did."

SOUTHERN REMOVALS   The removal of the southern Indians was much more difficult than the similar process farther north. The five tribes, numbering possibly 60,000 and occupying some 18 million acres of land, resisted strenuously. Active efforts by the federal government did not come until the 1820s, even though such action had been promised Georgia with its cession of 1802, but white pressures mounted during the 1820s when the normal flow of settlers was swelled by the news of the discovery of gold. The subsequent removal of the Indians was one of the least savory incidents in a long story of unhappy racial contacts; the sorry details were repeated with monotonous and depressing regularity.

Treaties of removal were frequent, but often unsatisfactory, being negotiated with whomever the government agents could round up and bribe or coerce. Often there were real differences of opinion within a tribe which could be exploited by white negotiators who dealt with the more amenable part of the tribe and then insisted that the resulting agreement bound the entire tribe.

Many of the treaties included provisions for distributing at least part of the homeland to individuals of the tribe—a sort of allotment process half a century before the famous Dawes Act of 1887, in fact, some of the treaties were superficially only land allotment acts, with no mention of removal. However, the land was in reality only a sort of bonus for moving, and the government had no idea that any considerable number of Indians would remain in their homeland. In so far as the land was allotted there appeared the same sort of fraud and injustice later apparent under the Dawes Act; many who should have received land did not, and vice versa. The Indian who received land often used it to pay an existing debt, or sold or rented it for a very small sum; seldom did his profit exceed the cost of a single spree. The general result was added confusion.

The Choctaw of Mississippi had up to this time been consistently friendly to the United States in spite of various provocations, including several fraudulently obtained land cessions. They had a fairly high civilization during the 1820s, including the outlawing of whiskey, which might have served as a laudable example to the whites. Efforts by the whites during the 1820s to buy more land failed even when various chiefs were bribed. Mississippi thereupon became impatient and attached the Indian land to adjacent white counties (1829), thus making the Indians citizens of the state and subject to its laws.

Spurred by the action of Mississippi, the United States obtained a treaty of cession in 1830, but the circumstances were so unsavory that even President Jackson agreed that the document was fraudulent. The Senate rejected it, but more because of the cost than because of the fraud. At a new council in 1830 the Choctaw remained steadfast in their refusal to sell their eastern land, even in the face of threatened military action. After this council had officially disbanded, the white commissioners bribed the few remaining Indians to sign the desired treaty, which was then ratified by the Senate and proclaimed by the President.

In spite of Choctaw resentment, a considerable share of the tribe migrated in the years 1831–1833; others remained in Mississippi permanently. The whites did not wait for Indian departures, but seized land, cattle, homes, and other property at once. Most Indians departed with no more possessions than the clothes on their backs. They were

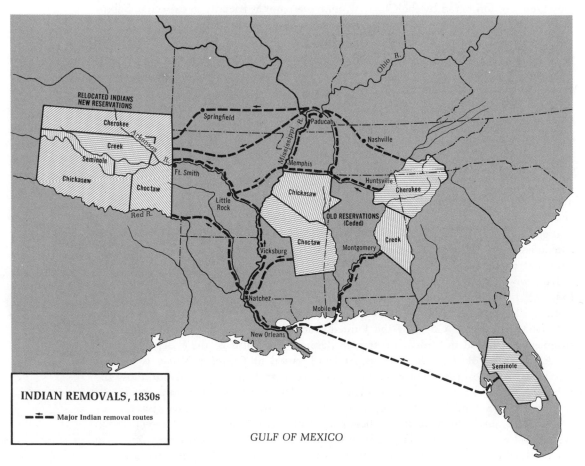

INDIAN REMOVALS, 1830s

━ ⚏ ━ Major Indian removal routes

GULF OF MEXICO

cheated unmercifully by merchants and ship captains, and encountered blizzards, near-starvation, and cholera and other diseases. In the West they found unimproved land, with no provision for their arrival, and were harassed by thieving settlers, dishonest traders, and wild Plains Indians. To the immense credit of the Choctaw was their construction of a fairly prosperous civilization including churches, schools, newspapers, and a constitutional tribal government. Understandable was their law that provided death for any chief who agreed to a further land cession.

Chickasaw removal followed much the same pattern; unsuccessful efforts to purchase land, the extension of Mississippi laws in 1830, and white appropriation of Indian land and improvements. Cession treaties of 1830 and 1832 were never put into force because of the difficulty of obtaining western lands, but the treaty of 1834 gave the basis for the migration that started in 1837. By this time the eastern Indians had become almost completely demoralized by white encroachments, whiskey salesmen, and the cholera. Arriving in the West they were greeted by a smallpox epidemic and a drought; moreover, they were outnumbered by the Choctaw, who were not as friendly as expected. Subsequent Chickasaw history is not a subject for the sensitive investigator.

The Cherokee had also been advancing rapidly in civilization during the 1820s. They had become a settled agricultural people, adopting white ways of life and even a constitution (1827) based on that of the United States. Cherokee policemen maintained at least as good order as that in the neighboring white communities, and taxes were collected at least as poorly. Most remarkable was the work of the Indian genius Sequoyah, son of a white trader and an Indian mother, who developed an alphabet of eighty-six symbols that made possible a written language. The *Cherokee Phoenix*, printed in both English and Cherokee, began publication in 1828.

An agricultural civilization meant Cherokee stability. Removal treaties could be obtained only by fraud, and then the Indians refused to move. Georgia became increasingly impatient, particularly because of the gold discoveries of 1828, and in that year annexed the Indian lands, after which it provided for their distribution by lottery among white Georgians. As usual, miners and settlers did not wait for the law, which was scheduled to go into operation on June 1, 1830, but began immediately to seize Indian land and property. President Jackson approved the Georgia action, feeling that the Indians would soon see the desirability of moving, and withdrew federal troops. The Indians on their part provided heavy penalties for anyone signing a treaty of cession, and appealed unsuccessfully to the federal government.

Even the Supreme Court of the United States became involved in the Cherokee troubles, and found difficulties of its own defining the status of the Indian. It finally labeled the Cherokee a "domestic dependent" nation in *Cherokee Nation* v. *Georgia* (1831), which meant whatever the Court wanted it to mean, and did not allow the tribe to appear as a litigant. In each case appealed to the Court the state of Georgia refused to appear, and in each, Georgia carried out the provisions of its own laws regardless of the Court's decision. In the best known of them, *Worcester* v. *Georgia* (1832), which concerned two missionaries imprisoned by Georgia, the Supreme Court held the pertinent Georgia law unconstitutional. Georgia refused to recognize the decision, but cautiously freed the missionaries by executive clemency. The federal executive supported the actions of Georgia rather than the decision of the Court. President Jackson is reported to have remarked: "John Marshall has made his decision—now let him enforce it!" Even if the words are apocryphal, they reflect accurately his sentiments.

The Cherokee refused defiantly to leave their homes. Treaties of 1834 and 1835, signed by a few Indians who had been bribed, were rejected by the tribe. A new treaty of 1835 was signed by some twenty men, none of whom was a chief, and then repudiated by the overwhelming majority of the tribe. The federal government, apparently despairing of anything better, ratified the document and declared it in force.

The mere assumption that a fraudulent treaty was binding did not move the Indians west, and General Winfield Scott was sent in 1838 with 7000 regulars to do the job. Detachments were ordered to round up the Indians; all too frequently, as white soldiers surprised and surrounded an Indian family, white adventurers stood ready to grab the property about to be abandoned. Because this summer was unbearably hot many of the removals were postponed—but winter removals proved even more unfortunate; more than a quarter of the 16,000 migrants died en route, and the remainder ended their trip in poverty and squalor, and suffering from disease.

Creek removals paralleled those of the Cherokee. The Creeks had been the most advanced of the southern tribes at the advent of the whites, with a settled agriculture and a reasonably stable government. Land cessions had been forced by Jackson at the end of his southern campaign, but no later ones were signed except through bribery, and the signers were frequently put to death. Conscientious President Adams disapproved of the fraud during his presidency, and was denounced vitriolically by Georgian authorities. Georgia then appropriated Creek territory. Whites overran the Indian country, seizing land and property, and debauching the natives.

All the eastern Creeks finally accepted a removal treaty in 1832, and started to move west the next year. Traders and contractors took advantage of them, and the militia fired on them—presumably by mistake. Some 1500 of the Indians were so angered that they went on the warpath, harrying outlying settlements. Immediately 11,000 troops were sent under General T. S. Jesup to put down the insurrection. Although most of the Creeks were corralled and sent west, a number evaded the soldiers; during the 1850s an additional 4000 were removed, part of them in chains. As a result of its troubles the Creek population was cut almost in half within a generation.

SEMINOLE WAR   A few of the Creeks who disliked moving west escaped to Florida, where they joined their racial brothers, the Seminole. These Seminole had always been exasperating, not only because they occupied desired land, but also because they raided outlying settlements, killing and plundering, and offered an asylum for escaped Negro slaves. After the American acquisition of Florida the Seminole agreed (1823) to confinement in a 4-million acre reservation in return for various gifts; migration to the West was not mentioned, but seemed to most people to be the next step. Conditions of the Indians did not improve. The land was reasonably good, but the

Indians were poor farmers, and were faced by a drought. As Indians continued to raid the surrounding countryside, white Floridians increasingly desired Indian elimination.

A Seminole removal treaty was signed in 1832, although probably a majority of the tribe opposed it. In accordance with its terms prospective migrants gathered at Tampa in the winter of 1832–1833, where they heard of an Indian raid and consequently dispersed because of the fear of white retribution. Then followed ten years of sporadic warfare between the United States Army and a handful of half-starved, poverty-stricken Indians. In defense of the army's performance it should be added that the Indians could find their way through almost impenetrable swamps, emerging only for short raids, and that pursuit was extremely difficult. The best-known Indian leader was Osceola, who ultimately died in captivity. A succession of white generals were not above treachery, but results were unimpressive.

THE SEMINOLE WAR, 1835-1842

■ Military outpost
△ Indian settlement
● Town
★ Battle

The last real battle of the so-called Second Seminole War occurred in 1842, at which time General Zachary Taylor estimated that some 3000 Indians had been removed at a cost of $20 million and the lives of 1500 soldiers, not to mention the losses of white Floridians. Further fighting of the 1850s reduced the Florida Indian population to about 100, and these Indians were generally invisible in the Everglades except as they emerged to trade, as at Ft. Myers. A century later the Indian population had increased to possibly 1000.

WESTERN CONDITIONS   The transplanted Indians ended their mournful hegira in present Oklahoma, where they were anything but happy. The Plains Indians, including the Osage, Kiowa, and Comanche, resisted their new neighbors, and the migrants fought back to the best of their ability. The federal government forced cession treaties on the western Indians to provide room for the eastern arrivals, established new forts to preserve the peace, and sent expeditions to overawe the Plains tribes. Several Indian councils, notably those of 1842 and 1843 sought to create amity between the old and new inhabitants of the present Oklahoma. Although they contributed to the settlement of grievances and the creation of friendships, they by no means eliminated all frictions.

Not least of the difficulties confronting the migrant Indian was that of leaving an agricultural way of life to enter a plains country without houses or barns or stock, and where the plow had not as yet broken the tough prairie sod. For the time being the Indians were entirely dependent on the bounty of the government as it trickled through the sticky fingers of private contractors. The Indian seldom received what the government had authorized, and the government was far from generous. Then, too, illegal traders entered the Indian country where they found the natives all too willing to trade anything they possessed for a few hours of forgetfulness. Furthermore, and quite unexpectedly, white settlers found the country attractive and became a perpetual source of friction.

Rumors of fraud and mismanagement in the West reached the War Department, which sent Major Ethan Allen Hitchcock to investigate (1840). The major filled nine fat notebooks with circumstantial stories of bribes, falsified accounts, short weights, spoiled meat, and similar deplorable situations. His report was duly filed, but the department took no action—some said because too many prominent men would have been involved. When Congress insisted on receiving this information, the War Department discovered very conveniently that the report had been mislaid.

THE PERMANENT FRONTIER   With the removal of both northern and southern tribes, except for a few fairly harmless groups, the Indian problem east of the Mississippi had been solved. The resulting Indian frontier was not a vague general region but a definite line that could be drawn on the maps of the 1830s. Starting from a point on northern Lake Michigan, it struck across Wisconsin to the Mississippi, with a little dip for the Menominee. It followed the Mississippi to the northern boundary of Missouri in 1830, but moved west in Iowa a little later because of the Sauk and Fox cessions. Then it followed the northern boundary of Missouri and the western boundaries of Missouri and Arkansas to the Red River. West of this line lived some 350,000 Indians in 1840, of whom possibly 100,000 had ancestors who had once lived east of the Mississippi.

The permanence that this frontier was expected to have was demonstrated by the provisions made for marking and guarding it. A road from the mouth of the St. Peters to the Red River was ordered surveyed by Congress in 1836; the surveys were not made, but some of the road was actually constructed and a long line of forts built. A commission suggested the creation of a no-man's-land between Indians and whites, to be controlled by rangers. General Gaines, who commanded in the West, proposed in 1838 the building of permanent stone forts that would at least outlive the century, but before his recommendations could receive favorable attention the frontier line had again advanced. This time the shortage of undesired land to which the Indians might be pushed necessitated a new and different "solution."

The administration of Indian affairs was strengthened during the early 1830s. General supervision was given to the office of Commissioner of Indian Affairs, with the commissioner responsible to the secretary of war. The entire country was divided into three superintendencies, and under each superintendent were numerous agents and subagents who dealt directly with the Indians, settling disputes, allotting rations, and presumably avoiding the necessity of using the army. The agency was not a new institution, but the functions of the agent were stated more specifically. Among these functions was the licensing of traders who could enter the Indian country. A new Indian Intercourse Act of 1834 made more stringent the licensing provisions for traders and the regulations excluding whiskey. Presumably all unauthorized persons were expected to stay east of the permanent frontier.

Some hope existed that in time the Indians could be persuaded to adopt white civilization, although a number of critics insisted that settled agriculture could not develop until the Indians were given individual rather than tribal ownership of their lands. The annuities provided by the federal government had long included agricultural and other implements, sometimes at the request of the tribes themselves. Furthermore, the government for many years aided missionaries in the establishment of churches and schools; thirty-eight schools were thus assisted in 1825 at the cost of $200,000, and the aid became more regular and extensive as the years passed. Many of the mission establishments had been moved west with the Indians and were concentrated particularly in the Southwest. The Congregationalist and the Presbyterians, acting mainly through the American Board of Commissioners for Foreign Missions, were most active, but other denominations also participated.

WESTERN ARMY   The main work of controlling the Indians remained basically with the army. Starting in 1837 the entire region west of the Mississippi was constituted the western department so that its administration was unified. The American army of the period grew from some 6000 in 1830 to 11,000 in 1841. Even though most of the men were stationed on the frontier, they did not constitute an impressive force for 1500 miles of border. Many of them were rowdy down-and-outers or immigrants trying to learn English. Their arms were rather nondescript and sometimes they had no uniforms. Supplies, such as overshoes and mittens, were often lacking. Altogether the army was seldom very intimidating.

Besides the regular army of the western department, a special western force was created in the 1830s. A corps of rangers was raised under authority of a law of 1832, but lacked both uniforms and discipline; it was replaced the next year by a regiment

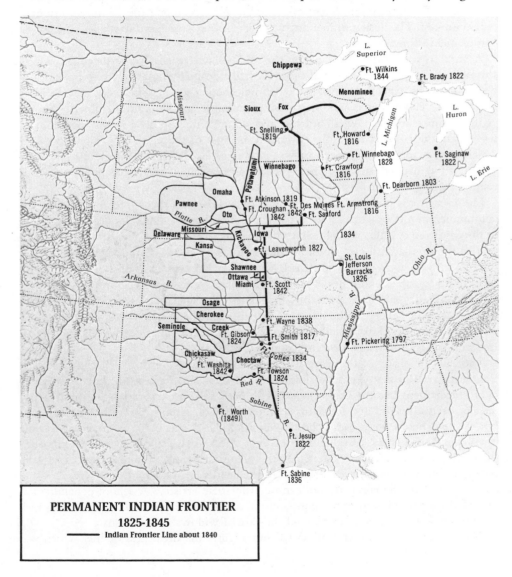

PERMANENT INDIAN FRONTIER
1825-1845
——— Indian Frontier Line about 1840

of 600 mounted dragoons. These men were never impressive in appearance, but they did good work in the wilderness; they comprised about a quarter of the western army. The colonel of the regiment was Henry Dodge, the lieutenant colonel Stephen Watts Kearny, and one of the second lieutenants was Jefferson Davis.

The western army spent a large share of its time in the various forts. Most important in 1830 were Forts Howard (Green Bay), Winnebago (Portage), Snelling (St. Paul), Crawford (Prairie du Chien), Armstrong (Rock Island), Leavenworth (Leavenworth), Gibson (on the Arkansas River in present northeastern Oklahoma), Jesup (Natchitoches), and Jefferson Barracks (St. Louis). During the decade a number of changes were made, including the establishment of several new posts among the Civilized Tribes of the Southwest. The busiest of the forts was Fort Gibson, which ordinarily had the largest complement of men.

A western fort, ordinarily built by the soldiers, was usually constructed of pickets, although sometimes of stone, and typically had two-story towers at diagonal corners. Inside the walls were the barracks for the men, homes for the officers, kitchen, dining hall, offices, school, storehouse, magazine, guardhouse, and hospital. Ordinarily a small civilian community sprawled nearby, and a fur-trading post was not uncommon; western towns liked nearby forts, primarily because of the soldiers' pay and the construction of roads. The frontier fort was impregnable to attack from the outside, even when badly manned and equipped. The wide spacing of the forts, however, made reinforcements difficult.

Life in a fort was above all monotonous, particularly in the winter, when the little community might be completely isolated for months at a time. Routine filled most of the day from reveille at daybreak to the reading of orders and taps at night. In addition to the regular drilling, cleaning, and guard duty the soldiers spent most of their time in farming and construction work, for soldier labor erected most of the buildings and grew vegetables and other crops as well as hay for the horses. During the summer the soldiers' diet might be palatable, thanks to vegetables from the post garden, but during the rest of the year the staples were bread and soup, neither very good. Special delicacies in food and drink and wearing apparel might be purchased from the authorized post sutler, but prices were high and pay was low.

The chief diversion of the army was gambling, whether on cards, checkers, or even the weather. Whiskey was a possible means of relieving the tedium, but in 1832 the War Department became abstemious and stopped the whiskey rations; a soldier's pay did not permit him to get drunk many times a month. A post library had possibilities, but the few books were badly chosen. For the officers and their wives there was the usual round of dinners, teas, dances, and calls, but the West Point graduates curtailed their enjoyment by a rigid insistence on the dignities of rank. Amateur theatricals were common, but women were excluded from the boards; men donned their wives' clothes and squeaked the female parts with more ardor than artistry. A school generally was provided for the children of the post, and the sutler devoted part of his income to such worthy projects as school, library, and the care of widows and orphans.

The few army amusements alleviated but slightly the dreariness of life, which was made even less bearable by the frequency of sickness; doctors were ordinarily either poor or nonexistent, and only the youth and resiliency of the men averted a high mortality rate. The inevitable results of boredom were many infractions of the rules, and desertions. From an army of 6000 in 1830 there were some 1250 desertions. The situation was not improved by the severe punishments visited on men for such minor offenses as a missing button or imbibing too much whiskey. An iron yoke, stocks, confinement on bread and water, hard labor, stoppage of pay, or extra guard duty while possibly carrying a log or a bag of shot, was common. Whipping was still in vogue, being done by the drummers taking turns. The man was stripped to the waist, tied to the flagpole, and whipped with a knotted instrument made of nine leather thongs.

The monotony of life at a western fort made any alternative seem attractive, and even Indian outbreaks were viewed with some enthusiasm. Periodically a detachment was sent into the wilderness to remind the aborigines that the United States had the power to enforce its desires. Such an expedition tried to remove causes of friction and to obtain promises of good behavior. Its commander had to be a man of both energy and discretion, who could double as explorer, strategist, and diplomat. The limited number of his troops and the wildness of the country necessitated extreme care, for even with great diligence he might lose much of his command through Indian attacks, accident, starvation, and disease. His negotiations with the Indians required both moderation and finesse, for his small force hardly permitted aggressive domineering.

Other special army details were also necessary. Sometimes a detachment was used to enforce the decision of an Indian agent, as, for example, to bring to the agency a native accused of theft or murder; such a mission had dangerous possibilities, since lack of tact might drive an entire tribe into open hostilities. From time to time men were sent on exploring expeditions. Sometimes detachments were used to guard the overland traffic, including the Santa Fe trade. This work was comparatively dull, with long hours of slow travel in the dust kicked up by the traders' mules. Even such a trip, however, had advantages over the dull routine of a fort.

The idea of a permanent frontier was delightful in theory, but disappointing in fact. The Indian problem was not solved but merely moved across the Mississippi, where all the old difficulties soon reappeared. The Indians never succeeded in living in permanent peace either with the whites or with each other. Indian agents found themselves without adequate power, and even the support of the army was sometimes insufficient.

The worst trouble with the so-called permanent frontier was that it failed to divide. Traders and trappers, both licensed and illegal, flowed across the border, and the Indian agents were powerless to stop them. Explorers and traders traversed the plains country in increasing numbers. The Oregon Trail received greater use, and soon miners were streaming across the plains. Even worse, the "desert" proved much less forbidding than had been expected. Before the outbreak of the Civil War settlers had begun to seep into the Indian country all the way from Minnesota to Texas. The frontier that had looked so permanent and useful in the 1830s had definitely outlived its usefulness by the 1850s, and treaty obligations proved no effective barrier to the advance of the American nation.

READINGS   *Paperbacks are marked with an asterisk.*

General   James C. Malin, *Indian Policy and Westward Expansion* (1921) is a good monograph, but see also William C. MacLeod, *The American Indian Frontier* (1928) and *Everett N. Dick, *Vanguards of the Frontier* (1941); the latter is particularly readable.

Army Life   Good are *Francis P. Prucha, *Broadax and Bayonet* (1953), on Mississipi Valley;* *American Indian Policy* (1962), more general; and *A Guide to the Military Posts of the United States, 1789–1793* (1964). But see also Edgar B. Wesley, *Guarding the Frontier* (1935), good monograph; and Henry P. Beers, *The Western Military Frontier, 1815–1846* (1935), monographic on campaigns. Individual forts are described by Evan Jones, *Citadel in the Wilderness* (1966), Fort Snelling; Bruce Mahan, *Old Fort Crawford* (1926), interesting. Contemporary accounts include Percival G. Lowe, *Five Years a Dragoon* (1965); Eugene Bandel, *Frontier Life in the Army, 1854–1861* (1932); Theodore C. Blegen and Philip D. Jordan (eds.), *With Various Voices* (1949), Fort Snelling.

Black Hawk War   The best complete account is William T. Hagan, *The Sac and Fox Indians* (1858); but see also Theodore C. Pease, *The Frontier State 1818–1848* (1918), concerning Illinois; Roger L. Nichols, *General Henry Atkinson* (1965); *Donald Jackson (ed.), *Black Hawk: An Autobiography* (1955), which was dictated.

Southern Removals   The general story is well covered by Robert S. Cotterill, *The Southern Indians* (1954). John K. Mahon, *History of the Second Seminole War, 1835–1842* (1967) is scholarly. Most work has been done by Grant Foreman in his books *Advancing the Frontier, 1830–1860* (1933), *The Five Civilized Tribes* (1934), *Indian Removals* (1932), and *The Last Trek of the Indians* (1946), which are informative but not exciting. Certain state histories are pertinent, as E. Merton Coulter, *A Short History of Georgia* (1933)—1960 edition titled *Georgia, A Short History*, and Sidney W. Martin, *Florida During the Territorial Days* (1944). For the receiving end the accounts tend to be dull, as Edward E. Dale and Morris L. Wardell, *History of Oklahoma* (1948).

Individual Southern Tribes   Marion L. Starkey, *The Cherokee Nation* (1946), excellent; Grace S. Woodward, *The Cherokee* (1963); Morris L. Wardell, *A Political History of the Cherokee Nation* (1938); Henry T. Malone, *Cherokees of the Old South* (1956), stops with the removals; Althea L. Bass, *Cherokee Messenger* (1936); Angie Debo, *The Rise and Fall of the Choctaw Republic* (1934) and *The Road To Disappearance* (1941), both good, with the latter concerned with the Creeks; Edwin C. McReynold, *The Seminoles* (1957).

Fulton's Steamboat *Clermont.* This early side-wheeler was the forerunner of later vessels that would make such rivers as the Ohio and the Mississippi "two-way streets"; in other words, upstream traffic was now possible for the commercial world. (New York Public Library)

Chapter 15 / STAGECOACH AND STEAMBOAT

The West of the early nineteenth century had no more perplexing problem than transportation. Most attractive were the rivers, but they had obvious limitations. They flowed only in one direction, often lacked water in the fall and froze in the winter, and were remote from much desirable land.

203

Consequently road travel was important from the time when the earliest trapper plodded over a blazed trail.

Any American road before 1790 was unpaved, and typically exhibited two deep ruts in dry weather and a sea of mud in wet. Streams usually had to be forded, although there was an occasional undependable ferry. After 1790 a few roads were improved along the lines suggested by the Englishmen McAdam and Telford. Such roads were not hard-surfaced but had ditches for drainage, bridges over the streams, and a roadbed of various sized rocks.

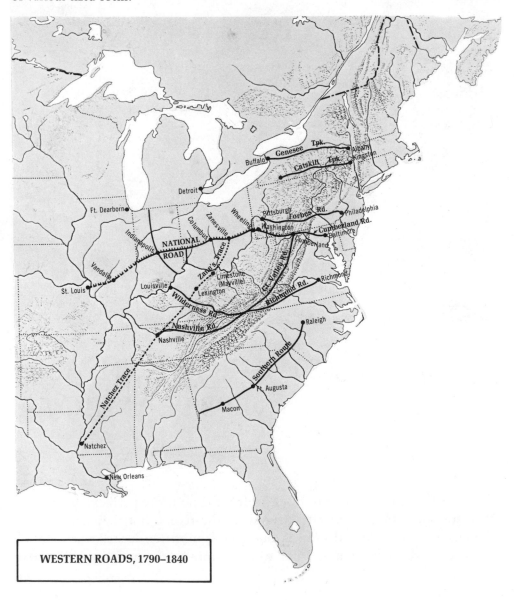

WESTERN ROADS, 1790–1840

WESTERN ROADS   Early western roads achieved the distinction of being even worse than eastern roads. Starting usually as Indian trails, they followed the uplands as much as possible. The whites blazed the trails (notched trees along the side) because they were poorer woodsmen than the Indians, and the paths became wider with more use. Here and there a few logs were placed to enable passage over the worst mudholes, and now and then a crude and erratic ferry seemed to the harassed traveler a gift from Providence. The average road was a partially cleared path on which the traveler wove back and forth among the stumps and felled trees, trying to avoid deep mudholes, which, it was rumored, could swallow both horse and rider at a single gulp.

Building good roads was almost impossible because of the great distances and lack of funds. The federal government felt responsible only for military roads in the territories. States legislated some main highways, but grandiose plans failed because of inadequate funds. Private businessmen now and then opened a toll road, which possibly was subsidized by the federal government. Counties and townships did most of the actual road building; taxpayers often worked out their taxes on the roads, but apparently with much less enthusiasm than when they worked for themselves.

In spite of the difficulties, a few main roads were at least partially improved before the War of 1812. Among the best known was Zane's Trace from Wheeling, Virginia, to Limestone (later Maysville), Kentucky. Its construction, aided by a congressional grant of 1796, consisted of felling the larger trees, but not removing their stumps, and clearing away the brush. Zane's Trace connected with a road to Lexington and Nashville. From Nashville to Natchez was the famous Natchez Trace, used largely by flatboatmen returning from New Orleans. Among other main highways was one directly over the mountains to Nashville, and another through Georgia to New Orleans, as described earlier.

Western roads seldom could accommodate anything as luxurious as a stagecoach. Passengers ordinarily rode in a farm wagon with the seats placed crosswise, and sometimes covered by a canvas top and curtains. Freight was carried in a Pennsylvania or Conestoga wagon. The Conestoga was distinctive in its curving upward and outward at each end, reputedly to avoid losing freight on the hills. A 16-foot box was covered by a 24-foot canvas top, the whole rig being hauled usually by six horses. The blue underbody, the red upper, and the white top exhibited a vivid and patriotic display on the road. The poorer road would hold nothing more than a wooden cart with two wide wooden wheels; the usual traveler was the man on horseback, his entire baggage contained in a pair of saddlebags.

ROADS BETWEEN EAST AND WEST   Bad western roads distressed all westerners except those in New Orleans, who profited. Farmers, merchants, and bankers looked longingly at eastern markets and at the more direct route to Europe. They also yearned for manufactured goods that would be available with cheaper transportation. Even more distressed were easterners, and particularly manufacturers, importers, and merchants, who were saddened as they saw western business floating down the river. The project of highest priority for both East and West was an improved road connecting the two sections, and as could be expected the yearning crystallized as a continuing demand for Congress to act.

Congress was perfectly willing to aid an East-West road provided the economy-minded administration did not have to advance cash. It provided in the Ohio Enabling Act of 1802 (as modified in 1803) that 5 percent of the proceeds of Ohio land sales should be dedicated to roads, three-fifths to be spent for roads within the state, and two-fifths for roads from elsewhere to the borders of the state. Similar provisions were made for other states as they were later admitted to the Union. The 3 percent fund soon permitted Ohio to build several roads, particularly to connect Lake Erie and the Ohio River; other states with smaller land sales were less lucky. The 2 percent fund was allowed to accumulate in the federal treasury for a future East-West road.

THE NATIONAL ROAD   The route of the new East-West road, as stated in the law of 1806, was picked after intense competition among dozens of communities with high aspirations. Baltimore was chosen the eastern terminus, although actual construction was begun at Cumberland. For the western terminus Wheeling won over many competitors, particularly Pittsburgh and Steubenville. Albert Gallatin of Uniontown, Pennsylvania, had sufficient influence to divert the road through his hometown. Immediately Maryland, Pennsylvania, and Virginia authorized construction. The first contracts were let in 1811, but actual work did not come until the end of the War of 1812. By 1818 the mails were being carried over the road from Washington, D.C., to Wheeling. The total coast was $1,700,000, or an average of $13,000 a mile, which was probably excessive.

The right of way of the National Road (often called the Cumberland Road) was 30 feet wide in the mountains and 66 feet elsewhere. Bridges were of solid masonry. The roadbed was raised in the center, with a ditch on each side to drain the water, and was composed of stones broken by hand hammers. The lowest stratum of the road was of stone broken to pass through a 7-inch ring, while the top stratum had stones that passed through a 3-inch ring. A layer of stones was put in place and after traffic had packed it down, another layer was added. The process was repeated until the desired depth had been reached.

The National Road was a great improvement, but it had serious deficiencies. Heavy traffic produced bad ruts that melted snows and heavy rains turned into deep gullies; at times portions of the mountain construction washed out completely. The eastern part of the road wore out before the western section was completed, and soon the whole road needed repair. Congress met the situation by a law authorizing the collection of tolls to provide for repair, but to the dismay of friends of the road President Monroe vetoed the bill on the rather complicated constitutional reasoning that Congress had the power to build and repair roads but not to collect tolls. Congress then refused to make appropriations from general funds, and a decade was spent in constitutional wrangling while the road deteriorated. Ultimately Congress provided for the repairs and then (1831–1834) turned the road over to the states through which it ran; these states thereupon erected tollhouses and used their collections for repairs.

TRAVEL ON THE NATIONAL ROAD   The National Road was immediately crowded with immigrants, salesmen, farmers, freighters, stages, and cattle being driven to market; both Wheeling and Baltimore grew in size and importance. The growing traffic necessitated considerable amounts of equipment, and in consequence there appeared large freighting and coaching companies. Most important of the stage lines was the National Road Stage Company; its chief competitor was the Good Intent Line.

Public Landing, Cincinnati, 1835. This riverfront scene was repeated innumerable times from Cincinnati to Fort Benton, Montana. During the nineteenth century it changed little. (Cincinnati Historical Society)

A stagecoach had to be well built to stand the rough usage it received. Ordinarily it was drawn by four horses, which were changed about every twelve miles. The stage itself had three seats, of which the front one faced the rear and the middle one had a strap for its back. Each seat held three passengers; another place, beside the driver, was much coveted in fair weather. The driver sat on top in front, and the baggage was placed in a "boot" in the rear. Leather straps were the only springs, and leather curtains were but partially successful barriers against rain and cold. A coach ride over the Alleghenies, with the coach rattling and jolting over the ruts and around sharp curves, with magnificent vistas in the distance and frightful chasms in the immediate foreground, was an experience not easily forgotten.

The aristocrat of the road was the stage driver. Every small boy knew the names of the drivers, and achieved an imperishable halo of glory if one of them condescended to speak to him. The importance of the driver did not depend on his pay, but on his courage and skill. Travelers often complained that he was "addicted to drunkenness," but even so he drove rapidly and well, averaging ten miles an hour, which was excellent for the sharp grades and abrupt turns of a mountain road. Driving was a dangerous occupation even under the most favorable conditions, but on a dark night, or in a heavy rain, or on icy roads it was so hazardous that only the most competent or the most foolhardy man would undertake it.

Stage fares were collected by the hotel landlords, who acted as agents for the various companies. The landlord gave the driver a bill of lading which told the next landlord the names of the passengers and the distances for which they had paid. The fare varied somewhat, with the average a little over six cents a mile.

The daily distance covered by a stage tended to increase, but varied with the time of the year and the condition of the highway. During the 1830s the trip from Washington to Wheeling could be made in a continuous thirty hours. The usual time with overnight stops was two and a half days. By then the construction of the road had been continued farther west, reaching Columbus, Ohio, in 1833 and being graded, but not surfaced, into Illinois. By 1837 the trip from Washington to Columbus could be made in forty-five and a half hours, to Indianapolis in sixty-five and a half hours, and to St. Louis in ninety-four hours. The usual times to these places were, respectively 3 days, 16 hours; 6 days, 20 hours; 10 days, 4 hours.

Freight, like passengers, was handled mostly by large companies, although farmers, with their teams and wagons, offered competition during the slack farming season. The usual wagon was of the Conestoga type. Wheels were continually made wider, for it was found that the broader wheel was more satisfactory on a gravel road. Brakes were poor, and on steep grades saplings were sometimes fastened around the rear wheels or heavy logs were tied to the back of the wagon to slow its descent. The average load was about 6000 pounds, although there is a record of as much as 10,375 net pounds carried by one wagon in 1835. Wages of the wagoneer were paid by the trip. The freight rate between Cumberland and Wheeling varied from $1.25 to $2.25 per hundred pounds, and the average daily trip was about 15 miles. Unlike the stages, the wagons always stopped at nightfall; the same horses were used throughout a trip.

Taverns lined the whole route of the National Road at frequent intervals, even in the mountains. Drivers of wagons were not given rooms in these hotels, but had to sleep either on the barroom floor or outside. Here and there were so-called wagon houses— rude shacks for the use of the teamsters; the teamster furnished his own bedding and food, and did his own cooking.

The National Road, in spite of its drawbacks, was a tremendous boon to the West. Year-round traffic was possible over an improved roadbed that permitted faster travel. Also the highway had numerous connecting roads, which further improved transportation for anyone who was anywhere close to it.

OTHER WESTERN ROADS   Most western roads tended to improve but slowly with the years. A so-called road was often no more than a single track through the woods, and at best an unimproved double track that was almost impassable in the early spring. A traveler on the road between Nashville and Memphis in 1831 reported: "Frightful roads. Precipitous descent. No regular highway. The road is only an opening cut in the forest. The stumps of the trees are not completely cut away, so that they form so many impediments over which we jolt."

Bad roads meant high freight rates. The Illinois farmer of 1820 would have lost money in hauling his corn even 20 miles at the cost of 50¢ a hundred pounds. One region might have a near famine while a neighboring area had an unmarketable surplus. One consequence was that prices varied tremendously from place to place. Wheat sold for 25¢ a bushel in Illinois in 1825 and for $2.00 on the eastern seaboard.

Coach travel was undertaken only by the hardy or under the pressure of dire necessity. The usual main road had one or more coach lines, but often there was no regular schedule and the passenger might wait days or even weeks for a connection. Travel might continue both day and night, but the traveler ordinarily stopped overnight. The usual day's trip was between 20 and 50 miles, although it might be as long as 100 miles. An ordinary day's trip might begin as early as three or four in the morning and last until ten or later in the evening, with stops only for meals. Three or four days exhausted even the strongest traveler, who would be glad to stop for a week or more to regain his strength.

A stage followed the meanderings of badly located roads, and dodged back and forth to avoid being "up against a stump." In dry weather the coach lurched, swayed, and bumped over the rutty roads, enveloped in dust from the horses' hoofs: at the end of a day many a traveler nursed a headache caused by bumping his head against the roof. During rainstorms the coach plowed through the water, with now and then a detour through a neighboring field to avoid a particularly menacing mudhole. If the coach stuck in the mud, the male passengers used rails or saplings to pry or push the vehicle to a drier spot.

Accidents were commonplace. When the coach swayed with the bad road, the passengers swayed in the opposite direction to keep the coach from tipping over on its side, but sometimes the coach lost its balance, anyway. The passengers then crawled out as best they could, bound their wounds, righted the coach, and proceeded on their way. A broken axle or wheel was more serious, even though the driver carried materials and implements for repairs. If the men could not make the necessary repairs, the driver would set out on foot for the nearest settlement while the passengers invited themselves to stay for the night at the most convenient log cabin.

The smaller streams were forded. Timid passengers might alight and walk, with appealing scenes of gallantry as the men carried the younger, more attractive, and lighter members of the opposite sex through the water. Floods might mean days of waiting until the water subsided; a premature effort at fording might result in the coach being washed down the stream. Ferries were operated on the larger rivers, but probably the ferryman had to be called from his farmwork; the coach was carried on the first trip and the passengers on the second.

The Port of St. Louis, 1832. St. Louis became the great commercial crossroads of the West. It harbored vessels from such remote points as Pittsburgh, Fort Benton, New Orleans, and the upper Mississippi region. (City Art Museum of St. Louis)

TAVERNS   The usual stopping place for a stage was a tavern. The driver raced the horses the last few rods, tooted the horn, set the brakes with a grinding roar, and leaned back on his reins pulling the horses to a sliding stop in a cloud of dust. The tavern might be anything from a commodious frame house to a small log cabin, where the travelers slept in the same room with the landlord's family. The keeper of the inn met his guests at the door, showed them to their rooms, and presided at meals, where he led the conversation. The largest and most attractive room was the bar, which had the only chairs, and in which the men gathered. Normal decorations would be a wooden clock, a map of the United States, a map of the state, a framed copy of the Declaration of Independence, a looking glass with brush and comb attached, and a few engravings or woodprints.

The rooms of the western inn were usually large and bare. Frequently the washing facilities were a pump and a tin basin outside the back door. Real luxury was a shallow tin pan, pitcher, and bucket in the room, the traveler using whatever water was in the pitcher, since there was no personal service. Bedding was usually scanty and filthy. A room often had several beds that were filled without regard to sex or previous acquaintance, except that a man and woman were not given the same bed unless they were married; the traveler was paying only for a place to sleep. In the smaller inn the first floor might be given to the ladies, while the loft was occupied by the men. The ordinary price for accommodations was a dollar a day for board and lodging.

Tobacco and liquor were everywhere. There was a cud of tobacco in nearly every male cheek, and the chroniclers have reported that the floors, coaches, boats, and great open spaces were all convenient receptacles for surplus juice. Drinking was equally universal among the men. The better hotels had long wine lists, but the smaller establishments concentrated on the cheap and potent whiskey, which was even used at meals in place of water.

Meals were served at regular hours and were eaten by everyone together, with breakfast usually at seven thirty, dinner at two, and supper at seven. Everything was put on the table in large dishes, and the guests helped themselves; a servant girl passed tea and coffee. Immense quantities of food were consumed rapidly and silently. Tablecloths were common, napkins rare. Spoons were frequently of silver, but knives and the two-pronged forks were likely to be steel, with horn handles. Eating with a knife was a fine art.

Western food varied with the type of tavern, the region, and the time of year. In the North the traveler might expect such viands as venison steak, bread, butter, honey, tea, coffee, beefsteak, eggs, applesauce, corn bread, chicken, and potatoes. In the South the common bill of fare included such items as beef, turkey, venison, chicken, sweet potatoes, corn cake, ham, and bacon. Pork was ubiquitous both North and South. Whenever feasible the food was fried in grease, and meat often was practically swimming in it. Coffee was poor, and any sugar was usually brown. The one typically American dish was corn on the cob. Usually lacking were green vegetables, which were scarce in the summer and even rarer in the winter. New Orleans was one of the few places where the traveler might hope to be served such vegetables as radishes, peas, asparagus, lettuce, and spinach.

EARLY WATER TRAFFIC Roads were desirable for the West, but only when water was not available. The Mississippi and its tributaries were the most significant western transportation until well after the middle of the nineteenth century. Before 1790 almost all water travel was by canoe, ordinarily a dugout and seldom a bark canoe. The dugout, hollowed from the trunk of a tree, was usually about 20 feet long, and could be constructed by four men in four days. A few were as large as 30 feet, with a beam of 3½ feet, and carried a square sail. Most of them were divided into four compartments formed by allowing portions of the tree to remain as partitions. The front and rear divisions were use for paddling and steering, respectively, while the center divisions contained the cargo. When used for commercial purposes the canoe was handled ordinarily by Indians or by French from Canada or Louisiana. The French Creoles were noted as hardworking, happy, and carefree; their songs rang loudly in the silence of the river and the neighboring forest.

Several modified forms of the canoe were called pirogues. The ordinary type of pirogue was a canoe with a square stern. Two canoes lashed together and floored over, and frequently using a sail for motive power, represented another type. West of the Mississippi were two other kinds of boats. The Mackinaw boat resembled a large rowboat possibly 50 feet long, with the cargo carried in a watertight compartment in the center; four oarsmen sat in the front to row, while the steersman sat on an elevated perch in the rear. An even more peculiar craft was the bullboat, which looked something like an inverted rimless hat, possibly 30 feet long; made of caulked buffalo hides stretched over a willow frame, it had the virtues of lightness, easy construction, large capacity, and very shallow draught. The bullboat was navigated by two men with poles and consequently was slow moving.

The increasingly popular boat of the whites was the flatboat, which obviously was flat-bottomed. Flatboats varied a good deal in dimensions, with common varieties anywhere from 20 to 100 feet long, and 8 to 15 feet wide; the depth was seldom over 3 feet, but might be much more. The crudest of the boats were little more than good-sized rafts, and when used by migrants might support a barn for the cattle and a small cabin for the family. A boat used for a comparatively short commercial trip might be partially roofed, but the New Orleans boats were completely covered and somewhat more sturdy.

Each flatboat had four oars, but not for motive power. On each side was a 30-foot oar to get the boat to shore or out into the current; because of them the boat was sometimes called a "Kentucky broadhorn." In the stern was a 40- to 50-foot oar used for steering, and in the front a smaller oar, called a gouger, to aid the steering in unusually rapid water. Since the flatboat depended on the current for motive power, it moved slowly except for those moments when it shot the falls of the Ohio at Louisville. Ordinarily the boat was tied to the bank every evening, since sandbars and others obstructions made travel dangerous at night.

The passengers on a flatboat had their living quarters aboard, with bunks instead of beds. Food was prepared in a rude fireplace. Migrants took aboard all their possessions, and one of the humorous sights of the river was a cow riding peacefully on a flatboat.

A migrating family broke up its boat at the end of the trip and used the boards and nails for the construction of a home on land. When a cargo was sold in New Orleans the boat was ordinarily torn apart and sold; the men returned overland by the Natchez Trace.

The principal upriver craft was the long, narrow keelboat, which usually measured about 50 feet in length and 7 to 10 feet in width. Being designed for longer use than the flatboat, it was better constructed, with pointed ends and a regular keel, which gave it its name. The draught varied from 20 to 60 inches, depending on the rivers on which it operated. In spite of this small draught the boat could carry between 20 and 40 tons of freight, which was protected from rain and sun by a roof.

The keelboat used every possible method of propulsion. Three to six oars on each side permitted rowing. A square sail of some hundred square feet was used in a favorable wind. A cordelle (tow rope) could be stretched from the top of the mast to the shore,

The Steamer *Okeehumkee* at Silver Springs, Florida. From Florida to the far northwest, before the coming of the railroads water transportation was predominant on the frontier. (Library of Congress)

with an auxiliary line to keep the boat from yawing; it was used to tow the boat through turbulent waters. This form of progress was slow and arduous, with twenty to thirty men scrambling over the rocks and through the water to drag the boat upstream; at times it was even necessary to employ a block and tackle. Because of the difficulties of towing, the method was used only when absolutely necessary. Whenever the water was sufficiently shallow, the boat was propelled by poles, and for this purpose a 15-inch platform was built on each side of the deck. Half of the crew took their places on each side. Each man thrust his pole into the bed of the river, put his shoulder against the socket at the end of the pole, and walked from fore to aft; as each man arrived at the stern he took out his pole, walked to the bow, and repeated the trip.

The only advantage of keelboats was that they could transport fairly heavy cargoes upstream. Trips were long, exhausting, and expensive, and so were practical only for valuable goods that would not spoil in transit. Since most western products were cheap and bulky, they could not be carried by keelboats. The model boat of the river was the galley, with dimensions of approximately 45 by 12 feet; it was propelled exclusively by oars and carried only passengers and mail.

River traffic grew rapidly as white immigration to the West increased. Down the river went such heavy and less perishable commodities as flour, potatoes, salt pork, bacon, linen, corn, and cordage. Up the river went such articles as molasses, sugar, coffee, and tea—all of comparatively large value in small bulk. One scholar has estimated an average of 3000 flatboats a year on the Ohio River between 1810 and 1820; certainly by the end of the War of 1812 the river was covered with these slow-moving craft floating with the current.

River traffic necessitated a "floating population" to furnish the labor on the flatboats and keelboats, and on the waterfronts. These rivermen, "half horse, half alligator," were poorly educated, restless, strong, rough, and tough. The semilegendary Mike Fink boasted that "I kin outrun, outhop, throw down, knock down, drag out, and lick any man in the country. I'm a Salt River roarer. I love the wimmen and I'm chock-full of fight." Men of the breed of Fink collected in such river towns as Cincinnati, Louisville, Natchez, and New Orleans. They roistered up and down the river, drinking, fighting, making love, and in the process created folklore and folk songs that have continued to live.

EARLY STEAMBOATS   Early western river traffic was slow; even more distressing, it could not move upstream without tremendous expenditures of capital and labor. The immediate answer was the use of steam. Robert Fulton demonstrated the commercial possibilities of the steamboat in his trip on the Hudson with the *Clermont* in 1807, and he and his backer, Robert R. Livingston, obtained a legal monopoly of steamship transportation in the states of New York and Louisiana. If this monopoly could have been maintained, it would have meant control of a large proportion of all the shipping of the United States. The breaking of the monopoly, including the case of *Gibbons* v. *Ogden* (1824), made constitutional history.

One of the earliest efforts of the Livingston-Fulton monopoly was to introduce and develop the steamboat in the West, since western commerce was large and the control of Louisiana was strategic. In May 1809 Nicholas Roosevelt was sent West to sound out steamboat possibilities. For Roosevelt the trip was a honeymoon as well as a business venture, so he built a flatboat at Pittsburgh, fitted it with luxurious appointments, and floated leisurely down the river. At each town he discussed his plans with the leading citizens. He spent three weeks at Louisville, for here were the dreaded falls, and the old-timers were skeptical of the ability of the proposed new machine to move against the current. The end of Roosevelt's journey was New Orleans, from which he returned to the East by ocean.

Roosevelt's report was apparently favorable, for in 1811 the steamboat *New Orleans* was built in Pittsburgh. The *New Orleans* was 138 by 26½ feet, burned wood, and cost $38,000. Whether it was a side- or stern-wheeler is still argued. It was launched in March 1811 and started down the river in October. On the second day it arrived at Cincinnati, where the people admired it but were not convinced that it could move upstream. The following day the vessel arrived at Louisville, where it inspired a big reception and dinner. Some of the leading citizens were taken on a short ride to demonstrate the boat's possibilities, and for the first time the skeptical were convinced

Marylanders Moving West, Fairview Inn. These boatlike wagons with their high bows and sterns and billowing canvas tops were the forerunners of the famed prairie schooners of the high plains country. They seem to characterize the westward movement in the mind of the artist. (Maryland Historical Society)

that progress could be made against the current, even though the maximum upstream speed was only about 3 miles an hour. After waiting for high water the boat shot the rapids at Louisville and continued downstream, arriving on January 10, 1812, at the city for which it was named. Its life was short, for while engaged in regular trips between New Orleans and Natchez it struck a snag and sank on July 14, 1814. Despite the briefness of its career, the *New Orleans* demonstrated the possibilities of steamboat traffic on western waters.

THE WESTERN STEAMBOAT   The advance of the steamboat was very rapid. Competition was introduced with the defeat of the Livingston-Fulton monopoly after a long court struggle. Steamboat machinery was improved, so that better speeds could be maintained. The side-wheeler was common on the Ohio and the Mississippi, but the stern-wheeler was the usual boat on the narrow and winding Missouri. Keels gave way to flatbottoms, which were so necessary for western rivers. More decks were added, and the decorations were elaborated. The prototype of later boats was the *Washington*, built at Wheeling in 1816 for Henry M. Shreve. By the 1820s the riverboat had reached the general form it was to maintain during succeeding decades.

Every steamboat carried its freight, machinery, and fuel at water level; the shallow draft provided no room below decks. The engines burned wood, producing multitudes of sparks and necessitating frequent refueling. The woodcutters' homes on the banks of the river soon became landmarks. Some of the wood was carried on board by the deck passengers, who traveled at lower rates and usually slept on the rear of the first deck. The second deck, the domain of the cabin passengers, had sleeping quarters, a dining room, a men's room and bar, and a ladies' parlor. The ladies' parlor was always in the rear—not because the ladies were considered unimportant but because the frequent explosions of the boilers in the front of the boat made the stern the safest place. The top, or hurricane, deck was occupied by the pilothouse and the officers' quarters, and was commonly known as the texas in later years.

The cost of steamboat travel varied with the amount of competition, but tended to decrease. In 1819 a cabin passage from New Orleans to Louisville was $125; the return trip, being with the current, cost only $75. A deck passage was, of course, much cheaper, since such a passenger furnished his own food and bedding, slept on the deck, and helped carry the wood. By 1832 the traveler could make the trip from New Orleans to St. Louis for $25 and return for $20; the deck passage was $5 either way. Freight rates dropped even more sensationally. The estimate has been made that just before the Civil War downstream rates were from 25 to 30 percent of those of 1815–1819, while upstream rates were only from 5 to 10 percent. Along with decreased fares went increased speeds. In 1817 the *Enterprise* made a record run of 25 days, 2 hours, and 4 minutes from New Orleans to Louisville; in 1853 the *A. L. Shotwell* covered the same distance in 4 days, 9 hours, and 30 minutes. Every boat cherished any record it made.

The effort to make speed records was one of the many factors producing frequent accidents. Part of the trouble, however, was due to nature and not to man. Even with the most careful navigation the Ohio and Mississippi were dangerous rivers. Snags and sawyers were omnipresent and difficult to avoid. A snag could, and often did, rip the wooden hull so that the boat would sink in a few minutes; effective snag removal did not come until the late 1820s with the work of Henry M. Shreve, who designed a twin-hull boat for pulling snags, which he called *Heliopolis*. In the summer and fall both rivers were low, and in a channel changed by shifting sandbars it was easy to go aground. In the spring the floods, carrying large quantities of debris, created other hazards.

Serious accidents were also caused by mechanical failures. Western steamboats used dangerous, high-pressure boilers to get more power with less weight. The metal of the boilers was sometimes poor and burst under the high pressure of steam or for lack of water. When the captain wanted a high speed a man might be ordered to sit on the safety valve to maintain an abnormally high pressure of steam—the pressure always went up, and sometimes the man and most of the passengers with it. Then, too, the wooden boats were highly combustible and the sparks pouring from the smokestack often set fire to the boat. The danger was increased when greater speed was obtained by the addition of such substances as pitch, oil, turpentine, and lard, which produced a hotter fire and more steam, but also a greater shower of sparks.

Another common cause of accidents was racing. Each captain considered his own boat the best on the river, and rival claimants frequently tested the merits of their respective crafts. Some of the races were planned in advance, with each captain placing a wager on his own boat. The races were particularly spectacular at night on the Mississippi, with the lights of the two steamers glowing against the surrounding darkness and the open furnace doors bringing into bold relief the muscular bodies of the firemen, stripped to the waist, as they rushed wood to the insatiable fires. The engines roared, the paddles churned, whistles shrieked, and the passengers gathered at the rail to lay odds on the outcome. Masses of sparks shot out of the funnels, and heavy black smoke indicated the addition of lard or turpentine to the fuel supply. Not infrequently the boat would catch fire or the boilers would burst, and the spectacle would end in tragedy.

The most noted race came after the Civil War (1870), when the *Robert E. Lee* and the *Natchez* sped up the river from New Orleans to St. Louis. The *Lee* stripped for action and made special preparations for refueling; it won the race even though the *Natchez*, under ordinary conditions, was probably the faster boat. Mile after mile they raced neck and neck, their progress followed all over the country by telegraphic dispatches. They arrived at St. Louis within a few minutes of each other, having covered the 1278 miles in 3 days, 8 hours, and 14 minutes—an average speed of 14⅙ miles per hour, including stops.

The height of the steamboat business came during the 1850s, at which time the Mississippi and Ohio were the most important rivers, although the Missouri and other tributaries carried part of the business. This was the period of huge, many-decked boats embellished with gingerbread scrollwork and bright paint. Rich carpets covered the floors, elaborate glass chandeliers multiplied the brilliance of the many lights, and luxurious furniture rivaled that of the best hotels. Excellent food was prepared by a corps of cooks and served by a host of well-trained black waiters. Elaborate bars and long wine lists were provided for convivial guests. Orchestras and brass bands added the romance of gay music. After the Civil War the splendor of the Mississippi steamboat waned as the traffic on which it was based was diverted to the expanding railroads, and taken directly east.

The development of the steamboat during and after the 1820s made it the home of many activities that in an earlier time had been confined to land. Photographers bought

The Old Stage Coach of the Plains, by Frederic Remington. Rugged terrain, reckless drivers, and the inevitable guard "riding shotgun" characterized western stagecoach transportation. Passengers found them far less glamorous than did the artists. (Amon Carter Museum)

their own boats and worked the river towns. Patent-medicine vendors traveled the river, presenting vaudeville acts as part of the sales pitch for their nostrums. Gamblers, saloonkeepers, and prostitutes also took to the river, either running their own boats or exploiting the opportunities available on regular commercial craft. "Showboats," with the dulcet strains of their calliopes and their bright lights beckoning, brought to many river towns their only touch of drama; in spite of the smallness of the showboat theater and the poor performances of the players, the showboat filled a very real need in the emotional life of the West. Even preachers sometimes navigated their own boats to bring salvation to the river population—which certainly needed it. Add to these itinerants the immigrant, the migratory worker, the riverman, and all the others who found water transportation desirable, and the diversity and size of the river traffic can be partially understood.

BOAT CREWS   Navigation of the riverboats was in the hands of comparatively well-trained and experienced men. Most skilled was the pilot, who sometimes received as much as $1000 a month. He was in absolute command of the movements of the boat, except that the captain ordered the time to start and stop. The knowledge of the Mississippi pilot can be estimated justly only when it is remembered that he had to know intimately 1500 miles of one of the more changeable rivers in the world. The channel varies continually with the shifting of sandbars; even the banks and cutoffs shift. There were no lights or buoys as there are today; consequently, the pilot had no guide except his own vision and experience.

The captain, frequently a part owner, was the master of the boat, except that he could not give orders to the pilot concerning navigation; he acted as host to the passengers, much as did the proprietor of an inn. Of slightly less importance was the engineer, who was absolute ruler of the machinery, obeying only the tinkling orders of the directing bell. A mate and a clerk had their chief duties in accepting and reckoning the charges on freight. A semiofficial person on most boats was the barkeeper, who usually made good profits by operating his bar as a concession. In early days simple drinks were favored, with whiskey ranking first and the mint julep second in popular favor, but later times brought more elaborate concoctions. Possibly also to be considered semiofficial were the professional gamblers who traveled on many boats; not infrequently they paid part of their profits to the captain.

Roustabouts did the common labor of cleaning the boat, carrying the wood, stoking the furnace, and loading and unloading cargo. A few of them were old rivermen who had drifted to the steamboats when the slower-moving vessels were driven off the rivers, and there were considerable numbers of Irish immigrants who were employed during the 1830s and later. By far the largest group, however, and the one that eventually monopolized this kind of work was the Negro, who gave much of the tone to the life of the river, and, like preceding boatmen, left a permanent record with his folklore, poetry, and songs.

The steamboat had only a relatively short period of dominance, but its impact on increasing transportation of freight and passengers, and on the growth of particular cities, has long continued. In addition it appealed romantically to men, as has every form of transportation from the oxcart to the jet plane.

READINGS   *Paperbacks are marked with an asterisk.*

General   By far the best account of transportational developments, although not limited to the West, is *George R. Taylor, *The Transportation Revolution* (1951, 1961). Also useful is *Everett Dick, *Vanguards of the Frontier* (1941), west of the Mississippi. State and regional histories normally include transportation; see the Readings for Chapters 6 and 13. See also Leland D. Baldwin, *Pittsburgh* (1937), very good.

Roads   Good in every way are Philip D. Jordan, *The National Road* (1948) and Norris F. Schneider, *Y Bridge City* (1950), which includes Zane's Trace. See also Paton Yoder, *Taverns and Inns in the Early Midwest* (1969), scholarly.

Water Transportation   Presteamboat transportation is described excellently in Leland D. Baldwin, *The Keelboat Age on Western Waters* (1941). Early rivermen are described in Walter Blair and Franklin J. Meine, *Mike Fink* (1933) and their *Half Horse, Half Alligator* (1956).

Steamboats   By far the best account is Louis C. Hunter, *Steamboats on the Western Rivers* (1949). Emphasizing the Mississippi are Walter Havighurst, *Voices on the River* (1964); Herbert and Edward Quick, *Mississippi Steamboatin'* (1926), somewhat factual; William J. Peterson, *Steamboating on the Upper Mississippi* (1937, 1968). For the Missouri the classic account is Henry M. Chittenden, *A History of Early Steamboat Navigation on the Missouri River* (2 vols., 1903); see also William E. Lass, *A History of Steamboating on the Upper Missouri River* (1962); Joseph M. Hanson, *The Conquest of the Missouri* (1909, 1946).

Junction of the Erie and Northern Canals, 1830. Water transportation, traditionally the cheapest way to move freight, played an important part in opening the frontier. During the period depicted here America went "canal crazy." (New York Historical Society)

The West of Steam and Steel

It is no exaggeration to say that the settlement of the West depended upon the coming of the railroad. High-yield ventures, such as mining, could be carried out using the wagon for transportation, but this was far too expensive for the farmer. Even before the coming of the ordinary farmer, the range-cattle industry required rail transportation to market cattle.

Building western railroads became a national project. Even persons not remotely connected with the undertaking watched with interest, as workmen graded, laid track, and sent steam locomotives ever deeper into the Great American Desert. They cheered as new construction records were set and showed pleasure when communities deep in the mountains of the West were freed from their economic prisons. Railroad building gave rise to visions of trade with the Orient, of connecting Asia and Europe with steel bands across this country, and of linking the frontiers to "civilized America."

Union Pacific Emigrant Train, about 1870. (Union Pacific Railroad)

Railroad Construction in Montana, about 1887. A typical view of iron rails cutting a swath through Whitman's "Sea of Grass." Note the wagons on the right hauling ties forward. (Minnesota Historical Society)

The Track-layers. Almost impatiently the engine awaits the "Gandy Dancers" as they lay rails upon ties that appear to have been simply laid out along the prairie without benefit of grading. Many a "record" was set by hasty construction. (Santa Fe Railway)

Construction near Cheyenne, 1868. Work slowed as the Union Pacific approached the foothills of the Rockies. Cuts and fills were time-consuming. (Union Pacific Railroad)

Preparing Tunnel Timbers, 1868. A great deal of wood was required in the construction of a railroad. Here timbers are being readied to shore up the tunnel seen in the background. (Union Pacific Railroad)

Tunneling Through the Mountains, Weber Canyon, 1869. These Union Pacific crews are working through solid rock. No speed records were set in this type of terrain. (Union Pacific Railroad)

Steam Shovel, Echo Canyon, Union Pacific, 1869. After the original construction was completed, "modern" equipment was used to haul ballast and widen cuts. (Union Pacific Railroad)

Chinese Coolie Labor on the Northern Pacific, 1880s. First brought in to complete the Pacific Railroad, Chinese laborers were used on other "transcontinentals." The Northern Pacific employed some 15,000. (Northern Pacific Railway)

Across the Rockies. Here the crews of the Colorado Midland Railway tunnel into solid granite near Manitou Springs. (Denver Public Library)

An Army Marches on Its Stomach. Napoleon's reference to the importance of food in a campaign is applicable here. A Union Pacific construction crew stops to eat while building through Wyoming, 1869. (Denver Public Library)

Emigrants, Early 1880s. Special low rates attracted thousands who entered the West faster and more cheaply than ever before. However, as Robert Louis Stevenson pointed out, these trains were unhesitatingly shunted to the sidetrack when first class or even freight trains demanded passage. (Southern Pacific Company)

Chapter 16/CANAL BARGE AND RAILROAD LOCOMOTIVE

The desire for improved transportation gripped nearly all Americans. Westerners and easterners alike pursued this hope. Better roads helped. Steamboats were fine, but were limited to navigable rivers, and could not connect East and West. Newer possibilities were canals, then railroads.

Every eastern seaboard town from Maine to Florida dreamed of its own route to the West that would make it great and prosperous. These dreams were temporarily shattered when the federal government gave Baltimore the nod for the National Road. Rival cities groaned unhappily, for even if they could raise the necessary money their own routes would be less attractive; for example, Boston and Charleston were almost without hope. New York and Philadelphia both had roads to the West, but neither merited boasting. Even Baltimore itself was not completely happy; it realized that high stage and wagon rates were sending business down the Mississippi, with New Orleans becoming the leading American port. In fact, all eastern cities realized that improved roads were not the final answer and that faster and cheaper means of transportation were necessary.

The great transportation innovation of the 1820s was the canal, which seemed the ultimate achievement. The canal would move traffic smoothly and cheaply; and each community closed its eyes to inconvenient, if not insuperable, obstacles and dreamed of itself as the center of a national network of canals. The wilder enthusiasts imagined canals linking navigable bodies of water to connect the Atlantic and Pacific, ignoring such obstacles as the Rocky Mountains. Public-spirited citizens gave and solicited funds, governments helped, and even the loafer at the grog shop came to speak learnedly of locks and water levels. This excessive enthusiasm ultimately was squelched by the panic of 1837. When men recovered a measure of financial stability, their eyes turned toward the newer railroads.

NEW YORK'S PRIMACY IN CANALS   The canal that fanned a small blaze of enthusiasm into a holocaust was the Erie Canal, the greatest engineering project of its day. Here was envisioned a canal 364 miles long to connect the Hudson River with Lake Erie when all the canals of the United States covered less than 10 percent of this distance. It was to run through a wilderness with no existing traffic along much of its route and little available from farther west. Financing was a big problem. Workers were difficult to obtain, even with the newly arrived Irish, and at times fever and ague almost brought work to a stop. That many people chuckled sardonically at this plan is understandable.

The Erie Canal was begun at Fort Stanwix (Rome) in 1817 and was opened for traffic in 1825. The opening was marked by the tour of Governor De Witt Clinton and his party from Buffalo to Albany, and then by steamship to New York. Each town along the way celebrated with parades, bands, dinners, speeches, toasts, and fireworks. Finally, on November 4, 1825, in a solemn ceremony at the mouth of New York harbor, the governor poured a keg of Lake Erie water into the Atlantic Ocean to symbolize the wedding of those two bodies of water.

The Erie Canal was in many ways unimpressive, being little more than a large ditch, 40 feet wide at the top, 28 feet at the bottom, and 4 feet deep. Locks were usually 80 by 14 feet, which meant that the largest boat could carry only about 100 tons of freight. And yet the effects of the Erie Canal exceeded the hopes of its most ardent supporters.

It was significant in the development of central and western New York, being directly responsible for such cities as Herkimer, Utica, Syracuse, and Lockport. Buffalo grew mightily, particularly with the harbor improvements that began in the 1820s. The canal was also vitally important in the growth of the Great Lakes country, including Michigan, Wisconsin, Minnesota, Iowa, and northern Ohio, Indiana, and Illinois. It brought an immense amount of business to New York City, helping it to achieve supremacy. Almost at once the canal's facilities were overtaxed; enlargement began within a decade of the opening. For a visionary scheme it had decidedly practical results.

PHILADELPHIA COMPETES   Philadelphia viewed with apprehension and alarm the building of the Erie Canal by its chief commercial rival, New York. Rather despairingly, Pennsylvania surveyed (1824–1825) possible water routes across the state, but even the strongest optimism could not carry water across the mountains. The ultimate answer was a marvelous combination of canals, inclined planes, and newfangled

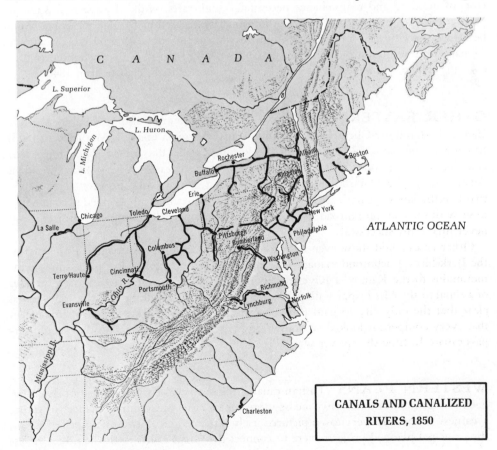

CANALS AND CANALIZED
RIVERS, 1850

railroads. Work was started in 1826, and completed in 1834, with the state shouldering the entire cost of $13.5 million, or almost twice that of the Erie Canal.

The Pennsylvania System was a mechanical marvel. In general its route was that of the later Pennsylvania Railroad. From Philadelphia to Columbia on the Susquehanna was one of the nation's early railroads, with the steep grade at either end surmounted by an inclined plane on which the cars were raised or lowered by a rope attached to a stationary engine; in the early years horses were used to move the cars on level stretches. From Columbia a canal with 18 dams, 33 acqueducts, and 101 locks followed the Susquehanna and Juniata rivers to Hollidaysburg. The mountains of the next 37 miles were surmounted by inclined planes with stationary engines; between the mountains were stagecoaches, which were soon replaced by horse-drawn railroad cars, and then by steam locomotives. At Johnstown the traveler again boarded a canal boat that encountered 64 locks, 10 dams, 2 tunnels, and 16 aqueducts before it arrived at Pittsburgh. The total length was 363 miles.

The Pennsylvania System was exceedingly ingenious, but not very practical. High costs of building and maintenance necessitated high rates, while the speed was unimpressive. Improvement came with the introduction of sectional canal boats that could be loaded piecemeal on railroad cars, but this was not enough. Income was inadequate to maintain the interest on the construction bonds, and the state was delighted to turn over the whole white elephant to the Pennsylvania Railroad, chartered in 1846.

OTHER EASTERN CITIES   The Baltimore area, also worried by the Erie Canal, chartered the Chesapeake and Ohio Canal (Virginia in 1824, Maryland in 1825) to connect the navigable portions of the Potomac and Ohio rivers. The project was considered so important that at the dedication ceremonies on July 4, 1828, President Adams threw the first shovel of dirt. Unfortunately the work progressed so slowly that Cumberland was not reached until 1850, and there the work stopped permanently, in view of the coming railroad. As a delayed and only partially completed project it was never financially successful.

Other cities could show even less success. Boston could never imagine a canal across the Berkshires. Richmond managed a canal as far as Lynchburg, but plans to cross the mountains to the Kanawha River never materialized. Charleston toyed with the idea of a canal to the Mississippi Valley, but got no further than talking. By the 1830s it was clear that the only city to gain through canals was New York, which in turn meant that every competitor looked anxiously for any form of transportation that would surpass canals. In time the answer was railroads.

WESTERN PLANS   Eastern canal enthusiasm was rivaled by that of the West. Each western community saw one or more canals as its outstanding chance for future greatness. Although every town pictured itself as the center of a vast network of canals, the principal planned projects were to connect the Great Lakes with the Ohio-Mississippi system. Eastern connections that already existed with New York, could easily be made with Philadelphia by way of the Pennsylvania System, and with Baltimore by way of the Chesapeake and Ohio Canal if it were ever completed. What was sought was an easy and cheap flow of goods between East and West.

The greatest difficulty facing the West was a lack of funds. Individual investors were solicited successfully, but were frequently too optimistic about their ability to pay. States borrowed freely, but their credit was limited. The federal government received earnest appeals. When Henry Clay proposed federal help for internal improvements as part of his American System he was expressing the opinion of much of the West. Unfortunately both Madison and Monroe had constitutional scruples about using federal money for local projects. John Quincy Adams was more generous, while Jackson had constitutional scruples, as shown in his Maysville veto (1830), but was willing to approve projects that were interstate and hence to his mind constitutional.

Western canal building was also limited by the very enthusiasm that characterized it. Each community was certain that its future prosperity depended on canals and, realizing the limited nature of the funds available, opposed any project that was not immediately to its own benefit. The obvious political solution was to combine several plans in a single proposal, closing one's eyes to the financing and sometimes even to the necessary water. The existence of too many of these projects brought delay in completing any of them.

OHIO   The first western state to build canals was, naturally, Ohio—the most populous. Inspired by the building of the Erie Canal, Ohio investigated (1822–1825) possible routes. Depending on its own resources and on promises of private eastern loans, it authorized two canals in 1825 to connect the Ohio River with Lake Erie. The estimated cost was $5,700,000, which was approximately a tenth of the value of all taxable property in the state, and, notoriously, actual costs always run above estimates—a magnificent gamble.

The first of these projects, called the Ohio Canal, ran from Portsmouth on the Ohio north along the Scioto, east to the Muskingum, and then along the Muskingum and Cuyahoga to Cleveland. Work started on July 4, 1825, when Governor De Witt Clinton of New York dug the first spadeful of dirt. In spite of difficulty in obtaining enough labor, of costs larger than the estimate, and of absconding contractors, the entire 308 miles were completed in 1832. The Ohio Canal had approximately the dimensions of the Erie Canal, and on the whole was built both well and cheaply.

The second project, called the Miami Canal, followed the historic Maumee-Miami route from Cincinnati on the Ohio to Toledo on Maumee Bay; largely because of this project Ohio was a little later willing to fight a war (see Chapter 17) for possession of the Toledo area. Work was begun in 1825, with the Cincinnati-Dayton section opened in 1829. Later, work went slowly because of the preference given the Ohio Canal, so that the complete canal was not opened until 1845.

Ohio was so enthusiastic about the advantages of improved transportation that in

1836 it authorized further roads and canals. The following year it provided state aid to any railroad, turnpike, canal, or slack water navigation that met state standards; in addition certain federal aid was available. However, the results of these magnificent efforts were disappointing, since the panic of 1837 soon made state funds too expensive to be practical.

OTHER WESTERN CANALS   Indiana, like Ohio, had canal schemes before 1820, but they did not assume vital importance until after Ohio began work. All the difficulties hampering Ohio were magnified in Indiana because of its smaller population and less wealth; the total taxes collected in Indiana in 1827 were $33,000. Congress gave some slight assistance through its land grant of 1827, but main dependence was placed on a $15 million state bond issue. Of this imposing sum, about $2 million was embezzled, $4 million was lost in worthless securities, and much of the remainder was frittered away.

The principal route upon which the Hoosiers looked with favor was from the navigable portion of the Wabash northeast to Lake Erie near Toledo—another historic portage route. A small part of the route lay within Ohio, which gave permission in 1829 to build, and then backed out of its agreement and had to be repersuaded. Work was begun in 1832, but was bungled from the beginning. Money was spent haphazardly, management was inefficient, and the Irish laborers were continually embroiled in fights between the partisans of northern and southern Ireland.

Despite these various troubles, the Wabash and Erie Canal was finished in 1842 and opened the next year from Lafayette to Toledo, a distance of 215 miles. Work was then pushed south, so that by 1853 boats could go all the way to Evansville. Several other projects were complete failures, but for a time in the early 1850s the main canal carried much traffic, while the Whitewater Canal in southeast Indiana was a fair success. Business then declined, particularly with the opening of the Wabash Railroad in 1856. The floods of 1875 stopped all traffic, and the canal was never repaired.

Illinois also had its pet project in the Illinois and Michigan Canal, designed to connect Lake Michigan with the navigable portion of the Illinois River. The idea was old, but not until 1820 was the route surveyed and a tract of land donated by Congress. One of the results of the survey was the platting of the town of Chicago near Fort Dearborn in 1830. Construction of the canal began in 1836, and it was opened twelve years later.

These four canals in the states immediately north of the Ohio River were the most important projects completed in the West. Of the smaller canals most significant was the two miles of the Louisville and Portland around the falls of the Ohio at Louisville; it proved moderately profitable after its opening in 1830. A modest original investment by the federal government led to complete governmental control by 1874. Other minor enterprises ranged from the portage canal at Portage, Wisconsin, built in the 1840s, to a number of waterways in the vicinity of New Orleans. For every canal built there were plans for a hundred others, and every western state toyed with at least eight or ten projects it considered important.

Most of the canals completed between 1820 and 1840 were in the Northwest rather than in the Southwest. The sparser population and lesser wealth of the South had their effect, as well as the prevalence of the plantation system, which precluded the urban centers so necessary for canal promotion.

CANAL TRAFFIC   To the modern observer the outstanding characteristic of canal traffic was its slowness, for the usual speed was between 2 and 4 miles an hour. This leisurely pace was satisfactory for the transportation of heavy nonperishable freight to a fairly stable market. Passengers were reasonably comfortable, at least as compared with travel on a stagecoach, and those who were interested in the country through which they passed had plenty of time to enjoy the scenery.

Most canal boats were painted in bright colors, and, except for those devoted entirely to freight, could be classified as either line boats or packets. The line boat carried only local traffic and did not provide sleeping accommodations; the usual charge was 1¢ a mile without food and 2¢ with food. The packet was larger and finer. It furnished both food and bed, and traveled both night and day, so that it could cover some hundred miles a day. The cost, including food, was about 5¢ a mile, which was much less than the rate charged by the stages.

Boats carrying passengers were arranged somewhat alike. In the front was a tiny cabin with five or six bunks for the crew. Next came a small room used by the women for washing and dressing. Then there was a women's cabin, where the lady traveler could retire from the prying eyes of the male passengers, and where all the women slept at night. In the center of the boat was a large apartment, which might be as long as 45 feet. In the day it was used as a general assembly room in which the passengers could entertain themselves or doze, and in which smaller parcels were kept (the larger baggage was stacked on deck). Here meals were served on planks supported by wooden trestles. At night the cabin served as sleeping quarters for the men. Bunks were suspended on iron brackets, of which the ends on one side were pushed into the wall and on the other hung by ropes from the ceiling. Such shelves were each 6 by 3½ feet, and were arranged in tiers of three so that there was little room between them. When all the bunks were filled the surplus men slept on the tables or floor. Small straw mattresses and filthy blankets completed the equipment; these bedclothes were piled in a corner of the room in the daytime and were seldom washed. Behind the large room were a bar and the kitchen; the cook generally doubled as a bartender, and worked both day and night. The usual crew consisted of a captain, two steersmen, two drivers, and a cook; the drivers and steersmen alternated in 6-hour shifts. Just which of the crew had any duty in caring for the wants of the passengers is not clear.

Most of the passengers spent the fine days on deck, talking, playing games, sewing, reading, painting. From time to time some would get off the boat to stretch their legs by walking along the towpath and chatting with the driver. The principal hazard was the bridges, which were encountered every mile in some areas and still more frequently in the towns; these bridges were so low that everyone had to duck to avoid being knocked into the water. On bad days most people went below to the cabin, which was close and stuffy under the best conditions, and almost unsupportable in warm weather. Since ventilation was very limited, and standards of personal cleanliness rather low, many travelers preferred to stay outside, even in the rain. Sometimes a traveling minister would seize the opportunity of a captive audience by holding a religious meeting.

One of the amusements of canal boat travel was to watch the manipulation of the vessel, which was usually drawn by one to three horses or mules. The towpath was on only one side of the canal and so when two boats met, one of them would let its towline go slack so that the other could pass over. When the towpath crossed the water, considerable agility was necessary. The horse would first go under the bridge and then gallop over it to arrive on the other side of the canal before all the slack of the line was taken up by the drift of the boat. Now and then a horse was too slow and was pulled into the water. Mules found a bridge a disastrous place on which to balk.

The canal was an exceedingly important factor in the development of the West, even though its dominance was brief. It afforded cheap and safe, although slow, transportation. Even when canals did not show a profit they helped to advance the economic well-being of the communities they served. Prices for farm products improved while the cost of imported articles decreased. Many towns traced the beginnings of their commercial importance to the influence of the canal.

One of the greatest services of the canals was to bring population into new areas. Often their very construction brought settlements of canal employees along their banks. When completed they attracted more people because of the improved transportational facilities, which increased land values. They carried thousands of settlers to the West.

As with similar enthusiasms, the canal mania was carried to excess. Plans were always greater than completed projects. More work was started than could be finished. Excessive loans were floated to complete waterways that had no chance of financial success. Many canals were built far in advance of any possible usefulness. The overexpansion helped to cause the financial panic of 1837, from which the canals never recovered.

The desire for canals represented the peak of a movement for better transportation that included all types of internal improvements. The canals were the latest and most desired form of transportation, but other projects such as building roads, removing obstacles from rivers, marking river channels, and placing lighthouses and buoys on the lakes, also received sympathy and support. While the canal was at the height of its popularity, an even newer idea found expression in the first experimentation with railroads. Eventually the railroad overshadowed its predecessor.

RAILROADS APPEAR   The transportational novelty of the late 1820s was the railroad, but most Americans had only the vaguest idea, if any, of what it was. Here and there a mining tramway existed, but the story is told that when the people of Baltimore first decided to build a railroad they sent a man to Europe to discover what it was. The attractiveness of the idea is easy to understand. Here was a new means of transportation that could be used anywhere, regardless of mountains or water supply, and that would permit a horse to draw a larger load more rapidly than was possible on a regular road, and would not freeze in winter.

The difficulties of building railroads in the United States were intimidating. Distances were tremendous, and there were few concentrations of population so desirable for successful railroads. Costs of construction far exceeded those of roads and canals, and no one could conceive that it would be profitable to parallel such a body of water as the Hudson River. Methods of construction involved speculation that ranged from the permanence of granite blocks to the resilience of wooden trestles. The tracks themselves were first made of wood, topped by iron strips. Later, rails of various designs were made of solid iron. Steel rails were too expensive to use until after the Civil War. Even the width of the track (the gauge) was a subject for argument, with preferences ranging from 3 feet to 6 feet. Also, there were variations in time standards—standard time was not adopted until the 1880s—and it is easy to understand why the interchange of traffic between railroads and passenger connections was difficult.

Equipment was also a matter of uncertainty. Some of the cars at first resembled stage-coaches, but soon became more like oblong boxes. Such matters as specialized cars, brakes, signaling devices, lighting, and heating were problems to be solved. Even motive power was a question. The first engine was a horse, used now and then on a treadmill inside the car, but other devices, including sails, were tried. Obviously the final solution was the steam locomotive; the first one was a stationary engine on a flat car, and subject

The Coming of the Railroads, 1832. This primitive train, a part of the Mohawk and Hudson Railway (Albany to Schenectady), was indeed a crude affair. The term carriages, used in Europe for railroad cars, is an accurate one. (Library of Congress)

to such frequent breakdowns that many people thought a horse would be more satisfactory. The development of an effective steam locomotive was far from a simple problem. In short, the amazing thing about early American railroads is not the slowness but the rapidity with which they were built.

Technical difficulties implied conditions of travel that today would be completely unacceptable. Cars were uncomfortable. A stove at one end roasted nearby people, while those at the other end of the car froze. Cooling in summer could be obtained only by opening a window, which admitted a shower of sparks from the wood-burning engine, forcing the passenger to extinguish small fires in his clothes and to wipe the cinders from his eyes. There were no vestibules. The cars rattled and bumped over the generally poor roadbed. Signal systems were not dependable, and frequent wrecks resulted. An engine often left the track or broke down, leaving the passengers waiting to be rescued, with whatever patience they could muster. Even the speed was not wonderful; anything over 20 miles an hour was considered good. But these conditions should not be overemphasized. As compared with the stagecoach, the railroad was somewhat more comfortable and considerably faster.

BUILDING FROM EAST TO WEST   Eastern cities, aspiring eagerly to western business, looked hopefully at the new gadget. First to enter the competition was Baltimore, which saw the National Road being outmoded, and quite properly had little hope for the Chesapeake and Ohio Canal, which provided only a branch line for the city. On the same day that President Adams inaugurated work on the Chesapeake and Ohio Canal (July 4, 1828) the venerable Charles Carroll of Carrollton, last surviving signer of the Declaration of Independence, performed a similar service for the Baltimore and Ohio Railroad, which was designed to reach the Ohio River and thus bring western business to Baltimore. Its first few miles of track, opening the following year, inaugurated commercial railroading in the United States, but were attractive mainly to travelers who enjoyed the novel ride. Construction proceeded slowly, but by 1853 had reached the Ohio River near Wheeling.

Other cities that had suffered, but not in silence, as they saw western business moving toward New York on the Erie Canal, also picked up hope. Charleston, although remote from the Ohio Valley, speculated that it could at least short-circuit a share of the western business that was floating down the Savannah River. The Charleston and Hamburg Railroad was built to the Savannah River, and when its 136 miles were opened in 1833 it was the world's longest railroad under single management. To the north, Boston revived its hopes for western business and built westward through Worcester, opening a line as far as Albany in 1841. Unfortunately there was no bridge at Albany, and most shippers and travelers preferred steaming down the Hudson to bumping over the mountains to Boston.

Philadelphia was in a difficult situation when railroads entered the picture. With the construction of the Pennsylvania System the state had strained its resources beyond the breaking point and had no funds to replace the canal system, even though it was losing in the competition for western business. The ultimate solution was to charter the Pennsylvania Railroad in 1846 and turn over to it the old canal property. By combining railroads already in existence and adding others, the Pennsylvania Railroad was able to open its complete line to Pittsburgh in 1852, and to look for further expansion as far as the growing metropolis of Chicago.

New York was slowed down in its railroad construction by the excellence of its water facilities. By 1842 seven independent railroad lines paralleled the Erie Canal, their main advantages being speed and the fact that they did not freeze in winter. Their drawbacks were that they were not well run and that the connections between them were bad. No railroad paralleled the Hudson River until 1851. The small lines through central New York State united in 1853 to form the future New York Central. In addition, the Erie Railroad completed its line through the southern tier of New York counties to Lake Erie in 1851, giving New York two railroad outlets for western business.

WESTERN RAILROAD HOPES   In the West enthusiasm for the railroad rose to fever pitch. Western optimists envisioned economic salvation if only their local communities could obtain the new form of transportation. Whereas steamboats were limited to navigable rivers, and canals to available water supplies, now every town could hope to obtain railroad facilities. Even a community in the middle of the prairie might entertain the beautiful picture of itself as an important railroad center.

The main problem of the West in building railroads as in building canals, was money. Many individuals had much enthusiasm but little capital, while others, such as tavern owners, looked with alarm at the possible demise of the stagecoach business. Many westerners were suspicious of all bankers, while the bankers both of the United States and of Europe were properly suspicious of large investments where traffic was just a gleam in the eyes of speculators, and where the defaulting on bond interest was far from impossible. Even a partial exemption from taxation, as promised by Ohio, produced no rush to buy railroad stocks and bonds. As for the federal government, it remained hobbled by the current interpretation of the Constitution, and before 1850 the best it could do for western railroads was to lower the import duties on iron and for rails.

Local and state governments did the best they could. Local governments frequently bought railroad stocks and bonds, and even more frequently provided land for depots and yards; after all, they were vitally interested in obtaining railroad facilities. Some states—for example, Georgia and Michigan—built and operated their own railroads, which they later sold to private groups, often at very low prices. Railroads were included in a number of general acts designed to promote internal improvements. An Ohio law of 1837 permitted the state to purchase one-third of the capital stock of any railroad after the other two-thirds had been subscribed by private parties; promoters found such "subscriptions" easy to get, and ultimately made off with some $3 million. An Indiana law of 1836 brought great state expenditures but produced only a few miles of grading. An Illinois law of 1837 projected plans for some 1300 miles of railroads, which would have reached practically every crossroad in the state, but the results were negligible. Viewed with later knowledge, such plans are seen to have been a mistake, but they were in accord with the ideas of the day. The newer West may well have been particularly optimistic, but it followed the general American pattern.

The plans of the 1830s did not materialize; only a few random miles here and there were constructed, as in Michigan, Kentucky, and Louisiana. Then followed the depression starting in 1837, and even aspiring westerners shelved their plans. One traveler in Illinois in 1845 described the state's longest railroad in this fashion: "This railroad . . . is another of the links of that endless chain that was to bind the State in love together, but has bound them in debt forever. It is already so dilapidated that mules have been substituted for locomotives, and as it fails to pay expenses, it must shortly go out of business for want of repairs."

HOPES REALIZED When prosperity returned in the 1840s, the West was ready to embark on a vast program of railroad building that was not to slow down until the depression of 1857. The North had a greater concentration of population, including cities, than the South, and hence did more building of railroads; but both sections of the country eagerly threw their resources into expanding their networks. At the outbreak of the Civil War, Ohio was said to be better covered with railroads than any other state in the Union.

Some of the newly built railroads were designed to connect the larger cities; although for the farmers the feeder lines were equally important, since any long wagon haul of corn or wheat or cotton was economically impractical. Examples of such roads were those between Springfield and Sandusky, Ohio (1848), Cleveland and Cincinnati (1850), and Louisville and Nashville (1859). Each city was of course anxious to become the center of as many lines as possible. Here was the real chance for such a place as Indianapolis, which depended on road travel. Here also was the opportunity for bustling, aggressive Chicago, which had fewer than 5000 residents in 1840, under 30,000 in 1850, and then jumped in the next decade to 109,000. One important reason for the growth of Chicago was the spiderweb of roads—the Chicago and Northwestern; the Chicago, Rock Island and Pacific; and the Chicago. Burlington and Quincy. The Rock Island was the first to reach the Mississippi (1854) and to bridge it (1855). In contrast, the city of St. Louis continued to depend more on the river and hence gradually lost ground to its ambitious Lake Michigan rival. The injury to river business caused by the Civil War was a hard blow; by 1870 Chicago population almost equaled that of St. Louis, and within another decade had far surpassed it.

Probably more important than the connecting of large towns was the completion of through lines from the east coast to the Mississippi. Such connections were made in the 1850s, although frequently a particular route would not be under a single management. The completion of the Michigan Central and the Michigan Southern across Michigan to Chicago in 1852, plus the building of the Lake Shore to the east (1854) and the Rock Island to the Mississippi, gave both the New York Central and the Erie railroads the connections by which freight might be carried entirely by rail from the Atlantic to the

Mississippi. The Pennsylvania opened its complete line to Chicago in 1853; the Baltimore and Ohio made connections with St. Louis shortly afterward.

While several lines were traversing the North, the South was having more difficulty, even though the merchants of Charleston, Richmond, and other cities were as eager for railroads as were their northern counterparts. With tremendous labor a series of connecting roads was finally completed from Charleston through Hamburg, Atlanta,

RAILROADS, 1860

and Chattanooga to Memphis; the final connection was made in 1857. Farther south a line was being built from Savannah through Macon, Columbia, and Montgomery to Vicksburg, but was not completed before the outbreak of the Civil War.

The lag of the South in railroad construction had important effects in the Civil War, but also had long-run implications. The corn and wheat of the Northwest, the bulk of which had formerly moved down the river to New Orleans, went increasingly by railroad to northeastern ports. New Orleans, which had outcompeted even New York in 1840, began to fade in importance. The North had not only better transportation but also better markets, as a result of its growing cities and improved connections with Europe.

ILLINOIS CENTRAL   One western railroad, the Illinois Central, deserves special mention because of its sectional implications and because it gave a preview of conditions and problems that were later to become widespread. The Illinois Central was the culmination of an old movement to build north and south in Illinois, say, from Galena to Cairo. Local people, such as the young Abe Lincoln, were enthusiastic; of course he later became a railroad lawyer. As usual, funds were lacking, and appeals were made to the federal govement. When Stephen A. Douglas entered the Senate in 1847 he sponsored such a line, with personal motives that were both political and economic. Intensive logrolling brought an expansion of the plan to carry the railroad to Mobile to attract southern support. The Douglas efforts brought a federal law of 1850 by which alternate sections of land within six miles of the track went to a railroad that was to originate somewhere between Galena and Chicago and run to Mobile; actually the northern terminus became Chicago. The grant was in fact made to two states, Illinois and Alabama, since there was no public land in the intervening states.

Illinois chartered the Illinois Central in 1851 and transferred to it the federal grant; in lieu of taxes the state was to receive 5 percent of the gross operating revenue of the railroad—a very profitable deal for the state. Work started immediately and was pushed strenuously because there was a time limit beyond which the road could not get the land grant. The difficulties of construction were immense; both labor and railroad iron were imported from Europe, and the construction camps were characterized by drunkenness, rowdyism, and sickness; a cholera epidemic was particularly disheartening. In spite of these troubles the road was completed—and completed well—to Cairo in 1856, at which time George B. McClellan was the chief engineer.

The land for the Illinois Central was acquired and sold as rapidly as possible. Under the terms of the grant the railroad had to wait for its land until the government had sold its alternate sections at $2.50 an acre, or twice the usual minimum price. As each section of the road was completed and as the government sold its land, the railroad received its grant; the first installment was made in 1854. The land was advertised widely both in the United States and in Europe. It was sold at prices that averaged about $10 an acre, and on fairly liberal credit terms. Considering the costs of sale and the difficulties of collection, prices were quite moderate. Soon settlers were flowing into the area, with such towns as Champaign and Centralia booming. The most significant aspect of the Illinois grant, however, was that it opened the way to future federal grants, first to states, and then to individual railroads.

READINGS   *Paperbacks are marked with an asterisk.*

General   See Readings for Chapter 15.

Canals   Madeline S. Waggoner, *The Long Haul West* (1958), reads easily; Harry N. Scheiber, *Ohio Canal Era* (1969), scholarly, informative; Harlan Hatcher, *The Western Reserve* (1949), covers the Ohio Canal; Grace L. Nute, *Lake Superior* (1944), describes the Sault Canal; Ronald E. Shaw, *Erie Water West: A History of the Erie Canal, 1792–1854* (1966). James W. Livingood, *The Philadelphia-Baltimore Trade Rivalry 1780–1860* (1947) is excellent.

Railroads   The best brief, general railroad history is *John F. Stover, *American Railroads* (1961). For the Illinois Central see Carlton J. Corliss, *Main Line of Mid America* (1950) and Paul W. Gates, *Illinois Central Railroad and Its Colonization Work* (1934), a careful study.

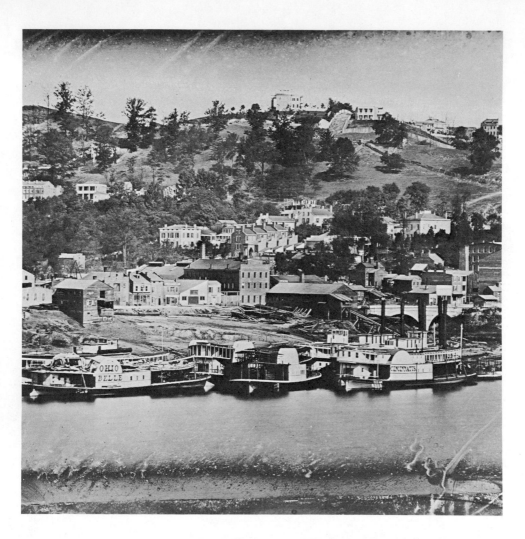

Chapter 17/A DELUGE OF PEOPLE

The flood of settlers that had ebbed after the panic of 1819 again swelled to magnificent proportions during the prosperous period of the late 1820s and early 1830s. Land sales of 1835 were over 12 million acres, or twice as much as those for any previous year; 1836 registered sales of 20 million acres.

Then history repeated itself as the number of newcomers declined with the panic of 1837.

The trans-Appalachian West grew rapidly, not only in absolute numbers, but also in comparison with the remainder of the United States. The West's 2.2 million in 1820 became 3.7 million by 1830 and 6.4 million by 1840, a rate of growth almost twice that of the United States as a whole. Westerners in 1820 were less than a quarter of the whole American population, but twenty years later they were a third. Ohio, Kentucky, and Tennessee, among the ten most populous states in all three census periods, were joined by Indiana in 1840.

The rapid growth of western population brought no great increase in the number of organized states and territories between 1820 and 1840. The only significant changes after the organization of Florida Territory in 1822 were the creation of the states of Arkansas and Michigan and the territories of Wisconsin and Iowa. However, by 1840 there were eleven states west of the mountains, which gave the West a considerable power in national politics, provided it could speak with a single voice.

Despite the increased foreign immigration of the period, the western migration of the 1820s and 1830s was predominantly of American farmers. Irish immigrants tended to stay in the East, although some toiled on western roads and canals and then settled in the regions in which they had worked. An increasing flow of Germans went to the Ohio Valley and as far west as Missouri and Wisconsin, where they were joined by early Scandinavian migrants. In spite of such foreign elements, however, the American West remained largely native born.

THE OHIO VALLEY   A good half of all westerners lived in the Ohio Valley. Kentucky grew only moderately, but the states north of the river boomed. Ohio's population almost tripled between 1820 and 1840; Indiana's increased more than four-fold, and that of Illinois more than eightfold—in fact, Illinois tripled within the single decade of 1830–1840. Not only were the river bottoms occupied, but people pushed into the prairie land of central and northern Indiana and Illinois.

Part of the population increase of the Ohio Valley was represented in the growth of its cities. Pittsburgh continued to dominate the upper valley in spite of the pretensions of Wheeling, but by the 1830s its title "Gateway to the West" had lost some of its pertinence because of the completion of the National Road farther south. Pittsburgh was known increasingly as a manufacturing center. "This city of smoke and mud, and ugly pavement" was all bustle and dirt and confusion, with commercialism rampant and ambitious businessmen grabbing their meals on the run. Shipbuilding included construction of both river steamboats and ships destined for the ocean trade. Coal mining and iron smelting were responsible for the general pall of smoke that was the despair of housewives; reputedly, Pittsburgh residents never saw white snow. Among the numer-

Cincinnati, 1848. This early daguerreotype indicates growth and development of a river town. Note the "permanent" type of architecture, cherished in all frontier settlements. (Cincinnati Historical Society)

ous Pittsburgh manufacturing industries were glass, rope, cotton, cloth, hardware, liquor, and books.

Farther down the valley was Louisville, which had become dominant in Kentucky, even though its commercial growth was slightly slowed by the canal that eliminated the need to transship goods around the falls of the river. The city had a varied assortment of young industries, but was most important as a distributing and shipping center. Here the state's agricultural products, particularly tobacco, were brought for shipment on the many steamboats that plied the Ohio. And here it was that the people from the backcountry did their shopping in the many stores of which Louisville was justly proud.

The commonly recognized "Queen of the West" was Cincinnati, seventh largest American city in 1830 and sixth in 1840, when its 46,000 residents displaced Charleston in the national ranking. Cincinnati was one of the most attractive of western cities, with clean, paved streets bordered by trees, well-tended houses, and good stores. Most visible was "Trollope's Folly," a bazaar constructed by Mrs. Frances Trollope (one of the least loved of American visitors), which reflected Greek, Roman, and Moorish influences. Cincinnati commerce boomed, the stores were well filled, and steamboats crowded the

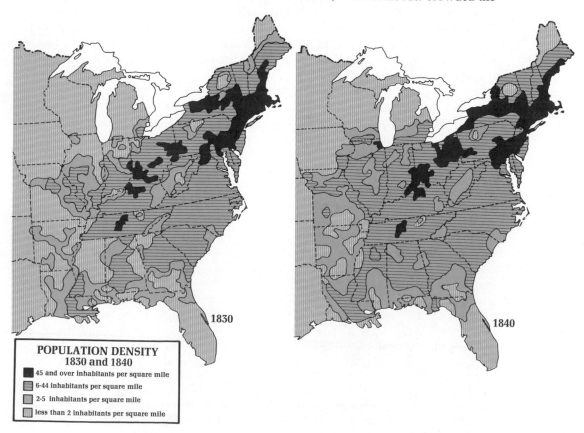

1830

1840

**POPULATION DENSITY
1830 and 1840**

- 45 and over inhabitants per square mile
- 6-44 inhabitants per square mile
- 2-5 inhabitants per square mile
- less than 2 inhabitants per square mile

wharves. The city was also distinctive as a center for the increasing German immigration that was coming in large numbers to central and southern Ohio. Cincinnati had German newspapers, clubs, and singing societies; German was commonly spoken on the streets, and peasant costumes could be seen here and there.

The principal industry of Cincinnati was pork packing; hence the city was frequently dubbed "Porkopolis." The squeal of pigs was the city's dominant sound—partly because Cincinnati, like other American cities, allowed pigs to roam the streets freely as scavengers. Cincinnati had the first packinghouse west of the mountains in 1818, and twenty years later some 182,000 hogs were processed in a single year. Pork packing involved the best contemporary division of labor, and utilized "everything but the squeal."

Cincinnati was not devoted entirely to business. It was also an important literary and cultural center. Books, magazines, and newspapers flowed in a steady stream from its presses. The city counted among its residents outstanding western authors and painters as well as numerous professional groups. Schools, hospitals, and libraries were comparatively plentiful and good; moreover, the city was the western center for such philanthropic organizations as the American Sunday School Union.

The growth of the Ohio Valley meant that by the 1830s the older sections along the river could no longer be considered a frontier. In most cultural traits it was more akin to the East than it was to the newer regions farther west, and consequently, it leaves the frontier picture.

NORTHERN OHIO AND MICHIGAN   To the north, there was a vast inflow of settlers along the Great Lakes, filling such cities as Erie, Cleveland, Sandusky, Toledo, and Detroit; Cleveland, for example, had a population of 1000 in 1830 and 6000 in 1840. Continuing west, migrants pushed into Michigan, northern Indiana and Illinois, Wisconsin, and even as far as Iowa. Travelers filled the boats, and crowded the roads. During the year 1833 some 60,000 people left Buffalo by water for the West, the next year saw 80,000, and the succeeding years brought still more. These figures did not include the greater number going by land; no one felt it worthwhile to count the wagon trains.

The city of Buffalo boomed with the opening of the Erie Canal, the improvement of its Lake Erie harbor, and the vastly increased migration; by 1840 its population numbered 18,000. The buildings that rose on every hand were usually large and cheaply constructed, with an extraordinarily large number of hotels and a theater that was considered one of the finest in the West. The streets were crowded with immigrants, land speculators, runaway slaves and their pursuing masters, Indians who were often drunk, merchants, canal drivers, and other elements of the heterogeneous population. Buffalo provided fine opportunities for the energetic and ambitious, particularly the speculators, but it was no place for a lady alone on the streets at night.

The great northern area of opportunity during the 1830s was Michigan, which was particularly attractive to Yankees.

Then there's old Varmount, well, what d'ye think of that!
To be sure, the gals are handsome, and the cattle very fat:
But who among the mountains 'mid cloud and snow would stay,
When he can buy a prairie in Michigania?
          Yea, yea, yea, to Michigania.

Detroit, the gateway to Michigan, remained as late as 1840 a rather small town with a population of about 9000, but it had large ambitions. It bulged with immigrants and merchants who stretched the available food and lodging to the breaking point. Streets were wide and unpaved, and sidewalks no more than a few random planks; in rainy weather a caller avoided being mired by driving his carriage directly to the front door of the house he was visiting. Yet Detroit was a city of the future, and as such attractive only to the man who kept his eyes on the new churches, banks, stores, newspapers, and homes, and transported them into a glorious future.

Many visitors saw only the drab present rather than the hoped-for future:

> O Detroit, what a barren and inhospitable City thou art! Thou shalt sit enthroned as the Queen of Muddy Streets, through which do saunter thy gaunt lean cows, which after feeding upon what thy generous inhabitants cast from their kitchen doors are killed and quartered to be cooked—but to be eaten—aye there's the rub—that is frequently an impossibility. Gristle, skin & bone, pervade the very marrow & boiled, baked, or fried one's teeth suffer in the attack.

Michigan settlers came largely from New York and New England and concentrated in the southern third of the state. The inland towns in this area had been established after the War of 1812 and now grew magnificently. Farther north such frontier settlements as Grand Rapids and Saginaw received their first growth in the 1830s. Land speculators practically monopolized available building lots. To the west the new towns of St. Joseph and New Buffalo considered themselves rivals of Chicago, with the speculators dreaming of the happy day when their towns and cities would outdistance the Illinois upstart. The Michigan boom was sadly injured by the panic of 1837, and then revived a little, only to collapse completely when depression finally hit the West with full force in 1839.

MICHIGAN STATEHOOD   The growth of Michigan led its inhabitants to talk about statehood. The census of 1830 had shown a population of only 32,000, but a new census four years later showed three times that number, which was more than sufficient for statehood. On the assumption that Congress would quickly grant statehood, a constitutional convention was called in 1835, which after arduous labors produced a document that was accepted by the voters. So assured did the inhabitants of Michigan feel of immediate statehood that they elected state officers and put them to work.

The admission of Michigan, however, was delayed by a boundary dispute with Ohio. The southern boundary of Michigan as stated in the Ordinance of 1787 was a line directly east from the tip of Lake Michigan. When Ohio had been admitted to the Union there had been some doubt as to where, if at all, such a line would strike Lake Erie. The matter did not at the moment seem very important, and merely as a precautionary measure the constitution of Ohio provided that if the line did not hit the western end of Lake Erie it could, with the consent of Congress, be changed to strike the most northerly cape of Maumee Bay.

The actual survey of the Michigan-Ohio boundary showed that the line did in fact miss the western end of Lake Erie. Moreover, the Toledo region was growing rapidly with the prospective building of the Wabash Canal. In consequence Ohio claimed the alternate line of its constitution, and Michigan promptly refused, positively and belligerently, to consider itself bound by a provision of the Ohio constitution. Both Ohio and Michigan rolled up their sleeves for a fight. Ohio raised troops and started them north toward the disputed area. Michigan likewise raised troops and sent them on what turned out to be a delightful junket while the legislature voted funds for "defense." Ohio surreptitiously held court in the disputed area, whereupon the Michigan patriots kidnapped some of the officials.

A potential civil war brought the intervention of President Jackson, although he was embarrassed by his desire to obtain the friendship of both sides in the coming presidential election. In this dilemma he followed good political practice by asking a truce, during which a federal commission would investigate the conflicting claims. The commission in time proposed a compromise that Michigan felt was dictated by the electoral votes of Ohio: Ohio was to receive the line it wanted, while in return Michigan was to receive the upper peninsula, which it did not in the least want. Presumably the only people who should have been dissatisfied were the few residents of the Wisconsin region; but their votes were insignificant, and by this time they should have been accustomed to losing territory to a neighboring state.

The proposed "compromise" was utterly unacceptable to Michigan and was rejected with considerable heat at a convention that met at Ann Arbor in September 1836. (Incidentally, the extralegal state government continued to operate during these troubled times.) After the delegates to the September convention returned to their homes, a small, unauthorized group of men anxious for statehood convened at Ann Arbor in December 1836 and voted to accept the compromise. Congress must have breathed a great sigh of relief when it heard of this latest vote, for immediately it turned a blind eye on the credentials of the members of the group and hastily admitted Michigan to the Union on January 26, 1837.

NORTHERN INDIANA AND ILLINOIS   Part of the settlers who had moved west by way of the Great Lakes ended their journey on the plains of northern Indiana and Illinois, where they merged with other streams of settlement from the south. The result was the appearance of thousands of new farms and of such cities as Galesburg, Springfield, and Chicago. The land rejected by early settlers as unfit for farming proved to be the most productive of the entire region.

Many of these new settlements came into existence on the relatively treeless prairies, and hence the pioneers faced a new set of problems that were later to become familiar beyond the Mississippi. Solutions were not found immediately, but at least the problems were recognized. The absence of trees eliminated the labor of girdling and chopping, but increased the difficulties of the first planting; at least four oxen were required to drag a plow through the tough prairie soil, at a cost of something like $2 an acre, or more than the usual cost of the land. The scarcity of trees also made it difficult to build houses and barns, fence the land, and find fuel. For the time being old frontier techniques were continued, but at a greatly increased cost because of the necessity of hauling wood long distances.

The wonder city of Illinois was Chicago, lying on Lake Michigan at the mouth of the Chicago River. The region had been fortified because it was on a trade route that ascended the Chicago River, portaged to the Illinois, and finally won through to the Mississippi. At the opening of the year 1830 the future Chicago consisted of one abandoned stockade, a handful of cabins, and large wastes of sand.

The Chicago boom started with the platting of the city in 1830 by the canal commissioners, and almost immediately the land speculators seized both rein and whip. Reports had it that although the town contained some 2000 inhabitants in 1834, it had

Chicago, 1816–1820. This barren scene hardly suggests the site of a future metropolis. But the availability of water transportation and the coming of the railroad led to development of the area. Chicago is a good example of a successful frontier town. (Granger)

surveyed building lots to provide for a population of 300,000 without crowding. Every male inhabitant bought and sold town lots, and eagerly transmitted the gossip of how someone else had made a profit of 20 to 30 percent within a few days or 100 percent or more within a few weeks. Every speculator could show amazing paper profits, and all the inns and stores were crowded with men just on the point of making their fortunes—at least until the pinprick of the panic of 1837.

Before the panic of 1837 Chicago had attracted some 6000 residents, with the customary variety of houses, stores, churches, taverns, banks, and newspapers, not to mention the considerable variety of industrial enterprises. Many people felt assured of the future greatness of Chicago, and, judging by the outcome, their prophetic vision was much better than that of many others who were equally certain of the future opulence of towns that never actually matured. Optimism was in the Chicago air, even though older and more important cities such as Cincinnati, St. Louis, and New Orleans as yet saw no reason for alarm.

WISCONSIN   North of Illinois, Wisconsin was receiving its first important settlements. Two areas had the preference. The first was the typical farming frontier stretching from Milwaukee west through Waukesha and north to Appleton. As was true in Michigan, a considerable number of the new residents came from New England and New York, but Wisconsin also received many foreign-born, particularly German, Swedish, Danish, and Norwegian. The northwestern Europeans were particularly enthusiastic over the new country, and their letters to their friends back home brought an ever-increasing flow of Scandinavians—first to Wisconsin and then to Minnesota and Dakota.

As on other frontiers, Wisconsin was a happy hunting ground for the land speculator. In most regions he was the first pioneer, occupying good agricultural land, millsites, and townsites. These early claims were generally respected without benefit of the law, and claim jumping was viewed askance even if done by a man who really wanted to farm. Later arrivals had to choose between paying for land already claimed, taking inferior land, or going to a more remote district.

The activities of the speculator were not considered bad as long as tremendous areas of the state were unoccupied. Men went west to improve their conditions, and any sign of farming or commercial activity was considered a hopeful portent for the future. Wisconsin wanted more people, and quantity was more immediately important than quality. It was the earliest state (1852) to give official encouragement to immigration, being followed by Iowa, Minnesota, Dakota, and other territories and states. Pamphlets were published in various languages, and an agent in New York tried to route the settlers to the region he represented. Unfortunately many of the migrants were badly swindled before they arrived at their new homes.

The metropolis of the infant Wisconsin was Milwaukee, which had its first speculative boom in the years 1835–1837. Quite appropriately its first newspaper (1836) was titled the *Advertiser*, and devoted its main efforts to attracting settlers. The Milwaukee of 1836 had fewer than 1000 inhabitants but great expectations. Houses were being built feverishly, living quarters were at a premium, wages and other prices were high, and speculation was rife. In other words, it was a typical frontier town.

The second important area of settlement in Wisconsin was the the lead district that straddled Illinois and Wisconsin, stretching roughly from Galena, Illinois, to Mineral Point, Wisconsin. The lead appeared near the surface and was comparatively pure; hence it could be extracted easily from pit mines and then smelted before being moved down the river to St. Louis and New Orleans. Desultory mining had existed for many years as far west as Dubuque, but the real development dated from the early 1820s. By 1826 there were an estimated 1600 miners in the region; during the following year there was a boom that was not equaled until the discovery of gold in California.

The lure of lead drew prospective miners mainly from the West and the South, but also attracted considerable numbers of Irish and French. Trial holes were dug all over the landscape, and rumors of new finds resulted in the overnight appearance of such mining camps as New Diggings, Hard Scrabble, Coon Branch, Fair Play, Platteville, Mineral Point, Dodgeville, and Blue Mounds. The miner first discovered a promising claim, then dug and smelted his own ore; he usually lived in a cave dug in the side of a hill. Now and then he attained wealth, but, as in most mining booms, the majority of searchers lived largely on hope. The mines lured farmers to the Rock River region and hence were responsible indirectly for the Black Hawk War, in which a good many miners fought.

The imminent admission of Michigan as a state led Congress to split off the western section as the territory of Wisconsin in 1836. It included not only the present state but all the land farther west between the Mississippi and the Missouri and from Canada to the northern border of Missouri, which had been a part of Michigan in the years 1834–1836. In 1838 Wisconsin was cut to its present limits except that it retained the region northwest of Lake Superior. The infant territory created in 1836 could boast some 22,000 inhabitants. The location of the territorial capital was a matter of bitter rivalry between Mineral Point and Milwaukee. A compromise produced the town of Madison in the wilderness of the Four Lakes region. Wisconsin attained statehood in 1848, and Minnesota became a territory the following year.

IOWA West of the Mississippi, settlement began to flow into the present Iowa during the 1830s. Earliest interest had been in the lead region near Dubuque, but with Indian land cessions after the Black Hawk War the way was opened for normal agricultural advance. Population first concentrated near the Mississippi, with the growth of such towns as Keokuk, Burlington, Davenport, and Dubuque. Quite properly the oldest of them, Dubuque, had the first newspaper—the *Du Buque Visitor* in 1836. The rapidly increasing flow of hopeful Hawkeyes resulted in the opening of local land officers at Dubuque and Burlington in 1838. The Iowa prairies presented no obstacle to the expansion of population, and Iowa City was founded as early as 1839.

Governmentally, Iowa had at first no independent existence, being only a small part of the vast region between the Mississippi and Missouri rivers and north of the state of Missouri. Its growth created problems because it was so remote from the center of administration at Madison; when the territory of Wisconsin was formed in 1836 it had 11,687 people east of the Mississippi and 10,564 west of the river. Under these circumstances the obvious solution was to create the territory of Iowa (1838), with Burlington as the temporary capital. Statehood was not to be long delayed (see Chapter 26).

KENTUCKY AND TENNESSEE   South of the Ohio River the slowing growth of Kentucky was almost as striking as the rapid expansion of the states to the north. Kentucky's diversified agriculture might have been expected to attract the same stream of settlers that appeared on the other side of the river, but several factors changed the outcome. Negro slavery deterred both northerners and foreign immigrants. The absence of public land brought a preference for the open spaces farther south. The very diversity of agriculture seemed unpromising to southerners interested in raising cotton. The consequence was that Kentucky grew slowly. Although in 1820 it was a close second to Ohio for the lead in western population, by 1840 Ohio had twice as many residents as Kentucky, and Indiana had almost come abreast of its southern neighbor.

Tennessee was quite different from Kentucky in that the fertile western part of the state remained open for settlement after 1820. The planters flooding into this section produced a great boom in Memphis, which was the first important town south of St. Louis. Memphis did a flourishing business as a shipping and distributing center. Farmers, traders, and migrating Indians crossed the river at this point. Cotton and other agricultural products were heaped high on Memphis docks. Planters, Indians, trappers, gamblers, and prostitutes rubbed elbows in the streets in typical western fashion.

THE LOWER SOUTH   Farther south the population of the new territory of Florida made little growth, the settled area being confined entirely to the northern parts of the territory. Neither oranges nor tourists were yet conceived as the basis of permanent prosperity. To most people Florida was a region of marshy land, scrubby trees, imposing wastes of sand, and hostile and dangerous Indians. Despite insufficient population Florida desired statehood, formulated a constitution, and applied for admission in 1838. The plea was refused.

The great bulk of southern migration moved into western Georgia, Alabama, Mississippi, and Louisiana. The older of these states, Georgia and Louisiana, almost doubled in the years 1820 to 1840, but the newer ones, Alabama and Mississippi, increased fivefold. The new settlements of the lower South attracted primarily planters moving their slaves to cultivate cotton, although Louisiana also had a very considerable sugar industry. A few of these migrants moved by water, either around the tip of Florida or by way of the Ohio and the Mississippi, but most of them started from Virginia or the Carolinas and moved overland through Georgia. Every night brought the twinkle of lights as the slaves prepared their evening meals over their campfires. Eastern planters who moved to the West frequently bought out the holdings of earlier frontiersmen who had cleared the land.

If current accounts may be believed, the southern frontier was even more boisterous and lawless than the northern. Indian troubles attracted the dissolute and vicious, who had splendid opportunity to seize Indian land and improvements as the natives were forced to move west. Furthermore, the fact that the towns were comparatively small, isolated, and badly policed made them splendid refuges for the lawless. Land speculators were as much in evidence as they were in the North.

Cotton culture in a region with navigable rivers that permitted shipping directly from the front doors of the plantations discouraged development of the hundreds of small, bustling communities so usual north of the Ohio. The larger commercial centers depended on water for their transportation. For the eastern part of the Deep South, Augusta and Savannah were both important outlets, since with existing forms of transportation Augusta's position on the river was but little inferior to that of Savannah. Farther to the west most of Alabama and a portion of Mississippi were tributary to the city of Mobile; the growing business of the rural regions was beginning to crowd the unpaved streets and wooden sidewalks of the Alabama metropolis. Mobile still con-

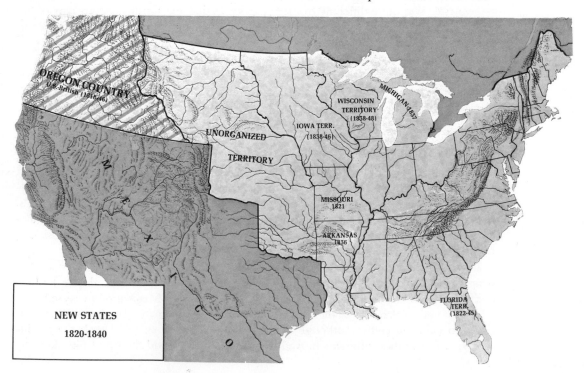

NEW STATES

1820-1840

tained French- and Spanish-speaking residents, but the dominant class was now Anglo-American.

Western Mississippi, Louisiana, and in fact the whole area bordering on the Mississippi looked to that river for transportation. Such cities as Vicksburg, Natchez, and Baton Rouge drew the business of their backcountries. Of these towns Natchez was the best, but not the most favorably, known because of its appeal to the more rowdy element of the river.

The dominant western city of the 1820s and 1830s was unquestionably New Orleans. Its location was such that it was expected to control the business of the two-thirds of the nation drained by the Mississippi and its tributaries, and few people doubted that New Orleans was destined to become and remain America's most important city. Its importance and prospects of growth attracted great numbers of people who aspired to wealth, and the population of New Orleans reached in the neighborhood of 100,000 by 1840.

Steamboats from the Mississippi and the Ohio lined New Orleans wharves, where they nudged oceangoing vessels from all over the world. As early as 1821 the city exported some $16 million of western produce in the year, while silks, French wines and brandies, British cutlery, rum, coffee, and other exotic imported products jammed its warehouses. Before the Civil War annual exports passed the $100 million mark despite the bad river channel, which inspired much moaning but no action. New York could well look to its laurels.

The most obvious drawbacks of New Orleans were its swampiness and its high morbidity, with the two of course related by more than the reputed necessity of weighting coffins to keep them underground. New Orleans suffered all the usual western ills, but in addition was a notorious center of yellow fever. The mosquito was considered a great nuisance, but was not connected in the popular mind with the disease. Every inhabitant who could find time and money went north during the "sickly season."

New Orleans continued to remain quite foreign in appearance, being somewhat Spanish, but more French. French architecture was in evidence, French was commonly spoken on the streets, a French theater operated successfully, and a magnificent Catholic cathedral served the Spanish and French. Across Canal Street was the American section of the town, slightly cleaner, and more bustling, with its own theater and hotels and stores. Some of the streets were paved with stone brought from the North as ship ballast. Most of the houses were constructed of wood, and some were covered with stucco.

New Orleans was famous for its gaiety, which visitors often identified with wickedness. Sailors gambled and brawled in the saloons, poolrooms, and gambling halls of the waterfront. Pickpockets jostled each other on the streets. In 1836, in a city of some 60,000 there were 543 licensed saloons, cabarets, and taverns, plus an unknown number of others not licensed. Brothels were numerous. The gaslights of the theaters glittered brightly; not only were the usual plays performed, but New Orleans was unusually cordial toward opera. The St. Charles Hotel, opened in 1837, was called the most imposing building west of the Appalachians. Balls (including masquerades) were held for every class of people, and some of them were quite rowdy. Music was received with enthusiasm, and some of the developments later gave direction to all American popular music.

Part of the city's reputation for sin came from its use of Sunday as a day for shopping, visiting, attending the theater, and giving parties. Northerners who arrived on business, and particularly conscience-ridden New Englanders, called these activities desecrations of the Sabbath, and were sure that they indicated general depravity. Northern visitors also expressed doubts of the virtue of Creole ladies, even though their evidence was extremely scanty. New Orleans women were noted for their dark, voluptuous charms; their soft, langorous drawls were enchanting to all but the most captious critics, who professed to detect a deplorable lack of animation. When feminine charms were combined with the peaceful and romantic beauty of a moonlit river, they erased even the unpleasantly monotonous music of the clouds of mosquitoes.

In addition to the Creole women New Orleans had many mulatto girls who seemed quite attractive to the white men. A whole section of the city was devoted to small houses inhabited by white men and mulatto (usually called quadroon) girls. The couples were prevented from marrying by both law and social custom. If the white man married one of his own race, the quadroon received the house and furniture. As for the white ladies, they met this delicate situation by ignoring it.

MISSOURI AND ARKANSAS   West of the Mississippi the great population center north of Louisiana was the state of Missouri, including the important city of St. Louis. The number of residents increased fourfold between 1820 and 1840 as settlers from both north and south of the Ohio River spread themselves over the greater part of the state, and as foreign immigrants began to arrive. German migrants were particularly numerous, even though they were frequently unhappy in a region that was aggressively proslavery. Older towns such as Cape Girardeau, Ste. Genevieve, Carondelet, and St. Charles retained considerable numbers of French Catholics, but the newer towns were entirely Anglo-American, and even the older towns were so overrun by English-speaking people that they began to lose their former ways of life.

The city of St. Louis dominated the Missouri area and much of the trans-Mississippi West, even though its population in 1840 was little over 16,000. Founded in 1764, it was old and well established in comparison with most cities of the newer West, and therefore looked with disdain on such young upstarts as Memphis, Milwaukee, and Chicago. Any St. Louis resident was completely confident that his hometown, situated near the confluence of the Mississippi and the Missouri, had command of the business of both those rivers, and that its control of the fur trade was a harbinger of a similar dominance of any business that developed in the upper Mississippi and Missouri valleys. Like other boom towns of the period, its wharves were jammed with steamboats, its stores crowded with purchasers, and its streets filled with the heterogenous population of the West.

Naturally the business section of St. Louis was close to the river, and this part of town was badly drained, filthy, and almost smothered by millions of flies. Some sections of the city showed evidence of French settlement, including an imposing cathedral, a Catholic college, and the Convent of the Sacred Heart. Other parts of the city were entirely American, with broader streets and many new buildings, including one of the finest theaters west of the Appalachians.

Lying between Missouri and Louisiana was the territory of Arkansas, which had been but sparsely populated upon its creation in 1819. In early territorial days Arkansas had extended as far west as the international boundary, but by 1818 it had been reduced to its present limits. The settlement of Arkansas proceeded slowly, in part because of the considerable swamps and mountains. As more easterly states were occupied, the overflow entered Arkansas, settling primarily along the Arkansas, White, Black, and Red Rivers, which was certainly a colorful collection. Development was hastened by the construction (1821–1833) of a military road between Memphis and Little Rock and by the removal in the early 1830s of the obstructions to navigation of the Arkansas River. The person responsible for the clearing of the Arkansas was Henry M. Shreve, a steamboat man even better known for his work in clearing the Mississippi.

Newly arrived Arkansans were not numerous but were vigorous in self-expression. A demand for statehood resulted in a convention at Little Rock in 1836; a constitution was formulated and an appeal for admission directed to Congress. Statehood came immediately, with Arkansas offsetting the northern state of Michigan. The population of Arkansas in 1840 was slightly under 100,000, but was spread so thinly that few areas could boast of as many as six inhabitants per square mile.

With the admission of Arkansas and Michigan, and the formation of the territories of Wisconsin and Iowa, the eastern half of the United States had almost assumed its present political form. East of the Mississippi only Florida and Wisconsin remained eligible for statehood. In the first tier of trans-Mississippi states, Iowa remained to be admitted, and Minnesota was still a matter for the future; otherwise, settlement had reached the latitude of the great bend of the Missouri.

READINGS   Paperbacks are marked with an asterisk.

North   See Buley, Havighurst, Holbrook, Wade, Esarey cited in Readings for Chapter 13. Madge E. Pickard and Roscoe C. Buley, *The Midwest Pioneer* (1946); Eugene H. Roseboom and Francis P. Weisenburger, *A History of Ohio* (1953); Francis P. Weisenburger, *The Passing of the Frontier 1825–1850* (1941), Ohio; William V. Pooley, *The Settlement of Illinois from 1830 to 1850* (1908); Rebecca Burlend, *A True Picture of Emigration* (1936), contemporary on Illinois; Bessie L. Pierce, *A History of Chicago* (3 vols., 1937–1957), scholarly; William Nowlin, *The Bark Covered House* (1937), contemporary on Michigan; Joseph Schafer, *Wisconsin Lead Region* (1932) and his *A History of Agriculture in Wisconsin* (1923); Bayrd Still, *Milwaukee* (1948), scholarly; David T. Nelson (ed.), *The Diary of Elizabeth Koren, 1853–1855* (1955); Ole M. Raeder, *America in the Forties* (1929), his letters; William J. Peterson, *Iowa* (1941); Irving Richman, *Ioway to*

Iowa (1931); Earle D. Ross, *Iowa Agriculture* (1951). Two good accounts of Norwegian immigration, largely in the Northwest, are Theodore C. Blegen, *Norwegian Migration to America, 1825–1860* (1931) and Carlton C. Qualey, *Norwegian Settlement in the United States* (1938).

South Francis G. Davenport, *Ante-Bellum Kentucky 1800–1860* (1943); Thomas P. Abernethy, *From Frontier to Plantation in Tennessee* (1932); Samuel C. Williams, *The Beginning of West Tennessee* (1930); Sidney W. Martin, *Florida During Territorial Days* (1944); Fayette Copeland, *Kendall of the Picayune* (1943), New Orleans; Harold Sinclair, *The Port of New Orleans* (1942); Henry A. Kmen, *Music in New Orleans: The Formative Years, 1791–1841* (1966), excellent; Lonnie J. White, *Politics on the Southwestern Frontier: Arkansas Territory, 1819–1836* (1964); John G. Fletcher, *Arkansas* (1947), mostly after the Civil War. See also Clark, Abernethy, Shoemaker cited in the Readings for Chapter 13.

Upper, A State Bank Note from Lecompton, Kansas, 1856. (Chase Manhattan Bank Museum of Moneys of the World) *Lower,* A Texas Bank Note. Another example of the varying kinds of paper money found on the frontier. (New York Historical Society)

Chapter 18 / THE MONEY PROBLEM

The West throughout its history was troubled by a lack of cash and credit. It was inevitably a debtor area. The migrant to the new lands of the frontier was not a rich man, and needed capital even for his original settlement. A horse and wagon had to be bought, provisions acquired, land and seeds and tools purchased, a house built, and the family supported until a first crop was harvested and sold. The usual frontiersman obtained as much funds as possible in the East. Possibly he had saved some money or had some property that he could sell, or relatives or friends who might advance needed capital; otherwise, particularly if he were young, he might work some years in the West and buy land before returning East to claim a bride or move his family. In any case obtaining funds was a personal matter, not involving commercial banking.

CREDIT BY MERCHANTS   After the migrant to the West occupied his new home, further financial requirements were satisfied largely by credit from local merchants. Surplus corn, tobacco, flax, honey, or cloth could be traded for tools or cloth, but also purchases could be made on credit. The result was that merchandising was a complicated and hazardous occupation, frequently involving travel to both New Orleans and the eastern coast to arrange sales, purchases, and credit. While many of his customers' products were sold in New Orleans, his stock came largely from the East; his hardware, for example, generally came from Pittsburgh. The lack of a two-way trade meant high freight rates, which often constituted a third of the final cost. Moreover, the merchant had the problem of selling a great variety of products, from copies of Thackeray to patent medicines such as Bateman's Drops. He frequently lacked ready money, and felt himself lucky if he was near an army post, where the soldiers were paid in cash. Currency was often lost in transit, and bills of exchange on the East were hard to obtain. Such difficulties of the western storekeepers measured their services to young and struggling communities. These merchants were an important source of western credit, even though their advances often came indirectly from eastern firms.

The obvious need of the westerner for credit did not imply that he was enthusiastic about banks and paper money; actually he seldom borrowed from a bank in the early days. The general attitude of the agrarian West before the Civil War was one of suspicion and hostility toward banks and paper money—an attitude which was to change in the late nineteenth century. The agrarians felt that banking produced speculation and instability; also they disliked large corporations, and of these, banks seemed the most objectionable. A number of states actually prohibited all banking for a time, particularly in the 1840s, or had all banking facilities limited to a state monopoly.

The pressure for banks and banking came largely from merchants and manufacturers who needed considerable amounts of credit. Also the states themselves desired banks to help finance their elaborate plans for public improvements, particularly transportation. When banks appeared farmers of course used their services; but the banks were reluctant to tie up any large part of their funds in farm loans, which were impossible to liquidate when economic conditions became bad.

EARLY BANKS   Organized commercial banking was unknown when the first frontiersmen crossed the Appalachians. Lending was in cash on a personal basis. But Americans soon learned that a promise to pay a designated person a sum of money might pass from hand to hand for a long time before being presented for redemption, and this knowledge opened the way to paper notes with relatively small cash backing; in consequence, several kinds of banks were established in the United States shortly following the Revolution. The first Bank of the United States (1791–1811) acted as fiscal agent of the federal government, doing private business as well. Local banks were incorporated by the states with unique individual charters; general and uniform banking laws did not become common until the 1850s. Finally, since there was no prohibitory legislation, private individuals and groups could engage in banking at their own discretion; sometimes such a private enterprise was so small that the entire bank could be moved from place to place in a trunk. The rapid growth of banking in the United States is evident from the fact that the 3 chartered banks of 1789 increased to 26 by 1800, and to 88 by 1811, in which year the charter of the first Bank of the United States expired.

WESTERN BANKS   The West as well as the East desired banks, but more to finance trade, business operations, and public improvements than to aid farming. Since there was considerable agrarian hostility to banking, many early banks took other names. For example the Lexington (Kentucky) Insurance Company (1802) did a banking business; the Miami Exporting Company (Cincinnati, 1803) was designed to finance New Orleans trade, but soon confined its business to commercial banking. Soon the word bank became common. The Bank of Michigan and the Bank of Kentucky started operations in 1806. The famous Nashville Bank opened its doors in 1807, and operated until the panic of 1819. Other small banks appeared throughout the West. Most of the organizations had short lives, but usually managed to circulate large quantities of paper money of varying value.

Restrictions on the transactions of early banks were few and comparatively ineffective. Chartered banks had various limiting provisions, but unchartered banks were left largely to their own devices. Some reliance could be placed on the honesty and good business sense of the owners of a bank, but this control was somewhat vitiated by the proprietors' lack of banking training and experience. A more effective and immediate check was exercised by the Bank of the United States, which felt some responsibility for banking conditions all over the country. This institution collected the paper money of banks that were rumored to be unstable, and then presented them for payment in cash in considerable amounts; the local bank then either gave convincing proof of its stability or was forced to admit its insolvency and close its doors. Even the threat of such action was sufficient to make many of the smaller banks follow a comparatively conservative policy.

The only real limitation upon irresponsible operations by the smaller banks disappeared when the first Bank of the United States was not rechartered, and conditions became still worse with the outbreak of the War of 1812. With the suspension of specie payments all over the country, the last vestige of control over the smaller banks disappeared. The field of banking was opened wide to all comers, with hundreds of men deciding that the easiest way to amass riches was to print their own money. As long as public confidence remained, any sort of paper money could be circulated, at least for a time.

Small banks under these conditions multiplied like rabbits. In 1811 there were only 88 state banks, but by 1816, the year of the chartering of the second Bank of the United States there were 246. Still the process continued and by 1820 there were 307 chartered banks in the United States, of which the West had certainly at least a reasonable share. In 1818 alone Kentucky authorized 40 banks with a total capitalization of $8 million, and other states were almost as generous. The country was deluged with paper money of varying trustworthiness. The recipient of paper money originating in his own area might have at least a general idea of whether the issuing bank was fairly sound, although he could be wrong. As the bank notes traveled farther and farther from home, the recipients had less faith in their credibility, with the result that usually they would be accepted only at a discount, and sometimes not at all: many people were suspicious and even hostile toward any paper money.

As might have been expected, many of the new banks were badly managed by their amateur owners. Usually a company was organized on the basis of a small cash subscription, with paper money supplying the deficit of metallic currency, or working capital raised by loans on the company's crisp, new stock. Metallic currency was a rarity and was kept mostly for purposes of display. Paper money was backed by little or no specie reserve. Most of the bank's loans were "frozen assets," that is, long-term loans that could not be collected in case of sudden need. Businessmen wanted long-term loans for plant and equipment. Government wanted long-term money for public improvements. Farmers were in a similar position.

The situation of the farmer was of increasing importance. Early farmers frequently disliked banks, and had relatively little need for loans, while the banks were very doubtful about tying up their assets in farm loans. But conditions changed as farmland became more expensive, and improved stock more important; the farmers looked increasingly toward the banks. The farmer needed money for at least a year at a time, and often much longer, so the rural bank had little option but to tie up its money in fairly permanent form. Even worse, the security for the loan was often inadequate. Sometimes the banker took the farmer's own optimistic concept of the value of his property, but even with an intelligent valuation, trouble still remained. Land tended to become practically worthless with economic depression and falling prices. When the farmer could not pay interest on his loan, the bank could of course foreclose; but then it was left paying taxes on land that was not worth the amount of the mortgage, while the borrower and his friends became extremely and bitterly hostile. The bank's only real choice was to continue the loan indefinitely, with slight prospect that payment would ever be made, and the excellent chance that the bank would go bankrupt in the meantime.

The evils inherent in western banking practices were worsened by considerable fraud. The "saddlebag bank" was notorious. A man would ride his horse into a small town with his saddlebags crammed with beautiful crisp new banknotes, based more on hope than on specie. Then he would set up an office and lend his paper money to all the neighboring farmers on easy terms and with but little security. After collecting all possible promissory notes, he disposed of them to the store owner or the innkeeper at a discount for cash and decamped with the proceeds. The local noteholder was thus left with the job of placating the irate farmers when they discovered that their attractive new bank notes were practically worthless. Another common fraud was counterfeiting. All bank notes were poorly printed and easily copied, thus offering great temptations to the dexterous man who possessed a printing press. The number of notes that were counterfeited became so large that anyone handling large sums of money bought a frequently revised "counterfeit detector," which described the most common frauds.

THE SECOND NATIONAL BANK OF THE UNITED STATES

Conditions were so bad that well-informed people were sure of the need for a federal bank; the result was the second Bank of the United States, chartered in 1816 for twenty years. The West had no great enthusiasm for this new federal agency, which exercised pressure leading to the closing of some of the less sound western institutions; holders of the notes of these defunct organizations were hardly pleased with the increase of sound banking. Furthermore the influence of the central bank was to decrease both the paper money issues and loans of the weaker banks; westerners resented these limitations, even though their big pressure for cheap money did not come until after the Civil War.

The obvious villain in the contraction of credit was the second Bank of the United States. Efforts to decrease the power of the federal agency included attempts to tax branches of the Bank out of existence. The western states of Ohio, Kentucky, and Tennessee were among those who acted, but they were stopped by a decision of the Supreme Court in 1819. Later that year occurred a general financial crash and the West looked for a simple explanation and a scapegoat. The answer was easy; conditions became bad only after the charter of the Bank, and hence it was to blame. The debtor part of the West was very bitter; Kentucky tried to relieve the situation by passing stay laws to prevent the collection of debts by the banks, but after a bitter political struggle the state courts declared the laws unconstitutional.

Returning prosperity reached its highest point during the middle 1830s, with prices rising sharply. New communities were established, property values increased, trade expanded, and western optimism revived. Along with the general expansion went an increase in the number of banks and in the paper money in circulation, which had declined between 1820 and 1830, and now rose between 1830 and 1837. Prices rose, and westerners were pleased. The enhanced value of the products they sold more than offset the increased cost of their purchases, while as debtors the "real value" of their debts in terms of things they sold declined with rising prices.

Growing prosperity enhanced the natural optimism of the West. Everyone bought all the land he could, and there was immense speculation in farms, townsites, city lots, and water sites. Much of this expansion was based on long-term loans, but no one worried. Times were good and would be better. A small investment today would return a fortune tomorrow. No speculation was too wild to be uninviting.

Individuals transmitted their enthusiasm to their respective states, and each state launched an immense program of public improvements. Canals were dug, rivers dredged, railroads constructed, harbors marked, and roads built; the future was to be glorious. The South was a trifle less involved than the North, but more from a lack of credit than a lack of desire. Nearly all public works were constructed (as in the East) on borrowed capital, with each state issuing its bonds to be sold at a discount in the East or in Europe, once again showing its confidence in the future by bonding itself far beyond its apparent capacity to pay.

JACKSON AND THE BANK   The only important brake on western banking optimism was the pressure of the second Bank of the United States, which held notes of country banks and forced these issuing institutions at least to approach solvency. The older and more developed portions of the West, as represented by Henry Clay, approved this concession to sound banking, but much of the younger West felt otherwise. Many hopeful farmers and businessmen wanted an expansion of credit, and resented the depressing effect of the Bank of the United States.

The man who dramatized western hostility to the Bank was Andrew Jackson. Emotionally he was antagonistic to all banks, for he remembered vividly the panic of 1819. At the same time he was no lover of paper money, much preferring specie. In addition he had specific grievances against the Bank—particularly that it refused to make appointments he desired—although the charge that the Bank was using its power to oppose Jackson politically was not justified until the fight was in full swing. Part of Jackson's support came from rising eastern businessmen, particularly from New York, who were anxious to decrease the financial power centering in Philadelphia.

Four years before the expiration of the Bank's charter Jackson made it known that he was implacably opposed to renewal. As a result the issue became political, with Clay and the Whigs supporting the Bank and Jackson and the Democrats opposing it. A recharter bill was passed by Congress in 1832 and immediately vetoed by Jackson in a vigorous message; whereupon the rechartering of the Bank became one of the most hotly contested points in the election of that year. Jackson won the election and interpreted the victory as a vindication of his policy in respect to the Bank. In 1833 he followed his victory by removing the governmental deposits from the national bank— even though he had to change secretaries of the treasury twice to do it—and placing them in "pet banks" in various parts of the country. This removal curtailed the power and usefulness of the national bank, which declined to insignificance by the time its charter expired in 1836. Jackson had "slain the octopus," and the American people were "free."

STATE BANKING   The opposition of Jackson and the West to the second Bank of the United States did not necessarily mean that they were opposed to all large banks or even to government banking. They hated this particular institution because it performed functions they did not like. Considerable feeling existed that the development of a proper system of credit was a legitimate government function, and several of the western states themselves engaged in banking ventures before, during, and after the 1830s. The results were partly good and partly bad, but at least the ventures showed that the West was not opposed to government banking.

State-owned and -operated banks were established mainly in the Northwest. Indiana was unlucky in establishing its first bank in 1819, the year of the depression, and it had a short life. Another state bank chartered in 1834 was quite successful, weathering the depression of 1837 to attain banking leadership of the state. A third bank was established later. Illinois also planned three banks, but with very sad results. The first was chartered in 1819, but not even organized. The second, incorporated in 1821, was run so badly that it lost half a million dollars in state funds before its charter expired a decade later. The third was chartered in 1835, but its early growth was stunted by the panic of 1837, which brought insolvency; it passed away in a long death agony during the 1840s. Missouri chartered a bank in the depression year of 1837 and gave it a monopoly position; the bank weathered its early difficulties successfully and was sound and prosperous during the 1840s and 1850s.

The southern states tended to subsidize private banking rather than to establish state banks. Louisiana, Florida, and Arkansas—all furnished such aid during the 1820s and 1830s. The usual plan was for the state to subscribe to the capital stock of one or more private banks, although sometimes it made further guarantees of other bank securities. The state subscriptions were financed by state bonds, which were sold mainly in the East or in Europe.

Western state banks were on the whole successful as compared with the many contemporary private enterprises that were notoriously badly managed and frequently insolvent. This success was particularly noteworthy in view of the strong political pressure to make state banks more lenient in their lending policies and thus to speculate on the future of the country. The use of state credit to furnish capital for private banks was not nearly so fortunate: the banks thus aided seemed to spend more time in trying to cheat the state than in doing regular banking business, and the inevitable results were poor banks and enormous state debts. In general this period of state banks and state aid, and of specially chartered private corportions, came to an end about mid-century, when general state laws provided for uniform incorporation and at least a minimum of regulation.

Even though state banks were reasonably conservative, they were few in number and therefore slight in influence. Other banks were less careful, especially when the restraining influence of the second Bank of the United States decreased. Less control plus the demands created by a rampaging prosperity brought new banks into existence daily, and each one issued large quantities of paper currency. Everyone had more money than he had ever had before. Prices rose steadily. By 1839 the West had spent on internal improvements possibly $50 million, of which the greater part had been borrowed from the East or from Europe.

FEDERAL FINANCES   The wave of prosperity brought the federal government more money than it had ever before collected. Land sales reached the staggering total of $25 million in 1836, exceeding even the substantial receipts of the compromise tariff of 1833. For one time in its history the federal government had more money than it well knew how to spend.

The flow of money into the treasury of the United States was so large in the 1830s that Congress became embarrassed. Legislative ingenuity in spending failed to keep pace with the flow of funds into the treasury, with the result that the legislature became worried. Some suggested that the surplus be spent for internal improvements, others talked of lowering the tariff or the price of land, while still others proposed giving the unused funds to the states. Each legislator had his pet scheme for disposing of the extraordinary receipts.

The result of congressional cogitations was the Distribution Bill of 1836, which provided that the secretary of the treasury take the balance that he had on hand (excluding a reserve of $5 million) and divide it among the states according to population. Payments were to be made in four quarterly installments. In theory these payments were loans, and were technically called "deposits," but in practice no one expected that the federal government would ever ask their repayment. They have in fact never been returned.

With the passage of the Distribution Bill the secretary of the treasury immediately notified the "pet banks" to turn over to the government funds they had on deposit to make the payments to the states. Then the trouble began. Most of the banks had lent all their available cash and when they tried to recall these loans, a cry of distress went up all over the country. Many debtors were forced into bankruptcy and the whole credit structure of the country showed signs of strain. The banks managed to meet the first and second payments in January and April 1837, but by that time they were in serious difficulties and on May 10 they stopped specie payments. This precautionary measure enabled them to meet the third installment on July 1, but the fourth was never paid.

The financial difficulties of 1837 were increased by an earlier maneuver by Jackson. He had always had an emotional preference for hard money rather than the paper variety, and had disliked the payment for large speculative land purchases with paper money borrowed from the banks. He tried unsuccessfully to persuade Congress to prohibit the practice, and ultimately (July 11, 1836) issued his famous "specie circular," an executive decree requiring that all payments for public lands be in gold or silver coin, with some possible exceptions for actual settlers. This order produced an immediate rush by land purchasers on the banks for specie. As this money was paid to the government for land, it was shipped east to the treasury, thus depleting the specie of the West and disorganizing the currency of the country. Land purchases fell drastically, since borrowed paper could no longer be used. Even more serious results became evident when the banks attempted to find money to carry out the terms of the Distribution Bill.

PANIC OF 1837 The financial difficulties of the country came to a climax with the suspension of specie payment in May 1837. The unsteady pyramid of currency and credit had long needed only a slight touch to cause it to tumble, and now that touch had come. Suspension by the banks brought a temporary eclipse of the earlier optimism about the country's future, and people became suspicious, economical, and conservative. Few bank notes remained at par, and many of them were refused under any circumstances. The banks became cautious, calling their notes as they became due, and refusing to make new ones. The resulting contraction of credit was a severe blow to all debtors, and western farmers were particularly hard hit; many of them could not pay their debts, and in consequence lost the products of years of labor through foreclosure. Moreover, the westerners were also adversely affected by a contraction of credit by the business houses with whom they dealt. Merchants tried to settle outstanding accounts and were reluctant to establish new ones. This was a bitter blow to the western farmer, who had long been accusomed to living largely on credit.

The results of the depression of 1837 were visible not only in the affairs of the banker, merchant, and farmer, but also in the business of government; the revenue of both federal and state governments declined as land sales fell to a minimum and the prices of all taxable property went down. With the exception of immediately necessary work, construction on public improvements came to an end; partially completed canals and roads were deserted, and machinery was allowed to rust beside the abandoned work. Most of the states had issued large amounts of bonds based mainly on overoptimism, and now found themselves hopelessly in debt. Often they had little to show for their large expenditures, and found difficulty even in raising the money necessary to pay the interest on the bonds. Taxes were hard to collect, since most people were in debt, and property values had gone down. In this extremity some of the states avoided their immediate financial troubles by exercising their sovereignty in stopping payments on their bonds.

One of the most easily visible effects of the panic of 1837 was the widespread unemployment that developed, particularly in the East, during the late 1830s and early 1840s. The closing of factories and the cessation of work on public improvements meant loss of jobs to many. The number of unemployed was swelled by the addition of the clerical employees of businesses that had found retrenchment necessary, by jobless farm laborers, and by farm owners who had lost their farms. The contrast with the prosperity of the early 1830s was startling, and the future looked black.

Rather surprisingly the panic of 1837 was at first not very severe in the West, and after the first necessary readjustment there came a period of improvement in which it seemed as though the West would weather the storm. This return of optimism proved premature, for a second collapse, coming in 1839, pushed the West into the depths of financial confusion. Prosperity did not return until well into the 1840s.

The panic of 1837 was but one of a long series of similar cataclysms that swept over the United States at fairly evenly spaced periods. Among them, the panics of 1819, 1837, 1857, 1873, and 1893 were the most important of the nineteenth century. Each panic was preceded by a crescendo of prosperity, enthusiasm, and optimism, to which the West contributed at least its proper share, and which found expression in public and private construction, rising land values, improvements in transportation, full employment, and large profits. Ultimately the prosperity bubble was pricked, with the prick frequently coming from abroad, since most periods of depression were worldwide. Then came a period of gradual recovery, leading to another boom and another recession. The tendency to feel that these people caused their own troubles and should have known better should be modified by the realization that the much greater social controls developed in the succeeding years still did not prevent men from alternating between optimism and pessimism.

READINGS   *Paperbacks are marked with an asterisk.*

National   The classic account of the national bank is Ralph C. H. Catterall, *The Second Bank of the United States* (1903); but see also Bray Hammond, *Banks and Politics in America from the Revolution to the Civil War* (1957). Every biography of Jackson covers the bank troubles; probably to be preferred is *Marquis James, *Andrew Jackson* (1937).

Western   Special, detailed studies include John R. Cable, *The Bank of the State of Missouri* (1923); George W. Dowrie, *The Development of Banking in Illinois, 1817–1863* (1913); Logan Esarey, *State Banking in Indiana, 1814–1873* (1912); Stanley J. Folmsbee, *Sectionalism and Internal Improvements in Tennessee, 1796–1845* (1939); James M. Primm, *Economic Policy* (1954), Missouri. An interesting account of retail trade is Thomas D. Clark, *Pills, Petticoats and Plows: The Southern Country Store* (1944).

Elementary Education. Corporal punishment was a part of the earlier education process. The victim's colleagues have varying reactions to the imminent administration of justice. (Granger)

Chapter 19/CULTURAL ADVANCE

The West of the 1820s and 1830s included both frontier communities struggling to conquer a wilderness and older towns that considered themselves rising cultural centers. Population ranged from illiterate criminal fugitives to a leisured few who read the latest European periodicals and wrote poetry Cities of the Ohio Valley boasted daily newspapers, theaters presenting outstanding stage stars, and authors of more than local repute, while more remote settlements were composed almost exclusively of hardworking farmers who thought themselves lucky to keep their families from starvation.

The general cultural level of the West was low, even allowing for the well educated and well informed. Large numbers of people were illiterate, with no other thought than making their fortunes. Speech was crude and actions direct. Jokes were coarse and amusements rough. The frequently seen pistol-carrying, swearing, tobacco-chewing, whiskey-drinking westerner cared little for the polite usages of eastern society. Many easterners and a few westerners feared that this reversion to the primitive would in time contaminate the entire nation.

RELIGION   Westerners were accused of irreligion because they frequently did not belong to or attend a church, or observe the Sabbath. Religious-minded easterners, and particularly New Englanders, were sure that the West was on the road to perdition and might well carry the East with it. One minister quite typically reported that the people of Green Bay in 1836 "seemed to be agreed in only one thing and that was to blaspheme God and indulge in all kinds of wickedness." Irreligion, according to the godly, led inevitably to improper speech and action, immorality, the degradation of women and the family, the failure of democratic institutions, and the collapse of patriotism. No descendants of Puritans could view these possibilities without serious concern.

Many Protestants also felt that a lack of religion was no worse, and possibly less bad, than the rapidly growing Catholic Church. New Catholic clergy were arriving, and Catholic schools and churches were being opened. European missionary societies were pouring money into the American West. Irish and German Catholics were flooding into the Mississippi Valley. Many Protestants were filled with foreboding and saw deep-laid plots to undermine American democracy.

In spite of Protestant fears, the Catholics actually faced serious difficulties. The flood of Catholic arrivals had little hope for help from a predominantly Protestant America, and suffered from a lack of funds. A typical priest wrote that his little church "can scarce accommodate all who come to worship," and that he found difficulty in raising funds for a larger church. Moreover, the Protestant minister might hold such a lay job as farming, but the Catholic priest had no such option.

The western irreligion that so alarmed the East was in part more apparent than real. The West may have attracted the irreligious and shown a lack of attention to the church, but in fact the appearance of disinterest was probably in the main the result of sparse population, poverty, and a diversity of sects. Even a basically religious westerner, struggling to attain wealth, parted reluctantly with the dollars necessary to build a church and pay a minister.

MISSIONARY WORK The obvious way of reclaiming the West was through home missionary work by pious Easterners; although extensive work was also undertaken by such groups as the American Education Society (1815), American Bible Society (1816), Sunday School Union (1825), and American Tract Society (1826). The most important home missionary group was the American Home Missionary Society (1826), in which Congregationalists and Presbyterians cooperated. Other sectarian groups included Presbyterian, Baptist, Methodist, and Episcopalian. These organizations combined and directed earlier state and local societies, which were now affiliated, although in some cases they continued their own independent work.

The new societies increasingly used their funds to provide settled pastors for regularly organized churches rather than to send missionaries on western tours. For example, the American Home Missionary Society encouraged appeals by western churches and then normally granted an applicant church $100 a year, which was presumed to be a quarter of the salary of a minister; in time the church was expected to assume the entire salary. Each society sent agents to encourage mission interests and collect funds, and to visit the aided churches to give advice and assistance. By 1835 the American Home Missionary Society had a budget of some $100,000 that went to over 700 representatives. Hundreds of churches were thereby brought into existence, or their continuance made possible. Various mission groups such as the "Illinois band," the "Iowa band," and the "Kansas band" helped the church to follow the population frontier rather closely; all these groups happened to have come from Andover Theological Seminary.

The home missionary movement was not without its opponents in the West. A certain number of westerners resented being considered a mission field. Some of the western clergy were also dissatisfied. The Baptists engaged in a bitter internal war on the subject during the 1820s, with ministers holding that the doctrine of predestination made a mission movement silly if not outright impious. Eastern replies suggested that the real opposition was based on the fears of badly educated western ministers that they would be overshadowed by better-trained easterners.

A lack of qualified western ministers reflected the absence of proper educational institutions, and to rectify this situation the church founded many western schools and colleges. Funds were raised in the East for western schools that would educate poor boys for the ministry. Best known was the American Society for Educating Pious Youth for the Gospel Ministry (1815) organized by the Congregationalists and Presbyterians, and becoming later the Education Society. A Ladies' Society for the Promotion of Education in the West (Congregational) took form in 1846, largely through the efforts of Catharine Beecher, to help western education but also to assist energetic unmarried girls to migrate to the West.

ELEMENTARY EDUCATION Westerners approved education in theory, but their main interest was in the elementary level. The elementary school generally remained private, with parents paying possibly a dollar or two a year for each of their children; the usual session was 13 weeks of 6 eight-hour days. Presiding over the ordinary ungraded one-room school was a man whose lack of training limited him to the most elementary subjects. Among the many shortages of the western school were proper textbooks, the children using a miscellaneous collection that had belonged to their parents. Most popular were Noah Webster's speller, Jedidiah Morse's geography, and Lindley Murray's grammar, all originating before 1800. The famous McGuffey readers were first published at Cincinnati in the late 1830s, and in the last half of the nineteenth century were used by most children.

The proportion of children attending school was low. It was estimated that in 1840 only one-eleventh of the western population of school age was in school, while the eastern proportion was one-sixth. In 1829 it was reported that of 2114 children of school age in Bullitt County, Kentucky, only 160 were in school; in the same year it was said that sixty families in the county had no member who could either read or write. Educational facilities were in general greater north than south of the Ohio, but were deplorable in both areas.

Interest in education grew rapidly in the West during the 1820s, with particular emphasis on providing free (not compulsory) public education to all those who might wish it. By 1830 a few cities such as Cincinnati, Louisville, Lexington, and Detroit boasted public schools, although of course insufficient to take care of the total population of school age. Public schools increased rapidly so that by 1840 Ohio, Illinois, and Michigan had at least the beginnings of state systems of education. By 1837 Cincinnati proclaimed proudly that it had ten public schools attended by 3300 of the 5500 children between six and sixteen. The average cost per child per year was $8, which was considered almost an extravagant amount.

Elementary education received impetus from the increase of professional-minded teachers. These men and women considered teaching to be a profession comparable to that of law or medicine, and not a stopgap until more profitable work could be found. They organized the Western Literary Institute and College of Professional Teachers in 1831, published the proceedings of the society, and founded an educational periodical, the *Common School Advocate*. Educational problems were discussed, new methods were given publicity, and increased educational facilities were urged. At no time during the period, however, were western teachers specially trained for their profession; the first normal school of the United States was opened in Massachusetts in 1839.

SECONDARY AND COLLEGE EDUCATION   Possibly 400 secondary schools, generally called academies, existed beyond the mountains in 1840. Almost all of them were private; for although the public high school movement developed in the East during the 1820s and 1830s, it reached the West slightly later. The usual secondary school either trained boys for college or "finished" the girls; none was coeducational. Entering students were frequently as young as ten or twelve and never had more than a common school education in the elementary subjects. Although the academies devoted much time to the classics, their graduates had little more than the equivalent of what the modern secondary school offers in the first two years.

The peak of the educational system was the college or university; here Transylvania University at Lexington, Kentucky, reigned as the most influential school in the West. Transylvania was founded as a seminary in 1783, and although it nominally became a college before 1800, it was really little more than an academy until Horace Holley became president in 1818. Under his guidance Transylvania became the outstanding college of the West, with a faculty including many well-known men. By the 1830s the medical department had come to overshadow the rest of the university.

Other colleges came into existence to challenge the leadership of Transylvania in the generation after 1815. The Presbyterians were particularly active, and in fact they controlled Transylvania until 1823, when they withdrew to found Centre. Presbyterian-founded colleges included the University of Pittsburgh, Indiana College (later the University), Muskingum, Wabash, Knox, and Ripon. In conjunction with the Congregationalists the Presbyterians were responsible for such institutions as Western Reserve, Beloit, and Illinois College. Other denominations did their part. The Baptists founded Shurtleff; the Episcopalians, Kenyon; the Catholics, St. Louis University; the Methodists, Augusta, Allegheny, McKendree, Lawrence, and Indiana Asbury (later De Pauw), and also took over Transylvania in 1841. State universities such as Missouri and Michigan were opened. Of considerable importance was Miami University (Oxford, Ohio), opened in 1824 under the presidency of R. H. Bishop, a former member of the Transylvania faculty; William Holmes McGuffey, author of the famous readers, was at one time on the Miami faculty.

Western colleges were generally small and poor, with one or two buildings for both classrooms and dormitories, two or three professors, and a handful of students. A considerable number of students actually did preparatory instead of college work. The instruction was generally poor, although a few good men drifted west from the better eastern institutions, notably Yale and Princeton. The rank of professor carried little social prestige, and its possessors were mostly recruited from the ministry; most men preferred farming or some other "useful" occupation to any form of teaching.

In addition to the regular colleges there were several western professional schools by 1840. Among half a dozen medical schools were the medical department of Transylvania, Louisville Medical College, and the Medical College of Ohio at Cincinnati. Three law schools presented the principles of Blackstone and Coke, and again Transylvania had the largest enrollment. Ten theological schools prepared candidates for the ministry; seven of these were Presbyterian, two were Baptist, and one was Episcopalian. Largest was Lane Theological Seminary (Presbyterian) at Cincinnati, of which Lyman Beecher became president in 1832. A secession from Lane on the slavery issue led to the establishment of Oberlin, near Cleveland, which soon became practically as large as its unwilling parent. Oberlin was particularly notable as being the first college to admit women as candidates for degrees.

BOOKS AND LIBRARIES   Educational progress in the West was continually hampered by the lack of cheap and easily accessible books. The publishing business of the West was of slow growth because of the difficulty and expense of obtaining necessary materials, and because the sparseness of western population made sales comparatively small. Prior to 1820 the publishing center of the West was Lexington, but most western books were actually printed in the East; after 1820 Cincinnati became the dominant literary center.

A lack of books meant a lack of libraries, both public and private. Here and there were libraries for the use of subscribers, but not open to the general public. Among the oldest of such libraries was one at Lexington, which was opened before 1800 and contained approximately 4000 volumes by the 1830s. Similar libraries in Cincinnati, Louisville, and other western cities could not boast as many books; anything over 1000 volumes was considered a noteworthy collection. Most of the colleges had libraries of their own, but they were small, consisted largely of textbooks, and were seldom used; the most impressive in 1840 was that of Lane Theological Seminary, which contained 10,000 volumes, and was the largest in the West.

OTHER TYPES OF EDUCATION   A less formal educational feature of the West during the 1820s and later was the lyceum. The lyceum was an association whose members were interested in the discussion of what they considered important problems, and had as its principal activity the presentation of a series of lectures during the winter. The subjects for discussion might vary from the abolition of capital punishment to the occupation of the Oregon country. Of much interest was phrenology, particularly because of its advocacy by Charles Caldwell, a member of the medical faculty of Transylvania; through his teachings Henry Ward Beecher and others were converted to this new medical "science."

First-rate work in the sciences was by no means unknown in the Ohio Valley of the 1820s and 1830s. William McClure and Robert Dale Owen did able work in geology; McClure has been called the father of American geology. The American-born Thomas Say was best known in entomology. John James Audubon published his epochal *Birds of America* in 1826, bringing him fame and fortune. Quite unique was C. S. Rafinesque, Transylvania professor, who did creditable work in practically every science, with sorties into the arts and social sciences. Some quarter of a century before Darwin he wrote (1833): "There is a tendency to deviations and mutations through plants and animals by gradual steps at remote irregular periods. This is part of the great universal law of perpetual mobility in everything."

History aroused much interest. John Filson wrote a narrative of Kentucky, although it was not well written. The ethnologist Henry Schoolcraft studied and wrote about Indian culture. A general interest in local history was demonstrated by the founding of such societies as the Vincennes Historical and Antiquarian Society (1808), the Antiquarian and Historical Society of Illinois (1827), the Historical Society of Michigan (1828), the

Historical Society of Indiana (1830), the Historical and Philosophical Society of Ohio (1831), and the Kentucky Historical Society (1838).

A discussion of religion always drew an interested crowd. Of particular note were the debates of Alexander Campbell, founder of the Disciples of Christ, and particularly his meeting in Cincinnati in 1829 with Robert Owen, who was visiting the United States to further his utopian experiment at New Harmony, Indiana, and held all religions to be bad and contrary to human nature. The Owen-Campbell debate continued hour after hour, day after day, with theoretical arguments that were often irrelevant, but the audience remained solemnly attentive. More exciting were the Lyman Beecher diatribes against popery. The West also listened to the feministic radicalism of "Fanny" Wright, who was then involved in an experimental Negro community at Nashoba, Tennessee. Westerners disapproved of Miss Wright's beliefs, but paid her respectful attention.

The lyceum and the lecture had an important rival in the museum, where for a small fee one could see Indian relics, old coins, collections of animals and plants, mummies, clothes and utensils from the Far East, and wax figures, as of great criminals committing their crimes. Particularly notable was Dorfeuille's museum in Cincinnati, where on the top floor was a "pandaemonium of hell," in which were dwarfs that grew into giants, imps of ebony with eyes of flame, large reptiles devouring youth and beauty; the surrounding railing, connected with one of the new electric machines, gave a shock to anyone who leaned on it. Most visitors satisfied their consciences that this exhibit was educational and told a good moral lesson.

The museum was closely allied to various types of traveling exhibitions. Minstrel shows were coming into favor, and a few of them toured the West. Traveling menageries attracted the curious, particularly when they were supplemented by the gyrations of acrobats. Automatons, of which the automatic chess player was best known, were viewed with great interest. Balloon ascensions were high in popular favor. The greatest American showman, Phineas T. Barnum, was beginning his career by tours through the West. All such amusements, however, were periodic in nature and enjoyed by comparatively few citizens.

MUSIC AND OTHER FINE ARTS The music of this new and growing West was usually primitive; the common instruments were the flute and the fiddle, with the latter much more popular. The fiddle (it attained the aristocratic name of violin later) was essential to all dances; the musician, almost always self-taught, frequently made his own instrument. Any attempt to cultivate good instrumental music was rare, although as early as 1807 a group of young men in Pittsburgh organized an Apollonian Society, and gave renditions of compositions by Haydn, Pleyel, Mozart, and Handel.

Vocal music was used largely as amusement for social groups. Few people could read music, and so most songbooks were printed with only the words and the names of the tunes, or with "patent notes" that showed their pitch by their shapes. Singing classes were popular, particularly with young men and women. Any one with even the vaguest knowledge of music would act as teacher, give the pitch, and sing the tune, after which the others would repeat the song. Singing in the churches was by the unaccompanied congregation. An organ would have been considered sacrilegious, even had there been funds to pay for one.

If western music was in its infancy, the other fine arts were newborn. A few westerners with artistic leanings, such as S. N. Clevenger and Hiram Powers, did a little sculpturing, but they were self-taught and their work was crude. It was Hiram Powers who made the figures for the representation of hell in Dorfeuille's museum, and this work proved so arresting that a patron of the arts subsidized him to study in Europe. Eventually he produced some fairly good work, but his best-known figure, the *Slave Girl*, probably attracted more attention for its nudity than for its artistry.

Architecturally the best building was the despised and derivative log cabin, which

The Jolly Flatboatmen in Port, by George C. Bingham. Inland water transportation was exceedingly important to American commercial life in the early part of the nineteenth century. (City Art Museum of St. Louis)

adapted western materials to western needs; certainly it was better than an octagonal house of fifty-seven rooms or an experimental concrete house, both of which appeared in Wisconsin during the 1840s. Homes and public buildings with pretensions toward style copied eastern forms, and the East was in the throes of a Greek temple craze. Most distinctive and challenging was Mrs. Trollope's bazaar at Cincinnati, which was described by an eyewitness as "Graeco-Moresco-Gothic-Chinese." Luckily for the viewer it was early covered by whitewash.

Painting had a slightly better reception than architecture or sculpture. A few artists, such as Charles Leuseur and Karl Bodmer, visited the West or moved to it, painted western scenes, and taught some appreciation of pictorial art. George Catlin, who came from the East, did hundreds of Indian portraits. Now and then a foreign artist would settle in a western city and give lessons in art; but although the West entertained him hospitably, it could not waste much time in viewing or acquiring this effeminate talent. The most that the average westerner would concede for painting was that a talented daughter of a well-to-do family might do worse than paint pictures on velvet.

A few westerners braved the absence of popular appreciation of art by teaching themselves the rudiments of painting, and then trying to exist on the dollar a head that farmers were willing to pay for pictures of their wives. Some evidence of an increasing interest in art came with the founding of the Academy of Fine Arts in the frontier town of Chicago in the late 1830s. However, for the West the business of making a living left little time for nonessentials. The few picture galleries were nearly all in the museums, and were sorry collections of paintings.

The West furnished a fair market for cheap portraits because of the unavailability of the camera. A landscape would now and then find a purchaser. Quite popular was the panorama, which at its most impressive might be a picture of the entire Mississippi, painted on three-quarters of a mile of canvas that could be rolled past the patrons. There was no western demand for still-life pictures, and portraits of nudes were banned by all polite society as fit only for barrooms.

Most important of western painters of the period was the Missouri artist George Caleb Bingham. Largely self-taught, he succeeded in making his living by doing portraits at some fifty dollars a head, including Clay for a political banner. In time he became sufficiently prosperous to visit the East and Europe. Best remembered are his descriptive paintings of local elections, pioneers, and river life, which were excellent both as paintings and as historical evidence. Very possibly he was correct in his claim that "I am the greatest among the disciples of the brush, which my native land has yet produced."

DRAMA The art that obtained the most secure foothold in the early West was the drama. Amateur theatricals were presented in Lexington before 1800, and appeared very early in such towns as Pittsburgh, Cincinnati, Detroit, and St. Louis. Military garrisons in the West produced their own plays in which soldiers usually took the feminine roles, with dubious results. Theaters did not exist in the early days; hence any large vacant room might be equipped with a rough stage and crude seats. Candles gave the necessary light, one or two small rooms provided dressing facilities for the entire cast; the scenery was entirely homemade. Plays produced under these circumstances were designed primarily for the amusement of the families, friends, and acquaintances of the amateur actors.

The first professional company to visit the West was recruited in Montreal and Quebec and opened in Lexington, Kentucky, in 1810. It was followed by other companies, notably those headed by Samuel Drake and N. M. Ludlow. The life of the traveling player was arduous and uncertain, for western towns were small and far apart, and the size of audiences was uncertain. Sometimes the town fathers considered the drama an immoral influence and tried to close the theater by heavy taxation. Audiences were mostly men, with a sprinkling of prostitutes; and rowdies were not averse to hurling overripe vegetables or breaking the furniture if displeased by either the play or the acting.

The theaters of the West remained poor and few before 1820. A traveling company might play one night in a regular theater, the next in a billiard hall, then in a brewery, in a vacant store, in the hall above the courthouse, or even in a clearing in the woods. The trip between stops was often long and always over bad roads. Poor receipts caused many a company to disband, leaving its members penniless in the wilderness. The chance of a western actor's becoming a star in the East was remote.

The western theater began to make progress in the late 1820s and 1830s, due largely to the efforts of the rival producers James Caldwell and Sol Smith. Caldwell favored New Orleans, but also worked more northern towns such as Natchez, Nashville, and St. Louis. Sol Smith preferred Kentucky but also made trips north into Ohio and south into Georgia, Alabama, and Mississippi, and had a theater in St. Louis. He was probably the most popular comedian in the West.

The best theatrical town in the 1820s and 1830s was New Orleans, with both an American and a French theater. Even grand opera was produced: *The Barber of Seville*, *The Marriage of Figaro*, and others. Cincinnati was next to New Orleans in dramatic importance, particularly after the opening of Caldwell's new theater in 1832. This structure held between 1300 and 1500 people. It was decorated elaborately and lighted with lamps instead of candles. Its magnificence was dimmed only by a new St. Louis theater of 1837, the most impressive ever attempted in the West. The stage was 55 feet wide and 73 feet deep, and the auditorium could hold 1400. The seats and floor could be removed to accommodate the equestrian performances so popular at the time.

Each theatrical company had a large repertory; otherwise, because of the smallness of most western towns, it would have been forced to move almost continuously. A certain amount of variety was achieved by the star system then in vogue. Outstanding actors and actresses appeared with one company after another in a limited number of plays. In this way the West was able to see such famous performers as Junius Brutus Booth, Edwin Forrest, Charles Kean, James H. Hackett, Fanny Elssler, "Jim Crow" Rice, and the Ravel family. Edwin Forrest, the most popular native-born actor, usually appeared in Shakespearean roles. Fanny Elssler, an Austrian dancer, was greatly admired, but she charged such high fees that theater managers were lucky to make expenses.

The usual dramatic performance consisted of a three- or four-act play followed by a one-act farce, with singing and dancing specialties between the acts to keep the audience from becoming restless. Acrobats, such as the Ravel family, drew good houses. Infant prodigies such as Master Burke were favorably received, and several of them toured the country profitably.

Most of the plays presented to western audiences were English in origin. Those of Shakespeare had the most performances, particularly *Richard III*, *Othello*, and *Hamlet*. Quite popular also were the plays of Thomas Morton, particularly *Town and Country*, *Speed the Plow*, and *A Roland for an Oliver*. Efforts by American actors such as Edwin Forrest to encourage American playwrights had only limited success. During the 1830s there were staged a few costly spectacles, including a battle in the war with Tripoli and the eruption of Mt. Vesuvius, as well as a wild horse in "Mazeppa," dogs, camels, monkeys, a Hercules, pugilists, and fireworks. These expensive treats were enjoyed by the audiences, but were not popular with the poor western producers.

NEWSPAPERS AND MAGAZINES   The most common reading material of the West was the newspaper, and a printing press was one of the first nonessentials of a new community. Before 1800 newspaper subscription lists were small, advertising was limited, paper, ink, and type were expensive, deliveries were uncertain, and news was hard to obtain, so that all papers were weekly and depended largely on the printing of public notices for their support. After 1800 they grew more and more rapidly. In 1790 there had been but one newspaper to each 75,000 people, but by 1840 the ratio had increased to 1 to 12,000, and the daily paper (six days a week) had become well established in larger cities such as Cincinnati. With all this growth, however, newspaper printing remained a hazardous business, and the mortality rate was high.

In addition to the newspaper there was the monthly magazine, usually literary or religious, but sometimes scientific. Usually it depended on exchange material, but several editors tried to encourage original western stories, sketches, and incidents. Timothy Flint failed in this attempt with his *Western Magazine and Review* (1827–1830). William Davis Gallagher did a little better with the *Western Literary Journal and Monthly Review* (1836), but best of all was James Hall's *Western Monthly Magazine* (1833–1836), possibly because he did most of the writing himself.

POETRY AND FICTION   Western poets were universally banal and uninspired. Probably the best was W. D. Gallagher, but even he could ruin fresh western themes with his dry and conventional treatment. Quite popular in the West was Richard Emmons, whose great work *The Fredoniad: or, Independence Preserved. An Epick Poem on the Late War of 1812*, published in 1827, received warm praise and earned a moderate financial return. To the modern reader, however, it is no better than the terrible *Columbiad* of Joel Barlow.

The two outstanding western authors of the 1820s and 1830s were Timothy Flint and James Hall. Flint was born in Massachusetts, attended Harvard, and entered the ministry. He went to the West in 1815 partly to improve his health, and there he undertook missionary work. For twenty-five years, in spite of ill health, he lived a very active life, traveling in the West, in the East, and in Europe; he died at Natchez in 1840. Among his many literary labors were editing the *Western Magazine and Review*, editing the far western travels of James Ohio Pattie, and a life of Daniel Boone. Other writings included an autobiography, descriptive essays, and several novels. Flint based his work almost entirely on frontier themes, but unfortunately he had a romantic imagination and an instinct for melodrama, so that he can not be trusted to depict western life objectively.

Much more important than Timothy Flint was Judge James Hall, the foremost western writer of his day. Hall was born in Philadelphia in 1793 of a well-to-do family and had just begun the study of law when the War of 1812 broke out. He joined the army, took part in the Niagara campaign, and fought against the Barbary pirates. Finally in 1820 he returned to Philadelphia, and after further law study moved to the famous Shawneetown in Illinois, where he became prosecuting attorney for twelve counties. His title of judge was not an honorary one: he held the office of circuit judge for twelve years. In his spare time he edited at least two newspapers, the *Illinois Gazette* of Shawneetown and the *Illinois Intelligencer* of Vandalia.

One of Hall's greatest contributions to the literary development of the West was his editing of the *Illinois Monthly Magazine* at Vandalia in 1830–1832. This, the first literary journal in Illinois, emphasized western material, of which Hall himself wrote the greater share. It was responsible for preserving many western figures such as Mike Fink. In 1833 Hall moved his periodical to Cincinnati, merged it with a new magazine called the *Western Monthly Magazine*, and continued to stress original contributions in order to increase western literary self-consciousness. It was he who discovered Harriet Beecher (Stowe).

Hall did not confine his literary efforts to editorial work. Novels, short stories, descriptive works, and texts flowed from his tireless pen in the prodigiously productive years 1828–1848. He was undoubtedly the greatest single advertiser and popularizer of the West, and did more than any other man to develop a real western literature. His graphic accounts of western life and customs were rivaled only by Albert Pike's *Prose Sketches and Poems Written in the Western Country* (1834), A. B. Longstreet's *Georgia Scenes* (1835), Mrs. C. M. Kirkland's *A New Home—Who'll Follow* (1839), and J. G. Baldwin's *The Flush Times of Alabama and Mississippi* (1853). The best Indian stories came from the pen of William J. Snelling.

EASTERN LITERATURE   The usual reading of the West was the literature of the East and Europe. British publications were widely reprinted and read, since they were in English, bore well-known names, and were not protected by copyright. The

West bestowed its favor on the sickly sentiments of Felicia Hemans and Hannah Moore, both of whom were well known in the East and in the West. Byron had a large and devoted following in the West as well as in the East in spite of some doubts about his personal morals; works like *Beppo* and *Don Juan* were reprinted west of the Alleghenies within a year of their publications in England (1818 and 1819). Best and most favorably known was Sir Walter Scott, whose works were republished and read eagerly in the West as fast as they appeared; western writers such as Hall, Flint, and Gallagher were influenced by Scott.

Eastern writers also had their western readers, but western taste was generally bad. Holmes, Whittier, and Longfellow were creating reputations, but Hawthorne, Emerson, and Poe were almost unknown. Irving had some following; but Cooper was viewed with distrust: most people felt that his stories would have been better if he had known more of the West. Bryant was known but little and liked less.

Eastern literary figures did not overlook the West as a rich source of material not only for works of travel and description, but also for short stories and novels. The situations particularly appealing to them were wilderness travel and Indian conflicts. Utilizing the travel theme, such books as Paulding's *Westward Ho!* (drawn largely from Flint), and R. H. Dana's delightful *Two Years Before the Mast* were outstanding.

Washington Irving, the dean of American writers, was attracted to western material partly through his friend John Jacob Astor. He wrote historically and descriptively rather than as a novelist. His *Astoria*, *Captain Bonneville*, and *Tour of the Prairies* were all published during the 1830s and dealt with the trans-Mississippi West. The first is the best of them, although the others are interesting for their style and for their descriptions of the western plains. All three are readable, but none is among the best of Irving's works.

Eastern writers generally found tales of Indian life and warfare more appealing to readers than stories of travel and exploration, which was also the attitude of the American public. George Catlin drew large crowds when he exhibited his collection of Indian portraits and curiosities. T. L. McKinney's *The Indian Tribes of North America*, largely pictorial, was said to have yielded a profit of $100,000 to its publishers. Innumerable plays used an Indian as either hero or villain. Best known was the prize play *Metamora* by John Augustus Stone, with Edwin Forrest monopolizing the part of Metamora from the opening of the play in December 1829. Realism flew out the wings as Forrest ranted, orated, and gesticulated, but thousands of Americans hung on the words of Metamora as this fearless lover of nature pursued his tragic life until he finally perished with his wife and child.

As for the novelists of the period, few before 1850 failed to produce at least one Indian story. Starting with Philip Freneau and Charles Brockden Brown, each author found occasion either to praise or to condemn his red-skinned brother. The main problem was whether to picture the Indian as a noble and tragic son of nature or as a lurking, cruel, bloodthirsty savage. A few of the efforts, such as Longfellow's *Hiawatha*, still retain currency, but most have disappeared. Among the best was James Kirke Paulding's *Koningsmarke, The Long Finne* (1823), written in a light vein, but giving a credible picture of the Indian as a human being.

Among the best-liked works of their own day were the novels of Robert Montgomery Bird and William Gilmore Simms. Bird's great work was *Nick of the Woods, or the Jibbenainosay* (1837), a dark tale of violence and bloodshed in Kentucky immediately after the Revolution. The Indians were the villains, and the Jibbenainosay was an avenging white who slaughtered them right and left. Simms did a more plausible job, particularly in his novel *The Yemasee* (1835). The scene is laid in the Carolinas of the early eighteenth century, and the book abounds in fights and hairbreadth escapes; and yet the Indian is given a sympathetic treatment as a social being with loves and hates, virtues and vices, who is being overwhelmed by a civilization more powerful than his own.

The writer whose Indian stories have had the greatest power of survival is James Fenimore Cooper. The five volumes of his *Leatherstocking Tales*, dealing with the lives and contacts of Indians and frontiersmen, appeared between 1823 and 1841. Cooper had lived in central New York State as a boy and considered himself an authority on the frontier, even though he actually had known no Indians except the deteriorated vestiges of once-powerful tribes, and had never visited the scenes he described. Even with these limitations his frontier stories lived.

In spite of certain errors in fact, Cooper's tales are not bad pictures of the frontier. They are primarily both masculine and juvenile in content and appeal; Cooper's women are always wooden and unconvincing, and his descriptions of love affairs are mawkish. The Indians tend to be types rather than individuals: either they are everything that is good and noble and true or they are a composite of man's less admirable traits.

Possibly these literary and psychological defects are the basic cause for the popularity of the volumes, both then and later. Many a small boy since the middle of the nineteenth century has marveled at the feats of the frontiersmen, has shuddered at the dangerous situations, has felt relieved at the miraculous escapes of his heroes, has applauded the good Indians and been angered by the bad.

Although the early nineteenth century made considerable use of frontier themes, much remained to be done. The emphasis on travel and Indian troubles meant that large masses of material were unexplored. The western thriller had not as yet appeared; its reputed originator, E. Z. C. Judson, published his first book in 1845, but it did not deal with the West. Even more important, there was as yet no fiction that the modern critic would consider realistic.

READINGS   *Paperbacks are marked with an asterisk.*

General   The varied material of this chapter is included in such regional accounts as *Everett Dick, *The Dixie Frontier* (1948); Roscoe C. Buley, *The Old Northwest* (2 vols., 1950); Francis G. Davenport, *Ante-Bellum Kentucky* (1943); Henry C. Hubbart, *The Older Middle West, 1840–1880* (1936). See the Readings for Chapter 8, 13, 17.

Religion   Particularly valuable are the works of William W. Sweet, *The Story of Religions in America* (1930), *Religion in the Development of American Culture*

(1952), *Religion on the American Frontier* (4 vols., 1931–1946), largely documents, *Methodism in American History* (1933), and *The Rise of Methodism in the West* (1920). Other useful studies include John F. Cady, *The Missionary Baptist Church in Indiana* (1942); Colin B. Goodykoontz, *Home Missions on the American Frontier* (1939); Theodore Maynard, *The Story of American Catholicism* (1941); Elizabeth K. Nottingham, *Methodism and the Frontier* (1941), Indiana; Walter B. Pusey, *The Development of Methodism in the Old Southwest* (1933).

Literature and the Arts   Careful literary surveys are Dorothy A. Dondore, *The Prairie and the Making of Middle America* (1926); Lucy L. Hazard, *The Frontier in American Literature* (1927); Ralph L. Rusk, *The Literature of the Middle Western Frontier* (2 vols., 1925). Albert Keiser, *The Indian in American Literature* (1933) is excellent even though filled with quotations. Good biographies are Frederick W. Allsopp, *Albert Pike* (1928); Randolph C. Randall, *James Hall: Spokesman of the New West* (1964); John T. Flanagan, *James Hall* (1941); John E. Kirkpatrick, *Timothy Flint* (1911); John D. Wade, *Augustus Baldwin Longstreet* (1924). James A. Shackford, *David Crockett* (1956) investigates primarily the legend; the Crockett autobiography is readily available. William G. B. Carson, *Managers in Distress: The St. Louis Stage, 1840–1844* (1949) is limited and detailed, but gives a good picture of the western theater. Rexford Newcomb, *Architecture of the Old Northwest Territory* (1950) contains many pictures. See also the writings of the authors mentioned in this chapter.

Chapter 20 / BEYOND THE MISSISSIPPI

Migrating frontiersmen found new problems as they moved west of the Mississippi. They soon encountered seemingly endless plains, flat or gently rolling, of the kind about which they had felt skeptical farther east. Annual rainfall became less and less until it averaged under 10 inches a year; beyond the 98th meridian eastern methods of agriculture became thoroughly hazardous if not impossible. Vegetation became limited largely to tough grass, which grew shorter and sparser as one traveled west. Trees were confined almost entirely to the river valleys, and the sound of the frontiersman's axe, so common in the East, faded away. Here the typical sounds were the thundering of buffalo herds as they swept across the plains and the fearsome crackling of prairie fires.

The Great Plains rose gradually as the traveler went west, ultimately giving way to the snowy peaks of the Rocky Mountains, which stretched from Canada to Mexico. Whereas the Appalachians had once been troublesome, they now looked small and friendly compared with the intimidating peaks of the Rockies. The one easy crossing of the Rockies led to the uninviting country of the Great Basin, dominated by the Great Salt Lake. Here the rainfall was so inadequate that part of the country was a complete desert; the salt water of the lake was cheering in appearance but unappetizing in fact. To the north the Snake River was a welcome relief—until the rapidity of the current and the cragginess of the banks brought the realization that it was anything but a parallel to the Ohio River in the East.

After plodding over the Great Basin, the weary traveler heading for California then encountered the majestic High Sierras, a barrier which some failed to cross. Descending to the valleys of the Sacramento and San Joaquin rivers, the traveler had the feeling of entering heaven. Farther north he could float down the Columbia, with some portages, through increasingly well-watered country; one branch of the Columbia, the Willamette, flowing generally from south to north, provided conditions nearly like those of the East. In general, the western halves of the present states of Washington and Oregon received reasonable amounts of rain, and the coastal strip even more. In California, except for a few areas, rainfall was inadequate by eastern standards.

PLAINS INDIANS   The Indians west of the Mississippi varied greatly in culture, from the lowly "Diggers" of California to the highly civilized Hopi; but the most important Plains groups had rather similar cultures. They were generally less agricultural than the eastern Indians. The open, treeless, semiarid plains offered far less encouragement to farming than did the well-watered country farther east, and in addition the western plains supported a seemingly inexhaustible food supply in the buffalo. The Indians depended for the greater share of their necessities of life on this animal. Its meat, which was preserved by smoking or drying, was the Indians' principal food. Its skin, after being tanned, with its brains as the tanning agent, made clothes, shoes, tepees, and blankets; its bones furnished implements such as knives and hoes, and at times bows, or children's sleds. Its tendons were used for thread and bowstrings. Even

View of the Rocky Mountains, by Karl Bodmer. The "breaks" in the foreground are typical of the land along the Missouri River. The terrain is characteristic of the Rockies, as seen from a number of points on the eastern side. (Joslyn Art Museum)

its entrails provided a part of the Indian domestic economy: the intestines were used in making sausages, and the bladder became a water bag.

Since the buffalo moved across the plains in huge herds, the Indians too were generally nomadic, even though they had a little agriculture. The usual Indian domicile was the temporary wigwam or tepee constructed of a framework of slanting, crossed poles covered with joined buffalo skins. Permanent wooden houses were rare. For traveling the Indian used a travois, an arrangement of poles with one end lashed to a horse and the other dragging on the ground; on these poles were fastened the tepee materials, clothing, sleeping robes, and cooking and eating utensils; frequently a young child or two perched on top. Horses were a necessity, and were used much more than

A Mandan Village, by Karl Bodmer. The Mandans and their neighbors (collectively called the Three Tribes) lived in huts, as opposed to the traditional tepee of the plains. The Indians in the foreground are utilizing "bullboats" made of a willow framework covered with buffalo hides, the seams sealed with pitch. (New York Public Library)

farther east. They were small and shaggy, the descendants of horses introduced earlier by the Spanish to the south. Every Indian was a good horseman; children were taught to ride almost as soon as they were taught to walk. The greatest use of the horse, except for traveling or fighting, was in hunting buffalo. In the usual buffalo hunt, horsemen rode into the herd and shot their quarry at close range. A miscalculation probably meant death under the hoofs of the frightened animals. Because arrows were hard to make and hence scarce, they were recovered at the end of a hunt; it was considered unfortunate if an arrow only wounded a buffalo, for then the arrow was lost. Buffalo hunts sometimes took the form of driving the animals into a corral where they could be killed at the hunters' leisure. At other times the beasts were driven over a cliff and thus slaughtered by the hundreds.

Many of the activities of the western Indians were similar to those of their eastern brothers. Chiefs obtained their offices by popular choice, and had but vague powers. War was the principal business of the men. These tribes were extremely powerful; their bows were probably more effective than muzzle-loading guns. Scalps taken in war proved that the brave had come sufficiently close to the enemy to touch him, while horse stealing conferred honor that was second only to touching the enemy. Prisoners were sometimes tortured, but they were usually either enslaved or adopted into the tribe; women captives were frequently taken as wives.

The division of labor between the sexes was practically the same in the West as in the East. The men hunted, fished, and fought, while the women did the rest of the work. In spite of white opinion to the contrary, the position of an Indian woman was comparatively good. She had rights that her husband had to respect; often she participated in ceremonial dances and tribal councils. Children belonged to the clan of the mother, and were well treated; unlike white children, they were seldom punished physically. Play and education were combined; the girls played with dolls and kept house, and the boys engaged in make-believe buffalo hunts and battles.

Marriage customs were similar over the plains, even though they varied in detail. A girl presumably remained chaste before marriage, although there were slips. She normally married young in a ceremony that involved some sort of purchase. Polygamy was accepted universally, but was practiced in most tribes only by a few of the wealthier men. Divorce occurred normally on the desire of the husband alone, though here and there either party could take the initiative. Infidelity by the wife was frequently punished by the amputation of the end of her nose by her husband. Infidelity by the husband was punished by the relatives of the wife; in fact the usual treatment of any crime was by vengeance. Women were ordinarily considered unclean during their menstrual periods, when they frequently lived by themselves in small temporary shelters. Childbirth was not allowed to interfere with the mother's regular activities. No assistance was given except in the case of the first-born child. Immediately after the birth the woman washed herself and her new baby, even if she first had to chop a hole in the ice, and then resumed her normal household work.

Medical care was furnished by medicine men, who mainly sought to drive out wicked spirits by elaborate ceremonials, although they also used simple herbs and sucking. Infection was beyond the power of the Indian doctor; white men's diseases such as measles, smallpox, and syphilis brought frightful mortality; the smallpox epidemic that swept the plains in 1837 killed over half of several tribes. Surgery was so primitive that a broken arm or leg was seldom set properly, and there was no assurance that the limb could be used in the future.

Utensils and weapons varied widely, depending on the materials and the customs of the particular group. Vessels might be simple wooden, horn, or bone receptacles, or they might be glazed clay with elaborate designs. Material for clothes, blankets, and tents ranged from poorly tanned buffalo hides to well-woven cloth and waterproof blankets. Bows, arrows, lances, clubs, shields, and knives varied from tribe to tribe.

Each Plains Indian tribe had elaborate dances and ceremonials. They were designed to ward off evil spirits or propitiate good ones, to ensure that corn would grow well, that the rain would fall, that buffalo would be plentiful, that the young men would be brave, that war would be successful, and that disease and accident would be absent. Frequently a dance was a mimicry of the things desired, as in a pantomime buffalo hunt, and took the form of short, jerky steps, together with a vertical movement of the body. Most of the dances were only for men, a few were specially for women, and some were for both sexes. Usually the dance was accompanied by singing and instrumental music; the drum was the most common musical instrument. The drummer and the singer made no effort to agree on their rhythms; each did a solo, with results that were weird and unearthly to the visitor accustomed to the musical traditions of the white man. In addition to all sizes and shapes of drums, the Indians used a varied assortment of rattles and simple whistles. The flute was a variation of the whistle, made only by a few tribes, used only rarely for love songs, and seldom heard by the white in its original Indian use.

The western Indians loved funny stories and practical jokes. They had strong family affection and were reasonably loquacious. They reveled in games of all kinds. A child had a sled and a hoop, bow and arrows, dolls, and other similar delights; he had dozens of games, including skating and snapping the whip. Adults also had many sports, including several ball games, guessing contests, the stick game, and various dice games; the dice were probably marked plum pits or bones. Both men and women participated, and betting was universal.

Each Indian tribe had its legends of spirits, mythological heroes, and animals who talked with humans, as well as fabulous tales of the origins of particular kinds of animals, parts of the country, and the human race. Many good and bad spirits were thought to inhabit the world; usually the Indians accepted a supreme good spirit and a happy hunting ground. Great credence was placed in dreams and visions. Most tribes had their mythical "culture heroes," about whom long tales were told. Other stories explained the making of the world, the appearance of people, the creation of the buffalo, and similar mysteries. Ordinarily such tales were told only at night, and then by a commonly accepted storyteller, who made an elaborate ceremony of the narration.

Despite their general similarities the Plains Indians were by no means a homogeneous people. Although they were grouped into tribes through similarities in descent, language, and geography, the tribe practically never acted as a unit; smaller groups within the tribe exercised complete freedom of action. Each tribe occupied a fairly definite portion of the plains, although periodic migrations changed the picture from time to time. Some tribes were traditionally friendly with each other, while others were ordinarily hostile. The idea of the Plains Indians acting together as a single unit does not correspond with the facts.

INDIVIDUAL TRIBES   The most powerful plains group was probably the Sioux, who numbered some 50,000. Originally located near the head of the Mississippi they had drifted west, so that when the whites arrived they occupied the country from the Minnesota region to the upper Missouri. They included seven well-defined divi-

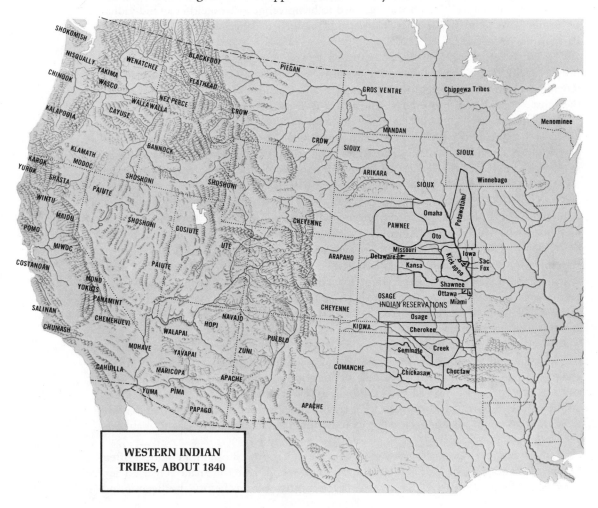

WESTERN INDIAN
TRIBES, ABOUT 1840

sions, which only infrequently met together; the chiefs in general did little more than carry out the will of the majority. In general the Sioux were typical of most Plains Indians; they lived in buffalo-skin tepees, were nomadic, and excelled as horsemen, hunters, and fighters. As with other northern Plains tribes they had an initiation ceremony for their young warriors which was very demanding physically; rather curiously, the most cruel of such ceremonies was that of the Mandan, who in general were peaceful, kindly, and friendly.

The Crows lived near the headwaters of the Yellowstone in present southern Montana. They despised the white men as inferior, and said so frequently and vigorously. Being warlike, they fought not only with the whites but with their red neighbors. A common plains rumor, difficult to check, was that their women were deficient in proper moral standards. Like other Plains tribes the Crows participated from time to time in a "sun dance" which was designed to bring vengeance on either an individual or group basis. The whole tribe participated in such a dance, and at times various participants had visions.

The Blackfeet, like other tribes, comprised several groups—in this case three—with similar backgrounds, inheritance, and customs, who lived at the eastern base of the Rockies from present northern Montana north into Canada. They may well have been the most aggressive and warlike of the Plains Indians, being noted for their ferocity, cruelty, and consistent hostility to the white man—a hostility that appeared as early as Lewis and Clark, and which later made many difficulties for the white trappers. They practiced no agriculture, but lived entirely by hunting; they were somewhat unusual in the extent to which they practiced polygamy—a useful practice for a tribe with a high war death rate among the men. Something over half of the tribe died in the small pox epidemic of 1837.

In the central plains region lived several powerful tribes. The Cheyenne tribe (in permanent alliance with the Arapaho) had been pushed west from Minnesota by the Sioux. During the 1830s it had split into two groups, with the northern Cheyenne occupying the upper branches of the Platte River, and the southern Cheyenne the upper Arkansas. Both were typical Plains Indians, having similar cultures, including the ritual of the sun dance. Their government, such as it was, consisted presumably of chiefs elected for limited terms, but in actual practice these chiefs tended to become hereditary, and they had no power to change the traditional ways of life.

Several other central Plains tribes might at least be mentioned. The Pawnee have received unusual attention because one of their ceremonies, practiced as late as 1838, included a human sacrifice. In the spring a young girl, a virgin, was shot, and her flesh and blood were used in an elaborate symbolic ceremonial to fertilize the fields of corn. South of the Pawnee lived the Osage, a small tribe roaming the region that is now western Kansas and eastern Colorado; its most unusual characteristic was probably its hereditary chieftainship.

Farther west, centering in present Utah, were various Shoshonean tribes, often known as "Root Diggers" or "Snakes" (the name coming from the Snake River). They were generally poor, miserable, and dirty, living mostly on roots because both game and agricultural products were scarce due to the lack of water. Usually they were peaceful. A bit confusing is the fact that the tribe known as Shoshoni was, in contrast, a normal Plains tribe.

In the Rocky Mountain region and along the Pacific Coast were many small tribes that by the early nineteenth century were for the most part poverty-stricken, filthy, and degraded; their early contact with the whites had at least not helped them. They lived chiefly on fish and roots, and now and then a delicacy like grasshopper pie. Their principal accomplishment was the weaving of baskets, some of which were so well constructed as to hold water. Some of the northern tribes flattened the heads of their children by strapping a board on the top of each new baby's skull—although this practice was not followed by the tribe known to the whites as Flatheads. Notable exceptions to the characteristic natives of the area were the Nez Percés, who actually did not have "pierced noses"; the Nez Percés lived on the lower Snake River and its tributaries, and were an extremely able and dignified people.

Among the most feared tribes of the plains were the Apache and Comanche, who lived in present Arizona, New Mexico, and western Texas; generally allied with the Comanche were the Kiowa, who lived in the Texas Panhandle and to the north, and who were almost equally dangerous to the whites. Both the Apache and Comanche elected their chiefs, but small groups tended to act independently, possibly because of the nature of the country which provided little food or cover. They were extremely warlike and did much raiding—certainly in part because they were usually hungry. They were intelligent and truthful, but also wild, warlike, and cruel. Prisoners were enslaved and sometimes tortured; if the prisoners were women, they were almost always raped. Both tribes were migratory, with no regular agriculture and no permanent villages; and both caused the whites much trouble because of their effectiveness in war.

Two minor groups in the South were notable for their high civilization. The Pueblo Indians, living for the most part in present New Mexico, were the remains of a highly organized and prosperous tribe; their stone, sometimes adobe, houses, excellent implements, and irrigated fields, all indicated a former state of opulence. West of them, on the lower Colorado, were the Navaho. Although the Navaho did not have permanent homes, they raised various grains and fruit, herded cattle, sheep, mules, horses and asses, and wove excellent blankets and coarse woolen goods.

These were some of the more important Indians the white frontier encountered as it pushed from the Mississippi toward the Pacific. They were proud and effective warriors, and their number, plus their lack of permanent villages, made them difficult to conquer. Their ways of life gave little promise that they might be converted into farmers after the white model. There was no region farther west into which they might be shoved.

EXPLORING LOUISIANA The Indian trans-Mississippi West was known but vaguely at the time of the purchase of Louisiana. Although the present Southwest had seen some Spanish exploration and settlement (see Chapter 23), the remainder to the north was known only as a region of great plains, beyond which were high mountains. Quite naturally, various adventurers were lured by the vast unknown. Jefferson had been scientifically interested in the West for many years before he had any thought of buying the territory. While serving as minister to France he talked in 1786 to the migratory John Ledyard, an inveterate wanderer of considerable ability. The two men planned that Ledyard would cross Siberia to Kamchatka, then sail across the Pacific, and finally make the overland journey through the Louisiana Territory. Ledyard started across Russia in 1786, traveling mostly on foot; eventually he was stopped and turned back by Russian officials. He moved on to Africa, where he died in 1788.

Other plans to explore the Far West soon followed those of John Ledyard. Captain John Armstrong made the attempt in 1790, but was thwarted by the Indians. André Michaux, the French botanist, started west in 1793, but was delayed by his involvement in the Genêt intrigue and did not travel beyond the Mississippi. Michaux was backed by America's most important scientific body, the American Philosophical Society, which acted on the recommendation of Jefferson. Other persons considered the long overland trip to the Pacific, but none of these projected expeditions was completed within the territorial limits of the United States before 1800. Of course there were a number of other expeditions with more limited objectives.

LEWIS AND CLARK   The interest in the Far West, particularly Jefferson's, made it almost certain that when Louisiana became United States territory during Jefferson's presidency, exploration of the whole area would be encouraged. Actually, even before the purchase of Louisiana Jefferson had requested and received permission from Congress to organize an expedition to explore the region west of the Mississippi (January 1803). For its leaders he chose Captain Meriwether Lewis (born 1774) and William Clark (born 1770). Lewis had been Jefferson's private secretary, and Clark was the brother of George Rogers Clark. These men were personal friends, and both were acquainted with the ways of the wilderness. Lewis started west shortly after his appointment, arriving at Pittsburgh in the summer of 1803. Both here and farther down the Ohio he gathered men and supplies. The party spent the winter of 1803–1804 in Illinois nearly opposite the mouth of the Missouri.

The expedition actually started on Sunday, May 13, 1804, when the ascent of the Missouri began. The party was composed of some 30 men, about half drawn from the army and the others hired for the duration of the trip; in addition there were 16 men to run the keelboat. Each man was expected to keep notes of all he observed, and oilskin wrappers were provided to protect the notes from the elements. In fact the expedition had been planned with great care, including provision of a vast variety of necessary equipment and proper training for the men.

The general aims of the Lewis and Clark Expedition, as stated in the instructions, were primarily scientific. The men were to explore the land, rivers, and mountains from the Mississippi to the coast, to make observations of all animal and vegetable life and all mineral resources, to observe the manners and customs of the natives, and to promote friendly relations with the Indian tribes of the region. These aims were far from modest for a small body of white men entering thousands of square miles of unknown country.

Progress up the Missouri was necessarily slow. A 55-foot keelboat carried most of the supplies and equipment: it had a large square sail, but most of the time the wind was unfavorable, and the vessel had to be dragged upstream at the end of a rope. Progress was still further delayed by the necessity of conferring with the Indians, informing them of their new masters, and trying to obtain their goodwill by means of presents. By

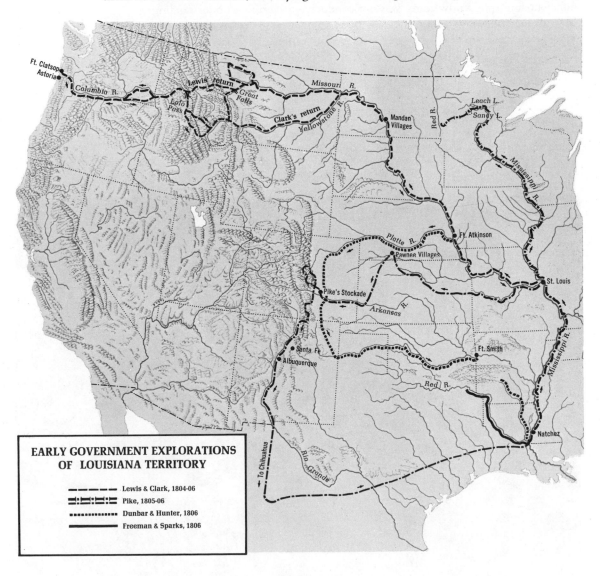

EARLY GOVERNMENT EXPLORATIONS OF LOUISIANA TERRITORY

- – – – – – Lewis & Clark, 1804-06
- ▰▰▰▰ Pike, 1805-06
- ▪▪▪▪▪▪ Dunbar & Hunter, 1806
- ——— Freeman & Sparks, 1806

the end of October the party had progressed as far as the Mandan villages, near the site of the present Bismarck, North Dakota. The winter of 1804–1805 was spent among the friendly Mandan. The men built a stockade and several log cabins, and then rested and collected provisions; they also added to their party a guide and an interpreter, a necessity for a trip farther west. Even with the interpreter, who was an Indian woman, there was great difficulty in communicating with some of the tribes. Sometimes a speech had to be translated a half dozen times before the principals could even begin to understand each other. Such a procedure, particularly when carried out badly by natives with insufficient linguistic knowledge, was not conducive to accurate understanding.

With the coming of spring the expedition sent the keelboat back to St. Louis and resumed its journey up the Missouri in pirogues and canoes. The party left the Mandan villages on April 7, and on April 26 arrived at the mouth of the Yellowstone, where some difficulty was experienced in determining which was the main stream. The next leg of

The Interior of the Hut of a Mandan Chief, by Karl Bodmer. This interior and its supporting log framework is characteristic of the "lodge." Although the term is often applied also to the tepee, the lodge was a more permanent structure, used by more sedentary Indians. (New York Public Library)

the trip had its worst period in the month that it took to portage the Great Falls of the Missouri, but eventually the party arrived (July 25) at the three forks, which diplomatically were given the names of Jefferson, Madison, and Gallatin. Any one of these branches, which combine to form the Missouri River, offered almost equal possibilities for the continuance of the journey, and consequently considerable time was spent in exploring all three. Finally the most westerly, the Jefferson was chosen, and the party followed it and then the Beaverhead to about the present Dillon, Montana. Then the men abandoned the river and prepared to make the next stage of the trip by land.

Lewis and Clark were in an unenviable position when they left their canoes and started forward on foot. They were then nearly two thousand miles from civilization, having crossed an untracked wilderness with its perils of starvation, accident, and disease. They had traversed an unfriendly country in which an unwise gesture might well have meant annihilation by the Indians. The hardest part of the journey still lay ahead, since the unknown Rocky Mountains had to be crossed in the face of approaching winter; supplies were running low, native guidance was poor, and hostile Indians occupied the country they were approaching. The decision to push farther west in the face of these obstacles required the highest courage and resolution.

The pedestrian part of the trip was begun in August under the leadership of unwilling guides who had to be watched to prevent their desertion. Snow fell by September 3, making the mountain passes exceedingly dangerous. On September 7 the party was near the present Idaho line at Grantdale, Montana, and from there it followed the Lolo Creek and Lolo Pass (Nez Percé Pass) through the mountains. Frequently the men floundered in the snow; most of the time they were wet and cold, and provisions were so scanty that hunger was an ordinary condition. In late September they passed the mountains and struck a branch of the Clearwater, where they built five canoes. The remainder of the westward trail followed the Clearwater, the Snake, and the Columbia, including a portage at The Dalles on the Columbia. The main objective of the expedition was attained when the Pacific Ocean was sighted on November 7, 1805.

Reaching the Pacific Ocean was a notable accomplishment, but from the standpoint of Lewis and Clark, a good half of the work remained. The homeward trip bristled with obstacles, and additional exploration was much to be desired. For the time being, the men constructed winter quarters (called Fort Clatsop) at the mouth of the Columbia, where they suffered through the fog and rain, and made preparations for the return trip. The eastward journey began on March 23, 1806, with the party retracing the path that had been followed westward through the mountains. Difficulties in obtaining food increased with the depletion of trading goods, and Lewis and Clark had to resort to posing as doctors to secure the needed supplies. After the mountains had been crossed, the group was divided, with half going north with Lewis and then descending the Marias River, while the other half under Clark followed the Yellowstone. The two parties were united at the mouth of the Yellowstone on August 12, and from this point the trip down the river was comparatively easy. The Mandan villages were passed on August 14, and on September 23, 1806, the party was back in St. Louis.

The Lewis and Clark Expedition was the first trip by non-Indians through the present continental United States to the Pacific Ocean. The magnitude of the feat is in no wise lessened by the even more marvelous trip of Alexander Mackenzie, who had reached the ocean through Canadian territory a full decade earlier, on July 22, 1793. It marked the beginning of accurate knowledge concerning the Far West, for the journals kept by the men were gradually published. Unfortunately some of the diaries were lost, but those that remained gave the only reliable facts thus far collected about the Far Northwest.

The expedition was also notable for the remarkably effective way in which it had been handled. Thirty men had been taken without serious mishap through 6000 miles of wilderness inhabited by potentially hostile Indians. For this service, Lewis was rewarded with the governorship of Louisiana Territory, a post he held until a bullet cut short his life in 1809. Clark entered the fur trade, and was governor of Missouri until it became a state. He then became Superintendent of Indian Affairs at St. Louis, holding the job until his death in 1838.

OTHER EXPLORERS   The expedition of Lewis and Clark was but the first of a long series of governmental efforts to obtain complete and accurate information concerning the country west of the Mississippi. Even before Lewis and Clark were well started, Congress authorized (1804) the exploration of a number of the rivers of the Great Plains—the Panis (Platte), the Paduca (Kansas), the Morsigona (Des Moines), and the St. Peters (Minnesota). Parties were picked for surveying each of these rivers but, although all of them did some work, the total results were disappointing. Most important were William Hunter and George Dunbar, both well-known scientists, who led a small party up the Ouachita of Louisiana in the winter of 1804–1805; they covered this river satisfactorily, but did not reach the Red River, in which Jefferson was particularly interested. A short time later (1806) Thomas Freeman ascended the Red River some 600 miles before he was turned back by a superior Spanish force.

Of the minor expeditions the most important were the two under the command of Zebulon Montgomery Pike, a young army officer who did his exploring under the orders of James Wilkinson, commander of the western army. By orders dated July 30, 1805, he was instructed to ascend and find the sources of the Mississippi, survey Indian conditions, and locate possible military routes. On his way north he stopped at the present St. Paul, Minnesota, where he bought a considerable tract of land just south of the falls of the Mississippi as a site for a future military post. Resuming his journey, he was much troubled by the difficulties of travel, for it was then midwinter. He found Canadian traders in control of the area, and made the noble and futile gesture of ordering them to pay duty on all goods brought across the international boundary, and to refrain from selling liquor to the Indians. Considering the smallness of Pike's force, its distance from effective support, and the nonexistence of an ascertainable boundary, such orders must have sounded ludicrous to Canadian ears.

Pike continued from Sandy Lake to Leech Lake, where he arrived February 1, 1806. Here he ended his advance to the north, since he mistakenly considered Leech Lake the source of the Mississippi. His return to St. Louis was slow and uneventful. The results of this first expedition of Pike were disappointingly meager. He had found what he thought to be the source of the Mississippi; he had bought land that was later to furnish the site of an important army post; he had made futile gestures toward the North West Company; but he had added little information to the slowly growing body of knowledge about the West.

Immediately upon his return (April 1806) Pike received new orders to explore the headwaters of the Arkansas and Red rivers. Leaving St. Louis on July 15 with twenty-two men, he ascended the Missouri and Osage rivers and then crossed overland to the Arkansas River, which he followed through what is now southern Kansas. His plan was

Title Page of *Sources of the Mississippi* by Zebulon M. Pike, Published in 1810. Accounts such as this were read with great interest by an expanding America. (New York Historical Society)

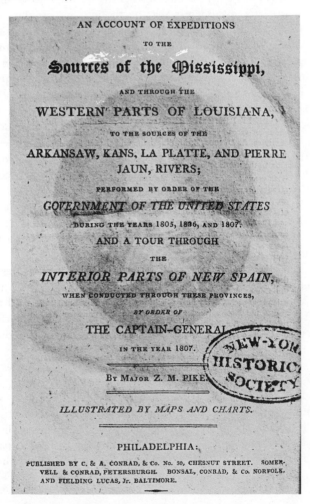

to ascend the Arkansas, cross to the Red, and descend the latter stream to its junction with the Mississippi. The farther west he moved the nearer he came to Spanish territory; and although the exact boundary line was as yet undetermined, the Spanish government became alarmed. A force of 600 Spanish dragoons under Lieutenant Don Facundo Malgares was therefore dispatched to keep Pike and his party out of Spanish territory. Pike heard rumors of the hostile Spanish expedition and so stopped and built fortifications on the site of present Pueblo, Colorado. Incidentally he took the time to start (but not complete) the ascent of the peak that now bears his name. As it happens his fears of the Spanish force proved groundless, for Malgares never found him.

In December Pike took a small part of his force and started south, ostensibly to find the source of the Red River. The weather was bitterly cold, and the men had a grim struggle with snow and hunger. Probably Pike had been instructed to do spying in Spanish territory, and to claim if necessary that he was lost. Whether he actually was lost is still being argued, but certainly he built a stockade on the Rio Grande, definitely in Spanish territory; his later excuse was that he thought it was the Red River. Unforunately the rude fort did not provide sufficient protection; when a hundred Spanish troops appeared on the scene, Pike was forced to give himself up as a prisoner.

After their capture of Pike the Spanish had the perplexing question of what should be done with him. If his party was considered hostile, the penalty might be severe; but if the presumed invasion of Spanish territory was actually an accident, then the invaders should be treated more leniently. The Spanish captain felt incapable of deciding the case and so took Pike first to Santa Fe and then south through El Paso to Chihuahua. Meantime Pike was making copious notes of the country through which he passed, hiding them carefully in gun barrels so they would not be confiscated. At Chihuahua it was decided to return Pike to the United States, and so he was escorted by way of San Antonio to Natchitoches and there handed over to United States troops (July 1, 1807). During the return trip he again took voluminous notes. The net result was that Pike, although not carrying out his orders to explore the Red River, brought home a great amount of information that added to American knowledge of the Southwest and stimulated interest in the Texas region.

All these governmental expeditions, as well as many private ventures, helped to push back the frontier of knowledge concerning the Far West. The main tribes of Indians were enumerated and their characteristics described. The animal and plant life of the western plains was reported. The principal geographical features became known, although much remained to lure other explorers to risk their lives in the wilderness.

READINGS   *Paperbacks are marked with an asterisk.*

General Accounts of Indians   See Readings for Chapter 7. Every history of any state or region has at least one chapter on the local Indians, and every travel account deals with them. Special treatments of the Plains Indians are John C. Ewers, *Indians of the Upper Missouri* (1968); George E. Hyde, *Indians of the High Plains* (1959); *Robert H. Lowie, *Indians of the Plains* (1954). The importance of the buffalo to the Indian is well covered in *E. Douglas Branch, *The Hunting of the Buffalo* (1929).

Specific Indian Tribes Apache: Charles L. Sonnichsen, *The Mescalero Apaches* (1958), excellent; Ralph H. Ogle, *Federal Control of the Western Apaches, 1848–1886* (1940), reads moderately well; Frank C. Lockwood, *The Apache Indians* (1938); Max L. Moorhead, *The Apache Frontier* (1968), scholarly 1769–1791. **Blackfeet:** John C. Ewers, *The Blackfeet* (1958). **Cheyenne:** George B. Grinnell, *The Cheyenne Indians* (2 vols., 1923) and *The Fighting Cheyennes* (1915, 1956); Donald J. Berthrong, *The Southern Cheyennes* (1963), fine; *Thomas B. Marquis, *A Warrior Who Fought Custer* (1931), interesting on the northern Cheyenne. **Comanche:** Rupert N. Richardson, *The Comanche Barrier* (1933), competent; Ernest Wallace and E. A. Hoebel, *The Comanches* (1952). **Cree:** Verne Dusenberry, *The Montana Cree* (1962). **Crows:** *Robert H. Lowie, *The Crow Indians* (1935). **Kickapoo:** Arrell M. Gibson, *The Kickapoos* (1963). **Kiowa:** Mildred P. Mayhall, *The Kiowas* (1962), fair. **Navaho:** Ruth M. Underhill, *The Navahos* (1956), anthropological approach; Oakah L. Jones Jr., *Pueblo Warriors and the Spanish Conquest* (1966). **Sioux:** James C. Olson, *Red Cloud and the Sioux Problem* (1965); *Mari Sandoz, *Crazy Horse* (1942); Henry H. Sibley, *Iron Face* (1950); *John G. Neihardt, *Black Elk Speaks* (1932); Luther Standing Bear. *My People the Sioux* (1928); George Hyde, *Red Cloud's Folk* (1957), *A Sioux Chronicle* (1956), and *Spotted Tail's Folk* (1961); Stanley Vestal, *Sitting Bull: Champion of the Sioux* (1932); Roy W. Meyer, *History of the Santee Sioux* (1968). **Ute:** Wilson Rockwell, *The Utes: A Forgotten People* (1956).

Exploration William H. Goetzmann, *Exploration and Empire* (1966). *John Bakeless, *The Eyes of Discovery* (1950), through Lewis and Clark. *John B. Brebner, *The Explorers of North America, 1492–1806* (1933, 1955) tries to be popular. Abraham P. Nasatir (ed.), *Before Lewis and Clark* (1952) concerns the upper Missouri. John F. McDermott (ed.), *The Western Journals of Dr. George Hunter, 1796–1805* (1963), Hunter-Dunbar expedition.

Lewis and Clark *John Bakeless, *Lewis and Clark* (1947), good in every way. Shorter accounts are included in *Bernard DeVoto, *The Course of Empire* (1952); James Monaghan, *The Overland Trail* (1947). For original material see Bernard DeVoto (ed.), *The Journals of Lewis and Clark* (1953), condensed version; Donald D. Jackson (ed.), *Letters of the Lewis and Clark Expedition* (1962); Ernest S. Osgood (ed.), *The Field Notes of Captain William Clark, 1803–1805* (1964). Also useful are *Richard Dillon, *Meriwether Lewis* (1965) and Burton Harris, *John Colter* (1952), a member of the expedition. Paul R. Cutright, *Lewis and Clark, Pioneering Naturalists* (1969), scientific contributions.

Pike and Mackenzie Excellent in every way is W. Eugene Hollon, *The Lost Pathfinder: Zebulon Montgomery Pike* (1949); Donald Jackson (ed.), *The Journals of Zebulon Montgomery Pike* (2 vols., 1966). Satisfactory on Mackenzie is Mark S. Wade, *Mackenzie of Canada* (1927); Mackenzie's journal is reprinted in Walter Sheppe (ed.), *First Man West* (1962).

Chapter 21 / THE FUR TRADE

The first large-scale business on any new frontier was the collection of furs, whether by catching the animal or by trading with the Indians. Preference went to fine furs such as beaver, otter, mink, and fox, but coarse pelts such as buffalo, bear, and deer were in demand for lap robes and heavy coats, while a few other commodities such as buffalo tongues, and buffalo or bear tallow, had markets. Not infrequently trappers and traders were ahead of the explorers. Lewis and Clark met trappers on the Great Plains, and Pike found them near the source of the Mississippi. The trapper was in the vanguard of white occupation and settlement.

SPANISH AND FRENCH The Spanish were the first European arrivals in the New World, but they dreamed of precious metals and stones rather than of the more prosaic furs. Spanish trappers and traders remained of very little importance until Spanish power had almost vanished from North America. Best known was Manuel Lisa, who in 1807 led the first commercial expedition up the Missouri River to the Rocky Mountains.

The French, more than the Spanish, were responsible for the development of the American fur business. They worked up the St. Lawrence and through the Great Lakes to the Mississippi Basin, establishing such remote trading centers as Kaskaskia, Cahokia, and Vincennes. The French adjusted well to wilderness life, often staying permanently in the wilderness, and apparently happy with their Indian wives and half-breed children. Even after French political power had disappeared from North America, the French trader and trapper continued to set the tone for the fur business of the entire West.

ENGLISH With the elimination of France from North America, England fell heir to the control of the fur trade of the new country. The business was transacted largely by English and Scottish merchants who used Montreal as their main American trading center and London as their chief distributing point. London set the fur prices of the Western world. In spite of English control, most men engaged in the fur trade in America were French, and the French influence remained dominant.

The most important of the English fur-trading companies was the Hudson's Bay Company, chartered in 1670 with absolute power over the vast and vague region of the Northwest that was tributary to Hudson Bay. The "Great Company" had only minor lapses in its enviable record of fair treatment of the Indian, on the principles of one price, no rum, and no violence.

Chief among the other but less important English companies interested in the fur trade was the North West Company, originated in the late eighteenth century by a group of Scottish Montreal merchants. The company's general field of operations was from the Mandan country to the Pacific and from the Hudson Bay territory to Louisiana. At the height of its power it employed some 2000 men. It not only had trading posts like those of the Hudson's Bay Company, but it also equipped expeditions to trade with the Indians in the more important Indian villages.

The Trapper's Return, 1810. This early engraving depicts a domestically inclined trapper. The life of trappers on the great fur frontier in later years was much more nomadic. (New York Public Library)

The proximity of the regions worked by the North West Company and the Hudson's Bay Company threw the two into a conflict that began almost with the organization of the younger concern. Geographical concepts were vague, so there was real doubt as to the proper limits of the jurisdiction of each company. Competition between them sometimes included such devious and objectionable practices as the excessive use of whiskey in trading, stealing furs, and inciting the Indians against rivals. In 1811 a settlement sponsored by Lord Selkirk at the present Winnipeg was encouraged by the Hudson's Bay Company as a buffer between the rival organizations; the object was attained, but at the expense of the settlers. Eventually, in 1821, the North West Company was absorbed by its older rival, and good trading methods were restored.

The most productive fur area in the West until a generation or more after the Revolution was the Great Lakes region. Here were the English and Scottish traders, whose operations were pushed rapidly north, south, and west. Here also were the Spanish and the French, operating from Vincennes, Kaskaskia, Cahokia, and St. Louis, and also pushing up the valley of the Missouri. Finally, here were the American traders who had come over the mountains with the hope of participating in the rich fur business farther west. With the appearance of the Americans, the greatest competition for western furs was between the English and American traders. This rivalry was largely responsible for the refusal of England to surrender its Great Lakes posts at the end of the Revolution, and also explained in part the campaigns around Detroit in the War of 1812.

FEDERAL REGULATION   One of the early problems faced by the federal government under the Constitution was the regulation of the western fur trade. The fur traders were the only white men seen by many Indians, and their behavior had a considerable effect on the attitude of the Indians toward the white government. The first attempt to deal with the problem was a long series of laws providing for the licensing of private traders and for the exclusion of all other persons from the Indian country. A trader was to be licensed only if he could show a good moral character and give a bond that he would not sell liquor to the Indians. These provisions looked fine on paper but were never enforced effectively; the small traders were a greater problem than the large companies. Licenses were easy to obtain, unlicensed traders were not ejected, and liquor sales and other undesirable practices continued to be widespread. The lack of necessary law enforcement personnel was decisive, and the Indians continued to be cheated unmercifully by many white traders.

A new attack on the problem came when the federal government itself entered the fur business, establishing its first "factory" in the Indian country in 1796; a total of 28 government trading houses were in operation at one time or another before the experiment ended. The hope was that a nonprofit-making organization providing first-rate goods at moderate prices would help the Indian, improve Indian–white relations, and force private traders to adopt better practices to meet the competition. At first the selling of liquor and the use of credit were outlawed. Although the first objective was at least approached, the second proved impossible. Private traders were still permitted to operate, but with the expectation that their number would decrease and that they would merely supplement the government system.

The small government establishments were never very successful. Their prices forced those of the private operators somewhat lower, but in the process the government faced steady losses. Among the reasons for this lack of success were the poor locations of government posts, the inability of the "factors" to travel widely among the Indians, less specialized and less efficient employees, bad judgment in the purchase of trading goods, poor furs that were improperly handled, and excessive credit to bad risks, including white soldiers of neighboring garrisons.

Private hostility to the government operations first became important after the War of 1812. The outstanding opponent was the American Fur Company, which went to

The White Trapper, by Frederic Remington. The trapper of the far west carried minimal equipment. (Granger)

the extent of encouraging Indian hostility toward the United States. It undercut the government on the staples it sold and advanced the prices of other articles; it lobbied vigorously. Among the politicians opposing government in business were Lewis Cass and Thomas Hart Benton, both friends of, and influenced by, John Jacob Astor of the American Fur Company. Cass was governor of Michigan, which had much fur trade and hence many traders. Benton's home state was Missouri, where the city of St. Louis was the most important center of the fur business. Political opposition was successful, and the government venture was abandoned in 1822, at which time there were 9 government factories and 126 licensed traders. The license system was continued, as were the violations.

The Americans, since they entered the fur trade rather late, found the most lucrative business monopolized by the English and Scotch companies. The long overland trip across the Appalachians was a serious handicap when competitors were using the easier St. Lawrence route; marketing and distributing facilities were underdeveloped until after 1800.

ASTOR   The most important single figure in the development of the fur business of the United States was John Jacob Astor, who was as far from being a frontiersman as can be imagined. Astor was born in Germany in 1763, and at sixteen left home to join a brother in the musical instrument business in London. During the winter of 1783–1784 he realized a long ambition by migrating to the United States. His only assets were seven flutes. He found work first as a baker's helper and then as an assistant to a fur merchant. After learning the fur business, he set up shop for himself, combining fur trading with the sale of musical instruments; eventually he dropped the musical side of his enterprise. At first he gathered most of his furs in central New York State and bought the rest in Canada; but gradually he developed an efficient collecting organization and was able to confine most of his attention to merchandising. About 1800 he expanded his operations to the Great Lakes region.

Along with his growing fur business, Astor combined trading with China, which was an excellent fur market, and by the beginning of the century had ships of his own engaged in trade with the Far East. Astor's strength and energy seemed inexhaustible, and everything he touched turned to gold. By the early 1800s he was one of the richest and most powerful men in the United States.

Then came the purchase of Louisiana, and Astor's mind was fired with the possibilities of the fur business in this new country. Why should he not monopolize the new region for himself? He thus envisioned a huge company with posts on the Great Lakes, and then along the Missouri and Columbia rivers to the Pacific Ocean. He dreamed of furs being taken to China to exchange for teas, silks, and spices, which would be returned to the United States to complete the circle of transactions. Included in the business would be the supplying of the Russian posts that stretched along the Pacific Coast of North America. Truly Astor had an ambitious dream embracing the entire world in its operations.

Astor's first move was to consolidate his existing position and obtain new capital by organizing the American Fur Company (1808) to control the region of the Great Lakes. Two years later he chartered the Pacific Fur Company, which was to be used in furthering his plans in the Far West. In practice it was difficult to distinguish the operations of these two companies, since Astor controlled both, and used their funds, supplies, and men interchangeably.

ASTORIA   The realization of Astor's dream of a series of forts along the Missouri and Columbia rivers was entrusted to the Pacific Fur Company. Partners were added to control field operations, and given approximately half of the stock. Astor himself advanced the necessary funds ($400,000) and agreed to assume any loss incurred within the first five years. Traders and *voyageurs* (boatmen) were hired from the North West Company.

The first planned fort of the projected chain was the most westerly one at the mouth of the Columbia. Two parties were to participate in its construction, the first to go west by sea and the second by land. The former started in 1810 on the trip around the Horn in the vessel *Tonquin*, commanded by Captain Jonathan Thorn, an able navigator but a stern, forbidding, and arbitrary disciplinarian. Thorn's attitude did not appeal to the extremely individualistic fur traders, who had ideas and wills of their own. The result was a series of misunderstandings and disputes, mostly personal, that marred the trip.

The *Tonquin* arrived at the mouth of the Columbia early in 1811 but had much difficulty in entering the river, losing a small boat with all on board before the entrance was finally effected. Upon entering the Columbia, Thorn discovered that the overland party had not arrived. After sailing up and down the river to pick a good place for a trading post, the men disembarked and built a small fort they named Astoria in honor of John Jacob Astor. The *Tonquin* and its crew left Astoria on June 1, 1811, to trade with the Indians along the coast. A surprise attack by the natives killed most of the crew; whereupon the remainder blew up the ship. The four men who escaped in a small boat eventually were killed.

Meantime the overland group under the leadership of Wilson Price Hunt had left New York in July 1810. Hunt first went to Montreal to engage *voyageurs* for the long trip, but difficulties were thrown in his way by the older companies and he had to do some of his hiring as he proceeded west. His route from Montreal was by way of Lake Huron and Lake Michigan, overland to the Mississippi, and then down that stream until he arrived at St. Louis in September. Ascending the Missouri to a point near the present St. Joseph, he established a permanent winter camp, and then returned to St. Louis to obtain additional supplies and an interpreter.

It was the middle of April 1811 before Hunt and his latest recruits joined the main group, and the whole party started up the Missouri. The plan was to ascend the river to the mouth of the Yellowstone, or as far as it was navigable, and then cut overland to a branch of the Columbia. Partway up the Missouri the men heard rumors of Blackfoot hostility and therefore changed their plans. Leaving the Missouri in present South Dakota, Hunt led his party through the Black Hills and ultimately across the Rockies to the headwaters of the Snake, which was descended by canoe until the river became impassable. The one large group was found to be unwieldy and so was divided into four, each group seeking its own route to the Pacific. Each of these small parties experienced terrible hardships and privations in its wanderings, and several men died. The last of the survivors reached Astoria on February 15, 1812.

The arrival of the overland party, together with the additional supplies brought by the ship *Beaver*, infused new spirit and vigor in the settlement at Astoria. The fort was strengthened, cabins were built, fish were caught and dried, trading was done with the Indians on the coast, and detachments were sent to deal with the tribes of the interior. Then came rumors of war between the United States and England, and the Astorians decided (1813) that because of their isolation and England's control of the sea their capture was only a question of time, so they might as well abandon the fort.

Before Astor's men departed, a force of North West Company traders arrived. To both groups the arrival seemed opportune. Many of the Astorians were Canadians, and in the fall of 1813 were easily persuaded to sell their post, particularly when they heard rumors of an approaching English warship. Some of them joined the North West Company. The Astorians were pleased to sell their property instead of having it captured by a British man-of-war, while the North West Company was glad to buy out a competitor at a moderate price. Within a month of the sale the British warship *Raccoon* arrived and "captured" Astoria. The commander was greatly disgruntled when he saw the insignificance of the small wilderness fort that he had crossed half the world to conquer.

The loss of Astoria ended Astor's plans in the Far Northwest, and he dissolved the Pacific Fur Company. The failure of the enterprise was not due to any fault in the overall plan, and only in small degree to the outbreak of the war. The decisive factors were the lack of adequate communications with the East, the failure to construct the series of forts originally planned to link East and West, and the mismanagement of the two groups sent into the field.

AMERICAN FUR COMPANY After his failure in Oregon, Astor concentrated his attention on the regions farther east. His operations in the Great Lakes country were strengthened until they became a monopoly; his control in the upper Mississippi Valley was almost as great. One estimate of the Astor company was expressed by Zachary Taylor, who commanded infantry in the upper Mississippi Valley in the 1820s: "Take the American Fur Company in the aggregate, and they are the greatest scoundrels the world ever knew." Later scholarly researchers have a different judgment, and have generally praised the company. In the matter of liquor, for example, the company preferred not to use it, but finally lowered its high standards to be able to compete effectively with smaller and less scrupulous operators; individual employees had always disregarded company policies.

The American Fur Company sent agents into the Missouri Valley in 1822, and during the same year established the headquarters of the western department at St. Louis. Gradually the employees of the company worked farther and farther up the valley, consolidating with or crushing competitors until it was supreme. In 1829 it established Fort Union at the mouth of the Yellowstone. Its boat, the *Yellowstone*, which ascended the river to Fort Union in 1832 and later to Fort Benton, was responsible for the opening of the steamboat business on the upper Missouri. Astor himself retired from the company in 1834, when its business was at a peak, but the American Fur Company remained dominant in the Missouri Valley for another decade.

The establishment of the western headquarters of the American Fur Company at St. Louis was one of the many indications of the increasing importance of that city as the center for the trans-Mississippi fur business. St. Louis, with its strategic position

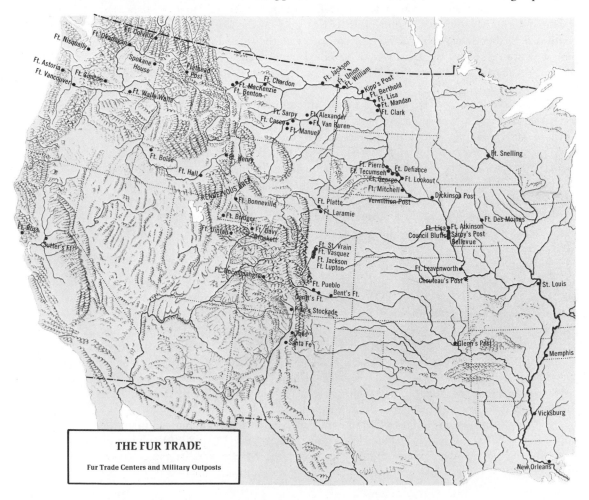

THE FUR TRADE

Fur Trade Centers and Military Outposts

on the Mississippi just below the mouth of the Missouri, was the natural outfitting point for traders and trappers and the logical place for them to market the furs they brought back. Here, quite understandably, were the headquarters of many companies doing business in the Far West.

MISSOURI FUR COMPANY The earliest important company with its main headquarters at St. Louis was the St. Louis Missouri Fur Company, commonly known as the Missouri Fur Company. The firm was started by prominent St. Louis men in the winter of 1808–1809, and included many of the best trappers, traders, and hunters in the West. Its first trading expedition, leaving St. Louis in 1809, was an imposing body: 160 men with their necessary supplies, materials for the establishment of four or five permanent posts, and outfits for equipping several smaller subparties. It ascended the Missouri River and built its first post on the Bighorn River. Then it continued farther west, constructing a second fort at the three forks of the Missouri; here it was attacked by the Blackfeet, who killed some twenty-five whites and caused the rest to abandon the fort. Farther west, a third post was established on the Snake River.

The first expedition of the Missouri Fur Company seemed pursued by an evil fate, for it met one misfortune after another. The attack by the Blackfeet was followed by other Indian encounters, physical obstacles proved unexpectedly difficult to overcome, some of the furs were accidentally burned, and all the forts eventually had to be abandoned. Nevertheless, the expedition showed a small profit. In 1816 a new method was adopted by which the company did not wait for the Indian to come to the fort but sent into the field parties that both trapped and traded. The Missouri Fur Company, like similar groups of the period, was reorganized frequently; in fact most of the fur companies changed their names and personnel so rapidly that it is almost impossible to follow consecutively the history of any one group.

ROCKY MOUNTAIN FUR COMPANY The Missouri Fur Company ended its precarious existence in the early 1820s and was succeeded by the Rocky Mountain Fur Company. The succession was not in any sense formal, but the same men who composed the earlier group were also active in the latter. The principal leaders of the new company were William H. Ashley, who had been born in Virginia, and Andrew Henry, who had come originally from Pennsylvania. Henry controlled operations in the field, while Ashley spent most of his time in St. Louis, arranging the financial affairs of the company, purchasing supplies, and disposing of the furs.

The first expedition of the Rocky Mountain Fur Company was announced in a little notice in the *Missouri Gazette & Public Advertiser* for February 13, 1822. One hundred "enterprising young men" were invited "to ascend the Missouri to its source, there to be employed for one, two, or three years." The expedition, which was away for two years, included some of the most famous trappers of the West. Among them was Jedediah Strong Smith, who later was responsible for the exploration of much of the unknown Southwest. There also was James Bridger, soon to become one of the best known of the mountain men. Not least was Hugh Glass, whose exploits were later described in the poems of John G. Neihardt. Glass, according to the usual tale, was at one time left for dead after an encounter with a grizzly bear, and crawled some two hundred miles without a gun, food, or adequate clothes to reach the nearest white habitation. Because of these many famous trappers, the first expedition of the Rocky Mountain Fur Company was notable in the history of the fur trade.

The later history of the Rocky Mountain Fur Company is difficult to follow since, like similar organizations, the company frequently changed its name, and at times lapsed completely or used no name at all. The title commonly given it is more a convenience than an exact designation. The company's field of operation was the upper Missouri Valley and the mountainous region beyond. A large part of its business was done in what is now the southern part of Idaho.

HUDSON'S BAY COMPANY   The chief competitor of the Rocky Mountain Fur Company in the Far Northwest was the Hudson's Bay Company, which had continued to push southwest after its absorption of the North West Company. Its chief agent in the Oregon country was John McLoughlin, who had established himself at Fort Vancouver, opposite the mouth of the Willamette, in 1825, and who became sufficiently powerful in the twenty years of his residence to deserve the title of "the King of Old Oregon." McLoughlin's power was absolute and he wielded it with choleric vigor. At the same time he was wise, generous, and hospitable, so that his monarchy was of the benevolent variety. Every traveler and trader who visited the region stopped at Fort Vancouver, where he was invariably well treated. The one exception was Hall J. Kelley, the Oregon boaster, whom he mistook for a cattle thief, but to whom he nevertheless gave shelter and care.

McLoughlin as representative of the Hudson's Bay Company was engaged in a three-cornered fight with the American Fur Company and the Rocky Mountain Fur Company for control of the Oregon region. In spite of the bitterness with which the contest was waged, McLoughlin's business dealings were fair and honorable; he treated the Indians generously and his own trappers justly. The profits of the fur trade of the region were only moderate, and one reason for maintaining the post was the desire of the Hudson's Bay Company to have an outpost to halt the advance of American trappers. Because of this situation McLoughlin was encouraged in his policy of trying to make the post self-sufficient. He fenced his fields, conducted a varied agriculture, raised stock, and built comfortable houses. When the first real agricultural settlers came to Oregon, McLoughlin was their friend, adviser, and helper—services for which he was later ill repaid. His control of Oregon was one of the brightest spots in the history of the fur-trading West.

NATURE OF THE FUR TRADE   The activities of the fur-trading companies were conditioned by the obvious fact that although furs originated on the North American continent the business was essentially European. Most of the furs were obtained in trade with the Indians in exchange for European-made articles. The furs themselves found their largest market in Europe, and European demand determined the American price. Even the traders, camp keepers, boatmen, and other participants in the trading were usually French and Spanish rather than American. The French language was in more common use than the English, and many of the terms of the business were French in origin.

The fur trade was also characterized by the large amount of credit involved in most transactions, and by the considerable element of hazard that produced either large profits or large losses. A period of approximately four years elapsed from the time the manufactured goods were shipped from Europe until the furs were returned and sold; almost every operation occurring in the interim was based on credit. The sale of goods, transactions of the middlemen, trading with the trappers and Indians, transportation, preparation, and sale of the furs were normally all credit operations. This emphasis on credit, when added to difficulties and dangers inherent in the business, produced a highly speculative industry. An annual profit of 50 percent was not unusual, and frequently the figure was much higher. On the other hand, the operations of a single year might result in total loss, often including the sacrifice of human lives.

PERSONNEL OF THE FUR TRADE   The personnel of the fur trade of the West was both interesting and distinctive, even though by no means inevitably ambitious or efficient. The most important individual was the "bourgeois," who was head of the permanent trading post and frequently a partner in the business, for employee ownership of stock is not a new concept. The position required considerable administrative ability, for it was the bourgeois who performed such functions as hiring hunters and trappers, supervising the trading, ordering the necessary goods and supplies, and setting the prices. Next in rank was the "partisan," who commanded field operations and held a rendezvous if there were no permanent post in the region. The first lieutenant of the bourgeois was the clerk, who was second in authority at the permanent post, taking complete command when his superior was absent; sometimes he held stock in the company.

In addition to the managerial force, an army of men performed the heavy manual labor. First of all there were two main types of white trappers—those who were hired by the year and those who had no direct connection with any particular company. The man hired by the year was paid a wage of about $400, for which he would give his entire catch to the company, while the "free trapper" disposed of his furs annually for whatever they would bring. Of lower social rank than the members of either of these groups were the camp keepers, each of whom received approximately $200 a year. The camp keepers performed all their duties in camp, where they tended the stock, and cleaned and dressed the furs. Another large group was that of the *voyageur*, who was usually a French Creole from Canada or Louisiana, and who did the arduous work of handling the boats. At the larger posts were artisans such as blacksmiths and carpenters. Unskilled labor went by the name of *mangeurs de lard* (pork eaters) and came principally from Canada. Not least in importance were the Indians who gathered a considerable proportion of the furs and traded them annually.

The most interesting and picturesque of these groups was the white trapping frater-

A Trader-Trapper. Stephen Bonga, born about 1789, lived in the Lake Superior region and on a photograph notation was called the "first white man at head of lake," meaning that anyone who was not Indian, was white or associated with the Anglo-Saxon group. (Minnesota Historical Society)

nity, which included such well-known men as Kit Carson, Jim Bridger, Jedediah Smith, Ewing Young, Bill Williams, and William Wolfskill. The white trappers were gaunt, brown, gloomy, taciturn men, with a dry native humor. Physical courage was essential for their existence; human life was not valued highly. They were the direct heirs of the Boone tradition, and knew the forest as intimately as the town dweller knew his front yard. They lived largely in the wilds, going to a trading post but once a year to exchange the season's catch for the necessities of life and for the ornaments so dear to their hearts. Most of them were improvident and were usually in debt to the trader; although it should be added that the trader's high prices, faulty measurements, and inaccurate book-keeping contributed to this situation. The trapper spent his earnings immediately, and then bought on credit as long as the trader would trust him. By winter he was penniless and had to go back to work.

The trapper favored a costume which was a curious mixture of Indian and white habiliments. Ordinarily he wore a light-blue cotton shirt, and over it a knee-length leather hunting shirt. Sometimes he wore breeches, but just as frequently he wore a breechcloth, allowing his thighs and hips to remain bare, Indian leggings and moccasins protected the feet and ankles, and a handerchief turban warded off insects and added a touch of color. Decorations were at a premium and included colored porcupine quills, feathers, and beads to fasten to his clothes, and feathers to thrust into his hair. His ammunition bag was attached to a belt that hung over his left shoulder in such a fashion that the bag came close to his right hand. In his belt were a knife, a hatchet, tobacco, sugar, and salt. A buffalo robe served for bed and cover, while a saddle made a high and hard pillow. Most of the trappers were excellent horsemen and very proud of their horses and equipment; the saddle and other gear were painted, embroidered, or decorated with feathers, beads, or silver. In the winter the trapper frequently lived in a rude hut, with an Indian wife to keep him amused and do his hard work; ordinarily he got along well with the Indians. His language was a medley of bad English, French, and Spanish. Rather curiously he had no interest in minerals except for decorative purposes; deposits of gold and silver were common knowledge, but no self-respecting trapper ever seriously considered descending to the ignoble work of mining.

TRADING POSTS   The permanent posts of the fur trade were notable landmarks in the wilderness of the West. Ordinarily they were rectangular or square, with sides between 100 and 400 feet in length. The walls were formed of pickets 12 to 18 feet high and 4 to 8 feet thick except in the South, where adobe walls were more common. Frequently a wooden path designed for defense was bracketed some 4 feet from the top. At diagonal corners were two blockhouses, each 15 to 18 feet square, two stories high, and surmounted by a roof. The blockhouse jutted out from the walls, so that it could command a clear view of the sides of the fort. The ground floor was designed for the use of cannon, and the upper story had peepholes for rifles. The strength of the blockhouse was attested by the fact that none was ever attacked successfully by the Indians. Somewhere in the picket wall of the fort was a heavy wooden door, well-buttressed, and usually with a small wicket to permit a view of the person desiring admittance without the need for opening the main gate. Indians were admitted only in small groups.

The buildings inside the stockade included barracks for the men, a storehouse, shops, the trader's house, and the clerk's house. Often there was a garden just outside the wall, and sometimes it too was barricaded. Livestock was ordinarily kept outside the walls, but in times of danger were brought inside. Life at the fort was slow and monotonous, but exciting moments came with the arrival of a caravan of goods from the East, a skirmish with the Indians, a hunting trip, or the departure of a trading expedition. In addition to the larger and more important posts were a number of smaller and less powerful stations scattered here and there throughout the West.

The alternative of the permanent trading post was the rendezvous, of which the first was held by Ashley in 1825 and the last by the American Fur Company in 1839. Its greatest use was in the region that is now southern Idaho and western Wyoming. The rendezvous was a specified gathering place for trading and had its principal advantage in obviating the necessity for a permanent post with a large personnel. A locality was chosen that had a good supply of grass and water, and to it would come the trappers, the Indians, and the traders from the East with their goods. The caravan left St. Louis early in the spring and arrived at the meeting place in late June or early July. Here it would stay and trade for the year's catch until either the furs or the goods were exhausted. Articles in special demand by both the Indians and the trappers were blankets, cloth, trinkets, beads, mirrors, jewelry, salt, sugar, tobacco, guns, ammunition, knives, and large quantities of liquor. Athletic contests, gambling, and drinking would occupy all of the days and most of the nights, and everyone was merry. Eventually the caravan would start its return trip in time to arrive in the East before winter.

Trading at all the posts was in goods and seldom in cash; the unit of value was the beaver skin. Manufactured goods were overvalued (from the standpoint of the trader), and whiskey was plentiful; consequently the trapper was ordinarily in debt and the Indian was impoverished, and considered a bad credit risk. The situation was on the whole favorable to the trader, who was thus assured that the trappers would be forced to work hard the next year, and that they would be likely again to do business with the same trader to whom they were in debt.

The fur trade reached the peak of its importance in the United States during the 1830s, after which it declined in relative significance, even though not in total value. The cream of the American fur supply had been skimmed, and advancing settlement was eliminating the trapper.

READINGS   *Paperbacks are marked with an asterisk.*

General   Hiram M. Chittenden, *The American Fur Trade of the Far West* (2 vols., 1954) is the classic account. Others of value include Paul C. Phillips, *The Fur Trade* (2 vols., 1961), encyclopedic; David S. Lavender, *The Rockies* (1968); Richard E. Oglesby, *Manuel Lisa and the Opening of the Missouri Fur Trade* (1963), good on early period; John E. Sunder, *The Fur Trade on the Upper Missouri 1840–1865* (1965), mostly American Fur Company; David S. Lavender, *The Fist in the*

Wilderness (1964), American Fur Company; *Lewis O. Saum, *The Fur Trader and the Indian* (1965), insists no single pattern; *Bernard DeVoto, *Across the Wide Missouri* (1947), mostly fur trade; *Harold A. Innis, *The Fur Trade in Canada* (1930), Walter O'Meara, *Daughters of the Country; The Women of the Fur Traders and Mountain Men* (1968). Regional histories almost always cover the fur trade. Government policy may be followed monographically in George D. Harmon, *Sixty Years of Indian Affairs, 1789–1850* (1941); Ora B. Peake, *A History of the United States Indian Factory System* (1954); *Francis P. Prucha, *American Indian Policy, 1790–1834* (1962).

Oregon and the Hudson's Bay Company John S. Galbraith, *The Hudson's Bay Company* (1957); *Oscar O. Winther, *The Old Oregon Country* (1950); D. W. Meinig, *The Great Columbia Plain* (1968). Richard G. Montgomery, *The White-Headed Eagle* (1934) is a biography of McLoughlin. Original narratives include Edwin E. Rich (ed.), *Letters of John McLoughlin* (1941), *Peter Skene Ogden's Journals* (1950), *Peter Skene Ogden's Snake Country Journal 1826–27* (1961); Alexander Ross, *Fur Hunters of the Far West* (1956).

Astor Good biographies are Harvey O'Connor, *The Astors* (1941); Kenneth W. Porter, *John Jacob Astor* (2 vols., 1931), scholarly; Arthur D. H. Smith, *John Jacob Astor* (1929), reads easily. Gabriel Franchère, *Adventure at Astoria* (1967) is an original account. The Stuart journal is reprinted in Kenneth A. Spaulding (ed.), *On the Oregon Trail* (1935) and Philip A Rollins (ed.), *The discovery of the Oregon Trail* (1935).

Trappers Good general accounts are Robert G. Cleland, *This Reckless Breed of Men* (1950); Bernard DeVoto, *The Year of Decision* (1943); *Harvey Fergusson, *Rio Grande* (1933); Stanley Vestal, *Mountain Men* (1937); Harvey L. Carter, *"Dear Old Kit"* (1968), Kit Carson; LeRoy R. Hafen (ed.), *The Mountain Men and the Fur Trade of the Far West* (5 vols., 1965–1968). Grace L. Nute, *The Voyageur* (1931) is excellent. Good biographies are J. Cecil Alter, *James Bridger* (1962); Levette J. Davidson and Forrester Blake (eds.), *Rocky Mountain Tales* (1947), Bridger stories; Alpheus H. Favour, *Old Bill Williams* (1936); Blanche C. Grant (ed.), *Kit Carson's Own Story of His Life* (1926); *Dale Morgan, *Jedediah Smith and the Opening of the West* (1953) and *The West of William H. Ashley* (1964); John E. Sunder, *Bill Sublette* (1959) and *Joshua Pilcher* (1968); Stanley Vestal, *Kit Carson* (1928); Donald D. Parker (ed.), *The Recollections of Philander Prescott* (1966), good on upper Mississippi Valley.

Forts Particularly good are David S. Lavender, *Bent's Fort* (1954); LeRoy R. Hafen and F. M. Young, *Fort Laramie* (1938); Erwin N. Thompson, *Fort Union: Trading Post* (1968).

Western Horizons. This William H. Jackson photograph successfully portrays the limitless sweep of the West that faced those traveling by wagon. (Geological Survey, National Archives)

Chapter 22 / FAR WESTERN EXPLORATION

Interest in the trans-Mississippi West increased steadily after the purchase of Louisiana and brought concern with the Louisiana boundaries that had originally seemed of little importance. The boundary between the United States and Canada was discussed in a desultory fashion, but hardly seemed vital as long as the questionable country was visited only sporadically by a few trappers. For a time there was talk of having the boundary follow the watershed of the Missouri, but ultimately it was found easier to agree on a straight line along the 49th parallel from the Lake of the Woods to the Rocky Mountains; such a line was at least comparatively easy to find and mark. The boundary west of the Rockies was not specified in the treaty of 1818, partly because both England and the United States had claims based on exploration and occupation. Provision was made that the Oregon country be left open to joint occupation for a period of ten years. In 1827 this provision was continued indefinitely until one of the parties should give notice of termination of the treaty. The boundary between Louisiana Territory and Mexico was settled in 1819 by the Adams-Onís Treaty, excluding the present American Southwest. Possibly the Texas region might have been included if the United States had been insistent.

The defining of western boundaries was necessary, but much less interesting to the general public than efforts to obtain accurate information about the soil, climate, physical features, flora and fauna, and native inhabitants of the Far West. The desire to obtain such information, coupled at times with the hope of monetary reward, lured a continuous procession of explorers across the continent, so that by the late 1830s the outstanding features of the Far West were reasonably well known.

The observations made by these explorers were remarkably keen and accurate, considering the difficulties of traversing an unknown wilderness and the usual lack of precise scientific instruments; many of the observations were made without the use of any instruments and represented only the experienced guesses of the explorers. The most obvious error of most explorers was the assumption that all of the western plains were semiarid or desert places that could never support a white agrarian population. This mistake was easy to make, since an explorer judged the fertility of the soil from the nature of its vegetation, and the trans-Mississippi country had but few trees and appeared to be very dry.

The expeditions going to the Far West were of every possible variety, but for convenience can be divided into three general groups. The first was the government party, moving under instructions from Washington, and usually commanded by a man who was interested in western exploration; its guide was ordinarily a westerner, frequently a former trapper, who had a firsthand knowledge of at least a portion of the country to be traversed. The second type was the trader who was motivated largely by the hope of personal gain, but who also in many cases was inspired by a desire for adventure in unknown parts of the country. The third group included the miscellaneous remaining expeditions of men going west to make their fortunes from salmon fishing, for the pure love of adventure, out of scientific curiosity, or for any one of the several reasons that lead men to perform new and dangerous exploits.

STEPHEN H. LONG The most noteworthy government explorer in the years shortly after the War of 1812 was Stephen H. Long of the Corps of Topographical Engineers. The Corps had been formed in 1777, but it had grown slowly. Its eventual dominance in western exploration, based largely on work done by men trained at West Point, came after the appointment of Colonel John J. Abert as its head in 1838. Long made his first trip in 1817, when he ascended the Mississippi River and built Fort St. Anthony at the junction of the Mississippi and St. Peter's (Minnesota) rivers. The expedition had little importance, except that the fort it established later became Fort Snelling and was on the site of the city of St. Paul.

Two years later Major Long was given command of the most pretentious expedition to be sent to the Far West since Lewis and Clark. Its aims were both scientific and military: the exploration of the region of the Missouri River, and a demonstration of power meant to impress the Indians, and the possible establishment of a fort which Calhoun hoped would in time be expanded to a whole series of posts for the control and protection of the West. The military section, under the immediate command of Colonel Henry Atkinson, spent the winter of 1819–1820 at Council Bluffs. Despite extensive plans the troops never advanced far beyond this point.

The scientific part of the expedition, under the direct command of Long, included a botanist, a zoologist, a geologist, an assistant naturalist, a painter and sketcher (for there were no cameras), and a topographical engineer in addition to the laborers necessary for moving the equipment and supplies. It was transported in the *Western Engineer*, a specially constructed 75-foot vessel that was one of the first steamboats to navigate the Missouri. The boat had its machinery hidden, and its bow was built to resemble a serpent's head; when the fires were burning, the smoke issued from the snake's nostrils. The vessel was better at frightening Indians than at carrying men and supplies; its speed was less than two miles an hour.

The scientific party made its way slowly up the Missouri, making observations as it went; it, too, spent the winter of 1819–1820 at Council Bluffs. By this time Congress was becoming impatient; the cost was great and the accomplishments were small. A congressional investigation led to the cutting off of financial support, and the expedition came to an end, which was unfortunate in view of its well-qualified personnel.

Long's failure did not prevent his being placed in charge of a new expedition in 1820 that was designed to explore the Platte, the Arkansas, the Red, and other rivers of the region. This was the same general task that had earlier been given to Pike. Long left St. Louis in June 1820 and made a leisurely trip up the Platte, arriving at the site of the present Denver on July 5. He failed to locate the headwaters of the Platte, but he viewed the peak that now bears his name, and one of his party climbed it. Turning south he sent half of his party home by the Arkansas; with the remainder he made a halfhearted effort to find the source of the Red River and then descended the Canadian River. By October he was back in St. Louis, having accomplished little and having added almost nothing to the knowledge of the region he had traversed. Like Pike, he classified the plains as a country unsuitable for farming.

In spite of Long's meager results to date, he was called upon to make another expedition in 1823, this time to explore the region between the Mississippi and the Missouri. Possibly because of his previous experiences he was able to accomplish more of importance on this expedition than he had in his former three expeditions combined. His party included a zoologist, a mineralogist, and a landscape painter, all of whom he recruited in the East.

The real start of the expedition was from Fort Snelling. During almost all the trip the force was divided, part going by boat with the luggage and the remainder exploring the shore; at night the parties joined to camp. The expedition moved down the Mississippi and then up the Minnesota, making careful observations along the way. The sources of the Minnesota and the Red River of the North were explored; then the party started the descent of the Red toward the town of Pembina in present North Dakota. Near Pembina the international boundary was located and marked.

Major Long's orders were to leave the Red River at the international boundary and follow the 49th parallel on his return trip to the East. Actually he found these orders impossible to follow because of the swampy nature of the ground, and so he continued along the Red River into Canada as far as Lake Winnipeg. Then he crossed to Lake Superior and followed the Great Lakes as far as New York State. He arrived at Philadelphia on October 26, 1823. The results of the expedition were satisfactory: a large amount of information was gathered about a hitherto comparatively unknown part of the country.

OTHER GOVERNMENT EXPLORERS   Although Major Long was the most outstanding of the western military explorers of the years 1815–1840, he was but one of many. Leavenworth, Atkinson, Dodge, and other western commanders who dealt with the Indians ranged far afield to collect both fact and rumor concerning unknown parts of the country. One of the best known of their expeditions was the demonstration of Colonel Henry Leavenworth against the Missouri River Indians in 1823, which resulted more in geographical information than in intimidating the Indians; Fort Leavenworth, named for the colonel, was established in 1827. Colonel Henry Atkinson led an Indian peace commission up the Missouri River in 1825; with his 476 men he made a great display of military force and obtained treaties of peace with the Indians whom he visited. On this trip, he traveled 120 miles above the mouth of the Yellowstone, but established no permanent posts. In the 1830s Colonel Henry Dodge led several Indian expeditions, of which the most important (1835) ascended the Platte and South Platte, returned along the Arkansas, and then went overland to St. Louis.

Probably the expeditions of Henry R. Schoolcraft, the Indian agent at Mackinac, should also be classified as military, or at least governmental. Most important was the expedition of 1832. With a party of thirty, including a geologist and a missionary, he skirted Lake Superior and ascended the St. Louis River. Portaging to the Mississippi Basin he eventually arrived at Sandy Lake, where there was an important trading center that had been visited by Pike a quarter of a century earlier. Continuing his trip he came to the farthest limit of previous exploration at Cass Lake, discovered and named by Lewis Cass. Here he reduced his party to those best able to continue the arduous trip upstream. Finally their hardships were rewarded by the discovery of Lake Itasca, that will-o'-the-wisp source of the Mississippi. Later, in 1818–1819, he made an extensive tour through the Ozark region of Missouri and Arkansas. His discoveries were important, but were overshadowed by his literary contributions to a greater understanding of the Far West. Schoolcraft had an immense knowledge of Indian ways and customs, and a facile pen; his writings greatly expanded the eastern knowledge of the western country and its inhabitants.

Best known of all military explorers in time became John C. Frémont, the "Pathfinder of the West." His first trip, a nonmilitary one, was an exploration of the Minnesota River in 1838. At this time he was only twenty-five, bright, quick, clever, hand-

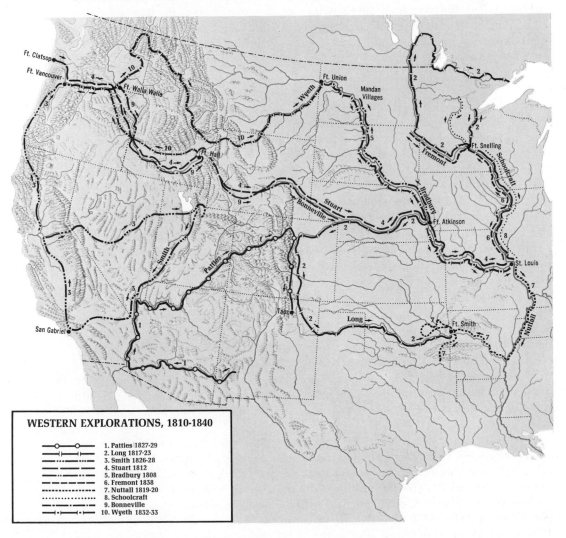

WESTERN EXPLORATIONS, 1810-1840

○—○—○	1. Patties 1827-29
├——┤	2. Long 1817-23
———————	3. Smith 1826-28
— — — —	4. Stuart 1812
—·—·—·	5. Bradbury 1808
–·–·–·	6. Fremont 1838
··········	7. Nuttall 1819-20
··········	8. Schoolcraft
—·—·—·	9. Bonneville
—┤—┤—┤	10. Wyeth 1832-33

some, and impetuous. The party of which he was a member was commanded by the eminent French scientist J. N. Nicollet, who gave Frémont much of the training he was to use on his later trips in the 1840s.

These and other minor military expeditions before 1840 increased vastly the information about the plains region of the Far West. The main rivers, such as the Missouri, Platte, Minnesota, Arkansas, and Red, had been explored and described. The outstanding physical characteristics of the plains had been recounted. Obviously the data still contained large gaps that would require many years to fill, but the essential information had been stated. But very little was known about the region west of the Rockies, unless vague rumors were to be given credence. No military expedition followed Lewis and Clark across the mountains until after 1840, partly because the United States had no exclusive possessions on the coast.

FUR TRADERS   Almost as important as the army men, and often ahead of them both geographically and chronologically, were the fur trappers and traders. The fur trade constantly opened new areas because of the normal expansion of the business, the push of settlement, and the depletion of eastern fields. The necessary expansion was by no means always unpleasant, for many of the trappers found pleasure and satisfaction in the exploration of new parts of the country. Frequently the trappers and traders went much farther than business required and often lost both time and money in their operations. Unexplored wilderness has always lured a certain type of man, whether he be a Marco Polo, a John Ledyard, a Robert Peary, or an Alexander Mackenzie.

The most active and able of the trader explorers was Alexander Mackenzie, a Scotsman operating in Canada. Fifteen years before the purchase of Louisiana and the exploration of Lewis and Clark, Mackenzie descended the river that now bears his name far enough to see the whales and the ice sheet of the Arctic Ocean at 69° 14′ north latitude (1789): one of the last unsuccessful efforts to find a Northwest Passage. Four years later he embarked on the adventure of reaching the Pacific Ocean overland. Ascending the Peace River he then crossed the mountains and descended the Fraser, finally painting his name on a rock on the coast on July 22, 1793. This feat was one of the most remarkable in the annals of the West. Mackenzie's small party was frequently without food, wet, surrounded by wild beasts, and faced by unknown natives. The trip was a monument to Mackenzie's endurance, to his mastery over men, and to his driving personality.

Other Canadian traders followed Mackenzie into the wilderness. David Thompson operated between Lake Winnipeg and the Mandan villages after 1795. He crossed the Rocky Mountains to the Columbia River in 1805, just failing to meet Lewis and Clark. Between 1807 and 1809 he traveled widely in the Oregon country. Donald McKenzie explored the Columbia and ascended the Snake River into present Idaho in the years just following 1818. Alexander Ross traversed much of the present northern Idaho in 1824. Peter Skene Ogden was also in the Idaho region during the 1820s, and later claimed to have discovered the Great Salt Lake in the winter of 1824–1825; probably the first white man to see the lake was Jim Bridger in 1825, although the matter is still in considerable doubt.

Traders of the Canadian companies moving southwestward were met by American traders moving to the northwest. Representatives of such companies as the Missouri Fur Company, Rocky Mountain Fur Company, and American Fur Company were pushing north and west from St. Louis during the early nineteenth century, with the Pacific Fur Company going the entire distance to the coast to establish Astoria. The American groups were particularly strong in the valley and near the headwaters of the Missouri, and in the southern Idaho region, where many a rendezvous was held in the 1820s and 1830s. Their greatest single discovery was the mountain route since known as South Pass, which was probably first used by the party of Robert Stuart returning from Astoria in 1812. This pass in present southern Wyoming is by far the best crossing of the mountains, since it has only a gradual grade all the way. After its discovery and popularization nearly all travelers to the Far West used it, and but few people traversed the more arduous passes near the headwaters of the Missouri.

The one great region that the traders had failed to explore by the middle 1820s was the Far Southwest beyond the mountains. This portion of the country was of course outside the boundaries of the United States; but international boundaries never hampered men searching for furs. More important to the trapper, it was an arid region of mountains and deserts, difficult to traverse and supporting relatively few fur-bearing animals. Moreover, it was far from any navigable rivers; the Colorado was impassable and the Rio Grande flowed through the inhabited part of Mexico. There seemed every reason why trappers would have no interest in this part of the country.

JEDEDIAH STRONG SMITH

In spite of the obvious drawbacks of the Southwest, several trappers became interested in it during the 1820s—probably more because of the excitement of prospective exploration than because of the opportunities for profitable trapping. Most important was Jedediah Strong Smith, who was responsible for the first exact information about the Far Southwest. In many ways Smith was an unusual man. He came from a New England family at a time when most traders were southern or western in origin, and he was deeply and sincerely religious. He drifted west in search of opportunity, and ultimately was attracted to St. Louis by the lucrative possibilities of the fur trade. He was a member of the first expedition of the Rocky Mountain Fur Company in 1822.

Smith accompanied William H. Ashley on the annual caravan of the Rocky Mountain Fur Company in 1826, but when Ashley stopped in present southern Idaho, Smith continued west. Following in general the later route of the San Pedro, Los Angeles, and Salt Lake Railroad, he eventually entered California, where he stayed throughout the winter. Early in 1827 he returned by the present Union Pacific route, leaving most of his party in California to await his return. He attended the rendezvous, where he joined two other men in buying out Ashley's business, and then persuaded his partners to trap in the Southwest.

Upon the completion of his business at the rendezvous Smith rejoined his party in California and started north along the coast. The trip proved unexpectedly difficult and dangerous, and a surprise attack by the Indians brought disaster. Only Smith and two others escaped with their lives; the furs which they had worked a year to collect were gone. After many trials and a vast amount of wandering, Smith finally reached Fort Vancouver, where he was received and kindly treated by John McLoughlin. In fact, McLoughlin went much further than the laws of hospitality required, recovering and paying for Smith's furs; in return Smith promised not to compete in the Oregon country. After Smith had rested he returned by way of the Missouri. At St. Louis he decided to give up trapping and to enter the Santa Fe trade. He died on the Santa Fe trail at the hands of the Comanche in 1831.

Smith's travels and adventures in the West were worthy of a Homer. Traveling thousands of miles through an unknown wilderness, penetrating forests full of wild animals, crossing raging torrents, paddling his canoe into unknown dangers, plodding across weary miles of sand, crossing snow-capped mountains, and continually evading hostile savages, his exploits in the decade that he spent west of the Mississippi verge on the miraculous. His own statement of motives is illuminating; "I of course expected to find beaver, which with us hunters is a primary object, but I was also led on by the love of novelty common to all, which is much increased by the pursuit of its gratification."

THE PATTIES   Two other trappers should be classed with Smith in the exploration of the Southwest during the 1820s. Sylvester and James Ohio Pattie, father and son, roamed the present states of New Mexico, Arizona, and California during the years 1824–1830 mining copper, hauling supplies, trapping, hunting, and fighting Indians (who nearly killed James on several occasions). In 1827 they gathered a small party and started down the Colorado River toward the ocean. Eventually they were forced to leave their boats and go overland, but the country was inhospitable and they nearly died of privation. Food gave out, and they ate their horses. Water gave out, and their mouths became so parched that they could speak only with the greatest difficulty. Sylvester, the eldest, collapsed first and begged to be left behind that the rest of the pary might be saved, but his son refused and they staggered on their way, partially supporting the old man.

When the Pattie company finally arrived at San Diego it received anything but a friendly greeting from the Spanish governor. The whole party was thrown into prison and fed spoiled food. Prison was unbearable for men who had been accustomed to vigorous outdoor life and who had just passed through a period of terrible hardship, and the older Pattie soon sickened and died. Shortly after his death a smallpox epidemic broke out on the coast; James Ohio, who was a jack-of-all-trades, offered to vaccinate everyone if he and his party were set free. The Spanish accepted the offer, and he vaccinated thousands of whites and Indians up and down the coast. For this service he was given his freedom, and eventually he made his way back through Mexico to the United States, where he arrived penniless and in bad health. The account of his travels, as edited by Timothy Flint, is a fascinating story of adventure and suffering.

PRIVATE EXPLORERS   The western exploration of governmental parties and of fur traders were but a few of the many trips to the region west of the Mississippi. Other travelers included private adventurers, observers, missionaries, sick men looking for health, and scientists in search of specimens. These men were largely responsible for the increase in eastern knowledge of the West, for they often kept and later published journals of their travels. Brief résumés of the travels of a few of these private adventurers will give an idea of what they accomplished.

John Bradbury, an English scientist interested primarily in botany, traveled up the Missouri River in 1809–1811; he published an interesting and illuminating account of his trip. Colonel John Shaw started in 1809 to go from Missouri along the 37th parallel to the coast; although he was turned back by the Indians before he attained his objective, he succeeded in reaching the mountains. The two years after his return (1809–1811)

Members of the Hayden Survey Resting in Camp. William H. Jackson, one of the best-known photographers of the West, left this view of one of the military surveying expeditions that criss-crossed the unknown land. (State Historical Society of Wisconsin)

Shaw spent in exploring a large part of Missouri and Arkansas. H. M. Brackenridge, an amateur botanist, published a good account of his trip up the Missouri River in 1811.

The best known of the many botanists who explored the Far West was Thomas Nuttall, who made numerous trips to the Northwest after 1810. Nuttall was the true scientist of fiction, and many stories are told of his care of specimens. After a hard day's work, when the entire company was wet, hungry, and exhausted. Nuttall would spend hours over the campfire, classifying and labeling with painstaking care the specimens he had collected during the day. At one time the party was caught in a sudden, savage storm on the Missouri and was saved from destruction only by Nuttall's presence of mind in grabbing a shrub on the bank, thus keeping the boat from being blown into the river; Nuttall's account of the incident consisted mostly of a classification of the shrub.

Only a few of the western travelers can be mentioned. Henry R. Schoolcraft explored for pleasure as well as for business and in 1818–1819 made an extensive tour through the Ozark region of Missouri and Arkansas. Prince Maximilian of Wied, one of many titled visitors, went a considerable distance up the Missouri in 1833–1834; his account of his observations was interesting, but even more valuable were the paintings of the excellent artist who accompanied him. Another painter, George Catlin, made several tours through the West in the 1830s and drew hundreds of pictures, mostly of Indians. An entirely different type of man was Father Pierre De Smet, a Jesuit priest who did very effective missionary work during the 1830s, particularly in the Idaho-Wyoming region. J. N. Nicollet, a scientist mentioned previously, made extensive surveys of the Mississippi and Missouri valleys between 1836 and 1840.

Another private adventurer, disproportionately publicized by the writings of Washington Irving, was Captain B. L. E. Bonneville, who received a leave of absence from the army from 1831 to 1833 to engage in trading. He outfitted at Independence and then journeyed over the Platte River route, trading as far west as present Idaho. As a commercial venture the trip was a failure; as a scientific enterprise it was unimportant, because the ground covered by Bonneville had been well known for two decades, and he had neither the knowledge nor the training for accurate scientific observation.

NATHANIEL J. WYETH The most spectacular of all the private trading expeditions were those of Nathaniel J. Wyeth, a solid and substantial New England ice merchant. Wyeth's interest in the West was inspired mainly by the enthusiasm of Hall J. Kelley, a New England schoolmaster who was so greatly impressed with the future of the Oregon country that he planned a colony on the Columbia River. Wyeth liked Kelley's proposals and so gathered a group of his friends and neighbors to join in the venture. Every Saturday night these prospective westerners met at Wyeth's house and made grandiose plans for their trip across the continent and for their operations when they arrived at the coast. In general they projected a trading expedition, but just what or where they would trade was left delightfully vague. Of course they expected to barter with the natives, but why not also do business with the white inhabitants of California, the Hudson's Bay Company, the Russian traders? Some talked also of salmon fishing on the Columbia.

Wyeth's group eventually got tired of waiting for Kelley's larger plans to materialize, and decided to go ahead on its own. The total membership of the Wyeth group was twenty-one, mostly farmers and artisans. Each man wore a sort of uniform of a coarse woolen jacket and pantaloons, a striped woolen shirt, and rawhide boots. Equipment included food, clothing, axes, beads, and trinkets. For the trip across the plains there were three amphibious monsters, part wagon and part boat. These transportational novelties were carefully fitted and caulked canoes with removable wheels, so that they could be used on both land and water. They were given the name Nat-wye-thium in honor of the leader of the expedition.

The Wyeth party decided that before it started its travels it needed some real wilderness experience, and so spent ten days on an island in Boston harbor. The people of Boston came in large numbers to view this curious group of explorers of the Far West.

The actual start for the West came in March 1832, when the party sailed to Baltimore and then rode on the newly opened Baltimore and Ohio Railroad to the end of the line. The journey over the mountains proved long and arduous, largely because of the necessity of dragging the wagon-boats over the hills. At one place the innkeeper refused to give the travelers rooms, alleging fear of Yankee shrewdness; possibly the curious appearance of the party played some part in his decision. Upon reaching the Ohio River the party continued its trip to St. Louis by boat. Here the wagon-boats were sold, since every westerner advised Wyeth that such vehicles could not be pulled over rough ground, or through forests and mountain passes, or paddled over the rapid streams of the West.

The expedition crossed the plains, attached to the trading party of Bill Sublette (1832). From time to time some members became so discouraged they went home. Eventually the more persistent reached present southern Idaho, but by that time everyone was thoroughly disheartened, and all would have started home except that the return trip was more difficult than continuing west and taking ship to Massachusetts. Wyeth and eleven others eventually arrived at Fort Vancouver on the Columbia River, where the party disbanded. Wyeth was back in Boston before the end of the year, defeated but not discouraged.

Wyeth certainly possessed the virtue of persistency; he immediately planned a second trip, which he made in 1834. He benefited from his former experiences, and although the expedition was a financial failure, it did not end as disastrously as the first. Wyeth trapped, and fished for salmon, but without profit. On the Snake River in present southern Idaho, he built Fort Hall, which was an important outfitting point for many years. Eventually he gave up his western dreams and returned to Boston, where he reentered the ice business and died fairly wealthy.

As a result of these and many other expeditions, by the end of the 1830s the Far West had become fairly well known. It was still considered generally uninhabitable; but the reports of government-sponsored explorations were printed, the journals of private travelers published, and the tales of the fur traders told and retold, so that the average easterner came to have fairly accurate notions of the main physical features. In addition, these many expeditions trained a considerable number of guides who later were able to lead other parties to the newer parts of the country with but a fraction of the difficulties encountered by their predecessors. The Far West was becoming known.

TRAFFIC ACROSS THE PLAINS The main distributing center for business to and from the Far West was St. Louis, which was strategically situated for commerce in the Missouri Valley, on the South Pass route, and to Santa Fe. For the usual traveler, however, the actual outfitting and jumping-off place was farther west, nearer the great bend of the Missouri. The town of Franklin, opposite present Boonville, was the busiest of such centers until 1818, when the river changed its course, and washed the town into oblivion. Its successors were most notably Independence and Westport (present Kansas City), but other towns also participated.

Traffic across the plains started in the spring as soon as there was grass for the livestock and the ground was firm enough to support wagons. To be ready for the earliest possible move, traders, trappers, soldiers, interpreters, hunters, guides, boatmen, and missionaries crowded the Missouri River towns for several weeks in the early spring. By the 1840s the addition of settlers migrating to the Pacific Coast brought a chaos of tents, livestock, wagons, and equipment, making bedlam of the towns. Whereas the bulk of early travel went over the Santa Fe trail, now the Platte River route, with its connections to both California and Oregon, took precedence. Each party was well organized—a sort of rolling republic—to provide for all sorts of contingencies, including attack, sickness, marriage, and crime.

Parties traveling across the plains varied in equipment and personnel. Traders bound for a mountain rendezvous or for Santa Fe carried an irreducible minimum of clothes and food, since they conserved all possible space for trading goods. A few staples such as flour, bacon, coffee, sugar, and salt supplemented a diet that consisted mainly of game shot along the route. The army expedition carried more food, although it hoped to vary its meals with game; if engaged in an elaborate survey, both the personnel and the equipment were exceedingly varied. Settlers carried the largest amount of personal possessions, since they needed household furnishings similar to those of their predecessors in the Ohio Valley. Their covered wagons were filled with everything that the owners felt could be hauled across the continent, but frequent errors in judgment were attested by the discarded equipment that soon lined the road.

Motive power was a matter of considerable differences of opinion. Horses were fastest, but most easily exhausted; they were most useful in the fur trade. Mules were more sturdy but not quite as fast; they were preferred in the Santa Fe trade, where speed was desirable but where long arid stretches made horses a poor gamble. Oxen, slow but hardy, were the choice of most settlers and freighters. The difficulties of travel necessitated more than one team for a wagon. Ordinarily the Santa Fe traders used eight mules; settlers, four to six oxen, with other animals in reserve for emergencies.

Travelers usually moved in groups to be able to cope with the natural and human dangers that might be encountered. A fur caravan might have fifty to a hundred men, with three or four times that many horses and mules. Other parties might range from five wagons to a hundred or more, with the larger groups becoming more prevalent as settlers increased in number. The smaller party could move faster and was less troubled by internal dissension, but the larger group was safer.

The usual practice was for individuals and families to leave the Missouri River in the early spring and then to stop at Council Grove in present eastern Kansas to organize

Surveying the West. This photograph, by A. J. Russell, was taken in the Uintah Mountains in connection with the building of the Union Pacific Railroad. (Union Pacific Railroad)

parties for the rest of the trip, whether to Santa Fe, California, or Oregon. Semimilitary organizations were created, and the various jobs such as cooking, gathering wood, feeding the stock, and standing guard were allocated.

The average day of travel on the plains was anything but exciting—a plodding, dusty trip broken only by lunch and by short rest periods in the middle of the morning and the middle of the afternoon. A campsite had to have grass and water, and if possible the caravan stopped early enough to complete all necessary chores before dark. The wagons were arranged in a circle and a guard was set, with the horses brought into the circle only in time of Indian danger. The usual day's trip was possibly fifteen miles, but the distances covered ranged widely from the two or three miles made by settlers confronted with adverse conditions to the thirty or forty miles made by professionals. Sundays were often used for rest and repairs.

The prevailing impression of plains travel was the slow pacing of countless miles in the scorching heat of the sun, the caravan enveloped by clouds of dust and the travelers suffering from parched, irritated throats. Fear of hostile Indians was less pressing than worry over cholera, and over the necessary minimum of water, grass, and game. A severe storm might flood the camp and stampede the animals. Sickness was common, particularly the internal upsets created by an improper diet. Accidents might come from an undesired contest with a bear, a snake, a mule, or a horse, by a misstep on a mountain, or from a bursting gun. The necessary human repairs were then as rough as wagon repairs. A snakebite might bring incision and searing with a hot iron, with the sufferer first fortified by whiskey taken internally; some men confined the treatment to the whiskey. An amputation might be performed with a butcher knife and a meat saw, but gangrene ordinarily cut short the sufferings of the victim.

Indians were normally friendly and hospitable, but there were important exceptions. Indians sought dignity and reputation by joining war parties to steal horses and collect scalps. In addition, the Indian was sensitive to personal slights and believed in personal retribution for any damage to himself or his family. When seeking revenge he was not always careful to harm the same man who had harmed him.

The whites were not without sin in the relations between the two races. White traders cheated the natives, white hunters drove off their game, and white government took their land. Like the Indians, the whites were not discriminating as to whom they punished for any trouble. An Indian raid frequently brought retribution to someone, but very possibly not to the person or group that created the original disturbance; all Indians looked very much alike to white eyes. In fact, most westerners were convinced that the only desirable Indian was the one who had ceased to breathe, and many were willing to help along the good work. Not infrequently a white took a shot or two at a stray Indian just for target practice.

Indian attacks were made but seldom on large white parties. Most Indians were armed with bows and arrows, and were not anxious to face white guns. Small white parties, however, might have their possessions stolen or even at times be attacked. The resulting engagement might be bitter and bloody, with each side employing every stratagem that generations of frontier warfare had developed. Mutilation of the dead was common for both Indians and whites, for plains warfare followed no strict military code.

Indian troubles tended to increase as the years passed. The first explorers and trappers found the various tribes generally peaceful, but as racial contacts increased so did frictions. In part the conflicts were caused by the less desirable and more headstrong of each race, but in part they were the inevitable outcome of an aggressive culture moving into control of a region occupied by a proud and warlike people. A completely peaceful removal of the Indian control of North America was difficult to imagine.

READINGS   *Paperbacks are marked with an asterisk.*

Secondary Travel Accounts   *William H. Goetzmann, *Army Exploration in the American West* (1959) and *Exploration and Empire* (1966), detailed; James C. Bell, *Opening a Highway to the Pacific, 1838–1846* (1921), scholarly; Robert G. Cleland, *A History of California* (1922); Gloria G. Cline, *Exploring the Great Basin* (1963); Leland H. Creer, *The Founding of an Empire* (1947), Utah; Harrison C. Dale, *The Ashley-Smith Exploration* (1918), monograph—1820s; Gordon C. Davidson, *The North West Company* (1918); *Everett N. Dick, *Vanguards of the Frontier* (1941), reads well; Le Roy and A. W. Hafen, *Old Spanish Trail* (1954); James Monaghan, *The Overland Trail* (1947), Wyeth; Dale L. Morgan, *The Great Salt Lake* (1947) and *Jedediah Smith and the Opening of the West* (1953), very good; Richard C. Wood, *Stephen Harriman Long* (1966); Allan Nevins, *Frémont* (1939); Richard A. Bartlett, *Great Surveys of the American West* (1962), 1867–1879; Mark S. Wade, *Mackenzie of Canada* (1927); see also biographies of fur traders in Readings for Chapter 21.

Original Accounts   Richard Glovey (ed.), *David Thompson's Narrative, 1784–1812* (1962); Dale L. Morgan (ed.), *Overland in 1846* (2 vols., 1963); Dale L. Morgan and Eleanor T. Harris (eds.), *The Rocky Mountain Journals of William Marshall Anderson* (1967), 1834; Philip A. Rollins (ed.), *The Discovery of the Oregon Trail* (1935), Stuart diary; Albert J. Dickson (ed.), *Covered Wagon Days* (1929), central route in 1860s; Matthew C. Field, *Prairie and Mountain Sketches* (1957), Wyoming in 1843; John F. McDermott (ed.), *Up The Missouri With Audubon* (1951); Lloyd McFarland, *Exploring the Northern Plains, 1804–1876* (1955); Philip P. Mason (ed.), *Schoolcraft's Expedition to Lake Itasca* (1958); Henry R. Schoolcraft, *Narrative Journal* (1953); Walter Sheppe (ed.), *First Man West* (1962), Mackenzie; Reuben G. Thwaites, *Early Western Travels* (31 vols. and atlas, 1904–1907), vols. V–VI, XIII–XVII, XXII–XXX.

Chapter 23 / MEXICO ATTRACTS

American advances toward the West met not only a wilderness to be conquered and red men to be brushed aside, but also a fringe of Spanish settlements. Spain had by accident entered the American continent in the Caribbean area, which led to the use of Mexico as a base of operations.

By 1540 Spanish expeditions had visited considerable parts of the present American Southwest. Men such as Cabeza de Vaca and Hernando de Soto should rank with Mackenzie and Lewis and Clark. Most impressive was the expedition of Francisco Coronado (1540–1542), which included three hundred horsemen in burnished armor, foot soldiers, hundreds of servants and friendly Indians, artillery, livestock, and provisions. The main goal of acquiring precious metals was not achieved, and after penetrating the continent as far as present Kansas, the expedition returned, bedraggled and discouraged.

The Spanish had visions of gold, silver, and precious stones, including the imaginary Seven Golden Cities of Cibola, but they were also interested in other sources of wealth and in the saving of pagan souls from damnation. In pursuit of these goals representatives of church and state plodded toward the north, establishing towns, garrisons, and churches. The last important Spanish expansion in the American Southwest came when the priesthood, led by Father Junipero Serra and backed by the army, advanced along the Pacific Coast. San Francisco was established in 1776, the year of American independence. Spain's ultimate failure to hold the Southwest was owing mainly to a lack of manpower. Probably the white population of the late eighteenth century was no more than 15,000, concentrated largely in the Rio Grande settlements, of which Santa Fe (1609) was capital and metropolis. Many of these 15,000 were of mixed blood, with divided loyalties.

SPANISH CIVILIZATION   Spanish control of the wilderness depended largely on the army, stationed in presidios (garrisons). These posts were few in number, and seldom manned by more than twenty or thirty men, who had difficulty in overawing the thousands of natives. Indian outbreaks and depradations were almost continuous; the worst of these was the Pueblo revolt of 1680, which brought death to a sixth of the whites, and drove most of the rest out of the area for the time being.

Even more conspicuous than the military were the Franciscan, Dominican, and Jesuit priests, who often arrived with, or even before, the soldiers. Church and state were indivisible, with the state preserving order to permit the saving of souls, and the church civilizing and Christianizing the natives to produce loyal subjects of His Catholic Majesty. The good friars had impressive results in the number of those baptized; as early as 1630 the New Mexico missions claimed 60,000 converts. Unfortunately these results came in good part from the lure of Spanish goods and the force of Spanish arms. From time to time the Indians deserted the Prince of Peace in favor of theft, arson, and murder, and when Spanish military power lapsed they tended to revert to their primitive ways of life.

The missions were by no means devoted exclusively to religion. They functioned as

---

The Prairie Schooners. Many a traveler in a wagon train talked about the day when another kind of train would move across the land more rapidly and in greater comfort. (Association of American Railroads)

inns, hospitals, and schools. They had large herds of cattle and horses, flocks of sheep and goats, great fields of grain. They did a certain amount of manufacturing, including wine and stronger liquors. After all, one of their prime objectives was to transform the Indian into a settled farmer or artisan.

Near each mission was an Indian town or pueblo, designed to make easier the supervision of the natives. Usually also there was a town of whites, sometimes created by force, as when soldiers were required to bring their families; in many cases the whites intermarried with the natives. Outside the towns were numerous cattle ranches, since cattle were cheap and land seemingly inexhaustible. But since there were few available markets, the average rancher lived in a crude log or adobe cabin, from which he dispensed open-handed but limited hospitality.

The golden age of the Spanish West occurred approximately from 1790 to 1810. The usual settlement involved a mission, a presidio, and a civilian town, and was worried mainly about the possibility of hostile Indians. Many of the missions were extremely prosperous. Spanish administration was not severe; many local officers were left largely to their own preferences. United States population was quite remote, and American energies seemed channeled to the north with the purchase of Louisiana.

INCREASING DISORDER   Peaceful stability declined rapidly as a succession of revolutions swept the land, including the successful revolt of 1821. Garrisons became less effective as they were reduced in size and paid irregularly. Among the more spectacular results was an increase in piracy. Jean Lafitte, after a checkered career in the United States, took over Galveston in 1817. His operations were efficient and profitable, and he became so strong that Americans appearing in the area felt that the course of discretion was to make their peace with him.

The faltering Mexican control also brought hope to Americans living near the Mexican border. They viewed with avarice the herds of cattle and horses, the millions of fertile acres, and the trapping opportunities, all of which stretched west to the Pacific Coast. Also attractive were the trading opportunities provided by the badly supplied and isolated communities, of which the towns of the Rio Grande seemed particularly promising.

Even before 1800 Americans began to seep into Mexican territory for trading and raiding; usually they ended in jail. Most spectacular of the early filibusterers was Philip Nolan, horse trader (and horse thief), friend of Jefferson, and protégé of Wilkinson. His last expedition (1800) got as far as the Brazos, and ended when Nolan was killed by Spanish soldiers and his men were imprisoned. His connection with Wilkinson was thought-provoking. Wilkinson was also involved in the Burr plans, which looked toward the Southwest. He gave Pike the order to traverse Spanish territory. His son was a member of the Gutiérrez–Magee expedition, and his nephew James Long led still another party.

The Gutiérrez–Magee expedition of 130 men invaded Texas in 1812 in the name of Mexican patriotism. Bernardo Gutiérrez de Lara was a Mexican patriot and Augustus

Magee a resigned American army officer. After occupying San Antonio, Magee died under mysterious circumstances, and the force was rent by internal dissension, where-upon a loyal Spanish army brought the final collapse, with neither side showing mercy. A somewhat similar expedition was that of James Long, formerly a surgeon in the United States Army. With seventy-five recruits from Natchez, Long captured Nacogdoches in 1819 and declared Texas "free." In time he was defeated, and suffered the usual punishment: he was shot, and his men were imprisoned.

American filibustering in Texas received no governmental support. The Florida treaty of 1819 had specifically excluded Texas from the United States, even though plausible claims might have been advanced. At the time of the Long expedition it must have seemed to anyone east of the Appalachians, including the king of Spain, that American colonization and acquisition of Texas were extremely remote possibilities.

SANTA FE TRADE   Conditions west of the Sabine changed markedly in 1820 when, as a result of a Spanish revolution, foreign settlement in the empire was permitted. Hardly had this news reached America when a successful Mexican revolu-tion (1821) inspired visions of possible American trade and settlement, dependent only on the attitude and strength of the new Mexican government.

The most important trade to be developed was that with Santa Fe, which involved other Rio Grande settlements, and extensions west and south. The trade began in 1821, with the somewhat accidental venture of William Becknell; after a rather tentative start it became regularly organized, so that each year a caravan moved west as soon as the ground was passable, and returned before the coming of snow. The usual jumping-off place was some town on the Missouri River, such as Independence or Kansas City. The early part of the trip was a helter-skelter affair, with the various drivers congre-gating at Council Grove (present Kansas) to organize for mutual protection. Officers were elected, guards and cooks appointed.

The trail from Council Grove went directly west to the great bend of the Arkansas River, up the river for some hundred miles, then across the Cimarron desert to the Cimarron River (a branch of the Arkansas), up the Cimarron, and finally cross-country to Santa Fe. The alternate way was to continue up the Arkansas to Bent's Fort, near the present La Junta, Colorado, and then turn directly south. The alternate route was safer but also longer, so it was used relatively little.

The dangers of the trip were considerable. Sometimes food was scarce, since the supply depended largely upon finding buffalo. Water was also a problem: rivers had to be forded, and one real desert had to be crossed. The Indians, particularly the Comanche, were dangerous. The import tax at Santa Fe was often intimidating, some-times going as high as 60 percent, but lessened somewhat by the customary bribing of officials. Despite such troubles the trade prospered, with an average trip bringing a profit of 10 to 40 percent.

The importance of the Santa Fe trade was not its dollar value. The average between 1822 and 1843 was $130,000, with the largest year (1843) totaling $450,000. The years after 1844 and through the Civil War saw larger amounts, but still not spectacular. In fact the American government provided only moderate protection (six military escorts between 1829 and 1845) on the grounds that the business did not warrant more; an incidental factor was that an American escort had to stay in American territory, as far as Bent's Fort, while most traders went across the Cimarron desert.

More positively, the Santa Fe trade appealed strongly to a nation nurtured on Cooper and Irving. Fighting Indians and forest fires, shooting buffalo and other game, fording rivers, crossing deserts, attending Spanish fandangos, and eating chile con carne, all seemed exciting. Then too there was the romantic appeal of the dusky, dark-eyed Mexican beauty with her high combs, her long black cigaret, and her alluring eyes and figure, while dirt and vermin were invisible over a space of a thousand miles. Even more important, the Santa Fe trade dispelled any illusion of Mexican power, while observation began to dispel the idea of a Great American Desert and worked toward the disintegration of the permanent Indian frontier.

AMERICAN SETTLERS IN TEXAS   If the Santa Fe trade disclosed Mexican weakness, the beginning of American migration to Texas proved the point beyond contradiction. In the vanguard was Moses Austin, Connecticut Yankee, who had long pursued unsuccessfully the will-o'-the-wisp of success. He received a land grant (1821) between the San Jacinto and Lavaca rivers under the newly liberalized Spanish policy. Moses died before he could profit by his good fortune, but his son Stephen obtained a reaffirmation of the grant, with supreme power for himself in such matters as distributing land, laying out towns, and administering justice. By the end of the decade he had attracted some 5000 Americans, enthusiastic about the cheap land.

Other Americans, including Wilkinson, tried to follow the Austin pattern. The Mexican government sidestepped any decision of its own by transferring most power to the individual states, and in 1825 the state of Coahuila and Texas authorized grants by which an empresario would be given a large tract of land if he attracted a proper number of settlers. Each colonist could buy land cheaply, with the payment spread over six years. Agricultural implements could be imported tariff free. Taxes were omitted for six years, and then levied at half the normal rates for the next six years. Under this liberal policy Texas soon became a patchwork of claims. The desirability of developing the area is understandable, but the examples of East and West Florida should have made Mexico more cautious; soon it would rue bitterly its generosity.

American farmers found Texas desirable. By 1827 their number was possibly 10,000, three years later it had doubled, and by 1835 it reached 35,000. Most of the newcomers were from southern states, but some came from as far as New England, and a few hailed from Germany and Ireland; later talk of a slaveholders' conspiracy was fantastic. Theoretically they were all loyal Catholic citizens of Mexico, but actually both their patriotism and their Catholicism were scarcely skin-deep. Catholic priests and Mexican soldiers were greeted with apathy. Some of the later arrivals married Mexican girls, which indicated not Pan-American unity but the scarcity of women and the larger land grants offered to married men. Here and there settlers expressed openly their desire for United States control, but most followed Austin's lead in preserving at least technical loyalty to the Mexican government.

One straw in the wind was the Fredonia revolt of 1826–1827. Haden Edwards had an empresario grant that included Nacogdoches, and that caused trouble with earlier grantees, mostly Mexican. When the government reacted by canceling the Edwards grant, Edwards revolted, and appealed to the United States for aid; the appeal was refused and the revolt was crushed. The trouble was unimportant in itself, but it gave pause for thought to informed and intelligent Mexicans. Clearly there were wide and deep differences between the Mexicans and the Anglos, particularly in government

Ezra Meeker and His Prairie Schooner. In 1852, Meeker with his young wife and child crossed the plains in this wagon. A half century later he retraced his steps in a rebuilt version of the wagon. Then in his eighties, he lectured along the way, charging 5 cents admission. In that modern day of speedy railroad trains many a youngster had never seen an ox-drawn vehicle of this type. (Union Pacific Railroad)

and religion. Each looked at the other with suspicion and even hostility. Each felt the other inferior. The final explosion came daily closer as American predominance in numbers increased, and as the interest of the United States government became apparent with the effort of President Adams to buy Texas.

STRONGER MEXICAN POLICY   Mexican fears inspired a severely restrictive policy in 1830. Further immigration from the United States was prohibited. Empresario grants were canceled whenever legally possible. Foreign ships were admitted to Mexican coastal trade in the hope that the traffic to New Orleans would be decreased. Texan garrisons were reinforced in 1830 and 1831. Finally, an effort was made (1832) to encourage immigration from non-American countries.

The Mexican reforms were too little and too badly enforced to be effective. A handful of poorly paid and badly equipped Mexican soldiers could not guard a thousand miles of frontier. Americans continued to arrive, while other nationals did not; in fact, the impossibility of excluding Americans was admitted in 1833, when the law excluding them was repealed. Trade with New Orleans continued. Obviously the colonists, including those formerly loyal to Mexico, were becoming more and more irritated. American settlers made belligerent demands for their "rights." President Jackson made a new offer for Texas, and talked also of California; his swashbuckling representative Anthony Butler suggested wholesale bribery of Mexican officials; but Old Hickory's morality was affronted, and Butler was recalled.

Just when Butler's mission was becoming hopeless (1832) a friend of Jackson's, Sam Houston, appeared on the scene; the coincidence may of course have been an accident. Houston had served with Jackson in the War of 1812, had practiced law, and had been a member of Congress. At the age of thirty-four (1827) he had been elected governor of Tennessee, and two years later he had married. Within three months of his marriage he had thrown up his job as governor, deserted his wife, and fled to the Indian country, where he assumed Indian ways, including an Indian wife, and drank to excess. Twice in the next three years he had been entertained by Jackson in the White House. When he entered Texas he was a marked man, both because of his friendship with the President, and because of his impressive build, deep voice, and engaging manners. His immediate involvement with groups favoring Texan independence can hardly be divorced from his friendship with Jackson.

During the very year of Houston's arrival a small Texan revolution occurred, although there is no connection between the two events. This revolution, precipitated by certain custom's restrictions, coincided with a successful Mexican revolution by Santa Anna. This leader dispatched an army to Texas, but more important to the outcome was Austin's conveyance of Mexican promises of reform, which led the Texans to lay down their arms and give three cheers for the "liberal" Santa Anna. The Texans were soon disillusioned when Santa Anna (1834) dropped his pretended liberalism, assumed dictatorial powers, and planned the military chastisement of Texas.

TEXAS REVOLUTION   Events moved rapidly to a crisis. General Martín Perfecto de Cos entered Texas in September 1835 and a month later Texas created a provisional government and gave Houston command of the army. Cos was defeated and driven south, whereupon Santa Anna took personal command; he crossed the Rio Grande on February 12, 1836, and on March 2 Texas proclaimed its independence.

Both sides to the conflict had obvious difficulties at the outset. Santa Anna, while having more men, was troubled by poor equipment and low morale. Sam Houston not only had fewer men, but these men were banded in small groups variously armed and equipped, and with little discipline; they insisted on following their own ideas of combat. Santa Anna took full advantage of his temporary superiority. A small group of Texans was defeated at San Patricio, and the survivors were executed. Another force was surrounded at San Antonio, and the battle ended only with the death of the last defender of the Alamo. A larger group surrendered at Goliad, whereupon the members were massacred. Santa Anna insisted that rebellion should be punished severely.

These slaughters had the effect of making Santa Anna less cautious, and of unifying and angering the Texans. Battle cries of "Remember the Alamo!" and "Remember Goliad!" became common as Houston started retreating eastward with his 350 men, gathering recruits as he went. Everyone agreed that the retreat was inevitable; but as Houston collected more men and still did not fight, many Texans became bitter and sullen, and some of them deserted.

The attitude of the United States was a matter of considerable importance. Public meetings demanded federal action, and sent supplies, munitions, and men to help the rebels. The government winked at these aids flowing across the border, but otherwise maintained a proper neutrality. President Jackson followed the fighting closely, and undoubtedly prayed for a rebel victory; he sent General Gaines to the border, perhaps hoping that he would follow the Jackson precedent of the invasion of Florida. More positive action might well have occurred if Houston had been defeated.

Ultimately Houston and Santa Anna confronted each other on the San Jacinto River near Galveston Bay. Rather surprisingly Houston waited until Santa Anna was reinforced, and then made a frontal attack on a superior position on April 21, 1836. The result was a total victory, perhaps in part because Mexican military tradition did not envision a frontal attack on a superior position by an outnumbered army. Santa Anna was himself captured, but then freed on his promise to support Texan independence—a promise he later repudiated on the grounds that it had been extorted by force.

TEXAS INDEPENDENCE   The Houston victory inspired Texan refugees to return. The constitution was given popular approval, and Houston was elected president. A minister was sent to the United States, and annexation was favored by an almost unanimous vote. Rather surprisingly Jackson was not only cool toward annexation, but lukewarm even about recognition; his attitude was probably influenced most importantly by domestic political considerations. At any rate he passed the buck to Congress,

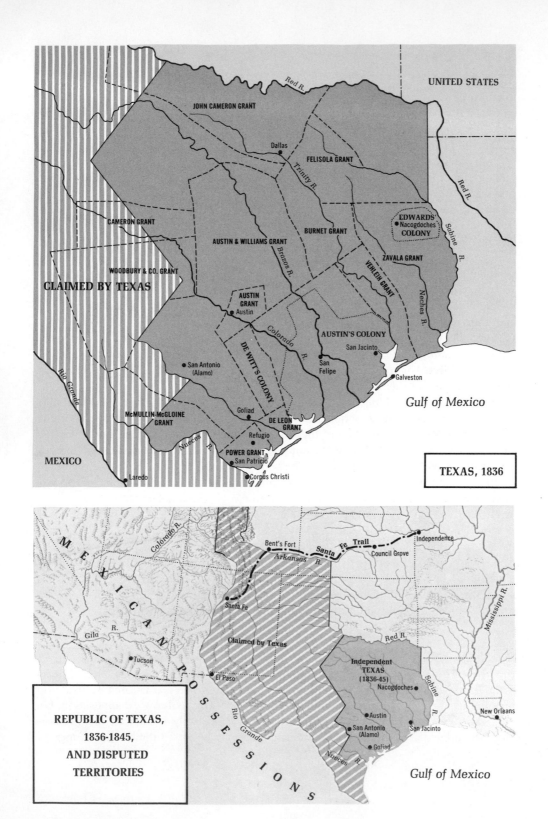

TEXAS, 1836

JOHN CAMERON GRANT

Red R.

UNITED STATES

Dallas

FELISOLA GRANT

Trinity R.

CAMERON GRANT

EDWARDS'
COLONY
• Nacogdoches

BURNET GRANT

Sabine R.

AUSTIN & WILLIAMS GRANT

ZAVALA GRANT

Brazos R.

VEHLEIN GRANT

Neches R.

WOODBURY & CO. GRANT

CLAIMED BY TEXAS

AUSTIN
GRANT
• Austin

Colorado R.

AUSTIN'S COLONY

San Jacinto

DE WITT'S COLONY

• San Antonio
(Alamo)

• San
Felipe

Galveston

Rio Grande

McMULLIN-McGLOINE
GRANT

Goliad

DE LEON
GRANT

Gulf of Mexico

Nueces R.

Refugio

POWER GRANT
• San Patricio

MEXICO

• Laredo

•Corpus Christi

REPUBLIC OF TEXAS,
1836-1845,
AND DISPUTED
TERRITORIES

M E X I C A N   P O S S E S S I O N S

Colorado R.

Bent's Fort

Santa Fe   Trail

Independence

Arkansas R.

Council Grove

Santa Fe

Mississippi R.

Gila   R.

Red R.

Claimed by Texas

Independent
TEXAS
(1836-45)

Nacogdoches

Sabine R.

• Tucson

• El Paso

Rio Grande

Austin

New Orleans

Nueces R.

• San Antonio
(Alamo)

• Goliad

San Jacinto

Gulf of Mexico

which immediately passed it back. Among his last official acts was the reception of the Texas minister and the sending of a chargé d'affaires to Texas. After his retirement he was an ardent expansionist, while Van Buren continued his predecessor's official policy of caution. As for Congress and the American people, the idea of annexation became mixed with the somewhat fantastic idea of the abolitionist Benjamin Lundy that the Texas developments represented a deep-laid plot by slaveowners.

Balked in its hope of annexation, Texas did its best to make independence work, even though hampered by a sparse population, a lack of variety in resources, and financial troubles. Efforts were made to obtain foreign recognition so that foreign trade might be promoted, and loans easier to obtain; recognition by the United States was followed by that of England and of France. The best that Mexico would offer was home rule, provided Texas returned to its Mexican allegiance.

Relations with Mexico quite naturally remained difficult. The unruly Texan army was deterred with difficulty from invading Mexico, while unauthorized groups crossed the border to try, unsuccessfully, to foment Mexican revolutions. Texas tried in 1841 to conquer Santa Fe, which it claimed; but the expedition was mismanaged, and its members ended in Mexican jails. Then Mexico tried, unsuccessfully, to reconquer Texas, after which there were raids by both sides. Incidentally, Texas had a small navy that refused to obey orders it did not like.

The Indians, and particularly the Comanche, were another problem as they raided across the border. Treaties were made with some of the tribes, and other tribes were expelled forcibly. Ultimately Texas adopted a policy similar to that of the United States. Garrisoned forts protected the less populated areas. All Indian trade was put under government supervision (1843), and sales of liquor and firearms were prohibited.

The greatest internal problem was raising money, which was difficult at best and almost impossible in the wake of the panic of 1837. Property taxes were often not paid. Tariffs were unproductive as trade languished. Efforts to secure foreign loans were lamentable failures. Texas bonds found few purchasers, even with interest at 10 percent. Paper money soon fell to about a tenth of its face value.

Land was in some ways the most important asset of Texas, and a local land system was developed that remained in force even after Texas was admitted to the Union. Individual land sales were few, but liberal grants went to revolutionary soldiers, to immigrants, to transportation, and to education. The empresario system was revived. One result was increased immigration, with the population of 1846 estimated at 100,000. All told, however, the period of independence was not happy, for most Texans were thinking of the United States as their country, and hoping for annexation.

CLAIMS TO THE PACIFIC COAST   Another focus of interest of Americans was the Pacific Coast. By the late eighteenth century the main competitors were Spain and England, which actually clashed physically (1790) in the wilderness of Nootka Sound at Vancouver Island. Spain, finding itself outclassed, limited its northern expansion to San Francisco Bay. A third competitor was Russia, which based its claims on the explorations of Vitus Bering, who had made his first eastward crossing to North America in 1725. Traders followed, and late in the century the Russian-American Fur Company was organized. The company's farthest expansion was Fort Ross (1812), a little north of San Francisco Bay.

The United States entered the picture with the development of a three-cornered trade between the United States, the Northwest Coast, and China. New England cutlery, textiles, and trinkets were exchanged for furs from the Northwest, which in turn were traded in China for such items as tea, spices, and silks—items that were attractive to Americans. The first American ship to enter the trade was the first American ship to circumnavigate the globe (1787–1790), and was commanded by Robert Gray. Reoutfitting after his memorable voyage, Gray sailed for the Northwest Coast, and entered the Columbia River (1792) slightly ahead of the English Captain George Vancouver. Gray's trip provided the basis for an American claim to Oregon, even though he actually had been preceded by a Spaniard.

American ships soon dotted the Pacific from Alaska to Mexico. At first the traders' main interest was seal and otter skins, but about 1820, when these animals almost disappeared, they turned to other furs in the north and to hides and tallow in the south. In addition they used California to reprovision their ships; the only more attractive place was Hawaii. Among their troubles were customs restrictions, which tended to change with the numerous Mexican revolutions, but the traders soon learned that their problems might be solved by greasing a few outstretched palms.

Close behind the sea merchants chronologically were the overland explorers and traders—the Canadian companies from the north, and Lewis and Clark and others from the East. The failure of Astoria left the Hudson's Bay Company dominant; its center was Fort Vancouver, opposite the present Portland, with the original fort built in 1825. Farther south, Spain and then Mexico was in control. As usual, aggressive American trappers and traders did not accept their exclusion with docility; they crossed into California, and operated on the fringes of the Hudson's Bay Company.

DIPLOMATIC NEGOTIATIONS   The United States government was obviously interested in the Oregon country. An English treaty of 1818 specified joint occupation for ten years. The Adams-Onís Treaty of the following year provided a northern limit of Spanish territory at 42°, the present northern boundary of California; the United States could then claim that it fell heir to all the more northerly claims of Spain. Then came the Monroe Doctrine, aimed partly at Russia, followed in 1824 by an agreement by which Russia limited its expansion to 54°40′. By these agreements the contested region was limited to the area between 42° and 54°40′, west of the Rockies.

Congressional interest was evident by 1820 with the consideration of a succession of measures aimed mainly at improving and guarding the route to Oregon. Such laws failed of passage, sometimes with small margins, since the distance was great, the costs were large, and there was some feeling that the area would in time become an independent nation. The one positive official action was that the State Department tried to get England to continue the 49° boundary to the Pacific Coast; England refused, and the ultimate decision was to continue the joint occupation agreement, with the right of either party to abrogate the understanding on twelve months' notice.

The significant factor was not the diplomatic maneuvering, but the increasing interest of Americans in the Oregon country. In fact, Oregon for many years was more attractive than California. Oregon had more fur-bearing animals, more fish in its rivers, more well-watered agricultural land; was closer to the Orient, and the overland route was a trifle easier. Possibly at least equally important was the somewhat accidental factor of more effective advertising.

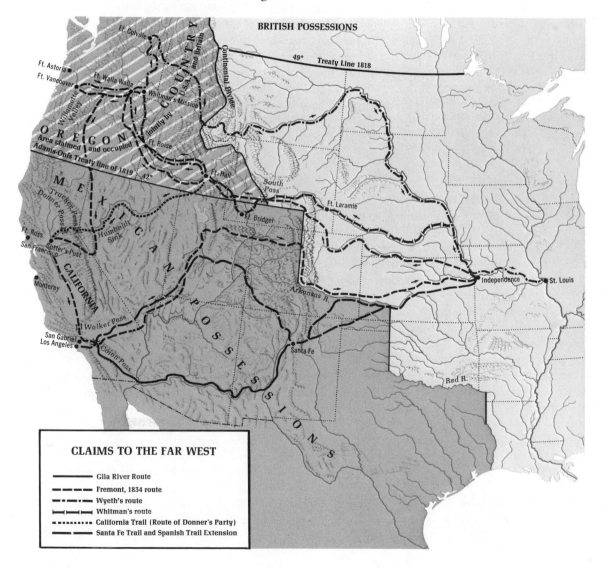

CLAIMS TO THE FAR WEST

———————— Gila River Route
— — — — Fremont, 1834 route
—·—·—· Wyeth's route
├──├──├── Whitman's route
·············· California Trail (Route of Donner's Party)
━━ ━━ ━━ Santa Fe Trail and Spanish Trail Extension

HALL J. KELLEY   The first great ballyhoo artist of Oregon was Hall J. Kelley, Boston schoolmaster, nervous, almost blind, excitable, deeply religious, lacking a sense of humor, and obsessed by a feeling of persecution. Excited by the Lewis and Clark Expedition, he felt that the loss of Astoria was a world-shattering tragedy. For Kelley, Oregon was supreme in every desirable quality, a veritable Garden of Eden. He memorialized Congress for help in establishing a great colony, but Congress was not enthusiastic, and potential settlers were slow in appearing; his most important convert, Nathaniel Wyeth, became impatient and started ahead with his own small group.

Ultimately Kelley started west (1832) with a small party. The trip was a complete fiasco. He arrived at Monterey penniless and alone, lost most of the cattle he tried to drive to Fort Vancouver, contracted malaria, and was greeted by McLoughlin as a cattle thief. He spent the rest of his life in writing justifications that were frequently incoherent and sometimes completely incredible, as when he claimed that "the colonization of Oregon was both conceived and achieved by me." On the other hand he stimulated American interest in Oregon, so that others wrote and spoke on the subject, with a common feeling that the acquisition and occupation of Oregon were only a matter of time.

OREGON MISSIONS   A new interest in Oregon appeared in 1831, when a party of four Blackfeet and Nez Percés traveled to St. Louis to see the white man's civilization and possibly to investigate the religion of the "black robes." Religious Americans were thrilled over the "wise men from the West," spoke and wrote widely, collected money, and enlisted missionaries to serve what they felt to be receptive natives. Actually, the idea of Oregon missions was not new; quite recently the American Board of Commissioners for Foreign Missions (Presbyterian, Congregational, Dutch Reformed) had turned down the idea as a wasteful use of its funds.

First in the field was a small Methodist party, headed by Jason Lee and his nephew Daniel, which crossed the plains in 1834 with the Wyeth party. Their deep enthusiasm was somewhat dampened by McLoughlin, who counseled against working with the Blackfeet. Finally they established a mission in the Willamette Valley near present Salem, constructing buildings, planting crops, and establishing a school.

The work of the Methodists proved disappointing. Finding Indian adults difficult they concentrated on the children, and particularly the children of French-Canadians who had formerly worked for the Hudson's Bay Company. Jason Lee himself blamed a lack of workers. He wrote fervent appeals for assistance, and then went east to obtain new recruits. He finally persuaded various people to come, including teachers, farmers, and artisans; but although several branch missions were established, the results remained unimpressive.

The American Board suffered from lack of funds and qualified missionaries. Ultimately it accepted reluctantly the elderly and ailing Reverend Samuel Parker, who missed the annual caravan, and then was joined the next year by another health seeker,

Dr. Marcus Whitman. Upon reaching the Green River the men decided they needed more help. Parker continued west by way of Fort Vancouver, and then by boat, while Whitman retraced his steps.

Finally a party of five, including Whitman and his bride, reached Oregon in 1836. They took the first wagon to reach Fort Boise, but actually the rough country deterred the ladies from doing much riding. Their first station was at Waiilatpu (near present Walla Walla), and they added two others as reinforcements arrived. Part of the reason for the new stations was to divide the missionaries, since the representatives of the Prince of Peace could not themselves live in peace and amity. Moreover, the Indians proved unreceptive to Christianity or any other phase of white civilization; a brave was hard to persuade to stick to one wife or to give up hunting for farming, which was a woman's work. The Board was discouraged and almost abandoned the whole project several times. Ultimately an Indian uprising (1847) resulted in the destruction of the central mission and the killing of a quarter of the mission population, including the Whitmans. Shortly later the other missions were abandoned.

The Catholics entered the field in 1838, working with both Indians and whites. Best known was the Jesuit, Pierre Jean De Smet, who came to the mountains in 1840; his greatest contributions were his many popular writings and his raising of money.

The Oregon missions did little to evangelize the world, but were highly effective in advertising Oregon. Even the family that confined its reading to the *Christian Advocate*, the publications of the American Tract Society, and the annual reports of the American Board tended to become interested in Oregon.

JOHN C. FRÉMONT   Last and greatest of the popularizers of Oregon was John C. Frémont, who did not really merit his title of the "Pathfinder of the West," but put his name to exciting books that stimulated a desire in men to go to the Far West —which at the time meant Oregon—and also described the best route and proper equipment. Frémont's first expedition left St. Louis in June 1842, guided by the famous trapper and hunter Kit Carson. The party went west by the well-known South Pass route as far as Wind River. It made few discoveries, but on its return Frémont wrote (or, rather, his wife wrote) a compelling and attractive description of his adventures and the country he traversed.

Frémont's second expedition (1843–1844) involved a large and well-equipped body of men. Frémont's superior, Colonel J. J. Abert, objected to the seeming military character of the party, and ordered Frémont to return, but Jessie Frémont withheld the Abert letter and wrote her husband, urging him to leave as soon as possible. Near the headwaters of the Arkansas Frémont was joined by Kit Carson, but an attempt to find a pass directly west failed, so the party used the South Pass. Frémont examined the Salt Lake area, and his later written description was important in the choice of this region by the Mormons. Then he swung as far north as the Whitman mission and Fort Vancouver, and back south with a marvelous crossing of the Sierras near Virginia City in February. Back in Washington he found himself a hero, and his written account of his adventures a best seller. Some of the readers were sufficiently impressed to pack their belongings and start west, while many used his account as a handbook of the proper route and equipment.

FARMING MIGRATION TO OREGON

Increasing Oregon attractiveness meant that farmers were interested; the first party set out in 1839 under the leadership of T. J. Farnham. Gradually the numbers increased, so that by the year 1847 some 4000 to 5000 left Westport and other Missouri River towns. The usual route was from the Missouri River slightly west of north to the Platte, which it followed. A stop was made at Fort Laramie for rest, repairs, and more provisions. Then the trail followed the Platte and the Sweetwater, and passed through South Pass, which permitted easy wagon travel. After South Pass the route followed the Green River to Fort Bridger, then north to Fort Hall, and ultimately went along the Snake and the Columbia to the ocean.

The South Pass route was normal for the great mass of travelers after the late 1820s. Traversing the plains part of the route was relatively easy, allowing of course for the ordinary hazards such as lack of good water and grass in certain areas, food shortages, sickness, and accidents. Indian troubles were few, since the travelers usually moved in large groups, put their wagons in circles at night, with sometimes the livestock kept inside the circle, and posted guards. The worst part of the trip was the Idaho region, where the rocky country, the hills, the forests, and the frequent lack of good water and grass made the trip unpleasant, and at times dangerous.

The Oregon settlers not only were isolated but suffered from a lack of established government, with neither England nor the United States acting. An appeal (1838) for an American government brought no reply, since the proper government for a region under joint control was uncertain. McLoughlin and the Methodist missionaries filled the void to some extent, and in 1843 the settlers followed good frontier precedent by establishing a government of their own.

Increasing Oregon settlement brought intensification of American interest in the area. Growing official concern was evident when Lieutenant W. A. Slacum was sent to the Pacific Coast (1836–1837) to obtain information for Jackson, and when Lieutenant Charles Wilkes was sent in 1838 for a survey that lasted almost five years. When Lord Ashburton arrived in the United States in 1842 to settle differences between Britain and the United States, Oregon was one of the matters discussed. Secretary of State Daniel Webster was willing at first to accept the Columbia River as a boundary, but he shifted his demand to 49° when Wilkes reported that sandbars blocked the mouth of the river. Ashburton would not accept this proposal, and ultimately the Webster-Ashburton Treaty did not mention Oregon.

CALIFORNIA

Interest in Oregon did not exclude interest in California, particularly because the white population gave immediate opportunity for traders, merchants, doctors and other professional men. Of course the related disadvantage was that Americans meant a certain amount of dislike and resentment; normally the Americans were well received, but sometimes they ended in jail. Another attraction was the climate, including the idea of California as being particularly healthful.

The Californians were themselves attractive to Americans, who talked of them as quaint or picturesque. The California man was impressive in rich jacket, velvet or silk vest, velvet or satin breeches slashed at the knee, and all decorated with gold and silver braid and embroidery; a broad red sash and a wide sombrero gave the finishing touches. The woman was loaded with jewelry, including conspicuous combs if she were married. Visiting New Englanders were shocked pleasantly at the absence of sleeves and corsets, and horrified when the women smoked cigarets. The ribald stories (generally untrue) told about the morality of California women did nothing to deter young men from going to California.

Governmentally, California was left largely to its own devices, particularly after Mexican independence, when national politics left little time for the outlying areas. Usually the governor was a Mexican appointee, and in most cases the results of a local revolution regularized by Mexico. Between 1820 and 1846 California was blessed

San Antonio Plaza, 1849. The primitive picture suggests the various kinds of industry that characterized not only Texas but all the Southwest in this period. (Witte Memorial Museum)

—or cursed —by fourteen administrations, including a short-lived period of rather meaningless independence.

Americans tended to jeer at the many Latin revolutions with their parades, bombastic proclamations, and maneuvers instead of battles, but actually they were only a rather exciting substitute for the Anglo-Saxon elections. A really bitter struggle would have depleted wealth and manpower, so the Californians quite intelligently made only a pretense of fighting, after which, victory was conceded to the stronger side. The Battle of Cahuenga Pass in 1845, for example, involved only the killing of one horse and the wounding of one mule, but was the decisive battle in a successful revolution.

Landownership was an increasingly complex problem in California. Land grants were made freely over the years, and conflicted with each other. Further confusion was added with the secularization of the missions, which began in the early 1830s and was completed in 1845. By law half of the mission land went to the mission Indians individually, and half to state trustees; but somehow it slipped into the hands of avaricious whites, causing added confusion. Ultimately, after American annexation, proof of ownership was placed on any man who had obtained his land before the American occupation—always difficult and sometimes impossible to obtain.

AMERICAN MIGRATION TO CALIFORNIA California of the early nineteenth century slumbered peacefully in the sun, except for the periodic political disturbances. Into this calm appeared an increasing number of foreigners, including Americans. The best estimate for California in 1840 was 380 foreigners, of whom possibly 50 had come overland and the rest by sea. Several American groups can be distinguished. Sailors had deserted their ships, seeking either health or economic opportunity. A scattering of trappers settled in California, either to do trapping or in some cases to become cowboys (vaqueros) or even ranchers. Other men sought specific opportunities, as in the hide and tallow trade, commercial business, or ranching. These arrivals adopted Mexican citizenship, embraced the Catholic faith, at least nominally, spoke Spanish, attended fandangos, and sometimes married native women. This group was important in obtaining control of most California business and the ownership of much of the land.

Several Americans were preeminent. Thomas O. Larkin, arriving in 1832, became wealthy as the leading merchant of Monterey; he was the first American consul to California, Polk's secret agent in promoting annexation, and in general a center of American influence. Isaac Graham had a successful distillery near Monterey, and he and his American riflemen were decisive in the successful revolution of 1836. John Marsh, a Harvard graduate, and also miserly and a misanthrope, was an important rancher and practiced medicine, even though he had no formal training; he did much to encourage American immigration.

John A. Sutter was born in Germany of Swiss parents and grew up in Switzerland, where after a shotgun marriage and amassing five children and a staggering mountain of debts, he ultimately left the country hurriedly just ahead of a warrant for his arrest.

Arriving in America in 1834 at the age of 34 he decided to try his fortunes in the Far West; after various travels he ultimately ended in California in 1839. He acquired Mexican citizenship, large tracts of land, and borrowed capital. In the Sacramento Valley he developed an impressive establishment which he called New Helvetia, with an adobe fort, shops, fields, orchards, and vineyards. He had his own coinage, his own artillery, and his private army of Indians in blue and green uniforms trimmed with red. His fort was the first settlement reached by the overland traveler, and he was very hospitable, particularly to Americans, including Frémont. For these services he was paid badly. Frémont viewed him with suspicion and even dislike, and later arrivals stole his property.

American agricultural settlers began to arrive in 1841. First was the John Bidwell group of 32; significantly, the larger part of the original party had seceded to go to Oregon. The number of arrivals increased year by year. They had no desire to adopt Mexican ways of life, and their arrival foreshadowed the end of Mexican control. While they came by various routes, including the Santa Fe Trail and the long swing around the Horn, most followed the Oregon Trail to Fort Hall and then turned southwest. Passing north of Salt Lake they followed the Humboldt River to the Humboldt Sink. Early travelers then proceeded along the Carson River, Walker Pass, and the Stanislaus, but the favorite route from 1844 went by way of the Truckee River and the Truckee Pass.

The trip to California was long and arduous. Wagons could be driven to Fort Hall with relative ease, but then came the arid stretches of Utah and Nevada, where water and grass were in short supply, where equipment wore out, where supplies ran short, and where tempers became frayed. Finally appeared the intimidating masses of the High Sierras, with no easy crossing. Progress was slow, difficult, and dangerous. A late start from the East, delays en route, or early winter in the mountains might bring snow that could easily be fatal. Most tragic was the fate of the Donner party, which was snowbound at Donner Lake in the winter of 1846 and was reduced to cannibalism before a fraction was finally rescued. It is not surprising that the green vegetation of California looked like heaven to the weary immigrant as he surmounted the last mountain range.

By 1846 California contained possibly 700 Americans, 100 British, 7000 Spaniards, and 10,000 Indians. Although the Americans were still a small minority, they were sufficiently numerous to give pause for thought to any Mexican administrator familiar with the past history of American expansion, and particularly with the events in Texas during the preceding decade.

READINGS   *Paperbacks are marked with an asterisk.*

Exploration   Satisfactory general accounts are Oakah L. Jones Jr., *Pueblo Warriors and the Spanish Conquest* (1966); Philip W. Powell, *Soldiers, Indians, & Silver, 1550–1600* (1952); *Bernard De Voto, *The Course of Empire* (1952); *W. Eugene Hollon, *The Southwest* (1961); Max L. Moorhead, *The Apache Frontier* (1968); Charles L. Kenner, *A History of New Mexican—Plains Indian Relations* (1968). Good accounts of individuals include *Herbert E. Bolton, *Anza's Cali-

fornia Expeditions (5 vols., 1930), vol. 1 is the biography and the other four are documents, *Coronado* (1949), (ed.) *Pageant in the Wilderness* (1950), *Rim of Christendom* (1936), Kino; *Arthur G. Day, *Coronado's Quest* (1940); Rufus K. Wyllys, *Pioneer Padre* (1935), Kino.

Santa Fe Trail   The classic account is *Josiah Gregg, *Commerce of the Prairies* (1967); see also Maurice G. Fulton (ed.), *Diary and Letters of Josiah Gregg* (2 vols., 1941–1944). Robert L. Duffus, *The Santa Fe Trail* (1930) is interesting, as is Stanley Vestal, *The Old Santa Fe Trail* (1939). Leo E. Oliva, *Soldiers on the Santa Fe Trail* (1967) includes a history of the trail. Original narratives, in addition to Gregg's, are *Stella M. Drumm (ed.), *Down the Santa Fe Trail, 1846–47* (1926), particularly good; John E. Sunder (ed.), *Matt Field on the Santa Fe Trail, 1839–1841* (1960). Pertinent material is included in David Lavender, *Bent's Fort* (1954).

Texas   Herbert E. Bolton, *Texas in the Middle Eighteenth Century* (1915) is the classic account of the Spanish-French conflict. See also Odie B. Faulk, *The Last Years of Spanish Texas 1778–1821* (1964), monograph. Of the histories of Texas, Rupert N. Richardson, *Texas* (1943) is probably best; Ralph W. Steen, *The Texas Story* (1948), scholarly; Owen P. White, *Texas* (1945), more informal. Shorter accounts are included in *W. Eugene Hollon, *The Southwest* (1961); *Paul Horgan, *Great River* (2 vols., 1954), Rio Grande; *Ray A. Billington, *The Far Western Frontier 1830–60* (1956); Rupert N. Richardson and Carl C. Rister, *The Greater Southwest* (1935). Lyle Saxon, *Lafitte the Pirate* (1930) has much on Texas. Filibustering is treated in Harris G. Warren, *The Sword Was Their Passport* (1943). Best on Austin is *Eugene C. Barker, *The Life of Stephen Austin* (1925); also valuable is his *Mexico and Texas, 1821–35* (1928), lectures.

Texas Revolution and Independence   Best on the revolution is William C. Binkley, *The Texas Revolution* (1952); Carlos E. Castañeda (trans.), *The Mexican Side of the Texas Revolution* (1928), interesting. For Houston see *Marquis James, *The Raven* (1929), which reads well. For Santa Anna see Wilfred H. Calcott, *Santa Anna* (1936). Best on the period of independence is *William R. Hogan, *The Texas Republic* (1946), but see also Joseph W. Schmitz, *Texan Statecraft, 1834–1845* (1941); Stanley Siegel, *A Political History of the Texas Republic, 1836–1845* (1956), detailed. Noel M. Loomis, *The Texas–Santa Fé Pioneers* (1958) is excellent on the expedition of 1841.

News of the Mexican War. Southerners, who were generally enthusiastic about the prospect of war with Mexico, probably were not as surprised at the report as the artist has shown them to be. (National Academy of Design)

Chapter 24 / SPOILS TO THE STRONG

New and attractive vistas opened before delighted American eyes during the 1840s. Americans had long been aggressively optimistic, but there had seemed to be insuperable limits to expansion. The presumed existence of a Great American Desert, the Spanish occupation of the Southwest, and the

English dominance in the Northwest had convinced many people that the ultimate limit of expansion of the American population was somewhere near the great bend of the Missouri River. Now the flow of settlers across the plains to the Pacific Coast, together with the obvious weakness of Mexico, gave new horizons to American aspirations.

MANIFEST DESTINY   Population expansion and an active desire for more territory went hand in hand. Manifest Destiny was the current ideal; the term came into common use during the mid-1840s. More and more Americans were convinced that the United States must inevitably own and occupy the entire region from the Mississippi to the Pacific Coast, including the entire area from Texas to the Pacific and north through Oregon. A vocal minority had even bolder visions and talked of all of North America and such neighboring islands as Cuba, and even Hawaii.

The American expansionist felt deep in his heart that the United States was the finest civilization in the world, and that his nation was destined by God to carry the blessings of democratic institutions and Christianity to less enlightened people. In the words of the time, the United States "is destined to manifest to mankind the excellence of divine principles; to extend on earth the noblest temple ever dedicated to the Most High—the Sacred and the True." In fact, "we should be recreant to our noble mission, if we refused acquiescence to the high purpose of a wise Providence." The idea of self-defense was seldom mentioned, and material advantages were stressed less than were religious and moral ones.

The idealism of a high mission foreordained by the Deity was sometimes buttressed by specific claims to desired territory. In the case of Oregon the joint occupation agreement was a recognition that the United States had plausible title to the drainage basin of the Columbia. As for Texas, its independence made annexation a distinct possibility, and after annexation the most extreme claims of Texas could be adopted. As for the Southwest there were no plausible claims.

The trend of American official opinion became clear as efforts of the late 1820s to buy Texas were expanded in the next decade to include the entire Southwest. Unfortunately for the expansionists, the annexation of Texas became overlaid with sectional antagonisms and the slavery issue, with even Jackson and Van Buren becoming cool publicly to annexation despite their strong personal enthusiasm. When Secretary of State Calhoun presented an annexation treaty to Congress in 1844, he maladroitly stressed the protection and expansion of slavery, and the treaty was defeated decisively.

The annexation issue took the center of the stage in the campaign of 1844. The Democrats nominated the expansionist James K. Polk, and the party platform favored what it called the reannexation of Texas and the reoccupation of Oregon, thus providing an offset for the slave area of Texas, even though Oregon was little discussed in the campaign. Public opinion favored annexation so obviously that Henry Clay, the Whig candidate, felt that he had to hedge on his original opposition to expansion.

The Polk victory, involving Democratic majorities in both houses of Congress, made certain that further American expansion was just around the corner. Tyler at once pressed an earlier proposal that Texas be annexed by joint resolution, which would avoid the necessity of the two-thirds Senate majority required for a treaty. This time annexation won, although by a very narrow margin. On December 29, 1845, the laws of the United States were finally extended over Texas, and in the following year Texas members were sitting in Congress. The annexation of Texas was manifestly an unfriendly act toward Mexico, which had never recognized Texan independence; and the Mexican minister in Washington immediately demanded his passport and left for home. The next years saw Mexico periodically threatening to reconquer Texas, and war with Mexico seemed constantly possible even though both countries had misgivings about taking up the sword.

OREGON   When Polk entered the White House, the more pressing part of his expansion program had already been completed, and he faced a potential war with Mexico. He desired to settle the Oregon dispute satisfactorily, but he did not want to risk two wars at the same time. The English negotiations that had been begun during the previous administration were continued by James Buchanan, the new secretary of state, who disregarded the increasingly violent demands of the extremists and suggested the compromise boundary of 49°. The British representative refused because although he had been authorized to accept 49° he had been instructed to insist on free ports to the south of that line. The British negotiator then suggested arbitration, which Buchanan refused.

Polk put pressure on the British government in his annual message to Congress in December 1845. Stating vigorously the American claim as far north as 54°40′, he asked Congress for power to give notice of the abrogation of the joint occupation agreement, which it promptly voted. By this time the British Foreign Office was in a conciliatory mood, as its bargaining power was being progressively weakened by the influx of American settlers into the disputed area. In fact, the Hudson's Bay Company had already recognized the approaching end of its Columbia River business and moved its main station to Vancouver Island in 1845.

The new British proposal accepted the 49° line, but stipulated that the entire Vancouver Island should remain British. This proposal was sent by Polk to the Senate without recommendation. The Senate passed a favorable resolution, whereupon a treaty embodying these terms was signed and ratified (1846). Although these provisions were not as favorable to the United States as some people had hoped, they actually represented an American victory. The American government had long desired the 49° boundary, and presumably had made the larger demands partly for political advantage and partly for bargaining purposes.

The acquisition of Oregon did not produce immediately the stable government that the people of the Northwest desired, for Congress was dilatory. Not until August 13, 1848, was Oregon made a territory, and its first governor did not arrive until the next year. At this time the white population of Oregon numbered approximately 9000. The original Oregon Territory included all the country west of the mountains between 42°

and 49°. The first division occurred because the people north of the Columbia were so desirous of a government of their own that they talked of statehood. The division of the territory was accepted by Congress in 1853 when the northern half of the territory was cut off and given the name Washington. When Oregon was admitted as a state in 1859, Washington was given all the country not within the present limits of Oregon. The present boundaries of Washington were established when Idaho was made a territory in 1863.

TEXAS AND THE MEXICAN WAR   With the fate of Oregon still in the balance, Texan troubles went from bad to worse. Not only was the United States confronted with the inevitable hostility arising from the annexation of territory claimed by a neighboring state, but the exact limits of the annexation were in bitter dispute. Mexico had long insisted that the western boundary of Texas was the Nueces River, with its outlet in Corpus Christi Bay. Texas insisted that its proper boundary was the Rio Grande, thus including a large section of New Mexico. Naturally the United States accepted the more favorable statement, and sent General Zachary Taylor with an army to occupy the region in dispute. A border clash seemed inevitable.

Sending an army seemed to promise direct military action, but Polk at the same time made another effort to obtain his desires by means of bullion instead of bullets. John Slidell was sent as United States minister with authority to release Mexico from paying admittedly valid claims if it would recognize the Rio Grande boundary. Furthermore, Slidell could offer $25 million and possibly more for the entire Southwest, which included approximately the region later obtained at the end of the Mexican War. Finally, if the latter proposal was not acceptable, $5 million could be offered for New Mexico. Unfortunately Slidell arrived in Mexico when a revolution was in progress, and neither side could risk the popular displeasure that would result from land cessions. In consequence Slidell was not even received, and in disgust he left Mexico in March 1846.

With the failure of the Slidell mission, Polk was in a quandary over his proper course. He definitely wanted to acquire the Southwest, not only for itself but also to block England; he felt that England might encourage an independent California hostile to the United States, or itself acquire California in payment of debts owed by Mexico. However, there seemed no way but war; and Polk was a peace-loving man. There was also considerable doubt whether Congress would be willing to declare and support a war for the acquisition of further slave territory. Polk presented his disturbing problem to his cabinet (all expansionists) and lengthy discussions ensued. Ultimately (May 9) the entire cabinet, with the exception of Bancroft, agreed that the only solution was war. Polk was left to determine the ways and means of starting such a conflict.

Even while the cabinet was holding its discussions, Taylor had moved his army as far as the Rio Grande and had seized ships carrying supplies to the Mexicans on the other side of the river. These actions were labeled aggressive by Mexico, which at the moment was willing to risk an American war under the delusion that it had a good chance of victory because of the division of American opinion. A Mexican detachment crossed the

Rio Grande in April 1846 with orders to harass the Americans. Almost immediately there was a small clash of patrols, unimportant except as a pretext for war.

The news of the engagement on the Rio Grande happened to reach Washington on the very day that the cabinet had decided on war; and even though Polk was a religious man and May 10 was a Sunday, he devoted himself to a war message that was delivered to Congress the next day. The message recited the wrongs suffered by the United States and the aggressiveness of Mexico, capped by the invasion of the United States and the spilling of American blood on American soil. "War exists . . . by the act of Mexico herself." Congress reacted properly and declared war. The entire country was aroused. The Mexican invader must be repelled. On to Mexico City!

Even after war had begun. Polk made one final effort to achieve his goal by peaceful means. It so happened that Santa Anna was then out of power and in exile; through a representative he promised that if he were slipped past the American blockade he would favor American desires. Polk was undoubtedly somewhat credulous to accept this proposal, but he was not sufficiently naive to withdraw the army. As might have been expected, the return of Santa Anna to Mexico merely added another Mexican general to be defeated.

CONQUEST OF CALIFORNIA   One of the first operations of the war was the dispatch of an overland expedition to capture Santa Fe and California; unquestionably the American negotiator at the end of the war would be in a stronger position if the United States were already in possession of the territory desired. The command of the overland expedition was given to Stephen Watts Kearny, an able and experienced officer. Kearny had started his army career as a private, and had seen considerable action in the West, learning the ways of the plains and their Indian occupants. He was a kindly man but a strict disciplinarian, which sometimes distressed the militia.

Kearny was stationed at Fort Leavenworth when he received his orders to move west, and his rank was raised from colonel to brigadier general for the occasion. He immediately sent supply trains ahead, and then departed with 1658 dragoons and 16 cannons. On August 18 he entered Santa Fe without opposition. For six weeks he acted as governor, keeping his men well in hand and being conciliatory toward the local residents, even to the extent of attending Catholic mass in spite of the fact that he was an Episcopalian.

When Kearny left Santa Fe he established a civil government with Charles Bent as governor; the choice was a good one, but unfortunately Bent was murdered early in 1847. Kearny obviously expected that the conquest of California would be easy because he took only 300 men, leaving the majority with Colonel A. W. Doniphan, who was soon relieved by General Sterling Price, and moved south into Mexico. Not far from Santa Fe, Kearny met Kit Carson, who was riding to Washington with the news that California had already fallen. Upon receiving this information Kearny sent back two-thirds of his troops and continued with the remaining hundred, arriving near San Diego in December 1846.

Following Kearny across the plains came the so-called Mormon Battalion, which had been enlisted from the ranks of the Mormons, who were just then starting their exodus across the plains. Leaving the Missouri River on July 20, the Mormons limped into Santa Fe between October 9 and 12. There they got their second wind for continuing their march to San Diego, where they arrived late in January 1847. The 1400-mile march was an impressive accomplishment, even though the battalion had no influence on the course of the war.

The situation that confronted Kearny when he reached California was so complicated that the story is difficult to reconstruct. A preview of California's annexation had come on October 19, 1842, when Commodore T. A. C. Jones, assuming that war had begun between the United States and Mexico, followed his orders for that contingency and seized Monterey. The next day he decided he was in error, so he returned the town with apologies and sailed away. His actions made clear, however, the expectation of the American government and the feebleness of Mexican control of California.

The California drama began to unfold when Polk assumed the presidency in 1845. His confidential agent in California was T. O. Larkin, who had been United States consul since 1843. Larkin was given the rather equivocal suggestions that he should not plot against the existing California government, but that an independent California would be welcomed as a part of the United States. Larkin's rather reasonable response was to plot a revolution scheduled for 1847 or 1848. The revolutionists were to include not only recent American arrivals but also native Californians.

The second marionette operated on a string from Washington was Commodore John D. Sloat, who was sent to the Pacific Coast with orders to seize Monterey in the event of war with Mexico; if he also had other and secret orders they remain unknown. The seizure orders were standard for the navy, and designed not so much to help win the war as to forestall possible British action. Not long after Sloat left for the West Commodore Robert F. Stockton was sent after him (October 1845) with sealed orders for Larkin.

A third actor in the coming drama was John C. Frémont, who probably had hopes of becoming the star of the production. Frémont was sent across the plains in the summer of 1845, ostensibly to explore the sources of the Arkansas, Rio Grande, and Colorado rivers, the Great Salt Lake, and the Sierra Nevada and the Cascade Mountains. The official orders of Colonel John J. Abert did not mention California. Later there was much dispute as to the exact meaning of the Frémont orders, and also whether he had additional secret orders or at least suggestions, coming possibly through his father-in-law Thomas Hart Benton, who had been in the inner circles of the Polk administration. Frémont's own evidence is inconclusive, since he apparently wavered between conflicting impulses, and his later recollections were somewhat different from the statements he made at the time.

Frémont's expedition had several curious characteristics, of which the first to become obvious was its unusual size and composition. Sixty-two men picked for their marksmanship and devoting their spare time to target practice were surely excessive for an avowedly peaceful exploration, even in a hostile wilderness. Then, too, they did no exploring on their way west, not even mapping the Oregon Trail, although this was one of their stated purposes. The party headed straight for California by the most practicable route. Frémont was at Sutter's Fort early in September and from this point rode down to Monterey, where he had a long and confidential talk with Larkin. Presumably this conversation did not deal entirely with the beauties of California scenery, and certainly Frémont's official instructions gave no authority to enter a foreign country.

Instead of replenishing his supplies and leaving California, Frémont obtained permission to settle down for the winter. The only restriction was that he should not approach the coast. When spring arrived he still showed no signs of leaving—in fact he moved closer to Monterey and started to construct a fort. By this time Governor José de Castro had become justifiably suspicious of Frémont's intentions and ordered him to leave Mexican territory; whereupon Frémont refused and began to fortify his

"Ridiculous exhibition, or Yankee-Noodle putting his head into the British lion's mouth." Oregon was far away from the British Isles and the people had little disposition to settle the boundary dispute of 1846 by a test of arms. "Yankee Noodle," as the cartoonist calls him, is not really doing anything very dangerous. (Granger)

position. In March 1846 one of his men raised the United States flag, but in justice to Frémont it should be added that probably the flag was not raised on his orders.

Just as an armed clash seemed probable Frémont apparently changed his mind, for he started north. At first his progress was slow and defiant, with his well-equipped and rested force making only some 6 to 8 miles a day, but after passing Sutter's Fort he moved more rapidly. Castro boasted of having driven out the Yankees. Just beyond the California border Frémont again seemed hesitant, for he slowed down and developed an intense interest in the painstaking exploration of a hitherto completely unattractive region. It almost seemed as though he were waiting for something or somebody.

While Frémont was loitering in the north, there appeared in California one Lieutenant A. H. Gillespie of the United States Marine Corps, who spoke fluent Spanish and had traveled across Mexico disguised as an invalid merchant. Gillespie brought new instructions from Buchanan for Larkin and Frémont. As published later these instructions were completely innocuous and certainly not worth the long trip to California; the most curious aspect of the matter was that Gillespie had considered the messages so damaging that he had learned them by heart and destroyed them before traveling through Mexico.

When Gillespie arrived at Monterey, he and Larkin talked long and earnestly. Then Gillespie hurried to find Frémont. As Frémont told the story almost a half century later, he heard that Gillespie was coming and galloped back 45 miles in a single day to meet him, for "then I knew the hour had come." The two men spent a long evening before the campfire, but what they said remains a mystery. The next day Frémont turned south.

The maneuverings of American officials coincided with a series of apparently unrelated events in California. The American settlers had grown progressively more hostile to Mexican rule and had started to talk revolution. Upon Frémont's return they did their plotting in his camp, but Frémont discouraged such talk; possibly his own plans were different. Despite this discouragement some thirty-five settlers, of whom the best known was William Ide, declared their independence (June 14, 1846) in an oratorial proclamation, and raised the Bear Flag of revolt.

The first stages of the revolution were considered by many native Californians as nothing but thievery by disaffected nomads, but the movement was taken more seriously after the occupation of Sonoma and the capture of several loyal Mexican citizens. Frémont talked to Ide and other revolutionists, but decided to maintain something that he could at least call neutrality. He did no actual fighting, but he gave the rebels advice and guarded their prisoners, which was certainly an unusual form of neutrality.

The ultimate importance of the Bear Flag revolt was negligible. In early June, with the news of the war with Mexico, Sloat landed and took possession of Monterey; he was soon replaced by Stockton. Frémont enlisted most Americans, including the Bear Flaggers, in his "California battalion," and Frémont and Stockton advanced jointly to the south and captured Los Angeles. The main American force then returned north to celebrate its victory by getting drunk, leaving a small detachment under Gillespie to hold Los Angeles. California had thus been conquered easily and almost bloodlessly, and it was this news that was carried east by Kit Carson and that influenced General Kearny to send most of his troops back to Santa Fe.

The only real fighting in California came after it supposedly had been conquered. Native Californians, finding the Gillespie rule of Los Angeles distasteful, revolted and drove him out of the city. Just at this time Kearny appeared on the horizon and was attacked by the Californians. The tired Kearny troops did the best they could, but their casualties were high and they were lucky to avoid complete annihilation; Kearny, with doubtful accuracy, reported the engagement as a victory. Luckily Stockton and Frémont returned and with the support of the Kearny force were able to reestablish American control of southern California.

The noisiest of the California battles was waged after the war by Frémont and Kearny as to who should be in supreme command. Stockton had placed Frémont in control and then sailed away. On the other hand, Kearny bore orders from Washington giving him the top command; in any case he outranked both Frémont and Stockton; Stockton was a commodore, a rank equivalent to a colonelcy in the army. Moreover, communications from both General Scott and the secretary of the navy gave control to Kearny. After a spirited exchange of insults, Kearny started home, taking Frémont along as a virtual prisoner. Frémont was then tried by court-martial and found guilty of mutiny, disobedience, and unbecoming conduct. The President approved this sentence, but remitted the penalties the court imposed. Frémont was so angered by what he felt to be injustice that he resigned his army commission. Much of his later activity reflected no credit on his abilities as an explorer, a businessman, or a public servant, even though his presidential candidacy showed his continued popularity. His historical reputation suffered particularly from his unsuccessful and almost disastrous fourth exploring expedition, from his doubtful financial ventures, and from his unsatisfactory record in the Civil War.

TREATY OF GUADALUPE HIDALGO   The first important action of the Mexican War was the southerly advance of Zachary Taylor. His capture of Monterrey and repulse of Santa Anna were due more to Mexican lack of proper leadership and equipment than to the ability of Taylor. Polk was displeased with what he considered Taylor's inconclusive operations, and distressed by the boom of Taylor for the presidency; hence he turned to General Winfield Scott, who landed at Vera Cruz in 1847. Scott defeated a new Santa Anna army, and after a completely victorious campaign entered Mexico City on September 14, 1847. At this point he could dictate whatever terms of peace he desired.

Before the Scott operations were completely successful, Polk sent a representative to Mexico to try to conclude a peace. For this mission he chose Nicholas P. Trist, chief clerk of the State Department. And a worse choice could hardly have been made. Trist was a man of integrity, scholarly and industrious, but of mediocre ability, chronic indecision, and great stubbornness. He had meticulous regard for the niceties of behavior, and was a virtuoso with the pen. His instructions were to obtain Texas, New Mexico, Upper and Lower California, and the right-of-way across the Isthmus of Tehuantepec. For this territory he might offer $30 million plus the cancellation of some $3 million of American claims. The least he was authorized to accept was a line up the Rio Grande to El Paso and then due west to the coast; for this he could offer $15 million.

Trist's first trouble was with Scott, for the two men disliked each other on sight and for a time refused even to speak to each other, confining themselves to writing home long letters of justification. Eventually they became close friends and Scott arranged an armistice to permit negotiations. Santa Anna encouraged the discussions

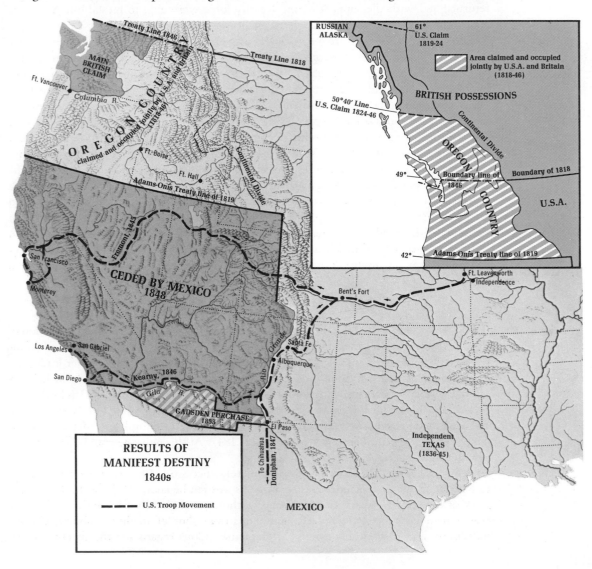

RESULTS OF
MANIFEST DESTINY
1840s

– – – – U.S. Troop Movement

because he hoped to get the $30 million to use on his army; but ultimately the armistice collapsed, Santa Anna fled the country, and Scott took the city of Mexico.

Polk was displeased with the Trist negotiations because he found, on the one hand, a growing Whig opposition to the war and on the other, a growing sentiment that Mexico disgorge more of its territory—an attitude approved by the President. Ultimately Polk ordered Trist to come home, but Trist disobeyed on the grounds that he saw a chance for a treaty and kindheartedly did not want to hurt Mexico more than necessary. The treaty he signed in 1848 fulfilled his minimum first orders by the acquisition of Texas, New Mexico, Arizona, California, and the region to the north for $15 million plus claims up to $3.25 million.

When the Trist treaty arrived in Washington, Polk was both angry and embarrassed. His term was coming to an end and he had renounced a second one. Opposition to the war raised questions as to whether Congress would vote adequate funds for its continuance. In consequence he tried to avoid at least major political tragedy by sending the treaty to the Senate, where it was ratified. As later events showed, the Treaty of Guadalupe Hidalgo marked the beginning of the end of American continental expansion. Subsequent additions were the small Gadsden Purchase of 1853 and the purchase of the detached Alaska in 1867.

LATER FILIBUSTERING   The end of continental expansion can be recognized today, but at the time it was not apparent. During the years after 1850 the old preliminaries of expansion continued as American settlers flowed across both the northern and southern boundaries and as filibusters went to the south; the only difference from the pattern of earlier years was that these activities did not result in annexation. Most famous of the filibusters of the 1850s was that "man of destiny," William Walker, slight, gray-eyed, dapper, cultured, well educated (including a law degree), and soft spoken; he is accused of having possessed a "Galahad complex" of purity. With an "army" of thirty-three men he established in November 1853 the Republic of Lower California, with the usual embellishments of president, flag, and constitution, and then "invaded" Mexico. The invasion failed, and Walker retreated to the United States, where he was hailed before a court for the violation of Mexican neutrality. The survival of the spirit of American expansionism is suggested by the story that the jury took but eight minutes to bring a verdict of not guilty.

Walker's next project showed greater ingenuity and met with greater success. In 1855 he sailed to Nicaragua, landed, and seized control of the government, which he operated for two years. His ultimate defeat and execution (1860) can be traced not so much to Nicaraguan patriots as to the efforts of "Commodore" Vanderbilt, whom he had antagonized. Walker's death was particularly sad when it is realized that he might well have been an American hero of the stature of Sam Houston if only he had lived a little earlier and so have fitted into the ideology and desires of the United States.

Most fantastic of the expansionists were the Knights of the Golden Circle, organized at Lexington, Kentucky, in 1854. The golden circle at which they aimed was a magnificent slave empire, centering at Havana and with a radius of some 1200 miles, that would include southern North America, northern South America, and everything between. The order had the three degrees of Knights of the Iron Hand (military), Knights of the True Faith (financial), and Knights of the Columbian Star (governmental). It was credited with helping to inspire such men as Walker. The Knights planned a Mexican invasion in 1860, but these plans fizzled, and the order itself finally disappeared during the Civil War.

COMPROMISE OF 1850   As a result of the Treaty of Guadalupe Hidalgo the United States was endowed with an immense new domain for which some governmental provision had to be made in view of the considerable white settlements. Texas, of course, was already a state, but its boundaries remained uncertain; New Mexico and California struggled along under military government; and the Mormon community of Utah (see Chapter 25) existed under a government of its own devising. The problem of acceptable governments was made more acute by the slavery issue, which Congress debated acrimoniously. Before the debate ended, President Polk's term of office had expired, President Taylor had died, and President Fillmore had assumed office.

The congressional debate concerning the government of the new territories involved complex factors and was highly significant for the future, but the men and women of the Southwest were hardly willing to sit passively and twiddle their fingers while congressmen and senators made oratorical reputations for themselves. The great interior basin, approximately present Utah and Nevada, was organized by the Mormons in 1849 as the state of Deseret, with the usual constitution and state officers. Statehood seemed unlikely for this area, not only because the population was inadequate, but also because of considerable doubt as to whether Congress would be willing to tolerate polygamy, which soon was to be linked with slavery as "twin evils."

The settlements of the upper Rio Grande had been organized by Kearny as the territory of New Mexico, which theoretically included the white population of Arizona; in fact, distance prevented any real control. A revolution early in 1847 was suppressed by the military, but in the course of it Governor Charles Bent was killed, which at least saved some future unpleasantness, since Kearny had had no power to establish a territorial government. During the congressional debate after the Mexican War the people of New Mexico petitioned for territorial government and then on their own initiative formed a state constitution (1850) that was accepted by the voters 8371 to 39.

The New Mexico situation was further complicated by boundary difficulties. The New Mexicans wanted a government of their own that would include the residents of Arizona, who were not pleased with the idea. More important, Texas had long claimed the area as far west as the Rio Grande, and that claim had at one time been accepted by the United States government. To reinforce its title Texas had organized the county of New Mexico and had sent county officials who had been prevented from functioning by the army. Incidentally, there still remained the unsettled problem of whether Texas itself should be divided into several states.

Californians were even more insistent upon an improved local government than were their eastern neighbors. American settlers had not been enamored of Mexican rule and were almost equally displeased with army control; moreover, their number had increased vastly with the gold rush. On a local level, most towns continued the office of *alcalde*, but here and there communities set up their own governments. On the state level the desire for a more responsive and effective government became so strong that the military governor finally bowed to the popular will and called a convention to devise a state government; he felt that if he could not prevent such a convention, he might as well have the glory of calling one.

The California convention met at Monterey in September 1849. The place of meeting was in itself an indication of the fact that it was more a creature of the old than of the new order. Three quarters of its members had arrived in California before the gold rush, and included not only such men as Larkin and Sutter but also a sprinkling of native Californians. The resulting constitution, ratified overwhelmingly by the electorate, produced a frame of government and also the present boundaries of the state. The first governor was Peter H. Burnett. The first legislature met at San Jose in December 1849, and among other actions elected John C. Frémont and W. M. Gwin as United States senators. Here was a full-fledged and active, although extralegal, government confronting the United States Congress.

The debate from which the Compromise of 1850 emerged was notable as the last public appearance of the three men who had so nearly dominated the American political scene during the preceding generation—Henry Clay, Daniel Webster, and John C. Calhoun. The final compromise was proposed by the aging Clay, supported by Webster, particularly in his famous Seventh of March Speech, and opposed by Calhoun, who, as usual, couched his arrogant demands in soft words. The original compromise was contained in a single bill, but failed of passage because of the combination of opponents. Ultimately the ideas in it were embodied in separate measures and passed.

The Compromise of 1850 provided for the admission of California under the constitution that was already in operation, which meant as a free state. Texas was paid $10 million to accept suitable boundaries, and of course remained a slave state. New Mexico, including present Arizona, became a territory, with statehood sixty years away. Utah also became a territory, with statehood to be delayed some forty-five years, primarily on the polygamy issue. In addition, slave trade was prohibited in the District of Columbia, and a more stringent fugitive slave law was enacted.

The Compromise of 1850 has long been recognized as a turning point in American history. In the East the old compromising spirit was ebbing rapidly with the passing of the conciliatory generation and the arrival of more aggressive younger men. In the West the formation of new states and territories marked very clearly the breakdown of the old concept of a permanent Indian frontier: no longer could men believe that the limits of white settlements had been reached at the great bend of the Missouri. Equally important, the total continental boundaries of the United States had been attained except for the small area of Gadsden's Purchase and the noncontiguous Alaska. The old and aggressive expansionism of the past, which had pushed the United States from the Atlantic to the Pacific was to recede for over a generation, after which it was to reappear only in terms of overseas aspirations. Much of the continental United States remained to be populated, but only a little remained to be acquired.

READINGS   *Paperbacks are marked with an asterisk.*

General and Trails   Good general histories of the Pacific Coast are Norman A. Graebner, *Empire on the Pacific* (1955) and John W. Caughey, *History of the Pacific Coast* (1933). Eugene Berwanger, *The Frontier Against Slavery* (1967), attitudes toward Negro. Marc Simms, *Spanish Government in New Mexico* (1968). Routes across the plains are described in James C. Bell, *Opening a Highway to the Pacific, 1838–1846* (1921); *William H. Goetzmann, *Army Exploration in the American West* (1959) and *Exploration and Empire* (1966); Bernard DeVoto, *The Year of Decision* (1943), reads well. The overland trail is described in James Monaghan, *The Overland Trail* (1947); George R. Stewart, *The California Trail* (1962), excellent; *Francis Parkman, *The Oregon Trail* (1943), contemporary. Standard on Frémont is Allan Nevins, *Frémont* (1939); see also Charles Preuss, *Exploring with Frémont* (1958).

Oregon   Useful general accounts include Oscar O. Winther, *The Great Northwest* (1947) and *The Old Oregon Country* (1950); David S. Lavender, *Land of Giants* (1958); D. W. Meinig, *The Great Columbia Plain* (1968); *Bernard DeVoto, *Across the Wide Missouri* (1947) and *The Course of Empire* (1952). Early travel to Oregon is described in Archer B. Hulbert (ed.), *The Call of the Columbia* (1934) and (ed.), *Where Rolls the Columbia* (1933); Ross Cox, *The Columbia River* (1957), contemporary. McLoughlin can be followed in Richard G. Montgomery, *The White-Headed Eagle* (1934); Edwin E. Rich (ed.), *Letters of John McLoughlin* (1941). Kelley is well covered in Fred W. Powell, *Hall Jackson Kelley* (1917) and (ed.), *Hall J. Kelley on Oregon* (1932).

California, General   Walton E. Bean, *California* (1968); Robert G. Cleland, *A History of California* (1922), *Pathfinders* (1929), travelers to California, *From Wilderness to Empire* (1959); Andrew F. Rolle, *California* (1963); Ralph J. Roske, *Everyman's Eden: A History of California* (1969); James A. B. Scherer, *Thirty-first State* (1942).

California, Early   The cattle business is described in Robert G. Cleland, *The Cattle on a Thousand Hills* (1941). William W. Robinson, *Land in California* (1948) tries to disentangle a complicated situation. The Donner party can best be followed in George R. Stewart, Jr., *Ordeal by Hunger* (1960) and (ed.), *The Opening of the California Trail* (1953). William H. Davis, *Seventy-two Years in California* (1967), contemporary. Outstanding early residents are described in Reuben L. Underhill, *From Cowhides to Golden Fleece* (1939), Larkin; Rockwell D. Hunt, *John Bidwell* (1942); Richard Dillon, *Fool's Gold* (1967), Sutter; Doyce B. Nunis (ed.), *The California Diary of Faxson Dean Atherton 1836–1839* (1964); Iris H. Wilson, *William Wolfskill, 1798–1866* (1965), trapper; James P. Zollinger, *Sutter* (1939), excellent.

California War Period For the Kearny expedition see Dwight L. Clarke, *Stephen Watts Kearny* (1961), a scholarly defense; George W. Ames Jr. (ed.), *A Doctor Comes to California* (1943); Robert L. Duffus, *The Santa Fe Trail* (1930); Erna Fergusson, *New Mexico* (1951); Blanche C. Grant (ed.), *Kit Carson's Own Story* (1926): David S. Lavender, *Bent's Fort* (1954). Parts of the story appear in Werner H. Marti, *Messenger of Destiny* (1960), Gillespie; Reuben L. Underhill, *From Cowhides to Golden Fleece* (1939), Larkin; William H. Ellison, *A Self-Governing Dominion, 1849–1860* (1950), statehood; Robert V. Hine, *Edward Kern and American Expansion* (1962), artist with Frémont; Allan Nevins, *Frémont* (1939). A later fourth Frémont expedition is well covered in William Brandon, *The Men and the Mountain* (1955); Solomon N. Carvalho, *Incidents of Travel* (1954), contemporary.

Manifest Destiny *Frederick Merk, *Manifest Destiny and Mission in American History* (1963). *Albert K. Weinberg, *Manifest Destiny* (1935), compiles the arguments. Albert Z. Carr, *The World and William Walker* (1963), best on filibustering.

Texas and the Mexican War General histories of Texas are listed for Chapter 23. Alfred H. Hill, *Rehearsal for Conflict* (1947), reads easily; Howard R. Lamar, *The Far Southwest 1846–1912* (1966); Leo E. Oliva, *Soldiers on the Santa Fe Trail* (1967), includes Kearny in New Mexico; Averam B. Bender, *The March of Empire* (1952), treats frontier defense after 1848; David Meriwether, *My Life in the Mountains and on the Plains* (1965), concerns largely New Mexico of the 1850s.

Chapter 25 / KINGDOM OF THE SAINTS

Even as Taylor and Scott were driving into Mexico the Mormons began their magnificent trek in 1846. This religious group represented an unusual type of frontier experience, and demonstrated that some of the country traditionally called "desert" could in fact be used by white farmers.

MORMON ORIGINS   The Mormons, or more properly members of the Church of Jesus Christ of Latter Day Saints, were Protestant Christians. The prophet and originator was Joseph Smith, born in 1805, the son of a poor Vermont farmer. Smith grew to maturity in central New York State, and even at an early age spoke of seeing visions and receiving revelations.

Mormonism was based on revelations to the prophet, and also on the sacred book of Mormon, reputedly dug from the ground near Palmyra, New York, in 1827 by Smith, acting upon revelation. The Book of Mormon was reputedly engraved on golden plates, and could be read directly in English by the use of spectacles that contained the magical stones Urim and Thummiom. It was a historical narrative telling how certain lost tribes of Israel had wandered to America, where the bad Lamanites (Indians) had destroyed the good Nephites about A.D. 400. Ultimately the only remaining Nephites were the prophet Mormon and his son Moroni; Mormon wrote the bulk of the book and his son completed the work. Smith's divinely revealed mission was to reconquer America, "the promised land," from the wicked Lamanites.

The faith taught by the Book of Mormon was generally democratic and optimistic. Free will was emphasized, with salvation free to anyone who repented and obeyed God. Eternal punishment was to be visited only on those who had heard the truth and rejected it. God was a real person who existed in both time and space; the traditional idea of the Trinity was rejected in favor of three separate personalities. Man was eternal, with a waiting soul coming into the world whenever a child was born. Progress continued after death through three degrees of glory.

After the publication of the Book of Mormon, Joseph Smith and his friends sold it from door to door. Purchasers were not easy to find, but some of the readers became believers and ultimately a formal church of six members was established on April 6, 1830. The new Saints were disturbed by the skepticism of doubting neighbors and consequently some of them followed Smith in 1831 to establish a group of their own at Kirtland, Ohio, near Cleveland. All property, as revealed to Joseph Smith in the Order of Enoch, was transferred to the church, with enough being lent to each individual for his own use; this practice was continued later. A magnificent temple, which even today remains impressive, was built. Houses were constructed, farms put under cultivation, and stores and a bank opened.

Extensive missionary work provided the basis for a spectacular increase in numbers. Indian missions were obviously desirable in view of the purposes of the faith, but in addition there were missions for white Americans, and before the end of the decade the work was extended to Europe. Missionaries were sent in pairs as part of their religious duties and were highly successful, particularly in England. Thousands of European converts were soon streaming to the New World. Britain alone provided some 55,000 between 1840 and 1890.

Most important of the early converts was Brigham Young, who saw the light in

Echo City, Utah, 1868. Shortly after this picture was taken by A. J. Russell, the Union Pacific workmen made their appearance. The three Mormon women then probably disappeared—if they were prudent. (Union Pacific Railroad)

1832, although at this time he had never seen Joseph Smith. Young, like Smith, was born in Vermont and reared in New York. By trade he had been a joiner, house painter, and glazier. By nature he had a forceful and attractive personality, a ready tongue, and excellent judgment concerning men and affairs. His most important early work was as a missionary, and he had tremendous success in England. He was sufficiently prominent to be named a member of the Council of the Twelve Apostles in 1835, but he never came in close contact with the prophet.

The Mormons were never happy in Kirtland. Gentile (non-Mormon) neighbors were suspicious and frequently hostile, accusing the Mormons of sacrilege, immorality, and polygamy—all denied indignantly by the Mormons. The Mormons also were rent by internal dissensions as various individuals claimed personal revelations, with each tending to become the nucleus for a small group of malcontents. Then too the panic of 1837 brought serious distress. Smith's investments in land, industry, and banking began to show signs of strain; in fact the prophet agreed that his best abilities were not in the field of business.

The solution of the Kirtland difficulties was to move farther west—a plan that had been in Smith's mind at least as early as his first western trip in 1831. The new "promised land" was Zion, Missouri, known to the gentiles as Independence, and to this place the Mormons had been moving during the 1830s in larger numbers than to Kirtland. Unfortunately the people of Missouri proved no more hospitable than those of Ohio. In 1833 the Saints were driven out of Independence and went to the Missouri counties to the north. Here it was that the prophet came when conditions in Kirtland became intolerable in 1838. But again the gentiles proved hostile, and mobs destroyed Mormon life and property. The crisis came in 1839, when the governor of Missouri not only refused to act against the mob but said: "The Mormons must be treated as enemies and must be exterminated or driven from the State if necessary, for the public good."

NAUVOO AND JOSEPH SMITH   The new Mormon haven was the town of Commerce, renamed Nauvoo, which lay on the Illinois side of the Mississippi, about halfway between Fort Madison and Keokuk. An impressive city was planned, and, as with each such settlement, one of the earliest activities was the beginning of a magnificent temple; this temple was never completed, and even the partially built section was later destroyed. Necessary homes and public buildings were erected and farming was begun. The people worked hard, and the community almost immediately became prosperous.

The Mormon community of the 1840s was dominated by the striking personality of Joseph Smith who considered himself a prophet, but laid no claim to divinity or even to personal perfection. Handsome and naturally impressive, he was over 6 feet tall and carried his 200 pounds easily and well. He had a magnificent physique, which he delighted to exhibit by wrestling with any and all visitors. A man of strong passions and lusty with life, he loved his friends and hated his enemies, worked hard, ate heartily, and sometimes drank to excess. His versatile mind embraced activities that ranged from the translation of Egyptian papyri to managing the combined grocery store and hotel named the Nauvoo House. His most magnificent gesture was to run for the presidency (1844) on a platform of territorial expansion, abolition, a national bank, and penal reform; Mormon missionaries did his campaigning. With all these activities he never lost an almost childlike love of display, whether of his own mental powers and religious authority or of his impressive uniform, lavishly embellished with gold, lace, and brass buttons which he wore as head of the Nauvoo Legion.

The Mormons always stressed the importance of the individual, but also held that the individual could only attain his maximum stature by working with others to develop both temporal and spiritual values. Each person should live an honest and abstemious life, avoiding such things as coffee, tea, tobacco, and liquor. A man should work hard and be frugal; poverty was a sign of sin. Property should not be a goal; all property really belonged to the church and was permitted to individuals only on the tolerance of the church. The church was active in all phases of life, including economic endeavor, philanthropy, and amusements. The individual went through elaborate rituals upon entering the church and upon getting married, performed some special mission for the church, and paid tithes throughout his life. These ideals were not far different from those of other Protestant faiths, but the Mormons were distinctive in the extent to which they applied their religion—on weekdays as well as on Sundays.

While the church was extremely paternalistic, it was also benevolent and democratic, at least in theory. Every male member of the church was also a member of one of the two priesthoods, and each higher office was elective; the catch in this procedure was that a church-preferred slate of candidates received almost unanimous votes. No individual would go unclothed, unhoused, and unfed if he were willing to work. Child labor was opposed, but every adult was supposed to work.

The basic Mormon institution was the family, not only to promote morality and to care for children, but also because the Mormons believed that for a woman marriage was necessary for salvation. Herein lies an important value for polygamy in a society that had a surplus of women. Also involved is the development of two kinds of marriage, of which one was for eternity only and did not include physical cohabitation on earth. The family was the only proper place for sex expression, and large families were much to be desired. The husband was head but not master of his family, for his wife was an individual and not a slave. In fact women were treated very well. They were allowed to vote in the early Salt Lake settlement, and Utah later became one of the first states to have woman suffrage.

Most discussed of Mormon practices was polygamy, which was based on a revelation to the prophet. Although the practice was denied publicly until after the migration to Utah, the original revelation had presumably come to Smith in 1831. Not until Nauvoo did the prophet divulge his revelation to a few of the leaders, by whom it was received with considerable consternation, since it violated deeply ingrained ideas of morality. Polygamy was but little practiced in Nauvoo except by Smith, who had a total of at least twenty-eight wives.

Plural marriage among the Mormons has properly been described as "Puritan polygamy." A second marriage was undertaken only after much prayer and also after consultation with and acceptance by the first wife. Elaborate ceremonies emphasized the gravity of the occasion. Sensuality was frowned upon whether inside or outside marriage, and adultery was punished severely. Marriage was a serious duty, both temporal and religious. By plural marriage the surplus women, many from England, were given the security of homes of their own, and an opportunity for salvation, while the number of children increased desirably. Of course only a relatively small proportion of Mormon men could afford more than one wife; one estimate is that about 10 percent of Mormon families were polygamous in the 1860s. The husband with more than one wife was supposed to treat his wives equally, but did not always do so. Frequently a man married sisters, possibly at the same time. Ordinarily the wives were good friends and enjoyed the companionship of living together and sharing the work. In fact the women gave little evidence of objecting to polygamy.

Along the Mormon Trail. The fabled handcart brigade, a courageous but somewhat foolhardy venture, indicates the determination of these settlers to reach the promised land. (Church of Jesus Christ of Latter Day Saints, Information Service)

Regardless of the possible justifications for polygamy, the gentiles near Nauvoo considered it as evidence of moral turpitude, and held that it was a fitting concomitant of the sacrilege of calling "Joe" Smith a prophet. These Illinois farmers may conceivably have been a little jealous of the pleasures they pictured in polygamy; they were certainly envious of the prosperity of the industrious Mormon community. In politics they also resented the Mormons. Nauvoo, at 15,000 in 1845, was the largest city of the state, and since the Mormons voted as a unit they carried considerable political force in the state and were able to obtain special favors. The enmity of the gentiles soon produced mob violence in the form of fires, thefts, malicious destruction, and personal attacks. Ultimately Joseph Smith and his brother Hyrum were charged with inciting a riot that had involved the burning of a critical newspaper, the *Expositor*. Ostensibly for their own protection they were placed in the Carthage jail, but a mob found only token resistance when it stormed the jail and murdered the two men in 1844.

BRIGHAM YOUNG AND THE MOVE WEST   The murder of Joseph Smith inspired several rival claimants to compete for his power as head of the church. Most picturesque was James Jesse Strang, who later had himself crowned "King of Beaver Island" in northern Lake Michigan. Most able and ultimately successful was Brigham Young, who luckily returned from a missionary tour at the psychological moment. Young first obtained the confidence of most of the Mormons and then consolidated his power by excommunicating rival pretenders. Several small groups, including one headed by Joseph Smith III, son of the prophet, went their own way, claiming to be the real depositories of the true faith.

Brigham Young faced serious problems. The death of Smith had removed the central figure of the group and hence reduced its cohesion. Internal dissension continued to be troublesome, even though the excommunication of rival leaders made it less effective. The hostility of the neighboring gentiles threatened annihilation unless the entire group moved. But where could the Mormons go? And could they find the depths of courage once more to abandon the fruits of years of hard work and start life again in poverty?

Young's answer to his problem was to start the evacuation of Nauvoo in February 1846, in the heart of the winter and with only a tentative objective. Groups of Mormons, led by a small party under Young, crossed the ice of the Mississippi and struggled through the roadless mud of Iowa. These people were leaving a settled and prosperous community with little more than the clothes on their backs and the few possessions that could be packed in wagons. Their farms and homes were conceded to acquisitive Illinois farmers; their furniture, crockery, and other personal possessions became the toys of future generations of Illinois children. Embarking toward the setting sun, they were hazarding their very lives for the attainment of an ideal—the right to live and work and worship God as they pleased.

The migration of 1846, like every Mormon undertaking, was organized effectively. Small groups went ahead to establish temporary camps, where cabins were frequently built and crops planted for the benefit of later arrivals. Then came the larger parties, which included the old and young, the sick and the infirm, for by fall the gentiles had ejected the last of the Mormons from Nauvoo. Even with the best possible planning, however, provisions soon became scarce. Some of the young men worked for the Iowa farmers along their route, others sold the products of their work; a brass band gave concerts to raise Mormon morale and to gather funds. But even at best, conditions were desperate. Only the magnificent faith of the people kept them slogging through Iowa mud, pelted by spring rain, subsisting on a meager and monotonous diet. Many a Mormon man or woman breathed his last on the Iowa prairie, and many a Mormon baby was ushered into the world on a blanket under a wagon box or in a leaky tent.

The principal winter quarters for the cold weather of 1846–1847 were near the present Omaha, although other communities were scattered through the surrounding countryside. Here it was that the Mormon Battalion was recruited for the long march to San Diego in accord with an agreement with President Polk by which the Mormons were to demonstrate their loyalty, and in return were assured—according to their understanding—of protection in the West. A forest of tents and crude cabins kept out at least a part of the elements. Food was scarce, and even the crude tools of the frontier were frequently lacking. The poor diet and exposure brought a dreadful mortality, so that at times the living had difficulty burying the dead. Brigham Young and other leaders exhibited day by day the tremendous courage that ensured the survival of the group.

WESTERN COLONIZATION The Missouri River was the first step toward a Zion far distant from hostile gentiles, but there is no evidence that the Mormons tried to get outside the boundaries of the United States. Brigham Young's only revelation (early 1847) was that the Saints should continue their march west. In April he took the road again, this time at the head of a party of 148, known as the Pioneers, which included 3 women and 2 children; the bulk of the party was composed of young men with the varied skills necessary to establish a new community. Guided by Frémont's writings, Young followed the usual Platte River–South Pass route, except that he took the north rather than the more frequently used south bank of the Platte. From Fort Bridger he cut directly toward Salt Lake, near which he reputedly announced: "This is the place." Immediately the party set to work to build houses and plant crops in preparation for later arrivals. As for Young, he again turned east to meet and direct later emigrants.

Although the Salt Lake area was described to eastern Saints in glowing terms, the actuality was exceedingly drab. The lake was beautiful but useless except for bathing parties. The land was treeless, and in fact had almost no vegetation except sagebrush. The ground was hard-baked by the sun. Everywhere was desolation and wasteland. Irrigation was necessary before the first crops could be planted with any hope of a harvest. The first buildings had to be closely packed and arranged as a fort to defend against hostile Indians.

Other parties immediately followed the pioneers, although it was five years before the entire population of Nauvoo reached Salt Lake. Each party was well organized, and experienced no more than the usual trials of wilderness travel. Part of the immigrants were foreign converts. Mormon agents planned their trips, met them on arrival (New Orleans at first and then Boston and New York), and superintended their overland journey. Special rates were provided. A Perpetual Emigrating Fund, started in 1849, loaned money to the migrants who were poverty-stricken; after reaching Utah they were expected to pay back from their earnings these advances, plus interest, and thus furnish funds for similar loans to later travelers.

To reduce the cost of the trip across the plains, the experiment was tried in 1856 of having some of the migrants pull handcarts. Five people were assigned to each cart, with the body of the cart some 3 to 4 feet long. The total baggage per person could weigh only 17 pounds. Other belongings and supplies were carried in regular wagons. The distance per day was between 10 and 20 miles. Tragic results occurred when groups started the trip so late that they were caught in winter weather. By the time the experiment was abandoned in 1860 ten companies had made the trip, with 2962 people pulling 653 handcarts.

The Mormon settlement was never confined to Salt Lake City. During the years 1847–1857 ninety-five communities were established, stretching from Idaho to south of the Colorado River, and as far west as the Pacific Ocean. Settlers for each "stake"

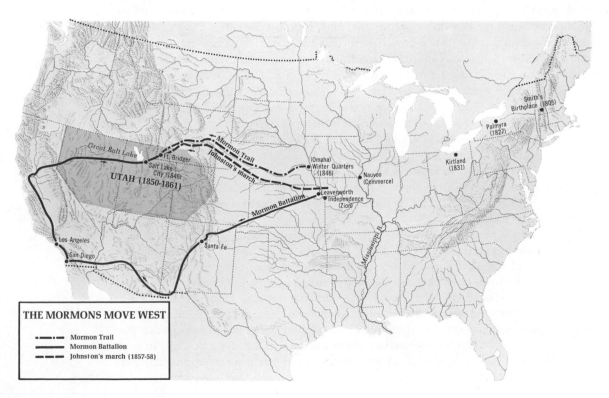

THE MORMONS MOVE WEST

- ·—·—· Mormon Trail
- ——— Mormon Battalion
- ▬ ▬ ▬ Johnston's march (1857-58)

were picked by the church authorities and went as a religious duty. Such careful attention was given to the general plans, the leadership, a proper distribution of skills, and necessary supplies that the communities generally survived. Plans existed as early as 1849 for lines of settlement to San Francisco and Los Angeles. The latter objective led to the establishment of a community at San Bernardino, California, but the church difficulties of 1857 brought its abandonment.

ECONOMIC DEVELOPMENTS The first years in the Salt Lake Valley were a time of extreme hardship for everyone. As new arrivals appeared by the thousands food became so scarce that it had to be rationed. The building of houses necessitated hauling wood with tremendous labor from the neighboring mountains. Clothes, tools, furniture, and other equipment were of the scantiest, for these consisted only of what had been salvaged from Nauvoo and hauled by wagon over the plains. Even Nature seemed hostile when the first crop failed because of the lateness of the planting. The crop of 1848 started well, but soon its destruction was threatened by swarms of locusts, and salvation came only with the providential appearance of large numbers of gulls, which today are commemorated by a statue in Temple Square. And then there was a drought in the winter of 1855–1856.

The future prosperity of the Mormons depended primarily upon irrigation. Irrigation canals were among the earliest ventures, being built and operated cooperatively under the supervision of the church; as early as 1865 they included over 1000 miles of ditches. Irrigation meant comparatively small farms, intensive cultivation, and closely packed communities. In Salt Lake City, for example, each resident was given a town lot and a farming lot; the farming lot of an artisan was quite small and near the city so that it could be used for garden crops. Everyone was guaranteed the right to the necessities of life if he were willing to work, with newer immigrants often being used on public works. No one has ever accused the Mormons of lacking industry.

In agriculture, as in every phase of Mormon life, Brigham Young had a dominant role. He urged new immigrants to bring all sorts of seeds, small trees, and shrubs. He sent parties to California to collect seeds and stock. He encouraged better agricultural processes by offering prizes for the largest crops of flax, hemp, wheat, and other grains to be grown on a single half acre. Sometimes he was unsuccessful, as with such newer crops as silk and sugar beets.

Young also appreciated quite early the necessity for developing as nearly a self-sufficient economy as possible. Iron mines were discovered and developed, but the manufacture of nails, other hardware, and machines was not successful. A sugar mill was also unsuccessful, producing nothing better than molasses. Cotton was introduced in the "Dixie" of southern Utah. Successful industries included tanneries, flour mills, lumber mills, potteries, and a woolen mill. Many industries, such as the manufacture of cloth, remained primarily in the home. The medium of exchange included a few locally minted gold coins but was mainly paper currency backed by gold dust; in general, however, Young discouraged Mormons from prospecting for gold; his ideal was a stable farming community. A special effort was made to attract a proper variety of artisans, particularly from abroad; while success was not as great as hoped, Utah could still soon boast of men who could make boots and shoes, watches, caps and hats, paper, carriages; in addition were stone masons, cabinetmakers and other skilled workmen.

Mormon enterprises were frequently inspired and not infrequently owned by the church. The tendency toward cooperative community enterprise developed at some places into outright communism, but this trend proved transitory. Merchandising was a particularly difficult problem. With the arrival of gentiles, the newcomers tended to monopolize retail selling; the common explanation was that Mormon merchants were expected to give unlimited credit to their fellow church members. The permanent answer was the cooperative store, with Zion's Co-operative Mercantile Institution (Z.C.M.I.) being organized in 1868 at Salt Lake City. For Mormons there was no distinct division between religious and nonreligious activities; the church had a vital part in all aspects of life.

Transportation and communication were also important because even with the greatest efforts the Mormons could not in fact become completely self-sufficient or be entirely indifferent to events of the outside world. The church early encouraged a Mormon freighting company that made connections with the East; later a mail route was established. When the transcontinental telegraph was strung in 1861 the Mormons were interested, and five years later completed their own connections. With the arrival of the Union Pacific, Brigham Young obtained a contract for grading part of the line in Utah, and this contract he sublet to other Mormons. Salt Lake City was disappointed in not being on the main line of the Union Pacific, and consequently the community had to build its own branch, which was completed in 1870; in 1883 connection was made with Denver by way of the Denver and Rio Grande Western Railroad.

SOCIAL DEVELOPMENTS
Material progress overshadowed but did not eclipse social interests. Education was always a matter of concern, and schools were opened even in the first year in Utah; like all Mormon schools they were coeducational. The elementary schools long remained private, largely because Young was opposed to the use of taxes for the support of schools. Higher schools were slow to open because only the most elementary education seemed vitally necessary for a young and poor community. In time academies were established and theological training was given. A college had been founded at Nauvoo, and the University of Deseret functioned at Salt Lake City for a few years starting in 1850, but this first effort failed, and the university was not reopened until 1867. Considered as a whole, Mormon educational efforts were not impressive unless allowance is made for the tremendous difficulties faced by early Mormon educators.

The amusements favored by Young and the church were drama, music, and dancing; as always the church was itself an integral part of most developments. As early as 1855 the church built a community center that was partly a theater. A magnificent theater was opened by the church in Salt Lake City in 1862, its elaborate decorations demonstrating the skill of local carpenters and painters. The actors included visiting companies and stars as well as local players, and Brigham Young could watch his own daughters perform on the boards. He thoroughly believed in the values of drama, music, and dancing, and felt, moreover, that they were closely related to religion; dances were generally opened with prayer. Music was common both inside and outside the church, with numerous choirs, bands, and orchestras of varying excellence.

Other cultural activities of the Mormons were less impressive. One or more newspapers were always published, with preference going to the *Deseret News*, which struggled desperately for existence during the two decades after its founding in 1850. Magazines were scarce, books were even scarcer, and decent libraries were almost nonexistent. Poetry was encouraged, but its quality was no better than mediocre. Considerable interest went to lectures that ranged in subject material from science and farming to history and morals. Museums were reasonably numerous. Artists were rare. Literary, musical, and other societies had somewhat tenuous existences. Here, as in all phases of life, the attitude of the church was the decisive factor as to what activities would succeed and what would fail.

One of the early advantages of Utah to the Mormons was that is was completely their own world, untroubled by skeptical or hostiles gentiles. The first arrivals in considerable numbers from the outside world came with the gold rush of 1849, but these Argonauts proved helpful rather than damaging; they stopped but briefly and had money and manufactured goods they were anxious to trade for provisions, an exchange that was mutually profitable. But increasingly during the 1850s and 1860s, and particularly with the desired opening of the Union Pacific, other gentiles moved into the Salt Lake area in search of wealth. Their reception was not cordial, since the Mormons were clannish, and had good reason to be suspicious of outsiders.

The Mormon hostility to non-Mormons was illustrated most extremely in the Mountain Meadows Massacre. In 1857, at the height of Mormon troubles with the federal government, a party of 140 Arkansas settlers passed through Salt Lake City on the way to California. At Mountain Meadows it was attacked by "Indians," some of whom were disguised Mormons. The emigrants prepared for defense by arranging their wagons in a corral and digging a protective ditch. A group of Mormons then appeared and persuaded the beleaguered travelers to give up their arms and be escorted to safety. After the emigrants were disarmed they were all murdered in cold blood except for seventeen children who were too young to remember. This cruel act of butchery has been admitted by the Mormons, with the only disagreement the extent of the participation, if any, of Brigham Young. The least possible complicity that can be claimed for him is that he had knowledge after the act but made little effort to apprehend and punish its perpetrators.

GOVERNMENT   Law and order in early Utah might have been comparable to that of California and Oregon except that the Mormons were an unusually orderly and obedient people, and that the church was a strong, controlling force. Almost at once the church made and enforced civil as well as religious rules. Enforcement was easily possible because the church not only could impose religious sanctions but also had the power of economic life and death.

As for civil government, the United States delayed in making provision and hence the Mormons, like other westerners, set up a state government of their own. A convention at Salt Lake City in 1849 wrote a constitution for the new state of Deseret, modeling it along the usual American lines. The infant state was not modest, including within its borders all the land between the Rockies and the Sierras, and south of Oregon. The constitution was at once put into effect, and to no one's surprise Brigham Young was elected the first governor. A delegate was sent to Washington to request Congress to recognize the new state, but Congress by the Compromise of 1850 made Deseret only a territory, with the name of Utah. Its limits were reduced, but still included approximately the present Utah and Nevada, with parts of Colorado and Wyoming. Later legislation continued to cut the territory until it attained its present boundaries.

Brigham Young was territorial governor, but other federal officers were gentiles, which made trouble. Some of the new appointees were definitely inferior and tactless men. A couple of them (and their wives) thought of the Mormons as a "gang of licen-

The Mormon War. This cartoon portraying Brigham Young charging the United States troops attempts to lampoon him with the reference to "breastworks" and a small army of offspring. Anti-Mormonism was in full swing during the 1850s. (Granger)

tious villains," and peeked through doors and windows to see what these peculiar people were doing. One judge left his wife at home and brought a Washington prostitute, who at times sat with him on the bench. But even the best possible officeholders could not have avoided all difficulties. The Mormons were sensitive, suspicious, proud, and dictatorial; under no conceivable circumstances would they have accepted the gentiles lovingly. The result was that even the best-intentioned federal officers found difficulty in performing their duties.

A crisis in federal relations came in 1857 when a territorial judge fled from Utah shouting that his life was in danger, and roaring diatribes against the Mormons, who, he said, were flouting federal authority with impunity. This incident occurred just as the practice of polygamy was receiving nationwide disapproval. The church had publicly accepted polygamy in 1852, and four years later the national Republican platform had linked polygamy with slavery as twin evils; apparently more people deplored polygamy than objected to slavery. With considerable public sentiment backing him, Buchanan decided to send a non-Mormon governor, backed by an army. The new governor was Alfred Cumming of Georgia, grossly fat, jealous of his power, and a difficult man with whom to do business. An army of 2500 was commanded by Colonel Albert S. Johnston, who later attained fame in the Civil War.

As the army moved across the plains the Mormons prepared for defense, with Brigham Young breathing defiance to the United States, which he labeled somewhat inelegantly "a stink in our nostrils." Outlying settlements were abandoned and their inhabitants drawn back to the neighborhood of Salt Lake City which was itself prepared for evacuation and destruction if capture threatened. The Danites, a Mormon militia, harassed Johnston by capturing wagon trains, stampeding livestock, and burning grass. As Johnston approached, Young threatened to destroy Utah and fight the invaders to the last man.

The federal army spent the winter of 1857–1858 in camp not far from Fort Bridger. It was characterized by rowdiness, gambling, fighting, and drinking, together with disobedience and some desertions. Cumming and Johnston disliked each other thoroughly. Ultimately mediation persuaded Cumming to visit Salt Lake City personally and without the troops; his position was recognized by Young. When the troops entered the city in the summer of 1858 there was no opposition; quite diplomatically they camped outside the city, and in a short time returned East. The Utah "rebels" were pardoned by the President. The entire episode had cost the federal government $15 million, without changing the basic situation.

The "Mormon problem" remained unsolved for a generation after the regrettable "Mormon War." No Congress could be found to accept an American state with polygamy while polygamy was frowned upon by the great bulk of American citizens. Public opinion was dominated by a flood of pornographic literature. Wildly improbable tales related how women were held in white slavery and how Brigham Young and other Mormon elders indulged in orgies at the Endowment House. Numerous "confessions" of ex-wives appealed to the prurient and morbidly curious. Many good Christians professed to see Salt Lake City as little better than an immense house of prostitution.

The Mormons quite properly answered their accusers that polygamy was an ancient and well-recognized form of family organization, used extensively in Old Testament days, and that it was highly moral, decreasing rather than increasing the amount of prostitution; even more immediately practical, it provided for surplus women. Such answers were completely ineffective because most Americans did not see them, and in any case would have rejected them. Furthermore, polygamy was becoming less desirable for the Mormons themselves. The surplus of women was disappearing. Outside opposition was harder to bear as communication and transportation improved, and particularly because it delayed the desired statehood.

Starting in the 1850s Congress passed a long series of laws designed to eliminate polygamy. The first laws were too weak to be effective, and their active enforcement was held up by the Civil War. With increasing experience Congress was finally able to pass effective legislation in the Edmunds Act of 1882. Plural marriage was forbidden, and living with more than one wife at the same time was made punishable by fine and imprisonment. All children born before January 1, 1883, were to be considered legitimate and those born in plural marriage after that date were to be held illegitimate. The real teeth of the act came in the provisions that no person practicing polygamy could vote, hold office, or perform jury duty, and that a presidential commission should be the final judge as to the beliefs of the voters, elected officials, and jurymen.

The Edmunds Act was enforced so vigorously that within five years five hundred Mormons had been jailed under its terms. The church then saw the handwriting on the wall, and the president of the church officially banned polygamy by an order of September 25, 1890. Polygamy of course did not actually end overnight, if for no other reason than that conscientious citizens were not willing to desert their wives, even though they were plural. Congress recognized the practical death of polygamy by passing an enabling act for the territory, and in 1896 Utah was admitted to the Union.

READINGS   *Paperbacks are marked with an asterisk.*

General   Among the many general accounts of the Mormons a few of the more useful are *Nels Anderson, *Desert Saints* (1942), scholarly; *Leonard J. Arrington, *Great Basin Kingdom* (1958), particularly good on economic aspects; Leland H. Creer, *Utah and the Nation* (1929); Gustive O. Larson, *Prelude to the Kingdom* (1947), quite sympathetic; William J. McNiff, *Heaven on Earth* (1940); *Thomas F. O'Dea, *The Mormons* (1957), particularly good on beliefs; Ray B. West, Jr., *Kingdom of the Saints* (1957). Kirtland is treated in Harlan Hatcher, *The Western Reserve* (1949); Nauvoo is described in Theodore C. Pease (ed.), *The Frontier State* (1918). Two good original accounts are Robert G. Cleland and Juanita Brooks (eds.), *A Mormon Chronicle* (2 vols., 1955), 1848–1876; and Juanita Brooks (ed.), *On the Mormon Frontier: The Diary of Hosea Stout, 1844–1861* (1964).

Portions of the Story   Juanita Brooks, *The Mountain Meadow Massacre* (1950) and *John Doyle Lee* (1962), by a Mormon; Klaus J. Hansen, *Quest for Empire: The Political Kingdom of God and the Council of Fifty in Mormon History* (1967). Wallace Stegner, *The Gathering at Zion* (1964), Mormon trail. Howard R. Lamar,

The Far Southwest (1966), government. Paul D. Bailey, *Sam Brannan and the California Mormons* (1943), interesting. Norman F. Furniss, *The Mormon Conflict 1850–1859* (1960), excellent on the "Mormon War"; Le Roy and Ann W. Hafen (eds.), *The Utah Expedition, 1857–1858* (1958), many documents. P. A. M. Taylor, *Expectations Westward* (1965), British converts. Le Roy R. and Ann W. Hafen (eds.), *Handcarts to Zion* (1960), includes good historical sketch. William Mulder, *Homeward to Zion* (1957), Scandinavian Mormons; see also William Mulder and A. R. Mortensen (eds.), *Among the Mormons* (1958). Brigham H. Roberts, *The Mormon Battalion* (1919) is written by a Mormon, as is Kimball Young, *Isn't One Wife Enough?* (1954), a sociological study.

Biographies   **Young:** Milton R. Hunter, *Brigham Young, the Colonizer* (1940); Morris R. Werner, *Brigham Young* (1925), reads easily. **Smith:** Fawn M. Brodie, *No Man Knows My History* (1945), excellent; John H. Evans, *Joseph Smith* (1933), very sympathetic. **Strang:** Oscar W. Riegel, *Crown of Glory* (1935), reads well.

A Land Poster. The Atchison, Topeka and Santa Fe poster typifies the promotional efforts of the roads. The center view—"Granger's Friend"—expresses a pious hope that soon evaporated before farmer complaints. (Atchison, Topeka and Santa Fe Railroad)

Chapter 26 / FROM PRE-EMPTION TO HOMESTEAD

The excitements of the Far West during the 1840s and 1850s should not obscure the more important but prosaic advance of the farmers. These men usually made no transcontinental treks, fought no revolutions, and founded no religious communities; but they pressed along steadily, settling new areas.

AGITATION FOR LAND LAW CHANGES Settlers after 1840 usually obtained their land under the law of 1841, which had been the result of much previous argument about the land system. One of the major objections of westerners to the earlier law of 1820 was that the auction system permitted a late arrival to bid against an original settler and at least push up the price. Westerners made stirring speeches describing the eastern speculator taking land from under the feet of the western farmer who was trying to support his family. In actual fact this protest was not really aimed at land speculation, since great numbers of westerners speculated—at least by claiming more land than they could farm. The real objection of the westerner was to a system which would force prices higher, and which would permit a well-to-do and nonresident easterner to bid land away from the man who had been there first.

The westerner expressed his sentiments in part by direct action through extralegal "claims associations" composed of farmers and speculators who had taken up land before it was surveyed and wanted to be sure to obtain it at the minimum price when it was offered for sale. When an auction was announced an interested association sent a bidder, usually the secretary, to act for all members. As each parcel was offered for sale the bidder consulted his little book of records; if the land was claimed by a member, the agent bid the minimum of $1.25 an acre. Now and then some bumptious or uninformed outsider bid on a member's land, which meant bad luck for the outsider. Some night he might receive a forcible invitation to be the guest of honor at a ducking, a whipping, or a tar-and-feather party. Competitive bidding was thereby discouraged. The association also settled conflicting claims between members, and failure to accept a committee award might bring the destruction of improvements or even physical harm to the noncooperator.

Westerners had no real desire to operate outside the law, and hence they deluged Congress with petitions for various land law changes. They were hopeful in the years after 1830, with Presidents Jackson and Harrison identified popularly with the West, and with considerable voting power in both houses of Congress. Western national power was further enhanced by the current split between Northeast and Southeast. The West followed no consciously opportunistic policy of pitting North against South for its own advantage, but found in fact that it frequently exercised the balance of power, and had a fine chance of obtaining any legislation which was approved generally in the West.

Congressional land legislation was delayed by its involvement with the moot problems of the tariff and of federal aid to internal improvements, but maybe even more important was the difficulty of agreeing on any one proposal. From the welter of debate there emerged with some clarity five possibilities of handling the disposition of land: cession, graduation, preemption, distribution, and an increase in prices. Most pleasing to the West was the idea of ceding the public lands to the states in which they lay. Senator Benton, as an influential westerner, gave it his rapturous support; but practically all the East was opposed, even though South Carolina's John Calhoun once favored the plan in a desperate effort to gain western support.

Next to outright cession, the West's favorite plan was graduation, which was Benton's pet. The idea of graduation was to reduce the price of unsold land year by year, and thus supposedly dispose of the poorer land to the less affluent purchasers. The East was unsympathetic because it visualized a progressive decline in federal revenue and an increased flow of industrial labor to the West. More moderate was the proposal for preemption, by which the bona fide settler could buy land at the minimum price before auction. The West liked the idea, but considered it at best a half loaf; the East was either noncommital or tepidly favorable. Preemption, like some of the other proposals, could be combined with other plans.

United States Land Office at St. Cloud, Minnesota, 1860s. Frequently long lines were seen outside these buildings giving rise to the expression "a land office business" to signify that trade is booming. (Minnesota Historical Society)

A fourth proposal, sponsored by Henry Clay as part of his "American system," was to retain existing land laws but to distribute the proceeds of land sales to the various states according to population. The idea appealed to the Northeast because its population would entitle it to most of the money and because the whole plan included a high tariff. The Southeast opposed the plan on the same reasoning. The West was interested because it provided some money for internal improvements even though it did not involve any basic land reform. Distribution became law in 1836, but the plan came to an early death with the panic of 1837 (see Chapter 18).

Possibly most appealing to the Northeast was the idea of raising land prices or even stopping completely all land sales; the latter proposal, as suggested by Senator S. A. Foot of Connecticut, produced the Webster-Hayne debate, which did nothing to clarify the land situation. Although such a plan was appealing, it involved political suicide, for it would push the West into the arms of the Southeast; hence it was not pressed.

While Congress was debating a permanent land policy, preemption was actually going into effect slowly and unobtrusively. The federal government had long recognized the impossibility of ejecting thousands of squatters as the law indicated, or of forcing them to bid in actual competition for their farms. Consequently Congress accepted the situation, and in a series of laws beginning in 1830 gave the right of preemption to particular regions within definite time limits. The passage of a general preemption law seemed only a matter of time.

PREEMPTION The land issue was prominent in Harrison's Log Cabin and Hard Cider Campaign of 1840, during which the Whigs talked preemption in the West and distribution in the East. With the Whig victory, a measure combining these two proposals was finally forced through Congress in a bitter fight, with the votes cast almost entirely on party lines. To ensure its passage was an amendment providing that there would be no distribution if the tariff went over 20 percent; this provision was deadly poison to distribution since the tariff of 1842 was well over 20 percent.

The law of 1841 has been known commonly as the Pre-emption Act. Its distribution feature provided that 10 percent of land proceeds go to the states in which the land lay, and the remainder, minus administrative costs, be divided among the states according to the number of senators and representatives each had in Congress. In addition, 500,000 acres were given to each of the public-land states. The preemption section provided that a man could settle on the public domain before it was surveyed. When the land was surveyed and offered for sale, a settler, upon evidence of having cultivated the land he claimed, could buy a maximum of 160 acres at the minimum price without auction, except that no man could qualify for a preemption claim who would thereby own over 320 acres. A settler was not prohibited from selling his claim immediately, but an amendment of 1843 prohibited any man from making more than one preemption claim.

Preemption established for the first time the principle that an actual settler should be given special privileges and consideration. Incidentally, Benton's idea of graduation was adopted in 1854, but apparently with no considerable advantage to the small farmer.

The West greeted preemption favorably, but was by no means enthusiastic since westerners felt that Congress deserved little praise for a long-delayed act of simple justice. Agitation continued for cheaper—preferably free—land, and also for larger and larger grants to aid internal improvements. When the pressure became sufficiently great, Congress acted.

MIGRATION AND NEW STATES   While Congress debated further modifications of the land laws, settlement continued to move westward. Migration had been large during the 1830s, declined with the panic of 1837, and then again increased during the 1840s. From 1840 through 1850 came the states of Texas and California, and the territories of New Mexico, Utah, and Oregon, as already described. Another product of the decade was statehood for Florida. This area was not yet acclaimed for its citrus fruit or sunshine, and few Americans felt enthusiasm for the Florida swamps inhabited only by hostile Seminole. Migration during the 1820s and 1830s had resulted in the establishment of many communities all the way from Apalachicola to Key West, the concentration being largely in the north. A statehood movement produced a constitution in 1838 and the beginnings of a compromise capital at Tallahassee the next year, but Congress was unsympathetic. Not until 1845 was Florida admitted to the Union, and then only to balance the northern state of Iowa. The Florida population of 1850 was 87,445, concentrated almost entirely in the north and north central sections of the state.

The main migration to the West during the 1840s and 1850s was to or near the fringe of the frontier. In the South, although there was movement to Mississippi and Louisiana, many more people went to Missouri, Arkansas, and Texas. Missouri increased over 75 percent during each decade, but Arkansas and Texas each increased over 100 percent. In spite of these impressive percentages the increase in the Southwest was less than that of the Northwest; this lag was accentuated during the 1860s, presumably because of slavery and the Civil War.

Part of the migration to the Northwest in the two decades after 1840 was to the older states of Illinois and Michigan, but the bulk was to the newer regions of Iowa, Wisconsin, and Minnesota. As usual, the peak of the migration came during prosperous times, in this case just prior to the panic of 1857. The new arrivals included an unusually large percentage of the foreign-born—notably Germans, particularly in Wisconsin, but also Norwegians, Swedes, Danes, Dutch, and others, mostly from northern and western Europe.

Iowa was the first of the new states of the upper Mississippi Valley after 1840. The first important white population had come after the Black Hawk War and had occupied the eastern fringe along the Mississippi, giving rise to the various river towns. Optimistic farmers started immediately to push farther west, where the open plains were ideal for such tools as steel plows, drills, reapers, and threshers, and where there was no obvious route of travel or place of settlement. These pioneers had the usual disregard for Indian landownership, especially since the Indians were by then impotent. Settling ahead of land surveys, they organized claims clubs to protect their holdings when the government finally caught up with settlement. The Indian cessions of 1837 and 1842 merely recognized white occupation. Early Iowa settlers grew considerable amounts of wheat, but the hog-corn economy so typical of later Iowa was evident as early as 1840.

In government the Iowa region had been attached successively to Michigan and Wisconsin; in 1838 it became a territory in its own right. At that time it included most of the present Minnesota and considerable parts of the Dakotas. Early talk of statehood was somewhat muted because of the increased costs involved. A constitutional convention finally met in 1844 and produced a document agreeable to the people of Iowa. Congress, however, refused to accept the boundaries that Iowa had drawn for itself with a lavish hand. A considerable wrangle over boundaries finally ended in a compromise, and Iowa was admitted to the Union on December 28, 1846; eleven years later the capital was moved to Des Moines. Iowa's population growth was magnificent; the 43,000 of 1840 increased to 192,000 in 1850, and to 675,000 in 1860.

Wisconsin antedated Iowa in becoming a territory but attained statehood later. Early arrivals tended to congregate in the mining districts of the south and in the lake towns of the southeast, but an ever-increasing number pushed north and west into the grain country, while a few hardy souls settled along the Mississippi and on the shores of Lake Superior. Vast reaches of the northern and western parts of the territory remained comparatively unpopulated for many years. The total growth of population

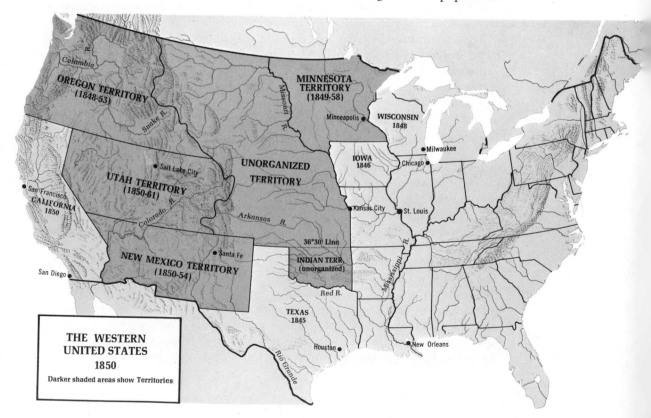

THE WESTERN
UNITED STATES
1850
Darker shaded areas show Territories

was spectacular—from 30,000 in 1840 to over 300,000 in 1850; the next decade brought another increase of 150 percent.

Wisconsin was apparently less anxious for statehood than were some other areas, for it took no positive action until Congress passed an enabling act in 1846; among other factors, many Wisconsinites were irritated by having lost to Illinois and Michigan two important areas that should have been theirs under the Ordinance of 1787. In time a constitutional convention was held, and the results were ratified by the people. Wisconsin was admitted as a state on May 29, 1848, leaving the Minnesota area without a government; but this defect was remedied the next year by the creation of the territory of Minnesota.

By the time the new states and territories of the 1840s were joined by the products of the Compromise of 1850, the organized territories of the United States had assumed the appearance of a horseshoe. The eastern leg was formed by Minnesota, Iowa, Missouri, and Arkansas. The southern base comprised Texas and New Mexico. The western leg included California, Utah, and Oregon. White settlement, of course, was sparse in many areas, with the Rio Grande and Salt Lake Valley settlements the only important ones between Texas and California. The remainder of the trans-Mississippi West continued to be the hunting grounds of the Indians.

KANSAS AND NEBRASKA   Frontier advance of the 1850s brought special difficulties in present Kansas and Nebraska—particularly in Kansas. Outfitting and distributing centers for plains travel had developed on the great bend of the Missouri, and during the 1850s farmers began to push west of them. The advancing whites brushed the Indians aside with relative ease, basing their rights to the land particularly on the treaty of 1854, by which the Indians ceded all land between 37° and 42°40′, or present Kansas and southern Nebraska.

Even before Kansas and Nebraska had enough settlers to disturb the coyotes, they entered national politics. As early as 1844 Stephen A. Douglas began urging the territorial organization of the area to pave the way for a transcontinental railroad, and with an eye on the honey of public approval to satisfy the bee of presidential aspirations that was buzzing in his mind. To lessen the obstacles of the slavery issue he proposed "squatter sovereignty," which meant the repeal of the Missouri Compromise, with each new territory deciding for itself whether or not it wanted slavery; his plan was enacted in 1854. Kansas as then constituted stretched west to touch Utah. Nebraska included roughly the immense area between the Missouri and the Rockies north of Kansas.

Early Kansas settlers were largely the ordinary frontier element from near at hand. They included swarms of speculators who utilized military land warrants, or bought Indian lands or railroad grants, frequently on credit. Quite naturally many of these early arrivals were from Missouri and hence were proslavery. To offset these proslavery influences the zealous abolitionists of New England organized an Emigrant Aid Society, which subsidized abolitionist settlers, even to the extent of furnishing them rifles. The abolition center was Lawrence and the proslavery center Atchison. The main fight was in Kansas rather than in Nebraska because even the most ardent proslavery man could not imagine Nebraska as anything but free.

The political history of Kansas during the middle 1850s is a depressing story of fraud and violence. Elections were frequently controlled by parties of armed men stationed at the polls, and in at least one case there were twice as many votes as there were qualified voters. Successive elections might produce almost unanimous votes on opposite sides, depending on which party dominated the voting places and did the voting. A steady stream of governors tried to achieve some semblance of order, but their successes ranged from moderate to negligible. At one time two rival legislative groups had simultaneous meetings.

Disorder and violence increased, including the depredations of bands of armed men who used the slavery issue as a pretext for raiding and theft. On May 21, 1856, a Missouri mob sacked the town of Lawrence, and a reprisal in the form of a free-state march toward Topeka was so alarming that the governor asked for federal troops. Among the least creditable episodes was the Pottawatomie massacre of the same year, in which the mentally unbalanced John Brown, four of his sons, and two other men, on the plea that they were fighting for liberty, killed and mutilated five proslavery men and stole their horses.

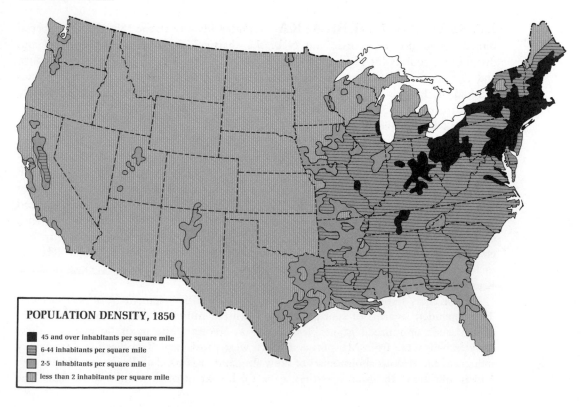

POPULATION DENSITY, 1850

- 45 and over inhabitants per square mile
- 6-44 inhabitants per square mile
- 2-5 inhabitants per square mile
- less than 2 inhabitants per square mile

Ultimately statehood became the vital issue, and in 1857 a proslavery constitution was adopted at Lecompton; the free-state men were suspicious of the governor and hence abstained from voting either for delegates to the convention or on the ratification of the constitution. This constitution was submitted by Buchanan to Congress (1858) and accepted by the Senate, but amended by the House to require another popular vote. This vote rejected the constitution by a ratio of about 10 to 1. A new constitution was then prepared, and Kansas was admitted as a free state in 1861. The population of Kansas by the census of the preceding year was 107,206.

Nebraska, the "twin" of Kansas, had no similar trouble: even the most moral and conscientious New Englander saw no reason to rush to "save" a territory that would obviously be saved in any case. A few settlements along the Missouri River, plus even fewer along the Platte, comprised almost the entire population of the 1850s; the figure given by the census of 1860 was 28,841. Congressional leaders who desired a few extra votes obtained the passage of an enabling act in 1864, but Nebraska residents promptly rejected increased responsibilities and expenses. The legislature of 1866 received a new proposal for statehood unenthusiastically and passed it along to the electorate, of whom only some 8000 voted, with a favorable majority of a scant 100. A constitution was then formulated and accepted by Congress, only to meet the veto of President Johnson. Congress showed its current respect for the judgment of the President by passing the bill over his veto in 1867; grudgingly he signed during the same year the paper making Nebraska the thirty-seventh state. By 1870 the population of Nebraska had reached 112,993.

MINNESOTA   Kansas was exciting during the 1850s, but the growth of Minnesota involved more people. The early white settlement, centering at Fort Snelling at the junction of the Mississippi and Minnesota rivers, was very small; as late as 1850 the federal census showed only 6000. As Wisconsin approached statehood, Congress toyed with the idea of government for this handful of whites west of the Mississippi; but apparently action was at least partially stymied by a difference of opinion as to the spelling of "Minnesota." At any rate, Minnesota was left without a government when Wisconsin was admitted. A convention met at Stillwater and sent Henry Hastings Sibley to Congress to present a memorial asking for the provision of a government. Congress solved the problem of how to treat a representative of a territory that did not exist by paying him as a delegate of the defunct territory of Wisconsin. Minnesota became a territory in 1849, with boundaries that extended as far west as the Missouri River.

Almost all of Minnesota was Indian country until the big accession of the Sioux treaty of 1851. Other agreements followed, so that within the succeeding decade nine-tenths of the present Minnesota was opened for settlement. In accordance with age-old frontier practice, the whites frequently took up land before the Indians had sold it. Theoretically the Indians were paid for their cessions, but the joker in the usual treaty was a provision that before any money would be paid to an Indian all traders' claims against him should be satisfied. The Indians were perpetually in debt and the traders kept the accounts, so there can be little wonder that very little treaty money ever reached Indian hands.

The rush to Minnesota in the 1850s was spectacular even for the American frontier. An unending procession of wagons poured into the territory, land being occupied much faster than it could be surveyed, and towns being planned hopefully at every promising location. St. Paul was the expanding metropolis, with the usual preponderance of land speculators, and with "gambling houses too numerous to mention." An actual count of the territory in 1857 showed 150,000 residents, an increase of 144,000 or 2400 percent in seven years. With the depression of 1857 the tide slackened somewhat, and the census of 1860 showed 172,000.

Minnesota attracted considerable numbers of foreign-born, particularly Danes, Swedes, and Norwegians, and, like Wisconsin before it, gave official encouragement to such settlers from abroad. But the great attractions, as always, were the wonders described by the older immigrants to their friends back home. Minnesota was portrayed as the center of the American continent, with an ideal climate. The letters spoke glowingly of the absence of social classes and the higher pay. They also advanced the remarkable claims that the United States was practically free of crime, drinking, profanity, and Sabbath-breaking. Fabulous stories were told of common pastures with cows free for everyone to milk, of grass so high that it concealed all of the cattle but the horns, of freedom from taxes, and of rivers that ran syrup.

Minnesota had sufficient population by the middle 1850s to warrant statehood, but the inhabitants showed no interest. They changed their minds when they realized that as a territory they could not borrow money to build railroads, but as a state they could. Congress passed the necessary enabling act in 1857. A constitutional convention found the Democrats and Republicans so bitter toward each other that they held separate meetings, but they ultimately compromised by accepting the same constitution, which

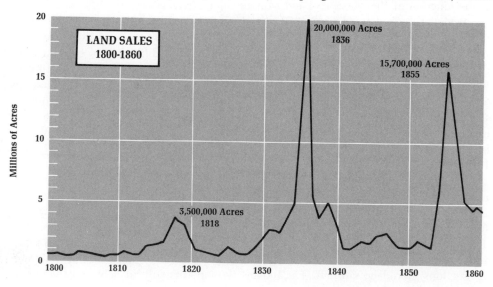

LAND SALES 1800-1860

The Mining Frontier

The mining of precious metals became the first great economic exploitation of the American West's many resources. The fur trade, it is true, preceded it, but compared with gold and silver the value of furs was minimal.

Placer, or "pick and pan," mining required little equipment. A pack animal to carry supplies and a few basic tools were all that was needed to collect the gold particles gathered in the sands of stream beds.

Later, quartz, or "hard rock," mining necessitated machinery and a great deal of labor. The search now turned to fugitive gold hidden away in the recesses of the mountains. Since there was more in the mountains than in stream beds this phase of mining lasted longer. In the end great mining corporations, supplied with capital and complicated machinery, dug away at the remote treasure.

Panning for Gold. The miner gently rocked his pan in which gold-bearing soil and water had been placed. The heavier gold particles sank to the bottom and were recovered as the water and dirt drained off. (Granger)

The Search for Gold. This photograph taken in Alaska, shows the importance of wood and water in gold mining. (State Historical Society of Wisconsin)

The Miner's Friend, Cripple Creek, Colorado. The burro, a durable if sometimes stubborn animal, was the mainstay of the prospector's transportation system. (Denver Public Library)

Quartz Mining. A laborious aspect of hard-rock mining was drilling holes preparatory to blasting. For the apparently unconcerned individual in the center of this scene there were certain occupational hazards. A small miscalculation and someone else would deal the cards that evening. (Minnesota Historical Society)

Hydraulic Mining. There were many ways of washing gold out of its hiding place. High-pressure streams of water were a part of more sophisticated methods that were developed. (Denver Public Library)

Men and Machinery. As the search for gold and silver became more determined, increasingly expensive machinery was used. The term miner began to take on its more traditional meaning as men worked far underground. (Denver Public Library)

Gold Dredge at Bannack, Montana. A few ladies inspect a gold dredge, that monster used to inch along worked-over placer sites to pick up the "tailings." There was a good deal of waste in placer mining and the dredge was capable of recovering much that had been missed. (Montana Historical Society)

The Ore Crusher. Machines were used to pulverize ore-bearing rocks. The desired product could then be extracted from the resulting pulp. (State Historical Society of Wisconsin)

Ore Carts, Ophir, Utah. This picture illustrates advances in the mining frontier. This particular horse was lucky. Many of his kind went down into the mines and never saw the light of day again until they were retired. (Utah State Historical Society)

The Miner at Play. The saloon at Telluride, Colorado was typical of mining camp dispensers of spirits, as was the "art work" on the back wall. (Denver Public Library)

Miner's Cabin, Sierra Nevada Mountains, 1860s. This particular cabin was rather elegant compared to many that were hastily erected hovels. (Library of Congress)

Helena, Montana, 1869. Narrow streets clogged with commerce were a common sight in mining camps. Wagon freighting sustained such places before the coming of the railroad. (Montana Historical Society)

was then adopted by the people of the territory. In Congress the southerners lost a fight to exclude a new northern state, and Minnesota was admitted on May 11, 1858. Just as the admission of Wisconsin had left Minnesota dangling, so the admission of Minnesota left unorganized the region between the western boundary of the state and the Missouri River; finally it was included in Dakota Territory upon the latter's organization in 1861. By that year all of the West, with the exception of the present Oklahoma, had been divided into organized states and territories.

GIFTS OF LAND BY CONGRESS   The same years that saw such important changes in the political map of the West witnessed an equally important revolution in the laws concerning the disposal of the public domain. Expanding settlement brought to Congress more westerners with any number of ingenious plans as to how the federal government could give away its land in desirable ways. And the federal government, prodded by land-hungry westerners and by speculators from all over the country, was but mildly reluctant to accede to such demands; for here was an easy type of bounty that might be used to lure votes without increasing taxes. Best of all was the argument that the wealth and prosperity of the country were thereby enhanced.

One class favored by the government was the soldiers, for Congress was both thankful for the services of the nation's brave defenders and mindful of their votes. The soldiers of each major war were given land warrants, and in 1850 a general act included Indian wars, so that practically any former soldier could obtain his 160 acres free. Then various near-soldiers, including teamsters and chaplains, were added (1855), and finally the navy was included (1857). In the early years specific land had been set aside to satisfy these claims—first in Ohio, and then in Michigan, Illinois, and other areas; eventually (1842) the claims could be located anywhere.

Military warrants provided the continuing basis for a tremendous amount of speculation, even though prior to the law of 1852 they could not be transferred legally; but they were always sold freely and in large amounts. Their price varied with time and place, the common price of 1857 being about 60 cents an acre. One expert has estimated that not over one in five hundred of the warrants was actually located by the soldier or his heir. No new grants were made after 1855 because at the time of the next major war land was free to everyone; but soldiers were given special privileges, such as the ability to homestead 160 acres of the alternate sections of railroad grants, as compared with the 80 acres available to other people, and a shorter term of cultivation before final title.

Education likewise received munificent grants. Starting with Ohio the states received gifts of land to aid all levels of education, from primary school through college, although with limitations on disposal of the land. Aid to higher education was at first sporadic, but was regularized in the Morrill Act of 1862; each state received land in proportion to its representation in Congress, with a maximum of 1 million acres, the proceeds to be used to establish and support agricultural and mechanical colleges. Direct money aid began in 1890.

Internal improvements, particularly roads, canals, and railroads, were a third occasion for lavish gifts of land. Grants for specific improvements really became imposing after the Illinois Central grant of 1850 opened the way. In addition to specifically designated gifts, certain other donations were expected to be used largely for public improvements. The Pre-emption Act gave a half million acres to each public-land state. The Swamp Act of 1850 gave outright to each state the swampland within its borders, and, reputedly, much land looked swampy to state authorities for the first time; some 80 million acres were transferred under the terms of this act.

These and other magnificent gifts of the land heritage of the United States were justified publicly as advancing the nation's prosperity; but cynical commentators have long noted that speculators were active in the passage of the laws, harvested a considerable share of the land, and pocketed a goodly proportion of the resulting profits. Quite clearly the military warrants were used primarily for speculation, and there seems little doubt that Benton's graduation measure was of greatest importance to speculators collecting large tracts. Railroad grants were at times manipulated to the disadvantage of actual settlers. Educational grants received notoriously bad handling and soon appered in private hands with little revenue accruing to the state or the schools. Swamplands were no better, since they also gravitated rapidly to the speculators, with little revenue to the state and no reclamation of the supposed swamps. All these gifts were at least disappointing, either in getting land to actual settlers or in providing revenue for public improvements. Whether they were dictated by the speculators or merely used by these gentlemen for their advantage remains a subject for investigation, but the ultimate results are unquestioned.

THE HOMESTEAD ACT   The various grants, no matter how munificent, did not satisfy the West, which wanted above all free land for settlers; and this proposition it kept before Congress almost continuously throughout the 1850s. The often repeated arguments in its favor were that such a measure would encourage the development of the United States by making it possible for every ambitious American to acquire a farm of his own, and that the increased prosperity and resulting taxes would more than compensate for any immediate loss of revenue from land sales. As time passed, free land seemed to many a natural right of each American.

Western ambitions came closer and closer to realization as eastern conditions changed. Increased immigration was taking care of the northern need for industrial labor, and Irish immigrants were more tractable than New England farm boys. The frontier was becoming so remote that by the 1850s it drew more migration from the farms of the Mississippi Valley than from the eastern seaboard. Eastern manufacturers were at the point of desiring markets even more than labor, and the expanding West meant a vastly increased market.

The demand for free land was buttressed by the arguments of a growing eastern labor and reform movement. Led by such men as Horace Greeley, numerous articulate minorities insisted that free land was one of the essentials for a rich and contented democracy. They argued that free land provided an outlet for the restless, the ambitious, the oppressed of the East. If industrialists offered low wages and bad working conditions, their employees could escape to the opportunities of the West, which in turn would mean less eastern labor competition and thereby a rise in wages. This argument was in fact not justified, at least in short-run terms, but it appealed to many.

Various homestead bills, designed to assure free, or at least very cheap, land were considered by Congress during the 1850s. Ultimately one of them passed both houses in 1860, only to be vetoed by Buchanan, who sympathized with the southern opposition. During the same year the Republicans linked free land with a high tariff to appeal to both East and West, and with the Republican victory free land was assured.

President Lincoln finally signed in 1862 the Homestead Act, which provided 160 acres of free land from the public domain to each American adult or head of a family who was a citizen or had declared his intention of becoming one; the only cost was a small fee of $10. The one important qualification was that each settler had to prove five years of continuous residence and cultivation before receiving final title. After six months of residence he had the option of commuting his claim and obtaining immediate ownership upon the payment of $1.25 an acre. Although these provisions were modified slightly in the succeeding years, the law remained the basic feature of the American land system. It superseded but did not eliminate the Pre-emption Act, which was not repealed until 1891.

The Homestead Act was the best advertised of many laws that threw open the public domain to land-hungry Americans. Although its importance was not as great as has

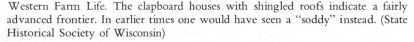

Western Farm Life. The clapboard houses with shingled roofs indicate a fairly advanced frontier. In earlier times one would have seen a "soddy" instead. (State Historical Society of Wisconsin)

sometimes been claimed (see Chapter 34), it was still a large factor during the following generation, which saw the great bulk of agricultural land that did not require irrigation transferred to private hands. The rapidity of the process was greater than anything that had gone before; the second half of the continent was occupied, even though sparsely in many spots, in a tenth of the time that the first half had taken. Inevitably there was much selfish grabbing, fraud, and waste. Whether a more deliberate process would in the long run have brought more desirable conclusions is one of the questions that historians will never be able to answer finally.

READINGS   *Paperbacks are marked with an asterisk.*

Land Legislation   *Roy M. Robbins, *Our Landed Heritage* (1942) is best. Two useful special studies are Raynor C. Wellington, *The Political and Sectional Influence of the Public Lands, 1828–1842* (1914) and George M. Stephenson, *The Political History of the Public Lands from 1840 to 1862* (1917).

Individual States   Wisconsin: see Readings for Chapter 17 under Still, Schafer; *Merle E. Curti, *The Making of An American Community* (1959), illuminating; Theodore C. Blegen (ed.), *Frontier Parsonage* (1947), the 1850s; Clarence A. Clausen and Andreas Elviken (eds.), *A Chronicle of Old Muskego* (1951), diary. **Minnesota:** Theodore C. Blegen, *Minnesota* (1963), very good, *The Land Lies Open* (1949), *Grass Roots History* (1947), immigration, *Norwegian Migration to America, 1825–1860* (1931); Theodore C. Blegen and Philip D. Jordan, *With Various Voices* (1949); Grace L. Nute, *Lake Superior* (1944), *Rain River Country* (1950), very good; Margaret I. Snyder, *The Chosen Valley* (1948), interesting; Merrill E. Jarchow, *The Earth Brought Forth* (1949), agriculture. **Iowa:** *Allen G. Bogue, *From Prairie to Corn Belt* (1963), Iowa and Illinois; Robert P. Swierenga, *Pioneers and Profits: Land Speculation on the Iowa Frontier* (1968), quite useful; William J. Peterson, *Iowa* (1941); Irving B. Richman, *Ioway to Iowa* (1931); Roscoe L. Lokken, *Iowa Public Land Disposal* (1942), factual; *A Century of Farming in Iowa* (1946), good; Thomas H. McBride, *In Cabins and Sod Houses* (1928). **Florida:** Sidney W. Martin, *Florida During the Territorial Days* (1944). **Kansas and Nebraska:** James C. Olson, *History of Nebraska* (1955), good; William F. Zornow, *Kansas* (1957), clear and factual; Samuel A. Johnson, *The Battle Cry of Freedom* (1954), good on Emigrant Aid Company.

Special Topics   Wyatt W. Belcher, *The Economic Rivalry Between St. Louis and Chicago, 1850–1880* (1947), fine study; *Stewart H. Holbrook, *The Yankee Exodus* (1950), New England migration; Carlton C. Qualey, *Norwegian Settlement* (1938).

A Young Miner. This westerner, who died fighting Indians in Dakota during the 1860s, poses for a picture that might be called the "American Dream" of that era. A few basic tools, a handy jug, a small arsenal to protect the returns, and the presumably inevitable result: a bag of gold. He appears to be more stunned than happy at his good fortune. (Minnesota Historical Society)

Chapter 27 / MINING ADVANCES

Miners of the trans–Mississippi West were often among the advance guard of the frontier. The most exciting mineral for which they searched was gold, partly because it was the standard of currency, but even more because it could often be found in a pure state, with large value in small bulk.

Probably more important for the development of an industrial state, however, were iron and copper. The greatest western iron find was by William A. Burt in the Lake Superior region in 1844. Development was begun immediately, with the ore being carried to Pennsylvania for processing; but large-scale operations did not occur until the 1880s.

Copper was distributed widely in the West, but the only area of exploitation before the Civil War was near Lake Superior. Here the deposits had long been known, but the first practical mining came in 1846. The mines were almost incredibly rich, and ore worth millions was removed before the Civil War. The famous Calumet and Hecla Consolidated Mining Company came into existence by consolidation in 1871, and by 1930 had paid dividends of over $170 million. Such operations needed outside capital, and the stockholders of the Calumet and Hecla included many of the social and financial elite of Boston.

CALIFORNIA GOLD RUSH   The best-advertised mining boom in American history was triggered by the finding of traces of gold on January 24, 1848, in the tailrace of a mill being erected for John A. Sutter on the south fork of the American River. Sutter tried unsuccessfully to suppress the news, but soon the cry of "gold" was heard on the streets of San Francisco, and the resulting enthusiasm spread with almost incredible rapidity. Sailors deserted their ships, cattle tenders left their herds, farmers abandoned their plows, and merchants closed their doors to search for the precious metal. Soon the news reached the East, and stores began to feature supplies ranging from shovels to Spanish grammars. Potential miners strutted along the streets in hip boots, talking grandly of placers, fandangos, nuggets, and Spanish beauties. They visualized a few months in the West and then an eastern palace, blooded horses, and a trip to Europe.

Many of the hopeful gold seekers who streamed west in 1849 went as individuals, but others, particularly New Englanders, formed organizations such as the California Mining Company for greater security in travel and group efforts in mining. Such a New England company inevitably had its full complement of officers, and strict rules on such moral matters as swearing and Sabbath-breaking. These moral goals tended to lose force as Boston receded in the distance, while the plans for joint work and the division of profits usually evaporated when California was reached.

Part of the migrants went by water around Cape Horn, which meant a tedious six months' trip, with monotonous food; the obvious occupations of reading, games, music, religious services, and communing with a diary soon lost their attractiveness. The trip could be made shorter but more uncomfortable by crossing the Isthmus of Panama by land, with connections at both ends by the Pacific Mail Steamship Company—whose ships were overcrowded and dirty, and served poor food. Travel across the Isthmus was difficult, filthy, costly, and unhealthful. Coast cities were so bad that most of the potential miners camped. Some improvement came with the completion in 1855 of a railroad across the Isthmus.

Most Argonauts went overland to California, using routes ranging from Mexico north. By far the most popular was the well-known Platte River route, which probably was more traveled than all the others combined. Evidence of the lack of experience in plains travel was apparent in the dead animals, jettisoned supplies, discarded furniture, and the graves of the weak, improvident, and unlucky that lined the trail. As in previous years there was a variety of possibilities west of the Rockies, with some of the travelers even making the sad mistake of going through Death Valley.

The great metropolis of the gold country was San Francisco, where the prospective miner waded through seas of mud or drifts of dust, garbage, and other filth. Saloons, gambling halls, and houses of prostitution were omnipresent; it was said that "virtue plodded through the streets bearing burdens, while prostitutes, lauded and caressed, became the leading conservators of social life." Prices were astronomical to the eyes of an easterner, with gold the usual medium of exchange. The footloose inhabitants

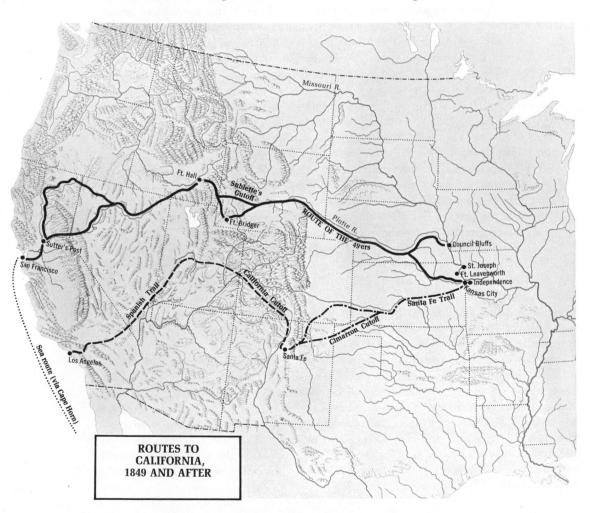

**ROUTES TO
CALIFORNIA,
1849 AND AFTER**

included the riffraff of four continents from Valparaiso to Hong Kong, and led to an outburst of crime: robbery, claim jumping, and murder were commonplace. Regular police were ineffective, so the job of curbing crime was taken over by self-appointed groups of citizens, who sometimes themselves shifted to criminal activities. In later years San Francisco remained not only the feverish center for trading in speculative mining stocks, but also the most important commercial center of the Coast, with responsibility for the financing of much of the business of the Far West.

GOLD MINING   The miners fanned out rapidly from the place of the original gold discoveries, and hundreds of camps such as Poker Flat, Slumgullion, Delirium Tremens, and Hell-out-for-noon-city had their brief moments of glory. Gold was sought in the form of nuggets to be pried from the rocks or as fine particles to be collected from the beds of streams. The simplest method was to rock a pan containing gold, mud, sand, and water until only the gold and sand were left, and then fan off the sand. Early improvements were only in the size of the operation, with a large, cleated box replacing the pan, possibly a sluice to provide more water, and mercury to catch the gold. Group operations became more common, even to the extent of changing the course of a river so that gold might be collected from its bed. Hydraulic mining, which began in 1852, brought no basic change in the process.

Stories of miners who made $1000 or more a day were widely publicized, but actually the average miner of the early days was lucky if he collected as much as an ounce of gold ($16) a day; this amount tended later to decline. With current California prices the average miner was lucky to be able to eat. The real profiteers were the merchants, the gamblers, and the saloonkeepers. When easily worked deposits were exhausted most miners moved on, leaving in control the rather inefficient mining companies with their stamp mills to crush the ore, and mercury to collect the gold.

The life of the miner was arduous, drab, and monotonous. He lived in a crude tent or cabin, sat on a cracker box, darned his own socks, and consumed a monotonous succession of simple, but expensive, meals. Washing of either person or clothes was often neglected. A high morbidity rate came from working so much in cold water, eating an unbalanced diet, and the lack of doctors. Minority groups were given little consideration. Indians were killed, Mexicans frequently driven out, and Chinese permitted only to work claims abandoned by the whites.

Regular law enforcement did not keep pace with the footloose miners, and so they acted for themselves. Rules were adopted for the making and holding of claims, and these rules were then embodied (1866) in United States law. Crime increased rapidly as undesirables were attracted from the rest of the world. The usual camp reacted by organizing a vigilance committee, which ordinarily used some form of jury trial, although a bit haphazard and not always fair. Since jails were not available, the usual punishment was whipping, exile, or death. Miners supported the California statehood movement (see Chapter 24), but the constitutional convention was composed mainly of nonminers.

Recreation tended toward the rough and crude. The favorite places of entertainment were the saloons and gambling houses, where a man could drink himself into a transient delusion of success, or chance his hard-won gold on roulette, faro, or poker, or dance with the hurdy-gurdy girls provided by the house. Singing to the accompaniment of a fiddle or flute, or tin can or dishpan, was always popular, with the songs ranging from such a nostalgic favorite as "The Last Rose of Summer" to ribald ballads not fit for polite ears. The absence of women was always a matter of regret, and stories were told of a man walking miles merely to see a woman's clothes hanging on a line. The thousands of prostitutes who came from all over the world tended to concentrate in the larger towns; in fact some of the smaller camps actually ejected them.

Hordes of hungry men had important effects on the California economy. Cattle- and sheepmen who had long had difficulty in getting funds for the gold braid on their jackets, suddenly rolled in wealth. Unfortunately the cattle boom was temporary because of improved transportation from the East, and bad times on the Coast—particularly the drought of 1863–1864. But various crops flourished. Wheat production increased spectacularly during the 1850s, by means of such machinery as the McCormick reaper, while the diversified California climate made possible an unusually wide variety of crops.

LATER GOLD RUSHES As placer mining became less profitable, there was an exportable surplus of miners. Some returned East or embraced other occupations, but many remained fascinated by the golden metal. They argued that if gold were present in California streams, it might be found in other similar streams or in the mountainous areas from which such water originated. Soon there came rumors of rich finds all the way from New Mexico to Alaska. Footloose miners were enticed by each new rumor, sometimes hitting it rich, but more frequently being disappointed and then following another promising rumor. One of the most obvious results of the scramble for quick wealth was the production of hundreds of communities which in time became ghost towns.

New finds came first, quite understandably, near the California field. Traces of gold were discovered in the present Nevada as early as 1849, but the supply was meager; the peak of early placer mining was a production of some $110,000 in 1855; a few miners recognized the existence of silver, but silver seemed less valuable and was in any case beyond the powers of the individual miner, with his scant equipment and lack of capital. In Arizona the situation was somewhat similar. The metals were usually copper and silver, difficult for the individual miner to exploit. Most important of the gold finds were those on the Colorado near the mouth of the Gila, and those south of Tucson. Tucson became the best known of the Arizona mining communities of the 1850s, being described as a "paradise of devils," a title that was not easily won; in fact, the claim was made in 1860 that only two residents of the Tucson cemetery had arrived there through death from natural causes.

Gold had been found in New Mexico in 1828 in the Ortiz Mountains south of Santa

Fe. Early production was small, but grew to about $3 million a year by the time of the American occupancy. After a lapse during the 1850s and early 1860s there were renewed efforts after the Civil War; Taos, for example, had a minor gold rush in 1867. Gold was found in two-thirds of the counties of New Mexico; but mineral production was not large, and it was 1937 before mining produced more revenue than agriculture. By 1958 mineral production accounted for about a quarter of the state's gross product.

MINING IN THE NORTHWEST   To the north the most important find was at Colville, in northeast Washington, but to the rush of 1855 the findings were disappointing; so when there were reports of easily available wealth on the Fraser River in Canada, there was a stampede to that region in 1858. Many miners had hopes for the northern American Rockies, particularly along the Columbia River, the Snake, and their tributaries. Among the important effects of the search in this area was the construction by the federal government of a road across the mountains from the Missouri River at Fort Benton, by way of Mullan Pass, to a branch at the Columbia River. Built between 1859 and 1863 at the cost of $230,000, this road made more accessible the entire area of the northern Rockies.

A succession of booms near the Snake River in modern Idaho started with gold discoveries on the Clearwater in 1860 and the establishment of Lewistown, Oro Fino, and Pierce City. The minors disregarded the guarantee of the country to the Nez Percé Indians, thus causing considerable trouble for the federal government. Shortly later there was a mad rush to the Salmon River (1861). One result of these booms was the creation in 1863 of the territory of Idaho, including the present Montana and Wyoming.

Pushing east over the Bitter Root Mountains, the miners produced a succession of boomtowns in the Montana region. Three areas attracted particular interest. Bannack City was the first, with James and Granville Stuart originating the excitement in 1862. Next came the Alder Gulch and Virginia City region, opened in 1863. Finally, in 1864, came Last Chance Gulch, later given the more melodious name of Helena. The growing population of these regions made necessary a governmental rearrangement, since Idaho could hardly care adequately for people living across the mountains near the headwaters of the Missouri. Montana, with its present boundaries, was made a territory in 1864; the unwanted region, later to become Wyoming, was given back to Dakota.

THE CENTRAL ROCKIES   The existence of gold in Colorado had long been known, but discoveries of 1858 triggered the first great rush. The panic of 1857 had lessened more prosaic opportunities, and Colorado was easy of access. Estimates have it that some 100,000 prospective miners crossed modern Kansas and Nebraska in 1859, with many displaying the slogan "Pike's Peak or Bust." The resulting boom spawned dozens of new towns such as Golden, Boulder, Black Hawk, Central City, and Idaho Springs. The metropolis was Denver, which had been born with the coalescing of several small towns; as early as 1859 it boasted the infant *Rocky Mountain News*. Ambitious and impatient Coloradans tried to organize a government as the State of Jefferson, which in 1861 emerged as the Territory of Colorado.

The Colorado placer boom was of short duration, and soon the miners were headed east with the slogan "Busted, by Gosh!" or leaving for more promising areas or settling down to more prosaic farming or ranching; population actually declined during the 1860s. With the coming of the railroad in 1870 farmers began arriving in large numbers, including the group migrations that produced Greeley, Longmont, Evans, and Green City. Colorado was admitted to the Union in 1876 as the centennial state.

One later important gold boom hit Colorado—at Cripple Creek in 1890–1891. Within three years the town numbered 10,000 people, and by 1901 the annual gold production reached $25 million, while the population climbed to 50,000. The Cripple

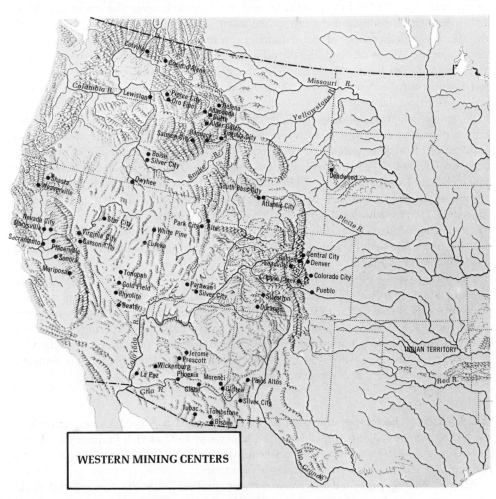

WESTERN MINING CENTERS

Creek boom was unusual in its duration, since as late as 1938 the region was producing over $5 million annually; the area included eleven different mining cities, or "camps," all connected by electrically operated tramways.

THE BLACK HILLS When the Colorado boom was declining in the 1870s, some of the miners followed the Custer expedition of 1874 into the Black Hills country of South Dakota, and their favorable reports attracted others. The peak of the boom came in 1876, with miners being drawn from all over the West— undeterred by the weak efforts of the army to keep them out of Sioux territory.

Center of the excitement was Deadwood, with its main street wandering along a gulch, to the sides of which houses clung precariously. The lower part of the town was sacred to the gambler and the prostitute, with no pretense to even the minimum of law and order that characterized the rest of the town. The Main Street was crowded with the usual conglomeration of booted miners, teamsters, gamblers, storekeepers, and casual visitors. Whips cracked like pistols as the ordinary ten-oxen, three-wagon teams lumbered through town. Twice a month the steel-lined treasure chest of Wells Fargo and Company rolled out of town; altogether it transported over $60 million before it was replaced by the railroad.

A boomtown such as Deadwood presented various leisure activities to absorb the time and money of the miners. Obvious were the saloons, gambling halls, and houses of prostitution. But there was also a very active theater. At the completion of a play the floor was cleared, a bar was opened at one end of the theater, a band installed at the other end, and dancing begun. The ladies of the chorus acted as dance partners, receiving a commission on each drink the man was expected to buy at the end of each dance, and earning additional income by ventures into commercialized vice, encouraged by the curtained boxes. The miners who roistered on a Saturday night might well appear in church the next morning, for by 1877 Methodist, Congregational, and Catholic services were available.

The boom days of the Black Hills rush declined as the free gold disappeared, causing some gold seekers to turn to quartz mining, which involved expensive machinery. Most profitable was George Hearst's Homestake Mine, which by the early 1930s had produced some $35 million in gold. Considerable outcry arose over the big profits of a relatively few capitalists, but it must be remembered that any production from relatively low-grade ore was possible only with large investments in technological improvements, and that there was real risk involved in the investment.

ALASKA The existence of gold in western Canada had been known as early as the 1830s, but the biggest rush came with the news in 1897 of rich findings near Dawson in the Yukon. The resulting boom was spurred on by the merchants of Seattle, who realized that they would be the greatest beneficiaries.

Alaskan mining presented extremely difficult problems for the farmers and clerks who comprised such a large part of the rush. The inland passage past Juneau was simple enough. The real troubles started at Skagway, for most miners preferred the overland trail to the longer sea and river route, which meant struggling over 600 miles of frozen waste, precipitous and ice-covered mountains, and boiling rivers to reach the goal of Dawson. Not the least of the troubles were clouds of man-eating mosquitoes, and the need for each man to carry a year's supply of food—not only for subsistence, but also because it was required by the Canadian police, which set a minimum of 1150 pounds; this, in addition to tents, tools, and other essentials.

Gold deposits near Dawson were rich, but the hazards were great. During the long winter the gravel had to be thawed before it could be dug into piles and then allowed to wait until spring when water was available for its working; at this point the miner might discover that his gravel contained no gold and that his entire winter's work was lost. Dawson claimed the title of the most wide-open town in the West; but actually the Northwest Mounted Police prevented the major disorders and loss of life that were customary in American towns such as Skagway, Nome, and Fairbanks.

PASSING OF GOLD MINING FRONTIER   The last of the American gold booms came about the turn of the century in Death Valley and to the north and east in Nevada. Rumors of gold in Death Valley had been spread as early as the days of the '49ers, but the real booms came in the 1870s and later. They turned out to be of little importance because of the cost of transportation. Considerable interest went to Walter Scott (Death Valley Scotty), who claimed a rich and secret gold mine. He lived in a two-million-dollar house with electricity, paneled rooms, a quarter-million-dollar organ, a glass-enclosed swimming pool, and other luxuries. When he traveled he attracted much publicity by throwing money out of his hotel window. But the really identifiable Death Valley fortune came from borax, discovered in 1880. F. M. Smith made a great deal of money, and at the same time gave national fame to the twenty-mule teams that hauled the borax across the 150 miles of desert.

A new center of excitement appeared at Tonopah in 1900, and for a time Tonopah could boast plate-glass windows, the latest French fashions, and dinners featuring champagne, caviar, and oysters. Next came Goldfield (1903), where Tex Rickard operated a popular saloon and gambling hall, and obtained experience for his later career of sports promotion by ballyhooing (1906) a boxing match between Joe Gans and Battling Nelson. Other towns followed in rapid succession; possibly most interesting was the construction in 1905 of the model town of Rhyolite, with concrete buildings, modern schools, attractive stores, large office buildings, electric lights, and paved streets. Its death by 1908 produced one of the most impressive town corpses in the history of the West.

SILVER AND COPPER—NEVADA   While gold was the first metal to produce large western mining booms, there was increasing interest in other metals, particularly silver and copper. Quite illuminating is the experience of Nevada. The first mining was the scraping of the surface for gold. Henry T. P. Comstock, for whom the

Comstock Lode was named, obtained his claim through fast talk, a blind horse, and a bottle of whiskey. Two months later he sold it for $10,000, losing potential millions in the transaction; for he did not know that rich silver ore lay a few feet below the surface.

By late 1859 analysis of the "blue stuff" (quartz), formerly discarded as worthless, assayed $1595 in gold and $4791 in silver per ton. Immediately there was a big rush from California, with population centering at Virginia City and Carson City, and with more interest in silver than in gold. The original discoveries seemed fairly well exhausted by the late 1860s, but then came new finds, bigger and richer than anything that had preceded them. Dividends began to flow in large amounts to the lucky owners.

The history of the big bonanza is largely a biography of a Scotsman and three Irishmen—James G. Fair, John W. Mackay, James C. Flood, and William S. O'Brien. The first two had been prospectors, which they felt qualified them as mining experts, and the other two had run a saloon in San Francisco, engaging in the usual mining stock speculation on the side. Their confidence in their own judgment led them to purchase mining properties as fast as funds were available. The four partners rode the crest of the boom of the 1870s, and each man became a multimillionaire. The Consolidated Virginia jumped from $1 a share in 1870 to $700 in 1875. It was united in 1884 with the California to create the Consolidated Virginia and California.

Silver mining presented new and difficult problems, both in prospecting and in mine operations. Everyone knew that silver existed in quartz rock, but not all quartz contained silver, while rich surface indications might disappear a little below the surface, or poor prospects improve. The result was rather hit-or-miss mining, and abandoned claims all over the countryside, even in the streets and under houses. The prospector looked for promising quartz, examined it with a magnifying glass for uncombined particles of gold or silver. If encouraged by what he saw, he pulverized a specimen, washed the light matter away, and dissolved the rest in nitric acid, which precipitated chloride of lime, which he then dried and heated with a little soda in a hollowed piece of charcoal by the flame of a candle; the result was a button of silver, which gave a rough indication of the richness of the ore. Sometimes he only collected samples, and took them to an expert for assaying.

Engineering problems were also difficult. Immense amounts of wood had to be hauled to feed the necessary fires and to support the mine shafts. When hauling became too expensive, huge flumes might be constructed down the mountainside and across the ravines to wash the logs to the mines. Since the veins often widened into large lodes, a new method had to be devised to support the roof and walls. Best known of the engineering innovations was the Sutro Tunnel, named for Adolph Sutro and completed in 1878. It permitted the draining of even the lower levels and at the same time provided for the transportation of the ore.

Because of the large cost of mining and processing silver ore, the individual prospector and miner was heavily dependent on the big company. He might work directly for such a company or sell his claims or do his own mining and have the company do the smelting. The whole process was highly speculative, particularly because profitable ore was a variable quantity. Most miners held considerable varieties of stock in such intriguing enterprises as "Let Her Rip" or "Gouge Eye." Most of such stock turned out to be worthless, but now and then one was fabulously rewarding. For example, the Gould and Curry mine with an investment of $200,000 took out $9 million of ore in the

Central City, Colorado. This collection of frame houses, with denuded hills in the background, is a classic illustration of what happened to Rocky Mountain forests as the mineral frontier advanced. (Granger)

two years 1863 and 1864, and paid a handsome $2.9 million in dividends. One spectacular result of the uncertainty of silver mining was that the selling prices of stock fluctuated madly; for example, a share of the Alpha mine brought $1570 in February 1868 and could find few buyers at $33 in September of the same year.

Most miners struggled to exist. They worked hard, wore cheap, coarse clothes, and often lived in tents because of the scarcity of wood. Here and there a man made a big strike, which he ordinarily spent with great speed. "Sandy" Bowers, for example, after a rich strike built a house worth $407,000, entertained lavishly, and traveled in Europe, where he bought everything in sight except the Tower of London; returning to Virginia City he hired a hotel to hold open house for the entire town. About this time his ore was exhausted, and so he went back to prospecting, while his wife told fortunes.

The boomtowns of Nevada were very similar to those in other mining areas. Theaters, newspapers, and churches appeared quite early. Prices were tremendously high. Saloons, gambling houses, and brothels were highly visible. The usual undesirable bad men, claim jumpers, gamblers, and prostitutes arrived very soon. The result was that many of the earnings of the miners went to freighters, storekeepers, and gamblers. Mining was itself a tremendous gamble, in which only a few won, and gave little incentive to frugality.

COLORADO   Colorado went through a process similar to that of Nevada. For example, California Gulch was on the point of becoming a ghost town from the exhaustion of gold when a metallurgist discovered (1877) the richness of the silver deposits, and another mining engineer representing a St. Louis smelting and refining company, built a successful smelter. The result was the reborn town of Leadville, which within three years had some 15,000 residents and was the state's second most important city. Among the aspirants for participation in the new silver boom were two railroads, the Denver and Rio Grande and the Atchison, Topeka and Santa Fe. They fought a "war" over the Royal Gorge route to Leadville, with the Rio Grande winning by 1880. H. A. W. Tabor, who had struggled to make a living in his small grocery store, grubstaked the right prospectors and became one of Colorado's most famous "silver kings." Tabor and some of his fellow "kings" died bankrupt, but others did not: Meyer Guggenheim of Philadelphia, for example, sold his holdings in 1888 for $10 million.

Before the declining price of silver ended the boom, such mines as Holy Moses, Last Chance, Amethyst, and Champion were names known all over America. By the end of 1892 the Amethyst had produced more than $2 million in silver ore, Last Chance $1.6 million, and others lesser amounts.

MONTANA   During the 1870s and 1880s the main mining interests of Idaho and Montana were diverted from gold—first to silver and then to copper. The main areas were near Butte, Montana, and Coeur d'Alene, Idaho. Silver finds in Montana brought a very considerable rush of miners in the 1870s; among the newcomers was an Irishman named Marcus Daly, who was disappointed when his silver mine turned out to have copper, but whose mood became one of unbounded optimism when he discovered that the copper was unusually pure. From this small start, made in 1876, Daly built a copper empire and became a millionaire. Another silver miner, William J. Parks, also found such large amounts of copper that "Uncle Billy" contended that the ore could be shipped "to hell and back" for smelting and still yield a profit. But he sold his property, which ultimately yielded $1 million in profit, for a mere $10,000 and did not become a "copper king." Another ambitious newcomer was William Andrews Clark, a precise, parsimonious, and ambitious little Scotsman, who arrived in 1872. He was a merchant and banker, but became interested in the great mineral prospects of Butte. Before long he and Daly became rivals, and the "war of the copper kings" was under way.

The Clark-Daly feud was one of the epic struggles of the day. Clark was in control of Butte, and advanced the fortunes of that young metropolis. His newspaper sneered at the pretentions of Daly who was boss of his own new town of Anaconda, where his rival paper returned with interest all the jeers thrown in his direction. Ultimately both men spent money freely in a struggle for political control of the state.

Clark's great ambition was to become United States senator, and in 1899 he spent some half million dollars persuading the state legislature of his merits. The ensuing scandal was so great that he resigned just before a Senate committee reported that he should not be seated. His place then being vacant, he was appointed to it by the lieutenant governor, an act that was later canceled by the governor, who had been absent from the state at the time of the appointment. In 1900 Marcus Daly lay dying, and a pro-Clark legislature voted to send their man to the Senate, where he served for six undistinguished years.

At about the close of the century Standard Oil money entered the copper industry and combined many firms, including the Anaconda, into the Amalgamated Copper Company, which later became the Anaconda Mining Company. Amalgamated failed in its effort to create a monopoly of the copper business, largely because of the power of Calumet and Hecla. It did manage, however, to play a dominant role in Montana affairs, and for years was known simply as "the company"; the cattle people could never compete effectively against the copper people. Much later, in the mid-twentieth century, "the company" sold its string of Montana newspapers and moderated the more obvious aspects of its political activities. By then the state's farm organizations were more powerful politically than either the cattle or the copper industries.

IDAHO   Idaho's placer mining enthusiasm passed its peak during the 1870s, and a silver rush was apparent by 1880; by 1883 the Wood River district had a railroad and a flow of capital from home and abroad. Northern Idaho witnessed a gold rush in the Coeur d'Alene area in 1883, with the usual boomtowns and the motley array of the footloose. But the available gold soon ran out, and interest turned to silver. The really big find (1885) was the Bunker Hill lode of silver and lead. In time the Bunker

Hill and Sullivan mine paid some $50 million in dividends. This and other mines seemed to have inexhaustible supplies of silver, lead, and zinc

The Coeur d'Alene mines attained national notoriety from their labor troubles, particularly in the 1890s and later. Mining was an arduous and dangerous occupation. Both operators and laborers were rough and tough, with neither side willing to make concessions. Labor troubles meant armed forces on each side, shafts and buildings dynamited, pitched battles, and sudden death. Here it was that both William Borah and "Big Bill" Haywood began their national careers. Here it was also that the Western Federation of Miners, with its Local Number 1 at Butte, had its baptism of fire and developed the ideology that a little later produced the Industrial Workers of the World.

ARIZONA AND UTAH   Arizona's mineral richness had long been known, but little developed, partly because the ores were easily exhausted, but mainly because an individual prospector found the desert country forbidding, and the Apache dangerous. The Indian problem was partially solved after the Civil War. Kit Carson's campaign against the Navaho in 1863 resulted in the removal of these Indians, first to a reservation in eastern New Mexico and later (1868) to a permanent location in the northwestern section of the territory. The Apache, who ranged both Arizona and New Mexico, were put under so much pressure by General George Crook during the 1870s that a great many were forced onto reservations. As was true in the North, all the Indians were not so corralled, and the Southwest continued in a state of turmoil during most of the 1880s because of raids by these nonreservation Indians.

The partial quieting of the Apache by Crook encouraged the miners to ply their trade, and more mineral discoveries were made. Outstanding were the numerous finds in the neighborhood of Globe, Arizona. The rich Silver King claim was discovered in 1875; rumor had it that some of the ore assayed as high as $1000 a ton.

Most famous of the Arizona boomtowns of the late 1870s was Tombstone, which originated in a silver find of 1877 by Edward Schieffelin, who had come to the territory determined to find a fortune or a tombstone for his lonely grave. From the discoveries in southeastern Arizona grew one of the roughest and most wide-open towns in the West. Old yellowed files of the Tombstone *Epitaph* recall but faintly the turbulent days of the Earps, "Doc" Holladay, Billy the Kid, and other exponents of western violence. The story of the Earps' encounter with the Clantons at the O. K. Corral is one of the stories of the frontier legend most often told.

The Tombstone deposits were exhausted within a few years. Today one passes through a country pockmarked with abandoned shafts to enter one of the most notable of the West's ghost towns; rows of deserted houses and stores and saloons attest its once numerous population, while an imposing "boot hill" cemetery gives mute evidence of the frequent use of the six-gun in its long-departed past.

More important to Arizona in the long run than silver was copper, and, recently, rarer metals. The Cornelia mine in southwestern Arizona has been worked fairly continuously but inefficiently since the 1850s. Rich new finds were made in other parts of the territory during the 1870s. Work in the Morenci area of east-central Arizona began in 1871 and provided an inspiration for other copper districts such as nearby Clifton. Copper mining had all the usual difficulties with transportation, water, and supplies, but there also were imposing technical problems of extracting the copper. The Bisbee and Jerome regions were both opened in 1877, and in time the mines near Globe came to be concerned predominantly with copper; the first copper was extracted at Globe in 1878. Since copper mining required large amounts of capital, it was particularly the domain of the large company. By the 1880s such organizations as the Calumet and Arizona Mining Company and Phelps, Dodge and Company were preeminent in copper production.

Utah's mineral development was slow. The Mormon Church recognized the importance of a balanced, self-sufficient economy, but was also anxious to avoid any rushes that attracted the human flotsam and jetsam that disrupted normal life. Mormon boys were encouraged, however, to take employment as mine laborers not only to bring money into the community, but also to prevent the necessity of importing large numbers of outside workers. After the coming of the railroads—which also furnished employment—the Church was less adament on its stand on mining and employment could be found in this field also. In Utah the farmer and stockman preceded the miner, which was an inversion of the usual development, and mining was carried on in a somewhat different setting.

Utah mining is also associated with the day of corporate mining, of big investments, of outside financial participation. By the 1870s word of the West's mineral wealth had circled the globe, and many were anxious to invest in the mines. Those mines such as the famed Emma were rich enough, but so much money was invested in them to find even more riches that many a stockholder was deeply disappointed in the result, and not a few were bilked. As was true in Montana and Arizona, copper became the leading mineral and provided the basis for a more stable mining industry.

INFLUENCES OF THE MINING FRONTIER   The long succession of western mining booms brought into sharp focus many picturesque persons and institutions as miners flocked from one rumored find to the next. The boomtowns resembled one another in their congested living quarters, astronomic prices, and imposing "boot hill" cemeteries. Traders, gamblers, and prostitutes trailed after the hordes of predominantly young and vigorous men. With each find a few men made their fortunes, others missed by an eyelash, and the majority moved to greener fields. The color, movement, and virility are obvious and spectacular.

In some respects the mining frontier made contributions of doubtful value. It was rapid, fluid, transitory, and wasteful. Many of its settlements were of only fleeting importance, as is evidenced by the trail of ghost towns. Some did not become ghost towns, but have continued as modern small towns, where the remains of the past have disappeared almost completely. Where buildings have fallen into decay or have been dismantled for use elsewhere, there are now pockmarked hillsides, a countryside stripped of trees to support mine shafts and to produce charcoal for ore reduction, and perhaps crumbling tombstones that mark the end of vain hopes of fame and wealth. From the pessimistic viewpoint mining is wasteful—it takes from the land and returns nothing.

Yet the mining booms made contributions that were much more than just picturesque episodes to be used later in novels and scenarios. The men who were searching for wealth produced large quantities of real minerals which had an important impact on the industrial life of the United States. Certain results are very obvious, such as the effects of vast new supplies of copper available at a time when American streets were being transformed into mazes of telegraph and electric wires.

Most important was the effect of new supplies of precious metals on the total economy of the United States. American industrialization expanded impressively during the late nineteenth century, which meant a proportionate increase in the number of business transactions. The result was a vastly greater need for money—a need that the banking system of the day could not satisfy. The corollary would normally have been deflation—a fall in prices. This fall actually occurred, but was tempered by the tremendous flow of precious metals from the West. Without the addition of this gold and silver the depressions of 1873 and 1893 might have been longer and more severe.

This gigantic injection of precious metals into the monetary system had some not altogether desirable side effects. The enormous increase in silver production destroyed the old ratio between the values of silver and gold that had been at least in accord with the facts. The immediate consequence was that when the farmers wanted inflation they talked of the "crime of '73" and the remonitization of silver. The farmers' reaction precipitated the "money question" that plagued the political scene in the latter part of the nineteenth century. Continuing discoveries of gold in Alaska and South Africa helped somewhat to redress the imbalance created by the "silver kings." During the late 1890s prices increased, and cries for the free and unlimited coinage of silver abated.

For the West itself, the mining rushes also had important implications. The movement of large numbers of miners into Indian country decidedly hastened the coming of white settlers and, as already mentioned, hastened the "solution" of the Indian problem. Each boom meant new towns with commercial opportunities attractive to storekeepers, bankers, artisans, laborers, and railroad men; and these new residents in turn provided opportunities for still other people, including stockmen and farmers. When the St. Paul or the Northwestern went into the Black Hills or the Denver and Rio Grande followed the mining booms into central Colorado, transportation improved not only for the mine owners but for everyone else. The farmer or the stockman was attracted to the area served by the railroad, and the result was more and faster western settlement than would have occurred otherwise, and often in more or less isolated spots. Although some of the western states waited much longer for statehood than their boosters thought reasonable, mining should be credited with their population increasing as fast as it did.

The chaotic conditions created by frontier mining have largely disappeared. Most mines have become stable enterprises, run much like factories, and surrounded by orderly towns that look and act much like other municipalities. But mining continues to be hazardous. A mine may be exhausted, but much more likely is a slight fall in the price of the metal, making operations temporarily or permanently unprofitable. There is always the possibility of new and financially rewarding discoveries. For example, in the 1950s occurred a brief uranium rush that faded when the quantity quickly outstripped the market. A few men became rich, a good many invested in stocks whose value fell drastically, and the boom was halted at least temporarily. Still, the West is a land of known mineral deposits, and even though it has been thoroughly prospected, a new find or a new metal or a new market may appear, and once more the hills will rock with excitement.

READINGS   *Paperbacks are marked with an asterisk.*

General Accounts of Mining   *Rodman W. Paul, *Mining Frontiers of the Far West, 1848–1880* (1963), excellent, stressing the technical; William S. Greever, *The Bonanza West* (1963); W. J. Trimble, *Mining Advances into the Inland Empire* (1914); Glenn C. Quiett, *Pay Dirt* (1936); W. Eugene Hollon, *The Southwest* (1961); Harold E. Briggs, *Frontiers of the Northwest* (1940), readable; Duane A. Smith, *Rocky Mountain Mining Camps* (1967); David S. Lavender, *The Rockies* (1968); Clark C. Spence, *British Investments and the American Mining Frontier* (1958).

California   General histories are listed in the Readings for Chapter 24. See also John W. Caughey, *Gold Is the Cornerstone* (1948); Owen C. Coy, *Gold Days* (1929); Octavius T. Howe, *Argonauts of '49* (1923); *Rodman W. Paul, *California Gold* (1947). Among the better acounts of travel to the gold fields are Owen C. Coy, *The Great Trek* (1931); Benjamin Harris, *The Gila Trail* (1960); James Monaghan, *The Overland Trail* (1947). Individual travel accounts include Robert Eccleston, *Overland to California on the Southwestern Trail* (1950); George W. B. Evans, *Mexican Gold Trail* (1945); Vincent Geiger and Wakeman Bryarly, *Trail to California* (1945), diary; Heinrich Lienhard, *From St. Louis to Sutter's Fort, 1846* (1961), just before the gold rush; Elizabeth Page, *Wagons West* (1930); John E. Pomfret (ed.), *California Gold Rush Voyages, 1848–1849* (1954).

Individual Accounts of the Mining Areas   A few of these many accounts are Rodman W. Paul (ed.), *The California Gold Discovery* (1966); Thomas D. Clark (ed.), *Gold Rush Diary* (1967), handsome book; Doyce B. Nunis (ed.), *The Letters of a Young Miner* (1964); Dale L. Morgan and James R. Scobie (eds.), *Three Years in California* (1964); Helen S. Giffen (ed.), *The Diaries of Peter Decker* (1966); Charles A. Barker (ed.), *Memoirs of Elisha Oscar Crosby* (1945); Doyce B. Nunis (ed.), *The Golden Frontier* (1962), 1851–1869; Franklin A. Buck, *A Yankee Trader in the Gold Rush* (1930); John W. Caughey (ed.), *Rushing for Gold* (1949) and (ed.), *Seeing the Elephant* (1951); Robert G. Cleland (ed.), *Apron Full of Gold* (1949), woman '49er; Carvel E. Collins (ed.), *Sam Ward in the Gold Rush* (1949); Le Roy R. and Ann W. Hafen (eds.), *Journals of Forty-Niners* (1954);

Archer B. Hulbert, *Forty-Niners* (1931), synthetic diary; Joseph H. Jackson, *Anybody's Gold* (1941), mining towns; *Francis S. Marryat, *Mountains and Molehills* (1952), 1850; George W. Read (ed.), *A Pioneer of 1850* (1927); Benjamin B. Richards (ed.), *California Gold Rush Merchant* (1956); Walker D. Wyman (ed.), *California Emigrant Letters* (1952), '49ers. Amusements are described in Edmond W. Cagey, *The San Francisco Stage* (1950); George R. MacMinn, *The Theater of the Golden Era in California* (1941).

Nevada   Gilman M. Ostrander, *Nevada* (1966) and Effie M. Mack, *Nevada* (1936) contain useful information. See also Carl B. Glasscock, *The Big Bonanza* (1931); George D. Lyman, *The Saga of the Comstock Lode* (1934), interesting; *Richard G. Lillard, *Desert Challenge* (1942); *W. Turrentine Jackson, *Treasure Hill: Portrait of a Silver Mining Camp* (1963). The story of John W. Mackay is in Ethel Manter, *Rocket of the Comstock* (1950); another pertinent biography is Robert T. Stewart, Jr., and Mary F. Stewart, *Adolph Sutro* (1962). Margaret G. Watson, *Silver Theater* (1964), 1850–1864.

Colorado   *Robert G. Athearn, *High Country Empire* (1960), brief on mining; Carl Ubbelohde, *A Colorado History* (1965); Le Roy R. Hafen, *Colorado* (1933), (ed.), *Colorado and Its People* (4 vols., 1948), vols. I and II, (ed.), *Colorado Gold Rush* (1941), (ed.), *Overland Route to the Gold Fields, 1859* (1942); Marshall Sprague, *Money Mountain* (1953), entertaining; Don L. and Jean H. Griswold, *The Carbonate Camp Called Leadville* (1951), detailed; George F. Willison, *Here They Dug the Gold* (1931), popular; Irving Howbert, *Memories of a Lifetime in the Pike's Peak Region* (1925); Louis E. Simonin, *The Rocky Mountain West of 1867* (1966), contemporary; Mabel B. Lee, *Cripple Creek Days* (1958), reminiscences. On early Colorado settlement see James F. Willard (ed.), *The Union Colony of Greeley, Colorado* (1918) and James F. Willard and Colin B. Goodykoontz (eds.), *Experiments in Colorado Colonization* (1926).

Montana and Wyoming   Merrill G. Burlingame, *The Montana Frontier* (1942), largely on original discoveries; Carl B. Glasscock, *The War of the Copper Kings* (1935), centers on Butte; K. Ross Toole, *Montana* (1959), stresses the author's interest in mining; Joseph K. Howard, *Montana: High, Wide, and Handsome* (1943); Larry Barsness, *Gold Camp* (1962), entertaining; Andrew F. Rolle (ed.), *The Road to Virginia City* (1960), mining camps; Lola M. Homsher (ed.), *South Pass, 1868* (1960), Wyoming; Helen M. White (ed.), *Ho! For the Gold Fields: Northern Wagon Trains in the 1860s* (1966).

Oregon   Oscar O. Winther, *The Great Northwest* (1947) and *The Old Oregon Country* (1950); Alice H. Ernst, *Trouping in the Oregon Country* (1961), interesting on amusements.

Idaho   The history of Idaho has been much neglected. Dorothy O. Johansen and Charles M. Gates, *Empire of the Columbia* (1957) touches briefly on mining.

Black Hills   *Bruce Nelson, *Land of the Dacotahs* (1946), popular; Watson Parker, *Gold in the Black Hills* (1966), mostly Deadwood—scholarly but reads well; *Agnes W. Spring, *The Cheyenne and Black Hills Stage and Express Route* (1948).

Arizona, New Mexico, Utah   Joseph Miller, *Arizona: The Last Frontier* (1956), only a little on mining; Ann M. Peek, *The March of Arizona History* (1962), several brief chapters on mining; Walter N. Burns, *Tombstone* (1917), boom town. Robert G. Cleland, *A History of Phelps Dodge* (1952), mining corporation. Warren A. Beck, *New Mexico* (1962) and Edna Fergusson, *New Mexico* (1951) are both general treatments; David Meriwether, *My Life in the Mountains and on the Plains* (1965) has much on New Mexico in the 1850s. *Leonard J. Arrington, *Great Basin Kingdom* (1958), fine economic study, including information about mining.

Alaska   Edward B. Lung, *Black Sand and Gold* (1956); Pierre Burton, *The Klondike Fever* (1958); William S. Greever, *The Bonanza West* (1963).

Death Valley   Neil C. Wilson, *Silver Stampede* (1937).

Chapter 28 / THE OVERLAND ROUTE

Early residents of the Far West were almost completely isolated from their friends and relatives back East. Correspondence was a precarious business. Books, clothing, hardware, and other attributes of civilization were as much as 3000 miles distant, while markets for western products were equally remote. Such conditions were unpleasant even for the fortune seeker who expected soon to return to the East, but were often intolerable for the man who realized that from either desire or necessity his stay was to be permanent.

EARLY COMMUNICATIONS WITH THE PACIFIC COAST

The best communication in the early days was by ocean, even though no planned service existed. The shipper of goods and the letter writer had the same problem: to find a boat going to the general area in which he was interested and then dicker with the captain. The journey around the Horn was time consuming, and the captain took little responsibility for deliveries; a letter might never reach the addressee, and goods might be dropped on the wharf to rot. Regardless of cost, such service was unsatisfactory. The Pacific Coast seemed as remote as Kamchatka or Capetown.

Transportation by land was even worse. Freight sent by wagon was slow, erratic, uncertain, and expensive; rarely were goods of sufficient value to be worth shipping. The delivery of letters depended on the kindness and memory of someone making the trip. Here and there along the overland trails was a primitive "post office," usually a deserted cabin or the crotch of a tree, where letters would be deposited in the hope that some future traveler would deliver them. No doubt some were delivered, but many merely served as reading material for other travelers.

OCEAN MAIL CONTRACTS   Regular communication depended on mail service, which was unprofitable unless subsidized by the government. The first mail contracts, utilizing the Panama route, were awarded in 1847. The successful bidders for the trip from New York to Panama organized the United States Mail Steamship Company, while those winning the Pacific section from Panama to San Francisco chartered the Pacific Mail Steamship Company. Both groups started operations in 1849, with the western part of the trip the first to be opened. The first boat, the *California*, reached California along with the first big mining rush, and all the crew deserted for the mines except the captain and one cabin boy. The original monthly mail service became semimonthly in 1851 with a government payment of $724,350 a year; the postage rate after 1855 was ten cents a half ounce. Passenger rates were high; a cabin from New York to San Francisco in 1849 cost $500, which of course did not include the trip across Panama. Not unexpectedly, the companies made large profits.

Both the eastern and western companies soon occupied the whole route and divided the business (January 1851). Cornelius Vanderbilt provided competition with his Accessory Transit Company, which in 1851 offered more comfortable boats by the

---

Ed Hawke's Bull Train, 1864. The wagons were loaded at Nebraska City for the long haul from the Missouri River to the mining camps of the Rockies. Despite their limitations, oxen were regarded as the most reliable means of motive power at the time. Within two or three years the iron horse would be pulling freight across Nebraska. (Nebraska State Historical Society)

Nicaragua route. Vanderbilt's partners doubled-crossed him and acquired his company while he was on vacation in 1853. Upon his return all three companies paid him a subsidy to keep his fingers out of their pie, and alternately maintained rates and fought each other bitterly.

The greatest improvement of the Panama route was the opening in 1855 of the Panama Railroad; the fare for its 47 miles was a profitable $25. Vanderbilt then regained control of the Nicaragua route, but his service was poorer, particularly because of his troubles with William Walker. Ultimately (1860) Vanderbilt controlled all the Atlantic business, and the Pacific Mail all the Pacific business; rates then rose. In time the transcontinental railroads were to bribe the steamship lines to avoid rate cutting.

Some efforts were also made to obtain mail service by the Tehuantepec route. An American concession, including the right to build a railroad, was granted in 1853. Five years later came a mail contract at $250,000 a year, but the service was never satisfactory and was seen abandoned. Although mail and passengers went through Central America, the great bulk of the freight continued to make the trip around the Horn.

OVERLAND MAIL ROUTES The Panama route left much to be desired. It was long and slow, passed through foreign territory, required two reshipments, and was extremely circuitous for all points east of California. Westerners continued to agitate for more direct overland service. Little consideration was given to the most northerly possibility by way of the Missouri and Columbia rivers; this route was long, passed through few settlements, encountered hostile Indians, and included mountain passes that were impossible to use in winter.

The central route, despite dangerous deserts and mountains toward the west, was mostly easy and well marked, had few hostile Indians, and benefited from passing through the Mormon settlements. The southern route might either follow the 35th parallel from Santa Fe, or, after the Gadsden Purchase, proceed farther south along the Gila River. The southernmost of these options had the advantages of few mountains and no winter snow; on the other hand, it was long and indirect, and crossed much desert country.

The beginning of overland mail service came in 1848, when a contract was awarded for the trip between Independence and Salt Lake City; service to Santa Fe was begun the next year. Even these comparatively easy hauls proved difficult, and deliveries were slow and uncertain. Provision was made in 1851 for the western section of the central route, but two years later, because of the tremendous difficulties involved, the terminus was moved from the San Francisco area to Los Angeles. Travel remained difficult, however, and mule packtrains were at the best slow.

More western population increased the demand for coach service, while more progressive citizens talked of railroads. A few ingenious persons speculated that as long as much of the Southwest was known as a desert, the right answer should be camels. The federal government was sufficiently impressed to detail an army officer to the Near East to buy the necessary camels, and 75 were delivered near San Antonio in 1856. To the disappointment of lovers of the picturesque, camels never became popular on the "American desert."

Whatever the means of transportation, more adequate geographical knowledge was essential to its success; between 1845 and 1853 at least twenty-five new exploring expeditions penetrated the less known parts of the West, to say nothing of thousands of reports from other travelers. The greatest single exploration of the West came in the years 1853–1855 under orders of Secretary of War Jefferson Davis, with the primary object of surveying possible railroad routes. Although these explorations produced a

STAGE AND MAIL ROUTES

|---|---|
⊢•⊣•⊢•⊣	The Pony Express, Telegraph, and Overland Mail
⊢•–•⊣•–	Butterfield Overland Mail
— • — • —	San Antonio to San Diego Line
··········	Kansas City and Neosho to Sacramento
–•–••–••–	Fort Abercrombie to Helena
——————	Salt Lake City to Los Angeles
⋈⋈⋈⋈⋈	Salt Lake City to Virginia City and Umatilla (Ben Holladay)
–⊢—⊢–	Sacramento to Portland
–⊢—⊢–	Independence to Santa Fe

great deal of useful, detailed information, they discovered no new routes; those available were the northern, between 47° and 49°; the central, between 38° and 42°; the southern, along either the 35th parallel from Albuquerque or the 32nd parallel following the Gila River. Davis, a southerner, not unexpectedly concluded from the vast amount of evidence that one of the southern routes was to be preferred, but Congress failed to act on his recommendations.

BUTTERFIELD   A speculative railroad for some unspecified date in the future was far from satisfying to westerners, who wanted immediate action. Their impatience produced results when in 1857 the postmaster general called for bids on a fast and continuous service by road to the coast. The contract that finally was awarded included a subsidy of $600,000 a year for a semiweekly service taking not over twenty-five days for a single trip. When the line opened, it started in the East from both St. Louis and Memphis, converged at Little Rock, and then passed through Preston, El Paso, and Yuma on its way to San Francisco, a trip of over 2500 miles.

The Butterfield Overland Stage Company marked an important advance in the development of rapid communication between the East and the Far West. The first stages left opposite ends of the line in September 1858, the eastbound stage covering the road in 20 days, 18 hours, and 16 minutes, or well within the specified time limit.

The elaborate equipment of the company was expensive, costing about $1 million. Concord coaches were used, with wide-rimmed wheels to make travel through the sand easier. Leather straps served for springs, and leather curtains attempted feebly to shut out inclement weather. The three seats were designed to hold nine passengers snugly, but more were sometimes crowded into the space. The driver was perched on the top in front, with now and then a passenger or two beside him. Mail and packages were placed in the "boot" at the back. An overflow of mail was frequently dumped on the side of the road to wait for a less crowded coach; passengers paid cash, whereas government mail was carried at a flat rate. Stages traveling long distances needed frequent changes of horses and drivers; stations were placed at distances of between 8 and 25 miles. "Swing stations" provided minimum care of the stock; less frequent "home stations" provided headquarters for company agents and served meals to travelers.

A trip on an overland stage was hardly a pleasure excursion. For over three weeks, day and night, the passengers jolted steadily on the most primitive of roads. Sleep in a moving coach filled with passengers was snatched sporadically if achieved at all. When the sun was shining the passengers roasted; during a rainstorm they were drenched; in dry weather the dust nearly suffocated them. Toilet facilities were nonexistent; hence bathing and shaving waited until the end of the trip. Little wonder the passengers drank large amounts of whiskey to keep up their courage. With little sleep, too much whiskey, and little water, overland travelers were a wild-looking group before the end of their trip.

One of the worst features of overland stage travel was the food. Of course each traveler might carry his own provisions, but food that could be carried in the hot sun for three weeks and then eaten without cooking was neither varied nor appetizing. The company provided food only at home stations, and even there it was far from tempting. The usual fare was rancid bacon, maggoty bread, and coffee that tasted like ditchwater. The price for this unappetizing meal was sometimes as high as $1.50. The care of passengers was always secondary to the care of livestock; horses and mules were expensive to replace.

The drivers on the overland stage were experts with the reins, but sometimes were drunk and always were profane. Divisional superintendents had to be sufficiently hard to control such drivers, and included a scattering of "bad men" who were making a little side money when their own business was slow. The fare varied with the amount of traffic and the business conditions of the country. A typical charge was that of 1859, which was $200 for the trip west and $100 for the return east, the difference representing the difference in the traffic in the two directions.

Butterfield did not confine his attention to passenger and mail service, but also did freighting. This portion of the traffic was the same as the freighting provided by others. The wagons, drawn by mules or oxen, lumbered across the plains with no effort at speed. There was no great rush to get freight across the continent; perishable commodities were not shipped. Many years were to pass before such products as fruits, vegetables, and dressed meat could be produced in the Far West for marketing in the East.

THE PONY EXPRESS   The Butterfield Overland Stage Company was the largest passenger and freight carrier on the plains in the late 1850s; but numerous other companies also operated, sometimes over many years and with United States mail contracts. Most important of these rivals was Russell, Majors and Waddell, the greatest freighting concern of its day, which operated along the central route. Its organization was much the same as that of its southern competitor. Its most important division point was Julesburg (in present Colorado), which was described as the toughest town in the West.

The company of Russell, Majors and Waddell added further speed to the trip across the plains by introducing the Pony Express. For some years Senator William M. Gwin of California had urged upon William H. Russell the desirability of giving the people of California faster communication, and had suggested the possibility of a sort of horse telegraph system. Among the advantages claimed for the plan was the advertising of the central route, with possible mail contracts for Russell, Majors and Waddell. Russell was impressed with the idea, and after an unsuccessful effort to obtain governmental assistance decided to go ahead on his own. Stations were outfitted across the plains at ten-mile intervals, and Russell himself picked out hundreds of the fleetest horses he could find and a highly selected group of expert riders.

Public announcement of the Pony Express created a great sensation. Russell announced his willingness to transport letters between St. Joseph, Missouri, and Placerville, California, at five dollars an ounce, and to do it in ten days, which was just half of Butterfield's best time. Later the fee declined to one dollar a half ounce. Many observers doubted whether this speed could be maintained, particularly in the winter. This doubt was still unresolved when the route was opened on April 3, 1860, the day on which the first rider left St. Joseph; the next day another rider went out of Sacramento. The first trip was made in ten and a half days. The future was to show whether this time could be maintained, or even improved.

The success of the Pony Express rested primarily on the ability and endurance of the riders. Care was taken to choose only light men and boys, and to reduce the weight of their clothes and equipment to the smallest possible minimum. The mail was wrapped in oiled silk to protect it from the weather; a normal load was between forty and ninety letters, depending on their bulk. No wonder the service was costly.

The rider was expected to average about 9 miles an hour, day and night, allowing no more than two minutes for changing horses. The usual "run" of a rider was between 75 and 100 miles, with a round trip twice a week. Sometimes, because of sickness or accident, runs were increased; at one time "Pony Bob" Haslam covered 380 miles with but nine hours of rest. The life of a rider was hard and dangerous; more than the usual courage and stamina were required for the fast riding on bad roads in all kinds of weather and in perpetual danger from the Indians. The pay of about $125 a month was considered high at the time.

The real test of the Pony Express and of the route over which it operated came in the winter of 1860–1861. The cold and snow perceptibly slowed the time, but still the men rode through; by the spring of 1861 they were averaging nine days for the trip. Even under extremely bad conditions, Lincoln's inaugural address was carried over the 1600 miles between the ends of the telegraph line in 7 days, 17 hours.

The Pony Express proved that the central route was rapid and feasible for year-round

Western Stagecoaching, 1867. By the time this photograph was taken the Union Pacific Railroad had penetrated deeply into the American Desert, and although the track shortly would be completed, the stagecoach acted as a "feeder" to this and other railroads for a surprisingly long time. (Library of Congress)

travel, but in the process of the demonstration Russell, Majors and Waddell went bankrupt. The Pony Express failed to make money, which was expected, but it was completely ruined by the completion of the first telegraph line across the plains in October 1861. No longer was there any real reason for the pony express; the type of message it carried could be sent more rapidly and cheaply by telegraph.

Even more disastrous to Russell's hopes was the failure of his company to receive government mail contracts. When the Confederates at the beginning of the Civil War captured a portion of the route and property of the Butterfield Overland Stage Company, Russell and his partners expected to receive the overland mail contracts for the central route. Instead, Butterfield himself moved to the central route and continued operations until his contract expired in 1862. By that time Russell, Majors and Waddell had become bankrupt and had been forced to sell their interests (1862) to Ben Holladay, who was shortly to become dominant in overland transportation.

BEN HOLLADAY   Ben Holladay was one of the best-known figures on the plains during the 1860s. Poorly educated, he was coarse, crude, and boisterous, with a taste for whiskey, gambling, and tall stories. He trusted no one, not even his wife, and his business and political morals were deplorable. He was greedy and ruthless, having little sympathy for either employees or passengers. On the other hand, he was congenial, lavish with his family, and beloved in the West as a champion of the underdog; he could be counted on to give land for a church or to grubstake a prospector. He lived with a flourish; he had an impressive mansion in White Plains, New York, but spent his winters in Washington when Congress was in session. He traveled widely to inspect his properties. His private coach, drawn by blooded horses, was gold trimmed, with silver door handles; it had coil springs, interior lights, a let-down bed, a food locker, and silver-topped decanters.

Holladay was born in Kentucky, but as a boy ran away to Missouri. Shrewd and energetic, he tried saloonkeeping, the job of postmaster, and running a general store before he gravitated to transportation; he freighted for Kearny and Doniphan during the Mexican War. His interest in transportation culminated in the purchase of Russell, Majors and Waddell in 1862. Holladay expanded rapidly, so that by 1866 he had over 3000 miles of stage lines under his control, plus vast amounts of freighting. In addition he had steamships running to Oregon, Panama, China, and Japan. Probably his was the greatest one-man business in the United States.

Ben Holladay's reputation throughout the United States was well expressed in a story told by Mark Twain: American tourists were visiting the Holy Land, and one of the boys of the group was told impressively how Moses had led the Israelites through 300 miles of desert in forty years. After listening patiently for a while he could contain himself no longer: "Forty years? Only three hundred miles? Humph! Ben Holladay would have fetched them through in thirty-six hours."

Hollady's supreme ability was the organization and control of men. The main line of his overland route across the plains had three divisions: from Atchison to Denver, Denver to Salt Lake City, and Salt Lake City to Placerville. A superintendent had immediate supervision over each division. A conductor, or messenger, rode with each coach on the seat in front with the driver, his "beat" being about 200 miles. The presence of an authorized representative of the company prevented many of the unfortunate incidents that had taken place on the Butterfield line.

The driver was the most interesting man in the employ of the company, since it was he who held the reins of power. His characteristics were different from those of his predecessor who drove for Butterfield. Usually he was a reticent, somewhat retiring individual, who interrupted his driving only to chew and spit, and who almost never drank whiskey while on the job. Properly approached, he told fascinating stories of holdups, accidents, and Indian attacks, stories that grew with each retelling. The coach he drove was the usual Concord type, except that it was a fiery red, with yellow running gear and black trim, and on its door panels were painted western scenes. Each coach was drawn by four or six horses picked for speed and endurance.

The stations along the Holladay route were similar to those formerly maintained by Butterfield, and were placed at intervals of from 10 to 50 miles. The drivers were changed about every 50 miles at a home station. Even the home station was crude—a central building of rough logs and dirt floor. Ordinarily it included a blacksmith shop, living quarters for the drivers, and facilities for serving meals. All supplies had to be hauled by team.

The price of the trip from the Missouri River to the Pacific varied widely because of the financial confusion of the period. Rates advanced along with other prices as the Civil War continued and paper money depreciated. In 1863 the fare from Atchison to Denver was $75, to Salt Lake City $150, and to Placerville $225. By 1865 rates had more than doubled, and a little later they were even higher.

The days of coach travel across the plains were few. By the middle 1860s farsighted men such as Holladay saw the end in view as they watched the Union Pacific creep westward. Holladay did not wait for the end, but sold out to Wells, Fargo and Company in 1866. The completion of the railroad three years later ended most of the transcontinental coaching, but the stagecoach continued to operate for many years in regions to which the railroad did not extend. The Deadwood stage of the 1870s and 1880s was particularly famous, probably because of its use in Buffalo Bill's Wild West Show.

The stage was more picturesque than the other forms of transportation across the plains, but it was no more important than the freighting done by individuals and by large companies; one of the larger customers for such freighting was the military. The business was conducted ordinarily in covered wagons drawn by ox or mule teams. It was estimated at one time that Russell, Majors and Waddell had 6250 wagons and 75,000 oxen in use; a little later Holladay was credited with 20,000 wagons and 150,000 animals, including 600 thoroughbred horses. A big wagon held 3 to 5 tons of freight; a standard "train" included 25 freight wagons, a mess wagon, reserve animals, and spare parts. Ordinarily oxen were the motive power, but sometimes mules were used for greater speed. The usual six yoke of oxen per wagon might be increased to ten or twelve if conditions were bad. The bullwhacker and the mule skinner were particularly noted for their picturesquely profane vocabulary and for their prowess with a 30- to 50-foot lash, which they could crack to sound like a pistol shot.

RAILROAD PLANNING   The successor of the stagecoach was the railroad, which was well adapted to conquer the long flat stretches of the plains, and which offered the best solution to the special needs of the western farmer, stockman, and miner. The first trans-Mississippi railroads were constructed in the 1850s, when American railroads were still in the first quarter century of their history. Connections were just being made from the eastern seaboard to such midwestern cities as Chicago, St. Louis, and Memphis. The first bridge across the Mississippi was opened in 1855. Population was sparse and capital scarce. The West lacked knowledge of the technical details of financing, construction, and operation, and was deficient in labor, whether skilled, unskilled, or managerial.

But westerners were never long intimidated by obstacles, no matter how insurmountable they appeared to others. During the late 1840s and early 1850s enthusiasm

Union Pacific Construction. The horse and the "iron horse" joined in hauling mountains of supplies needed to complete the railroad. Here materials are being loaded onto wagons that will precede the tracklayers. (Union Pacific Railroad)

for the railroad was aroused by the camp-meeting technique. Large and enthusiastic gatherings at such cities as Chicago, Iowa City, St. Louis, Little Rock, and Memphis stressed plans for a railroad to the coast, but the resulting interest also spurred the construction of local lines. Congressmen were urged to work for federal aid, and there was talk of state loans, county loans, city loans, town loans. Every possibility was canvassed hopefully. Railroads were supported as public improvements, much like the parks and museums of a later day. Their backers were considered public-spirited citizens. Not the railroad but the community was expected to profit. Costs of transportation would decline, property values would rise, profits of farmers would increase. The West would raise itself economically by its own bootstraps.

The basic requirement for the building of railroads was the collection of sufficient capital. The most obvious method of financing was to invite personal subscriptions, but although pledges were easy to obtain they were difficult to collect except in the form of land or labor. The West had little surplus capital, and the great bulk of funds had to come either directly or indirectly from the East or from Europe.

A second financial possibility was to utilize the credit of a small governmental unit, say, town, county, or city. A town, for example, would issue bonds to be exchanged for railroad stocks or bonds; the town bonds would then be sold by the railroad in the East, usually at a large discount. To obtain such assistance, the railroad might play one town against another by surveying two or more routes, even though the final line had already been decided upon. The towns thereby were encouraged to compete in offering assistance to obtain the road.

A third possibility was the state, which might use its bonds in the same way as the county or town. Missouri loaned some $19 million in this way and lost almost all of it. Minnesota hurried its admission to the Union so that it could lend $5 million to prospective railroads; no railroads resulted, and ultimately Minnesota paid off its bonds at 50 cents on the dollar without providing for accrued interest. California gave some assistance to the Central Pacific. Texas probably had the best record, getting more railroads for its money than did other states; in addition, Texas had its own land grant policy, for it controlled its own public domain.

Both states and smaller political units found difficulty in paying their bonds, particularly since many of them were twenty-year issues that came due during the depression of the 1870s. States were sovereign and hence could delay payment of their bonds or repudiate them. Towns and counties had no such option, and the courts held such debts collectible even if there had been minor irregularities in issue. Most notorious was the hide-and-seek played by the officials of Yankton, South Dakota, to avoid payments. Conservative easterners were so aghast at this display of what they considered the western temperament that they opposed statehood for the Dakotas. Ultimately, of course, the bonds were paid.

The fourth possible source of railroad funds was the federal government, which had earlier aided roads and canals. Cash loans would have been most welcome but were improbable. Land was different, and the West held that gifts of land would benefit the entire country by increasing western population and trade. Even the government would not lose, because alternate sections could be doubled in price, thus producing as much revenue as before. Congress remained reluctant because of sectional antagonisms until the Illinois Central grant of 1850 broke the jam. After 1850 all the first tier of states west of the Mississippi were given railroad grants, while specific projects farther west were aided.

All the grants of the 1850s were similar in terms. The railroad was given alternate sections within 6 miles on each side of the road, and if any of the land had been settled the railroad was allowed to make indemnity selections within 15 miles. The grants were to revert to the public domain if the aided roads were not completed within ten years. After 1860 grants were made only to such strategic roads as the Union Pacific, Santa Fe, Northern Pacific, Texas and Pacific, and Atlantic and Pacific; terms were usually more generous because of the lesser value of the lands farther west.

The administration of the railroad grants was in the hands of the General Land Office. As soon as a railroad filed its approximate route, all the land within the indemnity limits was withdrawn from sale so that settlers could not occupy regions that might be found to belong to the railroad. As fast as the road was located definitely, land selections were made, final patents were issued, and the remainder of the land was thrown back on the market.

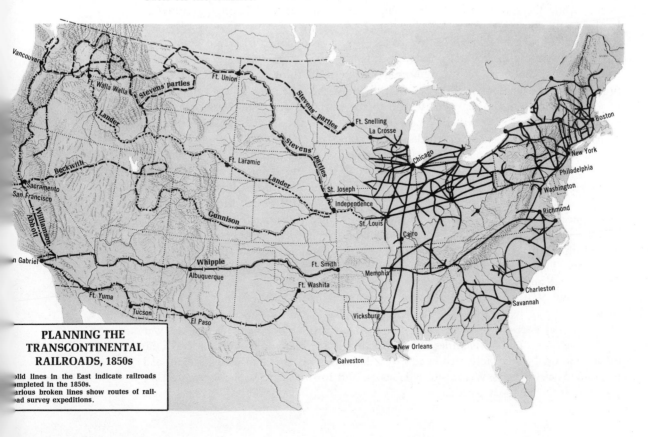

**PLANNING THE
TRANSCONTINENTAL
RAILROADS, 1850s**

Solid lines in the East indicate railroads completed in the 1850s.
Various broken lines show routes of railroad survey expeditions.

The policy concerning railroad grants was a constant source of annoyance to prospective settlers. Large areas, frequently including much excellent land, were closed to settlement. The settler felt that he should have the right to take any unoccupied land, and often did so in spite of all restrictions. The situation was aggravated when the Supreme Court decided that the reversion clause of the grants did not work automatically, but needed special legislation by Congress. The result was that land grants were often kept off the market for many years, even though the railroads gave no indication of building.

The last of the railroad grants was made in the early 1870s, for by then sentiment toward the railroads had changed, as was also evidenced by the Granger movement. Approximately 180 million of acres of the public domain were actually received by the railroads. The total value of these gifts, at the price for which the land was sold, amounted possibly to $500 million.

RAILROAD BUILDING Western railroad plans were of two general types. The first was the transcontinental project, which was completed later (see Chapter 33). Many roads that today are purely local at one time had hoped to build across the continent, while the transcontinental lines engendered enthusiasm that often resulted in local construction.

The second type of railroad project of the 1850s was designed to create state transportational systems, each state considering primarily its own interests and paying little attention to connections with neighboring states, except those to the east. Minnesota proposed several lines running east and west across the state, and others centering in St. Paul. Iowa planned almost every road to run east and west. The Missouri system, with the exception of a northern road across the state, centered at St. Louis, Arkansas roads at Little Rock, and Texas roads at Galveston Bay.

The first feeble beginnings of actual construction came in these states during the 1850s. Missouri, Iowa, and Texas acquired a few short, weak lines. Farther west, in California a short mining road was built. These early efforts were halted by the panic of 1857, and before the resulting depression ended the Civil War had further disrupted the finances of the country. Only two trans-Mississippi roads made important progress in these years. The Hannibal and St. Joseph was completed in 1859 between the two cities named in its title, thus connecting the Mississippi and Missouri rivers north of St. Louis. The Missouri Pacific, after many tribulations, was finally finished from St. Louis to Kansas City in 1865.

The Civil War proved more destructive to the railroads of the Southwest than to those of the Northwest. Some of the Missouri and Texas lines were used for military purposes, and portions of them were destroyed on various occasions. When the war ended, the South had fewer miles of railroad than at the opening of hostilities. On the other hand the North, motivated in part by a desire to replace the Mississippi, continued to build. Such states as Wisconsin, Minnesota, and Iowa made reasonably satisfactory progress during the war period.

With the return of prosperity after the war, railroad plans and construction once more moved to the center of the stage. The second bridge across the Mississippi was completed at Clinton, Iowa, in 1865, and others followed. Three main groups of lines, as classified by their objectives, were being built. The first was the transcontinental group, to be discussed later; it was exemplified by the Union Pacific, completed in 1869.

The second group, the so-called Granger roads, was being built from Chicago and St. Louis to the Missouri River. The two Missouri roads have already been noted. The Chicago and Northwestern, crossing the Mississippi at Clinton, was finished to Council Bluffs in 1867. The Chicago and Rock Island, crossing the river at Rock Island, reached Council Bluffs in 1869. The Chicago, Burlington and Quincy, crossing at Burlington, also arrived at Council Bluffs in 1869. The Illinois Central, crossing at Dubuque, was opened to Sioux City in 1870. The Chicago, Milwaukee and St. Paul, the other important road of the group, did not attain its objective of the Missouri River until the late 1870s.

The roads in the third group were built to connect the Missouri River with the Gulf of Mexico. Two of the lines were completed in 1873. The Missouri, Kansas and Texas, commonly known as the "Katy," extended from the end of the Missouri Pacific at Kansas City south to Houston. The other line was really a combination of four roads that together joined St. Louis and Houston: the St. Louis, Iron Mountain and Southern in Missouri; the Cairo and Fulton in Missouri and Arkansas; and the Texas and Pacific and the International and Great Northern in Texas.

Also during this period immediately after the Civil War occurred the first important effort to create a large and effective railroad system. The sponsor was James F. Joy, a Detroit banker who was president of the Michigan Central and who had a financial interest in the New York Central. Purchasing the Chicago, Burlington and Quincy, he pushed it as far west as Fort Kearny by 1873. Then he added the Hannibal and St. Joseph, which he connected with the Burlington in the east, and from which he built branches in the west to Kansas City and Atchison. To these lines he added the Missouri River, Fort Scott and Gulf, but his intention of reaching the Gulf of Mexico was never realized. Joy's plans were wide ranging and magnificent, but he had extended his investments too far for safety; with the panic of 1873 the "Joy lines" collapsed with a resounding crash.

CHANGING ATTITUDE TOWARD RAILROADS
The buoyant and enthusiastic optimism with which the West viewed possible railroads during the 1850s underwent a radical revision twenty years later. The first unbridled and rapturous enthusiasm cooled, and finally turned to bitter opposition. The basic factor was disappointment that the hoped-for prosperity had not arrived; hence railroad mistakes and abuses tended to irritate the farmers more and more. Railroad construction and finance had both been notorious. Many of the roads had been built badly, resulting in poor service and numerous accidents. Financial mismanagement was the rule rather than the exception. Many of the roads had been built entirely for the profits to be

derived from their construction, the original owners juggling the construction contracts so as to provide for themselves even though the roads were left hopelessly insolvent. Much of the misused money had been borrowed from states, towns, and private individuals who could ill afford its loss. When the debts contracted in the prosperity of the 1850s came due during the depression of the 1870s, the debtors quickly developed a burning hatred of the railroads as the cause of their impoverishment.

The reversal of feeling toward the railroads came in part from a change in the railroads themselves. Frequently they had started as small, struggling, local concerns, freighted with the hopes and desires of their communities. Now they had grown into vast impersonal organizations, the Chicago roads becoming dominant as they constructed western additions or bought and consolidated local projects. Most of the western roads moved their headquarters, shops, and yards eastward. The executives frequently never saw the country through which their lines passed except through the windows of their private cars. This lack of contact resulted in the almost complete absence of mutual understanding. Transportation charges had gone down as expected, but market prices had also declined; hence the farmer had failed to benefit as he had hoped. In fact, the small producer actually suffered from the railroads because special rates, including rebates for large shipments and the favoring of competitive points over noncompetitive points, had given the large producer an even greater advantage than he had possessed before the railroad arrived.

Changing conditions lessened the West's enthusiasm for the railroads, and opposition made its appearance. State aid came to an end. State constitutions prohibited local gifts. No more land grants were made by the federal government. Congress debated and almost passed regulatory legislation; certain states put control measures on their statute books.

Growing hostility by no means halted railroad construction. After a work stoppage in the half dozen years after the panic of 1873 came a revival in the late 1870s and early 1880s that produced the largest amount of construction of any similar period in United States history. At the end of the period the railroad network of the West had assumed approximately its present form.

The change of the Far West from the stagecoach to the railroad did much more than increase the rapidity of the movement of passengers and freight. The whole concept of the West was modified. Gone were the lumbering oxcart, the covered wagon, the long and dangerous trip across the plains, the nightly stop with its gleaming campfires. Gone were the jolting stage, the periodic station, the driver with his cracking whip. Gone were the trapper, the trader, the hunter, and the explorer. In their places appeared the modern and efficient, but impersonal, steam locomotive. The result was eventually a transformation in the characteristics and state of mind of the West.

READINGS   *Paperbacks are marked with an asterisk.*

Road Travel   State and regional histories are pertinent; see the Readings for Chapter 22. James Monaghan, *The Overland Trail* (1947); W. Turrentine Jackson, *Wagon Roads West* (1952), scholarly. Smaller areas are treated in Grace

R. Hebard and E. A. Brininstool, *The Bozeman Trail* (2 vols., 1922); Henry P. Walker, *The Wagonmasters* (1966); Ralph Moody, *Stagecoach West* (1967); Louis L. Simonin, *The Rocky Mountain West in 1867* (1966), contemporary; Roscoe P. and Margaret B. Conkling, *The Butterfield Overland Mail* (3 vols., 1947), detailed on route; Le Roy R. Hafen, *The Overland Mail, 1849–1869* (1926), scholarly; Waterman L. Ormsby, *The Butterfield Overland Mail* (1942); Raymond W. and Mary L. Settle, *Empire on Wheels* (1949), revised 1966 as *War Drums and Wagon Wheels*, Russell, Majors & Wadell: Ellis Lucia, *The Saga of Ben Holladay* (1959), a trifle fictionalized; Edward Hungerford, *Wells Fargo* (1949), rather random. Harlan D. Fowler, *Camels to California* (1950), easy reading; Lewis B. Lesley (ed.), *Uncle Sam's Camels* (1929), journals. Arthur Chapman, *The Pony Express* (1932), good. Robert L. Thompson, *Wiring a Continent* (1947), telegraph.

Railroads   Best general account is *Robert E. Riegel, *The Story of the Western Railroads* (1926). Exploration is covered in George L. Albright, *Official Exploration for Pacific Railroads, 1853–1855* (1921); there is good material in Leland H. Creer, *The Founding of an Empire* (1947). Robert R. Russel, *Improvement of Communication with the Pacific Coast as an Issue in American Politics, 1783–1864* (1948), scholarly. The railroad conventions are covered monographically in John G. Van Deusen, *The Ante-Bellum Southern Commercial Conventions* (1926). James N. Primm, *Economic Policy* (1954) concerns Missouri. The Illinois Central Railroad is treated in Carlton J. Corliss, *Main Line of Mid-America* (1950) and Paul Gates, *The Illinois Central and Its Colonialization Work* (1934), scholarly. Good histories of other railroads are scarce, but see Richard C. Overton, *Burlington Route* (1965); John L. Kerr, *Missouri Pacific* (1928).

Chapter 29 / THE CIVIL WAR IN THE WEST

The era of gold rushes, of Indian campaigns, of stagecoaches, river steamboats, the Pony Express, and of railroad planning was highly exciting to Americans of the 1850s. It was a time of inflation, of better prices—until 1857—and of harvesting the fruits of Manifest Destiny. The lengthening shadow of the "southern question" gradually dulled the frontier luster and, in 1861, the eruption of hostilities diverted national attention to the crisis at hand. During the war years there was a continued westward migration and a consciousness of that region's importance, but the ferocity of the conflict east of the Mississippi and the importance of its outcome prevented any serious development of new frontiers. Because events in the main theater of war were so dramatic, so critical, and so engrossing, historians generally have given them the attention they so justly deserve. By comparison, nothing appeared to be happening in more remote parts of the land.

THE WESTERN PROBLEM   From an immediate military standpoint there was no reason why there should be any concern about the great trans-Mississippi West, for the side that won the war was bound to fall heir to that portion of the country. The West of 1861 was very sparsely settled, was without any satisfactory means of transportation, and was dominated by powerful Indian tribes who were happy that the whites were annihilating each other. With no cities to be captured, transportation systems to be destroyed, or populations to be defended, it was obvious that military operations of the traditional type would not be conducted in that region. That this undeveloped backcountry would play no significant part in the war seemed apparent to the man on the street in both North and South.

However, some considerations made the West at least potentially significant. There was a possibility that Mexico, perhaps with the aid of some other nation, might take this opportunity to recover some of its lost possessions in the Southwest. The elevation of Austrian Archduke Maximilian—a puppet of the French—to be emperor of Mexico strengthened this notion. The Pacific Coast, particularly mineral-rich California, was of interest to other countries. Great Britain, once attracted by Texas, remained alert to the possible benefits of an economic penetration of the western hemisphere. The warm sympathy that the English ruling classes showed for the Confederacy, and the growing desperation at Richmond as the war progressed, added to the concern of the North that the West might be a pawn in the international game. From the standpoint of larger strategy, both sides understood the impact it would have on world opinion if the great western reaches were added to the Confederacy. The new land, not well understood as yet by Americans, was an even greater *terra incognita* to Europeans, who would be impressed by the acquisition of so much territory even though it was undeveloped.

CONFEDERATE INVASION OF NEW MEXICO   Behind any Confederate long-range strategic considerations lay the more practical necessity of finding a source of bullion with which to buy foreign goods and to support a shaky domestic

Empire, Colorado, During the Civil War. A detachment of Company "G", First Colorado Cavalry Volunteers, carries out a drill in a remote mining camp of the West. The activity frequently was more for recreation than for military preparation. In the main, the war was far away. (Denver Public Library)

financial structure. Southern planners had some reason to believe that they could successfully invade northern-held mining country and capture valuable resources they sorely lacked. They knew that after a brief period of indecision the West had generally declared itself for the Union, but there remained pockets of resistance to such a loyalty. For example, one spring day in 1861 the Confederate flag flew briefly over a Denver store; even though it was ripped down by Union sympathizers, the southern faction was not dismayed. Pro-Confederate elements openly advertised for ammunition and percussion caps to be used in the "war against the government." There was open talk among southern-born miners that the Denver minting establishment of Clark and Gruber would be an excellent source of gold for the Confederacy. Such attitudes encouraged the Confederates to organize a raiding force and send it into the West.

In February 1861 Texas adopted an ordinance of secession and at once began to take over federal forts within its borders. Military posts in New Mexico territory were next on the occupation schedule. Accordingly, in July Lieutenant Colonel John R. Baylor, C.S.A., led a body of troops into New Mexico by way of El Paso and quickly captured Fort Fillmore, situated a few miles to the north on the Rio Grande River. The fort's commanding officer and his men ignominiously fled upon the approach of Baylor's force. So rapid was the Confederate thrust that within a month most of the important population centers in the southern portion of New Mexico had fallen. On August 1 Baylor announced that the conquered province would henceforth be known as the

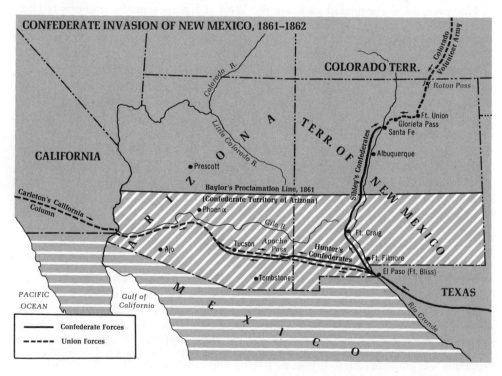

Confederate Territory of Arizona, its boundaries extending from Texas westward to the Colorado River and from the Mexican border northward to the 34th parallel. Its capital was located at Mesilla (across the river from Fort Fillmore), and Baylor assumed the position of governor. A few months later Jefferson Davis acknowledged the acquisition and proclaimed it as an officially organized Confederate Territory.

The sudden Confederate movement up the Rio Grande put such a place as Tucson in a difficult position. Its residents were obliged to decide whether their loyalties lay with federal officials at Santa Fe, or with the new government at Mesilla. After several meetings, held in August 1861, the people of Tucson voted to support the Confederacy and elected a delegate to the southern Congress. On paper, at least, the forces of Jefferson Davis were gathering in considerable western territory. Actually, the initial moves brought the Confederacy little in the way of material wealth, but it was hoped that such a beginning would lead to the conquest of Colorado and perhaps of California, both of which were rich in minerals. An even more optimistic belief was that the Mormons, angered by the recent Utah expedition against them, would make common cause with the Confederacy.

Late in 1861 the Confederate forces in New Mexico were considerably strengthened by the arrival at Mesilla of some 3000 troops, recruited in Texas. They were commanded by Brigadier General Henry Hopkins Sibley, who now assumed command of the invasion forces along the Rio Grande and prepared to conquer key federal installations to the north. Sibley, a graduate of West Point and a former major in the United States Army, had his eye on Fort Union, where he had once been in command and had superintended the building of arsenal and storage buildings.

Opposing Sibley were federal troops commanded by Colonel Edward R. S. Canby, a West Pointer who had graduated a year after Sibley and who had married Sibley's sister. Canby's force, of some 2500 troops, had been seriously weakened at the outset of the campaign when soldiers fleeing Fort Fillmore were overtaken by Confederates and were forced to surrender. At one stroke Canby lost nearly a quarter of his field strength. Later, as Sibley moved up the Rio Grande, more federal soldiers were immobilized when after a battle at Valverde the defeated federal soldiers took shelter at Fort Craig, only to have Sibley move on toward Santa Fe, leaving them behind. By February 1862, with Albuquerque and Santa Fe in Confederate hands, only Fort Union (east and slightly north of Santa Fe) lay between the oncoming invaders and the mineral wealth of Colorado. In a desperate situation, Canby called for help.

"GETTYSBURG OF THE WEST"   The first regiment, Colorado Volunteers, commanded by Colonel John P. Slough, marched nearly 175 miles in five days in response to Canby's plea. Pausing only a few days at Fort Union, Slough and his contingent of over 1300 men pressed on toward Santa Fe hoping to drive the Confederates from that city. On March 26, 1862, an advance element of the Volunteers, commanded by Major John M. Chivington (the presiding elder of the Methodist Episcopal Church in the Rocky Mountain district), encountered a group of Texans in the vicinity of Apache Canyon. The narrow defile, some 7 miles in length, was the western end of Glorieta Pass; through it ran the trail to Santa Fe, about 25 miles to the west. In a bold stroke the "Fighting Parson's" men circled the enemy, destroyed a supply train of 73 wagons, bayoneted some 600 mules and horses, and attacked rear elements of Texas troops. The main action, fought on March 28, was characterized by five hours of extremely bitter fighting. Then the Union forces were driven back and so badly beaten that it was feared for a time Slough's Volunteers would mutiny. However, the Confederates assumed that it was Canby who had destroyed their supplies; and the belief that his large force lay between them and Santa Fe, and because they were now without supplies, caused them to withdraw. Sibley began to retreat into Texas, his forces seriously diminished and his striking power weakened.

Critics of Canby charged that he did not pursue Sibley, his brother-in-law, as relentlessly as he should have, but Coloradans contented themselves with the idea that this "Gettysburg of the West," as they called the Battle of Glorieta Pass, had saved the day for the Union in the Southwest. Actually, the invading force had about reached its limit. A federal force of 5000 men was prepared to march from Fort Leavenworth to New Mexico in the spring of 1862 while General James Carleton was en route from the West with his California Volunteers. As he moved eastward Carleton mopped up isolated pockets of Confederate resistance in Arizona. For example, at Tucson he took into custody one Sylvester Mowry, a former United States officer who was operating a mine in the vicinity and who was said to be supplying guns to southern raiders in the region. Then Carleton pressed forward, anxious to join Canby in New Mexico. Had Sibley stayed on, he would have faced some 12,000 federal troops by autumn. Wisely, he left.

DEFENSE OF THE SOUTHWEST Carleton arrived in September and assumed command of the Military Department of New Mexico. He immediately began to repair some of the older posts and to erect new ones to guard the avenues of approach. Fort Sumner was built in eastern New Mexico, between the modern towns of Vaughn and Clovis, and a temporary encampment was established at Las Cruces, near the Texas border, to ward off any further attempts at invasion. Although the Texans did not return, that possibility always remained; in fact Colonel Baylor received instructions from Richmond to recruit four battalions of rangers for such an effort. Before he could carry out his orders the war came to a close.

The reoccupation of New Mexico by Union forces ended any threat to Colorado. Small and widely scattered raids occurred during the next two years but, in the main, there was little work for the Colorado Volunteers who had done service at Glorieta Pass. In the autumn of 1862 a group of southerners, including five members of the original Green Russell party that had made the initial Colorado gold discoveries, attempted to return home. Soldiers of the Second Colorado Cavalry arrested them. In February 1863, they were released and, after taking an oath of allegiance—which, it is said, they kept—the men were permitted to go south. A second Confederate effort in the fall of 1862 also failed. William P. McClure, one-time Denver postmaster who had fled at the outset of the war, tried to reenter Colorado, where he planned to recruit for General Sterling Price's Confederate army. This sally was cut short when Osage Indians, in the employ of the federal government, intercepted the party, killed all its members, and brought in the heads of the victims as proof that they had carried out orders.

James Reynolds was the best known of the Confederate raiders in Colorado. Having threatened that he would pillage Denver as the Confederate guerilla leader William Quantrill had pillaged Lawrence, Kansas, he returned to the mountains in the summer of 1864. With a force of about twenty-five men Reynolds plundered a wagon train on the Santa Fe Trail and then moved into Colorado's South Park region, robbing ranchers, miners, and stagecoaches—presumably to raise money for the Confederate cause. Before long a posse located the gang. Some of the members were captured and taken to Denver, where they were tried and condemned to death. The presence of southern sympathizers in the city, however, made an execution so risky that the men were ordered transported to Fort Lyon in the southeast corner of the territory. They failed to complete the trip. As the story went, the prisoners tried to escape and were killed; but it was generally understood in Colorado that the men were lined up along the way and shot.

The Confederate withdrawal from Arizona left southern supporters in that area isolated, although their delegate continued to sit in Congress at Richmond until the war's end. Baylor's establishment of a Confederate Territorial government in the Southwest appears to have drawn that area to the attention of legislators in Washington, D.C., for on February 24, 1863, they passed an act creating their own Territory of Arizona. Tucson, a hotbed of secessionism, was passed over as the capital in favor of Prescott, a new mining town that held the honor only until the war's end.

Arizona was typical of many areas of the West during the Civil War; for, although it was not the scene of large-scale battles, the Confederate thrust in that direction pointed up the divisions among its residents and altered the region's history. If the war, fought so viciously in the East, had its influence upon the outer reaches of American settlement, it is also true that shock waves from the West reached congressional ears at Washington.

UTAH'S WARTIME ROLE   The vast reaches of the West were connected by extremely weak transportation and communication threads. Hundreds of miles were served only by stagecoach and freight lines; a fragile telegraph wire, subject to disruption by Confederate raiders, by Indians, or even by buffaloes who scratched themselves on poorly placed telegraph poles, provided very unreliable service. It is no wonder that the Pacific Coast felt isolated or that Montana miners referred to the East as "the states."

The enormous task of guarding this lengthy roadway was given to Colonel (later General) Patrick E. Connor and his Third California Volunteers. With approximately 1500 men Connor was charged with keeping an eye on the Mormons. Although the latter saw some advantage in selling supplies to the Californians, who established headquarters at Camp Douglas near Salt Lake City, they were unhappy over the colonel's insistence that they first take a loyalty oath. Brigham Young said he would see the military in hell before he would subject his people to such an indignity, but there is no evidence to show that the troopers suffered from a lack of fresh vegetables.

Connor informed his superiors that Brigham Young had an active army of 8000 men that could be increased to 50,000 if necessary, and that in this hostile land the utmost diplomacy would have to be exercised by the Volunteers. He distrusted the Mormons, who, he asserted, publicly rejoiced at federal reverses "and thank God that the American Government is gone, as they term it, while their prophet and bishop

The Horse Soldiers, by Frederic Remington. This engraving of volunteers on the move captures the mobility and informality of western cavalrymen. (Denver Public Library)

preach treason from the pulpit." The forces of Brigham Young and those of Connor lived under an uneasy truce, one that both sides knew might easily be shattered, and this realization was of concern to the federal troops. Yet the Californian permitted his men to engage in mining precious metals—something church leaders had for the most part discouraged among their own people—and even actively promoted such enterprises. He reasoned that it would keep his poorly paid men, many of whom were former miners, in a more contented frame of mind, and also that the mineral wealth so obtained would be useful to the Union. In his official correspondence he also indicated that a mining rush would settle the Mormon question peacefully because it would attract a large, non-Mormon population whose numbers would make unnecessary the maintenance of federal troops in Utah. As if this were not enough, Connor founded an anti-Mormon newspaper, the *Union Vedette*, to "educate the Mormons" in what he called "American views." Despite a great deal of publicity, in which Connor invested considerable sums of money, the anticipated boom did not take place. Other western mining regions were much richer and drew off most of the prospectors; Utah was so isolated that ore transportation costs were prohibitively high; and, finally, the church exerted so much pressure on its members that few Mormons joined the Californians in the search for gold. Until the coming of the railroad in 1869 none of the efforts of the Volunteer miners showed a profit.

Although the war did not stimulate Utah's mining industry, it had a pronounced effect on the territory's efforts at economic independence. Just as the bitter conflict altered life in the northern states and in Great Britain, so did the disruption of the cotton trade have its influence on Utah. In 1857 and 1858 initial efforts were made to raise cotton in the southern part of the territory, in what became known as "Dixie," but by 1860 the entire production of the territory amounted to only 160 bales. At the outbreak of war church leaders made a great effort to increase migration into southern Utah and did all they could to promote the "cotton mission." By 1863 enough was raised to allow a shipment of 74,000 pounds to "the states" at a price that ranged from $1.40 to $1.90 a pound. In Utah the price was set at $1.25 a pound, and cotton was used as legal tender to pay bills or to make exchanges. The crops of 1864 and 1865 were a disappointment. By 1869 the coming of the railroad and the availability of cheaper southern cotton caused a rapid decline in this local industry. A cotton mill was built in 1867 and remained open until 1910, but the high cost of irrigating the crops made cotton culture in Utah prohibitively expensive.

Although Connor spent most of his time keeping an eye on the Mormons and promoting Utah mining he was called upon occasionally to stop Indian depredations along the overland trail. In 1863 there were scattered attacks, ranging from those made on travel in southern Utah to sporadic raids on the main routes. In that year Chief Washakie, a Shoshoni well known for his wisdom and friendship toward the whites, returned 150 stolen horses and mules, and shortly afterward Connor signed a peace treaty with this band at Fort Bridger. He also came to terms with a branch of the Ute and received pledges of peaceful cooperation in the Spanish Fork region of Utah. Further negotiations with the Shoshoni, Goshute, and Bannock relieved the pressure on wagon routes in southern Idaho. By an agreement reached in October 1863 some 8000 tribesmen agreed to remove pressure from white communications lines in return for annuities.

WARTIME CALIFORNIA The problem of isolation, felt so keenly throughout the West, was particularly apparent in California. The mining rush of 1849 and after had brought to that area a number of foreign-born persons who were much more interested in economic betterment than in the sectional question that had so long plagued the eastern part of the United States. Both Europeans and Orientals maintained closer sentimental ties with "the old country" than with faraway Washington, D.C., a place that was only a name to most of them. Nor could the federal government expect much sympathy from the Californians of Spanish or Mexican descent; they had long resented the cavalier manner in which their lands had been taken over and the disdain with which the Americans treated them as a minority group.

Led by miners of southern origin large segments of the California population frequently complained of the laxity of Washington officials in providing the facilities of government. The U.S. mails were irregular, the federal court system was badly understaffed and painfully slow, and talk of transcontinental railroads had petered out in the late fifties as the sectional crisis mounted in the East. These and many less immediate grievances grew in intensity west of the Sierra Nevadas until older loyalties to the Union wore thin. Coastal residents, who generally associated the outbreak of war with the slave issue, found it difficult to become excited over a deadlock in which they felt they had but a small interest. Those in Lincoln's administration who felt concern about the threadlike connection that held Golden California to its parent had adequate reason to worry.

The problem of disloyalty, of only a minor and transitory nature in such a place as Colorado, was much more evident in California. Newspapers in some of the more important cities were so hostile to the Lincoln administration that they were denied the use of the mails by the federal government. The injunction was lifted in early 1863, with certain exceptions, but by then at least one newspaper had been forced to suspend operations. The *Expositor* of Visalia, so unrelentingly hostile that it did not regain mailing privileges, was kept alive by contributions from the community. When troops were sent to suppress secessionists in Visalia, residents brazenly rode by a dress parade and loudly cheered for Jefferson Davis. Although they were promptly arrested, their confinement only stirred the opposition to more stubborn resistance. Meanwhile, all efforts to silence the *Expositor* of Visalia were in vain; it continued to attack President Lincoln openly and frequently. But when it referred to the state's volunteers as the "California Cossacks" the paper went too far. In March of 1863 soldiers stormed the paper's offices and threw all its equipment into the street. The editors decided not to resume publication.

In another attempt to halt the spread of subversion, teachers were required to take a loyalty oath. Those who would not sign were denied teaching certificates, and no warrants for the payment of their salaries were to be authorized. Apparently Californians believed that the classroom was only one nest of subversion, for they also passed a law denying any attorney the right to practice unless he promised his allegiance to the Union cause. Any backsliding cost an attorney a fine of $1000. The state itself felt obliged to reassure the federal government of its loyalty, and on two occasions—in 1861 and in 1864—the legislature passed resolutions endorsing the Lincoln administration.

Punitive legislation and the use of troops drove the secessionist movement underground. Such organizations as the Knights of the Golden Circle (originally organized in Cincinnati) and the Knights of the Columbian Star were so active that they claimed secret membership within the Union League and among the California Volunteers. As was true of their eastern brothers, members held that the war was illegal, having been initiated by Lincoln without the consent of Congress, and they insisted that all they were guilty of was an unflinching support of the Constitution.

THE NORTHWEST   In terms of population the Pacific Northwest was not significant as a factor in the Civil War. At the outbreak of that conflict slightly fewer than 65,000 whites lived there, most of them concentrated in the valleys between the ocean and the Cascade Mountains. However, since these pioneers represented the seed of the future, their attitudes were important. Highly nationalistic, they declared for the Union, and its preservation, at an early date. While they professed opposition to the institution of slavery, they were outspokenly anti-Negro. As early as 1857 the voters of Oregon simultaneously excluded both slave and free Negroes. When the war erupted, enthusiasm for the North's cause was so great that even a movement for an independent Pacific Republic, which had bubbled beneath the surface for a decade, was swept aside. Copperheadism, as evidenced in California, seems to have had little if any support in the Northwest.

Unlike the experience in California, where the number of volunteers was so large that they outnumbered the size of the entire pre-Civil War federal army, recruitment in the Northwest was slow and arduous. Labor was in short supply, and there was little attraction for men who could make good wages in the mines or elsewhere to volunteer for low-paying military positions. Somewhat belatedly Oregon raised six companies of cavalry, but in neighboring Washington there was difficulty in assembling even two companies of infantry. The latter territory had to call upon California for men, from which source it eventually raised eight companies.

Some of the soldiers raised by various means were dispatched to northwestern Washington; others were sent to Forts Walla Walla and Colville in the eastern part of the territory. In general, they carried out only patrol duties, having no one in particular to fight. However, people of the Northwest were aware that the Canadian boundary was undefended and that England was sympathetic to the Confederacy. Also, there existed a potentially dangerous dispute over the San Juan Islands in the Vancouver area, and the possibility of British intervention in that area was ever present in the minds of local residents.

In Oregon the local troops were used primarily to keep open routes of travel to the Idaho mines and to keep an eye on the Indians, who were growing restive over this traffic. New posts were established at Boise and near Klamath Lake in southern Oregon. Another post was constructed in Nez Percé Indian country, near Lewiston, Idaho, and in 1863 a treaty signed with those Indians opened a considerable portion of the country to miners. For a mere $262,500 they accepted a much smaller reservation; the dissatisfaction thus generated within the tribe later led to trouble. The neighboring Snake

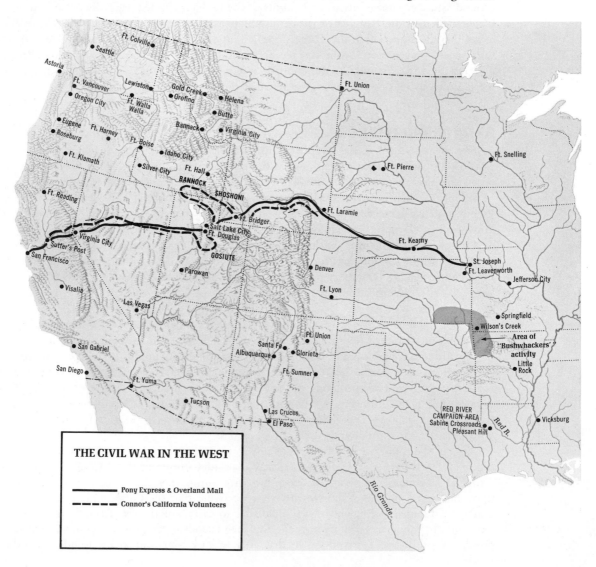

THE CIVIL WAR IN THE WEST

——————   Pony Express & Overland Mail

— — — — —   Connor's California Volunteers

Indians, having signed a treaty with General Connor the same year, remained generally quiet.

The mining camps of Montana were born during the war years, and that territory felt almost nothing of the great conflict taking place in "the states." A remark of a miner dramatizes the distance that separated his kind from the war. When he saw an account of the firing on Fort Sumter in a newspaper then three months old, he noted, "Bad news from the states. The North and South are fighting." He made no comment, showed no emotional reaction, but simply made a record of the event. That the new territory, so remote and undeveloped, could play no part in the fighting was obvious. However, the presence of a large number of southern miners—some of whom could ride by the territorial governor's residence firing pistols and cheering for Jefferson Davis without fear of punishment—had an effect on the political development of the territory. Montanans voted the Democratic ticket, and continued to do so, with the result that the territory remained steadily with that political faith and waited patiently for twenty-five years after its birth (in 1864) for the Republican party to grant it statehood. During the latter years of the war millions of dollars worth of much-needed bullion passed down the Missouri River to Union coffers. What the young territory could not offer in manpower it gave in gold.

THE BORDER STATES   Although the far-flung mountain and coastal regions were not absolutely vital to the Union cause, those westerners who lived closer to the seat of war were obliged to participate more actively. Missouri, whose outlook was western, did not belong to either the North or the South but, hanging in the balance, it was of importance to each side. Not only was it the most populous western state, but St. Louis was the greatest center of western trade and travel; its importance grew when the Butterfield route was moved north at the outbreak of hostilities. Superficially Missouri was southern, with legalized slavery and a governor (C. F. Jackson) who was clearly southern in his sympathies. On the other hand, Missouri actually had very few slaves and contained a large number of Unionists, notably among the antislavery Germans of St. Louis. This complexity explains why, though the state legislature almost unanimously declined to secede (March 1, 1861), Jackson flatly refused Lincoln's request for troops for the Northern Army.

Immediate and aggressive action by the wealthy and energetic Francis P. Blair made Missouri a Union state. St. Louis "home guards," mostly German, captured Jefferson City, put the state under martial law, and organized a loyal government. In reply, Jackson continued to insist he was the proper governor and in this capacity raised militia, called a state legislature into session, and on August 6 had Missouri declared a free and independent state. With aid from outside, Jackson forces overran most of the southern part of the state and defeated a Union army at Wilson's Creek on August 10.

Command of the Western Department of the Union Army was at this time most unfortunately in the hands of John C. Frémont, who at the least was dilatory and at the most was guilty of mismanagement, extravagance, favoritism, graft, and other sins.

Moreover, Frémont made the mistake of issuing on August 30 a very drastic order, freeing all slaves and confiscating the property of rebels in a region he arbitrarily designated. At a time when every effort was being made to win the sympathies of doubtful border areas, such an order was catastrophic. This turn of events put Lincoln in a very difficult position, since he was obliged to discipline the Republican party's first nominee, a man who had married the daughter of Missouri's famous Senator Thomas Hart Benton, and who was otherwise widely known. After some soul-searching Lincoln assumed the responsibility and on November 2 removed Frémont.

The political leaders of Missouri were able to maintain the connection with the Union, but there was a degree of geographical division. Western Missouri farmers did not agree with the sentiments of St. Louis businessmen and other eastern Missourians. Although no clear-cut distinctions between these two sections of the state can be made, the sympathies of those in the backcountry became apparent as the war proceeded.

Union forces took the offensive in 1862 and pressed Confederate defenders back into Arkansas. For the remainder of the war Missouri was in general under the control of the northern forces. A southern raid in 1863 penetrated as far as Springfield and another in 1864 advanced as far as Jefferson City, but neither had any real hope of adding the state to the Confederacy. Mainly they were bids for recruits; and here they failed most miserably, for more Missouri members of the southern armies deserted in order to go home than new recruits flocked to the colors.

Arkansas was of comparatively little importance to the war. It accepted secession, May 6, 1861, with but one dissenting vote. The military campaigns that touched Arkansas were concerned primarily with operations on the Mississippi River or in Missouri or Texas. Arkansas had little strategic value for either side.

Texas was in some ways the reverse of Missouri, for in Texas Governor Sam Houston was a Unionist, whereas majority sentiment was southern. An irregular convention, boycotted by Union sympathizers, passed an ordinance of secession, February 1, 1861, by a vote of 167 to 7, and this action was legalized by the legislature over Houston's veto. Union property was confiscated, and Union troops surrendered. A popular vote on secession late in February showed a 3 to 1 majority for that cause. Under these circumstances Houston was forced out of office.

JAYHAWKERS AND BUSHWHACKERS In Kansas and western Missouri an informal or guerrilla warfare harried the population but did not materially influence the outcome of the war. Although a good many Kansans were less interested in the plight of the southern Negro than they were in the preservation of the Union, their leaders tended to be abolitionists. Some of the more enthusiastic residents, fearful that Missouri might join the Confederacy and effectively isolate Kansas, joined local regiments and marched on their neighbors. In the autumn of 1861 James Lane, recently elected to the United States Senate, and subsequently commissioned brigadier general, led an expedition into Missouri ostensibly to suppress secessionist activity there and to challenge the Confederate general, Sterling Price. He accomplished little more than confiscating a considerable amount of "secesh" poultry and collecting some 600 Negroes whom he brought back into Kansas. The foray, followed by several more into nearby Missouri, only antagonized the residents and drove many of them into the gray uniform. The "jayhawkers" served the Union badly at a time when Lincoln was trying to soothe feelings in Missouri and keep it in the Union. General Henry Halleck became so concerned aboute the raids that he predicted a few more would make Missouri as Confederate as eastern Virginia.

As Halleck anticipated, Missourians did not submit to such invasions peaceably. They repaid the visits with forays into Kansas that left a trail of blood, burned homes, and disrupted communities. These guerrillas who "took to the bush"—hence the name "bushwhacker"—carried on the same kind of irregular warfare practiced by the Jayhawks. The most famous of them was William Clarke Quantrill, who had come to Kansas a few years before the war and had ridden with the jayhawkers for a time. Early in 1862 he formed his own band of Missouri bushwhackers and began to plunder Kansas towns. From a modest force of less than 30 his following grew until he commanded a small army of approximately 300. Under the guise of serving the Confederate cause, Quantrill, the James boys, and Cole and Jim Younger, to mention only a few, entered careers that ended in undisguised banditry. Outlawed by the Union forces, Quantrill came in time under Confederate suspicion and was arrested. He escaped to Texas and in 1865 evolved the fantastic plan of dressing his men as Union soldiers, making his way to Washington, and assassinating Lincoln. He left a trail of blood and destruction as far as Kentucky, where he was killed in a surprise attack.

At first Confederate officials did not complain openly about the disruption of parts of Kansas, but they did not approve of the bushwhackers' methods. Feeling that the raids did more harm than good, southern authorities tried to persuade the guerrillas to join regular forces. This had little appeal to men who wanted to fight for plunder and who often were deserters from the Confederate Army. On the other hand, such men as Quantrill received open support from the people of western Missouri who approved of retaliating in kind to the jayhawk attacks. In addition to these grievances, there was considerable resentment toward state authorities who tried to enroll sons of these Missouri farmers in the federal service. Although they had no real sympathies with the system of slavery, certain sentimental and cultural ties with the South remained.

THE RED RIVER CAMPAIGN
In the spring of 1864 federal forces embarked on an expedition in northwestern Louisiana aimed at an invasion of Texas. The purpose of the Red River campaign, as it became known, was to take advantage of Union sentiment among Texas westerners and to open new sources of cotton to hungry New England mills. The idea was as old as the war itself, General George McClellan having recommended it to Lincoln as early as the summer of 1861. The invasion of New Orleans, supposed to produce cotton in quantity, was given precedence, and General Benjamin Butler's troops undertook that assignment in 1862. As a growing number of cotton spindles came to a halt, the pressure for a strike against Texas mounted. Lincoln,

who viewed the Mississippi River as the "backbone of the Rebellion," found demands by representatives of the textile industry increasingly hard to put off. That he was able to do so until early 1864 was due in part to his personal abilities and to Union military successes in other parts of the South.

After elaborate preparations, nearly 30,000 men under the direction of General Nathaniel P. Banks and supported by Admiral David Porter's gunboats began the ascent of the Red River. Confederate General Richard Taylor's forces engaged a part of this army at Sabine Crossroads and again at Pleasant Hill (April 8 and 9, 1864) and sent it

John M. Chivington. The militant Denver minister yielded to the temptation of glory and donned the blue uniform for a rather inglorious career with the Colorado Volunteers. His exploits are still a matter of controversy in Colorado. (Denver Public Library)

back down river. Meanwhile, General Frederick Steele's federal forces marched out of Arkansas in an attempt to execute a pincers movement, in conjunction with Banks's troops, only to be driven back upon Little Rock by Confederate cavalry divisions.

The Red River campaign, which General Sherman called a disaster, not only strengthened Confederate morale but had a direct influence on other operations. A. J. Smith's command of 10,000 men, drawn off to aid Banks, did not participate in the famed Georgia campaign, and although this in all probability did not alter the outcome of that movement, it did diminish Sherman's army. Troops sent along with Banks also might have been assigned the task of reducing Mobile, whose capture was delayed nearly a year. Confederate troops scheduled to defend that port were diverted to General Joseph Johnston's army then facing Sherman's invaders. The expedition failed to liberate any cotton, the southerners burning any that was in danger of falling into Union hands. Just as the Confederates had been denied the mineral resources of the Southwest, earlier in the war, so the federal side was unable to capture any appreciable amount of the South's major resource—cotton.

THE WARTIME ROLE OF THE WEST   In general, the remote and sparsely settled West experienced many of the war-born problems that confronted Americans farther east: divided loyalties, subversive activities, questions over civilian rights, shortages of certain supplies, and the general disruption of civil life brought on by such a struggle. However, there were additional difficulties that did not plague more settled parts of the land. The vast distances, served only by threadlike communications, magnified the remoteness in which westerners lived. There was no rail connection with "the states" until after the war, and the stagecoach and wagon routes were subjected to such additional pressures as increased Indian hostilities and the danger of Confederate raiders. The Pacific Coast states, aware that they dangled as colonial appendages in prewar days, found this status even more marked in time of war.

To hold this vast area of land until the major question was resolved between North and South put an enormous strain upon both the federal officials and the people of the West. Volunteer troops, generally unseasoned and not always reliable, were called upon to defend vast sections of the country, not only against the Indian tribes and the Confederates, but against the possible invasion by outsiders. That the latter intervention failed to materialize did not lessen the concern of those who would have been involved, and their constant vigilance provided a certain degree of strain.

By maintaining its control over the West the federal government could claim two important accomplishments: it retained the source of supply of valuable minerals that were vital to wartime finance and eagerly sought by the Confederates; and it presented the world with a diplomatic achievement—a demonstration of the loyalty of all the nation except eleven states in the American Southeast. To assess the importance of these accomplishments is, of course, very difficult, and is filled with what-might-have-beens. That both sides thought the West important is apparent in the efforts each made to control all or part of it.

READINGS *Paperbacks are marked with an asterisk.*

General No satisfactory general study has been written about the trans-Mississippi West in the Civil War. Ray C. Colton, *The Civil War in the Western Territories* (1959) treats only Arizona, Colorado, New Mexico, and Utah. Oscar Lewis, *The War in the Far West* (1961) is largely about California. Aurora Hunt, *The Army of the Pacific, 1860–1866* (1951) treats the Pacific Coast, and is supplemented by her *Major General James Henry Carleton, 1814–1873: Western Frontier Dragoon* (1958). Flora W. Seymour, *The Story of the Red Man* (1929) has a chapter entitled "The Civil War in the West."

New Mexico A basic work is Ovando J. Hollister's history of the First Colorado Regiment of Volunteers, first published in 1863, and reprinted in 1949 as *Boldly They Rode*. Warren A. Beck, *New Mexico: A History of Four Centuries* (1962) has a chapter "New Mexico and the Sectional Controversy." Martin H. Hall, *Sibley's New Mexico Campaign* (1960) is best on the Confederate invasion; briefer is Robert L. Kerby, *The Confederate Invasion of New Mexico and Arizona, 1861–1862* (1958). An alternative is Arthur A. Wright, *The Civil War in the Southwest* (1964). Events leading to the outbreak of the war are described in Loomis M. Ganaway, *New Mexico and the Sectional Controversy, 1846–1861* (1944). Max L. Heyman, *Prudent Soldier: E. R. S. Canby* (1959) is helpful. See also W. W. Mills, *Forty Years at El Paso, 1858–1898* (1962), with an introduction by Rex Strickland; C. L. Sonnichsen, *Pass of the North* (1968), especially chapter 13.

Central There is little in print about the central plains and Rockies during the war. Fred B. Rogers, a former army officer, wrote *Soldiers of the Overland* (1938), telling the story of General Patrick E. Connor's role. Something of Connor's impact on Utah appears in *Leonard J. Arrington, *Great Basin Kingdom* (1958), which also describes the impact of the war on Utah's economy. *Robert W. Johannsen, *Frontier Politics and the Sectional Conflict* (1955).

Border A number of books describe events in the "eastern" West, or along the border. Jay Monaghan, *Civil War on the Western Border, 1854–1865* (1955) reads well and is informative. More particularized is Richard S. Brownlee, *Gray Ghosts of the Confederacy: Guerrilla Warfare in the West, 1861–1865* (1958). Also good is Albert Castel, *A Frontier State at War: Kansas, 1861–1865* (1958). Castel has also written *William Clarke Quantrill: His Life and Times* (1962); see also Carl W. Breihan, *Quantrill and His Civil War Guerrillas* (1959). Stephen B. Oates, *Confederate Cavalry West of the River* (1961) explores a subject little written about. The Red River campaign is well portrayed in Ludwell H. Johnson, *Red River Campaign: Politics and Cotton in the Civil War* (1958). William E. Parrish, *Turbulent Partnership: Missouri and the Union, 1861–1865* (1963).

The Military-Indian West. As these cavalry officers with General Nelson Miles studied the plains encampment of tepees that could disappear the next day, they saw at a glance the difficulty of solving the Indian problem militarily. (Library of Congress)

Chapter 30 / THE INDIANS AT BAY

The tribes of the high plains, those fierce, proud "horse Indians" so well immortalized in countless pulp and celluloid westerns, were pressed back again and again by white invaders until they could retreat no more. The beginning of the end was marked by the opening of the emigrant trails over which wagon trains made their way across the Great American Desert to the Pacific Coast. As travel over these crude roadways increased, and as little branches sprouted from them into unclaimed parts of the West, the Indians were aware that the tide was not to recede. Although the natives accurately foresaw the threat to their land and their livelihood, their own inertia or lack of organization, as well as the gradual nature of the white advance, delayed resistance until it was too late. By the time they mounted their horses and appeared on the field of battle, the numbers against them were too great.

During the latter half of the nineteenth century Americans talked a great deal about the "Indian problem." They referred to a dilemma of their own making: how to acquire the land held by the natives without assuming the role of bare-faced aggressors. Over the years administrators carried out a piecemeal program that alternated between kindness and cruelty to the natives, a course that indicated a basic ignorance of the problems at hand and a general helplessness in their search for equity. By and large the American public desired to treat the native races fairly, but how to do so while relieving them of their landed inheritance posed a question that was never satisfactorily answered. Seemingly the proper course was to make treaties with the Indians, by which they were compensated for losses incurred with each white advance. To the cynics this policy became known as one of "treat and retreat."

WESTWARD BY TREATY   One of the most significant Indian treaties ever formulated by the American government was the far-famed agreement made at Fort Laramie in the autumn of 1851. By its terms the various Indians involved revealed their conviction that the white man had come west to stay, even if he asked no more than passage across their lands. The whites, on the other hand, confessed that the inviolability of "Indian country" was one of America's most short-lived myths. The results of pipe smoking at Fort Laramie set the stage for the final struggle of the plains Indians, one that was to continue for about forty years.

The negotiations at Fort Laramie stemmed from the realization by white leaders that wagon trails of the 1840s ultimately must be superseded by iron rails. When that day came the westward rush of settlers would be enormous. As early as 1849 Secretary of the Interior Thomas Ewing foresaw this development and predicted it would necessitate the protection of such routes against Indian depredations. Father Pierre Jean De Smet, the Catholic missionary who had traversed the West so thoroughly, also anticipated trouble in the future. In 1851 he expressed his belief that western Indians would soon experience the fate of the eastern tribes, that their lands would also be overrun by settlers. Even as he wrote, the commissioner of Indian Affairs was worrying about moving farther west some of the removed eastern Indians "so as to leave an ample outlet for our white population to spread and to pass towards and beyond the Rocky Mountains." The expression of such sentiments forecast the necessity of the meeting at Fort Laramie, and in the late summer of 1851 the representatives from some of the western tribes began to drift into that famous western outpost. They were prepared to "make talk."

Agent Thomas Fitzpatrick, of the Upper Platte Agency, acted as host and chief white negotiator. Old "Broken Hand," as he was called, had known the plains country ever since the twenties, when he came west with William Ashley. Together with other whites, including the Jesuit missionary De Smet, these men sat down with chiefs from the Sioux, Assiniboin, Arikara, Crows, Grosventres, Shoshoni, Arapaho, and Cheyenne. Jim Bridger, dean of the mountain men, served as an interpreter. After lengthy speeches by members of both sides, an agreement was reached. For the right of their people to make the westward passage in safety from attack, the Americans promised to pay the Indian owners $50,000 a year in annuities for fifty years. These privileges were to include the building of military posts along western roadways. It was further agreed that any depredations by Indians or whites would be punished and that restitution of losses would be made. Tribal boundaries were marked off as additional insurance against collisions among the various signatories. The Indians then went to their various homes, and the American negotiators submitted the treaty to the Senate for approval. That body amended the document to read ten instead of fifty years, pending Indian agreement; but by now the natives were so scattered they could not be rounded up for the necessary quorum. Although the treaty was never ratified, the government paid annuities for fifteen years; in general, the Indians fulfilled their part of the bargain.

The negotiations at Fort Laramie gave official sanction to travel over the "Great Medicine Road" along the Platte River, but there was another western route that demanded equal consideration. The road to Santa Fe was still heavily traveled, and at least two proposed railroads were expected to pass that way. In the spring of 1853 Fitzpatrick arranged for a meeting at Fort Atkinson (near the present Colorado-Kansas line) with the Comanche, Kiowa, and Apache and in July he concluded an agreement with them for use of the route, including, again, the right to build forts and maintain military forces along the way. The latter stipulation required some persuasion on the part of Fitzpatrick, who reported that the Indians did not want military establishments in the area. He insisted, however, because "at no distant day the whole country over which those Indians now roam must be peopled by another and more enterprising race." This was, in effect, the point of the Indians' argument.

In addition to the Laramie and Atkinson treaties there were other pressures on the western tribes. The Kansas–Nebraska question loomed large, and those who were anxious to promote political status for the area wanted to extinguish its Indian titles. In 1853 Commissioner of Indian Affairs George Manypenny recommended the organization of what he called a "civilized government" in the new country. It was his belief that the opening of the area by "the enterprising and hardy pioneers" would be of benefit to both races, a point of view not shared by the original owners. Nevertheless, during the winter of 1853–1854, as Congress debated the controversial bill, government agents moved among the Plains Indians distributing money and harvesting titles. One result was the projection westward of a large wedge that tended to divide the tribes into two principal groups. The wagon-road treaties, the blossoming of transcontinental railroad plans, and the creation of new political subdivisions—all emerging nearly simultaneously in the early fifties—acted as a trip-hammer against an Indian domain so recently regarded as forever fixed and secure.

Even as Indian commissioners busied themselves acquiring land titles in Kansas and Nebraska, trouble was brewing out on the high plains. Late in the summer of 1854 some Brûlé Sioux killed a cow belonging to a Mormon emigrant train, and when the owners reported their loss, at Fort Laramie, a young lieutenant named John L. Grattan was sent out to apprehend the guilty. Supported by only thirty soldiers and a drunken interpreter, the young officer precipitated a fight in which the whole detachment of troops was wiped out. Undaunted by the disaster Grattan's immediate superior quickly called for a force sufficient to punish the offenders, arguing that this would persuade neighboring tribes to remain peaceful. It was a notion that would cost the lives of a good many troops before plains warfare ended.

Widespread raiding occurred along the Platte River after the Grattan affair. Young tribesmen, out to make names for themselves, tended to ignore the advice of their elders and to strike at isolated travelers when the opportunity presented itself. In the autumn of 1854 a small band of Brûlé Sioux ambushed the Salt Lake mail stage, killed three men, and made off with $10,000 worth of gold bullion. In general, the Indians from the Platte Valley north to the Missouri River country were in a sullen mood, one that caused the War Department considerable worry.

In the spring of 1855 General Winfield Scott, the commanding general, ordered Colonel William S. Harney to conduct a campaign against the Indians with sufficient troops to punish with extreme severity any who accepted the challenge of battle. By August the colonel had gathered a force of some 600 men at Fort Kearny, Nebraska, and to the announcement that he was ready he added, "By God, I'm for battle—no peace." Quickly he moved up the Oregon Trail looking for Indians who wanted to fight. On September 2 he found Little Thunder and his band of Brûlé Sioux encamped near the North Platte River in the vicinity of Ash Hollow. Lieutenant Colonel Philip St. George Cooke (later famous as a Civil War general) placed four companies of men behind the Indian camp while Harney confronted Little Thunder with the demand that he surrender his unruly young men. When the chief declined to meet such conditions, an attack was launched on the camp. Harney later reported that they killed 86, wounded 5, and captured about 70 women and children at a cost of 4 killed and 7 wounded.

After he had crushed Little Thunder's band, Harney moved on to Fort Laramie, where he laid down the law to other Sioux chiefs. In harsh terms he demanded that they surrender the braves who had struck the Salt Lake stage and that all stolen stock and property be returned. According to the colonel, his listeners "begged pitiously to be spared" and promised to comply with all his demands. Not yet satisfied that the natives were duly impressed by armed might, Harney struck off for Fort Pierre, where he received delegations from several Sioux bands. At a peace conference held during early March 1856, nine tribes agreed to hand over all Indians who molested travelers, the chiefs giving their word that the agreement was to be carried out to the letter. In turn, the United States government promised to protect the Sioux against white incursions and to provide agricultural implements to those Indians requesting them. Not much time elapsed before both sides broke the agreement.

During 1856, as Harney concluded his agreement with the Sioux, army officials were increasingly irritated at the conduct of the Cheyenne, particularly the northern band that ranged along the North Platte River. During the summer of 1856 they raided that well-known road, killing men, women, and children. Almon W. Babbitt, secretary of Utah Territory, was one of the victims. Spreading out from the Platte, they moved into Republican River country and impeded travel on that route. General Persifer F. Smith, in command of western troops, stated positively that "this tribe must be severely punished." Both sides knew there would be fighting when the grass grew in the spring and campaigning was renewed on the plains.

The men who received the assignment were Colonel Edwin V. Sumner and Lieutenant Colonel Albert Sidney Johnston, both of whom were to play important roles —on opposite sides—in the Civil War. Dividing his command, Sumner sent one body of troops in a circular movement to Bent's Fort, up along the Rockies to the South Platte and then eastward. Meantime he scouted the interior of this arc with another

Refugees in the Minnesota Sioux War of 1862. In most of the so-called Indian Wars civilians on both sides suffered in surprise attacks. (Library of Congress)

force, searching for Cheyenne bands. Late in July Sumner found about 300 of them along the Solomon River and promptly launched an attack. The Indians broke and ran, the troopers in pursuit. The next day a Cheyenne camp of some 170 lodges and nearly 20,000 pounds of buffalo meat was discovered and destroyed. Again, the Indians fled, preferring to conserve their strength to fight another day. This they would do, with great effect. As LeRoy Hafen wrote in his book *Fort Laramie*, "Thus ended the Sumner campaign against the Cheyennes. It had chastised a few Indians, embittered many more and overawed none."

THE CRITICAL YEARS, 1861-1865 By the time the United States was embroiled in the Civil War, the Indians of the high plains and the Pacific Coast region were becoming increasingly disturbed. The Indian mind was filled with bitter resentment at the arrival of caravans of emigrants, at the rumbling overland stages, at dozens of exploring parties, at railroad surveying crews, and at the succession of military expeditions. Most irritating of all were miners, who paid not the least attention to such scraps of paper as Indian treaties: where gold beckoned they went. A boom occurred here one day and a thousand miles away the next, any rush as likely as not taking place in the heart of Indian country. Legally the miners had no right in any region reserved to the Indians, but the government seldom had either the troops or the desire to eject good white voters, no matter how turbulent; in fact it might well act for the miners' protection in the very probable event of trouble with the Indians. Quite understandably the Indians vehemently resented such intrusions.

Of even more vital importance to the Indians were the hide hunters who methodically destroyed buffaloes, depriving the natives of their very livelihood. Early hunters and travelers had been prodigal of buffalo life, but the fewness of the hunters and the vastness of the herds had made the slaughter relatively unimportant. Now plains travelers were increasing, and they were all either hungry or imagined themselves mighty hunters. Railroad construction crews frequently depended on buffaloes for their meat supply, and by the late sixties special excursions from the East brought well-armed trainloads of men intent on shooting a few of the shaggy animals. In the seventeen months that "Buffalo Bill" Cody worked at supplying Kansas Pacific Railroad workers with meat he personally accounted for 4280 of the animals.

Even by the time of the Civil War the decrease of herds was evident, particularly in the Oklahoma area. After the war professional hunters armed with repeating rifles made the plains a slaughterhouse. Because of the ease with which a herd was approached, the hunter might kill as many as a hundred at a single stand; the carnage might be halted only by overheated rifles or by the physical exhaustion of the two skinners who usually accompanied the hunter. By 1870 buffaloes were being killed at the rate of about a million a year, and by 1875 the southern herd was virtually exterminated. Less than a decade later the northern herds suffered a similar fate. By the mid-eighties a representative of the Smithsonian Institution had difficulty in finding twenty-five specimens to preserve. Saddest of all, much of the slaughter was not even very profitable economically: most of the meat rotted on the ground and the plethora of buffalo robes drove their prices to unprofitable levels. In time a minor subsidiary occupation developed—gathering the tons of buffalo bones that lay over the plains. One wonders how many buffalo died to bring five dollars a ton for the bones collected later.

The dwindling buffalo herds provided the handwriting on the wall for the old nomadic life of the Plains Indian. The buffalo had furnished food, clothing, tools, and weapons; its elimination made impossible the traditional life on the plains. Even without the many armed conflicts that were to occur before the end of the story the fate of the Indian was inevitable. In some future day he must accept woman's work: in the terminology of his conqueror, he must practice the agriculture of the white farmer.

Many Indians were aware of the precariousness of their situation as early as the 1860s. The old men shook their heads sadly and talked with regret of the good old days in which game had been plentiful and in which there had been no demoralization from the white man's whiskey and the white man's diseases. The young braves grew increasingly angry as they saw white encroachments and heard rumors of white atrocities. Every year more Indians came to believe that if their race were to avoid annihilation, it must soon make a stand against white aggression.

The era of the Civil War provided an excellent opportunity for the Indians to roll back the white man's advancing frontier. Those far-flung western settlements, cut off from more settled regions and very thinly protected, would have been hard pressed to withstand any organized military effort during the war years. With the bulk of the federal army heavily engaged in the East, and most of its armaments in use, the plains and mountain West was obliged to rely largely upon volunteer troops armed with such weapons as were available in their own communities. Yet the Indians remained remarkably calm while the big fight was going on among Americans in the East. Except for the uprising of the Sioux in Minnesota during 1862, the natives showed no disposition to attack white settlements in any great numbers.

THE MINNESOTA SIOUX OUTBREAK   The origin of the Minnesota affair was typical of the frontier misunderstandings that had made Indian-white relations so unstable in the past. Its background included the underlying Indian resentment against white expansion, the sharp dealings of the traders, the seduction of Indian girls by unprincipled white men, and the demoralization caused by large doses of the white man's "firewater."

On August 18, 1862, six whites were murdered by a small band of Indians near New Ulm, Minnesota. The murders were unpremeditated and represented no general major attack, but the survivors became panic stricken and fled to the town, spreading exaggerated stories of a widespread Indian uprising. Most of the Minnesota Sioux seem to have been almost equally thunderstruck at the news of the murders. Knowing the ways of the whites, they concluded that they must either fight or flee toward the west. To remain peacefully in the lodges was to invite slaughter. Acting on this reasoning, part of the Indians prepared for war while the remainder packed their belongings and left that part of the country.

The band that remained to fight was led by Little Crow and included some 1300 warriors. Not waiting for a white attack, it immediately began offensive operations against the outlying settlements of the Minnesota River Valley. Men, women, and children were killed to the number of 737, barns and houses were burned, and the frontier was thrown into a fever of apprehension. The young state government called for volunteers and asked for federal troops.

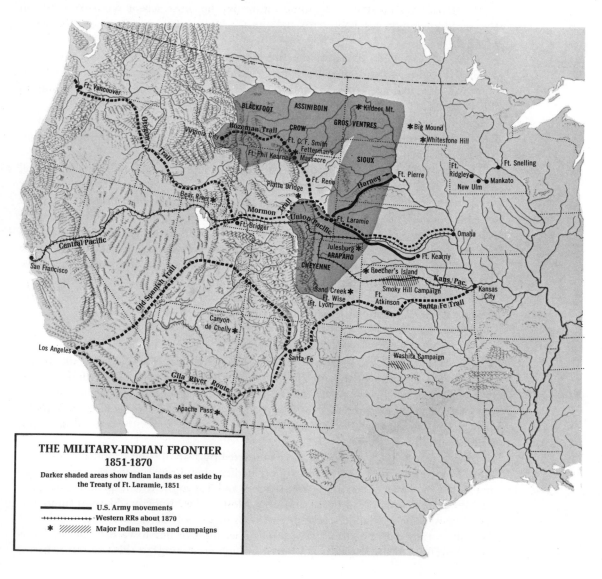

THE MILITARY-INDIAN FRONTIER
1851-1870

Darker shaded areas show Indian lands as set aside by
the Treaty of Ft. Laramie, 1851

━━━━━━━━━ U.S. Army movements
+++++++++ Western RRs about 1870
* //////// Major Indian battles and campaigns

With surprising force the Sioux routed the troops, nearly captured Fort Ridgley, and came close to overrunning New Ulm. However, by September volunteer troops under the command of Colonel Henry Hastings Sibley defeated the Indians. After rounding up over 1700 prisoners, the military staged a grand court-martial that condemned over 300 of them to death. Some were convicted of no other crime than being present at such battles as New Ulm or Birch Coulee, but Sibley was in favor of hanging the lot. Through the intervention of President Lincoln all but 39 of the death sentences were commuted. Toward the end of December residents of Mankato, Minnesota, witnessed a mass hanging from a single scaffold, signifying the conclusion of this particular phase of western Indian warfare. Little Crow, who escaped the noose, was shot not long afterward by a settler and his son who were deer hunting.

The punishment of the Minnesota Sioux had been swift and terrible, but more was to come. In 1863 a punitive military expedition was sent against them, and the rest of Little Crow's band met defeat. In the same year Congress confiscated all the Sioux land in Minnesota, and during the following year the dispossessed Indians were sent to Dakota, where they arrived too late to raise corn. Government supplies were few and poor, which meant a year of misery, with cold, disease, poverty, and starvation. If punishment could ever prevent further crime, then no new outbreak should have occurred after the disaster to the Sioux in Minnesota.

MASSACRE AT SAND CREEK   Another Indian-white engagement during the war years, one that had national repercussions, took place at Sand Creek in the southeastern part of Colorado Territory late in 1864. The conflict, which is still a subject of hot argument in Colorado, involved an attack of territorial volunteers on an encampment of southern Cheyenne said to be peaceful and friendly, in which a large number of Indian men, women, and children died. The massacre underscored the general lack of understanding between the two races and typified much of the ruthlessness displayed in the so-called Indian wars after the Civil War.

Central to the problem of the Indians was the federal government's policy of alternating peace with war. In this case the government had attempted to buy a considerable portion of the southern Cheyenne and southern Arapaho lands, the Indians signifying their agreement at the Treaty of Fort Wise in 1861. The new Indian home was to be a small tract of dry, sandy, almost gameless country in southeastern Colorado. The only virtue of the location was that it was so desolate and barren that it was unlikely to be the object of white cupidity.

The Treaty of Fort Wise made the Indians sullen and more resentful, and most of them refused to go to the designated land. War parties sniped at outlying settlements, plundered travelers, and struck at overland stagecoaches. Periods of ominous quiet were but uneasy interludes between frontier depredations. Governor John Evans of Colorado Territory, nervous over the Indian threat and hard-pressed by aggressive whites in his territory, ordered the "friendly" Arapaho and Cheyenne to report to Fort Lyon (formerly Fort Wise) in the spring of 1864. Some of the other tribes ranging Colorado's plains were told to report to posts designated by the governor. The implication was that the "friendlies" would be protected and those not reporting would be regarded as "hostiles," to be hunted down and punished.

The policy of separating friendlies from hostiles, to be practiced much more wisely in later years, did not stop depredations against stage lines or attacks on isolated settlements. The territorial militia prepared for action and a first-class Indian war appeared to be in the making. Then, whether because of sober second thought or because winter was approaching, the Indians began flocking to the vicinity of Fort Lyon on Sand Creek. Their move was an anticlimax to troops who were anticipating the excitement and the glory of killing a large number of Indians. Furthermore, whites had the uncomfortable feeling, coming from bitter experience, that the Indians would live peacefully on government rations during the winter, but in the following spring more Indian parties would be on the warpath. The majority white reaction was expressed by Major General Samuel R. Curtis, when he wrote from Fort Leavenworth: "I want no peace till the Indians suffer more."

Colonel John M. Chivington echoed the sentiment and marched his volunteers toward Fort Lyon. The colonel's subordinate, Major Jacob Downing, wrote: "I think and earnestly believe the Indians to be an obstacle to civilization, and should be exterminated." Meantime about 500 Indians under southern Cheyenne Chief Black Kettle were encamped peacefully at Sand Creek, under the impression that they had obeyed the governor's proclamation and were safe from harm. A white flag and an American flag were displayed to give evidence of their intentions.

Chivington and his troops reached Sand Creek late in November. Here they spied out the Indian village and prepared to win the glory for which they had enlisted. The attack of November 29, 1864, found the Indians completely surprised and unprepared. Their first reaction was to start to run, which gave the Colorado troops the opportunity to carry on the slaughter as they pleased. Both men and women were shot down, women were ripped up the body, children were brained, and every other conceivable mutilation was practiced. Here was Indian war at its worst: whites engaging in methods they had long condemned as uncivilized. When the carnage ended, the village had been destroyed and about a fifth of its inhabitants murdered. Black Kettle and the remnants escaped.

The action near Fort Lyon has often been labeled either the "Chivington massacre" or the "Sand Creek massacre"; Coloradans called it a punitive expedition and professed to be pleased with the results. They applauded when the victors returned to Denver with two women and five children as prisoners and agreed with Chivington's excuse for killing the young: "Nits make lice." The heroes of the battle also brought back to Denver over 100 scalps, some of which were stretched across the stage of a local theater by means of a rope, for between-the-acts viewing.

All in all it appeared to have been a satisfactory campaign, one that evened up the score for a number of past Indian crimes. Very shortly more treaties were signed with the natives—the Apache, Kiowa, Comanche, Arapaho, and Cheyenne, in particular—

and more land was ceded. For the southern Cheyenne, victims at Sand Creek, the story was one of surrendering their last vestige of land in exchange for a home in Indian Territory, or what would ultimately be the state of Oklahoma.

THE POLICY DILEMMA   The wartime troubles in Minnesota and at Sand Creek dramatized the fact that the return of peace, certain to bring a fresh wave of whites westward, would mean years of racial turmoil on the plains. As it had been before the war, the postwar era witnessed an undermanned army vainly trying to control thousands of shifting, ever-mobile bands of Indians. The plains military problem was primarily in the hands of General William Tecumseh Sherman, the war hero, who requested and was given command of the country lying between the Mississippi River and the Rocky Mountains. It was a task of monumental proportions: not only were the mounted tribesmen fierce, ever-dangerous enemies, but from the East came opposition both from the Department of the Interior—sponsors and guardians of the Indians—and from the humanitarians who saw the noble red man such as Cooper had envisioned him. This latter group, once fully occupied with the question of abolition, now devoted its literary talents to the plight of another minority and filled the eastern press with stories of injustice in the trans-Mississippi West.

In theory the Indian Bureau of the Department of the Interior had control of the Indians. In practice this was true only when the tribes were peaceful; when they got out of hand the army was called in to chastise the unruly, and this duplication of jurisdiction caused a good deal of friction between the two governmental departments. As a rule the Indian Bureau tried to be kind and beneficent, distributing goods, arms, and money, and settling Indian disputes in the hope that by kind treatment the Indian might be persuaded to be docile and peace loving. This policy irritated the War Department, which felt certain that the correct attitude toward the savages was a stern fairness, made effective by the frequent display of large and heavily armed forces, and severe punishment of any Indian who transgressed the white code of conduct.

Extremely controversial was the matter of arming the Indians. The Indian Bureau believed that the Indians needed guns and ammunition to kill the game necessary for their survival. But the army became vigorously profane when the same guns were turned against the troops—and it was particularly irritated when the guns of the Indians were better than those of the soldiers. In behalf of the Indian Bureau it should be added that comparatively few of the Plains Indians ever had guns and that the few repeating rifles they had usually came from white traders, not Indian agents.

The friction between Indian Bureau and War Department was further increased by indefensible acts by representatives of each. Certain Indian agents were notoriously inefficient and corrupt, lining their pockets with the gains from distributing shoddy clothing and blankets, moldy flour, and spoiled meat. Each unscrupulous agent created potential trouble for the army. On the other hand, the military sometimes interfered improperly—often with such highhanded and dictatorial methods that peaceful agreement was impossible. Military expeditions often created more trouble than they allayed, and an undiplomatic army officer could destroy within a few hours the effects of years of painstaking work by a good Indian agent.

Differences between War and Interior Departments reflected a national lack of agreement on the subject of solving the Indian problem. Westerners, in particular, held that the only possible way to keep the Indians in hand was to administer frequent and severe chastisement, and, if necessary, to kill off enough of them to tame the others. The extreme example of the application of this theory was Chivington's attack at Sand Creek. Perhaps a majority of easterners sympathized with the efforts of the Interior Department. Their remoteness from the problem, their overall ignorance of western Indian ways, and the great influence the humanitarians exerted over eastern minds explain this more peaceful point of view. The arguments, pro and con, were a part of the general clamor that followed the close of the Civil War and the renewal of white-Indian conflict in the West. Although scattered Indian battles beyond the Missouri frequently involved relatively few people and no significant amounts of land, the question was national in scope. Today, decades later, thousands of words are printed on the subject each year.

PLAINS WARFARE   As the Civil War drew to a close, the western stage was set for a drama that was to last for thirty years. With the coming of spring in 1865 and the appoach of peace talks at Appomattox there was evidence that full-scale violence would visit the high plains country. The Indians were concerned about the demands for more territory that followed the cessions at Laramie in 1851, angered by such transgressions at that of John Bozeman, who boldly marked off a shortcut between the Oregon Trail and Montana, and infuriated by the final aggression: the massacre at Sand Creek. When the northern Cheyenne heard about the treatment of their brothers at Chivington's hands, they spread the word among their friends, the Sioux and the Arapaho. The word was out: violence would be answered by violence. As a taste of things to come, a band of northern Cheyenne waylaid nine whites who were making their way east, in January 1865, and after dispatching them opened the dead men's baggage and found two scalps that had been taken in the Sand Creek affair. These veterans of the massacre were the first to pay for the fighting parson's attempts to solve the Indian problem. Their blood merely whetted the appetites of the braves, who were resolved that there would be no more Sand Creeks.

Widespread raiding now occurred along the line of communication between the Missouri River and the Rocky Mountains. In the early days of 1865 a Cheyenne party struck Julesburg, Colorado, and plundered it thoroughly. They streamed out of that little village trailing strips of cloth behind their ponies and brandishing captured articles of hardware. One piece of loot they found useless: an army paymaster's strong box yielded some $40,000 in currency, strange bits of colored paper that they scattered to the winds across the prairie.

Brigadier General Robert Mitchell assembled over 600 cavalrymen and set out to punish the raiders, but after a fruitless march of several hundred miles he came home empty-handed. The Indians scattered widely, striking at isolated points, and then gradually withdrew northward to the Powder River country. Before they moved on, they paralyzed travel along both branches of the Platte River, heavily attacked a group of soldiers at the Platte River Bridge (near present Casper, Wyoming), and frustrated the efforts of hundreds of soldiers.

Stung by these slashing attacks, a large body of troops commanded by General Patrick Connor plunged into the Powder River country in a determined effort to hunt out the warriors and punish them. An elaborate triple-headed strike was planned, a military vise in which the Indians would be caught and crushed. The story was one of rendezvous failure, uncoordinated attacks on scattered bands, and the near-starvation of two of the three units invading that unknown land stretching out toward Powder River. The whole expedition was a signal failure, and for it Connor was handed the blame. It was not the failure of one man, or of his subordinate officers, but simply a victory of a raw and unconquered region, and its wily natives, over inexperienced Indian fighters who had much to learn about fighting Indians.

PEACE EFFORTS   Government officials, concerned over the expensive but futile efforts to hunt down Indians and mindful of voter pressure to cut back expenditures, decided on an alternative course of peace since war seemed so unrewarding. An expedition headed by General J. B. Sanborn, and bound for the Arkansas River country to fight the southern plains tribes, was called off. Treaty conferences were conducted on the Little Arkansas and at Fort Sully on the Missouri River in the autumn of 1865. By the first of these treaties the Cheyenne and the Arapaho signed away the remainder of their lands; by the other a portion of the Sioux merely agreed to cease hostilities.

General Grenville Dodge replaced Patrick Connor and was instructed to parley with the northern tribes, not to fight them. In June 1866 some 2000 Sioux, mostly Brûlé and Oglala, assembled at Fort Laramie to hear what the peace commissioners had in mind. At about the same time the War Department ordered Colonel Henry B. Carrington to move into the Powder River country to establish a line of posts that would protect travel on the Bozeman or Powder River Road. He and his troops passed through Fort Laramie about the time the commissioners were trying to talk peace to the Sioux. It is unnecessary to elaborate on the thoughts that passed through the minds of the assembled Indians. Red Cloud and Man-Afraid-of-His-Horses promptly withdrew from the deliberations and headed for home, ready to stop white travel across what was some of the best remaining buffalo country on the northern plains.

Carrington carried out his orders and three forts—Reno, Phil Kearney, and C. F. Smith—appeared along the Bozeman Road. He made his headquarters at Fort Phil Kearney, named after the gallant Irish cavalryman who had lost his life in the recent war, and from this pivotal position (near the present town of Sheridan, Wyoming) he endeavored to carry out his assignment. From midsummer 1866 until late autumn his men labored at cutting logs, readying the headquarters post for winter, all of which went on under the careful scrutiny of the Sioux. From time to time the woodcutters were obliged to make a run for it as small parties tried to intercept them. After a close call early in December, in which the men were saved only by a timely arrival of troops from the fort, it became clear that such escapes would not always be made. The Indians were tightening the noose around the hated little outpost that bristled in their very midst.

On December 21 distress signals from a beleaguered wood train stirred the men at Fort Phil Kearney into action, and young Captain William J. Fetterman, who had boasted that he could ride through the Sioux nation with 80 men, begged for his chance to make the rescue. Cautious Colonel Carrington acceded to the request, but specifically warned his young cavalryman not to pursue the Indians over Lodge Trail Ridge. Fetterman saluted in acknowledgment of the instructions and led a force of 81 through the gates to what he imagined would be glory. The Indians—Cheyenne, Arapaho, and Sioux— stayed back in the hills and set up the oldest ruse in military history: the decoy. A few selected braves rode within rifle range, and when the troops failed to nibble at the bait they became more daring. At some undetermined point Fetterman's resolve to follow orders yielded to temptation and he took up the chase—beyond Lodge Trail Ridge. Quickly the main Indian force snapped shut the trap, and what amounted to an

The Buffalo Hunter. Here the upended monarch of the plains is surrendering his shaggy coat. In warmer weather the work was so malodorous that the hunter was socially ostracized in nearby towns. (Minnesota Historical Society)

execution took place. In less than an hour Fetterman and his command lay dead, most of the troops in an area about 40 feet square, the others scattered around it. By the time a relief party arrived the corpses lay frozen in grotesque shapes, presenting a grisly tableau of death. One of the surgeons in attendance wrote laconically: "We brought in about fifty in wagons like you see hogs brought to market."

Carrington at once dispatched the news east by means of a civilian courier who carried his message 236 blizzard-swept miles to Fort Laramie. His plea was simple: "Do send me reinforcements forthwith." Not only were additional troops sent but so was a replacement for Colonel Carrington, who spent most of the remainder of his life trying to vindicate himself. Although some army difficulties might be dealt with by a simple transfer of a commanding officer, it was not enough to silence the national outcry over such disasters. All across the country the outraged cries that the only good Indian was a dead Indian mingled with cries of insistence by humanitarians that the heartless Indian policy was causing such understandable reaction by the natives. Both sides fired a good deal of verbal ammunition at the War and Interior Departments, with the word "mismanagement" prominent in their salvos.

Once again violence on the plains brought renewed efforts at peace. In the spring of 1868 tribesmen and commissioners sat down to smoke the pipe of peace at Fort Laramie. It had been less than two years since Red Cloud and the others had stalked out of that place, deeply angered at the government's resolve to fortify the Bozeman Road, and determined to oppose the move with all possible vigor. Red Cloud's demands were unchanged: close this shortcut and oblige Montana-bound miners to use an alternate route. The abandonment was agreed to, and troops were pulled out of the contested region. It is understandable why a "cause-and-effect" construction should be placed on this incident and that contemporaries as well as later students of western history should say that the mighty Red Cloud had turned back forces of the federal government. There were several reasons for the decision: the Union Pacific Railroad, then nearing completion, would allow fast and relatively cheap transportation to Corinne, Utah, from which point goods could be hauled into Montana by wagon over a well-used road that did not pass through the land of powerful, determined Indians; no organized public transportation, either freight or passenger, ever used the Bozeman Road, which was employed chiefly by emigrant parties and one-trip freighters; the number of federal troops required to keep the road open made it unreasonably expensive in terms of financial outlay and manpower. In short, the cutoff had pretty largely served its purpose by 1868. The Sioux were only a persistent annoyance.

WAR ON THE WASHITA   While the federal government was inclined to make peace where such a course seemed profitable, it continued to press the Indians in other quarters. In April 1867 General Winfield Scott Hancock maneuvered against Sioux and southern Cheyenne bands in Kansas and finally burned a village of about 250 Indian lodges along Pawnee Fork. The action not only outraged the Indians, who lost much property, but infuriated the Indian agents, who thought Hancock's campaign absolutely unnecessary. In fact, the badly timed and inept actions of the military are generally credited with setting off a whole series of Indian depredations that followed. As one example, the Indians lashed out so frequently and so severely at Kansas Pacific Railroad engineering parties that construction was virtually halted for over a month. All along the Smoky Hill Road across Kansas, affairs became sufficiently turbulent to cut travel to a mere trickle.

In early 1867 there had been no war on the southern plains—only scattered raids here and there—but by autumn attacks had become so widespread and so bold that some solution to the problem had to be found. In October Indian commissioners, accompanied by a large body of cavalrymen, met with the Cheyenne and Arapaho at Medicine Lodge Creek (Indian Territory), where a treaty was effected. The terms were familiar: white passage through the southern and central plains was guaranteed; railroad crews would be undisturbed; more Indian lands were ceded; new homes for the dispossessed would be provided on reservations. For this the government promised individual land-holdings (320 acres per family head), issues of clothing, and $20,000 annually for the tribe for twenty-five years. Formalities concluded, some 2000 Cheyenne accepted presents from the commissioners (including ammunition) and headed south for winter camp.

In 1868 the Cheyenne warriors became restless and expresed their dissatisfaction with the recent treaty by renewing their practice of raiding. During August northern Cheyenne and Sioux came close to annihilating a small force under the command of Major George A. Forsyth along the Arikaree Fork of the Republican River in eastern Colorado. The Battle of Beecher's Island—named after Lieutenant Frederick H. Beecher, who died in the siege—became a part of the annals of Plains Indian warfare.

The axiom that war follows the failure of peace was again demonstrated as troops took the field for a major campaign. One prong of an elaborately planned triple-headed strike was composed of eleven companies of the Seventh Cavalry, commanded by Lieutenant Colonel George Armstrong Custer, and elements of the Nineteenth Kansas Volunteers brought into service during the emergency.

Custer was probably the most picturesque and magnetic army officer of his day. Six feet tall, with the broad shoulders and narrow hips of the cavalryman, he wore his golden hair to his shoulders and moved with a swagger. Most unusual for the period, he used neither liquor nor tobacco and swore but seldom. The great and abiding goal of his life was glory, and in pursuit of it he was brave to the point of recklessness, a characteristic General William Tecumseh Sherman called "a good trait for a Cavalry officer." His career was brilliant but erratic. A graduate from West Point at twenty-one, Custer found in the Civil War the opportunity to achieve high rank in a brief period. As an Indian fighter in the 1860s he was a lieutenant colonel, although he is often referred to by his wartime rank of brigadier general of the Volunteers. His command, the Seventh Cavalry, became one of the best and most famous units of its kind. Custer had that rare quality which, in spite of harsh discipline, attracted men who were willing to follow him to the death.

Custer left the rendezvous late in November, in bitter cold and in snow a foot deep, to search for Indians. He found Black Kettle's camp of southern Cheyenne along the Washita River, not far from the Texas border, and within ten minutes his troops had invested the place. Then the slaughter began. Over a hundred Indians, including the hapless Black Kettle, who had miraculously survived Sand Creek, fell before the troopers. Before neighboring Comanche, Arapaho, and Kiowa warriors could swing into action Custer marched his men out of danger. Part of the young officer's fame for this action came from an exaggerated and much-publicized report he wrote, one in which little mention was made of the women and children who died at the hands of the troops. Nor was much said about the fate of Major Joel H. Elliott, whose detachment was surrounded and dispatched by the Indians. Captain Fred W. Benteen was so outraged at what he regarded as a callous abandonment of Elliott by Custer that he wrote a bitter but anonymous letter to the newspapers. It was the beginning of a famous enmity that survived even the controversial Custer. An even more unsatisfactory outcome of the engagement was the fact that it did not intimidate the southern Cheyenne, did not stop the raiding of the frontier, and was in no way decisive.

THE GREAT ENIGMA   In the spring of 1869 General U. S. Grant was inaugurated as President. His hopes for the troubled South, writhing in the agony of Reconstruction, had been expressed in the words "Let us have peace." He felt the same way about the troubled frontier, a conviction that was shared by many Americans of his day. The early post–Civil War years yielded only turmoil in the West, where another American minority was struggling for its rights. Unfortunately for the Indians, they were powerful enough to fight for what they regarded as theirs, and their willingness to exert that power was costly to them. Federal government authorities were perplexed over the apparent insolubility of a problem that frustrated them but was not sufficiently critical to call forth more of the nation's resources to combat it.

A historian who lived during those trying years described the situation as he saw it. In 1903 Hiram Martin Chittenden wrote in his *History of Early Steamboat Navigation on the Missouri River* (II, 355):

> History will exonerate the government from any but the purest motives in its dealing with the Indians. It may have been unwise in some of its measures; it was certainly weak in carrying its purpose into effect; but it always sought, with the light it possessed, the highest good of the Indian. . . . It was the problem of how to commit a great wrong without doing any wrong—how to deprive the Indian of his birthright in such a way that he should feel that no injustice had been done him.

The American government, having treated with the Indians at Medicine Lodge Creek and at Fort Laramie between 1866 and 1868, and having fought northern and southern tribes alike during that time, faced a disturbing dilemma as the decade of the seventies approached. After experimenting with both war and peace on the plains, the government still had a problem that was no nearer solution; it was, in fact, growing worse. Unhappily, the fumbling was to go on for approximately a quarter of a century longer.

READINGS   *Paperbacks are marked with an asterisk.*

Crisis on the Plains   Robert G. Athearn, *Forts of the Upper Missouri* (1967); Robert W. Frazer, *Forts of the West* (1965), handbook of forts west of the Mississippi; Le Roy R. Hafen and Francis M. Young, *Fort Laramie* (1930), much on pre-Civil War period; Remi Nadeau, *Fort Laramie and the Sioux Indians* (1967); William S. Nye, *Carbine and Lance* (1937), emphasizes Fort Sill. General accounts are Harold E. Briggs, *Frontiers of the Northwest* (1940) and *Everett Dick, *Vanguards of the Frontier* (1941). Carl C. Rister, *Border Command* (1944) is good on Phil Sheridan; see also his *Southwestern Frontier* (1928). J. Cecil Alter, *James Bridger* (1962) includes something of the Indian pressure of the 1850s and 1860s.

Disappearance of the Buffalo   *Wayne Gard, *The Great Buffalo Hunt* (1959); *E. Douglas Branch, *The Hunting of the Buffalo* (1929); Mari Sandoz, *The Buffalo Hunters* (1954); Frank G. Roe, *The North American Buffalo* (1951); Donald B. Russell, *The Lives and Legends of Buffalo Bill* (1960), best on the subject.

Indian Uprising in Minnesota   *Kenneth Carley, *The Sioux Uprising of 1862* (1961); Theodore C. Blegen and Philip D. Jordan (eds.), *With Various Voices* (1949); Charles M. Oehler, *The Great Sioux Uprising* (1959).

Early Post–Civil War Disturbances   *Ralph H. Andrist, *The Long Death* (1964); William H. Leckie, *The Military Conquest of the Southern Plains* (1963); James C. Olson, *Red Cloud and the Sioux Problem* (1965); Douglas C. Jones, *The Treaty of Medicine Lodge* (1966), treaty of 1867; *Captain Eugene F. Ware, *The Indian War of 1864* (1911, 1960), firsthand account; Dee Brown, *Fort Phil Kearny: An American Saga* (1962). Most detailed concerning troubles on the Bozeman Road is Grace R. Hebard and E. A. Brininstool, *The Bozeman Trail* (2 vols., 1922). Custer's earlier exploits are treated briefly in Edgar I. Stewart, *Custer's Luck* (1955).

For a more extensive list of related readings see Chapter 31. For the individual Indian tribes see Chapter 20.

Plenty Horses, the Killer of Lieutenant E. W. Casey. The picture was taken at Fort Meade, South Dakota, in 1891, as he awaited trial. His crime was adjudged an act of war and he was freed. (Library of Congress)

Chapter 31 / THE INDIAN PROBLEM "SOLVED"

The troubled condition of the plains moved Congress to engage in an extended study of the matter. Since the legislators were generally ignorant about Indian affairs and since the better-informed members were as badly divided in opinion as was the public at large, the first job seemed to be to collect information. As early as 1865 a joint committee of seven was appointed to investigate and to make necessary recommendations for legislation. Headed by Senator J. R. Doolittle of Wisconsin, the committee took its duties seriously and traveled widely over the plains, interviewing Indians, Indian agents, settlers, miners, army officers, and, in fact, every available person with information or a grievance.

The report of the committee of seven was presented in January 1867. Its conclusions were that Indian troubles were caused by white aggression and the overly vigorous actions of the army, and that the Indians were dying off rapidly. The report suggested a small permanent committee to investigate further and to make specific recommendations to Congress. These rather modest proposals brought no action, but the investigations of the committee had provided a vast fund of information upon which future action could be based. In spite of the seemingly inconclusive results a more vigorous and better coordinated policy was in the making.

PEACE COMMISSION   The rather tentative efforts of the 1865–1867 investigations led to the formation of a new commission composed of four civilians, including the Commissioner of Indian Affairs, and three generals. Congress stated its purpose: removing the causes of friction between the two races; securing the safety of the overland routes; discovering permanent homes for the Indians; and finding ways of promoting Indian civilization without interfering with the rest of the United States. Moreover, the new commission was not limited to investigation and recommendations, but could negotiate any necessary treaties to put its program into effect.

During 1867–1868 the commissioners crisscrossed the plains and negotiated treaties with practically all tribes. These agreements provided for various reservations throughout the West, the most important of which was Indian Territory. This region, essentially modern Oklahoma, was to house all the tribes of the southern and central plains. A large area west of the Missouri River (primarily in modern South Dakota) was given to the Sioux. It was this group of men (including General William T. Sherman, commanding the military Division of the Missouri) that agreed to the abandonment of the Bozeman Road.

The final report of the "peace commission" was sympathetic to the Indian, but recognized realistically that the Indians could not be permitted to roam freely over the plains, and that their concentration in reservations was necessary. The friction between the War and Interior Departments was noted, and the suggestion was made that a new and independent Indian Department be created to eliminate the resulting difficulties.

Soon after the report was made, the troubles occurred that culminated in the Custer campaign on the Washita, and the commission then decided that complete control by the War Department would be the best solution. Noting that the Cheyenne and the Arapaho were raiding widely and that various treaties had been broken, General Sherman spoke for his colleagues when he said: "Spite of Indian Peace Commissions, and all our efforts to keep the rascals quiet, they have broke out simply because they can make more by war than Peace. We must not let up this time, but keep it going till they are killed or humbled." He advised the secretary of war to cut off all annuities to hostiles and give the Indians the war they had asked for: "I propose to give them enough of it to satisfy them to their hearts' content," wrote the crusty general. The affair at Washita was an application of this line of thinking.

THE QUAKER POLICY   Just when the national debate about Custer's raid on Black Kettle's camp was at its height, a new policy shift occurred. Grant took office in March 1869 and brought Sherman to Washington to fill the vacated position of general of the army. The President's stand on the Indian question did not agree with that of his old comrade-in-arms, Sherman, but rather looked toward pacification of the natives through peace overtures. Positions in the Indian service were filled by recommendations made by the various churches, the Quakers receiving a considerable proportion of the appointments; hence the name "Quaker Policy." Although the Indians registered no objections to the new approach, it was not well received by all churchmen. The Catholics especially resented the small proportion of appointees awarded them and felt that the new policy was anti-Catholic.

The employment of church people to work among the Indians appealed to the humanitarians and particularly to the radicals in Congress who were heavily engaged in promoting Negro rights. The Indians were another minority, one whose problems appeared to be much more important immediately after the Civil War. In 1870, and a number of times later, delegations of Indians were brought to Washington to visit the Great White Father. As a rule they were put on display in one or more other eastern cities before being allowed to return home. During the visit of 1870 Red Cloud and about twenty other Oglala Sioux were shown military parades, naval cannon, warships, and other examples of the white man's "thunder." Before returning home the visitors dined with the President and met with members of the cabinet and the diplomatic corps. When Red Cloud declined an invitation to dinner extended by the wife of Admiral Dahlgren, on the grounds that he was in Washington on business and not for pleasure, capital city society was titillated.

In another departure the old treaty system was abolished. By a law of March 3, 1871, the United States abandoned the fiction that the various tribes were sovereign powers. Agreements might still be made, but they were to be ratified by the entire Congress rather than merely by the Senate. The change was in the direction of political realism, since the Indians never had been foreign nations in the usual sense of the term; in practice the only important effect was to give the House a long-desired voice in any new Indian agreements.

Negotiating treaties for the creation of reservations was by no means equivalent to getting the Indians on the selected land and making farmers of them. Actually it was unlikely that they could be confined to the reservations as long as game was available on the plains. In the north the Sioux continued to roam as their desires dictated, with apparently not the least intention of migrating to their new homes. Those confined to Indian Territory showed similar inclinations, spending their summers in war and hunting parties and then returning to the reservation for winter rations.

While the reservation system did not solve the problem, and there was turmoil on the plains during the seventies and eighties, the trend was to limit the size of Indian landholdings. An army of plowmen was relentlessly marching westward, and its final occupation of the trans-Missouri country was easy to forecast. One by one the tribes were isolated and with each of these moves the chance of a general war diminished. In this light the predictions of contemporaries that the end of Indian resistance was in sight were well justified, although bitter resistance by the natives made their views appear to be questionable at the time. The question that remained was what to do with the tribesmen after they had been subdued. It was one that puzzled contemporaries as much as it did later generations.

MODOC REBELLION   The idea of negotiating with rebellious Indians, one that gained wide approval in the East during the early 1870s, had some serious drawbacks when put to a practical test. The disastrous result of diplomatic efforts with the Modoc of southern Oregon and northern California did not cause the peace advocates to abandon their theories, but it considerably modified their initial ardor.

A few months after Grant's inauguration in the spring of 1869 Alfred B. Meacham, a party worker and a great supporter of the general, was appointed Indian superintendent for Oregon. Meacham, a good Methodist and a long-time resident of the West, was regarded as well qualified to administer the President's "Quaker Policy." A good humanitarian, the new agent was properly appalled at conditions among his charges, and he at once set about uplifting their moral decline by issuing a number of prohibitions against such sins as polygamy, gambling, ghost-dancing, and slaveholding. The varying shades of color found among the Indian children suggested that the troops had anticipated the agent's desires for friendly association by some years, and he made great efforts to terminate such outward evidences of friendship between the sexes of the two races. Before long there were a number of objections to Agent Meacham's program, which appeared to be aimed at keeping the natives in a condition of paternalistic subjugation. It is not surprising that this tribe reacted as other American Indians had, and balked at the white man's efforts at civilization.

As always, in times of such trouble, there emerged a leader who became the spokesman for his people. In this case it was not the hereditary chief, who happened to be an old man, but a young subchief named Keintpoos, better known among the white settlers as Captain Jack. Meacham, who was somewhat taken in by Jack's initial display of cooperation, soon discovered that he was not as tractable as at first had appeared, particularly when Jack led his band off the reservation and refused to return peaceably.

By the autumn of 1872 the residents of Modoc country were clamoring for Jack's arrest. His men made nuisances of themselves, barging into farmhouses, demanding food, and trying to extort "rent" from the farmers whom they regarded as interlopers; moreover, Jack had killed an Indian medicine man in cold blood for failing to save two sick members of his family. Although the latter act was a tribal affair, the whites thought Jack should be tried for murder. General E. R. S. Canby, a career officer and a veteran of the Civil War, ordered his subordinates to arrest Jack and some of his henchmen to quiet the complaints of the settlers. The Indians resisted and what became known as the Modoc War ensued.

It now became the duty of Canby, who was sympathetic to the Indians and who had remarked that it would be "impolitic if not cruel" to make them return to the reservation, to round up the recalcitrants. It was a discouraging task, for the Modocs slipped into the lava beds of northern California and set up almost impregnable defenses. After a lengthy stalemate Captain Jack agreed to a parley to be held halfway between the lava beds and the encampment of the troops. Canby left his sidearms behind, and with

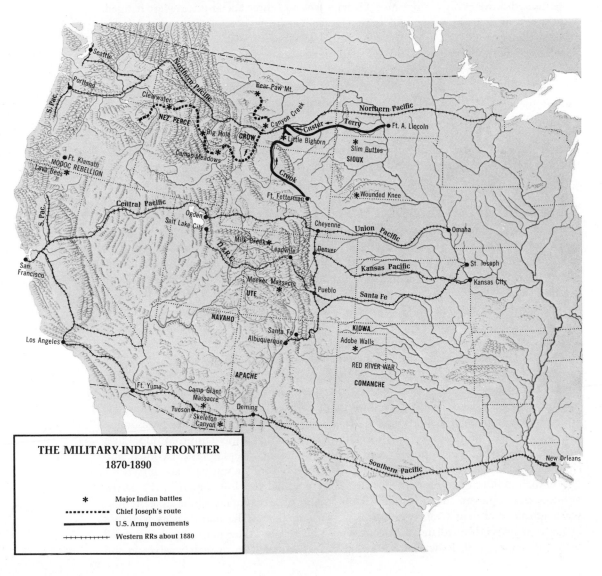

THE MILITARY-INDIAN FRONTIER
1870-1890

*	Major Indian battles
····	Chief Joseph's route
——	U.S. Army movements
+++++	Western RRs about 1880

several other white commissioners met with Jack and his followers. As the Modocs smoked the general's cigars and listened to him explain the federal government's Indian policy, they watched their leader for a prearranged signal. When it was given they drew revolvers and started firing. Canby was shot through the head; Reverend Elezar Thomas, a Methodist preacher acting as a commissioner, was also killed; Meacham was shot five times and left for dead; Commissioner L. S. Dyar escaped by outrunning the attackers. This affair, in which the first general officer of the United States Army to die at the hands of Indians was killed, thoroughly shocked the nation. The Modocs now were hunted down with a vengeance. Captain Jack and three accomplices were hanged, and the rest of the tribe was packed off to Indian Territory.

The rebellion of a small group of Indians, known as a "war," was typical of such disturbances in that it was costly in lives and money—considering the number of Indians involved—and was not a solution to the problem. When all the excitement had passed, some of the Indians were still off the reservation, the ghost-dancing had not stopped, and the manner in which Jack and a handful of his followers had stood off the troops made a deep impression upon other western Indians. Even more important, the government appeared to have learned nothing from the crisis. All during the decade of the 1870s it floundered with the Indian dilemma, applying alternate treatments of sweet reasonableness and force, a program that satisfied neither the Indians nor their white partisans.

TURMOIL IN THE SOUTHWEST

Making peace with the Indians was not so simple a matter as many churchmen believed. In the Southwest the Apache were cruel, cunning, elusive, and hard fighting. To westerners there was one answer: fight to the finish. An army officer reflected their sentiment in a remark he made to Kit Carson in 1862: "All Indian men of that tribe are to be killed whenever and wherever you can find them." Such notions were set aside as archaic by those who proposed to carry out the Quaker Policy. In 1870 Congress appropriated $70,000 to make peace with the Apache, and in the following year Vincent Colyer, secretary to the Board of Indian Commissioners, was sent to Arizona to negotiate with the Indians.

The Colyer mission was sparked by an atrocity against the Apache that rivaled the earlier Chivington affair in Colorado. A band of starving Indians had come to Camp Grant, Arizona, where they were fed by the commandant, who even encouraged them to send for their friends and relatives. A number of white and Mexican ranchers, annoyed by constant depredations against their herds, decided to administer punishment to any available Apache. At dawn, April 30, 1871, a group of these impromptu soldiers fell upon the Indian encampment near the fort, attacking sleeping men, women, and children. After a quick but bloody assault, they retreated to Tucson with about twenty-nine Indian children as prisoners, boasting that they had not lost a man in the battle. While western papers clucked mildly at the killing of women and children, easterners were aghast. President Grant acted firmly, warning that if the perpetrators were not brought to justice immediately, Arizona would be placed under martial law. To avoid such military control, leaders of the group were persuaded to turn themselves in and after a brief trial were acquitted. The result of this farce was the coming of Colyer, and of General George Crook.

Although the administration acted firmly, it also demonstrated, by what now took place in Arizona, that coordination in Indian affairs still remained only an ideal. Crook was ordered to cooperate with Colyer, who shortly laid off one reservation in New Mexico and three in Arizona. Many Indians were assigned new homes, with such notable exceptions as the Chiricahua and some of the Mescalero and Pinal Apache who ranged the countryside as hostiles. Fearful that Crook would pursue too severe a course with his Indian charges, the Grant administration sent out Major General Oliver O. Howard as the ranking officer in the Southwest. The gentle, one-armed Howard, recently involved in the southern Reconstruction program, negotiated several treaties, including a surprising agreement from the tough-minded old Cochise of the Chiricahua Apache in the autumn of 1872. However, despite real progress, scattered and sporadic raids continued. Crook, who had been drilling his men while Howard talked peace, now was brought into action with orders to crush the unruly hostiles.

Crook, a tall, slender, and muscular man who used neither liquor, tobacco, nor profanity, was as tough-minded as he was industrious. After expressing sympathy for the Indians he ordered them back to their reservations and promised the severest punishment for those who did not obey. Crook's words could be trusted completely, and when the Indians flouted his commands he took the field. By dividing his forces into comparatively small parties he harried the minor hostile bands unceasingly until, by April 1873, they were at his mercy. For the first time in 300 years Arizona knew peace from Indian depredations.

In 1875 Crook was transferred north, and his departure marked the renewal of trouble in Arizona. The Indians did not like reservation life, especially when they found themselves hungry. Denied the hunt, they were unable to subsist on inadequate and irregularly dispensed rations. Well-armed bands under such leaders as Victorio and Geronimo raided the countryside; when Arizona became too dangerous they crossed the boundary into Mexico, only to raid back across the border. Military expeditions found themselves hampered by the international boundary as well as by the methods of Apache warfare. Ultimately, in 1880, Victorio was killed, but it was another six years before Geronimo was cornered and forced to surrender.

NORTHERN PLAINS WARFARE The various southern Indian troubles were but sideshows to the main performance that was taking place on the northern plains during the seventies. The Sioux was the one important tribe that had never experienced a major defeat by the whites and had even won several minor victories. The Sioux harbored a number of grievances. Bad conditions on their Dakota reservation had reinforced their desire to roam the plains farther west, where they came into collision with miners, stockmen, and a scattering of settlers. More important, white miners had invaded country reserved to the Indians, particularly the Black Hills region, where rumor had it there was "gold in the grass roots." Early prospectors were ejected at Sherman's order, but a new group tagged along after the Custer expedition of 1874, and very soon the entire United States Army might have had trouble in freeing the country from white trespassers. Recalling earlier demands by volunteers to be allowed to retain all the loot they might capture from the Indians, the Sioux now made sarcastic inquiries about the possession of horses, wagons, and other equipment they might take from the white invaders. Grant's answer was an offer to buy off the Indians with $25,000 and hunting rights along the Platte River, an overture that was declined. The government now took the customary recourse of turning to force and peremptorily ordered all hostile Sioux back to the reservation by February 1, 1876, under the threat of punishment. This order was physically impossible to obey even if the Indians had so desired; consequently, when the specified date arrived considerable bands of Indians were still roaming the country to the west. No less a figure than Phil Sheridan believed the Indians would regard the order as little more than a joke.

General Alfred Terry sent word to Sitting Bull, of the Hunkpapa Sioux, that after the specified date he would move against the roving bands. "You won't need any guides," Sitting Bull is reputed to have said. "You can find me easily; I won't run away." Perhaps the noted Sioux did not say these words—he denied having done so in later years—but his actions were far from friendly. When the deadline passed and there was no acquiescence from the Indians, both sides resolutely prepared for war. A punitive expedition made ready to enter the country of the hostiles in force to punish both Sioux and Cheyenne, but particularly the former.

The favorite strategy—a triple-headed strike—was decided on: one column under General Crook was to move north out of Wyoming into Montana; a second under Colonel John Gibbon was to move eastward from Fort Ellis, Montana; and a third under Terry was to march westward from Fort Abraham Lincoln (Bismarck), Dakota. Terry, who had won distinction in the Civil War but had had no experience in Indian fighting did not relish the assignment and would have turned it over to the more experienced George A. Custer had Grant not prevented it. The President was angry at the flamboyant young Custer for having presented embarrassing evidence in the recent House investigation of Secretary of War W. W. Belknap. It was bad enough that the secretary was in trouble; even worse, the affair involved some of Grant's relatives. It was all that Phil Sheridan could do to get so much as permission for Custer to join the expedition.

Crook left Fort Fetterman, Wyoming, in March 1876. He marched his men slowly northward toward the rendezvous, penetrating hostile country cautiously, fully aware that a talented enemy lay somewhere ahead. In March they came across the village of Crazy Horse, a camp of over 100 lodges of Sioux and some Cheyenne. Although the troops were victorious, the affair was far from satisfactory to the military. General Joseph J. Reynolds, in immediate command, pulled his troops out of the fight so precipitously that one of Crook's officers could write: "We practically abandoned the victory to the savages." The disgruntled Crook later preferred charges against Reynolds and two other officers for misbehavior before the enemy. The discordant group, tired and cold, returned to Fort Fetterman to recuperate and prepare for further action. Late in May Crook again moved his forces northward and within two weeks he again engaged the Sioux, this time along the South Fork of the Rosebud River; after a fight that cost the general 9 of his 1325 men, both sides broke off the action. In the latter days of June Crook's little army went into camp, this time along Goose Creek near the Big Horn Mountains in northern Wyoming, where the men spent their time fishing and waiting for the next phase of the campaign to commence. During these days, when one of Crook's officers estimated that some 15,000 trout were caught and consumed by the troops, events of a much more critical nature were taking place not far to the north on the Little Big Horn.

Terry did not leave Fort Abraham Lincoln until the middle of May. The main element of his force was the Seventh Cavalry commanded by Custer. Late in the month, Terry's troops met Gibbon's Montana column on the Yellowstone, at the mouth of the Powder River, where the officers conferred. Reports of an "Indian sign" on the Rosebud stirred the campaigners into action. Terry at once sent Custer ahead to follow the trail, with orders that gave him considerable freedom of action but that urged caution in carrying out his mission, which was largely to permit the deployment of the remainder of the army to cut off any Indian retreat. No one conceived of an Indian victory.

When Custer left on his fateful march he was only thirty-seven years old, but his strenuous life had made him in some respects older than his years. His chances of winning great fame seemed to be lessening and he was in the mood to wager everything on the single throw of the dice, for he was utterly confident that his Seventh Cavalry could beat all the Indians on the plains. Sherman recognized the nature of the gamble when he made the comment: "I suppose now the Indians will lead our troops a will-o'-the-wisp circle, until some lucky turn may give one of the columns a chance." As Custer pressed forward he revealed his anxiety that the "lucky turn" would fall to his command.

Although his scouts reported large bodies of hostiles in the region, Custer tended to underestimate the threat. Even had he known the exact number of the enemy it is doubtful that he would have altered his tactics: he was convinced that a hammerblow against almost any group of Indians would scatter them. He had struck such a blow with great success at Washita; he was sure he could do it again. On June 25, 1876, he came upon an encampment of Sioux and Cheyenne, their tepees spread out along the valley of the Little Big Horn; characteristically he ordered the charge. Without waiting for the remaining elements of the proposed three-pronged attack and apparently fearful that he might have to share some of the glory, he led his men into a fray in which they were outnumbered perhaps 8 to 1. Major Marcus Reno, leading some 134 officers and men (plus 16 scouts), was sent across the valley floor in a direct attack, while Custer took some of the men along the low-lying hills in a circling movement. Reno, a fine officer with a good Civil War record but with no Indian fighting experience, broke off the attack despite the consternation he caused among the Indians, and retreated instead of charging on through the camp. For whatever reason—irresolution, extreme caution, or a long background in more formal fighting—Reno failed to carry out his assignment and took refuge in the timber along the Little Big Horn River where he could better defend himself.

Meanwhile, Custer attempted to complete his movements along the bluffs overlooking the Indian village. There remains great speculation today with regard to the details of his movements after he left the others, but since none of those in the group survived the day there exists no proof of what happened. Presumably he tried to move down from higher ground, cross the river, and join the attack on the village, but was obliged to retreat to seek a better defensive position. It was on a knoll that terminates a series of ridges that Custer made his famous last stand as the warriors of Sitting Bull, Crazy Horse, Gall, and others swept up the grassy slopes to ride down the troopers. Reno's indecisiveness in the valley was fatal to the whole daring plan.

The annihilation of Custer's 225-man force turned out to be relatively unimportant in the general campaign. Terry had been delayed but not stopped by this single action, and in a relentless pursuit of the Sioux and Cheyenne that ensued, the hostile bands were forced to surrender while Sitting Bull and a few of his Sioux escaped into Canada. Even he later returned and became a reservation Indian.

Ration Day at the Pine Ridge Agency, South Dakota. Though it has been argued that the handout ruined the American Indians, it is likely that the natives would not have survived without assistance. (Denver Public Library)

THE NEZ PERCÉ WAR   During the remainder of 1876 and in early 1877, as the blue-clad troopers were running down scattered Sioux and Cheyenne bands, there were reverberations farther west that would erupt into another Indian war. The source of trouble surprised some Americans, for it came from the relatively peaceful Nez Percé Indians of Idaho, who had lived a quiet, pastoral life all during the years that Plains Indians had caused so much commotion. In 1875 President Grant approved the opening of part of their reservation to settlement, but this raised no eyebrows in a nation where such actions had become almost policy. What generated comment was the fact that the Indians registered objections to such an old and time-honored practice of encroachment and presented their complaints in the tangible form of rifles and raiding.

The gentle O. O. Howard, who was in Idaho at the time of the trouble (1877), at once ordered troops into the field to put down any uprising. Under the very capable direction of Chief Joseph, a young but wise leader, the Indians began a retreat toward Canada that is one of the classics in the annals of American Indian campaigns. With some 200 warriors, but hampered by more than twice that number of women, children, and aged, he moved eastward across the Bitterroot Mountains toward Montana. The frightened residents of Missoula sent forth a hastily assembled group of volunteers, who erected a barricade in a nearby valley and prepared to stop the invasion. Joseph's advance scouts took one look, circled past what became known as "Fort Fizzle," and headed south toward Yellowstone Park. By now Colonel John Gibbon and about 160 troopers were in hot pursuit, marching as much as 30 miles a day, or twice the rate made by the heavily encumbered Nez Percé warriors.

On the morning of August 9 Gibbon came across the sleeping camp of Chief Joseph and at once launched an attack. Despite the element of surprise, the soldiers found themselves in a sharp fight that cost them heavily. As their ammunition ran low, they took up defensive positions and waited for reinforcements from Howard, who was in the Bitterroot Valley. The Indians, having lost 50 women and children and 30 warriors, according to Chief Joseph's account, took this opportunity to continue their flight. Once more they moved east, through Yellowstone Park, where they thoroughly frightened some of the tourists and narrowly missed encountering General Sherman, who was fishing there; they then headed north toward Canada.

The pursuing Howard covered 1321 miles in seventy days, but was outmaneuvered and outdistanced. Jeeringly the newspapers called his force the Indians' best supply line, and the general became so angered that Sherman had to remind him that he was fighting Indians, not newspaper reporters. General Nelson A. Miles, fresh from his pursuit of Sitting Bull's Sioux, was brought into the chase to cooperate with Gibbon, who was, in turn, trying to help Howard corner the elusive Joseph. Colonel Samuel D. Sturgis tried to make an interception along the Yellowstone River but was outfought and outmaneuvered. The chase went on as frustrated army officers cursed their luck and the red race in general, and the nation's newspaper readers followed the curious pursuit with mounting fascination.

By the time Joseph and his band were in the Bear Paw Mountains of north central Montana the leader decided it was time to stop and care for the sick and wounded. There is some reason to believe he thought he was in Canada. It was here that General Miles caught up with the group and after a five-day siege in which the Indians, particularly the women and children, suffered from cold and hunger, Chief Joseph decided to surrender. It was October. Of the 800 Nez Percés who had left Idaho in June slightly over half remained. About 100 had been killed, over twice that number escaped from the battlefield, and of the beleaguered group only 87 were fighting men. "Hear me, my chiefs," Joseph told his small band of warriors, "I am tired: my heart is sick and sad. From where the sun now stands, I will fight no more." Summarizing the affair General Sherman called it

> one of the most extraordinary Indian wars. . . . The Indians thoroughly displayed a courage and skill that elicited universal praise; they abstained from scalping, let captive women go free, did not commit indiscriminate murder of peaceful families which is unusual, and fought with almost scientific skill, using advance and rear guards, skirmish-lines and field-fortifications.

The wily Joseph and his followers were subdued at a cost of nearly $2 million, not including property destroyed. After receiving the due praise of Sherman, Miles, and others, the recreants were packed off to Indian Territory, in violation of a promise that they would be returned to Idaho. In a new, humid climate most of them died. It was an ironic end for those who had survived all kinds of weather, marches over unheard-of distances, and pursuit by several thousand federal troops.

The echoes of military-Indian strife in Montana had barely died out before a new struggle ensued in Colorado. The Ute Indians living on the White River Reservation were in a bad mood over the laxity of the government in providing them with supplies. In 1878 Nathan C. Meeker, once associated with Horace Greeley's newspaper, was appointed agent and he at once made the usual mistake of trying to reform the less fortunate natives. Not only did he push these nomadic hunters toward a new, agrarian life, but he tried to fit them into the white social structure as he envisioned it. Grudgingly the Ute took to the plow, with occasional unauthorized flights from the reservation, and the agent began to have high hopes for their salvation. However, like the stern parent, he pushed his charges too hard, and when he plowed up their racetrack, he made a grave mistake.

In September 1879 Chief Douglass and a small group of his followers attacked the agency, killed a dozen white men (including Meeker), and captured the agent's wife, daughter, two other women, and a small baby boy. Meanwhile, other Ute ambushed an army relief party of 160 men, commanded by Major T. T. Thornburg, killing the major and 13 of his men. Only the prompt march of reinforcements from Fort Steele, Wyoming, saved the remnants. What became known as the "Thornburg massacre" and the other events at the agency caused a great deal of excitement and, of course, brought a large body of federal troops. The result was familiar: the subjection of the Indians, a "treaty," and the removal of the Ute from Colorado.

RESERVATION LIFE   During the post-Civil War years, in particular, it was the general policy of the United States government to segregate whites and Indians by placing the latter on their own reservations. As the policy developed, various Indians were placed on a number of reservations, but in the early years after Appomattox a rather vague notion prevailed that the Plains Indians should be divided into two large groups, one north and one south of the main line of traffic up the Platte River, and that there should be no trespassing on them by the white population. As this idea took shape the northern Indians were gathered along the west bank of the Missouri River in Dakota Territory and those of the southern plains were assigned lands in "Indian Territory," or, in essence, modern Oklahoma.

There were several difficulties with the reservation plan. Ever since they had acquired the horse the Plains Indians had pursued a nomadic existence, following the buffalo herds, and living off the shaggy humpbacks. They were more than a source of food: following them became a way of life. The "hunt" was something that ran in the Plains Indian's bloodstream from birth and to deny him that was to make him give up all he knew and loved. To be forced to abandon the chase was catastrophic enough, but to be forced to till the soil was to be reduced to woman's work: it was humiliation piled upon deprivation. In addition, the government tended to send some of the northern Indians into Indian Territory, where they literally pined away their lives. The climate was humid and unhealthy compared with that from which they came, and the Indian's sincere love of the land of his birth added to his anguish when he was, in effect, deported.

One of the most dramatic examples of rebellion against the strictures of reservation life is seen in the heartrending efforts of the northern Cheyenne to get back to their homeland. This band had remained north when the southern Cheyenne moved down along the Arkansas River after the establishment of Bent's Fort. They lived in such a close relationship to the Sioux that the southern Cheyenne called them Sioux when they wanted to be insulting. After the violent campaign of 1876 General Miles had persuaded some of the northern Cheyenne to move south to Indian Territory, with the vague promise that if they did not like it, they could move back among the Sioux in Dakota.

One of the more important bands to accept the arrangement was one led by Chief Dull Knife. By 1878 his people were sick and dying; they were utterly unhappy with the amount of rations they received; there seemed to be little in common between them and the other Indians crowded onto the reservation. Interior Department officials were deaf to all pleas for a change of climate. Early one September morning Dull Knife and his people quietly slipped away from their encampment, leaving behind their tepees and all but the most necessary equipment, and commenced their flight home. After a running fight with pursuing soldiers, one that extended all the way across Nebraska, the fleeing Indians were overtaken and captured. The prisoners were held in log barracks at Fort Robinson, Nebraska, until early January 1879, when orders came to remove them to Indian Territory. With new desperation the band again broke away, this time under the leadership of Wild Hog, a younger chief, and plunged northward through snow and bitter cold. In the confusion that followed, the Indians were scattered, old Dull Knife eluding his pursuers, and in a few days those who were not captured were ridden down and killed. Dull Knife died a natural death at the Tongue River Reservation in Montana years later, an embittered man to the end.

MESSIAH CRAZE The Sioux War was the last important resistance of the Plains Indians against the United States government. As this realization came home to the tribesmen, restless in their new reservation homes, they began to turn increasingly to mysticism to recapture faded glories of their past history. The decade of the 1880s

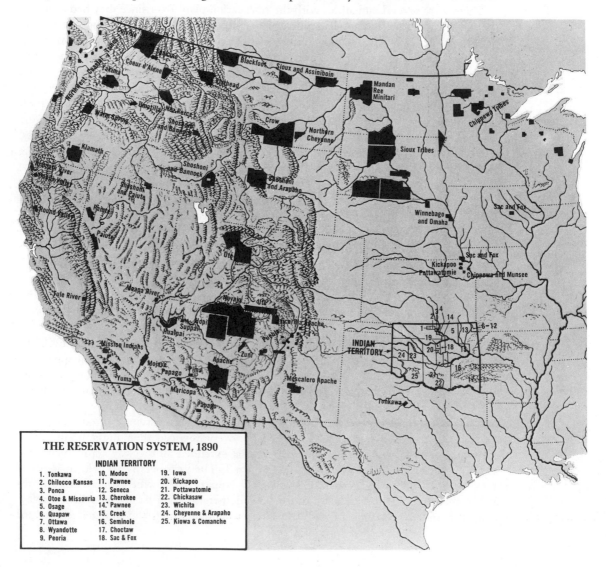

THE RESERVATION SYSTEM, 1890

INDIAN TERRITORY

1. Tonkawa	10. Modoc	19. Iowa
2. Chilocco Kansas	11. Pawnee	20. Kickapoo
3. Ponca	12. Seneca	21. Pottawatomie
4. Otoe & Missouria	13. Cherokee	22. Chickasaw
5. Osage	14. Pawnee	23. Wichita
6. Quapaw	15. Creek	24. Cheyenne & Arapaho
7. Ottawa	16. Seminole	25. Kiowa & Comanche
8. Wyandotte	17. Choctaw	
9. Peoria	18. Sac & Fox	

was particularly trying, for the imposition on the Indians of a new life not only shattered their old economy but caused a collapse of their traditional culture, which was based upon the earlier economy. Governmental attempts to break up the bands and to disperse the red plainsmen as ordinary farmers threatened to destroy the Indian as an Indian. Unable to combat the process openly, the northern reservation Indians, in particular, sought spiritual means of preserving what little remained to them.

Through all of Indian history certain individuals were thought to have peculiar and magical powers. Now, in their time of despair, rumor spread among the tribes that there was at hand the coming of an Indian messiah who would eliminate the whites and unite the Indians, both living and dead, in an earthly paradise where there was no disease and where buffalo would be plentiful. The prophets of the messiah were somewhat vague as to whether these idyllic conditions were to exist in actuality or only in the believer's mind, and whether on this earth or only in a future life after death. Most of the Indians who accepted the beliefs thought they would be fully realized in the near future.

The leading candidate for the role of messiah was a Paiute Indian named Wovoka, sometimes referred to as Jack Wilson because he lived with the family of a white rancher named David Wilson. It was through his studies of the Bible, while living with the Wilsons, that Wovoka learned about the great white medicine man, Jesus, and his miraculous healing powers. On January 1, 1889, during an eclipse of the sun, the young Paiute had a vision in which he visited heaven, saw God, and then returned to earth as the chosen Indian messiah. All he needed to establish his position was to perform a miracle. His rise to power among Nevada Indians was assured when he successfully predicted that he could cause ice to flow down the Walker River in the summertime. He did not go into details about the nature of the miracle, and the Wilson boys, who helped their adopted brother along in his profession by dumping a wagonload of ice blocks into the water upstream from the site of the performance, kept quiet about their part in the affair.

Word of Wovoka's fame spread, particularly the ghost-dance feature of his religion that urged nonviolence as opposed to the customary emphasis upon war, and before long the Dakota Sioux and Cheyenne heard of this new spiritual power. In their time of doubt and distress it appeared to answer many needs. These people, so recently defeated on the field of battle, who now fared so badly at the hands of venal agents and who suffered continually from disease and hunger, grasped at Wovoka's religion as one last hope. Many of them acquired "ghost shirts," the symbol of the new cult. The shirt was a sacklike affair, usually made of cotton, and highly decorated with designs having special mystical significance. Of great interest was the medicine man's assurance that wearers would be invulnerable to bullets. Although the idea was not new, the Indians having long worn "medicine shirts" of various kinds for protection in battle, there was great stress among the Sioux over this particular virtue of the garment. The importance of this detail lies in the fact that the Sioux used it to transform Wovoka's doctrine of peace into one of war and violence against the whites.

The ghost-dance religion probably would have burned itself out had not the Indian agents become frightened and called for help. When troops, or Indian police, came on the scene the Indians usually fled. However, trouble developed when an effort was made to arrest Sitting Bull in 1890. In the struggle that ensued, the old warrior was killed, and excitement immediately erupted among the others. In the last days of that December some 500 soldiers surrounded a band of 300 Miniconjou Sioux, two-thirds of whom were women and children, along a little Dakota creek called Wounded Knee. It was not a battle in the usual sense of the word, but a melee that occurred when the Indians refused to be disarmed, and in the shooting that followed 146 of them died in what amounted to an execution. A day or so later the frozen bodies were thrown into a mass grave. Commenting on this last great "battle" with the Plains Indians, a witness who watched the burial said: "It was a thing to melt the heart of a man, if it was a stone, to see those little children, with their bodies shot to pieces, thrown naked into the pit."

THE HUMANITARIAN VIEW The crushing of hostile Indian tribes and their isolation on reservations were but the first steps in the solution of the Indian problem. To consider the Indians as wards of the nation, to be cared for and protected, was satisfactory only on the assumption that some day they would reach maturity and provide for themselves like other adult residents of the United States. Previous efforts to give the Indians the white type of education and to teach them the trades of the whites had been far from satisfactory. Because the natives did not always share their white neighbors' views on how the good life should be lived, the attempts of both governmental and private philanthropic agencies to remodel Indian life had made an extremely small impression.

The desire to improve Indian conditions was demonstrated and reinforced about 1880 by the organization of several groups designed to study and assist the Indian: the Bureau of American Ethnology (1879), the Women's National Indian Association (1879), the Indian Rights Association (1882), the Lake Mohonk Conference (1883), and the National Indian Defense Association (1885). Not to be underestimated is the influence of Helen Hunt Jackson's books, *A Century of Dishonor* (1881) and *Ramona* (1884), which, overdrawn and romanticized as they were, had a powerful effect on the reading public. The end of any real danger from the Indians apparently inspired a more widespread tolerance and desire to help the vanquished.

To advance the Indians along the paths of white civilization two developments seemed at the time to be necessary: proper education, and the allocation of land to the Indians to be held individually rather than in a group. Such a plan offered the Indians the benefits of two highly prized American doctrines: improvement through formal learning, and an opportunity for economic betterment by participation in a program of private enterprise.

EDUCATION Indian schooling on the reservation was financed largely by the federal government. Education of the adult Indian held little promise, but many hoped that influencing the children would produce a new kind of Indian within a generation.

Unfortunately only one child in twelve was attending school as late as 1880. Moreover, the influence of the home often seemed more effective than that of the school for those children who attended day schools in the centers of Indian population. Parents tended to discount the importance of the school, and this attitude was reflected in the classroom by students who were frequently hard to discipline. About the only weapon the teacher had was the threat of expulsion, and that was an end so fervently desired by all the pupils it was seldom invoked. The answer appeared to be the reservation boarding school, where the young could be removed from home influences during the educational process. Even here, however, there was a considerable amount of failure: the boy or girl went home for vacations, found his new ways of life not in accord with the opinion of the home community, and nearly always relapsed into tribal customs.

A novel and more effective method of education was introduced by an army officer, Captain Richard H. Pratt. While in charge of Indian prisoners consigned to St. Augustine in 1875, he experimented with the idea of allowing his prisoners a measure of self-government and of encouraging them to undertake various kinds of work in the neighborhood. The results were so encouraging that Pratt was convinced that if younger Indians could be taken from their homes and given good training, at least for them the Indian problem could be solved. To realize this hope he persuaded some fifty children to go to the Negro school at Hampton, Virginia. Ultimately over a thousand Indian boys and girls attended Hampton, where they were quite successful in acquiring white customs.

But Pratt was not satisfied with anything short of an independent Indian school.

Indian School at Pine Ridge, South Dakota, 1891. As a rule Indian children did not like the white man's school. Since the parents, being exceptionally fond of their offspring, shared the view, truancy was high.

Having obtained the aid of Congress, he toured the West and collected over a hundred children, with whom he started a school in an old army barracks at Carlisle, Pennsylvania, in 1879. The children divided their time between school and farm or shop; during vacations they worked in homes of the neighborhood. At first the school was handicapped by a lack of funds and by the homesickness of the children, but ultimately it was successful and led to the establishment of dozens of similar schools. Carlisle itself never went higher than junior high school, and was finally closed when the army needed the barracks during World War I.

Nonreservation schools were effective in educating the Indians, but their facilities were limited and the long-range results were not always encouraging. Youngsters educated in the ways of the white man found themselves social and economic misfits if they went home after graduation. Their manner, dress, and attitudes were un-Indian and they found themselves socially isolated among their own kind. If the boy or girl had learned a trade, he often discovered that there was no place to employ it in the limited economy of the reservation. In this situation the young generally reverted to the old way of life.

LAND ALLOTMENT In addition to efforts to educate the Indian was the drive to make him a settled farmer. A nomadic, hunting Indian would never accept white ways—in fact he was bound to starve as the game disappeared. Most whites felt that the way to encourage the hunter to be a farmer was to divide the tribal domain and assign each individual a piece of land that would be his to cultivate and to improve. The idea of giving land in severalty was not new, but it had never been applied on a large scale. It was generally accepted by the late 1870s as inevitable; the only real questions were when and how.

The great piece of land allotment legislation was the Dawes Severalty Act of 1887, which applied to almost all Indians except members of the Five Civilized Tribes, who were not forced into line until 1898. The President was allowed to allot land whenever he thought desirable. Provided that the supply of tribal land was sufficient, the head of each family was to receive 160 acres with lesser amounts going to others; the size of these allotments was later changed. The beneficiary was permitted to choose his own land so that he might include any improvements made on particular pieces prior to the passage of the act. The land was to be held in trust for twenty-five years, after which time the Indian, or his heirs, was granted full ownership; within this period the land could not be alienated. The Indian became a citizen as soon as his land designation was confirmed. If any surplus land remained after allotment, it was to be opened for white purchase, with the proceeds going to the Indians.

From the standpoint of the Indian the Dawes Act did not work well. Often the wrong man received improved land, for Indian names were confusing to white clerks. Allottees were generally inefficient farmers living in poverty and filth and unprepared for complete ownership; as a result, when they received the final patents most of them either sold their land or lost it for debts—often fraudulent—and then became poverty-stricken dependents on charity.

Modifications of the Dawes Act brought little improvement. The permission to lease (1891) meant that allottees rented their land in order to live in idleness—and usually in comparative poverty. In 1902 the Secretary of the Interior was permitted to shorten the trust period if he thought such action was wise, which meant that in many cases the Indian lost his land in less time than the twenty-five years of the Dawes Act. The Burke Act of 1906 deferred citizenship until after fee simple title had been granted, and further legislation of 1907 and 1908 allowed the Indian to dispose of his allotment before the end of the trust period. Presumably such laws were approved by the whites who were impatient to acquire Indian land.

The process of allotment fluctuated in speed, but it was particularly rapid after 1916. By 1920 more than half the Indians had received their allotments. In round numbers, 175,000 Indians had received 37 million acres; of these allottees, 117,000 had obtained their final patents, with about 90 percent of them in Oklahoma; 35 million acres remained unallotted, the heritage of some 135,000 Indians. Presumably the end of the tribal system was in sight. In prospect of this conclusion all Indians were made citizens in 1924.

Although in theory the day was soon to come when the Indian would be a citizen and a landowner, according to white standards, conditions in the Indian country remained extremely bad. Division of the land was not producing economically independent farmers, for the Indian had not as yet achieved competence in farm management and hence was an ineffective competitor. The land soon went out of Indian hands and the former owner relapsed into poverty and squalor—the recipient of government charity. This increasing demoralization meant that the virtues of the old Indian culture were being replaced, not by a better white culture but by its worst traits. All friends of the Indian were distressed.

RETURN TO TRIBAL ORGANIZATION   In 1934, a decade after the citizenship law was enacted, the New Deal sponsored one of the most far-reaching pieces of Indian legislation ever passed by Congress. Under the Wheeler-Howard Act (or Indian Reorganization Act) of 1934, as expanded in 1936, a strong effort was made to turn back the clock and to foster the better traits of Indian culture. Land allotments in severalty were to cease, and existing trust periods and other limits on alienation were to be continued indefinitely. So-called surplus land awaiting sale was to be restored to the reservations, and new lands were to be acquired. The Indians were encouraged to continue their tribal organization; lands were to be revested to tribal ownership. The most important provisions of the act were those permitting the tribes self-government, for here the federal government explicitly recognized a principle followed by the courts since the days of John Marshall: that the Indians possessed the inherent right to rule themselves.

Although it may take several generations to assess fully the effects of the Indian Reorganization Act, several positive gains were apparent in the first three decades following its passage. During the first fifteen years after 1933 Indian-owned livestock increased from 171,000 to 361,000 head, and total agricultural income advanced from $1,850,000 to $49,000,000. Of equal interest is the fact that lands owned by Indians increased by almost 4 million acres, thus reversing a trend characterized by a steady relinquishment and diminution of holdings.

That the Indian "problem" was far from solved became apparent shortly after World War II, when the opponents of "big government" demanded that the period of federal trusteeship over the Indians come to an end at some foreseeable time. Legislation passed in 1953 provided that civil and criminal jurisdiction be transferred to specified states and, in general, allowed other states having Indian reservations to acquire such jurisdiction. In the same year a concurrent resolution made the sweeping declaration that the Indians should be released from federal supervision or control at the earliest possible time. Public reaction to such fundamental changes prevented a major uprooting of the course laid out by the New Deal, and during the late 1950s pressures against federal control of the Indians relaxed.

By the 1960s administrative planners had adopted the less radical view that assistance to the Indians ought to continue until it was much more certain that special aid to this particular group of Americans was no longer an obvious necessity. All the Indians asked was sufficient help to find for themselves, in a space age, "some measure of adjustment they enjoyed as the original possessors of their native land."

READINGS   *Paperbacks are marked with an asterisk.*

General   *Robert K. Andrist, *The Long Death* (1964), Plains tribes; William C. Macleod, *The American Indian Frontier* (1928); Jay P. Kinney, *A Continent Lost —A Civilization Won* (1937); George E. Hyde, *Indians of the High Plains* (1959), panoramic; Loring B. Priest, *Uncle Sam's Stepchildren* (1942, 1969), good on policy; Ralph H. Ogle, *Federal Control of the Western Apaches, 1848–1886* (1940); *D'Arcy McNickle, *The Indian Tribes of the United States* (1962) and *They Came Here First* (1949); William H. Leckie, *The Military Conquest of the Southern Plains* (1963); Henry E. Fritz, *The Movement for Indian Assimilation, 1860–1890* (1963); Richard H. Pratt, *Battlefield and Classroom* (1964), founder of Carlisle; Donald Jackson, *Custer's Gold* (1966), expedition of 1874; *Andrew Garcia, *Tough Trip Through Paradise 1878–1879* (1967), Montana.

Individual Tribes   See Readings for Chapter 20.

Indian Biographies   *Mari Sandoz, *Crazy Horse* (1942); *Thomas B. Marquis, *A Warrior Who Fought Custer* (1931), about Wooden Leg, a northern Cheyenne—reprinted as *Wooden Leg* (1962); Stanley Vestal, *Sitting Bull* (1932, 1957); *John G. Neihardt, *Black Elk Speaks* (1932), Oglala Sioux; Paul Bailey, *Wovoka: The Indian Messiah* (1957).

Indian Wars   No really good general study exists. Paul I. Wellman, *The Indian Wars of the West* (1947) is exciting but not penetrating. For the Nez Percés trouble see *Helen A. Howard and Dan L. McGrath, *War Chief Joseph* (1941), revised as Helen A. Howard, *Saga of Chief Joseph* (1965); Mark H. Brown, *The Flight of the Nez Percé* (1967); Lucullus V. McWhorter, *Hear Me, My Chiefs!*

(1952). D. L. Thrapp, *The Conquest of Apacheria* (1967), Apache; Edgar I. Stewart, *Custer's Luck* (1955) and *March of the Montana Column* (1961) concern the events of 1876. William A. Graham, *The Custer Myth* (1953), documentary; Robert M. Utley, *Custer and the Great Controversy* (1962); Stan Hoig, *The Sand Creek Massacre* (1961) and Marshall Sprague, *Massacre: The Tragedy at White River* (1957) are set in Colorado. A dramatic account of the flight of the northern Cheyenne is Mari Sandoz, *Cheyenne Autumn* (1953); the same story is told by a contemporary in *Edgar B. Bronson, *Reminiscences of a Ranchman* (1910, 1962). Sidney E. Whitman, *The Troopers: An Informal History of the Plains Cavalry, 1865–1890* (1962) and Don Ricky, *Forty Miles a Day on Beans and Hay* (1963) describe army problems in the Indian wars. See Hiram M. Chittenden, *History of Early Steamboat Navigation on the Missouri River* (2 vols., 1903) for comments on Indian problems. Best on the Messiah craze among the Sioux is *Robert M. Utley, *The Last Days of the Sioux Nation* (1963).

Personal Reminiscences of the Indian Wars   James H. Cook, *Fifty Years on the Old Frontier* (1923, 1957); Frazier and Robert Hunt, *I Fought with Custer* (1947); Martin F. Schmidt (ed.), *General George Crook: His Autobiography* (1946); Lucile Kane (ed.), *Military Life in Dakota* (1951), account of Philippe R. de Trobriand; Nelson Lee, *Three Years Among the Comanches* (1957); *John F. Finerty, *War-Path and Bivouac, or the Conquest of the Sioux* (1890, 1961).

Chapter 32 / THE CATTLE COUNTRY

The best-advertised feature of the post-Civil War West was the cattle business. A host of authors from Owen Wister to Zane Grey have given it a species of immortality. Painters such as Frederic Remington and Charles M. Russell have made it only slightly less vivid than did Buffalo Bill in his

Wild West Show. Movies and television have in turn made the "horse opera" a staple of American entertainment—all this in spite of the secondary economic importance of the cattle industry, and in spite of the fact that the distinctive period of the long drive lasted less than two decades.

The raising of cattle was always characteristic of the frontier. Surplus grain fed to cattle and transformed into beef could move to market under its own power, which was highly desirable in an era of poor transportation. The big cattle areas of the early nineteenth century were Ohio and Kentucky, from where stock was driven east over the mountains. As land became more expensive the center of cattle raising moved to Indiana, to Illinois, to Iowa, and eventually to the Great Plains. The more sparsely settled areas bred the cattle, which were then fattened and marketed farther east.

Far western herds appeared first in California and Texas, where millions of cattle increased as much as 25 percent a year. Before the Civil War these western herds had little value because of the lack of available markets. The California rancher could sell a limited amount of hides and tallow to the New England trader. The Texas cattleman now and then pickled some of the meat for export, and occasionally drove a few animals as far as New Orleans or even St. Louis, but such incidents were rare.

Following the Civil War, conditions changed radically as the expanding railroads reached the western plains and provided transportation to the growing cities farther east. The development during the 1870s of the tin can and of artificial refrigeration helped the big packers to dominate the national market, with locally raised and slaughtered cattle declining in relative importance. Cheap western herds, fattened on the grass of the public domain, were a good source of supply, even though they were replaced before many years with better-bred stock.

Texas cattlemen viewed the expanding railroads with hope, and in 1866 sent their first important herds over the long trail to the northern railroads. This first big drive was not very successful. Unfamiliarity with trail conditions led to the loss of many of the quarter million animals that started the trip.

ABILENE AND OTHER CATTLE TOWNS   Various men were impressed with the potential profits of $5 Texas cattle that brought $50 in the East, and speculated on the possibility of establishing points in the north from which the cattle driven from Texas could be shipped east on the newly building railroads. Most important of these speculators was the twenty-nine-year-old Illinois stockman James G. McCoy, who succeeded in obtaining special rates from the Kansas Pacific, and then chose for his center of operations the feeble little town of Abilene, Kansas, which the railroad was expected to reach in 1867. Energetic Texas advertising brought the herds to Abilene —only 35,000 in 1867, but then steadily more.

Social Hour in Cow Country. In the mining camp and cattle country, the saloon was a gathering place where refreshments were served, good fellowship sought, and occasionally long-standing grievances settled. (Library of Congress)

Abilene created the pattern of later cattle towns. The economic center of the community was the stock pens and railroad loading facilities, together with the three-story "Drovers' Cottage" and other hotels and boardinghouses necessary for visiting cattlemen. Almost equally vital were the amusements for the hundreds of cowboys who arrived from their long and tiring weeks in the saddle with a craving for bright lights and excitement, and with several months' pay in their pockets. For them the lights glittered in such saloons as the Bull's Head and the Alamo, for them the balls of the roulette wheel clicked and the cards fell in the gambling parlors, for them the Novelty Theater offered its tawdry entertainment, and for them the "Devil's Half Acre" on the other side of the tracks offered its shopworn feminine castoffs of the river traffic as a pathetic substitute for authentic romance. Drunkards and homicides were no news in Abilene in spite of sporadic and valiant efforts at law enforcement.

Although the lights of Abilene beckoned invitingly to the cowboy with money to spend, the prospect was not so pleasant for the farmers who arrived in ever-increasing numbers. They and their wives felt economic distress as the wild Texan cattle knocked down their fences, trampled their crops, and infected their stock with "Texas fever." But also they saw unhappily the streets ankle-deep in mud or dirt, the rough wooden sidewalks, the shabby store fronts, the drunkenness, the personal violence, and the prostitution. Their efforts at reform were supported in early years by various groups, including railroad management, but were opposed particularly by the merchants who stood to lose much of their profits if the town became too moral. As the number of farmers increased so did their power, but their ultimate victory was hard fought and depended greatly on the relative decline in importance of the cattle business. As early as 1871 Abilene was losing its appearance of a cattle town.

Important among the supporters of the new order were the hardworking wives of Abilene citizens. Such a woman must have felt bitter as the sun and wind of the plains dried her skin, and as hard work and excessive childbearing made her prematurely old. There must have been many days when she could have wept bitterly as she saw the few obvious pleasures monopolized by the young and immoral. Every fiber of her being called for a new and better social order where the usual social values were respected and where children could be reared without contamination from a crude and lawless society.

Abilene was but the first of a long succession of towns that utilized their railroad facilities to capture the cattle business of the plains. Although the gun-wielding Wes Hardin, an expert on the subject, has been quoted as saying of Abilene in 1871: "Have seen many fast towns, but I think Abilene beats them all," he may have changed his mind when he saw Ellsworth, Newton, Julesburg, Wichita, Hays City, Ogallala, and other plains settlements take their turn at attracting the cows and the wickedness of the West.

Best known of all the cattle towns was Dodge City on the Santa Fe, which ruled supreme as the "Cowboy Capital" in the decade 1875–1885. During the height of its reign a quarter of a million cattle arrived each year; in 1884 alone it shipped 3648 carloads to Kansas City and Chicago. Along with the cattle came the usual horde of reckless cowboys who filled the tills of the saloons, supported the gamblers in ease, patronized the disreputable houses south of the tracks, and filled the well-populated Boot Hill Cemetery. In its moment of glory Dodge City was better known than Denver or St. Paul or Kansas City.

GUN WIELDERS The cattle towns of the plains provided a fine setting for men fast with their guns, and who later dominated fiction dealing with cattle. Here congregated many men who found desirable communities where police authority did not keep pace with expanding population; United States marshals and their deputies were limited both in numbers and by political boundaries. The days of the gun wielder, however, were relatively short, his activities overadvertised, his abilities exaggerated. Frequently he has been remade into a sort of Robin Hood, with curious results when the title is applied to such a mentally inferior juvenile delinquent as Billy the Kid (William Bonney).

One peculiarity of the West was the faintness of the distinction between the lawful and the unlawful killer. Some of the most expert gun wielders, such as Wyatt Earp, were generally law-enforcement officers. Others, such as Wes Hardin, were outside the law. But consider Wild Bill Hickok, who by common knowledge was a professional gambler and a persistent murderer, and yet served at various times as an effective law-enforcement officer. Quite clearly he wandered from one side of the law to the other without the West finding this mixture of good and bad particularly unusual or deplorable.

The truth was that the western line between the law-abiding citizen and the criminal was not hard and fast. Many a cowboy lapsed now and then into cattle stealing, while not a few westerners were involved in holdups as the men with the handkerchiefs over their faces. Perhaps here is part of the reason that holdup men, including particularly Frank and Jesse James, were accorded a certain amount of sympathy. Even well-known killers were allowed to roam freely, since the western code of ethics did not always accord with statute law. Generally speaking, if one killer beat another to the draw, the bystanders merely nodded approval. If nonprofessionals were involved in the slaughter, the reaction might be one of decided disapproval that ended in an equally illegal lynching.

Any frontier town was an attractive rendezvous for men who depended on guns for their livelihood, but the mining and cattle towns offered special opportunities. Each was a predominantly male community filled with footloose and reckless men. Each was turbulent and unruly. Each emphasized the more boisterous, carefree excitement and revelry. Each had a plentiful supply of wealth that might be corralled without the usual legal niceties. Here congregated the riffraff of the West in a proper setting for the man highly skilled in the use of the six-shooter.

NATURE OF THE CATTLE BUSINESS The cattle towns existed because of the peculiar nature of the western cattle business from the late 1860s through the early 1880s. Each spring saw vast herds collected in Texas and driven north over the public domain, living on the free grass of the government. Most of the cattle, exclusive of those used to stock northern ranches, were shipped from such centers as Abilene and Dodge City. A few were fattened on midwestern farms before they were marketed. Others were wintered on the northern plains and then sent to market the following year. Conservative estimates held that some 6 million animals were driven north during the twenty years following the Civil War.

These Texas cattle that flooded northern markets were long-horned and muscular. They were able to fight their own battles and to survive bad conditions. No modern fat, stock-show prize cattle could have existed under plains conditions. The western beef of the generation after the Civil War was tough and stringy, and could be sold only because the price was low.

Sooner or later almost all Texas cattle ended at the large packinghouses of Chicago, St. Louis, Kansas City, and Omaha. Of these centers Chicago was clearly the most important. Such men as Armour and Swift had begun their fortunes with lucrative war contracts, and by the 1870s were cooperating to dominate the market and fix prices. The western cattlemen acting individually had no possible chance of fighting effectively against the packers acting in common.

THE COWBOY The best-known figure of the western cattle business was the cowboy, who has sometimes been considered as intentionally dressing in a picturesque fashion. On the contrary, his apparel was highly utilitarian. Loose, heavy, woolen trousers were sometimes covered with leather or wool "chaps" for protection against brush and cactus thorns. A woolen shirt was worn open at the throat; bright red or yellow sleeve garters ensured that the hands were free. A coat was seldom worn because it bound the arms and retained perspiration that might become dangerous with the sudden temperature changes of the plains; in its place an unbuttoned vest held watch, tobacco, cigaret papers, and matches. A large gray or brown Stetson hat had a variety of uses beyond protection from sun, rain, snow, sleet, and wind: folded it made a pillow, and in time of necessity it could be used to carry food or water. A bright kerchief knotted around the neck also was supposed to protect against cold, dust, and wind, but did not.

The cowboy took great pride in his gloves, boots, and saddle. Gloves were gauntlets of the best buckskin, usually embroidered. They were worn all year round, more as a protection against rope burns than against cold. Boots were black, tight, high-topped, and high-heeled—designed primarily for utility. A cowboy was vain of his feet, even though he hobbled awkwardly on foot. As for a gun, the usual cowboy found such hardware a nuisance, particularly since he was not a good shot. When he called on his lady friend or attended a dance he was likely to remove his gun and retain his hat.

The cowboy's saddle was designed not for fast riding but for comfort on long rides and as a stable seat for roping. It was large, broad, and heavy, weighing some 30 pounds. The stirrups were so long that the rider almost stood upright. Each man owned his own saddle, which might be highly ornamented, and in which he took great pride. For a man to sell his saddle meant that he was dead broke and had lost a measure of his self-respect. A cowboy's whip (quirt) had lashes of twelve inches or more and was carried by a thong around the wrist. His lasso (or lariat or rope) was an 18-foot, loose-running coil with which he was adept. Seldom did he practice fancy roping.

The cowboy's long solitary hours in the saddle may have been responsible for his quietness, which at times approached taciturnity. He seldom expressed his deeper emotions, and certainly never to strangers. Even in the bunkhouse among companions of long and tried friendship he was not likely to be loquacious. Typical is the story of the dude who turned to the cowboy Reddy to verify a long-winded tale of adventure. Reddy responded: "All that mought be so. But the true facts was. The bar [bear] there. The dude he stepped on a stick. Skiddoo."

The cowboy's limited conversation was couched in a vocabulary that was at once picturesque, profane, and obscene. "Damn" was only an adjective and not an expletive. Language was rich in the metaphor of the plains. " 'Bring me a rib steak about an inch thick,' I says to the waiter. 'Don't cook it too much, but just cripple the critter and drag 'er in.' " Or a man might be described as the surest shot "since a horse pistol was raised from a Colt." Or, describing a spree, one man contended that "I was so drunk that I couldn't hit the ground with my hat in three throws."

The ordinary life of the cowboy was usually dull. Riding herd by himself was not an exciting occupation. The exclusively male companionship of the bunkhouse was not thrilling. Possibly here lies the explanation of the cowboy's exaggerated courtesy

Cattle Trailing in Montana, the "Big Sky" Country. The open ranges were vast and millions of cattle were moved along or subsisted upon an empire of free grass. (Montana Historical Society)

toward the women he so seldom saw. To him a woman was either all good or all bad, and toward the "good" woman he was almost unbelievably respectful. Even the most attractive of the opposite sex could travel the plains unescorted in much greater safety than she could walk the streets of New York, Philadelphia, or Chicago. Any mistreatment of a woman might bring vindictively cruel punishment.

The typical cowboy was young and vigorous; a ranch was hardly a convalescent home for the old and sick. Being young and strong, the cowboy's ordinary ailments were seldom more than stomachaches or sore throats. Doctors were rare. The ordinary medical treatment was a dose of some patent medicine—"cholera cure," "pain killer," "Universal Liver Remedy," or even diluted horse liniment. An aching tooth was removed by the blacksmith. Surgical treatment was available, if at all, only at the nearest settlement.

The amusements of the cowboy on the ranch were necessarily limited. Horse races, roping contests, and bulldogging combined business with pleasure. Athletic contests on foot were pretty well eliminated by the high-heeled boots and by the bowed legs that came from many hours of straddling a horse. The library of the ranch was confined to a few patent medicine almanacs, mail-order catalogues, saddlemakers' catalogues, old newspapers of various dates and places, and possibly a few novels or books of travel. The cowboy ordinarily did his only reading when he was extremely hard pressed for amusement or when he wanted a new suit or Stetson from Montgomery Ward and Company.

In the evening in the bunkhouse when he got tired of slapping down greasy, dog-eared cards, the cowboy might be moved to express his soul in music. A banjo or fiddle would be dug out of hiding and everyone would join enthusiastically in the singing. High notes were given lingering vibratos; "barber shop chords" were dwelt on lovingly. Included in the repertory would always be such sentimental ballads as "Rosalie, the Prairie Flower" and "Annie Laurie." Ditties about home and death expressed sentiments impossible of ordinary statement: "I'm a poor, lonesome cowboy," "The dying cowboy," "The night my mother passed away."

Most interesting were the songs indigenous to the cattle business, and using local settings and vernacular:

> Whoopee, ti yi yo, get along, little dogies!
> It's your misfortune and none of my own.
> Whoopee, ti yi yo, little dogies,
> For you know Wyoming will be your new home!

Many of the songs of unknown authorship were extremely sad and had to be rendered with long-drawn-out pathos:

> Oh, bury me not on the lone prairie,
> Where the wild coyotes will howl o'er me;
> Where the rattlesnakes hiss and the wind blows free,
> Oh, bury me not on the lone prairie!

Unfortunately the poor cowboy's prayer was not answered, at least in the song, and "his bones now rot on the lone prairie."

When the cowboy made his infrequent trip to town, he tried to squeeze into a short time all the amusements he had missed most of the year. Poker, seven-up, faro, and keno brought the thrill of risking more money than he could afford to lose. Whiskey provided exhiliration up to the moment when he slid under the table. Prostitutes furnished a synthetic and commercialized romance. Such a spree, coming after payday or when cattle were being sold, afforded a much-needed relaxation from the usual humdrum life of the ranch. True, the cowboy drank to excess and lost his money at cards, but he was young and vigorous, and a good night's sleep brought him back to work little the worse for his experience unless he had contracted venereal disease. The worst effects usually were on the towns he visited and on his own reputation.

Most of a cowboy's life was spent on such routine occupations as riding range, caring for animals in trouble, mending fences, and repairing harness, but certain outstanding events broke the monotony. In the spring the horses had to be "broken" or "gentled" for the year's work. "Breaking" was a really descriptive word, since some of the horses actually had their spirits broken. The usual method of breaking was to snub, blindfold, saddle, and mount the horse. Then the blindfold was removed and the rider tried to keep his seat until the horse gave up the struggle. The occasion was something of a sporting event as the cowboys gathered around to see the fun. If the rider "grabbed leather" (the saddle horn) his reputation suffered; hence he held his hat in his hand to demonstrate mastery. To be thrown was unpleasant in several ways, but certainly was desirable in the rare event that the horse rolled over. Possibly one in a hundred horses was never broken to the saddle, and many remained so untamed that they bucked every time riders straddled their backs.

Controlling even the small horses of the plains was hard on the men and helps to explain why the average working life of a cowboy was estimated at seven years. Enough horses had to be broken to give each man a "string" of from six to ten, to be ridden successively and changed from time to time. Only rarely did a cowboy have a special affection for some particular horse. A good cow pony was trained to respond to the pressure of the knees rather than the pull of the reins, to cut a steer out of the herd, and to brace itself on its haunches whenever its rider threw his rope.

THE ROUNDUP   Most important in the cattleman's year was the roundup. The spring roundup was common throughout the country as a means of identifying and marking calves while they were still with their mothers. At this time cattle in Texas were segregated for the drive north. A fall roundup was less frequent in the South than in the North, where cattle were selected for the market in the autumn. Because of the unfenced country of the early days the herds were badly mixed and a roundup was a cooperative venture, crews from the various ranches dividing the territory and driving the cattle to some central spot. If this happened to be in open country, the cattle were held together by being made to mill (move in circles).

The real work of the roundup was branding the calves. Each calf was cut from the herd, roped, thrown, tied, and dragged to the fire. Cowboys sat on its head and feet while it was branded with a hot iron and sometimes had its ears notched. A tally man kept count for all ranches. When the calf was freed it ran back, bawling and frightened, to its mother. The whole operation seemed to be one of utmost confusion. The calves bawled and their mothers bellowed; dust billowed and the herd milled; the horses ran and the struggling calves were dragged; the fire gave out a fierce heat, and the cowboys sweat and cursed. But beneath this confusing surface the work actually proceeded rapidly and methodically.

Cattle brands were at first simple markings developed at the pleasure of the owners, but with the vast increase of both herds and owners the men formed associations which kept elaborate records. Certain markings were outlawed, as for example the so-called frying pan brand, which could be used to obliterate earlier markings. Common brands included the 4–28, called the four bar twenty-eight; the A2 or big A two; $\underset{\underline{}}{\geq}$ or lazy M bar; (G) or circle G; $\langle\!\langle S\rangle\!\rangle$ or diamond S; $\curvearrowright$ or flying 9. In addition some owners used various kinds of ear slits.

Many a western herd was marked by the bar sinister. On the plains there were always unmarked "mavericks" that became the property of the finders. Since a maverick was ordinarily the progeny of a cow that had met an untimely end, there was a tremendous temptation for the ambitious cowboy to help nature make orphans. Having started a herd this way, he might later be among the most ardent supporters of law and order. If he entered cattle stealing as a profession, he became an artist with a piece of hot wire or a "running iron." The $\curvearrowright$ (flying U) was not hard to alter to $\curvearrowright$ (seven up); E (big E) was easy to convert to $\dashv\!E$ (pitchfork). The early defense against such depredations was a vigilance committee, a dark night, a tree, and a coil of rope. Later the stockmen's associations hired detectives and depended more upon established law.

THE LONG DRIVE The other outstanding event in a cowboy's life in the 1870s and early 1880s was the "long drive" from Texas to the northern plains or to a shipping point in Kansas or Nebraska. The drive started in the early spring, immediately after the roundup. The most efficient size of the herd was some 2500 to 3000, accompanied by a dozen men and the necessary horses, mules, and chuck wagon. After a few days in which the herd was acclimated to the trail, the cattle moved at some 10 to 15 miles a day, or 300 to 500 miles a month. At this rate the cattle could gain flesh on the grass of the public domain.

A caravan on the long drive was headed by a trail boss, who was followed by the cook with the chuck wagon; the cook was usually an older man and the best paid of the party. Then came the herd, with the more experienced hands on either side to keep the animals from straying and to avoid collision with other herds. Also on one side was the horse wrangler with the spare mounts. In the rear came the remainder of the cowboys, who had the unpleasant job of swallowing the billowing dust from the herd so that they could round up any stragglers. All in all the work was hard, dusty, and monotonous. It did bring, however, a splendid appetite for the bacon, flapjacks, and

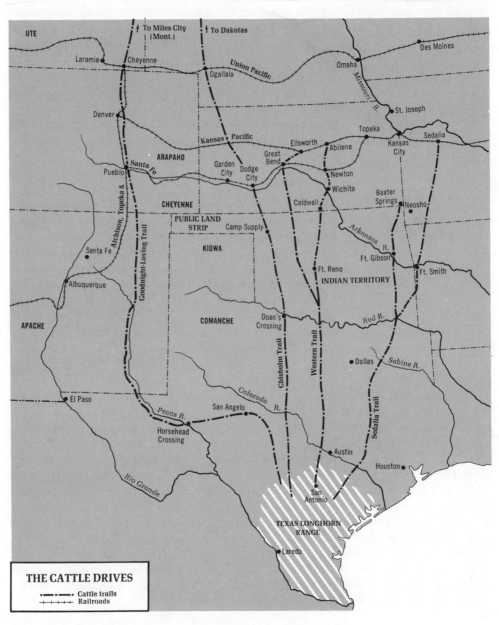

THE CATTLE DRIVES

-·-·-·- Cattle trails
+++++ Railroads

coffee that the "old lady" dished out at the end of the day. After supper the cowboy could not smoke his cigaret and roll into his blankets for a good night's sleep; he had to stand one of the three watches that prevented the herd from roaming during the night.

Numerous dangers confronted the men on the long drive. Cattle thieves and wild animals were possibilities. Swimming a river was dangerous because cattle were stupid and crowded enough to cause many deaths unless they were well handled. Worst of all was a stampede, which might be produced by any startling accident, as the shot of a gun or a flash of lightning. Cattle are easily frightened, which was one of the reasons the cowboy so frequently sang as he rode herd. Once a herd stampeded, the panic-stricken animals dashed wildly from the object of their fears. If they came to a cliff they fell to their death, if to a river they drowned, if to a mountainside they trampled each other to death. The cowboy's only hope was to head them off by hard riding and then cause them to mill. With this object in mind he took desperate chances, and not infrequently was himself trampled to death.

PERMANENT RANCHES
The striking character of the long drive tended to obscure the development of a more permanent and more important type of western cattle business all the way from Texas to Montana, and as far west as California and Oregon. As much as three-quarters of the drive from Texas has been estimated to have been used to stock the ranches of the northern plains, which in turn had large increases of their own. During the 1870s the cattle of Kansas and Nebraska increased from 500,000 to 2,500,000; of Montana from 36,000 to 430,000; of Wyoming from 11,000 to 520,000; of Colorado from 71,000 to 791,000. During these same years Henry Miller was building his cattle empire farther west in California and Oregon.

A cattle boom was evident on the western plains by the late 1870s, but even with the increasing herds the price of beef in Chicago had reached $9 a hundredweight, which meant that a steer on a Texas ranch, worth not over $5 or $6 in 1865, would bring around $35. Rumors were circulated of profits of 50 percent or more in a single year.

The boom of the late 1870s and early 1880s attracted large amounts of speculative capital, not only from the United States, but also from abroad, primarily from England and Scotland. The stockman of the past was being replaced by the corporation with capital from hundreds of small subscribers. Mammoth companies became frequent. The Swan Land and Cattle Company of Wyoming, largely Scottish, held half a million acres of land and had an investment of some $3 million. An American outfit, the J A Ranch of Charles Goodnight in the Texas Panhandle, comprised over a million acres. The Matador Land and Cattle Company was finally liquidated in 1951 for $19 million. The rapidly growing herds began to crowd the range, so that there was a mad scramble to obtain control of the available land, particularly the part of it that contained water. Land without water was useless, and there was always a lack of water. Bitter were the struggles to control springs and creeks.

Various stratagems were necessary to acquire large parcels of land, since most of it was part of the public domain, and the American land system had been developed primarily to provide small farms for settlers. Railroad land could sometimes be obtained, although the alternate-section pattern had disadvantages. Homesteaders could be bought out; in fact many men entered homestead claims in several names so that they could sell to the cattle companies. Cowboys were encouraged to acquire land by homesteading, preemption, or timber culture, and then assign it to their bosses. Of course such transactions were technically illegal, but punishment was unlikely. Only in Texas, which controlled its own land, could a large quantity be obtained legally. The most spectacular such acquisition was that of the Capitol Freehold Company, which in 1879 received a huge tract in the Panhandle in return for a promise to build the state capitol. The X I T brand soon appeared on some 160,000 cattle ranging 3,050,000 acres enclosed in 1500 miles of fence. Here was probably the world's largest ranch.

When all other methods failed, the cattleman merely fenced the needed land, regardless of ownership. The checkerboard of railroad sections might be fenced so that the alternate sections of public land were included. Fences might be strung around land to which the cattleman had no possible claim, and even across roads, so that the traveler had to cut the strands to continue his journey. This kind of illegal fencing amounted to a national scandal during the late 1870s and 1880s. President Cleveland made considerable efforts to enforce a law of 1885 that provided serious penalties, but was by no means entirely successful.

A permanent and fenced ranch, with its large capital investment, inspired efforts to produce better and hence more valuable beef. The low market value of small and scrawny Texas longhorns was not satisfactory to the large operator; hence the breed was improved by adding such blooded stock as Shorthorn, Polled Angus, and Galloway. Better stock necessitated more care, since the better the beef the fatter and more helpless the animal, and the greater the loss if it died. Water supplies were husbanded carefully, and natural running water was supplemented by wells. Hay was grown and the barns necessary for its protection were built, even though the cowboy was far from enthusiastic about digging postholes, watering stock, running a mowing machine, and pitching hay.

More competition for land and water brought a need for cooperative action by the owners. They subscribed to the cult of the self-made man and the superiority of rugged individualism, but like other contemporary businessmen were not hidebound in applying such principles. Cattlemen's associations were formed, of which the most important was probably the Wyoming Stock Growers' Association, founded in 1873; in time it operated in five states and controlled some 2 million head of cattle. Similar groups were soon created throughout the cattle country. They recorded the brands of their members, hired detectives to find cattle thieves, supervised roundups, settled conflicting claims, obtained railroad rebates, and did lobbying in both state and national legislatures. In time their various regulations were given legal authority by the several states.

The western cattle business underwent many changes during the middle 1880s. Most obvious to the casual observer was the end of the long drive. The railroads had made the drive possible, and now made it impossible by bringing thousands of farmers to the plains. These farmers naturally objected to the passage of cattle that broke their fences and trampled their grain, while local ranchers opposed outside competition. Since these farmers and ranchers were permanent residents, they could persuade the states by 1885 to pass a series of laws ostensibly designed to bar diseased cattle, which was entirely reasonable, but really aimed at the elimination of all cattle from the south. In consequence the long drive was at an end. The talk of a national cattle trail on the public domain never came to the point of action. In the future, cattle were raised on and shipped from their home ranches.

The omen of an even greater change came in 1883, when American beef exports dropped 50 percent. The next year saw a drop in domestic prices, which by 1887 descended to $2.50 per hundredweight. One drovers' magazine urged: "If you have steers to shed, prepare to shed them now." To make the stockmen even more unhappy, the year of 1885 was hard on the cattle and 1886 was even worse: a hot summer was followed by a very cold winter, and during 1886–1887 cattle died by the thousand. Some herds lost as much as 90 percent. The cattle boom was dead; the cattlemen, along with most of the West, tightened their belts to try to survive the bad times of the late 1880s and early 1890s.

The collapse of the speculative fever for cattle meant that many investors lost their money, with the mortality of large companies greater than that of small individual owners. Expenditures could no longer be on the lavish scale of the past, and the ranchers had to find cheaper and more efficient methods of operation. The trend was to sell younger animals, since the lack of local grain made fattening them too expensive. Many of the animals were sent to the corn belt for feeding before they made their appearance in the Chicago stockyards.

SHEEP   The same land that was suitable for grazing cattle could also be used for sheep, and as eastern land became more expensive, there was a tendency for an increasing proportion of American sheep to be raised in the Far West. Even before the Civil War large flocks had grazed the land of California and New Mexico, and after the war there was great expansion to the north and east. These sheep frequently were driven east, mainly to Kansas and Nebraska, to be fattened for market. The drive was at its height between 1865 and 1885; estimates have been made that some 15 million animals were driven east between 1870 and 1900. The trip normally took over seven months, a day's travel being about eight to ten miles. Sheep were more docile than cattle; the main hazard was that they might wander away and get lost.

Sheep trails, like cattle trails, were gradually closed by state action. Starting with Kansas in the mid–1880s all states acted by 1890, and in consequence sheep had to be raised without the aid of free public grass. The greatest concentration of the industry came to be in the mountain and coast states, the plains east of the mountains being dominated by cattle. By the end of the century such states as Wyoming, Montana, Colorado, Utah, California, New Mexico, and even Texas, were raising more sheep than cattle. Wyoming, the traditional home of the little dogie, discovered that although it could boast in 1886 that cattle outnumbered sheep 3 to 1, in 1900 sheep outnumbered cattle by an impressive ratio of 8 to 1.

The main activities of the sheep business were driving the flocks to good pastures, protecting them from wild animals and other dangers, caring for newborn lambs, dipping, and shearing. Shearing was done once a year and hence was a seasonal occupation, much like threshing; shearing crews worked north from early spring until late June. Ordinarily the animal was dipped before and after shearing. Wool was the only important product, since until the twentieth century mutton was hardly worth shipping.

The sheepherder compared unfavorably with the cowboy in the popular mind. No one thought of the herder as a man of romance and excitement. He lived a life of solitude, except for his dog and flock. If lucky, he might have a permanent cabin; but

Chicago's Union Stockyard. Much of the open range, formerly dominated by cattle ranchers, gave way to sheep-raising. After a certain amount of economic warfare, the "woolies" became an accepted part of pastoral America. (Chicago Historical Society)

more frequently he followed his woollies with a bedroll on his back, or possibly with a covered wagon if his employer were generous. Daily association with sheep was reported to make a man queer, although some said that the occupation attracted the odd personality. When in the cattle country you called a man a sheepherder, you had better be prepared to reach fast for your gun.

Cattlemen and sheepmen never wasted love on each other, since they competed for the same range. The cattleman insisted that sheep cropped the grass too close and ruined the range with their sharp hooves, so that no self-respecting cow would graze on land formerly used by sheep; this statement was not true except in the sense that the close cropping by sheep possibly necessitated a considerable time before the grass was tall enough to be accessible to cattle. Moreover, the cowboy looked down with disgust and contempt on the lowly, unmounted, and usually unarmed sheepherder surrounded by his dirty, smelly woollies, and in return the sheepherder deeply resented the arrogance of the cowboy. Bitter feuds resulted, with the greater number and mobility of the cowboys ordinarily permitting them to take the offensive; although the sheepmen could hire professional gunmen to make the odds more even. Outstanding examples were the Tonti Basin war in Arizona in 1887, and the struggle in the Green River country of Wyoming in 1901. Thousands of sheep were clubbed, dynamited, driven over cliffs, fed poisoned grain, or given saltpeter, which was fatal to them but did not hurt cattle; shooting was considered too expensive. At times the herders fought back by cutting fences and slaughtering cattle, and personal physical combat was far from unknown.

Vengeful clashes were not to last forever. By the 1900s the general place of cattle and sheep in the national economy had been fixed, and the days of violence were mostly past. In spite of the cattlemen's opposition to the introduction of sheep, many a rancher had actually changed from cattle to sheep. In the long run, economic forces won over sentiment.

READINGS   *Paperbacks are marked with an asterisk.*

Regional   Practically every regional history treats both cattle and sheep; see particularly Readings in Chapter 34 under Athearn, Briggs, Dale and Wardell, Howard, Johnson, Nelson, Olson, Richardson, Rister, Shannon, and Toole. *Everett Dick, *Vanguards of the Frontier* (1941); T. A. Larson, *History of Wyoming* (1965); Erna Fergusson, *New Mexico* (1951); *W. Eugene Hollon, *The Southwest* (1961).

Cattle Business   Robert R. Dykstra, *The Cattle Towns* (1968), excellent on Kansas; Lewis Atherton, *The Cattle Kings* (1961), rather miscellaneous; Edward D. Branch, *The Cowboy* (1926), reads easily; Dee Brown, *Trail Driving Days* (1952); Edward E. Dale, *Cow Country* (1942, 1965) and *The Range Cattle Industry* (1930), very good; Joe B. Frantz and Julian E. Choate, Jr., *The American Cowboy* (1955), literary image, with fine pictures; *Robert G. Athearn, *Westward the Briton* (1953), comments by British visitors; Joseph G. McCoy, *Historic Sketches* *of the Cattle Trade* (1940), classic account; *Ernest S. Osgood, *The Day of the Cattleman* (1929), a classic in the field; Louis Pelzer, *The Cattlemen's Frontier* (1936), fine study; William M. Raine and Will C. Barnes, *Cattle* (1930), interesting; Philip A. Rollins, *The Cowboy* (1922, 1936), literary flavor; Floyd B. Streeter, *Prairie Trails and Cow Towns* (1936), the long drive; Clifford P. Westermeier, *Trailing the Cowboy* (1955); N. M. Pearce, *The Matador Land and Cattle Company* (1964), Scottish company with various ranches; Gene M. Gressley, *Bankers and Cattlemen* (1966); Henry S. Drago, *Great American Cattle Trails* (1965).

Individuals   Of the numerous accounts, frequently autobiographical, a few may be mentioned. *Andy Adams, *The Log of a Cowboy* (1903), good; James H. Cook, *Fifty Years on the Old Frontier* (1959), reminiscences; L. F. Crawford, *Rekindling Camp Fires* (1926); Angie Debo (ed.), *The Cowman's Southwest* (1953); James E. Haley, *Charles Goodnight* (1936); Will James, *American Cowboy* (1942); Bruce Siberts, *Nothing But Prairie and Sky* (1954), the Dakotas. The X I T Ranch has extensive treatment in James E. Haley, *The X I T Ranch* (1953) and Cordia S. Duke and Joe B. Frantz, *6,000 Miles of Fence* (1961). Wayne Gard, *The Chisholm Trail* (1954), excellent.

Sheep   Edward N. Wentworth, *America's Sheep Trails* (1948); Charles W. Towne and Edward N. Wentworth, *Shepherd's Empire* (1945); Hughie Call, *The Golden Fleece* (1942), reminiscences; Harry J. Brown (ed.), *Letters from a Texas Sheep Ranch* (1959), good.

Bad Men   General accounts, to be read with caution, include Eugene Cunningham, *Triggernometry* (1934); Wayne Gard, *Frontier Justice* (1949); Walter P. Webb, *The Texas Rangers* (1935), good. Individual biographies need even more caution. Possibly worth mentioning are Burton Rascoe, *Belle Starr* (1941); Roberta B. Sollid, *Calamity Jane* (1958); Frank J. Wilstach, *Wild Bill Hickok* (1926); William A. Settle, *Jessie James Was His Name* (1966); *Wayne Gard, *Sam Bass* (1936); Brown Waller, *The Last of the Great Western Train Robbers* (1968).

Chapter 33 / TRANS-CONTINENTAL RAILROADS

The greatest single influence in the settlement of the trans-Mississippi West was the railroad, which made possible the settlement of the Great Plains. As the railroad extended into the wilderness the traditional life of the Indian was destroyed by the extermination of his game, and cattlemen were supplanted by farmers in all areas where farming was even only barely possible. The vast stretches of wilderness that had seemed to be the permanent home of the coyote, the buffalo, and the Indian were reduced to insignificance within a generation.

Railroads were the products of prosperity, when men controlling capital felt optimistic. The first small western boom in railroad building in the 1850s collapsed with the panic of 1857 and did not revive until the end of the Civil War. The postwar expansion was relatively short-lived because of the depression of 1873, but the decade of 1878–1888 saw the peak of American railroad building, with the bulk of construction west of the Mississippi.

EARLY TRANSCONTINENTAL PLANS   The outstanding railroad accomplishment was the completion of a half dozen transcontinental projects. The bridging of 2000 miles of plains and desert and mountain overshadowed the more humdrum business of lacing steel fingers across the level plains, although both were vital. The long roads needed feeders if they were to be profitable; the short roads were valueless without connections to more distant points. The farmer needed his connections to remote markets to be within hauling distance. Once the railroad net was completed the frontier vanished.

The idea of a transcontinental railroad went back to the early 1830s, when it was entirely chimerical; its great enthusiast of the 1840s was Asa Whitney, a New York merchant engaged in trade with China. Popular interest grew rapidly, being intensified by numerous conventions; notable were those that convened at Chicago, St. Louis, Memphis, Philadelphia, Iowa City, New Orleans, and Little Rock between 1847 and 1853. There was general agreement that any railroad across the continent was so speculative that construction entirely by private interests was highly unlikely; while construction by the government, although favored by a few, went contrary to the prevailing sentiment that business activities were run most efficiently by individuals. Hence the debate ranged around the amount and type of government assistance thought to be necessary.

During the 1850s the technical problems of building a transcontinental road were solved; but the chances of construction seemed to decline with the increasing heat of sectional controversies over its route, for the assumption was that only one road would be built in the foreseeable future. Northern interests favored a road from Chicago by the northern route. Thomas Hart Benton dreamed of a "national road" from St. Louis in his home state of Missouri. Senator Gwin of California talked of the southern route, with branches to St. Louis, Memphis, and New Orleans. Stephen Douglas advanced the obvious political solution of building along all three routes, which was suggesting the impossible.

A Section of the Early Union Pacific Railroad. Light iron rails, rough-hewn ties, and hastily made cuts such as these were not unusual along the first of the so-called transcontinentals. (Union Pacific Railroad)

The withdrawal of the South from the Union eliminated the southern route, while at the same time the desire of Congress to please the West was at its height. As between the northern and central routes, the central route was shorter, had fewer physical obstacles, and possessed a larger population. Hence the first federal charter and assistance went to the central route in the act of July 1, 1862. Charters and subsidies for other routes soon followed. The Northern Pacific (1864) was given the northern route from Lake Superior to Puget Sound. The Atlantic and Pacific (1866) was to build along the 35th parallel from Springfield, Missouri, through Albuquerque to the Pacific. The Texas and Pacific (1871) was to run from Marshall, Texas, along the 32nd parallel to San Diego. Other roads, such as the Southern Pacific, the Great Northern, and the Chicago, Milwaukee and St. Paul were built without subsidies; the Atchison, Topeka and Santa Fe had subsidies for part of its line.

THE PACIFIC CHARTER   The first transcontinental charter of 1862 did not give the entire project to a single company. The western part went to the Central Pacific of California, already in existence, largely through enthusiasm of Theodore D. Judah, a young engineer who had gone to California in 1854. Judah had become enthusiastic about railroad connections with the East, had made extensive surveys, and had interested the prosperous Sacramento businessmen Leland Stanford, Collis P. Huntington, Mark Hopkins, and Charles Crocker. These men chartered the Central Pacific, and Judah traveled to Washington, where he obtained the inclusion of the Central Pacific in the railroad plans being considered by Congress.

The eastern part of the new line was given to a group called the Union Pacific Railroad. To compromise the aspirations of Chicago and St. Louis, the eastern terminus of the main line was placed between the two cities and west of both on the 100th meridian in central Nebraska. From that point to the west the road was to follow the well-known California trail. To the east, five branches were to radiate to Kansas City, Leavenworth, St. Joseph, Sioux City, and some unnamed place on the western boundary of Iowa. This last place was ultimately fixed at Council Bluffs, although Omaha was the real terminus. This peculiar arrangement compromised various local interests. The first four of the branches were given to companies already in existence, but none was built along the route specified in the charter; most important was the Kansas Pacific, which was completed from Kansas City through Denver to Cheyenne in 1870. The fifth branch was given to the Union Pacific itself; since this was the most direct route it became for practical purposes part of the main line.

Each of the roads was given five odd-numbered sections of land on each side and within ten miles of the road, and also the right to use building materials from the public domain. In addition, a government loan was provided. It was to be $16,000 a mile over the greatest part of the route, but $48,000 in the Rockies and Sierras, and $32,000 in the region between the two ranges. Finally the act provided for organizing and financing the Union Pacific company; all its property should revert to the government if the road were not completed by 1876.

The chartering of the Union Pacific brought great rejoicing. One orator proclaimed grandiloquently: "It was said of the Nile that it was a god. I think the Pacific railroad project comes nearer being the subject of deification than anything else I have ever heard in the Senate. Everyone is trying to show his zeal in worshiping the road." But unfortunately for railroad hopes, enthusiasm did not lay tracks. Public meetings, glowing perorations, and enthusiastic newspaper publicity failed to drive a single spike. Potential investors looked dubiously at a wilderness railroad that might never pay dividends, and were not even tempted by the government loan and by land of doubtful value. Almost as soon as the company was organized, interested parties contributed $500,000 to a Washington "suspense account" to help persuade Congress to grant more aid. Their plea was effective, and in 1864 Congress doubled the land grant and reduced the loan to a second mortgage.

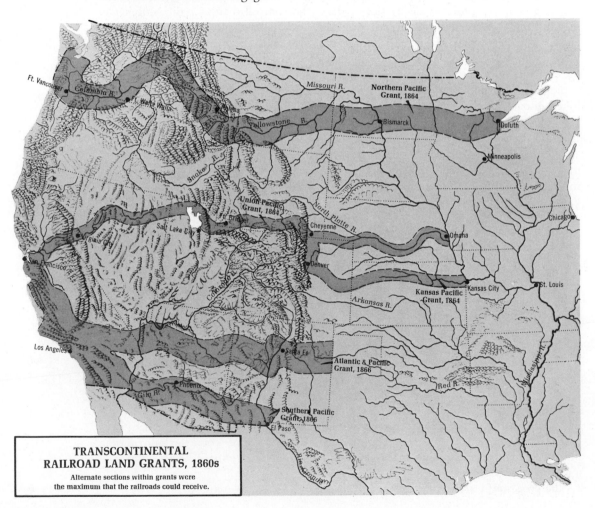

**TRANSCONTINENTAL
RAILROAD LAND GRANTS, 1860s**
Alternate sections within grants were
the maximum that the railroads could receive.

BUILDING THE UNION PACIFIC Actual construction of the Union Pacific was begun at Omaha in December 1863, but only 40 miles were completed by the end of 1865. The slowness was due primarily to the lack of enthusiasm by investors, but there was also difficulty in obtaining labor in wartime. The financial answer was finally found by T. C. Durant and his friends in the formation of a Pennsylvania corporation, the Crédit Mobilier of America, to handle construction contracts. Disregarding certain technical financial advantages of the new corporation, its main purpose was to profit by construction contracts, on the assumption that there would probably be no profit in running the completed railroad. The Crédit Mobilier was financed by advances from Durant and his friends and by short-term loans based on railroad bonds. Profits to the Crédit Mobilier on its construction contracts came, of course, from the railroad; and if they were too high, the minority stockholders suffered, but the insiders gained.

The amount of profit made by the insiders who controlled the Crédit Mobilier is still in dispute. A recent analysis by an economic historian is that congressional investigations and practically all histories have vastly overstated the profits, which actually were not unreasonable in view of the risks. On the other hand, as he points out, some of the financial and political manipulations of the men in the Crédit Mobilier were entirely deplorable. When Oakes Ames, a member of Congress interested in the Crédit Mobilier, distributed Crédit Mobilier stocks among his congressional friends with whom it would "do the most good," even the lax post-Civil War ethics were violated. When these transactions came to light, Ames was censured by the House for his conduct.

The first 40 miles of the Union Pacific were inspected and accepted by the government on January 24, 1866, and by July of the same year the road was completed 305 miles west of Omaha, forcing the overland stage to move its eastern terminus to Fort Kearny. The pace of construction increased during the summer of 1867, when a power struggle between Durant and Oakes Ames for control was settled, and when a railroad connection to the East was completed.

An adequate labor supply appeared after the Civil War, when discharged soldiers were available. The chief construction engineer was Colonel Grenville M. Dodge, a former army officer with extensive knowledge of western railroading and an unusual aptitude for handling men. The military training of these men was a real advantage, for there were many Indian depredations; and although there were troops on guard at times, the men usually had to fend for themselves. Each man was ordinarily armed, and the guns were stacked while work proceeded. When an alarm was given the boss called on his men to "fall in," and the workmen became an army. Isolated workers and men wandering off alone were always in danger of being ambushed by hostile Indians.

In the early days the Union Pacific had no rail connection with the East, and even after the completion of the Chicago and Northwestern to Omaha in 1867 many supplies had to be carried by wagon for crews working in advance of the track, a haul that might be as long as 100 miles. A special problem was the lack of wood for railroad ties, but this difficulty was partially solved by developing a method to harden cottonwood—a method that was not permanently effective.

The process of track-laying was described this way by an eyewitness:

On they came. A light car, drawn by a single horse, gallops up to the front with its load of rails. Two men seize the end of a rail and start forward, the rest of the gang taking hold by twos until it is clear of the car. They come forward at a run. At the word of command, the rail is dropped in its place, right side up, with care, while the same process goes on at the other side of the car. Less than thirty seconds to a rail for each gang, and so four rails go down to the minute! . . . The moment the car is empty it is tipped over on the side of the track to let the next loaded car pass it, and then it is tipped back again; and it is a sight to see it go flying back for another load, propelled by a horse at full gallop. . . . Closely behind the first gang come the gaugers, spikers, and bolters, and a lively time they make of it. It is a grand Anvil Chorus that these sturdy sledges are playing across the plains. It is in triple time, three strokes to a spike. . . . Twenty-one million times are those sledges to be swung—twenty-one million times are they to come down with their sharp punctuations, before the great work of modern America is completed.

The men who built the Union Pacific lived in tent cities that moved west with the road. Whenever a stretch of track was completed, all the equipment was moved to the next scene of operations. Rough streets were laid out, tents erected, and crude shacks built for the officers and the stores. To this hastily constructed town came the usual camp followers: land speculators, petty merchants, saloonkeepers, gamblers, and prostitutes. The bright lights of the saloons gleamed on streets that were ankle-deep in dust. The blare of cheap music and the allurements of the dancehall girls brought relief to the laborer after his toil. Drunkenness, immorality, and personal violence gave such towns the well-earned sobriquet "hell on wheels." More permanent cities would rise where work ceased during the coldest part of the winter, as at Julesburg, Cheyenne, and Laramie. But each spring the railroad-built houses were torn down, the tents, supplies, and furniture packed, loaded on freight cars, and moved to the next camp.

As Union Pacific construction crews approached Utah, they were given assistance by the Mormons who anxiously awaited the advent of rail transportation. Church leaders, who were also businessmen of the community, took contracts to grade and prepare the roadbed, while many of the farmers and their sons provided both labor and teams. Brigham Young, who for years has been charged with being opposed to the railroad was, on the contrary, extremely enthusiastic about it; he himself and three of his sons participated in construction. Further, during 1869, Young led the way in building a connecting line, about forty miles in length, between Ogden and Salt Lake City. This short road, known as the Utah Central, was later extended from Salt Lake City to southwestern Utah, finally to become a part of the Union Pacific line into Los Angeles.

THE CENTRAL PACIFIC   While the Union Pacific moved westward the Central Pacific was building eastward with equal vigor. The Central Pacific had even greater difficulties with finance and labor supply than had its eastern counterpart; the labor situation was finally met by importing Chinese. Even geography worked against the Central Pacific; the snow-clad Sierra Nevadas hindered the first part of the construction, while two-thirds of the Union Pacific was built on a beautifully level plain. By 1867 the Central Pacfiic had conquered its worst obstacles, and thereafter its building was rapid.

Of the Sacramento associates, Huntington was most important as financial and purchasing agent; the thrifty Hopkins was treasurer and business manager; the optimistic and energetic Crocker was in charge of construction; Stanford, who had been wartime governor of California, handled political problems within the state. This division of authority worked well, and affairs were handled with mutual confidence.

The building of the Central Pacific was done by construction companies, first Crocker and Company, and then the Contract and Finance Company. Both were owned by the men who controlled the Central Pacific, who hoped to garner the profits of construction, since they had no idea the road could be operated profitably. The methods of the Contract and Finance Company were similar to those of the Crédit Mobilier, but the accounts were muddled even more thoroughly. Huntington, Stanford, Crocker, and Hopkins held the capital stock, for which they paid with their personal notes. Then, as controlling directors of the Central Pacific they voted themselves lucrative construction contracts. The money for the construction was advanced by each man as he had the extra cash, and the only record of the transaction was his own memorandum. Profits were either put back into the business or divided equally. This scheme of bookkeeping had wonderful possibilities for preventing any close inquiry into the

Uintah, Utah. A water tank, a depot, and a scattering of tent houses usually were dubbed "cities" by optimistic westerners. (Union Pacific Railroad)

company's methods and accounts. The last bit of confusion was added with the "accidental" destruction of the company's books by fire in 1873, a date suspiciously close to the Crédit Mobilier scandal.

Both the Central Pacific and the Union Pacific were laying track furiously in 1868–1869, and then by the spring of 1869 the two construction crews came in sight of each other. The surveys began to parallel each other, and people ran to their copies of the *Statutes at Large* only to discover that although the legislation assumed that the tracks would join, there was no mandatory provision. What was to prevent each line from continuing to build and thus increase its subsidies from the federal government? Congress solved the difficulty by providing a meeting point at Promontory Summit, Utah, a little northwest of Ogden.

The final ceremony of connecting the rails took place on May 10, 1869. Governor Stanford represented the Central Pacific and Sidney Dillon, president of the Union Pacific, represented his road. Prayer was offered, congratulations were exchanged, and the last spike was driven. A report of the ceremony, including the blows of the sledgehammer, was carried to the rest of the country by telegraph. Then followed celebrations throughout the nation. Bells were rung, whistles tooted, guns fired, processions formed, banners hung, dinners held, and toasts given. The great project was complete. The West was linked with the East, and the trade of the Orient was ready for the taking.

Unfortunately for its reputation, the Union Pacific was immediately involved in all sorts of troubles. Much of it had been badly built and soon needed replacement. Financial troubles were omnipresent. The debt to the government was a source of seemingly unending trouble. Fraud, both public and private, emerged with distressing frequency. And yet the accomplishment had been great. Thanks to speculatively minded Americans, only approximately five years had been required to span the wilderness from the Missouri River to the Pacific Coast. The positive accomplishments should be given at least as much attention as the defects.

OTHER CONSTRUCTION BEFORE 1873   Other railroads with transcontinental aspirations started construction before 1873. The Atchison, Topeka and Santa Fe, chartered originally to connect Atchison and Topeka, had hopes of corralling at least the Santa Fe trade. Starting construction in the late 1860s, it was completed by 1873 to Granada, Colorado, and threatened to draw all the business of southern Colorado away from Denver. Denver's answer was the narrow-gauge Denver and Rio Grande, chartered in 1870 to build south and collect the rich minerals from the mountain area. The Rio Grande reached Pueblo in 1873, and planned to extend southward toward Santa Fe and westward to the mining area near Leadville.

Farther to the south lay the Atlantic and Pacific on the 35th parallel route. The Atlantic and Pacific was chartered only from Springfield, Missouri, and made its eastern connections by purchasing the Missouri Pacific. Construction was also started to the west, so that by 1873 the line had reached a junction with the Missouri, Kansas and Texas at Vinita in Indian Territory. Unfortunately the Atlantic and Pacific had expanded more rapidly than its financial resources permitted, and suffered keenly from the panic of 1873. Its control of the Missouri Pacific was lost and its further expansion to the west postponed indefinitely.

The Texas and Pacific, the most southerly project aided by Congress, had been preceded by a number of local Texas roads that had already done some building. It was the pet idea of president Thomas Scott, who was also vice-president of the Pennsylvania Railroad. Scott succeeded in building as far as Dallas by 1873, and to Fort Worth three years later. He was particularly anxious to reach the western border of Texas, which marked the beginning of the congressional land grant.

The most northerly transcontinental project was the Northern Pacific. Its eastern terminus was on Lake Superior so that it could draw the lake business, while its western outlet afforded a shorter route to the Far East than did the ports farther south. As a result the Northern Pacific was unusually attractive to businessmen interested in Far Eastern trade, and received more attention from the public at large than did any other road except the Union Pacific.

The Northern Pacific considered itself fortunate in having for its financial representative the famous Philadelphia firm of Jay Cooke and Company. Jay Cooke had had considerable experience in financing railroads and was also interested in western lands, notably in Minnesota. He had originally been skeptical of the prospects of the Northern Pacific, but changed his mind, partly because of a good contract of 1870 that gave him a handsome profit including a controlling interest in Northern Pacific stock.

Once Cooke entered Northern Pacific affairs he read and talked extensively, and apparently convinced himself that the road was a sound venture destined for a brilliant future. His enthusiasm for the land through which the road passed gave that area the name "Jay Cooke's Banana Belt," which accorded with the impression given by Cooke advertising that Minnesota and the Dakotas were almost tropical in their luxuriant vegetation.

The construction of the Northern Pacific began in 1870 at Pacific Junction, so named because it was the prospective meeting point for lines from St. Paul and Duluth. Three years later the road reached Bismarck, Dakota Territory, a new town named for the German chancellor. Unfortunately this construction exhausted all available funds. American investors had proved unexpectedly timid, and foreign sales almost stopped with the Franco-Prussian War. Construction and management accounts had been padded lavishly, and advertising had been excessively costly. The result was that Jay Cooke accepted the inevitable, and the doors of Jay Cooke and Company closed on September 18, 1873; the company had sufficient securities to meet its obligations, but was ruined by a lack of ready cash.

The closing of Jay Cooke and Company precipitated one of the worst financial panics in American history. Cooke had innumerable connections which suffered when he admitted his inability to pay. More important, other firms were also loaded with speculative paper, and Cooke's failure created a wave of suspicion and doubt. More banking houses closed, and commercial concerns all over the country had to follow suit. Business throughout the country was prostrated. Western railroads, being profitable only in times of great prosperity, collapsed almost simultaneously and all building stopped.

REVIVAL AND THE GOULD LINES There was little railroad construction in the West for the half dozen years after the panic of 1873, but then came the revival. For the first time the plains furnished enough traffic to make railroading profitable. The cattle business continued to expand. Mining had become a stable year-round industry conducted mostly by large companies that extracted all metals, not only gold; by 1880 the single town of Leadville, Colorado, was shipping a million dollars' worth of minerals each month. Wheat growing had become a large-scale industry in the Northwest. Such towns as Minneapolis, St. Paul, Sioux City, Omaha, Council Bluffs, and Kansas City were becoming important shipping, distributing, and packing centers. Furthermore, the railroads were learning how to eliminate violent and disastrous rate fluctuations by entering cooperative agreements that started with the "Omaha pool" of 1870.

The vast railroad opportunities attracted capable and energetic men. Railroad building, which was done by the thousand miles, and railroad strategy, which involved half a continent, brought forth bold, striking personalities—men who could lead, who could fight, and who had vision. Sometimes they were conscientious men and sometimes they were unscrupulous, but unquestionably they had capacity and genius.

Outstanding was the shrewd, capable, ruthless Jay Gould. Primarily a Wall Street operator, Gould had little interest in railroads as operating organisms, but looked on them as toys with which to play and as traps to catch the unwary. Never did he allow sentiment to interfere with the business of making money. Gould entered the western field when he purchased control of the Union Pacific in the early 1870s. He hoped to increase the price of the stock rapidly by establishing a sinking fund but was prevented by Grant's opposition, and so sold the majority of his stock—of course at a profit.

Gould saw another and more splendid opportunity in the late 1870s. He reasoned that if he bought the Kansas Pacific, he could hold the threat of competition over the Union Pacific and dictate his own terms. The Union Pacific refused to be intimidated, whereupon Gould decided that his plan had not been sufficiently comprehensive. Making one of his infrequent trips west, he bought half a dozen roads, including most notably the Missouri Pacific, the Missouri, Kansas and Texas, the Texas and Pacific, and the Denver and Rio Grande. This larger and more intimidating gun, together with Gould's connections with Vanderbilt's New York Central in the East, caused the Union Pacific to surrender. It consolidated with the Kansas Pacific and its subsidiary the Denver Pacific on terms of equality (1880). Kansas Pacific stock, being smaller in value, rose in price; whereupon Gould sold out.

Gould's speculations brought a handsome profit but left him with a number of fairly useless western roads. Further thought suggested the possibility of monopolizing the traffic of the Southwest, and so he disposed of the Colorado roads and consolidated his other holdings with the Missouri Pacific—a potentially strong road that could be held with a small investment because it had little outstanding stock. In addition to lines already in his possession he added, by complicated leasing arrangements, several others including the St. Louis, Iron Mountain and Southern, the International and Great Northern, and the Wabash. With these additions, the Gould lines made connections as far east as Buffalo; in the West they entered Chicago, St. Louis, Omaha, Kansas City, Galveston, and other important cities.

Gould was not concerned with good railroad service, and came to be one of the most hated men of his time. He was disliked both by those who worked for him and by those he served. Labor troubles (notably in 1885 and 1886) were frequent and severe and, together with the financial manipulations in which Gould was adept, led to the bankruptcy of most of the Gould roads in the middle 1880s. Before the crash came, Gould quite typically reduced his holdings to the vanishing point.

THE SOUTHERN PACIFIC The Texas and Pacific, under Scott, had made tremendous building efforts to obtain its promised federal land grant. At the same time, on the Pacific Coast, the Southern Pacific built south to Yuma, which was the prospective crossing of the Colorado River for the Texas and Pacific. The road to Yuma was of no value without eastern connections, so Huntington was sent East to see whether he could get congressional aid. Scott also went to Washington to ask for additional assistance; his funds were exhausted and his road was still on the plains of Texas.

The battle royal between Scott and Huntington for congressional support produced nothing for either man. Congress, loath to extend more aid to the Texas and Pacific, disliked helping a second line controlled by the California associates. At this point the Southern Pacific crossed the Colorado and the Yuma Indian Reservation without authority, obtained charters in Arizona and New Mexico, and continued to build east. Scott then knew he was beaten, and was glad to dispose of his stock to Jay Gould.

Gould, no Don Quixote to tilt at windmills, immediately entered an agreement with Huntington by which the two lines were to be joined near El Paso, the traffic was to be prorated, and the Texas and Pacific land grant transferred to the Southern Pacific. The lines were joined in 1882, but Congress refused to permit the transfer of the land. The joint line was entirely satisfactory to Gould, but did not realize the dream of the Southern Pacific for its own complete road to New Orleans. Continuing work east of El Paso, and utilizing Texas roads already constructed, the Southern Pacific was able to run its through trains over its own tracks from San Francisco to New Orleans late in 1882.

THE ATCHISON, TOPEKA AND SANTA FE The only other southern road to complete a line to the Coast was the Atchison, Topeka and Santa Fe, since the Texas and Pacific was never completed west of El Paso. The Santa Fe had

entered Colorado in 1873 on its way to Santa Fe, while the Denver and Rio Grande—
a narrow-gauge road—was building south toward the same place. The critical point
was Raton Pass, which the Santa Fe reached first, thus forcing the Rio Grande to confine its attention to Colorado.

The two roads also found themselves in conflict in Colorado over the Grand Canyon
of the Arkansas River (Royal Gorge), which was not wide enough for more than a
single set of tracks beyond Canon City. The Leadville boom of 1878 inspired both
roads to rush crews to the Royal Gorge, and again the Santa Fe arrived first; it was

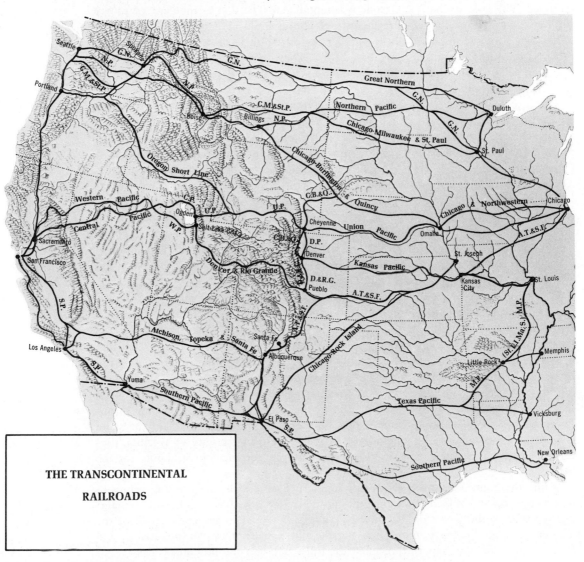

**THE TRANSCONTINENTAL
RAILROADS**

supported by irate local citizens who resented what they felt to be unnecessary delays by the Rio Grande. The Santa Fe consolidated its position by laying its track immediately, and by threatening to parallel the entire Rio Grande line to Denver with a standard-gauge road. The Rio Grande apparently threw up its hands in surrender and leased its entire line to the Santa Fe.

The Rio Grande continued its fight in the courts, and suddenly, in 1879, won all along the line. The courts gave the Rio Grande prior rights to the Arkansas gorge, and enjoined a Kansas road from operating a Colorado road. Finally, a compromise was arranged. The lease of the Rio Grande was repudiated. The Rio Grande agreed to pay for the construction along the Arkansas and not to build competitively toward the south. The Santa Fe promised not to parallel any of the tracks of its rival, but in return received the right to run its trains directly into Denver, which meant the laying of a third rail. Half of the through business of the Rio Grande was to go east by way of the Kansas road.

The agreement between the Santa Fe and the Rio Grande made certain the direction of future expansion of both roads. The Rio Grande expanded in Colorado and built toward the west, being completed to Salt Lake City in 1883; it was then able to compete for the entire haul of the Union Pacific, although by a somewhat roundabout way, by using its eastern connection with the Santa Fe, the Burlington, or the Kansas Pacific. These connections became more practical when the Rio Grande changed most of its line to standard gauge by 1890. As for the Santa Fe, its exclusion from Colorado directed its attention entirely to the south and west. In 1881 it joined its tracks with those of the Southern Pacific at Deming, New Mexico, thus completing the first transcontinental route to be opened after the construction of the Union Pacific. This junction was a landmark in western railroad construction but only incidental to the expansion of the Santa Fe, which wanted a line of its own to the coast.

When the Santa Fe considered building to the coast, its eye fell upon the Atlantic and Pacific, which had been chartered and given a land grant by Congress on the very route that was most desirable to the Santa Fe. It so happened that the Atlantic and Pacific was in bad financial circumstances, and had had to stop construction at Vinita in Indian Territory. During the latter 1880s it was owned by the St. Louis and San Francisco, popularly known as the Frisco. But the Frisco was not rich, and listened eagerly to overtures by the Santa Fe. An agreement of 1880 provided that the two roads would build jointly the western part of the Atlantic and Pacific, which meant a continuation of the existing Santa Fe line. Furthermore, the eastern parts of the Santa Fe and the Frisco were to be joined by a short link from Pierce City to Wichita, thus furnishing through connections for the Frisco and an entrance to St. Louis for the Santa Fe.

While the Santa Fe moved west, the Southern Pacific took defensive measures to maintain its control of California. First it built to Needles in California, the only remaining crossing of the Colorado River. Then it joined Gould in buying control of the St. Lous and San Francisco, thereby giving the allies a half interest in the Atlantic and Pacific. Of course the Santa Fe retained the other half and the building contract, but it was obvious that the future of the wesern part of its line could be made to suffer.

For the moment the Santa Fe seemed to abandon its dream of an independent line to the coast, for it built a connection with the Southern Pacific at the Colorado (August 1883), although the bridge was not opened until the following year. But soon it was evident that the submission of the Santa Fe was more apparent than real, for it started to rush a line that would pass through Mexico to an outlet on the Gulf of California. At this point the Southern Pacific felt compelled to compromise, and gave the Santa Fe a controlling interest in the Atlantic and Pacific, a half interest in and lease of the line from the Colorado River to Mojave, and trackage rights to San Francisco. The first big inroad had been made on the Southern Pacific control of California. Subsequently the Santa Fe built other lines in southern California, and particularly to Los Angeles. It also made connections with Galveston (1887), Denver (its own line in 1887), and Chicago (1888), and thus by the end of the 1880s was one of the strongest roads in the West.

THE NORTHERN PACIFIC   Even before the southern lines completed their through connections, the Northern Pacific had recovered from its prostration of the 1870s and showed new virility under Frederick Billings, who became president in 1880. Its development came to be linked closely with that of the Oregon Steam Navigation Company, which had been chartered in the 1860s to improve navigation of the Columbia River. The Oregon Steam Navigation Company introduced steamboats on the navigable portions of the river and short railroad lines on intervening gaps. It was obviously the best entry to Portland, and hence a controlling interest was purchased by Jay Cooke when he dominated Northern Pacific affairs. With the failure of Cooke, control reverted to the West.

When the Oregon Steam Navigation Company was badly affected by the panic of 1873, its numerous German bondholders sent Henry Villard to investigate the situation and to protect their interests. Villard was impressed by railroad possibilities in the Northwest, and began to acquire stock in companies he felt to be potentially important. Lacking sufficient funds of his own, he approached Jay Gould, who was then in control of the Union Pacific, and asked for his assistance in joining the tracks of the Oregon Steam Navigation Company and the Union Pacific along the general route of the Oregon Trail and thus give the Union Pacific an independent line to the coast. Gould agreed, but soon retired from Union Pacific affairs, and the plan was dropped.

After the Gould plans collapsed, Villard went ahead on his own initiative. Chartering the Oregon Railway and Navigation Company (1879) to combine the Oregon Steam Navigation Company and the Oregon Steamship Company, he started to build eastward. At the same time the Union Pacific moved toward the northwest, and the two roads joined their tracks at Huntington, Oregon, in 1884, thus producing a new transcontinental connection.

Just as Villard began to feel that he had the situation well in hand he received the shocking news that the Northern Pacific had resumed construction. Its completion to the coast would offer bitter competition for much of the traffic hitherto handled by the Oregon Railway and Navigation Company. Villard's first reaction was to try to induce Billings to use the Oregon road for his western connection, but Billings refused to make a definite promise. Then Villard conceived the boldest stroke of all. On the basis of no tangible security he advertised for subscriptions to a "blind pool" that he could spend as he pleased. The desired $8 million was quickly oversubscribed. Villard used the proceeds to charter the Oregon and Transcontinental Company, which took over his old roads and also bought control of the Northern Pacific. Work on the Northern Pacific continued, and the last spike was driven in September 1883 in central Montana. The main line to Seattle was completed in 1887.

Railroad Advertisement, 1867. As the Union Pacific crossed the high plains, its land department flooded the country with posters such as this. (Union Pacific Railroad)

OTHER LINES   North of the United States a Canadian road was completed during the same period, and one marvels at the persistence and energy required to cross the wide, uninhabited spaces of that country. The idea of the Canadian Pacific was conceived during the 1870s, and construction was started in 1880. Certain American bankers, such as Kuhn, Loeb and Company and J. P. Morgan, had a hand in the undertaking. The last spike was driven on November 7, 1885.

These roads were all the transcontinental projects completed by the end of the 1880s. A few others were added later. The Great Northern was completed in 1893 under the guiding genius of James J. Hill. The Chicago and Northwestern attained a junction with the Northern Pacific in Montana in 1894. The San Pedro, Los Angeles and Salt Lake City was opened between Los Angeles and Salt Lake City in 1905, and later became part of the Union Pacific system. The Chicago, Milwaukee and St. Paul finished its road to Seattle in 1909, and was particularly notable for its long electrified section across the mountains. The Western Pacific connected Oakland with Ogden in 1911 as one of the links in the dream of George J. Gould for a railroad from ocean to ocean.

The transcontinental lines completed by the middle 1880s can be summarized briefly: first (1869), the Union Pacific-Central Pacific over the central route; second (1881), the Santa Fe-Southern Pacific combination; third (1882), the Texas and Pacific-Southern Pacific combination; fourth (1882), the through line of the Southern Pacific; fifth (1883), the complete Santa Fe line; sixth (1883), the Northern Pacific; seventh (1885), the Canadian Pacific. In addition were the important fragments of the Kansas Pacific (1871), the Denver and Rio Grande (1883), and the Oregon Railway and Navigation Company (1884), to say nothing of thousands of miles of connecting and contributary links. Forty thousand miles of western railroads had been built within a decade.

The immediate and inevitable result of the building of railroads was the closing of the frontier. Population was scattered broadcast over the prairies, actually going farther into the Dakotas, Kansas, and Nebraska than the average annual rainfall warranted, and forming islands of settlement wherever the land was available farther west. The frontier that had moved so steadily across the continent was no longer visible in the new population maps of the census of 1890.

READINGS   *Paperbacks are marked with an asterisk.*

General   Accounts involving several railroads are *Robert E. Riegel, *The Story of the Western Railroads* (1926); *John F. Stover, *American Railroads* (1961); Stewart H. Holbrook, *The Story of American Railroads* (1947), popular; Glenn C. Quiett, *They Built the West* (1934); Ira G. Clark, *Then Came the Railroads* (1958), Far Southwest; Oscar O. Winther, *The Transportation Frontier: Trans-Mississippi West, 1865–1890* (1964); Julius Grodinsky, *Transcontinental Railway Strategy, 1869–1895* (1962), scholarly; practically every regional history includes some account of the railroads of the area.

First Transcontinental Railroad Robert W. Fogel, *The Union Pacific Railroad* (1960), new interpretation by an economist; Wesley S. Griswold, *A Work of Giants* (1962), satisfactory; John D. Galloway, *The First Transcontinental Railroad* (1950), emphasizes engineering; James McCague, *Moguls and Iron Men* (1964), reads well; Stanley P. Hirshson, *Grenville M. Dodge* (1967); George Kennan, *E. H. Harriman* (2 vols., 1922), detailed; Oscar Lewis, *The Big Four* (1938), Central Pacific associates; Neill C. Wilson and Frank J. Taylor, *Southern Pacific* (1952), eulogistic; David Lavender, *The Great Persuader* (1970), Huntington.

Other Roads **Denver and Rio Grande:** Robert G. Athearn, *Rebel of the Rockies* (1962). **Atchison, Topeka and Santa Fe:** Lawrence L. Waters, *Steel Rails to Santa Fe* (1950), popular; James L. Marshall, *Santa Fe: The Railroad That Built an Empire* (1945); William Greever, *Arid Domain* (1954), excellent on land grant. **Northern Pacific:** James B. Hedges, *Henry Villard and the Railways of the Northwest* (1930), scholarly; *Henry Villard, *The Early History of Transportation in Oregon* (1944), contemporary. **Missouri, Kansas and Texas:** Vincent V. Masterson, *The Katy Railroad and the Last Frontier* (1952). **Great Northern:** Joseph G. Pyle, *The Life of James J. Hill* (2 vols., 1917), best to date. **Chicago, Burlington and Quincy:** Richard C. Overton, *Burlington West* (1941), *Gulf to Rockies* (1953), and *Burlington Route* (1965), all excellent. **Gould lines:** Julius Grodinsky, *Jay Gould* (1957); Richard O'Connor, *Gould's Millions* (1962).

Nebraska Sod House. The "soddy" was the first home of many agricultural frontiersmen. Such huts were cool in summer, warm in winter, and dirty all the time. (Denver Public Library)

The Day of the Cattleman

The cattle story is an old one in American history. The Spanish utilized their vast holdings in what is today the Southwest and California to raise large herds. Most of the westward moving "Anglo" farmers kept small herds for domestic use.

However, it was not until after the Civil War, when the Great American Desert was invaded, that cattle became big business. At first it was believed that this great national pasture was good only for grazing. The day of the sod-buster was in the future. As the plowman waited behind the redoubts of the great Missouri River, herdsmen pushed their droves up the long drive from Texas. In the process the legend of the American cowboy was born.

The Long Drive. Herds such as this, leaving a snakelike trail behind them, moved across the limitless distances of the West. While on the move, the cowboys searched for open range upon which to graze and fatten. (Denver Public Library)

Branding on the Range. Before the herds moved up along the trail from Texas they were "road branded," or given a temporary identification. (National Cowboy Hall of Fame)

Branding. Identification of cattle was important. A number of methods were tried, including painting on the owner's label, but the only indelible way was to burn off the hair and leave a permanent scar called a brand. Even this was subject to "forgery" by rustlers who altered brands to suit their needs—a practice frowned upon in the West. (Library of Congress)

A Montana Cattle Ranch, about 1871. A small piece of land—the home ranch—was used as headquarters. Living quarters, sheds, and corrals usually were made of logs, or poles, of cottonwood, the only wood available in many localities. (Montana Historical Society)

The "Line Shack." Temporary dwellings, often half-dugouts, were used on the range as occasional shelter for the cowhands. Here one of the "hands" is performing a tonsorial operation on his partner, perhaps in preparation for a visit to town. (E. E. Smith Collection. Library of Congress)

The Leisure Hour. Cowboys enjoyed action and display. Frequently their arrival in town in a dead run, gave notice of brief but violent "relaxation" among the residents who patiently put up with the uproar in exchange for the money spent. (E. E. Smith Collection, Library of Congress)

Black Horsemen. Although the Negro cowboy has been only recently "discovered" by writers, he was a part of the western scene from an early date. (E. E. Smith Collection, Library of Congress)

Working the Herd. The cow pony, a highly trained animal, was an expert in helping to control the cattle. As with the sheepdog, the horse came to know instinctively what was expected. A well-trained animal made the rider's work much easier. (E. E. Smith Collection, Library of Congress)

"Nooning." On the drive, or during the roundup later on, the noon stop was welcome. Often it lasted a couple of hours as the men ate and rested before resuming their work. At night a temporary camp such as this one was set up and the night watch kept track of the herd until morning. (Library of Congress)

Crossing the Herd. Small rivers, such as this one in Montana, could be forded with relative ease. Larger and more turbulent rivers occasioned swimming, and often livestock losses were suffered in the action. (National Cowboy Hall of Fame)

End of the Trail. The ultimate destination of the cattle was the stockyard where the animals were sold to packers who processed beef for table use. (Library of Congress)

Chapter 34 / THE GREAT PLAINS

American farmers hesitated many years before occupying the Great Plains that stretched so impressively from Montana and the Dakotas south into Texas. The flat or gently rolling plains had little vegetation other than coarse grass, lacked water and wood, had few animals that could be used to supplement the pioneer's diet, and were harassed by perpetual winds. Little wonder that the farmer accustomed to more rain and more luxurious vegetation was intimidated by what he considered the "Great American Desert." The main problem that had to be solved if farming was to become possible was the lack of water, which involved also a lack of wood.

PROCESS OF SETTLEMENT   The first prairie settlements had come to eastern Kansas in the 1850s, but central Kansas and Nebraska were occupied only after the Civil War. The boom stopped temporarily, checked by the panic of 1873. A new flood came in the late 1870s and early 1880s, inundating the country from the Dakotas to Texas. Some of these newcomers were lured by the comparatively good rainfall of the early 1880s, and some by belief in the optimistic theory that increasing rainfall accompanied increasing settlement. This theory was exploded by the drier years of the late 1880s and early 1890s, and thousands were driven off their land by the specter of hunger: "In God we trusted. In Kansas we busted."

The first arrivals were often speculators, who were looking primarily for potential towns. As soon as the speculator saw a good prospect he obtained the land if possible —at times by fraud—and laid out streets and building lots, picking an impressive name such as Eureka or Garden City. Imaginative lithographed posters depicted impressive buildings, busy streets, and a river front crowded with boats even though the actual stream was no more than a small trickle. A weekly newspaper sounded the clarion call to settlers to come to a western metropolis that was to be a national railroad center. A few lots might be given as bait, as to the first woman or the first child. The promoter might make his fortune, but more frequently went broke, whereupon he tried to borrow money for a new venture. The speculator has been called a parasite, but certainly he helped produce the booms of the 1870s and the 1880s.

Most of the plains pioneers came from nearby states, as had been traditional. A good many foreign-born appeared, particularly in the North, coming either from nearby regions or from Europe. Practically every state and territory had a publicity agent or bureau to sing its attractions, both at home and abroad. Railroads also were active, selling their land and at the same time creating future traffic. They offered favorable installment terms for their land, and their agents carefully shepherded groups of the foreign-born lest some rival divert them. Special rates were given, free seeds were sometimes provided, and even temporary living quarters were arranged.

One unusual experiment in subsidized religious migration was made by the Catholic Bishop John Ireland, coadjutor bishop of St. Paul. Bishop Ireland planned to transport some of the poorer of his coreligionists from eastern United States and Europe with the objectives of improving their economic status and of reinforcing their religious faith. Buying his land from the railroads, he established ten rural village and farming communities in western Minnesota during the years 1876–1881. The results were disappointing but illuminating. Very few poor people were attracted to make the trip, and for most of those who did the experience was generally bad; for example, poverty-stricken Irish proved shiftless, and continued to demand charity for many years. The bishop had greater success with people who had some capital and had had farming experience; in other words, not with people escaping poverty but with people looking for better farms.

LAND LAWS The man who wanted to farm the western plains could theoretically homestead 160 acres, but actually found most of the available land claimed, particularly if it was blessed with fair transportation, or even prospective transportation facilities. The Homestead Act, while important, can easily be overrated, since most of the western land was never homesteaded. Entries under the Homestead Act were by no means always farmed by the original entrants; in fact, only about a third of the homestead entries between 1862 and 1882 were ever made final. Presumably many entries were made with the object of selling the claims to later comers, or, as in Wisconsin and Minnesota, holding the land only until the lumber could be removed. How many completed claims were in fact fraudulent is anyone's guess, but no one doubts that the number was considerable.

The land laws of the 1870s and 1880s seemed designed to encourage fraud. The carrying out of provisions of the Homestead Act needed close supervision that the undermanned land office was unable to give. Men "settled" by placing four stones at the corners of a prospective house, and "cultivated" by running a short furrow. With even less conscience, a man might use a toy house on wheels or erect a stick with a piece of glass to represent a wall and a window, or he would not even bother to make these gestures. If the man had money he could enter a preemption claim, which was still permitted, and he could then take up unsurveyed land; but the man who made a homestead claim had to wait until after the surveys.

Various other laws were open invitations to fraud. The Timber Culture Act of 1873 gave 160 acres to the man who planted and kept healthy 40 acres of trees not over twelve feet apart. These modest requirements were reduced five years later to 10 acres of trees; in actual fact many claims were fraudulent, with no trees planted. Also available was the ridiculous Desert Land Act of 1877, which provided up to 640 acres in various dry states at $1.25 an acre if the claimant irrigated parts of it; the amount of claimed land was considerable, but the amount of irrigation was negligible. Then too an ambitious man might buy directly from the states land they had been granted for swamp reclamation or education.

Illegal entries were a public scandal. Secretaries of the Interior asked continually and fruitlessly for a larger corps of inspectors, and pleaded for at least the proper classification of the public domain. Even the railroad land grants presented unexpected problems. Each provided that the land be forfeited if the road was not completed in a specified number of years, but the courts held in 1874 that such forfeiture required additional and specific legislation. A general forfeiture act for all unearned land grants was passed in 1890, but again the courts limited its application. The next year Congress passed a general reform act, which repealed the Timber Culture and Pre-emption Acts, modified the Desert Land Act and the commutation feature of the Homestead Act, and authorized the President to set apart forest reserves for conservation purposes. Unfortunately these reforms came too late to be of much value.

The government land available for homesteading was estimated in 1894 at 600 million acres, but because most of it was unfit for general farming, many people considered homesteading as largely a thing of the past. But land-hungry Americans were not easily discouraged, particularly when they were lured by the attractive advertising of railroads with land to sell. Montana alone saw 93 million acres filed between 1919 and 1922. Much of this land was in regions of inadequate rainfall, and many settlers went bankrupt. In the process, however, the public domain was further reduced, so that by 1929 less than 200 million acres were available for homesteading. Practically all of this land needed irrigation.

The government recognized the difficulties of homesteading in the acts of 1909 and 1912 that increased homestead claims to 320 acres and decreased the time of cultivation to three years. The results were not good. As one man put it: "The government bets title to 320 acres against your filing fee that you'll starve before proving up—and the government usually wins." Frequently the small farmer merely destroyed the good range grass, while the cattleman had no way of obtaining adequate amounts of grazing land from the government even by leasing. Very belatedly the Taylor Grazing Act (1934) improved the situation a trifle.

As early as 1878 John Wesley Powell, director of the United States Geological Survey, had made suggestions that, if adopted, would have avoided many later troubles. He insisted that general farming needed rainfall of a yearly average of at least twenty inches, and that farmers should not feel encouraged by short periods of exceptionally heavy rainfall; in fact, he located the exact areas of inadequate rainfall. For dry land he held that irigation districts should be formed with grants of 80 acres per person; otherwise the dry land should be used for stock ranches of not less than 2560 acres. Only by long and bitter experience did the nation discover that Powell was right.

Powell was also interested in conserving the natural resources of the West, but not until after 1890 did the conservation movement gain any considerable acceptance. Even then the West was generally opposed, feeling that conservation lessened economic growth and kept tax income low. Each succeeding President added more land to the forest reserves and to the national parks. Various irrigation projects have redeemed much land that otherwise would have remained useless.

FINANCES   In at least one respect the plainsman had the advantage over the earlier frontiersman. He found money easier to borrow because post-Civil War prosperity in the Northeast produced surplus funds for investment, and people raised on eastern farms looked favorably on farm mortgages as sound investments. European capitalists also showed great interest in investments in the American West. Much of this money was handled by mortgage companies, which had to raise the funds in the East or in Europe, to discover good risks, and to handle the details of the investment. During the period immediately after the war, interest rates tended to be the maximum permitted by each state, which was usually 10 to 12 percent. In practice the rate tended to be nearer 15 percent because of commissions and other fees. As the century approached its end, interest rates dropped decidedly. These high rates seemed reasonable to the western farmer, who was confident that prosperity was near.

Many farmers who contracted loans so eagerly were in time hard pressed to meet the payments, whereupon lenders came to be regarded as bloated capitalists who rolled in luxury by squeezing unmercifully poor and hardworking farmers. This point of view tended to obscure other factors. Many farmers made their first "improvement" by acquiring a mortgage, which they considered the first rung to success, as it often was. All too frequently they estimated unrealistically the prospects of the future. Sometimes the borrower had no real intention of farming, and decamped as soon as he got the mortgage money; many a New Englander saw the plains drink up his life savings as thirstily as they absorbed the inadequate rainfall. The lender was in trouble if payments were not made; usually he made every possible effort to avoid foreclosure, since he was in the business of lending money and not farming. In many cases the answer was tenancy. Although both mortgaging and tenancy might lead to a prosperous future, they might work the other way. No doubt most lending groups made profits, but they were reasonable and by no means as large as their critics later contended.

WATER   The basic problem for the plains farmer was the lack of water. As one moved west, annual rainfall contracted to a pitiful 10 to 20 inches, or even less. Not only did crops receive inadequate moisture, but the surface water which was used in early homes was polluted by cattle, and tended to be grossly inadequate or entirely lacking at certain times of the year. As for the rivers, they were not very helpful. They ran in the wrong direction to carry settlers to their new homes. In the spring they were vast, raging torrents that carried away barns, houses, and livestock. By midsummer they tended to die away to thin trickles, with no value for transportation; in fact they had little value of any sort.

Some believed that the way to get more water was to pray for rain, but many devout congregations were disappointed in the results. Another method, suggested at least as early as the 1830s, was based on the observation that rain often fell during battles. The conclusion was drawn that large explosions might produce rain, but experiments during the 1880s brought mainly frustration. The problem of aridity was generally met in later years by one of three plans of attack.

One plan, of which Hardy W. Campbell was the most important pioneer in 1883, was to get along with less water. Special varieties of wheat, barley, rye, corn, and later, other crops that required less water, were discovered. Deep plowing, sparse planting, frequent cultivation to keep down the weeds, and allowing the land to lie fallow frequently—all helped to preserve the limited moisture. Even at best, however, such "dry farming" was hazardous, and might end in complete tragedy.

A second possibility was to use subsurface water, which had long been known to exist. The main problem was that much of the water was quite deep, and that while a 20- or 30-foot well could be dug by pick and shovel, a 500-foot well was not similarly possible. The answer was drilling, which became common during the 1870s at about a dollar a foot; well-digging crews toured the country, since specialized knowledge and expensive equipment were necessary. Raising the water from a deep well was another problem. A bucket was practically impossible, and a hand pump was extremely inefficient. The answer was to harness the indefatigable wind, and during the 1870s windmills became common. Used first by stockmen and railroads, they dotted the entire landscape by the 1890s, with Fairbanks and Morse the great producer. A single mill meant one farmhouse; a group indicated a town. Of course the windmill had limited functions. It could provide for household uses, possibly a vegetable garden, and help water the stock, but not even the most optimistic farmer considered seriously cultivating 160 acres of farmland with well water.

The third possibility was irrigation, but, again, this method had limited value. Irrigation can conserve and spread water, but not create it. Estimates have been made that possibly a sixteenth of the dry land of the West can be irrigated if every drop of avail-

Breaking the Land. The "sod-buster," as cattlemen contemptuously called the prairie farmer, found the grassy surface of the land tough and resilient. But once the breaker-plow had turned the sod, plowing was easier. (Minnesota Historical Society)

able water were used, which certainly was not possible in the 1870s and 1880s. The only American experience with irrigation had been that of certain Spanish missions, of the Indians of the Southwest, and of the Mormons. When farmers experimented after the Civil War, the first results were unimpressive. Most farmers did not have the necessary capital, while capitalists were skeptical of the chances of profits. The few ventures by private companies were so costly that farming became unprofitable.

Farmers in trouble looked to the government for relief, and the government responded with the Carey Act (1894), which provided that the proceeds of sales of arid lands in several western states were to go to those states to be used for irrigation. The results were negligible. The funds were not large and the states were dilatory, possibly in part because many of the better projects were interstate in character.

The most important irrigation law was the Newlands Act of 1902, by which the federal government itself was to build irrigation projects from land sales in the arid states. The costs of such construction were to be met in time by the users of the water, the money then to be spent on other projects. By 1920 some 20 million acres had been irrigated under this program, and considerable tracts were added later. Few of the projects touched the Great Plains, however, and, all told, they served only a small part of the region deficient in rainfall.

A part of the whole water problem was the disposition of the water of western streams. Should abutting cattlemen and farmers be permitted to use the water, and to what extent? Under the English common law, accepted by most of the United States, the riparian owner could use all the water he desired as long as he did not pollute the stream or perceptibly lessen its flow. With western watercourses such a rule was folly. The water was small in amount, and anyone who used it lessened its flow perceptibly. The common law rule, if applied literally, would mean that no one could use the water.

Western reaction was to change the common law. The arid states ruled that anyone on a stream could use all the water he pleased, unless he had forfeited the right by a considerable period of nonuse. In some ways such a regulation was disastrous. Men down the stream could expect that for much of the year they would be without water. On the other hand, however, there seemed considerable virtue in allowing someone rather than no one to benefit. The immediate result was a rush to control the sources of the streams, particularly when the sources were springs.

FARMING ON THE PLAINS
Plains agriculture in the early years copied the methods and grew the products customary farther east, but modifications were necessary. The tough prairie sod required a special steel plow pulled by at least three yoke of oxen, which could break possibly one or two acres a day, but the effort required was possibly somewhat less than the Herculean efforts it took to clear forest lands farther east.

A special problem was the building of fences with inadequate supplies of wood. Unfenced land permitted the farmer's cattle to trample his corn unless perchance the Texas herds got there first. Wooden fences, with wood often hauled long distances, were estimated to cost about $500 a quarter section, which was altogether too much for the homesteader, or even for the large farmer or cattleman with his thousands of acres. Various alternates were tried. Here and there, as in Texas, stone could be used. Hedges were tried, but cattle failed to show them proper respect. Ordinary wire was also unsatisfactory because cattle soon learned that it was harmless and that a hard push would topple an entire fence.

The solution of the fencing problem came with the marketing of good barbed wire, starting in 1874. The rapidity of the use of barbed wire was amazing. In 1874 only 10,000 pounds were sold at $20 a hundredweight. In 1884 sales passed the 80 million mark, while the price had been cut in half. This rapid use of barbed wire did not mean that every farmer accepted it immediately and enthusiastically. Some were naturally conservative, others had extremely unpleasant experiences in trying to untangle and string badly rolled wire, and many a farmer cursed feelingly as his valuable stock ran into the wire and cut itself unmercifully. Ultimately the enthusiasm for barbed wire passed all reasonable bounds and men strung it not only around their own land but around railroad and government land and even over the public highways.

Special conditions provided special problems. Blizzards were dangerous on the northern plains. Prairie fires were hazardous everywhere. The particular pest was the grasshopper, notably after 1874. At times grasshoppers filled the air like a dirty snowstorm and ate all the plants but native grass and a few trees. Still hungry, they consumed every available object, including the clothes on the line. Chickens became sick from gorging on them, and livestock was reluctant to drink the water the insects had polluted. Trains were stalled by the carpet of grasshoppers that made the track as slippery as if it had been greased.

Transportation was another great problem, since rivers were unusable most of the year, roads were impassable bogs in wet weather and could hardly be improved without gravel, and canals were impossible without water. The solution was railroads, which could be built on a flat plain at 5 to 10 miles a day. Not that railroad construction was without its problems. Funds were hard to raise in sparsely settled areas, and eastern capitalists found difficulty in imagining profits for a line that was only a streak on a map that failed to show towns. Both stone and wood had to be hauled considerable distances, although a process was developed for treating the native cottonwood to retard its rotting.

The open plains country presented an excellent opportunity for the large-scale farm, concentrating on a single, simple crop such as corn or wheat, and where operations were mechanized much as in a factory. The farm machinery invented by ingenious Americans before the Civil War was improved, supplemented, and put into use on a large scale. To the harvester was added a self-binder that at first used wire, and then twine by the early 1880s; by then threshing was done with a straw-burning engine. The combine was the invention of a Michigan man, Hiram Moore, and the twine binder was the idea of a Wisconsin resident, J. F. Appleby. The early steel plow developed into a plow capable of turning four furrows at once and then into a disk gang plow. Planting came to be done by machine rather than by hand. A corn cultivator appeared before 1860, and a self-dump rake was in use during the 1880s.

The greatest concentration of large-scale farming was in the Red River Valley of the Dakotas. Much of the land was bought from the Northern Pacific, even though the railroad preferred small farmers. During the 1880s over two hundred highly mechanized farms in this district contained 1000 acres or more apiece. Such a farm might have an absentee owner or owners and a resident manager. It hired its labor, which did not need farming experience, just as a city factory did. Impressive pictures appeared of half a dozen huge harvesters in operation at one time on a single farm. Actually, the advantages of such large-scale production were not great, since most farmers could use approximately the same machinery if they worked cooperatively; moreover, there were certain inherent inefficiencies in absentee ownership. Many of these huge farms failed to weather the hard times of the late 1880s and early 1890s.

HOMES The first home of the pioneer might be a cave in a convenient hillside or a rough board shack covered with tar paper; the problem was the scarcity of wood. Finally native ingenuity hit on the use of sod; pieces of sod were cut and laid much like oversize bricks, and wood was used only for door and window cases, and for rafters.

The Harvest. Western farming depended much on the use of machinery. The reaper was used, then the grain was shocked (stacked) waiting the threshing machine. Here black and white workers gather bundles of recently cut grain. (Minnesota Historical Society)

The inside of the house might be whitewashed or plastered roughly, but it was always dark. Many a sod house backed into a hill, and with dandelions growing from the sod of the roof the family cow might wander on the roof and crash into the house. After a rain, mud might drop on the dining room table for weeks. Sometimes the walls weakened, the roof timbers slid, and the roof collapsed. Even a prolonged drought did not prevent the house from being damp. Obviously Americans were not enthusiastic about dirt houses, which may have been picturesque but were also filthy. As soon as possible they replaced them.

The furnishings of the plains house were much the same as the simple, rough articles customary for a century or more. Crude beds, tables, and chairs served until the family became more prosperous. A favorite rocking chair or a cherry table might be a reminder of a more comfortable life in the East. Lighting tended to be furnished by kerosene, which became plentiful and cheap after the Civil War. Heating and cooking were more difficult because of the lack of wood. The old-fashioned fireplace was sometimes retained, but the cast-iron stove was more usual; in any case, the hauling of wood for twenty miles or more was quite a morning chore. Buffalo chips were soon exhausted, and the hauling of wood or coal was expensive. Most easily available were sunflowers and straw, but straw burned out in one great flare that hardly baked bread or cake satisfactorily. Corncobs or stalks were often used, and quite frequently the cooking was done on a cookstove that burned corncobs and was the center of family life. An ingenious development was a stove that burned cylinders of pressed straw, which could easily be replaced as they were emptied.

The daily life of the average pioneer farmer on the prairies was not far different from that of his eastern predecessor. His clothing continued to be homemade, although more frequently from homespun (wool) than from linsey-woolsey. The cold of the northern plains led to the use of somewhat more bulky clothes. The frontier wife commonly wore calico, including a calico sunbonnet. Her dress was high-necked, long-skirted, and shapeless, with some ten yards or more of cloth draped over four or five petticoats. Her labors in making the family clothing were lightened somewhat by the use of the sewing machine which became fairly common in the 1880s. Shoes continued to be made sometimes at home, and the family went barefoot whenever possible to save leather and labor. Food emphasized pork and corn, with the traditional surplus of grease in its cooking.

While some people felt that the higher plains were quite healthful, the more common observation was an excessive amount of sickness coming from poor food, bad cooking, improper sanitation, and hard work. Common diseases included notably dysentery, ague, cholera, smallpox, and typhoid. In the more isolated districts a doctor was frequently unavailable, and dependence was placed on home remedies, patent medicine, and prayer. Such doctors as could be reached were frequently badly trained and overworked. Dentists were rare and but little consulted.

Although the life of the frontier farmer was difficult, special sympathy should go to his wife. Laboring to the limit of her strength in every waking hour she was perpetually tired, and the fatigue was not lessened by a succession of children, born usually without the benefit of a doctor. Her entire life was spent in a bare shack, which was infested by fleas, gnats, flies, and various types of vermin—and without a tree, a flower, or even a blade of grass to brighten the environment. The work, the hard water, the heat, and the perpetual wind combined to make her look old by thirty. For months on end she might not see even her closest neighbor. Little wonder that many a pioneer wife sat down and cried bitterly at the memory of her lost girlhood days spent in the East.

Religious observance tended to become less as population became more sparse, even though many families remained devout, with family prayers customary, and even though such churches as the Methodist, Christian, Presbyterian, Congregational, Catholic, and Episcopal followed the frontier closely. Communities were often rough and crude, with a high proportion of the ungodly. It was commonly said in Kansas that "there is no Sunday west of Junction City and no God west of Salina." The arrival of a church was important, not only for bringing religious consolation to men confronted by a stern Nature, but also for bringing a moderate amount of social contact in such forms as church suppers and "sociables" to people greatly in need of relaxation.

Education meant the typical one-room ungraded school, built and supported by private funds, and stressing the McGuffey readers. Not until after the frontier period did the government find itself able to take over the function of education. Texas was the first of the states to give state aid to education, but actually the Texas educational system grew slowly. A sprinkling of secondary schools and colleges was evidence of a firm belief in the values of education, although the training they offered was anything but first-rate.

No one could work every waking hour, and the prairie settler found amusement in church suppers, dinners, bees, square dances, poker and other card games, spelling matches, stereoscope and magic lantern shows, visiting, candy pulls, picnics, barbecues, and buggy rides; kissing games were common. Reading was a minor occupation as compared to such current fads as croquet and bicycling. Unfortunately some of the sports were not so innocent. On his visits to town the farmer's interests were not confined to the handful of poor stores, the tawdry traveling show, or the lyceum lecture. Saloons, gambling halls, and brothels, established mainly for the cowboy trade, proved to be not without attraction to the farmer.

NEW STATES   The settlement of the western plains made necessary further governmental changes. When Colorado became the centennial state in 1876, the greater share of the vast region beyond the Missouri remained in territorial status. Although mining rushes had brought pockets of settlement here and there, although the Union Pacific had inspired a few such towns as Cheyenne and Laramie, and although a few settlers had pushed elsewhere, as into southeastern Dakota, population in general remained sparse.

By 1880 conditions had changed. Washington, bristling with large hopes based in part on the approach of the Northern Pacific, had sufficient people for statehood, as had Dakota. But Congress failed to act. The new areas were supposed to favor the Republican faith, and for years the Republicans had not been able to control the presidency and both houses of Congress at the same time. The Democrat felt no glow of pleasure at the prospects of increasing their own handicaps. Furthermore, all conservative easterners were alarmed at the repudiation sentiment of the West.

Early in 1889, when complete Republican control of both houses was assured, Congress passed an Omnibus Bill to enable North and South Dakota, Montana, and Washington to form state constitutions preparatory to admission to the Union. All four states were admitted before the end of the same year. While these events were occurring, Wyoming and Idaho could see no good reason why they too should not become states, and so they followed their neighbors' example in adopting state constitutions, although of course without the blessing of Congress; Wyoming was unusual in providing woman suffrage. When these two new constitutions were presented to Congress, that body was not loath to acquire more Republican members, and so the two states were admitted in 1890.

After 1890 only four potential states remained in continental United States exclusive of Alaska—Utah, Indian Territory and Oklahoma, New Mexico, and Arizona. Utah

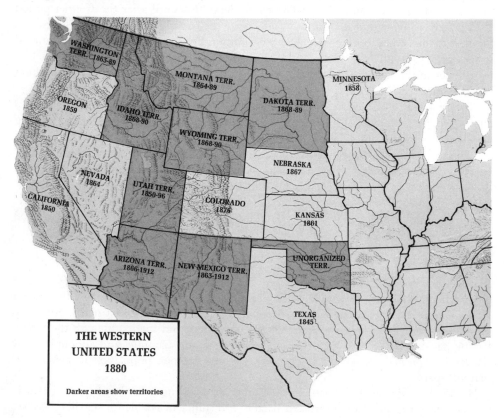

THE WESTERN
UNITED STATES
1880

Darker areas show territories

statehood had been held back by the polygamy controversy, but this situation was remedied in the early 1890s and the state was admitted in 1896.

Indian Territory presented a much more confused case. Presumably it was the exclusive domain of the Indians, but as other parts of the West were filled with white farmers, men began to look longingly at the sparsely settled Indian country. White cattlemen entered the country by leasing grazing land, which may have been illegal but was highly acceptable to the Indians. Other whites married Indian girls, apparently with some thought of the land they might thereby attain. Unauthorized traders slipped into the territory, and a few settlers edged past the army posts.

The prince of the Indian Territory "boomers" was David L. Payne, six-foot-four, handsome, jovial, and aggressive. Although Payne had had but little luck at farming in Kansas, his personal popularity had sent him to the state legislature and had then obtained for him the job of assistant doorkeeper for the federal House of Representatives. Forming a "colonization association" in 1879 he was undeterred by President Hayes's threat to eject white trespassers. Whether he really thought himself legally justified or whether he was only the paid agent of the railroads is still being argued. In any case, each year found him heading a body of settlers that would elude the soldiers for a time, only to be surrounded and ejected, after which Payne yelled persecution and planned a new party. After his death in 1884 W. L. Couch continued his work.

A new factor appeared in 1887 with the passage of the Dawes Severalty Act. Although this law was conceived by men who had the best interests of the Indians at heart, it was supported by more selfish individuals whose eyes were focused on the surplus land that would be available to whites after the allotments. The first offerings of such land came on April 22, 1889. At least 100,000 people lined up, ready for the gunshot that marked the opening. Then came the mad rush by carriage, horseback, train, and even on foot. Such towns as Guthrie and Oklahoma City came into existence overnight. Inevitably a few "sooners" had beaten the rush and picked promising tracts, whereas many of the "boomers" never did get Oklahoma land. Oklahoma Territory was created in 1890.

The first land opening was followed by others, even though the Five Civilized Tribes opposed allotments with sufficient force to prevent the division of any of their land until the late 1890s. By 1910 the allotments had been practically completed, although no one could say that whites and Indians had been amalgamated into a unified and homogeneous society. As the territory of Oklahoma expanded, governmental process kept pace, mainly because of the wishes of the rapidly increasing whites; actually the relations of the two races brought a multitude of difficulties. An enabling act of 1906 inspired a constitution, and the state of Oklahoma was admitted to the Union in 1907.

The last two states to be admitted at this time were New Mexico and Arizona. This entire area had been included (1850) in the territory of New Mexico, but this situation became increasingly objectionable to the people of Arizona as their number grew. Arizonians were far distant from the towns on the Rio Grande and were vastly outnumbered. The movement for an independent territorial status was successful in 1863, and was followed in both Arizona and New Mexico by agitation for statehood. Both regions were supposedly Democratic, but the Democrats were practically never in control of all branches of the government; moreover, Arizona's population was insufficient. When the Omnibus Bill of 1889 was passed, the Democrats tried to include New Mexico but failed.

Matters dawdled along during the succeeding years, with seemingly an indefinite delay because the Republicans had control of Congress. In 1906 there was talk of joint statehood, but although the proposal was acceptable to New Mexico it was rejected by Arizona. Ultimately separate statehood was accepted by Congress, and the two were finally admitted in 1912, Arizona being the forty-eighth state.

The settlement of the Great Plains was impressive in both speed and effects. In earlier days settlers had plodded across half the continent to settle the Pacific Coast, leaving the plains largely to the Indians, and isolating the western communities very effectively from the East. But within a generation white settlers overflowed the plains, the Indians were practically eliminated as a deterring force, and steel rails had bound together East and West. The distinctive frontier appearance of the nation seemed to disappear almost overnight.

READINGS *Paperbacks are marked with an asterisk.*

Regional The following accounts treat portions of the plains area, and include political developments for their particular regions. Gilbert Fite, *The Farmer's Frontier, 1865–1900* (1966); *Robert G. Athearn, *High Country Empire* (1960); Harold E. Briggs, *Frontiers of the Northwest* (1940), good on northern plains; Rupert N. Richardson, *The Frontier of Northwest Texas, 1846–1876* (1963); H. M. Drache, *The Day of the Bonanza* (1964), Red River Valley; W. Eugene Hollon, *The Great American Desert* (1966); Elwyn B. Robinson, *History of North Dakota* (1966), text; T. A. Larson, *History of Wyoming* (1965), text; Lewis E. Gould, *Wyoming* (1968); Edward E. Dale and Morris L. Wardell, *History of Oklahoma* (1948); Angie Debo, *Oklahoma* (1949), *Prairie City* (1940), composite picture, and *Tulsa* (1943)—all well done; Joseph K. Howard, *Montana* (1943), well written, and (ed.), *Montana Margins* (1946); Merrill Burlingame, *The Montana Frontier* (1942); Vance Johnson, *Heaven's Tableland* (1947), Texas and Oklahoma; *Bruce O. Nelson, *Land of the Dacotahs* (1946); James C. Olson, *History of Nebraska* (1955), good; William S. Prettyman, *Indian Territory* (1957), good pictures; Rupert N. Richardson, *Texas* (1943); Rupert N. Richardson and Carl C. Rister, *The Greater Southwest* (1935); Carl C. Rister, *Land Hunger* (1942), *No Man's Land* (1948), Oklahoma, and *Southern Plainsmen* (1938), good essays; Howard P. Lamar, *Dakota Territory* (1956); Herbert S. Schell, *History of South Dakota* (1961), good; K. Ross Toole, *Montana* (1959), interpretive; Stanley Vestal, *Short Grass Country* (1941); William F. Zornow, *Kansas* (1957), clear, factual; Paul F. Sharp, *Whoop-Up Country: The Canadian-American West 1865–1885* (1955); Edgar I. Stewart (ed.), *Penny-an-Acre*

Empire in the West (1968), newspaper argument over value of land on northern plains.

Plains Settlement *Walter P. Webb, *The Great Plains* (1931) is the pioneering account; Everett Dick, *The Sod House Frontier* (1937), also excellent; Edward E. Dale, *Frontier Ways* (1959), fine on plains life; A. B. Wallace, *Frontier Life in Oklahoma* (1964); Carl F. Kraenzel, *The Great Plains in Transition* (1955); *Fred A. Shannon, *The Farmer's Last Frontier* (1945), a broader focus; Merrill E. Jaschow, *The Earth Brought Forth* (1949), Iowa agriculture. More limited accounts, usually first hand, are Theodore L. Blegen and Philip D. Jordan, *With Various Voices* (1949), contemporary; Seth K. Humphrey, *Following the Prairie Frontier* (1931); *John Ise, *Sod and Stubble* (1936), Kansas; Martha F. McKeown, *Them Was the Days* (1961), Nebraska homesteading; Aagot Raaen, *Grass of the Earth* (1950), the Dakotas; *Mari Sandoz, *Old Jules* (1935), Nebraska; Zack Sutley, *The Last Frontier* (1930), the Dakotas; Ernest V. Sutton, *A Life Worth Living* (1948), Minnesota and the Dakotas; Arthur E. Towne, *Old Prairie Days* (1941).

Land Disposition *Roy M. Robbins, *Our Landed Heritage* (1942), best general account; Harold H. Dunham, *Government Handout* (1941), factual; E. Louise Peffer, *The Closing of the Public Domain* (1951), concerns 1900–1950. *Vernon Carstensen (ed.), *The Public Lands* (1963) is an excellent collection of published articles. Margaret B. Bogue, *Patterns from the Sod* (1959) treats Illinois, but with parallels elsewhere. Two accounts of Powell are William C. Darrah, *Powell of the Colorado* (1951) and *Wallace E. Stegner, *Beyond the Hundredth Meridian* (1954).

Chapter 35 / THE FAR WEST

West of the Great Plains lies almost a third of continental United States—
the Far West, comprising the Rocky mountain region and the Pacific
Coast. Like the Great Plains, most of the Far West, with some exceptions
such as western Washington and Oregon, suffers from inadequate rainfall.

During the frontier period a considerable part of the Far West was impossible to cultivate because of the absence of a constant water supply or the presence of mountains.

In the coastal area were rapidly growing cities such as Seattle, Tacoma, Portland, San Francisco, and Los Angeles, which hoped to achieve increasing commercial importance through railroad connections with the East and steamship connections with the rest of the world.

The majority of the transmontane West followed the almost stereotyped historic process of white expansion—white entrance into Indian country, racial friction, war, Indian land cessions, and finally white land acquisition under the national land laws. Typical was the white occupation of western Colorado: white arrivals, conflicts with the Ute, the Ute war of 1879, Indian cession and removal, and the land opened to white entry. Here and there were minor variations. Utah had been occupied for many years without proper titles; as a result, the opening of the first regular land office in 1869, brought a mad rush and much confusion. In Washington and Oregon special provision was made for the early settlers by the Donation Law of 1850, a sort of early Homestead Act, by which each adult could obtain a maximum of 320 acres if he were a citizen or if he had announced by December 1, 1851, his intention of becoming one.

LAND TITLES   The normal process of land disposition was impossible in much of the Far Southwest because large grants made by the Spanish and Mexican governments had been guaranteed by the United States in the Treaty of Guadalupe Hidalgo. Obviously there were problems: grants were often vague, and grantees or their heirs had in many cases lost the necessary papers. Mexican revolutions had played havoc with the original records. From time to time large claims had been asserted, and the land was resold without proper title. Some of these cases may have been legitimate mistakes, but others were certainly deliberately fraudulent.

During the years immediately after the American acquisition of the Southwest, the only important problems concerned California. Texas managed its own land, and the vast spaces between Texas and California were largely grazing land which was used without regard to ownership. California, and particularly the central part of the state, was a different matter. Into this area poured the usual horde of speculators and the equally usual horde of aggressive white farmers holding the then traditional attitude that unoccupied land should be available to anyone who wanted to use it. These men had considerable contempt for the Mexican grantees, and were not even impressed by such earlier American arrivals as Frémont, Sutter, and Bidwell. They occupied any land that appealed to them, without regard for legal ownership, and sometimes, as happened with the holders of John Bidwell's land, they had to be bribed to leave. Even the city of San Francisco had difficulty in retaining enough of its grant to establish the present Golden Gate Park.

The California Mountains, 1866. The long line of wagons was proof of the need for a railroad, which was shortly to come. (Library of Congress)

The California mess was placed in the hands of a committee of three, appointed under a law of 1851. The committee worked five years (1852 1857), trying honestly to clarify the situation justly. It listened to over eight hundred cases, and decided in favor of the original claimant in three out of four of them; but despite this record, the situation was far from satisfactory. The law placed the burden of proof on the claimant, who frequently understood English imperfectly, had paid no attention to records, and had no funds to hire a lawyer or to make the necessary trip to San Francisco, where most of the meetings were held. An additional cost was involved for all but nineteen of the cases when the decisions were appealed to higher courts, either by the original claimant or by his defeated rival. The best estimate is that the average case took seventeen years to reach a final decision, and that during these protracted and expensive proceedings many a claimant went bankrupt or was forced to sell to speculators.

CATTLEMEN AND FARMERS   The mountain West, with its supply of furs, first attracted whites, but the fur trade involved few men and no permanent settlements except a scattering of forts. Next came the miners, which meant larger numbers of men and some permanent towns, even though the average miner was footloose. The miners in turn opened the way for cattlemen and farmers. As on earlier frontiers, the raising of cattle was important, and settlement was sparse. In the early days cattle herds, as in California, had no value as meat, but this situation changed radically with the flood of miners after 1848. Cattle that had gone begging at $5 a head soared to an astronomical $500 in Sacramento in 1849; and although this highly inflated price was temporary, the demand still remained good. Not only were local cattle in demand, but new herds were attracted from Texas and the Mississippi Valley. All the way from Idaho to New Mexico the cattle business boomed, particularly after the expanding railroad network provided more adequate transportation.

As on the Great Plains, the cattleman was soon replaced by the regular farmer, since the growing of grains and vegetables was more lucrative per acre than the cattle business. In a few places such as the Willamette Valley rainfall was adequate for varied farming, but as with any frontier, and particularly one with a deficiency of water, the main early crop was wheat. The future states of Idaho, Washington, and Oregon particularly emphasized wheat culture, with the business extending as far south as the Sacramento and San Joaquin valleys of California; high mechanization was practiced by the 1880s. Some areas, such as the Pendleton–Walla Walla region, remain important for wheat production even today. Irrigation was not used in the early days; even the Sacramento Valley did not have it until after 1900.

IRRIGATION   Water for farming in the Far West came in time very largely from irrigation, with supplies drawn from streams; the digging of wells was tried, particularly in New Mexico in the 1870s and Oregon in the 1880s, but this method met with limited success and in many cases outright failure. The Mormon example of successful irrigation was available; but non-Mormon farmers did not have the backing of a theocratic state, and hence their first ventures could be no more than small, privately dug ditches during the 1850s. Such efforts had various limitations, depending on knowledge, money, and manpower, and the farmers were limited to the areas close to a few rivers, such as the Rio Grande, San Joaquin, or South Platte, or their tributaries. Some of the more important rivers were not useful, as, for example, much of the Colorado and Columbia, because of their deep gorges. Long ditches were economically impossible. In consequence the early results could only be considered even moderately successful on the premise that a little water was better than none.

Successful irrigation was necessarily a group effort, as the Mormons had demonstrated with their thousands of miles of communal ditches, and the inclusion of water rights in every land transfer. Various kinds of group efforts were possible. A town might take action; a famous example was the effort of the Greeley colony in Colorado in the 1870s; incidentally, the colony's efforts were entirely empirical, and there is no evidence of being influenced by information from Utah even after the first failure. One object of any town was to obtain water for domestic use, but neither the Owen River project of Los Angeles nor the Hetch Hetchy project of San Francisco came until after 1900.

Another irrigation possibility was the incorporated company that sold water for a profit, just as another company might sell steel or kerosene; a variant came when a railroad such as the Northern Pacific organized and financed irrigation companies, presumably in the hope of increasing railroad traffic. Still another possibility was the company organized by the farmers of an area to provide for their own needs; in many cases, such as the important "76 Land & Water Company" of the 1880s in the San Joaquin Valley of California, the company might also sell water to nonmembers.

Almost inevitably, and despite the highly touted individualism of the American farmer, government was finally brought into the picture. California was the leader in this field. The legislature of 1875 authorized a West Side Irrigation District that could issue bonds for the construction of a canal in the lower San Joaquin Valley, but the courts threw out the law as unconstitutional. A dozen years later the Wright bill authorized the formation of water districts with elected officers and with the power to issue bonds and to levy taxes. The act was not immediately successful, even though the courts held it to be constitutional. There were continual fights between large and small owners and between old and new projects; of the fifty districts created under the law, only four were successful. Despite these difficulties, however, other arid states soon copied the idea.

The federal government also was soon involved. Its first action was the Desert Land Act of 1877, which gave a man the right to occupy up to 640 acres of dry land if he made a down payment of 25¢ an acre; he could complete his claim within three years if he showed irrigation of part of the land and paid an additional $1.00 an acre. Why a bona fide settler would want to pay $1.25 an acre when he could get 160 acres free under the Homestead Act, and another 160 acres at $1.25 an acre without improvement under the Pre-emption Act, is not clear. The later presumption has been that the Desert Land Act was essentially a gift to the cattlemen, who had their cowboys enter the land

and do the smallest possible amount of irrigating, such as throwing a pail of water on the ground. Only slightly over a quarter of the land entered under the law was finally purchased, and the amount of irrigation was negligible.

The federal government entered the scene more directly with the Carey Act of 1894, but with disappointing results. Then came the Newlands Act of 1902, under which considerable progress was made. (See Chapter 34 for a discussion of the Carey and Newlands Acts.) Although the federal projects were profitable for the farmers who benefited directly and for the states in which such farmers lived, there was increasing question about the desirability of increasing farm production at the very time when farm surpluses were depressing prices.

Irrigation naturally was concentrated in the areas of the main rivers and their tributaries, including the basins of such rivers as the Colorado, Sacramento, San Joaquin, Rio Grande, and Columbia. The Colorado has been particularly interesting because of the long-drawn-out contest between California and Arizona over its control, and also because of the rather curious history of its harnessing. Observant men were impressed in the 1890s by the fact that the Colorado River was higher than the desert, and argued that merely scraping a ditch would permit its water to flow into what its promoters

A California Mission, 1835. The endeavor was to convert the Indians and to improve their lot. (Bancroft Library, University of California)

called rather grandiloquently the Imperial Valley. The first water arrived in 1901, along with the flood of opportunity-seeking farmers; the most optimistic hopes of the promoters were realized, and the Imperial Valley became one of the garden spots of the nation. Unfortunately the river did not cooperate with proper docility. First it threatened to cut off all water by filling the ditch with sand, and then in 1905–1906 it threatened to change its course and put the entire valley under water. A two-year fight, with E. H. Harriman—who temporarily controlled the Southern Pacific—furnishing most of the financial ammunition, was necessary before the river was confined to its present channel. The newer, All-American Canal, was completed in 1941. By the 1890s a large share of the agricultural land west of the Rockies had been irrigated.

UTILIZING THE WARM WEATHER   The prevailing heat in the area from Texas through southern California was regarded as nothing but a handicap by each early visitor as he plodded across the arid countryside. With the passing of time, the beginning of irrigation, and the improvement of transportation, men began to speculate that what grew in semitropical regions in other parts of the world might also grow in the American Southwest. An olive boom of the mid-1800s soon collapsed but later revived. Figs and avocados were tried, but they were not important until after 1900. Cotton booms occurred periodically, particularly as Mormons seeking self-sufficiency moved south into Arizona. Cotton was grown in California as early as the 1840s, but was not successful for many years. Several other experimental crops were less dependent on warm weather. Sugar beets were grown successfully by the Mormons, although they had trouble with the refining. Tobacco aroused much interest in the 1870s, but apparently the curing process proved a failure. One ever-recurring mania, both East and West, was silk culture. California went slightly mad on the subject during the 1860s, with the legislature in 1864 offering bounties, and with 10 million mulberry trees reported being grown in 1869; obviously the industry failed of permanent success.

Outstanding among the warm weather crops are citrus fruits. Most important have been oranges, cultivation of which began in earnest with the work of William Wolfskill at Los Angeles in the 1840s. Early development was hampered by the lack of proper varieties of fruit, inadequate knowledge of methods of cultivation, and the absence of the necessary transportation; the number of producing orange trees in 1860 was only 4000, and by 1870 no more than 40,000. Expansion was rapid after that year. Railroad construction solved the transportation problem, the first carload lot being shipped in 1877. Also during the 1870s the navel orange from Brazil was introduced by way of a missionary and the Department of Agriculture. The most serious insect pest was brought under control in the late 1880s by the introduction of the ladybird (or ladybug) from Australia, and oil heaters were in use to combat frost by the late 1890s. The Sunkist Fruit Growers' Exchange, organized to provide uniform sorting, packing, grading, and promoting, came into existence under a different name in the 1890s.

Although the center for citrus fruit was for a long time in southern California, other areas gradually took up citrus culture. The industry spread as far north as the Sacramento Valley in the 1870s. Moving east it gradually entered Arizona and New Mexico. Most important of the Arizona agricultural areas was the valley of the Salt River, a branch of the Gila. Irrigation began in the 1860s, bringing into existence the City of Phoenix, which in 1871 boasted proudly of 300 residents. Phoenix in time became the largest city and the capital of the territory, taking the latter honor from Tucson, which was far from happy at being left with the second prize—the state university. The commercial growing of citrus fruit in the Phoenix area did not begin until the early 1890s.

A quite different value was attached to winter warmth by ice-bound northerners, who viewed with enthusiasm the absence of cold weather, and who, after 1870, included many health seekers. The focus of interest was the Los Angeles area; such places as the desert communities of Palm Springs and Las Vegas and the "sun valley" of Arizona and New Mexico came later. The added attractions of open gambling and easy divorce in Nevada did not make their appearance until the twentieth century. Although the delights of the climate of southern California had been extolled even before the gold rush, any considerable influx of visitors and permanent residents waited for the completion of railroads. Retired Iowa farmers could hardly be expected to visit southern California by stagecoach. Estimates have it that by 1900 at least a quarter of the residents of southern California had originally come for their health.

The greatest southern California boom of the nineteenth century occurred in the Los Angeles area in the years after 1880. Hordes of people were lured by what was described as the nearest approach to the Garden of Eden since the beginning of the world. They inundated the streets of Los Angeles, trading enthusiastically in the city's many newly opened lots, and often boasting of large wealth—at least on paper. Suburban areas expanded rapidly, with the enthusiasm for Pasadena rivaling that for Los Angeles; when Azusa was opened, eager buyers stood in line all the preceding night, and it was reported that the second in line refused a thousand dollars for his place. Burbank, San Bernardino, Santa Barbara, and dozens of other towns shared the general excitement, even though some of them, such as Sunset, Gladstone, Chicago, and La Ballina, failed to remain for posterity. This particular boom soon collapsed, but the total growth of the region continued with greater and greater acceleration.

FRONTIER WAYS The newer frontier areas of the Far West were very small spots in a very large country. The population map of 1870 showed that west of the Rockies there was little population until one reached the San Joaquin and Sacramento valleys of California, the Willamette Valley of Oregon, and the Puget Sound area. The one exception was the Mormon settlements stretching north and south from the Great Salt Lake. Although settlement expanded during the next decade, the greatest impression conveyed by the population map of 1880 is the large white areas that indicate fewer than two inhabitants per square mile. Even the map of 1890 showed but little concentration of population, thus demonstrating the greater difficulties of settlement than was true, for example, of the Ohio Valley.

The frontier of the Far West repeated in many ways the developments farther east,

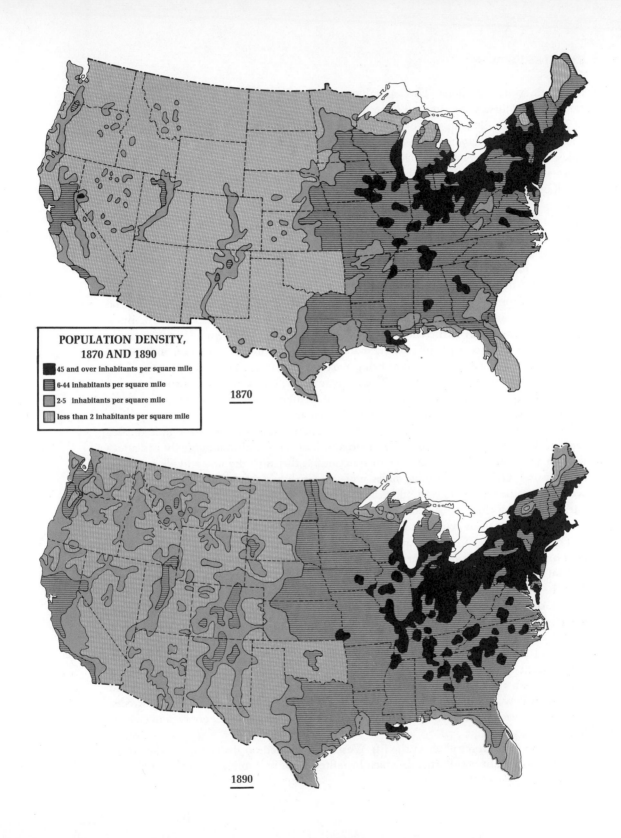

POPULATION DENSITY,
1870 AND 1890

■ 45 and over inhabitants per square mile

▨ 6-44 inhabitants per square mile

▦ 2-5 inhabitants per square mile

▯ less than 2 inhabitants per square mile

1870

1890

but with some variations. The log cabin, crude homemade furniture, limited foods, candles, and horse transportation were just as typical of frontier Idaho as they had been of frontier Ohio. Health was precarious because of improper diet, lack of knowledge, and poor medical services; the usual family depended on home remedies, patent medicines, and superstition. Small children were in particular danger from the time they were ushered into the world by a midwife until they managed to survive the usual childhood diseases.

Like other frontier areas, the Far West had a great preponderance of men over women. One result was that women had scarcity value and were usually treated with exaggerated respect—that is, the "good" women were treated with adoration, for the West distinguished clearly between "good" and "bad." Good women were supposed to be as delicate and modest as their eastern sisters, and there is something humorous in the long discussions of how women could with modesty negotiate the mud holes that existed on every street, or in the fulminations of an early Oregon editor who protested the sight of a woman riding astride a horse, holding that it caused "the blush of shame to mantle even the cheek of manhood." The scarcity of women at least partly explains why women were given certain advantages, as in higher education and voting. The shortage led Asa S. Mercer to bring parties of New England girls to Oregon in 1864 and 1866. These "Mercer girls" came as teachers, but to no one's surprise proved in even greater demand as wives; unfortunately their number was not sufficient to supply even a perceptible part of the western demand.

The scarcity of women did not mean that the farm wife could sit back in luxurious ease while her husband waited on her hand and foot. Husbands undoubtedly had affection for their wives, but the division of functions at that time did not provide for feminine leisure. The man's farming duties were seasonal, but the family ate its meals and wore its clothes every day of the year. Furthermore, the wife usually cared for the garden and the chickens, acted as family doctor and nurse, and arranged most social events. The fiction of women as the weaker sex had little supporting evidence.

The towns of the area were quite similar to earlier plains towns, though they probably originated in mining rather than in the cattle business. They were few in number and small in size, with nothing that could be called a city between Denver (population 4749 in 1860) and the Pacific Coast, except Salt Lake City. The western town, like its eastern predecessor, was characterized by unpaved streets, wooden sidewalks, hitching posts for the horses, inadequate and polluted water, and periodic epidemics, particularly smallpox. The streets of the mining town were lined with saloons, gambling halls, and brothels; every man went armed, life was held cheaply, and efforts at law enforcement were only the most cursory. Just as had happened in the East, the town changed with the arrival of the farmers. Sometimes the mining town disappeared and sometimes it was transformed into a more orderly community, with improved streets, less blatant vice, and ultimately a better water system, streetcars, telephones, and electric lights.

Naturally, the larger cities in the Far West were located on the coast. To the north, the most important was Portland, which benefited from its dominance of the Columbia

Valley; theoretically it should have been an extremely important port, but actually it was greatly handicapped by the sandbars at the mouth of the river. On Puget Sound were Tacoma, which advertised itself as "The Second Greater New York," and Seattle, whose site was apparently something of an accident. All the northern cities grew rapidly after the completion of the Northern Pacific and the Great Northern, and all had great hopes of trade with the Orient because they were closer to Asia than the cities farther south; these hopes were never realized completely.

Southern California had an excellent harbor at San Diego, but unfortunately San Diego had little useful backcountry and poor connections with the East, and failed to grow satisfactorily. Los Angeles had several disadvantages; it had no natural harbor, there were no early railroad connections to the East, and it was too far south for trade with the Orient; its population in 1880 was only 11,183. In time an artificial harbor was constructed at San Pedro, and railroad connections were made; the Southern Pacific was finished from San Francisco in the 1870s, and both this road and the Santa Fe made connections from the East in the 1880s; a boom resulted, but still the Los Angeles population of 1890 was only 50,395. Farther north the old capital of Monterey, with its modest harbor, failed to grow.

San Francisco was supreme among the coastal cities. Situated on one of the finest harbors of the world, it was the natural outlet for the large part of California's agricultural production that came from the San Joaquin and Sacramento valleys, and was the nearest point for eastern railroads; quite naturally the first transcontinental railroad had its western terminus at Oakland, across the bay. Then, too, San Francisco had the luck to be near the first gold discoveries and the rich Nevada finds. It is not surprising that the city of the Golden Gate was the financial, industrial, transportational, and cultural center of the Pacific Coast. It was the largest manufacturing center of the Far West and had the most imposing labor troubles. The dynamic, rabble-rousing Dennis Kearney centered his activities at San Francisco during the 1860s and 1870s when he and his co-workers, shouting "the Chinese must go," inspired mob action all the way from Puget Sound to San Diego; the San Francisco riots involved the looting of the Chinese district. The Kearney groups, operating under the name of the Workingmen's Party of California, ultimately obtained such measures as changed taxation, a railroad commission, banking control, and restrictions on the Chinese, but the results were somewhat less utopian than had been hoped.

CULTURAL DEVELOPMENTS   The Far West in the generation after 1850 was primitive in many ways, but no one desired that it remain that way. Most of the men and women had come from older communities farther east, and longed for the advantages of a more advanced civilization. Basic in everyone's mind was the advantage of education. Even the mining camps and the early farming communities established schools; obviously most of them were poor, but really surprising was the willingness of parents to part with some of their hard-earned money to provide education for their children. One of the first acts of each territorial legislature was provision for a public school system, although New Mexico was somewhat delayed by language difficulties. Free schools were developed rapidly and early; for example, Arizona authorized free schools in the early 1870s when the total population of the territory was certainly less than 20,000.

Education above the elementary school level was largely private in the early years, as had been true in the East under similar circumstances; but the public high school appeared in San Francisco as early as 1856, and by the end of the century was replacing the private school everywhere in the Far West. Teachers colleges generally came into existence by the 1880s and 1890s. Schools that called themselves colleges were opened as early as the 1850s, but were usually in fact preparatory. Private colleges—frequently church-connected, as Whitman and Gonzaga—soon lost their precedence in favor of the state universities. The University of Utah (1850) experienced many vicissitudes before it became prosperous. The University of Washington was opened at Seattle at the surprisingly early date of 1861. The University of California admitted its first students in 1869, and in a few years moved its campus from Oakland to Berkeley; its second president was the well-known Daniel Coit Gilman. The University of Nevada was established at Reno in 1874, when the territory had a population of not over 50,000. The University of Oregon opened its doors at Eugene in 1876, being helped in its early years by gifts from Henry Villard. The University of New Mexico came into existence at Albuquerque in 1889. The University of Idaho was opened at Moscow in 1892, when the population of the state was no more than 90,000. The University of Arizona opened its agricultural school at Tucson in 1890 and the university proper a year later, at a time when the population of the territory was no greater than that of Idaho. Such developments, no matter how feeble in their early years, showed the very real concern of the West with education.

Religion was also a matter of vital concern to the early settlers, who considered it the basis for proper morality—the foundation upon which society rested. The Catholic Church had been dominant in the Southwest when the United States took possession, and had also worked in the Northwest, but Protestant faiths, such as the Methodist, Baptist, Presbyterian, Episcopalian, and Congregational, were carried along by the farming frontier. As on earlier frontiers, the diversity of sects made the building of churches and the paying of regular ministers difficult; hence early meetings were often held in local schoolhouses or in private homes. The basic religious aspirations of the people received testimony in their willingness to deny themselves luxuries, even necessities, to support a settled minister.

Among the first cultural institutions carried west of the mountains was the printing press. The first newspaper was the *Oregon Spectator*, a four-page, semimonthly publication that began its ephemeral existence at Oregon City in 1846. The famous *Alta California* was first published in San Francisco in 1849. The *Deseret News* appeared in 1850 in Salt Lake City. As early as 1859 the *Weekly Arizonian* started publication at Tubac, but it soon moved to Tucson. The number of such early papers is surprising. In addition there were pioneer magazines, such as the *Golden Era* (San Francisco) in 1852 and the *Utah Magazine* (Salt Lake City) in 1868. Best known was the *Overland*

Monthly (1868), particularly when it was edited by Bret Harte. Among the western writers to obtain national recognition were Bret Harte himself, Mark Twain, Helen Hunt Jackson the novelist, and Joaquin (Cincinnatus H.) Miller the poet; none was a native of the area—hardly surprising in view of the proportion of Far Westerners born elsewhere.

Leisure-time activities were numerous. Horse racing, candy pulls, barn dances, singing schools, church sociables, and baseball were among the dozens of amusements available to even the poorest farm family. School exercises were attended regularly

The One-room Schoolhouse. Millions of Americans learned the three R's in such surroundings. The young scholars may well be laboring through McGuffey's readers, used by several generations. (Denver Public Library)

by parents who glowed with pride at the recitations of little John or Jane. The Fourth of July was celebrated with more enthusiasm than discretion. Although most of the amusements were simple, there were numerous choirs and orchestras, serious lectures, and other more demanding cultural activities. A Philharmonic Society appeared in Portland in 1859, and a California Art Association made its bow at San Francisco in 1871. Preconceptions of the lack of cultural aspirations in the West should be severely jolted by the fact that a presentation of *The Messiah* at Salt Lake City in 1875 attracted an audience that paid $1200 for the concert.

Dramatic performances were also received with enthusiasm. In the earliest days all performers were amateurs, and the results are best left to the imagination. Regular theaters were opened early, even during the gold rush in the larger towns; for example, at Sacramento in 1849 and at San Francisco in 1850. Despite the rough audiences a considerable proportion of the plays came from the pens of such classic playwrights as Shakespeare, Knowles, Bulwer-Lytton, and Payne. The star system then current permitted the Far West to see such well-known actors as Edwin Booth, James H. Hackett, Caroline Chapman, and Ellen Tree. Particularly identified with the West were the beautiful Adah Isaacs Menken, the notorious and fascinating Lola Montez, and Lotta Crabtree, who started her stage career as a child prodigy touring California. Since most of the West was sparsely settled, and the bigger towns were far apart, most theatrical productions in the early years were by third-rate touring companies playing in poor surroundings. Not until the 1880s and later did large cities and improved transportation permit more adequate presentations. A little later Chautauqua and the motion picture made their contributions to filling the western demand for drama.

The Far West repeated in general the developments of more easterly frontiers, but a semifrontier status was often retained for many years. Long after the frontier had theoretically "disappeared" large sections of the Far West had so few people that they showed on population maps as white areas indicating fewer than two to the square mile. In consequence many a farmer, stockman, or sheepman remained in fact a frontiersman long after most of the United States was absorbed by a high-speed, mechanical civilization.

READINGS   *Paperbacks are marked with an asterisk.*

General   Accounts involving more than one state include Earl Pomeroy, *The Pacific Slope* (1965); *W. Eugene Hollon, *The Southwest* (1961); Gilbert Fite, *The Farmer's Frontier, 1865–1900* (1966); Oscar O. Winther, *The Great Northwest* (1947); Sidney Warren, *Farthest Frontier* (1949), all phases of life in the Pacific Northwest; John W. Caughey, *History of the Pacific Coast* (1933), good.

Individual States   The material for this chapter has widely spread sources. **California:** Walton E. Bean, *California* (1968); John W. Caughey, *California* (1953); Andrew F. Rolle, *California* (1963); Ralph J. Roske, *Everyman's Eden: A History of California* (1969); Leonard Pitt, *The Decline of the Californios* (1966),

Spanish-speaking Californians; Robert G. Cleland, *From Wilderness to Empire* (1959), *The Cattle on a Thousand Hills* (1941), southern California, and with Osgood Hardy, *March of Industry* (1929), economic history; William W. Robinson, *Land in California* (1948), scholarly; George R. McMinn, *The Theater of the Golden Age in California* (1941), scholarly; Mary B. Ritter, *More Than Gold in California* (1933), reminiscences of a woman physician. **Oregon:** Alice H. Ernst, *Trouping in the Oregon Country* (1961), amusements of the 1850s and 1860s; Arthur L. Throckmorton, *Oregon Argonauts: Merchant Adventurers on the Western Frontier* (1961), scholarly, centering in Portland; D. W. Meinig, *The Great Columbia Plain* (1968); Nellie M. Young, *An Oregon Idyl* (1961), wife of Presbyterian minister, who made a trip to Oregon 1883–1884. **Washington:** Archie Binns, *Northwest Gateway* (1941), popular on Seattle; Paul L. Beckett, *From Wilderness to Enabling Act: The Evolution of the State of Washington* (1968). **Nevada:** Effie Mack, *Nevada* (1936); *Richard G. Lillard, *Desert Challenge* (1942), interpretation rather than history. **New Mexico:** Warren A. Beck, *New Mexico* (1962), brief and clear; Erna Fergusson, *New Mexico* (1951), reads well. For Utah see the Readings for Chapter 25. For fringe states see the Readings for Chapter 27 for Colorado and those for Chapter 34 for Montana.

Water and Health   For irrigation see Albert N. Williams, *The Water and the Power* (1951), largely after 1900. Earl Pomeroy, *In Search of the Golden West* (1957) is good on the tourist business. John E. Baur, *The Health Seekers of Southern California, 1870–1900* (1959), good monograph; Billy M. Jones, *Health-Seekers in the Southwest, 1817–1900* (1967), scholarly.

Chapter 36 / WESTERN PANACEAS

The westward-moving farmer had strong beliefs and desires. He was working to acquire wealth, and although he expected to advance on his own individual merits, he did not allow this individualism to prevent him from joining in various group efforts, as for example in building a home or

538

forming a claims club. He was quite willing to use the government if such action seemed desirable. In many states he was sufficiently numerous to be dominant, and even in the federal government he had considerable power, as witness his support of Jeffersonian and Jacksonian democracy, of Manifest Destiny, of internal improvements, and of reforms in land legislation. The West never had a congressional majority, but could often be successful by alliance with other groups.

During the generation after the Civil War the West threw its support to several political movements that were based primarily on economic aspirations. Such actions did not mean that the farmers were all going broke. Actually, the real income of farmers rose between 1865 and 1900 despite a decline in farm prices in the 1870s and 1880s. Technological improvements were great, interest rates declined in the 1880s and 1890s, and foreign markets were good.

Farmers may have been doing satisfactorily according to abstract and general economic analysis, but there were nevertheless difficulties. Many an individual farmer did badly, possibly because of conditions over which he had no control, such as insect pests or drought. Then too he often felt frustrated that wealth came to him so slowly, while at the same time the pleasures of an industrial society became increasingly evident. Newer writers such as Hamlin Garland and Ed Howe registered distress over the monotony and lack of beauty in farm life, and farmers' children were drawn in increasing numbers to the alluring opportunities and pleasures of the city.

Dissatisfied farmers could not believe that any lack of success was due to their own failures. A more palatable theory was that the rules of the game had been developed by selfish and privileged easterners, and should be changed by law to open the way for a rosy future for the western farmer. The political protest movements that developed from this belief were naturally greater in times of depression, when the number of the discontented was greater, and declined in periods of prosperity.

Western protest movements were geared mainly to farmers' desires; manufacturing and commerce were growing, but the dominant way of life was farming. The West was of course not the only farming area of the United States. Every state had important agricultural interests; and even if the state were Maine, Pennsylvania, or Alabama, these interests might be supreme part of the time. As a result the West might expect considerable sympathy and support from other sections of the country. Stated differently, the West had a high concentration of the very widespread industry of American agriculture.

Western protest movements were not only farmer-oriented, but, more specifically, directed in behalf of the farmer who was in debt. The West was consistently a debtor area. Few rich people moved to the frontier, and the meager capital of the West was strained to the limit to buy land, stock, and machinery. Additional funds were sought in the East and in Europe through mortgages, held not only by individuals but also by states and municipalities to provide such improvements as railroads.

The Granger Movement. The Patrons of Husbandry, more commonly known as Grangers, represented an early effort on the part of the farmers to achieve a national organization. (Granger)

GRANGERS   The first national farm organization to arouse enthusiasm in the West after the Civil War was the Patrons of Husbandry, organized in 1867 by a clerk in the Department of Agriculture. The local unit of the organization was known as a grange, which led to the members being called Grangers, and the whole agitation the Granger movement. At its beginning it was secret in nature, with a ritual modeled on that of the Masons or of the Odd Fellows. Socially, it was designed to alleviate the isolation and loneliness of farm life by encouraging such activities as parties, picnics, lectures, and concerts.

On the economic side the Grange emphasized cooperative enterprises in such fields as creameries, warehouses, insurance, purchasing, and manufacturing of farm machines and equipment such as plows and threshers. The troubles of the farmer were presumed to come partly from poor methods of production and high prices of what he bought, but even more from excessive costs of marketing. The feeling was that farmers acting individually had little control of the market as against manufacturers, elevator operators, packers, and railroad men, who tended to monopolize their products or services. The farmer cooperative enterprises were generally unsuccessful, partly because of inefficient management and partly because of the severe competition by larger business corporations intent on maintaining market control. One incidental but positive result was the establishment in 1872 of the Mongomery Ward Company, endorsed by the Grange, to sell goods more cheaply by mail.

The Patrons of Husbandry grew slowly until the farmers were struck by the panic of 1873, whereupon the membership hit its peak of over 1.5 million. The center of the movement was the upper Mississippi Valley, particularly Illinois, Wisconsin, Minnesota, Iowa, and Missouri; but there were widespread repercussions so that even today one can find Grange halls as remote as New England. The original idea of staying out of politics proved impractical, and the Grangers supported new small parties with such names as Independent, Reform, or Anti-Monopoly; these appeared in eleven western states, and usually allied with one of the older parties as a balance of power. Various public officials with Granger sympathies were elected to both the federal and state legislative bodies.

The Granger movement coincided with a growing disenchantment with the railroads and a widespread effort to regulate them. The idea of regulation was far from new, and went back not only to railroads but to other such common carriers as turnpikes and canals. Supporters were not limited to farmers, but included important groups of commercial and other business interests. Obviously, everyone who used the railroads desired lower rates except the relatively few who were granted special reduced rates. The general idea was to buttress private ownership and competition rather than to limit it. One of the main objectives was to give the various localities what they considered "fair" rates and which would allow them to compete effectively.

A series of "Granger laws" was passed in the years 1871–1878 by Illinois, Missouri, Wisconsin, Minnesota, California, and Iowa, and other states followed later. They were supported by business interests as well as by farmers. Two general provisions were common. Included in each law except that of California was a schedule of maximum rates for the railroads of the state. Each state provided a commission to inspect the roads of the state, prosecute violators of the law, and recommend needed legislation; only Missouri, however, gave the commission the power to adjust the specified rates of the original law. In addition to these major provisions there was usually the prohibition of certain specific types of railroad discrimination.

The railroads quite naturally felt no enthusiasm for such laws. Their particular unhappiness was owing not so much to an objection to a measure of control, but to its diversity. In fact the railroads after the panic of 1873 were not doing well financially, and wanted stability above all else. They tried unified action, as with pools, which did not work well, and ultimately by the end of the century moved toward consolidation. Immediately, however, they made their rate structures as ridiculous and unjust as the law permitted. They supported efforts to repeal the laws. They brought court cases on the plea that public control of private property was unconstitutional, and that only Congress could regulate business that was primarily interstate. The Supreme Court, however, in several cases of 1876, notably *Munn* v. *Illinois* and *Peck* v. *Chicago and Northwestern Railroad*, ruled that state legislatures had regulatory power, even over rates of goods shipped across state lines.

Regardless of the courts, state laws had real problems. Rigid laws became troublesome as conditions changed. Railroad commissioners were often better prepared to play politics than to control railroads. Interstate hauls that were extremely important could be regulated only inadequately by individual states. Railroads were foreign corporations for most regulating states, and there was difficulty in persuading them to produce understandable records. State controls varied, as for example a railroad crossing state lines might be forced to change its headlights three or four times on a single run. As early as the 1870s it was recognized that there was need for federal control.

Congress considered regulation of the railroads during the 1870s. The Windom report (1874) was submitted by a special Senate Committee, headed by William Windom of Minnesota, advocating competitive routes to the seaboard, development of waterways, and the establishment of a statistical bureau. The Reagan Bill (1878) sought the prohibition of railroad pools, rebates, and discriminatory rates. Numerous other regulatory bills were considered, but Congress failed to act. This inaction became untenable in 1886 when the Supreme Court in *Wabash, St. Louis and Pacific R.R. Co.* v. *Illinois* (usually referred to as the *Wabash* case) somewhat changed its attitude. The Court ruled that the individual state did not have the right to regulate railroad traffic moving in interstate commerce. Under the Constitution only Congress had such power. Whereupon a general demand for federal regulation received the support not only of farmers but also of businessmen in many parts of the country, and to a great extent of the railroads themselves. In response Congress enacted the Interstate Commerce Act of 1887. The immediate results were disappointing, but with amendments the Interstate Commerce Commission ultimately became an effective regulating body.

GREENBACKERS The Granger movement declined during the late 1870s. Its decreasing importance was due in part to an increasing prosperity that made people forget to some degree the supposed sins of the railroads, and in part to the disastrous failure of the Grange cooperative enterprises. During its latter years the Grange shared the center of the stage with another reform movement, which supported large issues of paper money as the correct answer to economic troubles. Although the Greenback movement developed at the time the Granger movement was declining, the only tangible connections between the two agitations were that large numbers of each group supported the program of the other, and that the leaders of one tended to move to the other as popular support veered.

The Greenback movement represented a demand for a managed currency. Green-

An Anti-Greenback Cartoon, 1878. Inflationary movements occurred at intervals throughout frontier history. The "money question" dominated late nineteenth-century western politics. (Granger)

No. 73.-VOL. III.   JULY 31, 1878.   Price, 10 Cents.

"What fools these Mortals be!"
MIDSUMMER-NIGHTS DREAM.

Puck

PUBLISHED BY
KEPPLER & SCHWARZMANN.   NEW YORK   OFFICE N° 13 NORTH WILLIAM ST.

THE NATIONALISTS AND THEIR PAPER JACKASS.
(Slightly altered from Exodus, Chapter XXXII.)

backers pointed accusingly at the decline of the per capita amount of money in circulation and the corresponding decline in prices. They contended that an increase in paper money would help to restore prices to what they considered a proper level. They held that prices might be stabilized by the proper manipulation of the nation's circulating medium, although the cynic suspects that they would never have desired to lower prices.

The average western Greenbacker was not a profound theorist on monetary matters, but he realized that large issues of paper money were good for debtors, and that the West was largely a debtor community. An increase of cheap currency, according to Gresham's law, tended to drive out the more expensive medium; no one would spend gold when the cheaper paper money did as well. The paper money tended to drop in value because of its very profusion, and the visual evidence of such a drop was a rise in prices. With the rise in prices any given amount of money would be worth progressively less in purchasing power. This outcome would be unfortunate for bankers and other possessors of money, but would be good for farmer-debtors, whose dollar income would increase while their debts remained the same. An added factor was that farm prices tended to move more rapidly than other prices, thus giving the farmer another advantage in a period of rising prices.

A very considerable inflation of the American currency had come during the Civil War, when large quantities of unredeemable greenbacks were printed and put into circulation. The result was a rapid rise in prices, which was good for the debtor but a burden on the creditor. After the war the majority feeling was that paper money should once more be made redeemable in gold. Congress felt that this process should occur rather gradually; hence in 1866 it authorized the retirement of $4 million of greenbacks each month. Debtors throughout the country were distressed as they looked forward to a period of deflation, with falling prices, and ultimately the resumption of specie payments. Their mutterings rose to a crescendo that brought the repeal of the act of 1866 two years later, when there were still over $356 million of greenbacks in circulation.

The problem of the resumption of specie payments continued to agitate the public mind in the years after 1866. In the presidential campaign of 1868 the Republican party was generally understood to favor resumption and the Democratic party to oppose it; although the Democratic candidate, Horatio Seymour, did not agree with this principle of his party. In spite of the Republican victory no resumption act was passed until 1875, and then it was not to go into force for another four years. As the time for resumption approached, the price of greenbacks gradually rose; at the date of the change they had attained par and consequently there was no rush to the Treasury to exchange them for gold.

As paper money rose in price the mutterings of the debtor class again became a loud roar. Monetary policy that added to the effects of the panic of 1873 brought prices down precipitously, with the result that the farmer was receiving less and less money to meet the debts he had contracted in a time of high prices. Protesting groups met all over the country, while larger conventions also gave expression to the existing dissatisfaction. Out of this rising wave of feeling came the call for a national convention to represent all who wanted more paper money. When it met in 1876 it took the name of the National Independent party, but by popular consent it was more usually called the Greenback (or Greenback Labor) party.

The convention held at Indianapolis in 1876 was attended by 240 delegates who represented eighteen states and the District of Columbia. After a long debate in which everyone had the opportunity to free his mind of his own pet grievances, a vigorous and oratorical platform was adopted. Then Peter Cooper of New York was nominated for the office of President of the United States. Cooper was a picturesque and appealing man who had made a fortune in iron, first at Baltimore and then at Trenton. More recently he had retired to New York to spend his money in philanthropy, his most notable achievement being the establishment of Cooper Union (to which he gave a total of $800,000) to aid workingmen by providing a free library and reading room, and by offering regular night classes. Mr. Cooper was an attractive figure, but in spite of his benevolences it still seemed inappropriate for this rich, elderly philanthropist to lead a movement composed primarily of farmers who wanted more paper money.

The Greenbackers were particularly fortunate in their choice of a man to organize clubs throughout the country. Recognizing the power of advertising, they chose Marcus M. ("Brick") Pomeroy, a journalist by profession. According to Pomeroy's own claims he organized 4000 clubs; even allowing for a modest 50 percent of error, the figure is impressive. In addition he found time to write many propaganda tracts under such appealing titles as "Meat for Men" and "Hot Drops."

The election of 1876 was a disappointment to the new Greenback party, which received only 80,000 of 8 million votes. Its principal support in the West came from Illinois, Indiana, and Michigan, and in the East from Massachusetts. The Greenbackers consoled themselves over this failure by reminding themselves that they were a new party. Additional work brought many new recruits, and in the local elections of 1878 the party was able to cast a million votes. As later events showed, this election was the high point of the numerical strength of the movement, voting power ebbing with the return of prosperity. General James B. Weaver of Iowa was nominated for the presidency in 1880, but managed to attract only 308,000 votes. In 1884 the Greenbackers joined the Anti-Monopoly party in nominating General Benjamin F. Butler of Massachusetts, who, needless to say, did not win the election.

POPULISTS   The early 1880s were a period of prosperity, which led to the disappearance of the Granger and Greenback movents. Labor experienced the pleasure of rising wages and falling prices. Farmers deplored the falling prices, but were consoled by bumper crops. Farmer specialization, together with improved machinery, increased and cheapened production; better processes of marketing, including the grading and inspection of grain, were helpful. Transportation improved remarkably, increasing demand, particularly from the East, but also from the rest of the world; the ever-expanding market slowed down the price drop. In fact the United States was the greatest exponent of farm productivity in the world, and representatives of other nations visited the United States to observe and to benefit by American methods. The result of the advances made in production, in marketing, and in transportation was that farm income increased markedly in spite of the price decline, while goods purchased by the farmer became cheaper. Under such conditions a party of protest was an anachronism.

Smaller groups continued to struggle along the path of reform, for no situation conceivably satisfies every one. Labor groups maintained at least nominal existence. Socialists and anarchists talked loudly to generally hostile audiences. Small farmer groups talked of being milked by the railroads, by manufacturers, by grain and cattle dealers, and by others; but while many farmers agreed that there were abuses, they were not carried along by the excessive claims of the reformers. Among the farmer groups the more important were the National Farmers' Alliance and Industrial Union, the National Farmers' Alliance, the Agricultural Wheel, and the Farmers' Mutual Benefit Association. Although wielding little influence they at least had organizations in a position to take advantage of any period of depression that might occur.

Economic conditions became worse during the late 1880s. Wages began to decline and unemployment to increase. Stockmen were hard pressed to survive. Crops failed in the West, especially in western Kansas, Nebraska, and the Dakotas, while prices continued to fall. Once again the farmers were sure they were being mistreated through a conspiracy of easterners rolling in wealth and plotting to take the land away from hardworking, honest farmers. There was talk of interest rates of 50 percent and of widespread foreclosures. Although such charges were in general untrue, many farmers were certainly getting along badly, and in terms of potential action beliefs were more important than facts.

Distressed farmers turned toward political action, and many of the small protesting groups suddenly were deluged by new members; here and there some of them combined. The organizations receiving the greatest benefit, both from attraction of new members and from the absorption of other groups, were the Farmers' Alliances, Northern and Southern. Their most radical proposal was that of the Southern Alliance: the government should lend the farmers money at 1 percent on nonperishable products stored in government warehouses. Neither group constituted a political party, but each threw its strength toward whatever candidates were most favorable to its views, and this method of action brought many local successes by 1891.

The development of numerous protest movements about 1890 suggested to various leaders the possibility of combining them into one great political party that might have a chance of winning a national election. The main difficulty was to formulate a program sufficiently broad to include all the reform elements without antagonizing anyone of importance. Obviously the task of reconciling such divergent elements as those favoring easy money, antimonopoly, protective legislation, woman suffrage, single tax, socialism, and temperance, to name only a few, was a Herculean one.

The most important and difficult problem in producing such a combination, then as later, was to reconcile the opposing viewpoints of the farmer and industrial labor. Labor desired high wages and low prices. The farmer, on the contrary, wanted high prices for what he sold and low prices for what he bought; but in a choice between prices that were all high and prices that were all low, he preferred the higher level. Furthermore, the farmer favored a more modest wage scale, since he was an employer of labor. The fact was that the two groups had little in common except their objections to the existing economic system in a period of depression.

The Farmers' Alliance was at least willing to attempt to unite all protesting groups, and called a meeting of all dissatisfied minorities at Cincinnati in 1891. The convention met as scheduled, with its 1400 members representing so many varieties of reform that it was nicknamed the "conglomerate conference." Its chances of success were greatly reduced by the absence of various important farmer and labor groups, and particularly by the abstention of the Knights of Labor.

The platform adopted at Cincinnati showed the nature of the reform movements represented. It included economy in government, a perennial prayer almost never answered. It asked for government ownership of railroads, telegraphs, and telephones, which seemed a natural next step after the Granger movement. Landownership by aliens was to be prohibited, and no land was to be held speculatively; these demands had a long history, and illustrated vividly the disappearance of the good land of the public domain. The circulating medium was to be plentiful, both paper and silver, and silver was to be coined freely at a ratio with gold of 16 to 1. The last plank was a logical continuation of the Greenback agitation, the only difference being in the increased emphasis on silver rather than on paper.

Other provisions of the platform of 1891 also reflected the state of mind of the reformers. The national currency of the United States was to be loaned liberally at an interest rate of 2 percent. A graduated income tax, postal savings banks, the Australian (secret) ballot, liberal pensions for veterans, the 8-hour day, and the initiative and referendum were to be adopted. The President of the United States was to be allowed only a single term. United States senators were to be elected by direct vote of the people.

The platform was obviously the combination of many proposals, including some designed to appeal to such groups as veterans and industrial labor. Read in the light of the present day, few of the demands seem extreme, and many of them have been put into practice. At the time the platform was adopted, however, it seemed radical if not revolutionary. The more conservative elements of the population were so alarmed as to appear panic-stricken. They shook their heads dolefully and lamented loudly the degeneracy of the times. The principles of the Constitution were being undermined. Such a program, if adopted, would destroy the civilization that generations of patriotic Americans had constructed through their unremitting zeal and toil. Particularly dangerous were the proposals to put the government into business and thus reduce that individual competition that was "the life of trade." Dire calamities were predicted if even the least of the proposed reforms was put into practice.

By the time the new party held its most important convention at Omaha in 1892 it had acquired a name—the People's party—and its members were called Populists. Attending the convention were 1336 hopeful reformers. The spirit of the convention was well expressed by the platform's preamble, written by Ignatius Donnelly, which began oratorically: "We meet in the midst of a nation brought to the verge of moral, political, and material ruin," after which followed a bill of particulars; then came the convention's proposals which resembled those of the Cincinnati convention.

The Populist candidate for President was General James B. Weaver of Iowa, who was nominated among scenes of wild confusion. Weaver illustrated very well the type of westerner who was leading the drive for reform. He came from a westward-moving family, and although he had been born in Ohio he migrated as far as California before he settled permanently in Iowa, where he practiced law. His first political affiliation was the Democratic party, but later he was attracted by the Free Soil party and then by the new Republican party. During the Civil War he served in the army. In 1877 he became a Greenbacker, and was elected to Congress on that ticket. Nominated for the presidency by the Greenbackers, he waged a magnificently energetic campaign, but obviously did not convince all of the half million people who heard him speak, for his vote was 308,578. During most of the 1880s he sat in Congress as a Greenbacker. With the

Grange Meeting in Ohio, 1873. While the Grangers organized primarily for social purposes, they soon turned their gatherings into political rallies where agrarian statesmen found new audiences for their orations. (Brown)

decline of the Greenbackers he followed his electorate into the Populist party. Ultimately he returned to the Democratic party (he supported Bryan), where he stayed until his death in 1912. He therefore ended in the same party in which he had started, but in the process his own views had remained fairly consistent, while those of the party had changed.

Weaver waged his usual vigorous campaign in 1892, traveling widely and speaking continuously. When the votes were counted, he had attracted about 1 million as compared with the approximately 5 million each for Cleveland and Harrison, most of Weaver's support coming, as expected, from the South and West. This result constituted an unqualified success. Even the wildest optimist had no expectation of Populist victory, and a million votes was a splendid omen for the future of the new party: a national victory four years later seemed possible.

CAMPAIGN OF 1896   The major political parties also were impressed by the million votes, and the minority Democratic party saw a splendid opportunity to win the presidency if only these votes could be acquired. When the Democratic convention met in 1896, many of its members favored the Populist views, either through personal conviction or for political expediency, and many elements of the Populist program were inserted in the party platform. The greatest fight of the convention was over the Populist demand for the free coinage of silver, and here the Democrats seemed hopelessly split. The westerners in general supported the idea, and the easterners opposed it. The debate was long and heated. Unity was desirable, and at the same time free silver was necessary to win Populist support.

At this dramatic moment the stage of national politics received a new actor in the person of William Jennings Bryan, a young lawyer from Nebraska. The "boy orator of the Platte" delivered the closing speech in the debate on the platform, and ended it with the most famous utterance of his long career: "we will answer their demand for a gold standard by saying to them: You shall not press down upon the brow of labor this crown of thorns, you shall not crucify mankind upon a cross of gold." At the conclusion of the "cross of gold" speech pandemonium broke loose. Men stood on chairs, stamped, waved, whistled, and shouted. The silver plank—in fact the entire platform—was adopted with a rush, and Bryan himself was nominated for the presidency. The Bryan speech killed the Populist party, for its chief appeal was gone. The only possible thing the Populists could do was to support the Bryan candidacy.

The campaign of 1896 was a spirited contest, during which Bryan performed prodigious feats in miles traveled, number of speeches made, and hands shaken, while McKinley campaigned in dignity from his front porch. For some still unascertained reason "the producing masses of this nation," to which Bryan had appealed, failed to see that their hope of economic salvation rested with the Democratic party. Great numbers of them voted for the many minor parties in the field, or for McKinley, who won easily.

As prosperity returned, Populism disappeared and the demand for the free coinage of silver passed into the realm of historical relics. Bryan ran for the presidency twice later, and although he still believed in free silver, he listened to councils of discretion and placed a continually decreasing emphasis on it, not even mentioning it in 1908.

WESTERN POLITICAL INFLUENCE   Western political influence did not stop with the Populist movement. Support for such democratic measures as woman suffrage, direct primary, popular election of senators, the initiative, referendum, and recall was greater in the West than in the East. Theodore Roosevelt received much western support in 1912 because of his acceptance of such "progressive" measures. The Wilson nomination of 1912 depended in part on the influence of a westerner, William Jennings Bryan, and the West was an influential factor in the elections of 1912 and 1916. The National Non-Partisan League (formed in 1915) was western, and the La Follette campaign of 1924 looked largely toward western support. Such illustrations merely reinforce the obvious statement of western influence in national elections.

More important in the long run to the West than its impact on national elections has been its influence in Congress. Because of the constitutional provision that each state shall have two senators, the less populated agricultural states have always had important voices in the Senate, and these voices have been loud in support of the desires of their farmer constituents. Even during the "businessman government" of the 1920s, the farm bloc was able to obtain concessions, and with the coming of the New Deal its powers vastly increased. The various agricultural support acts passed since the days of the New Deal have reflected convincingly the political power of the farmers, even though the number of farmers has been declining.

To speak of the political power of the farmers as a manifestation of the West is technically correct, but at the same time misleading because it implies a direct connection with the frontier. The result is to classify Illinois as a frontier state in the 1870s because it had an influential Granger movement. In no reasonable sense were many of the Granger states of the 1870s frontier states. The mere fact that they had many railroads would make that possibility doubtful. The Wisconsin of Robert La Follette was no more a frontier state than William Jennings Bryan was a later-day Daniel Boone.

The proper statement about western political sentiment seems to be that it was the sentiment of an area that was primarily agricultural. The important fact is that farmers were dominant and not that geographically the region was western; large areas in other parts of the United States were also farmer-oriented, and the western complexion existed only because so many states of the Mississippi Valley were agricultural.

In only one sense can the western reform movements of the past century be given a frontier interpretation. The frontier was composed predominantly of farmers who believed in political democracy and in governmental control of large aggregations of wealth; hence their point of view was similar to that of farmers in other sections of the country. Possibly the fairest attitude is to consider the frontier farmer as a special case of the universal farmer. But the caboose does not push the train. Any farmer confronted with certain conditions is likely to have predetermined responses, and the important fact is that farmers occupied the frontier and not that a few farmers were at one time frontiersmen.

READINGS   *Paperbacks are marked with an asterisk.*

Farmer Protest Movements   Among the better of the more general accounts are Russell B. Nye, *Midwestern Progressive Politics, 1870–1950* (1951); *Theodore Saloutos and John D. Hicks, *Agricultural Discontent in the Middle West* (1951); *Fred A. Shannon, *The Farmer's Last Frontier* (1945); Mary Wilma M. Hargreaves, *Dry Farming on the Northern Plains, 1900–1925* (1957); Chester M. Destler, *American Radicalism, 1865–1901* (1946); Thomas Walter Johnson, *William Allen White's America* (1947); Solon J. Buck, *The Agrarian Crusade* (1920). The classic account of the Granger movement is *Solon J. Buck, *The Granger Movement* (1913). Railroad control is described in *Robert E. Riegel, *The Story of the Western Railroads* (1926); Gabriel Kolko, *Railroads and Regulation, 1877–1916* (1965) gives less credit to the farmers in railroad regulation. Populism can be followed in *John D. Hicks, *The Populist Revolt* (1931), excellent; Martin Ridge, *Ignatius Donnelly* (1962), very good. *Allen G. Bogue, *Money at Interest* (1955) is a careful study of the validity of some of the farmer protests.

Mark Twain. Stories with western settings became enormously popular in both the United States and Europe in the nineteenth century. Twain was one of several who made great reputations abroad. (Brown Brothers)

Chapter 37 / THE WEST ENTERS FICTION

The West provided a tremendous store of material for people who earned their bread and butter by writing. What is remarkable is that early writings using frontier themes were limited in variety and involved little imagination. The one frontier theme that appealed to the writers of the early nineteenth century was the conflict between Indian and white. Here obviously was high adventure. Most authors saw the Indian as either a cruel and bloodthirsty savage who held back the progress of civilization, or a brave, noble, and virtuous primitive man who fought against overwhelming odds to protect his family and friends. Seldom was the Indian pictured as a credible human being. Here and there a novelist saw interesting material in other frontier topics such as banditry, but practically none saw opportunity in the ordinary struggle of the farmer to subdue the wilderness. Conflict between men seemed exciting, but conflict between man and nature seemed dull unless it involved great feats of exploration.

Frontier stories increased in number and variety as population moved west. A frontier at one's own back door was visibly dirty, uncouth, vermin-ridden, and dominated by dull and backbreaking labor. A frontier became more romantic and colorful in the hazy distance where unsavory details softened or vanished. The difficulties and hardships changed from unpleasant experiences to be forgotten to obstacles to be overcome by brave men and women. Day-by-day monotony was so telescoped that what was left was the picturesque incident, the heroic episode.

By the time the frontier reached the Great Plains there existed east of the Mississippi a large book-buying public to whom the West was remote, colorful, exciting. To the average farmer or factory worker the West became a magic word, conjuring up alluring pictures of an open, wind-swept plain over which roamed bold and romantic riders to whom adventure was a daily experience. The West appeared a land of freedom, where a man was his own master, bold and self-reliant, meeting human and physical challenges with heroic bravery and unvarying success.

And in truth the Far West of the late nineteenth century had certain elements of color that the more eastern frontier had possessed to a lesser degree. The 2000-mile trek of covered wagons inspired the imagination more than did the floating of flatboats down the Ohio River. The mad rush to gold fields hundreds of miles from civilization was more spectacular than the exploitation of the Georgia gold deposits or the lead outcroppings of Wisconsin and Illinois. Custer and Chief Joseph seemed more exciting than Harrison and Tecumseh. The cowboy had had no eastern rival. The Pony Express and the overland stage made the traffic on the National Road seem dull and plodding. The construction of the Union Pacific decisively outclassed the building of the Ohio Canal in its appeal to American imagination.

LOCAL COLOR FICTION   One outstanding literary trend in the generation after the Civil War was the exploitation of sectional peculiarities. This "local color" writing was accurate about geography, language, and customs, but often highly romantic in its attitude toward life. Naturally certain authors saw opportunity in describing the West, even though some had had no personal experience with frontier conditions. One of the earliest was Edward Eggleston, a native of Indiana, who wrote of pioneer life in southern Indiana in *The Hoosier Schoolmaster* and other novels published in the early 1870s. Eggleston's continued reputation is hard to understand; his characters are so badly drawn as to be almost caricatures, are sentimentalized into becoming heroes and villains, and are frequently mawkishly religious.

Standing head and shoulders above all other men who wrote about the West in the generation after the Civil War was Samuel L. Clemens, better known by his pen name Mark Twain. As a small boy Clemens lived in a Missouri River village that some romanticists have tried unsuccessfully to present as part of the frontier. He was steeped in the life and traditions of the river, and as a young man worked for some years as a steamboat pilot; his pen name was the call of the man who used the lead to plumb the depth of the river. Clemens' first experience with the Far West came in 1862, when he went to Nevada at the invitation of his brother, who was secretary of the territory. Although Clemens tried a little unsuccessful mining, as did almost all Nevada residents, his major occupation was as a writer for the *Territorial Enterprise* of Virginia City.

Clemens' first national reputation came with a jumping frog story, which was not original with him. The tale described a jumping match between two frogs in which one outleaped the other because his owner had the foresight to feed lead to the frog of his opponent. Journalistic and literary success brought invitations to lecture, at which Clemens was very effective, and soon he acquired a national reputation. Clemens' angular body and eccentricities made him an American institution, and he became the most easily recognizable man in the United States with his luxuriant thatch of white hair and his preference for white suits. His thoroughgoing pessimism did him no harm, which was surprising in view of the childlike optimism so characterstic of the American public.

Clemens' one book on the Far West was *Roughing It* (1872), concerned largely with life in Nevada. Its humor was typically American and typically western, depending heavily on exaggeration and unusual juxtapositions. Such incidents as the author's dinner with Brigham Young and his family, and the effort of a rough miner to persuade a recent graduate of a theological school to preside at the obsequies of a pal are in the best Mark Twain tradition, and remain as funny today as when they were written. But in addition, *Roughing It* is a fine description of mining life in Nevada during the 1860s, provided that allowance is made for exaggeration.

Ranking well behind Mark Twain, but still with considerable claim to fame, comes Bret Harte, an easterner by birth and education, an infant prodigy with a yearning to write. His father died when Bret was nine. His mother took her family to California upon her remarriage, and when Bret was seventeen. On the coast Harte tried various jobs, but gravitated toward journalism, becoming in 1868 the editor of the *Overland Monthly*, a West Coast effort to exploit western material and western writers. In this magazine appeared some of his best short stories, including "The Luck of Roaring Camp" and "The Outcasts of Poker Flat."

Growing fame drew Harte to the East in 1871, where the *Atlantic Monthly* offered him a magnificent $10,000 for anything he might produce in a year. Success had an unfortunate effect on Harte. He wrote less, he wasted time on ineffective playwriting and lecturing, and he always outran his income with lavish living. Worst of all, his short stories repeated earlier ideas and settings at a time when such material was losing popular appeal. He spent his last years in Europe, partly to avoid his wife, and when he died in 1902 most Americans were probably surprised that he had not died long ago.

Harte's fame rests on his short stories of the West, masterpieces of craftsmanship and the results of years of painstaking literary experimentation. Typically they deal with such human paradoxes as the self-sacrificing gambler, the crude miner with the soul of a child, the prostitute filled with motherly love. The climax of each story comes with some curious twist of fate. For some readers the Harte stories are exaggerated and artificial; for others they represent a peak in the art of the short story.

DIME NOVELS   The real literary bonanza was the western thriller. Increasing masses of people were now able to read, but the majority of them were not enthralled by the *Atlantic Monthly*, nor could they afford a clothbound volume that might cost two day's pay. For them a cheaper and more sensational type of writing was desirable. The man first to exploit this profitable possibility as it related to the West was Edward Zane Carroll Judson, who wrote under the pen name of Ned Buntline.

Judson wrote from the background of varied and exciting personal experiences: serving as a common sailor, as a soldier in the Seminole War, traveling up the Yellowstone for a fur company, fighting and being imprisoned in the Civil War, and lecturing extensively for the temperance movement about the delirium tremens he had known. Just prior to the Civil War he had written for the New York *Mercury*, a fourpenny thriller, and had established his weekly, *Ned Buntline's Own*. In both sheets he had exploited thrilling material, particularly related to the West. While in prison during the war, he had used his spare moments to write three blood-and-thunder novels. These activities had failed to make Judson wealthy, but they had demonstrated the existence of a wide market for rapid-action stories, particularly of the West.

The man who profited most from the Judson idea was Erastus Beadle, who published America's most famous series of "dime novels." The first of the series (1860) was *Malaeska, the Indian Wife of the White Hunter*, written by Mrs. Ann S. Stephens, well-known editor and novelist. Laid along the Hudson in the early days of Dutch settlement, it was a pathetic tale of the disastrous results of an Indian-white marriage: the son commits suicide, his bride-to-be remains in lifelong celibacy, and Malaeska herself fades away into a lonely grave. In spite of its sadness, the novel had a notable sale of some 65,000 copies, and opened the way for later books in the series.

During and immediately after the Civil War Beadle sold his dime, half-dime, and quarter series literally by the million. They were more truly a gold mine than most of the mineral discoveries in the West. The type of book is indicated but feebly by such titles as *Carson the Guide, California Joe*, and *The Prairie Rover*. Many of them were written, or at least signed, by men who could claim competence in the subjects they handled. Among the presumed authors were such well-known westerners as William F. Cody and Major St. Vrain.

The Beadle novels were read by soldiers in the army, by small boys in the woodshed, and by anyone else seeking a vicarious thrill. In general they were considered somewhat immoral and reprehensible, at least for others to read. Parents used a hickory stick or the flat of the hand to persuade their progeny of the error of their ways. Actually the books were violently and blatantly self-righteous. No expressions were used that might shock even the most prudish, and sex was almost entirely excluded. The hero was everything a hero should be, and the unbelievably bad villain was confounded in the end. The sin committed by the small boy reading them was more that of wasting his time than of being demoralized.

The vogue of the Beadle novels declined during the 1890s, the last one being published in 1897. The later ones dealt less frequently with the West, and more often with detectives and train robbers. Their place was filled by the western story magazine, including such titles as *Frontier Stories*, *West*, *Pioneer Tales*, *Western Story Magazine*, and *Cowboy Stories*. Hundreds of such magazines have vied with the "art" and "movie" magazines for popular favor. Quite understandably they have sold well in such industrial areas as New England, but apparently they have also been read by ranch employees in the West; if their publishers are to be believed, a considerable proportion of their readers are not virile, red-blooded "he-men," but members of the opposite sex.

The western story magazine has been devoted exclusively to tales of rapid action, with a little sex interest to add spice to the story. Guns spit fire, and redskins drop. Bloodstained fists strike yielding flesh. Wild rides through storm and danger bring rescue in the nick of time. Desperate bands of cattle thieves are defeated by the forces of right on the last page. The hero is brave, keen, farsighted, strong, and loyal. The villain is blackhearted, mean, cruel, and entirely despicable. The heroine is brave, beautiful, pure, and strong, but entirely feminine. Wickedness is always crushed at the last moment, right is triumphant, and the hero and heroine fall into each other's arms to live happily ever after. No wicked sex tangles or marital problems mar the pure and simple heroism of these tales.

WESTERN PLAYS   The West has also been given dramatic interpretation, and here again E. Z. C. Judson was an important factor. A play, *Buffalo Bill, the King of the Border Men*, based on a Judson story, was produced successfully in New York in 1872. There it was visited by no less a person than Buffalo Bill himself. Cody, with his childlike naivete, his love of admiration, and his keen sense of the dramatic, was enchanted. Persuaded to mount the stage, and being given an ovation, he decided he wanted to become an actor.

Judson realized the financial advantage to be gained from the appearance of Buffalo Bill and of other noted plains characters. Immediately he wrote *The Scout of the Plains*—reputedly in one evening in Chicago, which is not unlikely considering the character of the play and Judson's facility with a pen. The cast of characters included Buffalo Bill, Texas Jack Omohundro, and a group of "Indians" gathered from the streets of Chicago.

Within a year *The Scout of the Plains* was revised as *Scouts of the Plains*, Buffalo Bill had acquired a stage presence, Wild Bill Hickok was added to the cast, Judson was dropped, and New York crowds were receiving the presentation enthusiastically. Indians were killed wholesale, and the heroes and the beautiful heroine were rescued from all kinds of terrifying situations. Wild Bill's opening speech, as he galloped on the stage shooting a few Indians, ran: "Fear not, fair maid; by heavens, you are safe at last with Wild Bill, who is ever ready to risk his life and die if need be in defense of weak and helpless womanhood." In addition to rather obvious flaws in the realism of this speech—particularly in view of Bill's reputation with women—it should be noted that the words came at the beginning of the play, and not with the final dramatic incident.

Efforts to put the Far West before the public in plays led to the opening of a real dramatic field. High points came in operatic presentations; particularly notable have been *The Girl of the Golden West* by Giacomo Puccini, which has become standard, and the more recent and excellent *Ballad of Baby Doe* by Douglas Moore. In this connection, the popularity of western themes in music has been notable. While much of the so-called western music is of doubtful authenticity, various fine modern composers such as Aaron Copland have used western material successfully.

WILD WEST SHOW The meteoric rise of Buffalo Bill was due primarily to the work of his devoted friend and press agent Major John M. Burke, and secondarily to the writings of that dime novel expert Prentiss Ingraham. Thanks to these two boosters Buffalo Bill became one of the best-known men in the world. The idea of a Wild West Show probably did not originate with Cody, and the immediate formation of the show was due in large part to the enthusiasm of the veteran actor Nate Salsbury, who later became Cody's partner. After the dramatic season of 1882–1883 Cody returned to the plains and gathered large numbers of cowboys, Indians, ponies, buffaloes, and other symbols of the West. With these he opened his first outdoor show at the Omaha Fair Grounds on May 17, 1883, calling it "The Wild West, Rocky Mountain and Prairie Exhibition." For a time the show was in perpetual danger of financial failure, largely because Cody was always a much better showman than business manager. Cody was frequently drunk, was generous to relatives and old friends, and embarked on many outside, and expensive, ventures; no matter how much the show brought in, he was always in debt.

By the mid-1880s the Wild West Show was a brilliant success. Playing in England in 1887 it gave two command performances attended by the queen and other members of royalty, and was the fashion. The Prince of Wales rode in the Deadwood Stage, and Buffalo Bill was presented to the queen. Two years later the show was acclaimed on a tour of the Continent. Playing opposite the main entrance of the Chicago Fair in 1893, it rivaled the fair itself in drawing power.

The Wild West Show was attractive in presenting phases of American life that most people had met only in fiction. At first it was purely western, with pony races, Indian dances and battles, bucking broncos, steer roping, the Pony Express, and the attack on the Deadwood Stage; the emphasis was on riding and shooting. By the early 1890s it had become a "Congress of Rough Riders of the World" and by the late 1890s it had added circus sideshow attractions such as snake charmers, midgets, fire-eaters, and jugglers. By 1908 it had definitely become less profitable, and when Buffalo Bill died in 1917 he was poverty-stricken.

One of the chief attractions of the Wild West Show was the shooting. Buffalo Bill's own most admired shooting performance was from horseback. His protégé, Johnny Baker, was a boy prodigy. Best known and most admired was Annie Oakley, who although not a westerner could pass for the real article when dressed in a buckskin suit. By all reports Annie was a fine and modest woman, well liked by other performers. Annie Oakley's reputation as a marksman was so widespread that a punched ticket became known popularly as an "Annie Oakley" because of its similarity to a playing card at which the lady herself had shot.

In spite of Buffalo Bill's excessive drinking, his lack of business judgment, and his exaggerated reputation coming largely from press agent publicity, he did much to personify the West for Americans. For every child living in the years near 1900 one of the great thrills of life was to see Buffalo Bill ride his white steed at the head of the procession; his movements were dramatic as was the great shock of snowy-white hair, which in his last years was replaced by a wig. Always somewhere in the program was the exciting Indian attack upon the Deadwood Stage. As Buffalo Bill grew older his marksmanship declined, but even in the last of his "farewell tours" he was as impressive and picturesque as ever.

MOTION PICTURES   The year 1910 saw the arrival of the motion picture. It was in this year that Goldberg made his magic lantern slides of Buffalo Bill, that Powers made his motion pictures of Buffalo Bill, and that the Esaney Company started its weekly one-reel releases of *Bronco Billy*. As the motion picture developed, one of its staples was the western story, which included such spectacles as *The Toll of the Desert*, *The Taming of Texas Pete*, *The Iron Horse*, and *North of 36*. Such names as Tom Mix, William S. Hart, Hoot Gibson, and Harry Carey were known to every small boy of the country, and, for that matter, to his mother, father, and sister.

More recent motion pictures have included notable attempts at realistic backgrounds, as in the building of the Union Pacific or the migration of the Mormons, but the usual production has been aimed at creating an imaginary and idyllic West. Every farmhouse seems to contain a beautiful and well-dressed daughter, with nails manicured, hair curled, and speech well chosen. For each lovely heroine there is a handsome hero who is an excellent horseman, a first-rate shot, careless of personal danger, clever with his fists, and with a cat's proverbial nine lives, for no western hero, as far as the record goes, has ever died, with the one sad exception of Davy Crockett. The idyllic peace of the beautiful West is marred only by the villain and his evil gang. The villain is an evil, ill-favored, sardonic chap who spends his time concocting plans for stealing the old ranch or waylaying the hero. Luckily he is always outwitted and foiled by the hero before the play comes to an end.

The coming of television provided a new market for old westerns that otherwise would have passed to their well-merited deaths. Television also developed dozens of serials under such titles as "Gunsmoke," "Wagon Train," "Rawhide," "Wyatt Earp," and "Bonanza." Some of these various productions have been described as "adult," which generally means that the plot is more complex, and that a group such as the Cartwrights of "Bonanza" is given considerable emphasis as compared with the individual. Action may be less vigorous in some of the motion pictures, but there are seldom any involved psychological analyses, and there is no question as to who are the heroes and who the villains.

Dramatic presentations, particularly motion pictures and television serials, must have heroes. Many of them are completely fictitious, but often they are historical personalities such as Wyatt Earp, Billy the Kid, and Wild Bill Hickok. Since many of these characters were in fact rather dubious people, they must be heroicized—their physical appearance improved, their speech cleaned up, and all their actions transformed to the desirable. A bandit such as Jesse James becomes a philanthropist, taking from the rich to give to the deserving poor. Violations of the law are always for "good" causes. These phantasies appeal to the young of all ages in much the same way as did the Robin Hood stories of a previous generation. The plethora of violence may well have no more effect than had old fairy stories such as Jack the Giant Killer. Of course they are not to be trusted to describe the Old West accurately, but possibly they give some concept of the ideals and interests of their viewers—a rather unhappy thought. Rather curiously, parents seem to object less strenuously to the vivid color picturizations of violence than they did to the earlier and duller dime novels—again possibly a comment on current ideals.

The West of the motion pictures and television is at least fascinating. Each cowboy has a bright and shining gun, which he carries continuously and uses on the slightest provocation. Also he always has a favorite horse to which he is passionately devoted. Indians are perpetually either saying "ugh" or engaging in war dances preparatory to attacking settlers. A continual series of overwhelming and seemingly inescapable dangers is matched by an equal series of hairbreadth escapes. Right always triumphs eventually, and villainy is crushed to earth. And so the younger generation is encouraged to build a beautiful and heroic myth of the West.

LITERATURE AFTER 1900   Books about the West sold more widely after about 1900. The literary trend of the period was toward the rather nostalgic type of novel about rural and small-town life, for example, *David Harum*, and the historical romance of the type of *When Knighthood Was in Flower*. The western novel combined the simple, unlearned virtues of the characters of the first type with the glittering romance of the second. Much of this new literature was concerned with the cowboy, who only recently had become an exciting and romantic figure; for most of the nineteenth century the stock tender had been more a drab and pedestrian figure than the potential hero of a novel. One of the earliest to exploit the field was Emerson Hough, who in 1895 published his descriptive *Story of the Cowboy*, which was reasonably informative.

Later he published such novels as T*he Covered Wagon* (1922) and *North of 36* (1923), which at least were not dull. Hough was exceedingly impressed with the heroic nature of the western experience, and viewed with nostalgic sadness the passing of the good old days.

Owen Wister was responsible for one of the better of the western novels of the early twentieth century— *The Virginian* (1902). Wister was born and reared in the East, graduating from Harvard in 1885. His interest in the West came from a trip to Wyoming for

The Dime Novels. Westerners, and a great many other American readers, demanded action stories in preference to novels of literary excellence. The result: an avalanche of low-priced books such as those of Beadle's Dime Library. (Denver Public Library)

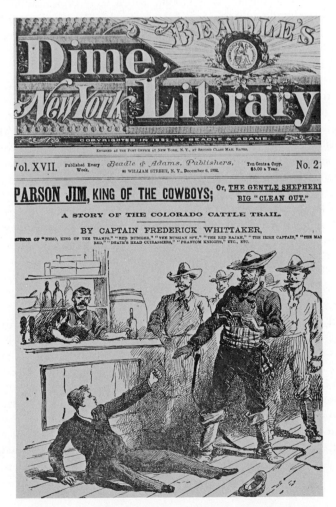

his health, and he became so enthusiastic that he returned several times, and talked about the West incessantly. Although his profession was the practice of law in Philadelphia, he affected loose-tied bow ties, short sleeves, and felt his real mission was to bring the West into American literature. In *The Virginian* he described interestingly life in Wyoming during the late 1870s and 1880s. Although the Virginian is himself an unusual cowboy, the atmosphere and most of the incidents are admirable.

Other writers on western themes have been legion, but most of their work has been ephemeral. Jack London had great popularity for a time with such tales as *Call of the Wild*, which described the raw passions and the struggle for survival in the Far North. Harold Bell Wright depicted western scenes in such books as *When a Man's a Man*, and profited thereby. B. M. Bowers (Bertha M. Sinclair) contributed the enjoyable Flying U stories, such as *Chip of the Flying U*. C. E. Mulford created the unforgettable character Hopalong Cassidy. A little later the best-seller lists included Max Brand's *Destry Rides Again* (1930) and *Singing Guns* (1938), which were typical action stories. Most spectacular of the popular successes was Niven Busch's *Duel in the Sun* (1944), which concerned cattle raising in the Southwest during the 1880s. Early sales were poor, since the book was but one of a long series of action westerns; but suddenly sales boomed, and then the film was extremely popular.

Two exceptional men, Andy Adams and Will James, both former cowboys, re-created the cattle country in a series of semiautobiographical descriptive books. Adams wrote vividly in his inimitable slang; his best work was probably *The Log of a Cowboy*, although other volumes were almost as good. Will James did similar work in his *Cowboys North and South* and *Cow Country*, and in addition illustrated his books with his excellent action drawings. Unfortunately the public taste in western literature had become quite standardized before Adams and James appeared on the scene, which meant that their sales were not as great as their works merited.

Adams and James belonged to the small group of westerners who grew up in the West of the frontier and who, with a minimum of formal training, managed to produce work that was acceptable in a literary sense. Possibly the California poet Joaquin Miller should be included in that group. In the field of painting, the Montana cowboy Charlie Russell deserves an important place. With only slight if any allowance for Russell's lack of formal training, his work compares favorably with that of his better-known contemporary, Frederic Remington.

Undoubtedly the best of all spinners of western yarns, if popularity is the proper test, has been Zane Grey. Grey, a dentist, received his D.D.S. from Pennsylvania in 1896, and started his practice in New York City. His literary labor began in 1904 and found immediate popular favor. In time he became convinced that the public would always recognize and buy a good book with a strong appeal, by which he meant his own. His novels have been described by one commentator as grim stories of sadists who are supermen, and of strongly sexed but virginal women. The reading of Zane Grey is an experience that should not be missed. Any of his books will do, since it is hard to distinguish one from another. A copy should be easy to obtain; in his heydey Grey was producing about a book a year and most of them ended on the best-seller lists.

LITERARY REALISM   The West has inspired hundreds of books of action and romance, but the literary historian has been particularly interested in efforts to create accurate pictures of the West, and particularly of the farming West. The great landmark of western realism was E. W. Howe's *The Story of a Country Town* (1883), which described the less pleasant aspects of a small and unlovely town in the wheat country of Kansas. Four years later Joseph Kirkland, son of Caroline Kirkland, herself a writer, published his *Zury* (short for Usury), which did a similar job for frontier Illinois.

Howe and Kirkland were early practitioners of realism, but the popularizer was Hamlin Garland, who was born (1860) and reared in the upper Mississippi Valley at a time when that area was not far removed from frontier conditions. Garland worked long and hard as a farm boy, and managed to obtain an education in the face of severe handicaps. Little wonder that he was critical of the world about him and became active in the Populist movement. As a radical young man with literary aspirations he naturally evolved a philosophy of life that he tried to apply to his writings. In his own words, he developed "two great literary concepts—that truth was a higher quality than beauty, and that to spread the reign of justice should everywhere be the design and intent of the artist."

Garland's first book was *Main Traveled Roads* (1891), but his best-known works were the various semiautobiographical *Middle Border* books, which tell of the pioneering in his own family. Garland told here of the dirt and vermin and fleas, of the monotonous and backbreaking drudgery, of the drabness and meanness of western life; but he also described hilarious parties, gorgeous sunrises, and the smell of sizzling sausages on a cold morning. Because of these latter and more pleasant incidents, certain literary highbrows profess to feel that he was really a romantic at heart.

Garland stated a point of view that was important and tried to exemplify it in some of his short stories, but his longer novels such as *The Spirit of the Sweetwater* and *Her Mountain Lover* tended to be nothing more than thin love stories. In spite of such failures to realize his literary goal, he had tremendous influence by his recognition of the literary and dramatic values of a fight for existence by the frontier farmer pitting his brain and brawn and endurance against the forces of a reluctant nature. Furthermore, he influenced and assisted important young writers, notably Stephen Crane and Frank Norris, both of whom were significant in American literary development. Crane was somewhat concerned with western themes, but Norris was more important in this connection.

Frank Norris was more versatile than Hamlin Garland, but less intimately associated with the West, even though part of his education was obtained at the University of California. Among his varied works, *McTeague* (1899) was an attempt to treat the San Francisco area realistically; unfortunately for the western historian the background was contemporary, which made it remote from the frontier. Just before his early death, Norris was engaged in a trilogy to show the importance of wheat. *The Octopus* (1901) pictured the growing of wheat in southern California; *The Pit* (1903) described the Chicago grain exchange; and *The Wolf* (never written) was to treat the use of wheat to stop a European famine. *The Octopus* was an impressive story in which wheat dominated the canvas, with individual characters dwarfed by the immensity and power of the inanimate grain; the action was the struggle between the wheat growers and the railroad, which was the octopus.

Time brought an ever-increasing number of novelists who used western themes with attention not only to accuracy of detail but also to the larger truths. Among the better works may be mentioned Herbert Quick, *Vandemark's Folly;* Mari Sandoz, *Old Jules;* A. B. Guthrie, *The Big Sky* and *The Way West;* H. L. Davis, *Honey on the Horn;* Vardis Fisher, *City of Illusion;* Walter V. Clark, *The Ox-Bow Incident;* Edna Ferber, *Cimarron.* Outstanding was the work of Willa Sibert Cather, born in Virginia but educated at the University of Nebraska. Her writings about the West included *O Pioneers!, My Antonia,* and, above all, *Death Comes for the Archbishop,* which is considered her masterpiece. Miss Cather was not interested in plot in the usual fashion, but used the historical chronicle to describe the reaction of man to his environment.

High on any list of realistic novelists should be the Norwegian-born C. E. Rolvaag, who came to the United States as a young man. His best novel was *Giants in the Earth,* written first, as were his other books, in Norwegian, which recounted the experiences of Norwegian immigrants on the northern plains. The main character and the central theme of the book was the prairies, which dominated the lives of Per Hansa, his wife Beret, and their children. When the prairies smiled, life was happy and prodigal. When the locusts came or the snow descended, the prairies became malevolent, seeking whom they could destroy. The book ends as Per Hansa, traveling in the middle of the winter to get a minister for a dying man, loses his way in the snow and freezes to death. The last chapter is entitled "The Great Plains Drinks the Blood of Christian Men and Is Satisfied."

Western novels have tended to idealize the West and westerners in spite of the growth of "realism" after World War I. The male pioneer hero continues strong, attractive, aggressive, ingenious, freedom-loving, patriotic; the profit motive is seldom emphasized. On the other hand, he is more frequently a farmer than a trapper, trader, miner, or cowboy, and his prosaic hard work is described more frequently. He is shown more usually as an average man rather than an eastern aristocrat who had fallen on bad times. The women have changed frequently from ornamental prudes to understandable human beings. They have become stronger and more hardworking. Sex has become more permissive, with the women no longer so "pure" as in the Victorian sense. The Indians are described variously, but in general are treated more kindly than in earlier novels. All told, the novelist has been doing an improved job in presenting his picture of the West, even though a great deal of escapist and completely unrealistic trash still remains.

READINGS   *Paperbacks are marked with an asterisk.*

Literature   Nicholas J. Karolides, *The Pioneer in the American Novel, 1900–1950* (1967), based on a great variety of books; Kent L. Stockmesser, *The Western Hero in History and Legend* (1965); John Greenway, *Folklore of the Great West*

(1969); Percy H. Boynton, *The Rediscovery of the Frontier* (1931); Dorothy A. Dondore, *The Prairie in the Making of Middle America* (1926), scholarly; Albert Keiser, *The Indian in American Literature* (1933); Lucy L. Hazard, *The Frontier in American Literature* (1927), scholarly; Ina H. Herron, *The Small Town in American Literature* (1939), good; Edwin W. Gaston, Jr., *The Early Novel of the Southwest* (1961), critical, based on forty major novels; Charles L. Sonnichsen, *The Southwest in Life and Literature* (1962), representative writings. Dime novels are well covered in Edmund L. Pearson, *Dime Novels* (1929); see also James Monaghan, *The Great Rascal* (1952), excellent on "Ned Buntline." Cowboy literature is well covered in Edward D. Branch, *The Cowboy* (1926) and Joe B. Frantz and Julian E. Choate, Jr., *The American Cowboy: The Myth and the Reality* (1955); see also *Wilson M. Hudson, *Andy Adams* (1964). Humor is treated in *Thomas D. Clark, *The Rampaging Frontier* (1939) and *Mody C. Boatwright, *Folk Laughter on the American Frontier* (1949). For Bret Harte see Richard O'Connor, *Bret Harte* (1966); George R. Stewart, *Bret Harte* (1931). For Mark Twain see *Bernard DeVoto, *Mark Twain's America* (1935); Effie M. Mack, *Mark Twain in Nevada* (1947); Edward C. Wagenknecht, *Mark Twain* (1935). See also the works of the authors mentioned in this chapter.

Buffalo Bill and the Wild West Show   Don Russell, *The Lives and Legends of Buffalo Bill* (1960), concerns the sources of stories; *Henry B. Sell and Victor Weybright, *Buffalo Bill and the Old West* (1955).

Other Topics   Ramon F. Adams and Homer E. Britzman, *Charles M. Russell* (1948), excellent. *Robert G. Athearn, *Westward the Briton* (1953), interesting on British travelers. Western stories and songs have been collected in Levette J. Davidson and Forrester Blake (eds.), *Rocky Mountain Tales* (1947); John T. Flanagan (ed.), *America Is West* (1945). Robert Taft, *Artists and Illustrators of the Old West, 1850–1900* (1953) contains largely biographies and pictures.

Chapter 38 / THE HISTORIAN
DISCOVERS THE WEST

Historians are a conservative species. Not until the frontier had disappeared
did they recognize it as an important factor in American life. The epochal
volumes of George Bancroft were concerned with the West only as it was
involved in notable legislation such as the Northwest Ordinance. Francis

Parkman wrote of the West as the scene of a struggle between European empires. Johns Hopkins, our first important graduate school, was overwhelmingly concerned with the Germanic origins of Anglo-Saxon political institutions. Early historians were usually eastern by birth and training, and knew Charlemagne much better than Lewis and Clark. They tended to have roots in New England, which appeared to them as the most important part of the nation, with Boston the hub of American culture. Other parts of the country were neglected.

EARLY INTEREST IN WESTERN HISTORY   New currents appeared in American history as more historians came from the South and West, and translated their sectional pride into historical interpretations. These newcomers found oceans of material in the local historical societies, which increased so rapidly from the mid-nineteenth century that some two hundred were in existence when the American Historical Association was formed in 1884. Of these the state societies were the most important, since they avidly collected raw material for the historian, often provided mediums of publication, and always enthusiastically pushed the interest in local history. For each state the period of its frontier origins was of first interest, and for those of the western half of the United States the frontier period was so close that original material was comparatively easy to obtain.

The new historical trend became visible during the 1880s, especially with the work of Hubert Howe Bancroft and Theodore Roosevelt. Bancroft was one of America's most diligent collectors, scouring the Far West to acquire thousands of letters, diaries, and other documents that probably would otherwise have disappeared; in this work he was doing privately what Lyman Draper was doing at the same time for the Wisconsin Historical Society. Between 1874 and 1890 Bancroft signed his name to some forty volumes of history of the Far West, and his documentary collections provided in time a seemingly inexhaustible source for later publications. Bancroft was primarily a regional historian and made little effort to relate the West to the remainder of the nation or to find basic significances of the western experience.

Of greater national popularity than Bancroft's writings were those of Theodore Roosevelt published between 1889 and 1896 under the title of *The Winning of the West*. Roosevelt had gone west in 1884 to escape reminders of the death of his wife and of the nomination of Blaine, and had been fascinated by western life. *The Winning of the West* concerned the early trans-Appalachian frontier, and was confined largely to such dramatic incidents as Indian fights and the American Revolution. Although Roosevelt contributed largely to an interest in western history, he was little concerned with the peculiar contributions of the West, if any, to national culture, and described only a single frontier, limited in both time and place.

Frederick Jackson Turner. This great exponent of the role of the frontier in American history made history with his highly controversial thesis concerning America's move west. (Huntington Library)

FREDERICK JACKSON TURNER   The real beginning of the modern history of the West came with the reading of a scholarly paper by Frederick Jackson Turner in 1893 at a small meeting of historians convened at the World's Columbian Exposition in Chicago. Its title was "The Significance of the Frontier in American History." Turner was a Wisconsin product, who had received his graduate training at Johns Hopkins, where he was dissatisfied with the lack of interest in his own part of the country. Teaching history at the University of Wisconsin, he had access to the files of the Wisconsin Historical Society, which, as collected by Lyman Draper and Reuben Gold Thwaites, were the best in the West. Naturally he became interested in the westward movement of population, and as a keen young college professor was also aware of the current speculation concerning the importance of free land and of population distribution; for example, the important books of Josiah Strong and Henry George appeared during the 1880s. When the census of 1890 showed for the first time no clear population frontier, Turner was ready to indicate what he thought had been the importance of the frontier in American history.

Turner's influence grew rapidly, and within a generation his ideas had become thoroughly embedded in historical writing, in other fields of research, and even in general literature. This effect came from relatively little writing, being based more on the enthusiastic championship of the Turner concepts by hundreds of students at Wisconsin, and later at Harvard. Above all, Turner was a teacher with the gift of inspiring his students with a deep affection for himself and an abiding interest in the subject he taught. These students carried the torch to all parts of the country and transmitted the Turner ideas, even though at times exaggerated and overly dogmatic, and at other times diluted and modified, to their own students.

Turner's general theories were almost all advanced in his first paper; later publications restated but did not change them significantly. When the original essay was republished in 1920, Turner saw no reason for altering as much as a footnote in what he had written twenty-seven years earlier. Presumably the generalizations he had first expressed somewhat tentatively had turned out, in his judgment, to be accurate and sufficiently complete.

For Turner "the existence of an area of free land, its continuous recession, and the advance of American settlement westward, explain American development." The influence of the frontier had been decisive in welding an American nation and in making it different from other nations. The seeds of American ideals may have existed in Europe and on the Atlantic seaboard, but without the environment of the frontier they could not have developed into full-blown plants.

The frontier of which Turner spoke began with the Atlantic Coast and ended with the Pacific, but he noted that only "from the time the mountains rose between the pioneer and the seaboard, a new order of Americanism arose." Then for the first time were the pioneers thrown on their own resources to develop distinctively American traits. Of the vast area west of the Appalachians, Turner stressed the log cabin frontier of the Old Northwest, even though he was aware of other regions.

The frontier meant to Turner a region of sparse settlement, "the meeting point between savagery and civilization," although now and then he spoke of the frontier as a line or a process of change or even a state of mind. The important attractive force was cheap land; freedom was a secondary objective. The great conditioning factor was the richness of that land, with little emphasis on minerals, climate, rainfall, and other environmental factors.

The process of settlement was described by Turner largely in economic terms. Each new region recapitulated the general growth of society as well as the experiences of former frontiers. In succession came the hunter and trapper, the trader, the rancher, the pioneer farmer, the specialized farmer, and the manufacturer. The frontier stage ended with the pioneer farmer. Little attention was paid to artistic, educational, and intellectual factors, and Turner never spoke of such a concept as a literary or an educational frontier.

The traits that Turner saw as characteristic of the frontier were democracy, individualism, freedom, coarseness, strength, acuteness, inquisitiveness, ingeniousness, materialism, exuberance, laxness of business morals. The West was a region of great individualism ("society became atomic"), even though westerners cooperated effectively for what they wanted. Westerners were impatient of restraint, even though they developed and were willing to follow strong leadership. They were ingenious innovators in material things and radicals in social and political thought. They were optimistic and nationalistic, believers in Manifest Destiny.

As to the importance of the West—or of the frontier, since Turner never distinguished the two words clearly—in the history of the United States, the West above all created and made firm American democracy. By democracy Turner meant not only certain political forms but also a consideration of the good of the common man, which implied programs of social amelioration. Westerners were fairly equal in wealth and social status, and hence believed in political equality and in programs to assist the average citizen. Democracy came not from the *Mayflower* but "from the forest."

Along with democracy went individualism and freedom of opportunity. The frontier prevented the development of class lines by providing opportunity for the ambitious who felt circumscribed by European or eastern conditions. It was a "safety valve of abundant resources open to him who would take."

Moreover, the frontier was the region that effectively took various European stocks and welded them into one nation. The wilderness stripped the European of his customary clothes and habits, and forced him to adopt the garments and usages of the frontier if he were to survive. In time he became entirely American, which meant not only that he adopted American habits but that he became an ardent patriot.

The frontier, held Turner, produced an aggressive nationalism as the pioneers dreamed of new frontiers and sought to attain them. It favored more lenient land legislation, internal improvements at federal expense, and a protective tariff—all of which meant loose construction of the Constitution and a growth in the power of the federal government. The West was but little interested in European affairs, and indicated its expansionist nationalism by backing the purchase of Louisiana and the War of 1812.

When Turner announced in 1893 that "the frontier is gone," he spoke partly in regret, for instead of the sectional struggles of the past, in which the West in general supported true Americanism, he envisaged an increasingly bitter class struggle. And yet he was basically optimistic, for he felt that frontier ideas as they were retained in the Middle West would be the salvation of the nation. To accomplish this end the individualistic drive must be sacrificed, at least in part, to uphold the democratic tradition of the rights of the common man as against the power of the large corporation. The great task of the future, according to Turner, is to adjust democracy to an industrial nation, and here the Mississippi Valley will be decisive: "The social destiny of this Valley will be the social destiny, and will mark the place in history, of the United States."

Later historians have done but little systematic checking of the Turner theories, although many have accepted them. The one really important effort at testing them has been Professor Curti's study of Trempealeau County, Wisconsin (Merle Curti, *The Making of an American Community*, 1959). Curti and his co-workers covered exhaustively all phases of life, but emphasized situations that could be examined statistically. One conclusion was that Turner had been correct in holding that the frontier increased economic equality, which in turn led toward political democracy. Some of the other conclusions, such as the slowness of the Americanization of the foreign-born, did not accord so well with Turner. As Curti cautiously observed, the study of one specific area for a limited number of years (mostly 1850–1880) can produce no universal generalizations, but only a method that if applied more widely might lead to important results. Unfortunately, the Curti methodology has not been followed by others.

One other piece of work based on the Turner ideas is worthy of special consideration. Professor Walter P. Webb, accepting the Turner generalizations, described the American frontier as but one part of a European frontier that expanded magnificently between 1500 and 1900 (Walter P. Webb, *The Great Frontier*, 1952). According to Webb, such concepts as individualism and democracy were the products of the vast increase and turmoil of ideas that accompanied European expansion. The end of the "great frontier" has meant a more socialized world, with emphasis on collective action to allocate known products. Webb resembled Turner in his imaginative approach to history, but his particular point of view has been received with more reluctance than have the Turner ideas.

CRITICISM OF TURNER'S IDEAS

The Turner ideas have met increasing criticism, which in turn has inspired vigorous defense; at times the discussion has become vitriolic, with Turner admirers even contending that the ideas are beyond discussion. One enthusiast asserted in respect to the Turner thesis that "its soundness . . . must in large measure be gauged by its effect on the men of its generation." This idea of estimating truth on the basis of contemporary agreement is at least novel.

Criticism of the Turner ideas starts frequently with questions as to Turner's use of the word frontier. At various times he talks of a frontier as a line, an area, a process, and a state of mind. Also confusing is Turner's interchangeable use of "frontier" and "the West," especially when a reference to the West concerns an area that has long ceased to be a frontier. The serious investigator pleads for a more consistent and clearer use of words; on the other hand, the point is not tremendously important, for Turner's writings make reasonably clear in most cases the way he is using a specific word.

Turner's concept of the frontier has been challenged as being too limited in time and place to merit generalizations of presumably universal application. Did the frontier traits Turner described appear in Russia or Brazil or South Africa, or even in Hawaii with the American occupation? Increasing studies of such places as Canada and Australia indicate important differences between various frontiers. Certainly one can not properly assume that a given frontier will inevitably produce the same characteristics as another frontier.

One variety of opinion is that the real originating factor for such American traits as equality, democracy, social mobility, aggression, and expansion has really been the existence of large resources, so that Americans have been wealthy in comparison to others elsewhere in the world. Of course Turner emphasized the importance of rich and relatively free land, but the point is that the agricultural frontier described by Turner was but one part of a generally rich environment and should not be given too much credit in the formation of American character.

Turner was preoccupied with the frontier of the pioneer farmer, which meant that he spoke little of the land speculator, the miner, the artisan, the mill owner, and other westerners. Similarly, he devoted almost no attention to the rise of towns and cities. Even more important, he minimized such developments as of the arts, education, amusements. His critics insist that these segments of life are as important as the growing of hogs and corn, and that no analysis of the frontier that omits them can be valid.

Several modern writers have speculated that the physical is but one type of frontier for the ambitious and adventurous. An energetic man of 1830 might have emigrated to Illinois, but also he might have entered a textile mill at Lawrence, experimented with rubber, or become involved in the temperance movement. In more recent years he might find no good, free land, but he could climb mountains or investigate outer space. One of these critics (James C. Malin) labels the Turner reasoning "unsound and vicious methodology and philosophy," and holds that all sorts of nonphysical frontiers remain inviting if only the government would permit private initiative and individualism to express itself.

Turner was also criticized for his analysis of the reasons why men went West. His description of a "westward marching army of individualistic liberty-loving democratic backwoodsmen" has been accused of misemphasis on the ground that the desire for liberty, if it existed, was infinitesimal in comparison with the desire for wealth, and that motives ranged widely, from the hope of adventure to the desire for better fishing. Most migrants were merely taking farms in less congested areas. They were doing roughly the same work they had left in the East, but under more difficult conditions and expecting greater financial reward. The freedom to work harder with the object of later prosperity and freedom from labor was not the kind of liberty Turner had in mind.

Practically no critic has had the temerity to doubt that the frontier was crude, materialistic, unlettered, exuberant, and lacking in artistic development. But some doubts have been expressed that these and other traits were distinctive of the frontier. The West tended to emulate the East. Very possibly these western characteristics were only a slightly primitive reflection of the culture prevailing in the East.

The proposition that the West was a great innovator in both material things and in social ideals—a "region of revolt"—has met great opposition. The western farmer—for example, the farmer on the open prairies—clung tenaciously to traditional methods of farming long after they were shown as obviously inadequate. Comparatively few inventions came from the West, even though a list can be compiled that would include most notably certain types of farm machinery as well as the typewriter and the solar compass. But almost no novel political, economic, or social ideas emanated from the West. The usual westerner was basically conservative, striving to make his fortune so that he might obtain the good things of life as defined by eastern society. He had neither time, strength, nor desire for anything strange and new. Social conformity was as great in most of the West as in the East, with no remarkable differences between the sections in the styles either of politics or of women's clothes. So-called radical proposals—cheaper money is an example—have long been traditional with agricultural groups and represented no distinctive frontier contributions.

Turner's great thesis that democracy was a product of the forest has been discarded entirely by his critics, who point out that for Turner democracy was a vague term, including at least such diverse elements as the beliefs of Jefferson and of Theodore Roosevelt. They insist that the frontier in many respects was not highly democratic; for example, until near its end it never gave the suffrage to women, to Negroes, or to Indians. Turner himself held that southern expansion was the influence that fixed the slave system securely in the South, but certainly slavery and democracy were not highly compatible bedfellows. His critics insist that democracy is an idea of long development, with roots deep in European history, and that even specific devices, such as the secret ballot, were not American in origin.

Democracy in the sense of helping the common man, state the critics, was primarily eastern. Whether it was the antislavery movement, missionary enterprise, railroad control, or prison reform, the West copied the East, which in most cases had taken the ideas from Europe. From this point of view the West produced no new trends in social reform, in literary endeavor, or in religious belief. The only way in which the West might be considered radical is that it was enamored of certain politico-economic concepts, such as the free coinage of silver, that seemed desirable to an agricultural population.

Individualism, to the man who views Turner skeptically, was no more western than steamboats. As one writer has said, the West contained many individuals but little individualism. The average westerner conformed to the general ideas of his time, including a minimum of social control over private enterprise, which was a product of the Industrial Revolution. But in contradiction to this general theory, the West, like the East, was quite ready to encourage government interference whenever the government could be helpful, as in the building of canals and railroads, the establishment of banks, and the control of railroads. Westerners were close to their governments and had no objection to using them, and their ingenuity in this respect was to increase with the years.

Regarding the Americanization of the foreign-born by the frontier, several criticisms have been raised. Comparatively few immigrants went to the raw frontier, which was occupied mainly by native-born farmers. Turner specifically and correctly repudiated the leapfrog process of settlement by which each frontier was settled by a new group of frontiersmen from the East or from Europe. When the immigrant did go to the frontier, he was not usually Americanized rapidly. German, Scandinavian, and other customs clung tenaciously; for example, the German frontier was markedly different from that of the Anglo-Saxon. Some question is thus raised as to whether the more eastern states did not modify European customs more rapidly than did the West.

The critics have accepted the Turner statement that the frontier produced vigorous American expansionism, but have added the corollary that such sentiment was almost entirely continental, stretching no farther than the West Indies. The forces favoring expansion during the 1890s and later were very little western, not to mention frontier. The Middle West actually contributed notably to isolation sentiment during the twentieth century. In addition, nationalism did not necessarily mean a loose construction of the Constitution. True, Clay wanted his American system, but Jackson, at least as good a westerner, opposed the Bank of the United States, and vetoed the Maysville bill. And on what evidence is the West depicted as giving strong support to a protective tariff?

Possibly the most debated of Turner's points has been his suggestion that the frontier has been a "safety valve of discontent." Although he made a similar statement several times, he never elaborated on it and apparently did not consider it of first importance. His exact meaning is therefore open to some doubts. Probably he was speculating that the opportunities afforded by cheap western land averted severe class conflicts in the United States because the discontented could find outlets for their dissatisfaction and aspirations without trying to overthrow existing institutions. Unhappy easterners became happy westerners rather than bitter reformers.

As expanded by other men, this safety-valve concept came to mean that the most distressed eastern classes, particularly factory workers, provided a large share of western migration, and that they moved in the periods of their greatest distress, that is, in periods of depression. In this form the idea is demonstrably false. No reasonable doubt exists that western migrants were predominantly eastern farmers. Detailed studies have been made of specific areas, both urban and rural, at different times. The conclusion is always the same; farmers, and not industrial laborers, moved to the frontier. Only a few artisans were attracted by the higher western wages, and factory workers were almost entirely absent. An unemployed factory worker on the frontier, even if he could have reached it, was a candidate for either charity or starvation.

Even less doubt exists that the westward movement was greater in prosperous than in depression times. Census figures, including special state enumerations, bear out this statement. New states tended to be admitted after their first big booms in population, and the dates of admission concentrate in the latter parts of periods of prosperity. Land sales reached their peaks just before the various panics, and again the evidence is suggestive, even after making allowance for the gap between settlement and land sales and the excess of speculation in prosperous times. Finally, all accounts by people who witnessed the migration agree that its peaks came in periods of prosperity; just before the panics of 1819, 1837, 1857, and 1873, and during the good times of the early 1880s.

The most drastic critics of the safety-valve theory insist that there never has been such a safety valve in either short-run or long-run terms. They argue that the westward movement could have lessened eastern discontent only if it had created a real eastern labor scarcity, with resulting higher wages, but that in fact such an event did not occur; more migration merely produced a vacuum filled by immigrants and women workers. They agree that wages were higher in America than in Europe, but explain this situation as the result of American ingenuity and cheap raw materials rather than of a scarcity of labor. Hence the so-called safety valve was no more than a suction pump to attract new labor, and produced no relative change in eastern classes. Professor Fred A. Shannon suggested that the real American safety valve was the city because it furnished an outlet for rural discontent.

The Turner critics have been useful in raising doubts about generalizations that many people were accepting without adequate consideration. On the other hand, some of the criticism was ill tempered, bad intentioned, and irresponsible, shaking the foundations of perfectly valid ideas by innuendos and suggestions that had little if any merit. In some cases the criticisms were really designed to glorify the authors' own sections of the country as against Turner's West. The extent of the criticism led in some cases to throwing out all that Turner wrote, the good with the bad, the baby with the bath water. This point of view apparently denied that the West had any specific influence, which was ridiculous. No one of intelligence can really believe that the conquering of 3000 miles of wilderness failed to leave some sort of stamp on American history and on the American character.

CHARACTERISTICS OF THE WEST

The frontier clearly attracted some people but not others. The economically successful easterner seldom moved west. The migrant was presumably unhappy economically, socially, or emotionally, but possessed of sufficient energy and initiative to break home ties and start a new life in the wilderness. In intelligence he probably represented a cross section of American life, but in aggressiveness he was above average, which implies that among the migrants to the West were holdup men and claim jumpers as well as solid, substantial, law-abiding citizens. Basically these men and women were choosing between trying their fortunes in the West or in the factories and shops of the growing eastern cities.

The characteristics of the West varied somewhat with time and place. The outer fringes of the frontier—explorers, traders, trappers, miners, and the earliest speculators and farmers—were composed almost entirely of vigorous young men. Of necessity they were hardy and brave; no others could have survived. They made an important contribution by opening the way for the mass of settlers, but they were relatively few, and their influence on the rest of the United States was slight. The main significance of the frontier depended on the larger number of later arrivals who occupied the more sparsely settled areas to the east of the outer fringe of the frontier.

For the average migrant to the West—and by the West is meant the sections of lesser population—life was above all a continuous round of hard work, with a minimum of conveniences. The average man was a farmer fighting against a reluctant nature, and suffering from inadequate and monotonous food, flood, drought, grasshoppers, and vermin of all kinds. Lice and bedbugs were more prevalent than feats of valor. The average pioneer farmer seldom saw an Indian, although now and then the frontier was ravaged by Indian raids. He seldom performed any heroic exploit, unless washing in cold water could be put in that category. His health was not good, for he was scourged by ague, malaria, typhoid, and other ills.

The West cannot be considered primarily as a region in which guns flashed, redskins bit the dust, and fair maidens were rescued from a fate worse than death. Such incidents were rare, and seldom affected the average farmer-settler. But on the other hand, the courage to meet adverse conditions and monotonous routine should not be underestimated. Starting life anew in the West was a tremendous gamble that increased as the distance from home grew. The gamble might well fail, forcing the gambler either to try again or to return ignominiously to his friends and relatives—a failure. Virtue may inhere more in the ceaseless effort to overcome large hardships than in the dramatic willingness to sell life dearly on the Little Big Horn. Forty years of drudgery to provide increasing comfort for one's family may be more admirable than forty days of heroic exploration.

Western life was endurable only to people who were basically optimistic. Men moved west because they were hopeful of the future, and that hope sustained them throughout life. The men who planned a New Buffalo as the metropolis of the Midwest were typical of the hopefulness of the frontier. And for each such optimist, exaggeration and bragging were as natural as breathing. Western stories were taller than eastern, partly because the West itself was a region of exaggerations, but some people unkindly call them lies. Neither optimism nor exaggeration can be labeled exclusively western, but the West certainly gave both a favorable environment.

Optimism had its corollary in aggressive nationalism. The emphasis should be on the aggressiveness even more than on the nationalism. Westerners gave little respect to Indians, Spaniards, or Mexicans when they desired new land—and they always desired new land, even when its necessity was remote. Generally the westerner was a patriot and linked his expansionist sentiment with his patriotism, but there were exceptions. Separatist sentiment all the way from Vermont to California was also a well-known point of view.

Western expansionist sentiment was limited to the continent of North America and its adjacent islands, for the West was concerned primarily with agriculture, mining, and stock raising. Missionary opportunity in Hawaii or textile markets in the Orient were more an eastern than a western interest. Profits for eastern businessmen were never a major ambition of westerners.

The very motives of western migration guaranteed that the West would be highly concerned with the material aspects of life. Men moved west to make their fortunes, not to obtain themes for novels or to educate their children. Success was measured in acres, in cattle, in buildings, in cash. This materialistic attitude toward life was common throughout the United States, and the West did no more than to underline a trait that every foreign visitor observed as common to Americans.

The emphasis on materialism implied less attention to noneconomic activities. The West had neither time nor money for such inconsequential pursuits as landscape painting. And yet this frame of mind should not be overstated. A visitor to a log cabin might find its owner immersed in George Bancroft's *History of the United States* and eager to discuss the latest European scientific discoveries. Parents wanted their children to be educated. A primitive St. Paul could boast a theater, and a cotillion party was not unknown in the cruder parts of the West. All that can be said is that the West was somewhat behind the East in the noneconomic interests of life, but not that the two sections were utterly different. Presumably the West exercised some sort of retarding influence on the cultural advance of the United States.

As an individualist, the westerner was not perceptibly different from his eastern contemporaries. Few Daniel Boones continued to search for elbowroom. Roads, canals, banks, steamboats, and stores were possible only as group activities, as also were theaters and Paris fashions. The westerner, a sociable creature who wanted the good things of life, was no hermit. He gave a vague support to laissez faire, as did all Americans, and objected strongly when the government thwarted his desires. Who did not? But when the government could help him he was wholeheartedly enthusiastic about the assistance.

The frontier may be considered individualistic in its willingness to use personal force, whether in a gouging match or in a vigilance committee. Yet this trait has been visible throughout American history in all parts of the country. The American Revolution is possibly the most striking example, but the long-continued practice of dueling or the use of violence in labor movements is equally typical. The West was somewhat more vigorous than the East, possibly because of the lack of policemen, but basically the sections were not vastly different.

Socially the westerner was a conformist. Generally he lived in a farming community or in a small town where everyone knew and was interested in his neighbors, and where standards of acceptable conduct were fairly rigid. Western communities should not be considered as lacking class distinctions; the wife of the village banker seldom exchanged calls with the wife of the livery stable handyman, but the gulf was by no means impassible. The clerk of one day might be the proprietor of the next. A common code of conduct and a common test of success produced a general feeling of equality.

Politically and economically the westerner was not radical. His criterion of individual wealth as the measure of success agreed with the ideals of the easterner, and hence his political and economic thinking was not original. In general the West functioned inside the traditional two-party system. As a predominantly agricultural area it had certain desires that were sometimes labeled radical by their opponents; although by the time the West supported the Populist movement in such radical innovations as the direct election of senators, some question was possible as to whether any important frontier influence was represented. The Wisconsin of Robert La Follette had little in common with the Kansas of Wild Bill Hickok.

Much more important than any specific political, economic, or social program was the basic desire of all westerners to attain the values that were held in esteem farther east. The Ohio farmer who moved to Iowa had no idea of creating a new and glittering utopia. Rather, he desired heartily to attain as commodious a house as his richer Ohio neighbor, as smart a horse and carriage, as good clothes for his wife and children. Western culture was basically and almost inevitably imitative.

IMPORTANCE OF THE FRONTIER   The importance of the frontier in American history has been great. Most obviously, the frontier was the first step in the occupation of the continent. Without it presumably we would all still be living in Europe and Africa and Asia today. The energy and aggressiveness that carried Americans across the continent are living parts of the American tradition; whether or not they have made the nation unduly egocentric and self-righteous, they certainly have been important.

Frontier expansion meant that until late in the nineteenth century a major part of American energy and wealth was devoted to internal development. Not until toward the end of that century did the United States have important amounts of capital or manufactured goods to export. The lateness of American overseas expansion and interest in world politics must be credited largely to the frontier, and this point is emphasized by the long-continued isolationism of the Middle West as compared with the Atlantic Coast.

Not only did the existence of the frontier lessen American interest in world affairs, but it slowed the industrial developments on which such interests are based. If the United States had been confined east of the Appalachians, its magnificent birth rate, regardless of immigration, would soon have produced a population density sufficient to bring a mechanical development similar to that of England. With slower industrialization such attendant problems as those of labor were naturally delayed.

An expanding frontier meant a deficit of workers in terms of available resources. The existence of such a situation was indicated by the high American wage scale. High pay attracted immigrants, which meant a yearly crop of new citizens to be absorbed. Consequently the frontier may be credited with having slowed the production of a uniform American culture by attracting new stocks that have been a source of strength to the United States.

Insofar as the frontier slowed industrialization it delayed the development of class warfare, particularly the struggle between capital and labor. American society was slow in solidifying, its fluidity being the result of great opportunities of all kinds, notably agricultural and industrial. Although there was no safety valve in the sense of an outlet for the industrial unemployed in time of depression, a real safety valve was operating indirectly over a long period of time: migration to the West reduced eastern concentration of labor, which in turn kept wages high as compared to those in Europe, which in turn lessened industrial discontent.

A preoccupation with material goods slowed other developments. In this respect the West merely reinforced a trend existing throughout the nation. Americans have seldom been impressed by the virtues of starving in an attic for the love of art. A man's first job has been to make a comfortable home for his family. The body must be fed before the soul is free. The West clearly emphasized, although it did not create, this point of view.

The frontier did, however, produce at least a few effects on noneconomic culture. No student of American literature can fail to note the varied use of frontier themes, and in particular the development of realistic writing concerned with western material. Exaggeration as a literary device has a definite western twang. In education, the introduction and increase of coeducation had western, and even frontier, implications. Singing schools, barn dances, quilting parties, and many other old American customs retained their popularity, in part because of the influence of the frontier.

Politically, the frontier influence is linked inextricably with the economic. The frontier produced a large and lasting agricultural area that has been entrenched through the American system of representation. Farmers have at one and the same time been capitalists and hand laborers. They have favored moderate wages, and at the same time high prices for farm products. They have believed in the control of large aggregations of capital, manufacturing, and distribution, and in low and easy terms on loans. Traditionally, the satisfaction of their desires was forwarded by giving more people the vote; hence farmer support for an expanded suffrage, direct election, and similar democratic measures. The frontier, by retarding industrialization, permitted the farmer to remain an extremely important political influence for many years. That situation has been changing rapidly within the past half century with increasing urbanization.

Any generalizations as to the importance of the frontier should be considered as largely tentative. They are based on data that have been filtered through the minds of individuals who have their own personalities and points of view, regardless of how impartial they try to be. In general, the frontier seems to have had its greatest importance not in originating new trends, but in throwing its weight in one direction or another, and even more in exaggerating national traits such as economic and social mobility, faith in progress, democracy, individualism, wastefulness, the value of hard work, and respect for women; some of these concepts obviously have eroded during the present century, but at the same time the frontier has been important in the development of the distinctive culture of the United States, and its influence is bound to continue into the remote future.

READINGS   *Paperbacks are marked with an asterisk.*

Frederick Jackson Turner   Every student of the American West should read *Turner's *The Frontier in American History* (1920), including the famous essay; Wilbur R. Jacobs, *The Historical World of Frederick Jackson Turner* (1968) and (ed.), *Frederick Jackson Turner's Legacy* (1965), which includes a good biographical essay. Very perceptive is Merle E. Curti, *Frederick Jackson Turner* (1949); *Curti's book *The Making of An American Community* (1959) generally supports Turner ideas, as does *Ray A. Billington, *America's Frontier Heritage* (1966). John D. Barnhart, *Valley of Democracy* (1953) uses the Ohio Valley to illustrate Turner ideas. *George R. Taylor (ed.), *The Turner Thesis* (1949) has both sides of the story. Walter P. Webb, *The Great Frontier* (1952) expands the Turner idea. Generally critical are Jeanette P. Nichols and James G. Randall (eds.), *Democracy in the Middle West* (1941).

Other Interpretations   *Henry N. Smith, *Virgin Land* (1950) is stimulating. *Louis B. Wright, *Culture on the Moving Frontier* (1955) emphasizes western culture. Somewhat varying interpretations appear in Laurence M. Larson, *The Changing West* (1937); John C. Parrish, *The Persistence of the Westward Movement* (1943); Frederic L. Paxson, *When the West Is Gone* (1930). John W. Caughey, *Hubert Howe Bancroft* (1946) concerns the most prolific of western historians. Discussions of frontier theory appear for the most part in periodical articles, which are extremely numerous.

INDEX